W9-BKP-895

LORD BYRON'S WIFE

Also by Malcolm Elwin:

LANDOR: A Replevin
THE STRANGE CASE OF ROBERT LOUIS STEVENSON
THE LIFE OF LLEWELYN POWYS
THE LIFE OF THOMAS DE QUINCEY
THE FIRST ROMANTICS: Wordsworth, Coleridge, Southey
OLD GODS FALLING
VICTORIAN WALLFLOWERS
THACKERAY: A Personality
CHARLES READE: A Biography

ANNE ISABELLA MILBANKE

From the miniature by George Hayter, 1812
In the possession of the Earl of Lytton,
by whose permission it is reproduced

Lord Byron's Wife

MALCOLM ELWIN

HARCOURT, BRACE & WORLD, INC.

New York

first American edition 1963

Library of Congress Catalog Card Number: 63-8083

Printed in the United States of America

To

THE EARL OF LYTTON,

owner of the Lovelace Collection of Byron Papers,

and to the memory of

THE 2nd EARL OF LOVELACE,

who assembled the Collection

CONTENTS

THE NOELS

Sir Edward Noel, 6th Bart., 9th Baron and 1st Viscount Wentworth, 1715–74,
m. 1744 Judith (*d.* 1761) dau. of William Lamb

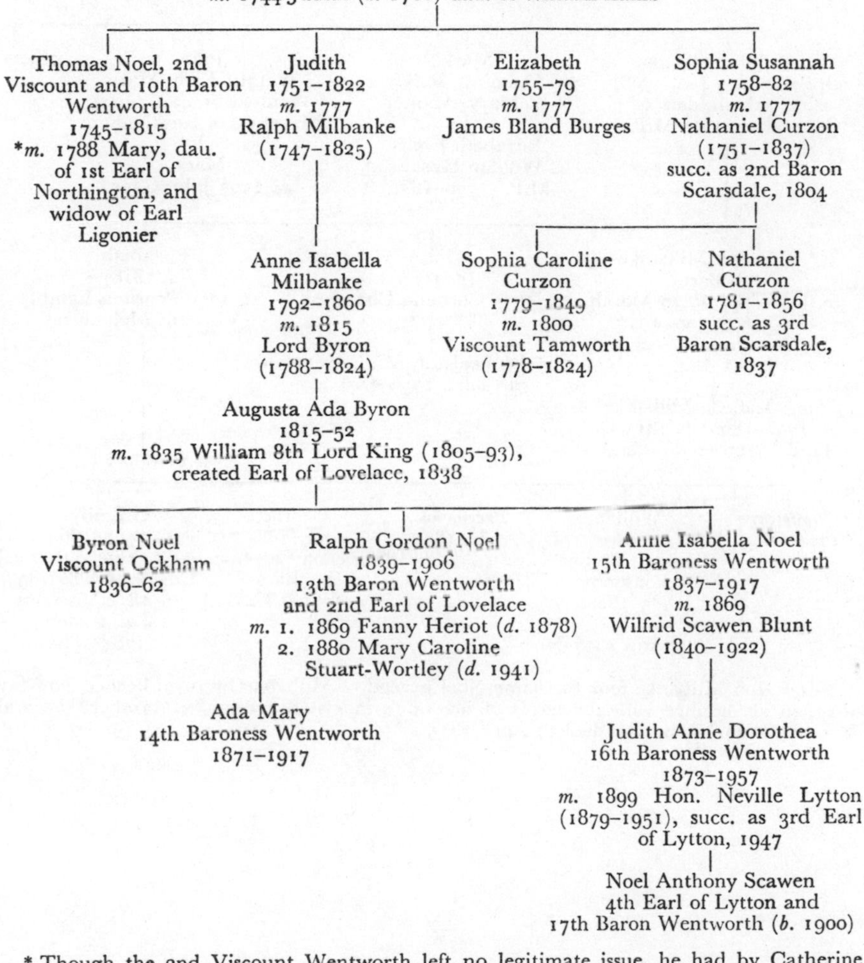

* Though the 2nd Viscount Wentworth left no legitimate issue, he had by Catherine Vanloo (*d.* 1781) a daughter, Anna Catherine, who married Vincent Hilton Biscoe in 1790, and a son, the Rev. Thomas Noel Noel (*b.* 1775) who married Catherine Smith in 1796.

THE MILBANKES AND THE MELBOURNES

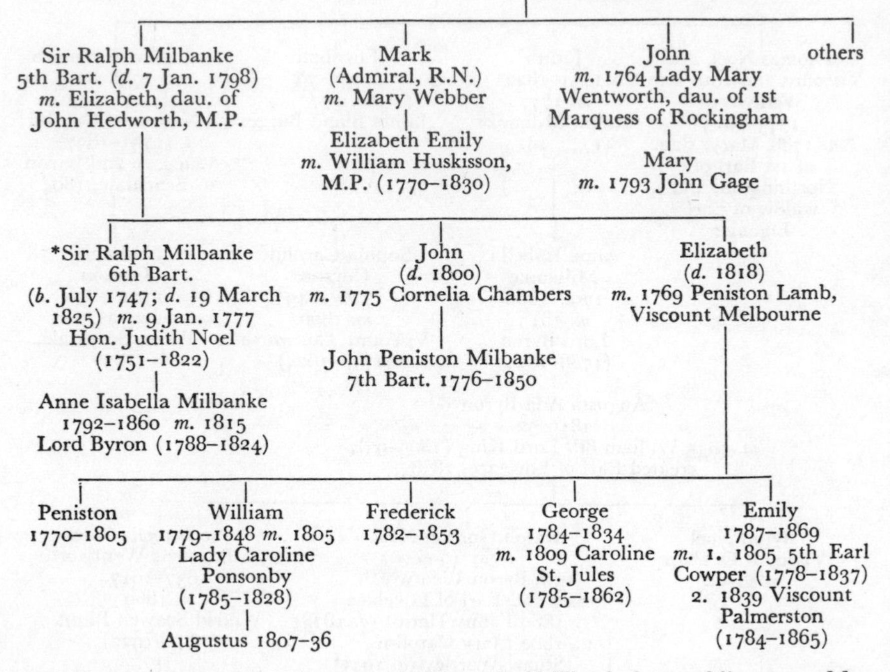

*Sir Ralph Milbanke took the name Noel instead of Milbanke by royal licence, 20 May 1815, in accordance with the terms of his wife's inheritance from her brother, the 2nd Viscount Wentworth, who died 17 April 1815.

AUGUSTA LEIGH'S FAMILY CONNECTIONS

Robert, 4th Earl of Holdernesse and 8th Baron Conyers, 1718–78,
m. 1743 Mary Doublet (*d.* 1801)

Amelia Baroness Conyers, 1754–84
m. 1. 1773 Francis Marquess of Carmarthen, 1751–99, succ. as 5th Duke of Leeds, 1789, divorced 1779.
2. 1779 John Byron, who *m.* 2ndly 1785 Catherine Gordon of Gight

George Gordon
6th Lord Byron
1788–1824

1. George, 6th Duke of Leeds, 1775–1838, *m.* 1797 Charlotte, dau. of Marquess Townshend

1. Francis Godolphin Osborne, 1777–1850, *m.* 1800 Elizabeth Eden, dau. of 1st Lord Auckland

1. Mary Henrietta Juliana (*d.* 1862) *m.* 1801 2nd Earl of Chichester, 1756–1826

3rd Earl of Chichester, 1804–86

2. Augusta Mary Byron, 1784–1851 *m.* 1807 her cousin, Col. George Leigh

Georgiana Augusta	Augusta Charlotte	George Henry John	Elizabeth Medora	Frederick George	Amelia Marianne	Henry Francis
b. 4 Nov. 1808	*b.* 9 Feb. 1811	*b.* 3 June 1812	*b.* 15 April 1814	*b.* 9 May 1816	b. 27 Nov. 1817	*b.* 28 Jan. 1820

THE

William, 4th Lord Byron, 1669–1736,
m. 3rdly, 1720, Frances, dau. of Lord Berkeley of Stratton*

- William
  5th Lord Byron 1722–98
  ("the Wicked Lord")
  m. 1747 Elizabeth Shaw
  - William 1749–76
    m. his cousin,
    Juliana Elizabeth Byron
    - William,
      killed in Corsica,
      1794
- John
  Admiral R.N. 1723–86
  ("Foulweather Jack")
  m. his cousin,
  Sophia Trevanion*
  - John 1756–91
    m. 1. 1779 Amelia, Baroness Conyers, divorced w. of Marquess of Carmarthen, later 5th Duke of Leeds
    2. 1785 Catherine Gordon of Gight (*d.* 1811)
    - 1. Augusta Mary Byron
      1784–1851
      m. 1807 her cousin,
      Col. George Leigh
      - seven children
    - 2. George Gordon
      6th Lord Byron
      1788–1824 *m.* 1815
      Anne Isabella Milbanke
      (1792–1860)
      - Augusta Ada Byron
        1815–52
  - George Anson 1758–93
    m. 1779 Henrietta Dallas
    (*d.* 1793)
    - George Anson
      7th Lord Byron
      1789–1868 *m.* 1816
      Elizabeth Chandos-Pole
    - Julia
      m. Rev.
      Robert Heath
  - Frances
    m. Gen. Charles Leigh
    - Col. George Leigh
      m. 1807 his cousin,
      Augusta Mary Byron
- Isabella (*d.* 1759)
  m. 1. 1743 4th Earl of Carlisle
  2. 1759 Sir William Musgrave
  - 5th Earl of Carlisle
    1748–1825
    m. 1770 Caroline
    Leveson-Gower, dau.
    of 1st Marquess of
    Stafford

*Lord Berkeley of Stratton had two daughters; the elder married John Trevanion, of Carhays, Cornwall, the younger the 4th Lord Byron.

BYRONS

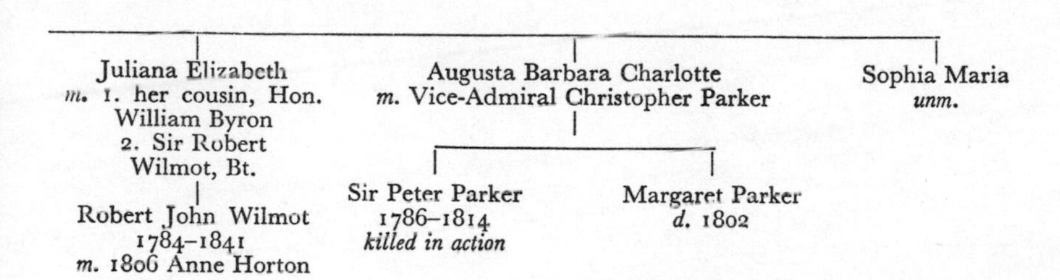
Juliana Elizabeth
m. 1. her cousin, Hon. William Byron
2. Sir Robert Wilmot, Bt.
Robert John Wilmot
1784–1841
m. 1806 Anne Horton
Augusta Barbara Charlotte
m. Vice-Admiral Christopher Parker
Sir Peter Parker
1786–1814
killed in action
Margaret Parker
d. 1802
Sophia Maria
unm.

INTRODUCTION

On the publication of *Childe Harold* in 1812, Lord Byron became the lion of London society. He was only twenty-four, of great personal beauty, and the holder of an ancient title—incredibly a fitting hero for his own romantic poem. Immediately he became a subject of scandal when Lady Caroline Lamb, daughter-in-law of the celebrated Lady Melbourne, fell so desperately in love with him that she visited his rooms in disguise, paraded her passion at public assemblies, once attempted suicide as an emotional gesture. When her family succeeded in removing her, Byron drifted into other amours only less notorious till in 1815 he married Annabella Milbanke.

Their married life lasted almost exactly one year; after the birth of a daughter, Annabella returned to her parents and demanded a legal separation. Husband and wife never met again; Byron left England never to return, living scandalously in Italy with a series of mistresses till he died at Missolonghi in 1824 as a martyred hero in the cause of Greek independence. Within a few weeks of his death his friend and executor, John Cam Hobhouse, met representatives of his wife and his half-sister at the office of his publisher, John Murray, and allowed the manuscript of his autobiography to be burnt.

The truth of his marriage and separation has remained ever since a subject of speculation for his many biographers. Nine years after Annabella's death in 1860, Harriet Beecher Stowe, author of *Uncle Tom's Cabin*, asserted that the cause of separation was Annabella's discovery of an incestuous relationship between Byron and his half-sister, Augusta Leigh—a charge that seemed substantiated when Byron's grandson, the 2nd Earl of Lovelace, published *Astarte* in 1905. But Byron's partisans found proofs wanting; more theories and speculations were evolved, and as recently as 1957 Professor G. Wilson Knight, in *Lord Byron's Marriage*, argued that the story of incest was merely a mask to screen the true cause of the separation—that Byron's wife discovered his practice of homosexuality. In 1958 Professor Leslie A. Marchand published a three-volume biography of Byron, imposing a lasting debt on all students of Byron by assembling the known documentary facts of his life, and many critics assumed somewhat impetuously that the last word had been written on the Byron mystery.

Professor Marchand lacked access to the Lovelace Papers, the vast collection of family letters and documents assembled by the Byrons' grandson, the 2nd Earl of Lovelace (1839–1906). On the death of Lovelace's widow in 1941, when the collection was valued for probate, the compilers of the inventory declared that it not only constituted "one of the finest collections of Byron letters known," but contained "a complete history of the Byrons' marriage and separation."

For Annabella, having condemned herself to widowhood at the age of twenty-four, devoted the remaining forty-four years of her life to self-justification. She preserved, not only every letter addressed to her with any bearing upon the subject of her marriage, but copies—often attested by witnesses—of her own letters and of letters shown to her by others. She also kept journals at irregular intervals and compiled many reminiscent statements, the most valuable of which were intended for possible legal use in the event of her being required to sue for custody of her child. No scrap of memoranda was too trivial for preservation.

Though the desirability of preserving correspondence as evidence was impressed on her by her lawyers, Annabella inherited from her mother the habit of cherishing old letters. We are told by his biographers that Byron disliked his mother-in-law and blamed her for the part she played in the separation, but there has been little indication of the forceful character that necessarily influenced the moulding of her daughter's personality. The full story of Annabella's parents, Sir Ralph and Judith Milbanke, appears in the first section of the Lovelace Papers, comprising several hundred letters in a correspondence of thirty-five years from 1767 to 1802 between Judith Milbanke, her brother, the 2nd Viscount Wentworth, and their aunt Mary Noel. Apart from a few sentences quoted in *Astarte* and by Ethel Colburn Mayne in her *Life of Lady Byron* (1929), these letters are unpublished and furnish the material of the first chapter in the present book.

The second section of the Lovelace Papers comprises correspondence of the Milbanke family and friends during Annabella's girlhood and her own correspondence and journals before her marriage. Her correspondence with Byron before their marriage and some extracts from her journals were published in Ethel Colburn Mayne's *Life of Lady Byron*, but much of this material remains unpublished and selected passages—as indicated in the Notes on Sources at the end of the book—are now quoted for the first time in Chapters 2 to 4 and 6 to 8.

A third section of the Lovelace Papers comprises documents and correspondence relating to the Byrons' separation, providing a day-to-day record of the four months from January to April 1816, with sometimes as many as twelve letters in a single day. Besides some letters from Byron to his wife only partially published, the unpublished material includes letters from Byron's half-sister Augusta Leigh, Annabella's letters to and from her parents, to and from her chief legal adviser Stephen Lushington, and correspondence with many close friends and confidantes—the Hon. Mrs. George Villiers, Lady Melbourne and her daughters-in-law Lady Caroline and the Hon. Mrs. George Lamb, Selina Doyle and her brother Francis Hastings Doyle, her former maid Mary Anne Clermont, Byron's cousins R. J. Wilmot and George Byron (afterwards the 7th Lord), her former suitor Hugh Montgomery and his sister, Lords Holland and Brougham, Sir Samuel Romilly, and Lady Liddell. Besides Annabella's own several statements, there are attested statements by her mother and by Mrs. Clermont, as well as legal correspondence and documents from the files of the family attorneys, Wharton & Ford. Only a fragment of this material—which supplies the basis of the last four chapters of this book—has been previously published and that incompletely.

The mass of letters and documents accumulated during Annabella's later life belongs largely to a continuation of her story beyond the period of the present book, showing how her policy of self-justification impelled her interference in Augusta Leigh's affairs till Augusta's death in 1851, inspired her sponsorship of Augusta's daughter Medora, despoiled her relationship with her daughter and son-in-law, and unbalanced the upbringing of her grandson. In her will she left elaborate provision for preservation of her papers by three trustees. Stephen Lushington was still living, and—significantly—he influenced the trustees to withhold Annabella's papers from her grandchildren.

Brought up by his grandmother, her grandson Ralph had been infected with her hostility towards his own father; rather than bear the courtesy title of Viscount Ockham as his father's heir, he successfully claimed the barony of Wentworth through his grandmother's title. On securing the papers from the trustees in 1868, he was inclined to feel less reverence for his grandmother and much sympathy with his grandfather. But during the last decade of her life Annabella had been injudicious in her choice of confidantes; when Harriet Beecher Stowe made her sensational revelations in 1869, Ralph Lord Wentworth resented the newspaper criticism of his grandmother. Assiduously he sought out all his grandmother's correspondents whom he could trace, and acquired from them all her letters that had been preserved. He made a friend of Hobhouse's daughter, Lady Dorchester, and copied Byron's letters preserved by Hobhouse as his executor, as well as passages from Hobhouse's journals.

Stung by a slighting reference to his grandmother in an article by Leslie Stephen for the *Dictionary of National Biography*, he printed in 1887 for family circulation thirty-six copies of *Lady Noel Byron and the*

Leighs, containing a long sequence of letters relating the history of Annabella's relationship with Augusta Leigh and her children after her separation from Byron. Succeeding as 2nd Earl of Lovelace on his father's death in 1893, he found among his father's papers another box of Annabella's letters relating to her marriage and separation. He then compiled the first version of his book *Astarte*, in which he told the story of the marriage and separation by setting forth a selection of the letters and documents in chronological sequence.

Unfortunately, he did not publish this version, which remains in typescript among the Lovelace Papers. In 1898 John Murray began to publish Byron's *Letters and Journals* under the editorship of R. E. Prothero. Lovelace had been on friendly terms with Murray, and had allowed him to copy some of Byron's letters to his wife and half-sister; on finding that Murray had allowed Prothero to publish these letters from what he regarded as confidential copies, he refused further co-operation with Murray, and instead of publishing the first version of *Astarte*, wrote the account of the separation which he issued in the privately printed edition of 1905, so offending Lady Dorchester that she revoked her intention of leaving the Hobhouse collection of Byron letters and papers to him and his heirs, and bequeathed to Murray the letters from Byron to Lady Melbourne, which were published in *Lord Byron's Correspondence*, 1922.

After his death in 1906 Lovelace's collection remained in the custody of his widow till her death in 1941. In 1921 she reprinted *Astarte*, with the addition of many unpublished letters. Subsequently she allowed a limited use of the Lovelace Papers to Sir John Fox for his book, *The Byron Mystery* (1924), to Ethel Colburn Mayne for her *Life of Lady Byron* (1929), and to M. André Maurois for his *Byron* (1930).

On the death of Mary Lady Lovelace in 1941, the Lovelace Papers passed, according to the terms of Lovelace's will, to his niece Lady Wentworth, the only child of his sister Lady Anne Blunt by her marriage to Wilfrid Scawen Blunt, the poet and diarist. In 1957, shortly before her death, Lady Wentworth agreed to allow Mrs. Doris Langley Moore to examine the Lovelace Papers on condition that she compiled a catalogue of them. But before Mrs. Langley Moore could complete her examination and proceed beyond beginning a catalogue, Lady Wentworth died, and possession of the Papers became a subject of dispute between her son, the 4th Earl of Lytton, and the executor of her will, Mr. Gladstone E. Moore. In pursuit of his claim, Lord Lytton engaged the present writer as his literary adviser, subsequently appointing him to assemble and catalogue the collection (the last section of which passed finally into his possession only in January 1962) and to write or edit books based on the material of the collection.

Himself the author of a memoir of his maternal grandfather, Wilfrid Scawen Blunt, Lord Lytton has required only that the full and complete truth about Lord and Lady Byron shall be told so far as it can be ascertained from the vast collection of letters and documents known as the Lovelace Papers, which he has inherited under the terms of the will of his great-uncle, the 2nd Earl of Lovelace. He has therefore allowed me complete liberty of quotation for *Lord Byron's Wife*, which is thus the first fully documented account of Byron's marriage and separation based on unrestricted use of the Lovelace Papers.

While I am thus indebted to Lord Lytton's generosity in entrusting to me an opportunity exposing me to the envy of all Byron scholars, I must acknowledge an overwhelming obligation to his great-uncle, the 2nd Earl of Lovelace, who has been esteemed far beneath his merits by many of Byron's critics and biographers. No less than a hundred and seventy volumes of typewritten transcripts of letters and documents survive as a testament to the diligence of his scholarship, and I have found him a meticulously exact transcriber of handwriting often very difficult to decipher. He has been accused of "suppressions," but any scholar aware of the scope of the Lovelace Papers must recognise that his problem was one of selection—that he may well have suffered from an embarrassment of riches after a lifetime spent in their accumulation and annotation. I shall be happy if my use of his materials leads to just recognition of his gifts and of his virtue as a conscientious scholar.

Like all other writers about Byron, I am indebted to Sir John Murray, the owner of the Byron copyright in the two-volume *Correspondence*, 1922, and to him and to the firm of John Murray, who, as the sole personal legal representatives of Lord Byron's literary estate, control the copyright in his unpublished letters or letters still in copyright, and examined four chapters of the book in typescript, as well as the Notes on Sources.

For permission to quote unpublished passages from the journals of John Cam Hobhouse, I am indebted to Sir Charles Hobhouse and to the Curator of the Berg Collection at the New York Public Library which now owns the originals of the journals for 3rd January to 1st July 1814 and 29th March 1815 to 5th April 1816. I am grateful to Mr. Gladstone E. Moore for allowing me the use of many volumes of Lovelace's transcripts while ownership of the relevant originals was still in dispute, and to Mr. Kenneth H. Callow and Miss Stokes, of Messrs. Coutts & Co., the trustees of Lovelace's will, for their co-operation in the task of assembling and sorting the Lovelace Papers. I am also grateful to my publishers—especially to E. R. H. Harvey, W. F. Parrish, and John Foster White—for much patient consideration and helpfulness.

Where an explanatory footnote may be required by the general reader, it appears on the page containing the relevant passage. Sources of all quotations and of statements of fact will be found in the Notes on Sources beginning on p. 473. Deploring the modern practice of defacing pages with frequent numerals so that the text tends to look like a problem in algebra, I have given in the Notes on Sources the page number with the number of the last line of the quotation down the page. Students and scholars, in identifying a source, will thus have to run a finger down the page to count the lines, but this inconvenience to the curious few seems preferable to defacement of the text for the majority.

In fulfilment of Lord Lytton's wish that the truth should be told so far as it may be ascertained from the evidence, I have avoided controversy and concentrated on presenting the evidence. If I seem sometimes to sympathise with Byron by drawing the reader's attention to his point of view, it is because the evidence presented emanates from Annabella and we have been deprived of Byron's interpretation by the destruction of his memoirs. Those who would weigh the balance should bear in mind that both the principals were very young—Byron was only twenty-seven and Annabella twenty-three during the year of their married life. Byron may be reckoned to have been his own worst enemy; he saw an audience in everybody—preferably in an attractive woman or in one disposed to be attracted—and it was unfortunate that his eloquence about himself seems to have been too much coloured during his married life by brandy-drinking.

Yet, in reading Annabella's remorseless evidence of what jurists would now define as "mental cruelty," it should be remembered that Byron's kindness and love of laughter won the heart of Augusta. By contrast with Augusta, who loved him the more for his weaknesses, Annabella fell in love with a character of her own conception formed upon a very slight acquaintance and cultivated by her own narcissism.

Selection may have compelled too little quotation for an adequate portrait of Augusta. Lovelace was the first to point out the falseness of the inference that Augusta was not personally attractive from the evidence of those who remembered her in her declining years as "a Dowdy Goody." Her letters show that it was a misconception to suppose that she was a silly woman because Byron affectionately played on the abbreviation "Guss" to call her "Goose"; she was perhaps too easily moved to tenderness, but she could maintain grace in adversity, and always there was a pervasive charm that rendered her eminently lovable.

I

MOTHER-IN-LAW

1751—92

"My only objection (supposing of course that ye Lady's was got over) would be to my *Mamma*, from whom I have already by instinct imbibed a mortal aversion."[1] So wrote Lord Byron to Lady Melbourne, his prospective father-in-law's sister, on 21st September 1812, when first contemplating his disastrous marriage to Annabella Milbanke. Nine years later, on 22nd June 1821—the year before the death of his mother-in-law, who had changed her name from Milbanke to Noel on the death of her brother, the second Viscount Wentworth—Byron wrote on hearing of Lady Noel's recovery from illness at the same time as news of the failure of *Marino Faliero* on the London stage:

> Behold the blessings of a lucky lot!
> My play is damned—and Lady Noel *not*.

Enclosing these lines to his sister, he added, "I will reserve my tears for the demise of Lady Noel, but the old b – – – h will live forever because she is so amiable and useful." He always believed that his mother-in-law's influence was responsible for his wife's insistence on a legal separation little more than a month after the birth of their only child.

Though Judith Milbanke was turned sixty when Byron met her, she was only a year older than Lady Melbourne, with whom he enjoyed such confidential intimacy that a wish to call her his aunt by marriage directed his inclination to marry her niece. But Lady Melbourne was a professional charmer, who had established herself as a leader of fashion by a series of well-chosen gallantries, the paternity of whose many children was a subject for speculation, and whose own son, who became Queen Victoria's first Prime Minister, remarked on contemplating her portrait in his old age, "A remarkable woman, a devoted mother, an excellent wife—but not chaste, not chaste." At sixty she retained the charm of an accomplished courtesan, allied to the glamour of high social position.

[1] Sources of quotations will be found at the end of the book, beginning on page 473.

By contrast Judith Milbanke had outlived the impulse to please. In her life there had been only one man. While her sexual attraction and impulse lasted, she adored her husband, recognising his limitations with affectionate tolerance but flying to his defence immediately he was criticised or threatened by others. In her middle age he had given her a daughter, and when Byron met her, she had been single-mindedly for twenty years devoting all her energies to educating the child she adored as exclusively as she had formerly adored her husband.

At sixty she was the victim of her own concentrated emotions. The intimates of her domestic circle, who had reason to recognise her virtues and had benefited from her generosity, could excuse her impetuous temper, tolerate her volubility, feel amused tenderness for her eccentricities, as when her elaborate wig became unsettled under stress of excitement to reveal the wisps of white hair beneath. Byron had youth's intolerance of a woman grown graceless and tiresome with age; his close relationship by marriage prevented even the qualified appreciation of John Cam Hobhouse, who recorded his impression when he went to Seaham to be best man at Byron's wedding: "My lady who has been a dasher in her day, and has ridden the grey mare, is pettish and tiresome, but clever."

She had always been clever enough to convince others of her cleverness, which was enough to insure success in the practical business of social life. She also had the advantage of belonging to "the top drawer" or "upper ten thousand" of English society in an age before social credentials became tainted by the Industrial Revolution with purely commercial values. There was a subtle but important difference between the cash values of the nineteenth century and the property values of the eighteenth century: the marriage settlements of women like Judith Milbanke reveal a shrewd regard for property, but birth and lineage were still indispensable assets in a woman's dowry. Assuring Lady Melbourne that he had duly considered his choice of Annabella Milbanke as a wife, Byron declared that he admired her "because she is a clever woman, an amiable woman & of high blood, for I have still a few Norman & Scotch inherited prejudices on the last score."

Judith Milbanke was the eldest daughter of Sir Edward Noel, sixth baronet of Kirkby Mallory in Leicestershire, who succeeded a distant cousin as ninth Baron Wentworth in 1745 and was created Viscount Wentworth in 1762. As he left small mark on history, Lord Wentworth doubtless owed his promotion in the peerage to the level carriage of his political dish; he owed his advancement to George III's favourite minister, Lord Bute, of whom Lord Stanhope wrote, "Has any Minister, with so short a tenure of power, and, I may fairly add, with so little of guilt in his intentions, been the cause of so great evils?" The Viscount also made a worthy marriage—to Judith, only daughter and sole heir of William Lamb of Farndish in Bedfordshire. She produced four children—a son Thomas (1745–1815), who succeeded his father as second Viscount and tenth Baron Wentworth in 1774, and three daughters, Judith, Elizabeth, and Sophia Susannah.

Shortly before her daughter became Lord Byron's wife, Judith began for her benefit an autobiography, in which she wrote:

> The first *Event* of which I retain a perfect recollection was the birth of my sister Elizabeth when I was 3½ years old, wondering *how* she came and *whence* she came. It was the fashion to tell Children in those days, that Infants where found in the *Parsley Beds*. This was told me of my Sister when I was first shown her in her Cradle, and did not *satisfy* me. I had seen my Mother very large, I had seen my Cradle again introduced into the Nursery and had observed bustle, preparation and expectation, that the *Doctor* was sent for, and when I again saw my Mother, she was in bed in a darkened room and appeared ill. Some vague conjectures floated in my mind, of which I longed to ask the explanation, but the Mystery observed, deterred me from enquiring, yet I was not so completely deceived as was imagined, but I well remember drawing this inference—that it was a *wrong thing* to have a Child, and that people were *ashamed* of it, therefore it was *not to be talked of*—and tho' I was pleased with the Infant, I felt a shyness of noticing it, for a long time, as if it was some thing wrong to do so.
>
> The earliest impressions on my mind were the cold austerity of my Father's manners, the more affectionate tho' *at times* severe conduct of my Mother. Yet I loved them both, but they never encouraged that Love to *expand*, by gentle affection. I was early taught to ask blessing night and morn—God bless you! with perhaps a kiss (but not always) chilled my manner, when nature prompted me to climb their knees and hang about their necks. This caused the whole warmth of my affections to center in my Aunt Mrs. Noel, a maiden Sister of my Father's who always lived in the house. She doated on *me*, from the hour I was born, and truly may I say her love was returned sincerely. Yet I *feared her*, but it was not punishment to myself I dreaded, but *giving her pain*, by my doing wrong.

When Lady Wentworth died in 1761 at the early age of thirty-five, this maiden aunt, Mary Noel (1725–1802), took charge of her brother's household and children. Judith was then in her tenth year, having been born at Kirkby Mallory on 14th November 1751 (3rd November Old Style); her sisters Elizabeth and Sophia Susannah were born respectively in 1755 and 1758. Her autobiography sketches her aunt's character and history:

> Endowed by nature with a superior understanding, a warm and affectionate heart, she was early left an orphan with a small fortune, and to

the care of a maternal Uncle,[1] who thought he did a great deal, in allowing her to reside in his house, and at the usual age to sit at the head of his table. He was a Batchelor, a violent Tory (perhaps in heart a Jacobite as many were in those days) and thought he promoted the Cause by making himself and those about him drunk on all occasions in his power. He lived in a large house adjoining the City of Oxford, of which City he was the *Tory* & popular Member. This situation, together with the famous contested Election for Oxfordshire in which he took a very active part, brought a vast concourse of people to his house—no Female resident in it but his Niece, who was constantly subjected from sixteen, to this motley drunken society, and to do the honors of the table dinner and supper constantly, as also to the wives and families of these persons when they accompanied the Gentlemen in their visits—and too frequently did she find herself treated as the dependent humble relation, instead as the Lady of the House. Her good sense and discretion steered her thro' this perilous situation free from blame. When my Father married, my Aunt came to reside with him—a more respectable, but not more independent home. She and my Mother were the same age, and my Mother was about 20 when she married—was handsome, somewhat determined, and in most points was the Lady Parramont. My Aunt had with resolution and activity cultivated her mind; she was self-educated, having received little assistance from others and unable to procure or pay for Instruction. She had acquired French and Italian, read *much* and *well*, her epistolary stile was *peculiarly* lively, clear and elegant, and at this moment I am possessed of letters and other writings of hers, which prove her talents.[2]

In one respect she was a singular character. She never for an instant considered her own interest and welfare whenever it came in competition with those of others, but was ready at all times to sacrifice her time, health and happiness for those she loved, nor did she ever complain of ingratitude and oppression, tho' she too frequently experienced them. Exemplary herself in the theory and practise of moral and religious principles, she was never severe or censorious about others, and if I have any good I owe it to her, for she was my early Instructress and my only one, except in some trifles which then came into the routine of a childish education . . .

I had a Maid, who used me very ill, unknown to any body. She taught me *my letters*, and when either she or myself were wrong, she was accustomed to lay me on my back in a closet and shut me up for a considerable time. I was a passionate little Devil, and used to cry and kick and scream till she let me out again, and then revenge myself by *grinning* at her, which trick

[1] Thomas Rowney, M.P. for Oxford. His sister Elizabeth, who died in 1743, married in 1714 Sir Clobery Noel (1694–1733). Besides the first Viscount Wentworth and his sister Mary, their children included two parsons: the Rev. John Noel (1719–89), rector of Steeple Aston, Oxfordshire, and vicar of Aston, Warwick, who officiated at the weddings of his nieces, and the Rev. Rowney Noel (1726–86), a doctor of divinity, rector of Elmsthorpe and Kirkby Mallory, and afterwards Dean of Salisbury.

[2] Mary Noel preserved all the letters written to her by her nephew and nieces from 1767 till her death in 1802, when the collection passed to her niece, Judith, who had kept all her aunt's letters to herself after her marriage in 1777. The letters passed from Judith to her daughter, Lady Byron, and from her to her grandson, the second Earl of Lovelace, who—in *Lady Noel Byron and the Leighs*, 1887—announced his intention of publishing them. But Lovelace worked slowly and his long labours on *Astarte* prevented his giving further attention to the letters before his death in 1906.

she cured me of, by running the dirty comb brush against my teeth. Tho' it stopped my grinning it did not correct my temper, as I was bursting with suppressed passion, and became obstinate. My Aunt discovered and put a stop to these proceedings, which if continued would have [made] my temper worse instead of better—and when I got a little older, I was her Tyrant, for after I was in bed and believed asleep, she used to admit her lover, one of the footmen, into the nursery—and when I wanted her to do anything, I threatened to tell of this.

That the fragment of autobiography ends there is as characteristic of Judith as the fragment itself; she was too busy with practical affairs ever to settle to writing for longer than the composition of a good letter. She remained always "a passionate little Devil," and if she did not "cry and kick and scream" in later life, she made everything uncomfortable for those around her till she got her own way. Just as she blackmailed her maid with her knowledge of the footman's visits, she never scrupled to use her power over others, and the grey mare proved herself much the better horse at intriguing to secure Ralph Milbanke's seat in Parliament.

The adulation of her aunt was also characteristic; Judith admitted no fault in those she passionately loved, and when she discovered the difficulties of her daughter's married life, she defended Annabella as an injured angel and vituperated Byron as a monster. Her letters show Mary Noel to have been a much livelier and more amusing character than the benevolent paragon sketched by her niece; if she was never "severe or censorious," it was because her views on morality were those of a society woman of Fielding's age, and she habitually practised a malicious wit at the expense of all her acquaintance except her favourite niece. Like her niece, she was devotedly loyal in time of trouble; when her nephew's mistress died in 1781, leaving an illegitimate son and daughter, she undertook the upbringing of the daughter, whom she eventually married with reason for satisfaction to a gentleman of good family and landed property in Kent.

When the first Viscount Wentworth died of cancer on 31st October 1774, all his four children were still unmarried. Dividing his time between Leicestershire and London, where he cut a figure as a man of fashion well received in court circles, the second Viscount, at the age of twenty-nine, had handicapped his chances of advantageous marriage by attaching himself to a mistress, Catharine Vanloo, by whom he already had at least one daughter. So far from assuming respectability with the responsibility accruing from his father's death, he had a son by Mrs. Vanloo in 1775—Thomas Noel Noel, who became the clergyman officiating at the wedding of Lord and Lady Byron. Apart from over-indulgence at cards and the bottle, he was a good-natured man of modest vices whose ambition was limited to a post in the royal bed-chamber, which he achieved only after marriage in middle-age with a well-endowed widow. The only male in a family of women, he varied a habit of defensive apology by occasional pompous plaintiveness when sensitive that his efforts on behalf of the family had been insufficiently appreciated. Mrs. Vanloo was not of course invited to Kirkby Mallory when his aunt and sisters were there, but her existence was resented by the sisters, who seldom spoke without disparagement of their brother's intimates—the eccentric Edward Rouse Yeo, latterly known as Count Yeo; Major Bowater, familiarly called "Bow"; their kinsman and neighbour at Newnham Paddox, the sixth Earl of Denbigh, whose ebullience was often disconcertingly reminiscent of Fielding's Squire Western.

Besides having her own house in London, Mary Noel had maintained her Oxfordshire friendships, notably with the Macclesfields at Shirburn Castle, the Clerkes of Waterstock, and the Dashwoods of Kirtlington Park. She was thus enabled to cast a wide net for suitors to her nieces, all three of whom were suitably married during the first eight months of 1777—Judith to Ralph Milbanke, elder son and heir to Sir Ralph Milbanke, fifth baronet of Halnaby in Yorkshire; Elizabeth to James Bland Burges, Lord Somerville's nephew; Sophia, who was only nineteen, to the Hon. Nathaniel Curzon, eldest son and heir of Lord Scarsdale.

It was while staying a month at Kimbolton Castle with the Duchess of Manchester, a sister of Sir Henry Dashwood, that Judith met Ralph Milbanke, whose aunt by marriage, Lady Mary Milbanke, lived within easy visiting distance at Harrowden. During the rest of the summer of 1776 Milbanke addressed to his "dear Miss Noel" whimsical accounts of social events at Richmond in Yorkshire, where he was a serving officer in the North Riding militia, ending always with the assurance that he was "ever sincerely & affectionately" hers. On 3rd September her aunt congratulated Judith that "you have drawn a happy lot, for Mr. Milbanke's character & behaviour are such as all your friends must wish, & when you can prevail upon yourself to shake off a little of that very unnecessary fear you have of him, I am sure he will be able to discover very many more *good* qualities for which he may like you, than those he has already seen."

When the courtship was protracted by legal difficulties over the marriage settlement, Judith applied the spur to her brother, who on 7th November felt so "much uneasiness on account of your health" that "I desire you will not make yourself worse by giving way to melancholy ideas," though "thro' the villainy of Mr. Hartley (ye Factotum of the Milbankes) your affairs are in but an awkward situation, but as the whole fault is on their side you need be under no apprehension that the least blame can affect you—as you may be assured I will take care the Saddle be laid on the right Horse." He communicated immediately with Ralph Milbanke, who took in Kirkby on his way between London and Yorkshire to inquire personally after his betrothed's health, and so effectually remonstrated with the factotum that the wedding took place at Kirkby Mallory on 9th January 1777. The Milbankes received £8,000 by the settlement.

Whatever fear Judith may have felt of Milbanke as a lover was quickly dissipated after marriage. The first part of their honeymoon was spent at Harrowden, whence she wrote to her aunt: "Nothing but Mr. Milbankes goodness to me & the entire Love & Esteem I have for him could have kept up my Spirits at quitting a Family every individual of which was dear to me and I have always flatter'd myself I was no less so to them." On arriving in Yorkshire, she had no time for homesickness in wholeheartedly applying herself to the duties of a wife, ingratiating herself with new friends and enjoying her social obligations, opening balls at the races and the assizes, spending the summer season at Scarborough, and making her mark in the great houses of the north. By October she felt secure in possession of "the best of Husbands (who by the way tells me I am the best of Wives & fancys I bestow a great obligation on him by being commonly grateful for the greatest kindness & attention ever shown a Woman)."

In the same letter of 29th October she confided a consultation with her doctor, who "thinks my illness is owing to impoverished Blood & a Nervous Habit, but is at present rather cautious about giving me much Medecine, as there is a possibility that there may be a reason for being careful, it being just eight weeks today since any appearance of a certain affair." Her hope was dashed two months later; her aunt wrote on 6th January 1778 her consolation "for your disappointment," which she believed "all for the best," as their own doctor at Kirkby told her "he did not think you would be able to go on, if you were Breeding, wh. he could hardly believe, your not being as usual proceeding from the extreme poorness of your Blood." Mary Noel was then at Kirkby with her nephew, who, with his three sisters now happily married, felt inclined to despond over the contrast of his own state in an illicit connection, and his aunt reported:

> You will guess nothing but the old inexhaustible could have kept us so long out of our Beds. I advised Marriage as a cure for all *Other* Missfortunes, but your Brother very gravely said he was glad he *was as he was*, since poor old England was in so bad a condition, that he should dread the thoughts of what might befall his Posterity, upon wh. I *rang* the bell & retired.

To this Judith replied on the eve of her wedding anniversary:

> Notwithstanding my Brothers fears for *posterity*, I cannot help wishing it may be my Lot to leave some even to run the Risques that threaten the next Generation; I condemn myself for repining at the late disappointment I have had, but cannot help it however wrong it may be . . . I was fearful you would not make out the whole of Mr. M's Letter which is a pity as it resembles himself in being the more liked the more known. I thought some months past I could discover no more perfection in him, but every Day convinces me more & more of his superior excellence. As to his kindness to me, it is without bounds & I have the great & inexpressible happiness of being fully persuaded he loves me more at this Hour than he did this Day twelvemonth . . . my Heart is so filled with Gratitude & Love to him, that I must unburden it to some one or it will burst . . . Tomorrow is our wedding Day & I can safely say (if we do not fall out before Sunrise) that not one wry word or look has passed between us during the Year.

Two months later, during a visit to London, Ralph Milbanke sat for his portrait by Sir Joshua Reynolds—though Sophia Curzon, the belle of the family, thought that fashionable painter wanted "more money than my ugly face & head put together is worth." The portrait was so successful that Lord Wentworth also sat to Sir Joshua—with a less happy result, as Wentworth reported in 1782 that "a great connoisseur" declared "Milbanks Picture to be one of the best he has seen & mine the *very worst*."

Nearly thirty-seven years later young Hobhouse found Ralph Milbanke "an honest red-faced spirit—a little prosy, but by no means devoid of humour;" Elizabeth, Duchess of Devonshire called him "old twaddle Ralph," and his daughter told him in 1812, "You are the best nonsense-monger I ever knew." The Reynolds portrait shows him to have been a handsome man at thirty-one, with a glint of humour in fine dark eyes and a full mouth ready to break into a good-natured smile in rebutting raillery with a waggish retort. He fancied himself as a wag, probably assuming the character defensively against criticism of his easy-going temperament by a family little given to disinterested affection—his brother John was a careerist as tough as their sister, Lady Melbourne, though the accident of sex denied him her success. Often he delighted Mary Noel by adding in his atrocious handwriting a humorous postscript to Judith's letters, sometimes taking the pen in the middle of a letter to comment facetiously on his wife's preoccupations or to suggest that their correspondent's elderly dignity was not deterring her enjoyment of fashionable frivolities. Much liked if too little considered, he was—as Gay said of Congreve—"a friendly, unreproachful man."

Judith's conduct reflected her happiness. During this first London visit after her marriage, her youngest sister Sophia was in town and wrote to their aunt on 7th March 1778:

> Mrs. Milbanke is grown quite wild with spirits & is not contented with being so herself but strives to make every body else so. I being *very* sober & prudent did not intend to go to the Masquerade last Monday but she absolutely made me by getting my dress entirely for me which was exactly the same as hers, we went in men's Dominos & were I assure you two very smart Beaus.

After such liveliness following her indisposition, Judith was ordered to Tunbridge Wells for the waters. As Milbanke had to return to his military duties in Yorkshire, she endured her first separation from her husband; on 27th April she informed her aunt that Milbanke was proving "a much more diligent Correspondent as a Husband, than he was as a Lover":

> Indeed nothing can exceed his goodness in every respect, & a falling Tear of tender Gratitude at this moment bears Testimony of the Sense I have of it; how small a time is elapsed since he left me! only a Week today! but sure the longest I ever past! but so will every one appear till we meet again.

Already she was planning that her being "in a *particular way*" should not coincide with her arrival in the north, "as that affair generally lasts me 6 or 7 Days." During her journey she wrote from Newark on 9th June:

> Oh! my dear Aunt, do you know I begin to suspect my Love for my Husband borders a little upon Romance for I cannot help pleasing my self with the Idea that I am nearer to him by 124 miles than I was this morning—fye, fye, to be romantic about a Husband is too bad, particularly when the Honeymoon has been expired a Year & half.

Milbanke had received his commission as lieutenant-colonel the previous February, and his wife was ingenuously proud of him in his new dignity, writing on 14th June after witnessing the regiment's entry into the town of Darlington:

> I wish you could have seen my Colonel marching at the head of his Men, in Sash, Gorget, & his Musket on his Shoulder; the Colours flying & Musick playing.

Meeting her sisters and brother in London had revived her interest in her family's affairs; indignant on hearing that Curzon, deep in debt from gambling, had urged the expenses of married life in excusing his embarrassment to his father, Judith commented to her aunt, "laying the blame on his Wife, when he must know she is not deserving of it is ungenerous—every man is not an *R.M.*" Thus far her happiness had only one alloy, as she told her aunt on 25th September 1778:

> Mrs. John Milbanke is brought to Bed of a Daughter & they have desired me to be God-Mother, which I have no objection to, but had rather leave out the first Syllable & be only the second & third, but that I fear I never shall be Heigh-ho!—but one must not expect *every* blessing & I have very many already.

She received a sharp reminder that maternity was no unmixed blessing under current conditions of medical science when her sister Elizabeth, after two miscarriages, died of a complicated childbirth on 21st January 1779. Her letters show Elizabeth Burges to have been a flighty, vital young woman, enjoying fashionable life in London and Bath while intelligently looking forward to helping her husband's political advancement. Her death afflicted the family so painfully that no correspondence was preserved during the following six months.

The summer of 1779 found Judith much concerned with her brother's affairs. In the previous December Wentworth had reported enthusiastically on a party at the Curzons' town house, where "Lady M. Fordyce & her Sister were the Syrens of the Night, & sang *à ravir*." Lady Margaret Fordyce's elder sister, Lady Anne Lindsay, was a woman of talent who—as Walter Scott revealed after her death in 1825—had written in her youth the celebrated ballad, *Auld Robin Gray*. Five years younger than Wentworth, she was still unmarried, apparently because her father, the fifth Earl of Balcarres, had died when she was only seventeen and left her inadequately dowered for her rank. Wentworth paid her attentions, and she was so attracted by him that, hearing his mistress was likely to inveigle him into marriage, she ignored the conventions and went down to Kirkby to interview Mrs. Vanloo. The consequent scandal reverberated in Yorkshire, and Judith wrote impetuously to her aunt on 27th June 1779:

> Whilst I have the least affection for my Brother I cannot hear without great concern of his exposing himself so dreadfully as he has done already and of the probability of his taking a Step that will be utter ruin to him and a great affliction to all the Family. Your intelligence was the greatest surprize to me, as from a Letter I received from Lady Anne the day before yesterday I was firmly persuaded Vanloo was discharged, but if he can be reconciled to her after being *beat* by her & her Maid & her assuming his Name to insult any Lady, I shall not be surprised if he very soon gives her an undoubted right to it, & it is for many years what I have so greatly feared that tho' it will be great grief to me it will not be an unexpected one . . . I answer'd Ldy Annes Letter, as she begg'd I would immediately

. . . as it was rather more favorable to herself I really concluded it was very likely he would marry her, not that I thought he wished it, but many concurring circumstances seemed to be drawing him into it: I never thought Ldy Anne a very eligible Woman, but imagined she was good temper'd, had rather a good heart & was much attached to him & tho' she would bring no fortune, would not by extravagance farther involve the small one he has left & I looked on her as the last resort to save him from the Snare he is I fear too certainly falling into; but her late conduct has been forward, foolish and unaccountable, but seems to me to have more of folly (or rather madness) than any thing else, as she must be totally unknowing not to discover that it must disgust beyond measure, & I am not surprized at his disliking *her:* but how he can endure the sight of that other horrid Wretch is astonishing & too well shews his infatuation . . . I doubt this affair has been too public not to be much talked of & I blush for the figure he will make in the Story. However inexcusable Ldy A—— might be for writing to him he did not act very honorably to let Vanloo have her letters & you (whatever she may think) have saved her Character from being utterly blasted by getting her Letters for her . . . as to myself I would give the World to restore my Brother to a Sense of honor & Virtue, but till that is the case shall not *seek* any Connection with him as I never can wish Mr. Milbanke such a Companion. Perhaps you may think I speak too harshly, but indeed I am excessively hurt at his conduct for which he has no excuse & nobody so severe on the folly of others as himself: tomorrow possibly I may think more coolly, but have been in great agitation ever since your Letter came . . . My Dearest Love is much hurt & thinks he certainly will marry her. Was all the world to take example by him what a good one it would be. If ever Man was formed without a fault it is him & my Dear Aunt reflect for your comfort on the happiness I enjoy in our little Cottage, which is a most lovely place & we are thank God! perfectly well & the days seem too short for all the amusements we have here.

She was minded "to write a *strong* Letter" to her brother—was exhorted by her sister Sophia to do so; that she did not was probably due to Milbanke's tactful dissuasion, though she would not admit her husband's interference in a family matter. By 5th July she was inclined more to sorrow than to anger:

As to my Brother it grieves me to say, I fear he has *already* suffered too much in the opinion of the World ever again to be looked on in an honorable or respectable light & there is but too great reason to dread his involving himself in still further Misery, for doubt he has but little chance of escaping the Clutches of that *Wretch*, who is destined to be his Ruin.

Her indignation returned two days later when she heard that Wentworth seemed unconscious of any reason for excitement:

My Brothers perfect unconcern about his conduct and situation is indeed astonishing. One should think he was totally devoid of feeling both for

> himself and others; I think I am decided to write to him, not that I hope any good effect *to him*, from my Letter, but I know when we meet again he will be as easy and familiar as if nothing had happened, which is what neither of us desire, and if he knows *my* opinion of his conduct . . . he will also know that an intimacy, till he changes it, will not be agreable, & to write will be better than to come to an explanation when we meet, but you shall have a Copy of whatever I write.

Fortunately she had many distractions. She had "sensible pleasure in dating from a House we can call our own," for after living in lodgings and visiting ever since her marriage, she had settled for the summer in what she called "a cottage" on the Milbanke estate at Seaham, then an unspoilt seaside village. She warned her aunt that Wentworth's crony, Major Bowater, was "a *Croaker*," and she needed "be in no Alarm about the French coming, for we are twenty miles from Newcastle & six from Sunderland, & should we discern a White Flag even thro' the Telescope, we will certainly decamp before it becomes visible to the naked Eye."

> I had an Idea that we should be quite retired here; & see no Soul, but I was quite mistaken, as we had Company every day last week, & most probably shall this, as every body within reach of a Dining visit comes to pay their *Devoirs* . . . The County in general seem very well affected to us & our coming here has caused much Speculation, & designs attributed to us for it, which we never thought of, till they were put in our head, viz: a design on the Town or County; I will tell you a great Secret, that should the present Members not be unanimously chosen again, or if by any means there should be vacancy, M—— will make a push to fill it, tho' not quite mad enough to stand a violent opposition, but if none happens he is determined to pay the market price for a Borough having a great inclination to be a Parliament man. He passed two entire days in looking into his affairs & had Hartley & all his Agents over here & a pretty tribe they were truly! But he had the satisfaction to find himself in a much more flourishing Situation than he had any idea of.

When they attended Durham races, Milbanke was appointed steward for the following year and opened the ball with "the beauteous Countess of Strathmore," while Judith was partnered by Sir John Eden, one of the two M.P.s for the county: "I was caressed & courted to the greatest degree and mio Marito was treated as a *great Man* by all partys." Arriving to stay with them at the end of July, the Curzons

> found the Milbankes dress'd out very fine & going to the Assize Ball though they had been two nights before at the Balls & had danc'd till four in the morning . . . They have been in a constant hurry for this 3 Weeks with the Races & company & the Assizes . . . My Sister never look'd better in all her life & seems to enjoy herself here vastly.

By the autumn Judith was so far mollified by her brother's imperturbability that, having received an invitation to visit him, she informed her aunt on 15th September, "we will take Kirkby in our road to London; but we shall not make any stay there, as he pushes the Bottle too much to make it comfortable." On 5th December Sophia Curzon reported: "I find that Vanloo is far from being in high favor which I am heartily glad to hear of . . . My Brother has *of himself* made Ly Anne a great many concessions on account of what happen'd last Summer, so now they are to meet on civil terms."

In the summer of 1780 Wentworth behaved so discreetly that, after meeting them at Tunbridge, he was invited to join the Milbankes at Scarborough in August, by which time Judith's attention was diverted to their sister Sophia, whom she considered to have behaved indiscreetly with a Mr. Gordon:

> altho' I am firmly persuaded it would have dropped of itself in a very short time, as I am sure she would never have permitted him to exceed the bounds of respect due to a married Woman, what made me rather uneasy was my knowing that the people she is a good deal with at present viz: Lady B[ridge]t Tollemache, the right honble: Scotch Sisters [Lady Anne Lindsay and Lady Margaret Fordyce] & Mr. H[ulse] would be the first to notice the least attention on either side & to buz it about with great exaggerations & I know they *had*, the Women on a levelling principle & the Gentleman out of pique from meeting with a very ungracious reception to his gallantry last year . . . I shall write to her by tomorrows Post, & mention the Subject in an ambiguous manner for fear of accidents as it is *possible* altho' *improbable* that the Letter might fall into Mr. C[urzon]'s hands & on such a Subject one cannot be too carefull . . . no Sister ever loved another better than I do her. I sometimes doubt whether it is returned with equal affection, but believe she has not that warmth of temper that I have, and I believe it is a happier thing to be without it, as God knows it often causes me uneasiness enough.

Eleven days later, on 19th July, Judith reported to their aunt Sophia's reaction to her interference:

> She is exceedingly offended at my mentioning the Affair to her & says "as She is neither fool or Child She shall give an account of her conduct to nobody but her Husband, & shall think those very impertinent who interfere with it & shall treat them as such," but if she knew how much it was observed she would think those who told her did her a kindness; however I shall pass over what she says of my interfering, as if one was always to quarrel when one had an opportunity one might be quarrelling with somebody or other every day in the Year.

Displeasure with her sister made her more disposed to sympathy with her brother by 23rd October:

> I am really very unhappy about my Brother, he looked very ill at Scarborough & my Sister says was far from well at Kirkby & that he was taking the Bark, but so much Wine with it that it was impossible it should be of any use to him. His Temper & Heart are by Nature so good and affectionate, that one must regret most deeply their being so far depraved by the Life he leads. I believe he took to Wine at first as a refuge from thinking, being dissatisfyed with his Situation tho' he wanted Resolution to quit it, & now drinking is become so habitual to him I fear he will never leave it off tho' he must be conscious he is ruining his constitution by it. I could not forbear giving him a little Sermon about it the other day; tho' almost certain it would have no effect.

Her concern inspired no eagerness for his company, as she wrote a fortnight later, "I have not heard from my Brother lately & hope he will not repeat his invitation for Xmas, as I am sure a drinking fortnight would make M—— very ill." After another week she was again in arms on hearing from Sophia, with whom Wentworth was staying in London,

> of an Extraordinary intrusion of Ldy Annes on a comfortable Quartetto at her House; her Ladyship is the most intrepid Woman I ever met with, it is said "*Faint heart* never won *fair Lady*," were Men of my mind *bold Woman* would never win *fair Lord*, but one does now & then see an attempt of that nature succeed, but then the Battery is in general masqued, not so open as Lady Annes. She told Mrs. Davison last Spring it was to my influence on my Brother that she attributed the change in his behaviour to her.

Wentworth ceased to be a bone of contention between his mistress and Lady Anne on 11th September 1781, when Mrs. Vanloo died suddenly, as he related to his aunt on the 13th:

> An express was brought me to Kirkby from Wootton late on Tuesday night to acquaint me Vanloo was dying. I set out immediately but did not arrive in time ever to see her more. This event so unexpected has shocked me much, it is allways painfull to part with an old acquaintance, particularly one with whom for many years I lived happily . . . With many failings I am convinced she has allways acted honestly & faithfully to me. The situation of her effects & her Will is a proof of it. My chief anxiety is about the poor Children, which are truly dear to me, & as fine ones as can be. However it never was or is my intention to do for them in such a manner as more legal Heirs to my Estate (if they have a spark of generosity) can grumble at. The Boy I shall educate well, & inculcate into him that his future livelihood must depend on some profession he may chuse. The little Girl is my greatest concern. She is of the most amiable disposition, but with so great sensibility that great care ought to be taken of her. Poor little soul she is allmost now broken hearted. With what her Mother has left her & a 1000 I settled on her, she will have £3000, this I shall by all

means keep secret from her . . . I wish I knew any proper person to put her to for tuition & care in the country . . . I wish you & the rest of the family to say as little to me on what is past as possible, *condolence* I do not desire, *congratulation* I shall not like . . . I have not wrote to any of the family but you. I wish you to hint some of my wishes in this to Mrs. M. & C.

His aunt responded immediately to the implied appeal by undertaking the upbringing of the eleven-year-old girl, Anna Catherine; the boy Tom, then aged six, was brought up by his father, who sent him to Rugby and Christ Church. Mary Noel also tactfully forwarded his letter to Judith, who took the hint to offer neither condolence nor congratulation, but warmly invited her brother to her home at Aycliffe Heads, near Durham.

The Milbankes had moved to Aycliffe in the summer of 1780. "Visiting is the business of the Mils life," remarked Sophia Curzon in October 1781, but the restless round of country houses required some return of hospitality. As Judith explained to her aunt, "Whilst Sir R—— lives, even was he willing to give it up, it is impossible we could afford to live in so large a House as Halnaby"; they were therefore considering enlargement of the "cottage" at Seaham before they moved to Aycliffe.

With an election pending, this move to the threshold of the city was doubtless dictated by Milbanke's parliamentary aspirations. On 5th September 1780 Judith was consequently furious on hearing that "that good for nothing John Milbanke is come down to Durham & intends Standing . . . acting totally against Sr Ralphs inclinations." Eight days later, on the 13th, she announced with satisfaction:

Mr. John Milbankes schemes have faild, he has exposed himself greatly, came down to Durham with his Wife & Child & no Gentleman or Lady took the smallest notice of them. Finding he had no chance on Saturday Even: he gave it up & quitted the place sufficiently mortified, which does not grieve *me* much.

Despite his prompt discomfiture, Judith never forgave her brother-in-law's attempt to forestall his elder brother; thereafter she permitted no pretence of fraternal relations and never mentioned John Milbanke and his wife without asperity.

At the time of Mrs. Vanloo's death the Milbankes were away on a month's tour of Scotland. The exertion of this tour, following the summer's usual energetic round of visiting, may have caused a second disappointment to Judith's hopes of maternity, for Sophia Curzon wrote on 17th January 1782:

I knew of my Sisters miscarriage sometime ago. If it was so she was monstrous Silly to go that tour; if she had been gone any time she could not have taken a Journey [free] from consequences; at least I know I was gone only three months & was forc'd to keep my Bed some days.

Sophia was then herself seriously ill. Already the mother of two children—a girl Sophy, born 11th February 1779, and a boy Natty, born 15th January 1781—she was pronounced pregnant again in September 1781. On 30th November her London doctor examined her,

& he almost confirms my suspicions which were that my child has been dead some time. He won't say that he is certain of it but that it is *most* probable. But he assures me that I shall continue very well till the time & then he says I shall be in no more danger than if the child was alive & shall recover afterwards faster than usual. I told him that if he apprehended I should be particularly ill I beg'd he would say so . . . but he said I had nothing to alarm me or fret me but the not having a live child.

When, a week later, she developed sickness and swellings, a second doctor[1] was called; the two together decided that she was not after all pregnant, but offered no further diagnosis and prescribed only the popular remedy for all ills, James's Powders. She wrote to her aunt from her bed on 8th January 1782:

If you was to see me you would not think my chief complaint lowness of spirits. I am indeed very, very ill & have undergone a vast deal & have *no* prospect of getting better. Consider a stoppage of now near 9 months, my body very hard & large, my legs swell'd exceedingly, no breath, *violent sharp* pains all about me but mostly in my breast & side—am oblig'd to be lifted up in Bed, hardly any sleep & very little appetite & my Bowels in so dreadful a state that I almost faint away myself at the smell of my Stools.

Her husband offered small sympathy:

As for Curzon he don't know what it is to be ill therefore he can't believe I am so bad or suffer so much as I really do. I am not angry with him as I am sure he loves me & would be really concern'd if he had the smallest idea of what I feel.

It was Wentworth who brought her most comfort, as she wrote on 1st March in the last letter of hers that has been preserved:

My Brother comes here very often & sits with me tete a tete both morning & even: sometimes he meets my friends of an even: I think it is very good natur'd of him as he comes to divert me & tells me the News of the day &c.

[1] This was Dr. Turton, who rose so high in his profession that he was one of the consultants who attended George III during his mental breakdown in 1804.

He continued to visit her regularly, though once "She cried & was so low when I talked to her, that I was obliged to stop ye conversation." He wrote frequent bulletins to Judith till she and their aunt arrived in town to take charge: "I hardly think there remain much hopes of her recovery," he wrote on 25th May. She was buried at Kedleston on 8th July 1782, aged only twenty-four.

Judith immediately adopted the three-year-old Sophy, writing to Lady Scarsdale of her sister's "dying Request to Mr. Curzon that he would permit me to have the care of Sophia, which he then complied with." By the time Lady Scarsdale received the letter, Judith was already posting to the north with her charge, writing to her aunt news of the child's behaviour on 10th July: "the first field of Wheat she saw she said what nice Grass it was, which proves her to be a Person of Observation." Thenceforth her letters to her aunt included always enthusiastic accounts of Sophy's charms and progress. At Scarborough on 27th August:

> I took Sophy a few nights since to the Rooms to see the dancing & she was quite delighted with it, particularly with *Uckle* Mils dancing—a Criterion of her Taste! She has a little playfellow in the House with her, Miss Pilkington, a Girl about five years old, they are now with me & making such a Noise I scarce know what I am writing.

Arriving at Kirkby from Sir John Eden's at Windlestone, she wrote on 18th November following:

> Our journey here was a very slow one for we were five days coming from Sr John Edens on Sophys account, so that we never came more than two or three Stages any one day, which Mr. Milbanke with his usual goodness complied with, with the greatest good humour, but he is very fond of Sophia and repeats her *bon mots* as if he was her Father.

When the child had "the Thrush . . . her Mouth being so dreadful sore that it was quite impossible for her to eat . . . I have made my heart ake several times with being obliged to exert a little authority to make her take her Medecines, which was a great pain to her, but it would have been a cruel kindness to have omitted to do it." It seemed that Judith could hardly have been fonder if the child had been her own. Nor did she for many years receive much contribution to the child's support from its father; leaving his son Natty with his own parents, Curzon was soon driven by his creditors to take refuge on the continent, where he remained in exile for more than twenty years till his father's death in 1804.

Bereavement drew the surviving sister closer to her brother. In the preceding January Judith had apparently wished her brother luck in his pursuit of Lord North for a post in the royal bedchamber, but hinted something she had heard of his pursuit of Lady Anne Lindsay, and Wentworth replied not without tartness on the 22nd:

> I thank you sincerely for your kind wishes for my success in the pursuit I sent you word of. I have heard nothing of it since I came back, indeed there is now no vacancy. As to the other pursuit you intimate I have not acquainted you of, your intelligence comes from people who know *better than the man himself*, consequently at least must be premature. When such a thing shd happen, I shall be sincerely sorry if I am not the first to apprize you of it.

Sadness over their sister brought a softer mood by 25th May:

> I am afraid, my Dear Sister, you have thought me unkind to you in not making a Confidante of you as to the terms I have long been on with Lady A.L. Uncertainty, & seeing things in a different kind of light at different periods has been ye reason, & besides I know ye absurdity of asking advice in those matters, when it is ten to one if it is followed afterwards. As the present state of affairs make us both see that our marrying would be next Door to Madness, & probably making us *both* miserable, for ever, it is unnecessary for me to let you know what has passed before. But this I must tell you, that I heartily repent I did not know my own mind sometime ago, for I am convinced that we should have been happy together, and that her attachment to me was & has allways been real & disinterested —of which I have the strongest proofs, & was it not for the conviction which prudence & reason give me, that misery to both must be the consequence, it would now not be *my* fault if I did not make her your Sister. We are now the best *friends*, & I have received the strongest marks of her friendship, ever since another sort of connection has been quite out of her view—& which would demand my most gratefull friendship, even had I not before both *loved* & *esteemed* her. When I tell you this I am sure you will bestow yours on her, I know she has been anxious to gain it, & I rather think (tho' I never heard her *say* so) that she thinks you have been rather cold to her advances.

On 6th June he thanked Judith for "your long & very affectionate letter, which I will not now answer as I hope so very soon to converse you on all the subjects of it in person." On 27th September following she graciously accepted his invitation to Kirkby, writing to her aunt, "I like visiting him too well to have any objection, *save one*, & he assures me now he only drinks like a *Gentleman* not like a *Lord*." The warmth and regularity of his letters show that he was well satisfied of his sister's affectionate goodwill, but if she pleased him by extending a semblance of friendship to Lady Anne, she maintained her hostility to a marriage between them. Worried that her brother seemed "much at a loss how to dispose of his time this Summer," she wrote to their aunt on 15th

July 1783, "I hope he won't marry Ldy A—— *pour passer le tems*, but I have lately been a little stagger'd about it."

Aware of her attitude, Wentworth never again confided as openly on the subject as at the time of their sister's death. When he wrote on 3rd January 1784, "I shall go for two days tomorrow to Yorke's, where the Lindsay family have been for sometime—before I came to town," the final clause was designed to allay suspicion that he was seeking Lady Anne's society. He was not always so guarded; Judith cannot have been pleased when he replied to an inquiry about some new acquaintances she had made in Yorkshire, "I asked Lady Anne about ye Durhams, she says they are honest good sort of people, tho' not of ye first water—& you need not be afraid of knowing them." By this time he had relieved his financial embarrassments by a mortgage on property inherited from his great-uncle Thomas Rowney, so Judith had reason to fear that Lady Anne's lack of money might seem a less potent deterrent. While a fellow-guest with her brother that summer at Kimbolton Castle, she wrote on 10th July:

> Lady Bridget [Tollemache] *roasts* him all day long about Lady Anne by *hints* he understands. Talking of Dress the other day my Brother said he loved plain, neat things. She very drolly expressed her surprize as she said she thought he admired a Gaudy, Shewy Stile of Dress. He understood her & his face was instantly Scarlet. I fear there is more between him & Lady Anne that I once suspected & I do fear it will be a Match at last & that under a pretence of giving him a time of probation about gambling, she is only keeping him in hand to try for a better Match which not being likely she should meet with, she will at last *condescend* to accept him.

Next day she wrote again to inform her aunt of a conversation with Wentworth, which she had begun by congratulating him on his illegitimate daughter Anna's being "a very good girl":

> I then went on to say I was sorry to find she had a bitter Enemy. He immediately said, you mean Ldy Anne. I told him I *did* & related the history of the Meuseum Gardens, which he owned he had been told & asked me how it was; I then gave *Miss Meynells* account of the Conversation that passed there between her & Ldy Bal[carres]—& I also told him Lady Annes behaviour to me at the Opera & also that *you* thought it better to say nothing to him, but that on consideration *I* had determined to do it. And as I find Lady Anne has told all these histories her own way, I own I am glad I did. I made no comments of any kind & Stuck to plain matter of facts. He appear'd greatly agitated & has looked distressed ever since. Indeed it would give me great concern for him to marry Ldy Anne—her Character *entre nous* being entirely gone & She is spoken of amongst Men as slightly as any Woman can, but unfortunately this my Brother never hears, as people would as soon abuse a mans wife before him, as Ldy Anne

before my Brother. Pray tell me in your next if he takes any notice to you.

Mary Noel's letters of these months are not preserved, but Judith further confided from Harrogate on 25th July:

> I believe he is bound by some promise or other, which keeps him in Lady Annes power and that *at times*, when he reflects seriously, that he is unhappy at it. I am sure he was quite miserable after what I said to him at Kimbolton. It is a pity he will not open his Eyes to her conduct, which is infamous. I wish to God he was married to any Woman on Earth so that he was out of her Clutches, for it is a sad thing to marry a Woman who has no reputation.

By 31st July she had persuaded her aunt to write in tactful protest to Wentworth:

> I *think* my Brother has too much honor to shew Lady Anne your letter. If he does *not*, no harm can arise from your writing it & very likely it may do good. But her Ladyship is the *devil in Scarlet* & we know by woeful experience how much my Brother may be duped and influenced by artful females. The more I consider it the more am I certain that he is strangely in her power, that the Yoke *galls* him, but that he is either unable or wants resolution to throw it off. If Lady Anne ever knows of the Step you have taken, you will experience some ill-humour from him, for which he will hate himself at the time—but I hope you will not be *silly* enough to let it *vex* you as it will be the consequence of your acting right & in a very short time he will repent & see things in a right light. His letter to you I think an indirect confession of Some connection with Lady Anne, but I do not think it a *Matrimonial* one.

Satisfied that for the present she had done all she could to frustrate Lady Anne's supposed designs, Judith devoted her energies to entertaining the friends of her girlhood, Di and Sukey Clerke. She was determined to make a match between Di Clerke and a respectful admirer of her own, the Rev. Christopher Wyvill, a middle-aged widower who was not merely a parson but squire of Constable Burton, near Bedale; only after causing embarrassment to both parties did she discover that Miss Clerke already had an "understanding" with a parson named Willes, who had to realise his expectations from an uncle before he could marry her.

If sensitive perception was not her strong suit, Judith possessed charm, which she capitalised as readily in the interests of husband and family as for her own pleasure. One summer at Scarborough she courted a wealthy old woman in her eightieth year, because she discovered her to be a cousin of Curzon's; with her niece Sophy in mind she reported, "the Old Lady & I parted such good friends that I do not despair of making her come down with something handsome before I leave Scarborough." She was a favourite with old Lord and Lady Ravensworth, and when Lord Ravensworth died in 1784, leaving his estates to his nephew, Sir Harry Liddell, she was soon on terms of friendship with Lady Liddell as intimate as with Mrs. Davison of Blakiston, the earliest close friend she had made on coming to Yorkshire. A good friend, she usually kept her friendships; though those with Mrs. Davison and Lady Liddell—as with Mrs. Chaloner of Guisborough, Lady Milner of Nun Appleton, and Lady Hildyard at Sedbury—were nourished by regular meetings in the same country houses, long intervals of absence did not deprive her of the affection of Millicent Acheson, a girlhood friend who had married Lord Gosford's heir. Much in love with an inconsiderate husband who frequently left her to fight his battles with his father—with whom he was on bad terms—even for the maintenance of herself and her children, Mrs. Acheson never forgot Judith's warm sympathy during her years of difficulty and always wrote to arrange a meeting when she crossed from Ireland for a visit to London.

Judith's charm did not depend entirely on personal attraction and gaiety of manner; she had the intelligence to equip her mind, so that her conversation was well-informed and entertaining. She was an early admirer of Sterne—"inimitable Sterne"; she considered Lord Kames's *Elements of Criticism* "amusing & instructive & I think lets one very much into the causes of ones own feelings"; she did not hesitate to explain her reasons for disliking de Sade's biography of Petrarch; of "Horace Walpoles Tragedy of the Misterious Mother" she declared "the language is fine & the Characters well drawn, but the plot is so *diabolical* that I think it can never please on the Stage." When Milbanke read Gibbon aloud to her during a winter's evenings, she resorted to Bishop Watson's *Apology for Christianity* as a corrective to the last two chapters of Gibbon's first volume. She had more tolerance than Dr. Johnson, who rudely refused to meet the Abbé Raynal because he would not shake hands with "an infidel"; after reading Raynal, she confided to her aunt:

> He is a most entertaining Author, as far as I am a Judge his Philosophy Politics & Morality are excellent, but had I my Religion yet to chuse (which thank God is not the case) it would puzzle one to adopt one from him as he seems to hold *tous les Cultes* equally cheap. People in reading or writing of the Atrocious Actions committed by *soi-disants* Christians, are apt to forget the Excellence of that Religion, which in bad hands has been made a Cloke for actions the most criminal, & when they consider a Hernando Cortes &c destroying Idols & exterminating Millions of their harmless but ignorant Worshipers under the spurious pretence of Zeal

> for Christianity, will not recollect that the Religion they so wrongfully profess is one that teaches humanity, charity & forbearance & forbids the love of Gain, the proposed end of all their Cruelty and Oppression. For had not America afforded Gold, its Temples might have remained unmolested without the Cross being erected on their Ruins & Multitudes of Slain.

The liberalism of some of her views was far in advance of her time; "the Executions are quite dreadful," she wrote after the Gordon Riots of 1780, "I wish they would give over hanging."

"As to your Politics I by no means accord to them," wrote her brother, who—though he abominated the French long before the Revolution, delighted in any discomfiture of "his Most Christian Majesty," and even expressed himself wryly about the policies of "Rex", as he called George III—was the most conservative of Tories, firm against all reform. Milbanke was naturally a Whig, since his sister, Lady Melbourne, was one of the most fashionable Whig hostesses, and his aunt by marriage, Lady Mary Milbanke, was a sister of the Whig Prime Minster, Lord Rockingham; after Rockingham's death in 1782, he attached himself to the left wing of the party led by Charles James Fox. Wentworth's letters show that his sister had fully absorbed her husband's politics and was accustomed to debating them freely with men; telling her aunt on 25th July 1784 that Milbanke "goes to York on friday to meet the *Foxites*, who hold a Club there," she added, "I shall go with him & dine with them."

Notoriously devoted to her husband, she could enjoy men's company without embarrassment to them or offence to their wives. In her determination to accompany her husband on all his pursuits, she acquired the rare feminine accomplishment of being a good shot; her reputed prowess was often doubted by men, including her brother, till they had seen her perform, and on one occasion Sir Harry Liddell

> in a fit of bravery offered a Wager that I should shoot more than them. Accordingly the Bet was made of a Guinea that I shot a brace in one morning. He escorted me himself & I got four Shots, killed three birds & wounded the fourth—& the Baronet was so delighted at winning that he was as happy as a King.

A skilled whist-player, as she liked playing for high stakes, she preferred playing with men; at Cheltenham in the summer of 1787 she related:

> I play at Whist every night, with George Damer, Mr. James & Mr. Colman & have won 7 or 8 Guis:—a Mr. Praed who is reckoned a famous player, came & stood over the table some time & told somebody afterwards I played the best of the four.

Normally she was too busy to be bored, but she wrote from Harrogate on 17th July 1784:

> Harrowgate consists of six large Public Houses, standing scattered on a bleak desolate looking common, & some few small Houses and Shops sprinkled amongst. Every House is now brim full of the most consummate vulgars I ever saw . . . Last night we had a Ball at our House to which the company from the other Houses came. I did not dance, but played three Rubbers at Shilling Whist. I had on one of the Spanish Hats, and I saw them *stare* as if I was an Angel from Heaven or Devil from Hell, but which they thought me I know not . . . Pity me for being in this Purgatory where I have no Woman I can talk Scandal with or Man that I can flirt with or party for Whist that will play more than Shillings.

Like most men of his time, Milbanke ate and drank too much, so was frequently ordered by his doctor to take the waters. "Bath is a wicked place & allows one no time to do what one ought to do," wrote Judith in 1779, and in later years avoided that resort, perhaps on account of its sad associations with her father and sister Elizabeth. She always enjoyed Cheltenham and Tunbridge, but when Milbanke was ordered a second visit to Harrogate in the summer of 1784, she preferred even a brief separation to a repetition of boredom. "Mil: goes tomorrow by himself to Harrowgate," she told her aunt on 19th August; "you will exclaim this is wonderful! So I think it & marvell at my resolution." She devised excuses: it would "save the *Argent*" and "give me time to attend to Sophy," and "should he want me I can be with him in four hours with ease . . . perhaps I may take a Cantor over for a day or so, which will cost nothing." Though admitting no stir of conscience, she ended her letter, "Mio Sposo is just going to Harrowgate and I am *very cross*, so believe I had better end here." Twelve days later: "I rode over to see him, stayed all night & returned yesterday evening . . . I live as happy as I can do when he is absent."

Concern with "the *Argent*" did not interfere with her pleasures. While his father lived, Milbanke's income derived from the Durham estates—including Chester-le-Street, Harraton, and Seaham—inherited from his mother, the co-heiress of John Hedworth of Harraton. Whenever there was ill news of the collieries, Judith had moments of compunction about expenses, as she wrote on 6th November 1780:

> I do not owe *one Letter*, would I could say as much in the *Bill* way! but *that* is a happiness I never expect & indeed have no right to from my abominable extravagance . . . why then not *mend?* I do intend to set about it & to shew you I have began would not buy a Winter nightgown tho' I have not one to my back. To be sure Milbanke to encourage me in my saving resolutions has presented me with one of ten shillings a yard, tho' I very modestly fixed on a Sattin of half the price, but as he took a fancy

to the rich one (which to be sure is beautiful) you know it was my *Duty* to *obey* him in having it.

When the collieries proved a "*total failure*" for two years and Milbanke borrowed £1000 on mortgage in January 1785 "to pay our Bills & make ourselves more comfortable," she resigned herself cheerfully to "remaining here quiet this year," though "I hope we may indulge the next without inconvenience," adding, "I only wish Mil: was as well satisfied with the Country as I am—but certainly Men have not half the resources to amuse themselves that we females have." Always watchful that her aunt should not be worried for money, she wrote on one occasion, "I hope you will not suffer yourself to be really distressed or uncomfortable for any trifle that may come within my ability to remedy, as tho' not very rich God knows! yet I trust it would be in my power to furnish you (at least for a time) with a little Cash." She and Milbanke frequently contrived means of delicately helping the old lady without compromising her independence.

After economy had confined them to the north in 1785, the promised indulgence the following year included not merely a London season but a continental trip to spend August and September at Spa. They travelled in the grand manner, the Milbankes with Sophy in a chaise, Lady Liddell and a friend named "Snug" Adams in a phaeton, and the servants in a coach. The most important visitors at Spa were one of George III's brothers, the Duke of Cumberland, and his Duchess, travelling as Earl and Countess of Dublin, and Judith exerted her charm so effectively that she reported after only a fortnight:

> I dance with the Duke of Cumberland every night, besides various other Princes, Counts &c. &c. His Royal Highness is so *very gracious*, that we see quite as much as we wish of him, as he takes his Breakfast here about three times a week *sans ceremonie* & sits for an hour or two after. We all supped at his House the other night & on tuesday next we give a Supper to them, at which we shall be about eighteen—this I look on as a bold stroke.

It turned out that "we were four & twenty" at the supper—"you would have been much amused to have heard the various Consultations we had about settling the Etiquette of who was to go out first & who was to hand who." Though "we go on here most gaily, Balls, Breakfasts, dinners & Suppers, *never ending still beginning*," Judith found time for tactful attentions to the Duchess when the Duke was laid up for three weeks with such "a very violent attack of the Family complaint" that his physician was sent for from London:

What time I could spare from our gay Party I have passed with the Dss, who says the handsomest things both of me & to me. I have dined several time with her quite in Famille, we did today & we do again tomorrow.

The Duke of Cumberland was one of the royal brothers whose marriages to commoners inspired George III's controversial Royal Marriages Act of 1772, having married in 1771 Anne Horton, a pretty young widow who had been born a Luttrell. The Duchess was about forty when the Milbankes met her—in the same year as Nathaniel Wraxall wrote of her in his memoirs:

Her personal charms fully justified the duke's passion. No woman of her time performed the honours of her own drawing-room with more affability, ease and dignity. The King held her in great alienation, because he believed that she lent herself to facilitate or to gratify the Prince of Wales' inclinations on some points beyond the limits of propriety.

If the Duchess of Cumberland was not of the inmost royal circle, Judith's charm prevailed equally with the King himself two years later. The Milbankes had taken Lord Fauconberg's house at Cheltenham in the summer of 1788 when they had to move into lesser lodgings to accommodate a visitation by the royal family; their concession to the royal convenience was graciously recognised, and returning from church on 3rd August, Judith "met the King & was detained near an hour by him."

Having received their Majesties commands to go to the Worcester Music Meeting . . . we intended to have *shirked* on the pretence of *no Lodging to be had*, but we were *nabbed* there, for the King had ordered one to be taken for us by his Factotum, so *go we must*. Nothing can to me be *more surprizing* than the very great attention & condescension shewn me by the King, Queen and Princesses. I am looked on *here* as a *Favorite*, & am imagined a *great Personage* by the *Cheltenhamites*. There is certainly nothing so precarious as the favor of Princes, therefore I do not suffer myself to be *elated* by it, tho' I must acknowledge nothing can be more flattering than the distinction paid me, which is to *me* & not to my *rank* as I have none to demand their attention—& also the handsome things said both *to me* & *of me*.

A week later:

The King sent us Tickets for all the Performances at Worcester & also paid our Lodgings—very gracious—& saved us sixteen Guins:—but I think the honor was more than the profit . . . I am just come from spending two hours with their Majesties—in a *quiet family* way. I can tell you I am quite a favorite—they all like me very much—especially the Princesses Augusta & Elizabeth who have each given me *keep*-sakes—& really without being biassed by their rank, I never met with more pleasing young Women—& the King is extremely chearful & her Majesty gracious & agreable. In short I never was in a more easy pleasant Sunday Circle & I *chatter'd* away, just as I should have done to *you & Anne*. You must allow the *Protection* shewn me is at least a Feather in a Cap—& something to boast of. I hope you tell all the *old Cats* of it, as being the *Aunt* of a *favorite* will give you Consequence with them. My *Aunt Rowney* looks on me as the greatest of all people & asked me the other day "Do ye now tell us what place you are to have. Jenny & I have been talking of it—can ye be Lady of the Bedchamber!!? Well to be sure you will have some great place, Do ye now tell us what it is to be?" I in vain assured them I expected & indeed could have nothing—they thought it was only *secresy* & that I would not tell them.

After a decade of married life her social success and security in domination of her husband developed arrogance in Judith. After the death of her uncle the Dean, she wasted little kindness on his widow; when that lady attracted a suitor who sought to ingratiate himself with her niece, Judith found him "so disgusting I can scarce be civil to him —tho' I hear he says vastly fine things of me." While she had cause for congratulation on the care of her niece Sophy, she grew increasingly self-confident in prescribing cures for ailments; she had wisely had Sophy inoculated against small pox, and when Curzon spent some time with them at Spa in 1786, she persuaded him to insist on his son Natty's being inoculated. Not unnaturally, being old enough to be Judith's mother, Lady Scarsdale resented the interference and wrote to ask her son if he wished her grandson "to be taken out of our hands & put into those of Mrs. M——." Receiving in this mood a letter in which Judith not only proposed when and where the boy's inoculation should be performed, but elaborating reasons from her superior knowledge why "inoculation is a thing so well understood at this period," the older lady bridled in a letter comprising a thousand words of outraged dignity. Judith replied even more sharply at the same length, and though each then proposed to "trouble" the other "with no more letters," both were stung into adding further fuel to the fire till silence followed the seventh letter. Judith preserved copies of her four letters with the originals of Lady Scarsdale's three; she had the last word, but the concluding paragraph of her last indicates a shrillness of vituperation unbecoming a younger woman to her dead sister's mother-in-law:

You accuse me of wishing to make a division between your Son & you —so far from it—that I most sincerely lament he does not experience from you any of the Sentiments of affection that ought to engage a Son to his Parents by the ties of Gratitude & Love.

She won her way some months later, as Lady Scarsdale was induced by her exiled son to make an approach to reconciliation through Judith's aunt, who tactfully contrived that Natty's inoculation was carried out under Judith's direction.

In the same year as her correspondence with Lady Scarsdale, Judith showed herself capable of the same arrogance in dealing with the opposite sex. At the general election of 1784 there was again no vacancy for Milbanke. Sir John Eden's colleague in representing the county of Durham was Sir Thomas Clavering, who—according to Judith—was "strongly urged" by Sir Harry Liddell to resign in Milbanke's favour, "but the old Fool swears he will (if opposed) stand the Poll to the last Man." Though confident that "my Sposo is the most popular Man both in Town & County," Judith informed her aunt that "Milbanke does not wish to disturb the Peace . . . but should Sr: Thomas be rejected as improper he is ready to step forward should the County honor him with their approbation." Sir Thomas retained his seat, but Milbanke was informed of a gentlemen's agreement among the local potentates that he should be put forward at the next election.

In January 1786 Sir Thomas Clavering intimated his readiness to resign, but immediately General Lambton, one of the members for the city of Durham, suggested his son as a candidate for the county, and Sir John Eden, as chairman of a public meeting, had to announce that young Lambton would offer himself as a candidate in the event of Clavering's resignation. "I am not at all amazed to hear the Bart: behaved like a Scrub," wrote Wentworth to Judith, who, conceiving that Sir John Eden's announcement amounted to a proposal of Lambton and a breach of his pledge to Milbanke, expressed her opinions so plainly that Eden wrote in indignant protest that he had made the announcement only in his capacity as chairman of the meeting. Without thought of leaving the matter to be settled by her husband, Judith on 15th January lost "not a moment to answer it as there seems at present some strange misunderstanding between us best ended one way or another without delay." Having related what she had heard of the circumstances in which young Lambton's candidature had been announced, she continued:

> I understood this (as surely every one must) as *your* naming Mr. L: and acknowledge it struck me as not consistent with a perfect Neutrality, and considering the friendship and intimacy in which we have lived for years it hurt me the more not expecting it. I certainly did mention these circumstances to more than one and as certainly did express warmly that I was hurt by it, but I never did assert in a general way that you proposed Mr: Lambton as a proper person nor that you voluntarily did it undesired by him.

If you as Chairman of the Meeting did it *officially* and would have done the same for any other Gentleman my reasons for feeling hurt at your Conduct fall to the Ground. If I have been misinformed of the matter of fact, I shall expect you will take the trouble to acquaint me how it really was & in that case hope you believe I have too much Candor not to acknowledge I have been *misinformed.*

You may observe I pass over the undue warmth of your Letter supposing your Expressions dictated by the first impulse of Anger & on that account allow for it. On revising the matter in my own mind I really feel clear of blame in this business and believe if you will give the above Statement a cool consideration you must acquit me too. On your answer depends the Terms on which we meet in future.

Sir Harry Liddell—whose wife was in close correspondence with Judith on the subject—held firmly to the gentleman's agreement that his interest was pledged to Milbanke, and when John Tempest proposed to vacate his seat for the city to stand against Lambton if he competed for the county, the Lambton candidature was withdrawn, Sir Thomas Clavering saving their faces by changing his mind about retiring. Apparently Sir John Eden expressed himself to Judith's satisfaction, for her intimacy with the Edens increased. When Ralph Milbanke eventually entered parliament as member for the county of Durham in 1790, his colleague was not Eden but another new member, Rowland Burdon.

Judith also triumphed eventually in her campaign to prevent her brother's marrying Lady Anne Lindsay. After her mischief-making at Kimbolton in the summer of 1784, her fears revived a year later when Lady Anne inherited a fortune on the death of Richard Atkinson, an M.P. and alderman of the city of London. "I was much surprized at the immense Legacy Atkinson has left Lady Anne," wrote Judith on 9th June 1785; "the Connection between her, Mr. Atkinson & my Brother formed the most mysterious Trio I ever heard of & I have ideas concerning it I do not chuse to commit to paper." On 1st July she felt she "must continue to wish the 35000£ may never come into *our* family as riches cannot neither purchase happiness or a good name—yet I have my *suspicions* that it will be so." She demanded of her brother an account of his intentions, but only the concluding sheet survives of a letter in which Wentworth evidently explained the terms of Atkinson's will:

I am persuaded the *ready* he left our friends will be forthcoming, & perhaps in time much more. I will freely tell you I was a little hurt at Lady A's not being explicit with me on this head, but I happen to know as much of it as she does, & I might have given her some useful hints . . . You will I am sure not divulge any part of what I have opened to you in this, except

> to Ralpho, for married Women should have no secrets from their Husbands, & his *discretion* I can depend on.

Apparently he satisfied Judith that he had no immediate intention of marrying Lady Anne, for his next letter of 19th August began,

> Your most affectionate letter which I received yesterday gave me the greatest pleasure as you approve of my Conduct & the motives which have actuated me on the subject of my last to you. As I shall see you so very soon I will not now again renew that topic.

Disliking trouble as much as he detested lawyers, Wentworth pursued an aimless and erratic existence that often irritated his aunt. "As for Ld W he is in a continual fit of Perplexity thinking of nothing," she wrote in one moment of exasperation; again, when she was seeing him regularly in London, "he looks ill, but that is no wonder as he is up all night, & in Bed half the day." But she was frequently touched by his affectionate kindness and his sense of duty to his family. After his uncle, the Dean of Salisbury, had died in his arms in June 1786, he undertook settlement of all his debts, and Judith herself wrote, "I loved my Brother very tenderly before but indeed my Dear Aunt his behaviour to my Uncle, to Mrs. Noel & to myself has been so exemplary good & kind that it has made me love him better than ever." His other uncle, the Rev. John Noel, fell into scrapes unbecoming his cloth, and when Mary Noel discovered that, unknown to the rest of the family, Wentworth had been helping him, she exclaimed to Judith, "he is so good, you must allow me to love him a *little* my dear Mil:, yet you need not be jealous, tho' I have not lately repeated the oft told but certain truth, that I love you better than myself, & a thousand times better than all the rest of the World."

Judith's fear of Lady Anne ended when Wentworth, in his forty-third year, married in February 1788 the widow of the second Earl Ligonier—a daughter of Lord Northington, a former Lord Chancellor, and younger sister of that Lady Bridget Tollemache who had "roasted" him about Lady Anne at Kimbolton. Except his sister's opposition, no reason appears why he did not marry Lady Anne after her windfall from Atkinson dispersed the prospect of poverty that had previously deterred him. He cannot have refrained from reluctance to relieve his own embarrassments with a wife's fortune, for Judith wrote on 21st December 1787, "I find Ldy Ligoniers fortune is greater than I supposed & feel assured that they may not only have a *Competence* but be in Affluent Circumstances—as surely my Brother will now entirely give up Play."

As Judith suspected, there was some "understanding" between her brother and Lady Anne, for Lady Ligonier wrote in an undated letter to Wentworth concluding with mention that she was writing to her sister to announce their engagement:

> I have waited with the most anxious expectation my dearest Friend the event of your negotiation with Lady Anne, and am happy to find it has terminated so much to her honor and Our mutual satisfaction. Can you doubt I look forward with equal anxiety to a Union I am assured will conduce to my happyness.

Judith did not withhold her friendship after Lady Anne married Andrew Barnard in 1793; when government service took her husband to the Cape of Good Hope, Lady Anne wrote long and affectionate letters which Judith preserved, and in her latter years she was regarded as such an old family friend that Judith's daughter confided to her some account of her married life with Byron.

Less than two years after his marriage Wentworth achieved his ambition in being appointed a Lord of the Bedchamber. In the same year of 1790 his daughter Anna Catherine—thenceforth known in the family as Kate—married Vincent Hilton Biscoe after Judith had made a clumsy attempt to involve her with Wentworth's rich friend Storer, the owner of Purley Park. Milbanke at last became one of the two members of Parliament for the county of Durham, after Judith had played a busy part in the election campaign. Of "a most successful Canvass" at Sunderland she wrote:

> think of me parading the Lanes & Alleys of a seafaring Town! ! ! shaking hands with the honest *Tars*, & saying civil things to their Wives & Daughters. I declare they are a very civilized Race of people & perfectly sensible of the deference due to a Lady.

In the midst of her triumphs Judith suffered a jar from her sister-in-law, Lady Melbourne. During the first years after her marriage Judith's references to her sister-in-law were few but amiable. On 29th October 1777 "Lady Melbourne was brought to Bed at seven months of Twin girls, one had been dead it is supposed some time, & the other dyed three days after its Birth; she herself is as well as can be expected." After staying "three days at Lord Melbournes" in January 1778, Judith remarked shrewdly, "As to Lady Melbourne the more I know her the more I like her & think her very much too good for her *Lord & Master*." After another visit to Brocket, on 12th September following, she found Lady Melbourne "very agreable en Famille; she is again with Child and I hope will be more carefull and have better Luck than she had last year."

At that time Lady Melbourne's only surviving child was her son Peniston, born eight years before. Evidently Judith had then no suspicion that Lady Melbourne's philosophy was that ascribed to Lady Besford in Georgiana Duchess of Devonshire's novel, *The Sylph*—that "you can do what you please once you have done your duty by your husband, but not till then." The son born to Lady Melbourne in March 1779 was William Lamb, who succeeded his nominal father as second Viscount Melbourne in 1828 and was Prime Minister at Queen Victoria's accession in 1837. Judith must have soon heard the rumour that the third Earl of Egremont was this child's father, for thereafter no mention of Lady Melbourne or of visits to Brocket appears in her letters. She could tattle cheerfully of scandal among her acquaintance, but her attitude to her brother's entanglements with Mrs. Vanloo and Lady Anne Lindsay, and to her sister Sophia's apparently harmless flirtation with Mr. Gordon, indicates her intolerance of laxity within her family. In view of her behaviour to Lady Anne, Wentworth doubtless felt satisfaction in reporting on 20th November 1783 that "Ld. Melbourne has got the Prince of Wales vacant bedchamber," and on 13th July 1784, "I enquired after Lady Melbourne today, she & your Neice are both as well as can be expected";[1] at this time Lady Melbourne was the dominant influence on the Prince of Wales, who was ten years her junior, and thus impressed the memoirist Wraxall: "A commanding figure exceeding the middle height, full of grace and dignity, an animated countenance, intelligent features, captivating manners and conversation; all these and many other attractions, enhanced by coquetry, met in Lady Melbourne."

For some years Judith's hostility towards an adversary so formidable was limited to avoidance of her society, but on his election to Parliament Milbanke presumably found impossible such avoidance of a leading Whig hostess and wrote to complain of his sister's coolness. Lady Melbourne replied from Brocket Hall on 20th March 1791:

> My Dr. Brother
>
> I have not answered yr last Letter sooner because I was in hopes that by giving you a little more time to consider, you would find out that neither you or Mrs. Milbanke can have ye least reason for being out of humour with me as differing in opinion only can not justify either side for being so—& I only write now that you may fully understand that I am determined not to dispute or quarrel with either of you about any thing that has past, as I should think myself extremely absurd if I did—& as I know that there has been no Coldness on my part or the most distant intention to show either of you any Slight I feel that I am just as good

[1] Apparently Wentworth was misinformed about the sex of Lady Melbourne's child; her fourth son George was born on 11th July 1784 (*In Whig Society*, by Mabell Countess of Airlie, 1921), and according to Lord David Cecil (*The Young Melbourne*, 1939), was "universally supposed" to be the Prince of Wales's son.

friends with both of you as I ever have been & if you are not the same it is not my fault.

I am yr most affecte. Sister

E. MELBOURNE

Judith's rejoinder ignored the example of brevity, extending to more than a thousand words, of which she preserved a copy. After explaining how "Milbanke introduced the Subject on which he wrote by saying he was sorry to have observed *a coolness* between You and me," she went on:

As You might *imagine* I continued ignorant of the groundless suspicions which were entertained in regard to my conduct, and I readily allow nothing in your outward manner to me gave room for the Assertion. But your disapprobation of things you have *supposed* or been *informed* I was capable of has been too frequently expressed and too strongly marked for it not from *various quarters* to have come round to my knowledge . . . had You under these impressions taxed me openly and upbraided me ever so warmly, it could not have hurt me like the insinuations you have dropped to *others* . . . whilst to my face you observed the appearance of civility if not even friendship. To a mind of the least sensibility it became almost impossible to acquiesce in Silence to such conduct, I acknowledge my temper is too warm and my heart too sincere, to submit to it, being extremely hurt by it, being conscious I have never deserved to incur such suspicions or merit such treatment. In the common intercourse of the World it is idle and foolish to regard what is said by people indifferent to one, but with my Husbands family, especially with a Sister he loves, it becomes more interesting & I have longed for nothing more ardently than to come to an explanation with you regarding certain points in which I could have convinced you . . . You say You cannot even guess at any reasons I may have for coldness on my Side—do you think it *none* to be perpetually hinted at as wishing to deter Milbanke from doing what is right? *none* as being the Person who advises measures that You deem unjust? *none* as supposing it necessary to exclude me from every consultation to induce Milbanke to do what is kind by his family? Ask your own heart whether You should not be wounded by such insinuations in regard to yourself from any of Lord Melbournes family or friends . . . I have suppressed resentment on various occasions which would fully have justified me shewing it, but it has been the Interest of *some* to deceive you . . . ever since I married it has been my sincere wish to conciliate the good opinion of Mr. Milbanke's family & perhaps to that wish I have sacrificed too much. I have every reason to believe these endeavours have not met with the Success permit me say they meritted. Nothing however shall deter me from persevering in what I deem just & right and if I meet with no other return the consciousness of doing so must be my reward. No other return have I *yet* met with.

I must now request of You that if You either believe or have been informed of any thing that appears to you reprehensible in my Conduct in regard to any family transaction that You will fairly and openly avow it . . . After a forbearance of some Years under Circumstances I cannot but think injurious you may wonder at my coming forwards in this open manner but there is a point in every thing which turns the Scale . . . I need hardly say it will give me the truest pleasure to find *myself mistaken* in regard to your Ideas about me, because it is very unpleasant to be thought so unjustly of.

Lady Melbourne was not drawn, like Lady Scarsdale, into an exchange of recrimination. No reply from her is preserved. She may have replied briefly to her brother, who tactfully suppressed the letter, for she held firmly to her resolution to remain "just as good friends with both of you as I ever have been"—meaning an appearance of cordiality with prudent avoidance of any approach to intimacy. Till his death in 1800 she remained always sympathetic towards her younger brother John, with whom Judith was never reconciled after his abortive attempt to forestall Milbanke's parliamentary ambition in 1780. After more than another twenty years of such "coolness" it was not surprising that Lord Byron received from Lady Melbourne an unfavourable impression of her sister-in-law.

"Today we dine at Ld Melbournes and go to Vauxhall, where I never was but once in my life and that sixteen years ago," wrote Judith on 18th July 1791. She was then in London for a brief visit between a stay at Cheltenham and returning north for the usual festivities at Durham assizes. With more important preoccupations intervening, she was well disposed to meet Lady Melbourne on her own terms.

From Aycliffe Heads in the autumn of 1783 the Milbankes had moved to a larger house at Richmond, just over the Yorkshire border, but Milbanke's election to Parliament made desirable their residence within the county of Durham. The "cottage" at Seaham had been their first home, both Milbanke and Judith enjoyed sea-bathing, and Sophy's health always flourished there, so they decided to build a house at Seaham—according, of course, to Judith's design, as described on 21st August 1791:

We shall have a Parlor 31 by 19–6 inches—a Drawing Room of the same size—the Staircase uncommonly pretty—a Study for Milbanke 21 by 16—a small Room beyond to dress in—a very good bed-room for ourselves, with a small dressing Room out of it for me—a *large* Butlers pantry and over it a Bed-room for Sophy, which with a large light Closet for my Clothes and a Water Closet forms our own end of the House, which has also the advantage of a back Staircase. The other end consists of a Bed Room, dressing Room and small bed room beyond it—below, and the the same over it. All these Rooms (except Sophy's and the Pantry) to the Front—no Garrets. Then behind on one Side will be a Servants hall, Housekeepers Room, Kitchen, Back-Kitchen and Larder wet & dry, with

> Rooms over for Servants. These included in a Court Yard; on the opposite side of which will be Wash House and Laundry, Cellar for Coals, Ashes &c. with Servants Rooms over, the whole Court Yard to shut up with Gates, so that we shall see nothing of the Offices. The Building is all of rough Stone, but is to be Stuccoed and there is a hewn real Stone Base, and Stone Band under the Windows. The Stables are built before and stand quite away from the House. All the miserable Cottages you remember are removed, and the road turned, and the Green before the House will be made quite level & the Garden go quite down the Dean you may recollect was in front of the House, with a small brook in the Botton. We mean to plant Poplars, Limes & Firs to conceal the Court Yard in front and all together it will really be a pretty Spot. Our Builder undertakes it by *Contract* & you will be surprised to hear all this *Magnificence* is for 1100£, except painting and Papering.

The building was "entirely covered in" by the end of September, but on 12th October Judith's aunt received news which "agitates me very much but surprizes me very little for you may recollect that *I* too prophesied when at Cheltenham & the reason I gave you was that both your health & Mr Ms were so much alter'd for the better that I should not be surprized if such an event should take place." Convinced that Judith's symptoms indicated pregnancy—"as for change of life I cannot think it is that for you are but forty next birthday & I believe it never leaves any body so soon unless occasion'd by Illness or fright—the Common notion is that it never stays less than thirty years & I think you were sixteen at least when it began"—she was concerned lest the childless Lady Wentworth, with whom she was then staying, should hear of it before Judith's condition was certain:

> you may be very sure I shall not tell it to any Soul as I sd be very sorry that even a hint of it sd arrive here untill it was past all doubt & that you had felt the little fellow kick for I believe the great Ldy notwithstanding her violent declarations of not wishing for a child wd be very envious & not sorry to make a very good joke of it if it was not so.

She warned Judith "not to ride on horseback," but "to use moderate exercise & live as near as you can in your usual way for if you are with child I dare venture my life you will not miscarry without some uncommon accident & as you are accustom'd to so active a life I fear you will be ill if you are too sedentary."

Every week or ten days came letters from the old lady, apologising for boring Judith with her "silly fancies", relating the devices by which she prevented Wentworth's seeing Judith's letters, as he always inquired on seeing her handwriting, repeating her admonitions and inquiries—"pray let me hear immediately of the first *Kick* for which I would submit to be kick'd downstairs." The news came to Lady Wentworth on 26th November from Wentworth's daughter Mrs. Biscoe, who had it from Mrs. Bland,[1] as Mary Noel related:

> As for your Brother he said, with that look one has when one dares not believe a thing one wishes, that he did not believe it, upon which I hinted my hopes, as the News came from Mrs. Bland, who must have her intelligence from Mrs. Baker, who is your particular friend & near Neighbor, & one from whom you keep no Secrets, upon which he express'd himself in the most friendly & affectionate manner, but Ly. W was not present, being gone up Stairs to tell her Maid, who immediately told mine, to whom to say the truth it was no secret, but she was too well tutor'd to betray me, & acted the astonishment & joy to the life.

On hearing from Judith, Wentworth wrote his congratulations to Ralph Milbanke on 30th November: "I shall certainly consult you as a most Skillfull & powerfull Physician, & if you recommend Cheltenham shall certainly try the Efficacy of those Waters."

As the new house at Seaham could not be ready for Judith's confinement, it was debated in December whether she should go to her aunt in London, but preferring to run no risk from travelling or from changing the routine of her country life, she welcomed an invitation from Mrs. Baker to stay with her at Elemore Hall, near Durham, while Milbanke went to London for the parliamentary session, taking Sophy with him to stay with Mary Noel. Though a kinsman of Milbanke's on his mother's side, George Baker had played no very friendly part in the dispute about Sir Thomas Clavering's parliamentary successor in 1786, threatening himself to stand against Lambton, but by 1789 he was associated with Sir Harry Liddell as foremost among Milbanke's supporters, and Judith recorded herself "quite charmed with Mrs. G. Baker," who "is one of the pleasantest women I ever met with & they seem so truly happy it gives one pleasure to see them—she seems as much pleased with me as I am with her & I think we shall be great friends." Wentworth wrote in January 1792, "I am quite in Love with your friend Mrs. Baker for her friendly attachment to you," and announced a month later, "Your Royal friend the Duchess of C. told me She was ready to answer for Godmother if wanted."

Since he could not have expected that Cheltenham or other waters would induce fertility in Lady Wentworth, who had failed in her youth to perpetuate the Ligonier earldom, Wentworth hoped for a male heir

[1] Mrs. Bland, as Mrs. Davison, had been the earliest of Judith's close friends among her neighbours in Durham and the North Riding. She was Jane, one of the three daughters of Godfrey Meynell, and married in 1776 Thomas Davison (1744–94) of Blakiston, who assumed the additional surname of Bland in 1786 on inheriting the estate of Kippax Park from his cousin, sister of Sir Hungerford Bland, last baronet of that name. Their son, Thomas Davison Bland, of Kippax Park, was one of the trustees of Lady Byron's marriage settlement.

from his favourite sister. "Altho' you say you will be as well pleased with a Girl," he told her, "I cannot in this respect pay a Compliment to the Sex at the expence of my veracity." He was the first with congratulations on the birth of "the little Lassie" at Elemore Hall on 17th May 1792.[1] Already referred to as Annabella in June by both her cousin Sophy and her uncle Wentworth, the child was baptised at Seaham on 10th August with the names Anne Isabella—Anne for her godmother the Duchess of Cumberland, Isabella for Mrs. George Baker.

[1] "Seaham.
Anne Isabella daughter of Ralph Milbanke esq. (son of Sir Ralph Milbanke of Halnaby) and Judith his wife (daughter of Lord Viscount Wentworth) was born at Elemore Hall May 17th 1792 and publicly baptized at Seaham Aug. 10th by me.
Richard Wallis, Rector."
Produced as a "correct Copy" of the entry in the register in the Wentworth Peerage Case before the House of Lords, 1863–4.

2

THE SPOILT CHILD

1792—1810

An only child born to a woman of forty after fifteen years of married life was likely to be spoiled. Those who had witnessed Judith's extravagant fondness for her niece Sophy must have been prepared for her absorption in maternity. Annabella's inoculation in October 1792 provided an excuse for not leaving Seaham before Christmas. In the new year Wentworth regretfully acknowledged Judith's further excuses for not accompanying Milbanke to London, but her old friend Lady Gosford[1] ventured a protest from Dublin on 4th February:

> I feel sorry you dont go to London. I can not bear your giving up the world which I think you in a straight road to do. I think you have greater inducements than ever to mix with it, the Education of your little babe is concerned in it, if once you quit it you will not be equal to the task of taking it up again, & the time will imperceptibly steal upon you when the consequence will be great to your Anna Bella. Neither do our children like us so well when always at our chimney corner, our minds contract, we are always plotting their substantial good as we then think it, whereas there are many points not judg'd *substantial* that I am convinced are of much importance. I could write a quire on this subject, but you are much more capable of judging the matter than I can be, provided you suffer yourself to argue the Subject fairly without allowing yourself to lean to your love of living every hour with your child.

In April her aunt—who had been staying with Judith since Annabella's birth—became so seriously ill that her life was despaired of. The tough old lady recovered in May, but attending her convalescence prevented Judith's accompanying Milbanke to Cheltenham, and her first absence from Annabella was in visiting Lady Liddell at Ravensworth in July 1793. "Dear Mrs. Baker . . . stayed here the whole time I have been absent which made me very happy as I was assured of her care," but this did not prevent the servants' conveying to Annabella "the *Itch*." Judith found all the servants "extremely culpable" for

[1] Millicent Acheson's husband succeeded as second Viscount Gosford on his father's death in 1790. He was created Earl of Gosford in 1806 and died in 1807, being succeeded by his elder son. His widow survived till 1825.

keeping "it a Secret when by disclosing it the mischief might have been prevented," but she was especially annoyed with her personal maid Clermont "because she was *Saucy* & when I returned from Durham, she would insist upon it that it was not the *Itch*, tho' both Eden & Doctor Brown said positively it was." When Clermont expressed contrition "from knowing herself wrong & my being angry," Judith vainly sought to fasten the blame on another of the servants:

> They have done nothing but quarrell amongst themselves from morning till night & the House has been an Eternal Scene of confusion ever since & we are forced to get our Beds made & our Rooms swept as we can & I must be at the expense & trouble of having every blanket scoured—besides the ridiculous Story it will make in the Country.

The storm quickly abated when, after her spots had been treated with brimstone, Annabella was found to be "perfectly well & now the weather is cooler has more Rosy Cheeks than ever."

Feeling disinclined again to trust the servants, Judith took Annabella with her on an autumn tour of visits. Fourteen years before, her sister Sophia had found "many inconveniences attending travelling with a Child & having them in other people's houses," but no such inconveniences troubled Judith, who wrote from Boroughbridge on her way to Kippax Park on 31st August:

> Annabella is the best traveller that ever was & as jolly as possible all the way in the Coach, except when asleep & she takes her nap as comfortably as if in her Crib—which by the by I have brought with me & had it set up for her last night, but what with the Crib & other matters, I find the Coach is compleatly filled, so that Milbanke brings the Chaise.

The stay at Kippax was not "*so gay* as I expected, for poor Mrs. Bland miscarried the day after I arrived . . . attended with dreadful Floodings." Moreover, "Sophy has had a rash which was preceded by a good deal of Fever, and as Augusta Bland was ill of the same complaint I was apprehensive that it might be *infectious*, so I sent Annabella with Nurse to the Inn at Ferrybridge, where I have seen her every day and she is perfectly well, indeed I think improved in her looks by the change of air." At the inn "I saw the Archbishop of Canterbury and Mrs. Moore and she admired Annabella *very much*."

Silence followed during three weeks at Kirkby in the company of both her aunt and her brother before Judith resumed her tale on 12th October from Lord Fitzwilliam's at Wentworth, where the heir, Lord Milton, then aged seven, "quite *doated* on Annabella, I wish he may do the same sixteen years hence"—he "saw Miss *naked*, therefore he can tell whether he will like her or no."

> They insisted on *Miss* coming down to the Desert every day, indeed Lady Fitzwilliam would have her almost constantly in the Room with us & I assure you Annabella behaved herself very well and we all agreed she ought to be Lady Milton.

After Wentworth followed a week with Sir William and Lady Milner at Nun Appleton and nine days with Sir Robert and Lady Hildyard at Sedbury, where "it was almost ridiculous how all the Country flocked in to see Annabella as if she had been something miraculous."

Back at Seaham at the end of October, Judith was soon devising excuses for refusing to leave home and Annabella:

> She has again got fatter and indeed has been perfectly well ever since her return, and I am convinced this air agrees better with her than any other & that travelling does not *entirely* agree with her.

In December, "Annabella keeps her good looks and gets a new word every day and calls *Mama* whenever she wants any thing and you may be pretty sure she gets it." By 2nd March 1794:

> She can say every thing, is grown very fat & very tall at the same time. She has just had her Sunday dinner of *Roast Beef* & I am sure eats more at one Meal than Bell Baker does in three or four. I think she has an Eye-tooth now coming, as her Cheeks were hot last night and she cryed a little. She is extreamly altered since you saw her—her Features are more formed and expressive & when she *frowns* she is the Image of *Milbanke*—when she *smiles* she is like *me*. Mr. Lambton (who has often seen her) always quotes *her* as the finest Child *he ever saw*—this I have been told by several people & he has said to those who he could have no Idea I should hear it from again.

Unfortunately too many friends recognised that Judith's estimation of themselves might be measured according to their praise of Annabella: "Lord & Lady Fauconberg sounded her praises at Newcastle after their visit here *most nobly* & her Ladyship, who loves some Relations of Mils *almost* as well as you do, says she shall have great pleasure in informing *them* how fine a Child she is."

Announcing that she would not be accompanying Milbanke to London after Easter and "my going to Town next Winter . . . will depend on Circumstances and my inclination at the time," Judith found it necessary on 21st March to defend her new domestic habits to her aunt as already to Lady Gosford:

> You must recollect that many things endear Annabella to me in a particular manner, her being given me so late in life, when I had ceased to hope for such a Blessing & her being an *only one.* The first Spirits of Youth have also subsided, which makes the gayeties of life a less tempta-

tion, & I can truly assert I had never so good health & Spirits as since Annabella's Birth & that I lived here—and now every day she gets more amusing . . . but do not imagine I am going to turn *Misanthrope.* I like to see my Acquaintance & can enjoy Society—but *quiet* Amusements are now most to my Taste.

A month later, on 20th April, after the usual praise of Annabella's progress, she admitted:

She gets very Saucy & is *Governess in Chief* of Papa, Mama & the Whole Family & does not seem inclined to give up her Authority. As to me she makes me her *humble Slave* & fags me well. It is her Royal Will & pleasure that I should lug her about half the day, and she gets so heavy that it is all I can do to carry her. She says every thing & speaks remarkably plain.

Fortunately for Judith, besides sharing her devotion to Annabella, Milbanke had a faithful heart, or trouble might have ensued from the contrast of her present conduct with her habit for fifteen years of accompanying him everywhere, always tireless in pursuit of pleasure. Conscientious in his parliamentary duties, he continually lamented having been induced to serve on another "damned Committee." He was an enthusiastic theatregoer, but his favourite actresses were Mrs. Jordan, who was the property of the Duke of Clarence, and Mrs. Siddons, whose virtue was impregnable and who was favoured with Judith's friendship. Moreover, when he went to London without Judith, he let their town house and lodged with her aunt.

From the time of Judith's pregnancy, he found increasing pleasure in the company of their niece Sophy, at fifteen an attractive girl of precocious tact and charm. Returning from a visit of duty to her friend Mrs. Bland, Judith found "Sophy & her Uncle have been very happy together during my absence, eating Supper & drinking Negus every night & ten thousand indulgences I do not allow when I am at home."

Judith's doating on Annabella did not detract from her fondness for her niece. During their stay with the Hildyards at Sedbury in October 1793, "there was an Assembly at Richmond which I was so entreated to let Sophy go to that I could not refuse."

She danced without ceasing, from nine at night till half past one in the morning . . . & had all the best Partners, being admired enough to turn her little head. She was extremely well dressed . . . and when she got a Colour and was animated with *dancing* and *delight*, looked *beautiful*. You may imagine how happy she was, playing the Woman, amongst those who remembered her only as a meer Child. I have watched her more narrowly than she suspects during our round of visits and am happy to observe that she is neither awkwardly shy nor pertly forward, and the large & mixed Companies we have been in, has been a good Trial of her *manners*.

Sophy's confidence in her relationship with her aunt appears in a letter of 26th May 1794 to Judith at Seaham while she was in London with Milbanke:

> I call'd today upon Lady Liddell from whom I have a long *string of messages* for *you* . . . In the first place she receiv'd your letter telling her that she was *a bad Woman* and *no Christian*, now this she desires to tell you is a great *L*, as she continues to vaunt Annabella's praises as she deserves *but* she does not *ever deny* that if it is possible to spoil a very fine Girl, *Annabella's Mama is determined to do it.*

As Judith's contemporary, the mother of five children, and a close friend of ten years' standing, Lady Liddell felt herself in a position to speak her mind thus plainly. But Judith resented the criticism; Sir Harry Liddell having died untimely of hard living in 1791, there was no longer the influence of his generous good-nature to over-ride differences, and on 14th June Judith was already venting her spleen:

> When I tell you that Lady Liddell, after Spunging her two Daughters and their two Maids on Mrs. Baker, has refused to discharge a Bill of six Guineas for her in London, you will not wonder at any thing else she does. I have long seen she is afraid we should *Steal* Sir Thomas, but she need not *Alarm herself*, for tho' he is a very goodhumored well disposed Young Man, my Sophie shall have some body more polished and Clever than him.[1]

Sophy now went frequently unaccompanied to stay with Judith's friends. After a visit to Nun Appleton in March 1794 Lady Milner spoke "in a very high stile of Sophy", who became a close friend of Lady Milner's "lovely Daughter" Diana, afterwards the wife of Francis Hastings Doyle, who played a leading part in the burning of Byron's memoirs. While Judith's friendship with Lady Liddell precariously survived the criticism of her spoiling of Annabella, Sophy continued to visit Ravensworth Castle, and in the summer of 1795 she was accompanied by her illegitimate cousin, Tom Noel, who had been proudly described by his father as "grown a *devilish handsome strapping fellow*" during his last half-year at Rugby. His looks had since been praised by both Judith and her aunt, and now completing his third year at Christ Church, he was as susceptible as handsome. Lady Liddell's eldest daughter Bessy had in the previous year suffered a frustrated romance with a Mr. Cogan, which was "entirely off on account of his bad Character—at all Events it would be a wretched bad Match for

[1] Lady Liddell's eldest son, Sir Thomas Henry Liddell (1775–1855), succeeded his father as sixth baronet in 1791 and was created Lord Ravensworth in 1821. He married in 1796 Maria Susannah, daughter of John Simpson of Bradley, who had eight sons and eight daughters. This lady, accidentally encountering Lord Byron on the roof of St. Peter's at Rome in 1817, ordered her eldest daughter (afterwards Marchioness of Normanby) to keep her eyes down, saying, "Don't look at him, he is dangerous to look at".

her." She now fell in love with Tom Noel, who readily responded; apprised of the situation by Judith, Lord Wentworth lost "not a single Post" before pointing out that "it will be impossible for them on their income ever to live up to the Ideas of life which she must have of necessity imbibed, & as most likely a total breach with her family would be ye consequence of her marriage with him, her Life could never be an happy one." A long letter was kindly considerate and reasonable:

> Nothing could make me happier than seeing Tom so very respectably settled & his forming so enviable a connection, but surely I could wish that no Step might be taken without giving time & *particularly to the Lady to reflect* on future consequences.

Presumably Miss Liddell considered that, as Lord Wentworth had no legitimate heir, he might be expected to provide handsomely for his only illegitimate son, for, writing again ten days later, Wentworth thought she should be warned "she is doing for herself an imprudent thing" and "if *she objects* to the Line I have marked out for him she is most unwise in so doing—a Character of Life in some profession is more essential to him than to almost any one—from various circumstances it is now too late, nay utterly impossible, for him to pursue any other with any hopes of either profit or comfort to himself."

Wentworth had not in fact fulfilled his sister's hope that he would "entirely give up Play" on his marriage; on the contrary, Lady Wentworth liked the faro table herself, and Judith discovered in July 1791 that her brother had lost "in one night seven hundred Guineas . . . in all during the Winter £2000." His Rowney inheritance, out of which he eventually provided for his two children, was heavily mortgaged, and he could have done nothing immediately for his son without drawing upon his wife's money—as he explained to Judith, "it would be most wrong in me if I, by adding to *imprudences* I cannot defend, further straightened or embarassed the most liberal & the best of Women My Dearest Mary."

Unluckily Judith as intermediary could not explain her brother's embarrassments, and she was likely to have been more eloquent than tactful; perhaps Lady Liddell expressed a suspicion that Judith was more concerned with cherishing Annabella's prospects of inheritance from her uncle than with doing her best for Tom Noel. The disappointed lover withdrew to Kirkby, where two months later (18th October 1795) his father "very soon . . . discovered his vanity was the only part much hurt by his dismission"; in the following May came the news that "Tom has Stole a Match with Kitty Smith" and "must lie in the bed he has made for himself." The breach between Judith and Lady

Liddell endured for two years, Judith informing her aunt on 16th July 1797:

After what you remember to have passed, it seems *somewhat odd* that Lady Liddell & us should have been together a month, with the exception of three or four days. We first met them at Ravensworth, then at Sir Henry Vanes & they returned here with us, where they have taken up their abode very contentedly since last friday was se'nnight, but they go tomorrow, very well pleased with their visit.

Tho' I certainly thought her very wrong two Years ago, yet *You know* & have often said that my temper is not *very irascible* & I cannot forget Old days, therefore on the Whole feel rather glad that we are again on terms of civility at least. Miss Liddell is not improved in looks or manner, but is out of Spirits & very much out of health.

Neither Lady Liddell's admonitions nor Lady Gosford's deterred Judith from her spoiling of Annabella, of whose progress she wrote regular bulletins to her aunt, as on 22nd June 1794:

In spite of an Enormous Bonnet She is *Sadly tanned*, but so much as She is out in the Sun & Wind it is impossible to prevent it. *I* think She looks much prettier without her Cap, but some people think not . . . She eats Meat of all kinds *but Veal* with different Sorts of Vegetables & fruit when She can get it, which She often does, as Mr. Baker has no greater pleasure than furnishing her from his Hot-house & this day Sent a Cart Load of Grapes, with three Dozen fine Peaches & Nectarines. She never misses having a *Do Do* as soon as She is up, and hardly ever more . . . She can tell twenty different Flowers & Weeds by name. If You shew her Honeysuckle, Cowslips, Daiseys, Plaintain . . . She can tell them all . . . Asparagus, She calls *Taileys* . . . She tells such long Storys & so eagerly!

In May 1795 Judith accompanied her husband to London:

I never wished any thing so earnestly as to be at home, being anxious to be with my Darling and also quite tired of this busy Town. I was at the Drawing Room on thursday & most graciously received. I found it was *too bad* not to make my appearance, as their Majesties were Spying at me at St. Margarets the tuesday before. The Princesses asked a great deal about Annabella & said they heard she was a *very fine Child.* The King said he saw me at the Musick, so all the fat would have been in the fire if I had not paid my Duty.

Few letters of 1795 and 1796 survive, but the year 1797 is lavishly documented. Returning from a visit to the Bakers at Elemore, Judith "found Annabella blooming & well & she has delighted her Papa by repeating five Stanzas of his favorite Poem, beginning 'Come Shepherds we'll follow the Hearse'." When a footman broke a lamp in cleaning it, "the Glass cut the large Vein across the Wrist & he had like to have bled to Death . . . the Stair-Case Passage & Pantry looked like the Description in one of Mrs. Ratcliffes Novels, & Annabella said they *swarmed* with Blood, but she was not the least frightened tho' she saw the Blood on the Floor." While staying at Seaham, Mrs. Baker gave Judith a letter to enclose with hers to her aunt, in which she tactfully remarked:

> Annabella grows very much, and is without partiality one of the finest Girls of her Age I ever beheld—her reading and Spelling quite astonished my Miss Walker.

In April Annabella accompanied her parents to visit the Hildyards at Sedbury "& shewed herself off to great advantage—I believe she will be calculated for *Society*, for it is really wonderful how the little Monkey sets out to figure in Company & before Strangers." Already, a month before her fifth birthday, "she reads very well"; a week after her birthday she was "*very desirous* of beginning a little french, which she reminded me I promised her she should do when she was five years old." One Sunday,

> tho' we have not been at *Church*, yet we have had the Psalms read to us in a most proper manner by Anne Hoar & Annabella, Verse & Verse like Parson & Clark, Annabella never missing her part once . . . and last Sunday she read all the Psalms herself & did not even boggle at *Melchisedeck*, which word I thought would have puzzled her.

In July Sir Henry Vane-Tempest had "a very large party" at Winyard:

> I took Annabella at Sir Henry's particular request & she was very happy & had a fresh Bottle of Claret opened for her every day—indeed she asked Sir Henry for it, to his great amusement.

In August:

> As to *the Angel* she is now an *Angel on Horseback*, as I have been fortunate enough to meet with the prettiest & quietest Poney that ever was seen & she is highly delighted with it, & rides without the least fear, with Edward walking by her with a Leading Rein. She rides in the *French* Fashion, which is safest & best whilst she is so young, & she trots away as upright as a Dart and as happy as a Queen. She . . . is sadly tanned, which I know would annoy you, but it will go off in Winter—I believe it is the bathing makes the sun & air catch her skin so much.

A few days later Annabella had "been in the Sea this morning & looks like a little Venus arisen from it." In October she had her first dancing lesson; the dancing master said "that since he taught, he never saw *such a first Lesson*, that her Strength & comprehension surprised him, as well as the attention & desire to learn," and "Mrs. Bland is quite delighted with her, tho' a little jealous that she so far exceeds Godfrey in every thing."

In November she had scarlet fever, and Dr. Fenwick "says he never saw such a Child, so patient, so sensible & so tractable; when she was in pain, she said to me, "go Mama", & when she was easier she would send for me back again—Clermont never left her night or day nor would the Child suffer any one else to touch her." "I never saw so patient or so good a Child when unwell as she is," wrote her cousin Sophy to their great-aunt; "if she has the nastiest mess in the world to take she swallows it without saying a word." She quickly recovered, "thanks to her excellent constitution," was soon "as well as ever she was," and it was Judith who felt "certainly a good deal shook by the anxiety I was under" when she took Annabella "a junketting" to Elemore, planning to go before Christmas to the Hildyards at Sedbury "and perhaps as far as Kippax and Harewood, having frequently had most kind and pressing invitations from the Harewoods & they insist on my taking the Child."

During the first six years of Annabella's life, persevering in her determination to be separated from her as little as possible, Judith went rarely to London and continued her usual round of visits only to those houses where Annabella was also welcomed. While receiving frequent visitors—especially Mrs. Baker, Mrs. Bland, and Mrs. William Hoar, who all had children slightly older than Annabella—she developed new interests at Seaham to occupy her abundant energy. She took up spinning as an alternative to embroidery as easier on her eyesight, but such feminine pursuits merely amused her leisure on winter evenings. She managed her own farm and corresponded with Arthur Young, the secretary of the Board of Agriculture, about crops most suitable to the soil. Diligent in her duties as lady of the manor, she took a personal interest in her tenants, though she failed in her efforts to persuade the village women to have their babies inoculated against small pox at her expense. Late in life Annabella recalled:

> Among the many interests that engaged the zealous good offices of my Parents, I never saw any preferred to the comfort of the labouring poor. It then seemed to me a matter of course that the best horse should be sent many miles for the best Doctor, to attend on Rustics, who are usually consigned to the Parish medical officer—that the finest Claret should be taken out of the Cellar to be applied to the exhausted Patients in a Tenant's house. I did not think that property could be possessed by any other Tenure than that of being at the service of those in need. It was all so simple! Yet my Mother put a spirit into it. She did not leave it to Servants. She saw that the execution was as good as the Intention.

When any of her servants became pregnant, Judith investigated the allegations of paternity; seducers were immediately discharged unless they agreed to make honest women of their victims, in which cases they were assisted to establish themselves in married life. Annabella recalled:

> The Moral standard by which they were judged was very indulgent. A girl's first false step was, in some cases, considered as a claim to greater instead of less kindness. "We must make the best of what can't be undone" was the spirit in which Transgressors were treated, with the exception only of the Savage & hypocritical classes. *Labour* had not then been placed at the top of the Social Pyramid, but *respect* was always shewn to the rustic labourer.

Judith's political views moved even further leftwards than Milbanke's as a supporter of Charles James Fox. At the end of March 1793 Lady Liddell wondered satirically if the reason why she had not heard from her recently was because Judith had taken Annabella to join the victorious General Dumouriez in Flanders, but as the latest news was of Dumouriez' evacuation of Brussels, she supposed that "no reinforcements have gone to him from the North as yet." She proposed not to

> provoke you by any more saucy *reflections* upon your republican politics but take it for granted that you rejoice in common with the rest of the world at the happy prospect there *now* seems to be of a speedy termination of the War and that you will at least allow that our *Interference* has done some service. There are *few, very few here* who do not think ours is a War of *Justice* if not of *Necessity*.

When Pitt's government was pursuing repressive measures against Horne Tooke and the members of the Corresponding Society, Judith wrote to her aunt on 31st May 1794:

> I wish any thing to put an End to the War for my part. I suppose some few of these *Conspirators* will be hanged & doubt not but several of them deserve it, but cannot think the Alarm was of that serious nature to justify the very extraordinary measures taken by Mr. Pitt, nor so serious as he wishes them to be thought. It appears to me that the good people of this country are so afraid of Republicanism that they are running into the jaws of absolute Monarchy—undoubtedly Mr. Pitt has carried Measures triumphantly that Lord North would have been impeached for proposing.

Three years later, on 24th May 1797, she reported that the regiment of Sir John Eden's son-in-law, General Seddon, had been "ordered out to quell the poor oppressed Irish, who are driven desperate & now must be subdued at all Events," adding caustically:

I think it probable as so many Troops are going to Ireland that the Supplementary Militia will be called out & then some of the Gentlemen who were so forward to accept of Commissions will be finely taken in, Sir Robert Hildyard for instance. What her Ladyship will do I know not, but she was in Tears whenever the Subject was named when we were at Sedbury & thought her Dear *Bobby* would certainly be Shot by the French —but she is so ridiculous an Aristocrat and Pittite that I cannot pity her. The distress of this part of the Country is dreadful! Sunderland is in a state of almost general Bankruptcy, no Trade, no Credit, no Money— People breaking every day . . . A Peace would set all afloat again.

She was reactionary only in resisting the convention—usually supposed to have been introduced under Queen Victoria—that Sundays must be destitute of amusement, writing on 2nd April 1798:

We are all in a bad way and unless our *Godliness* as proposed by our Bishop & Wilberforce, draws a blessing down on the Nation we are in a fair way of ruin & misery. I daresay you think with me that nothing can be so absurd & ridiculous as the proposed regulations for the Sabbath day. Nay, it is even cruel to debar those who have only one day in seven for a little recreation. *Yesterday* was an instance of the effect of so much *godliness*, because Sir Robert would not do so *wicked* a thing as play at half Crown Whist, the Gentlemen sat in the Parlour till 10 o'clock & came up as drunk as Owls.

The unpopularity of her opinions lent asperity to her comments, while advancing middle-age made her less patient of her juniors than she had been in her youth of contemporaries and seniors. She assessed Tom Noel's young wife Kitty as "a poor timid low-spirited Creature" who "does every thing they all bid her," and Sir Thomas Liddell's wife "is the merest Cypher I ever saw & her husband does not allow her the least sway on any one subject." At the time of the Powderham scandal in the winter of 1784–5 she had exclaimed:

What an infamous wretch is Beckford! & what a disgrace to the Age that he should be suffered to walk about! it is suspected that the Grandemonde mean to protect that vice *sourdement*, as in Italy, & if B is not universally shunn'd (is he?) it is too strong a confirmation of it.

But of heterosexual indiscretions she had been formerly tolerant, so long as they were outside her family circle; by 1797 she was censorious at least of those who philandered with social inferiors:

Lord Darlington . . . has had a shocking thing happened to him in Scotland—his *Footman* would have been hanged for it, but great folks may do things with impunity—he went into the Chamber of some young Servant Girl & attempted to violate her, but she got out at Window &

> *broke her Back.* It is some weeks since this happen'd & I conclude he has payed hush money . . . His *low Debaucheries* are something degrading to human Nature.

Three months later, on 20th October 1797:

> Lord Erroll is the greatest Beast I ever saw—his manners to the Ladies gross & unpleasant & to the Abigails, if he chanced to meet with any, brutal & indecent.

Evidence of the dissension she had fostered in the Milbanke family emerged at Sir Ralph Milbanke's death on 8th January 1798. During twenty-one years Sir Ralph's name had occurred rarely in his daughter-in-law's correspondence, probably because his household could not be visited by a woman of reputation. Though still in the prime of life when his wife died in 1767, he had remained a widower; during the first years of Judith's married life, he seems to have been associated with a Mrs. Demar, latterly with a Mrs. Ridley. Eleven days after his death Judith wrote to her aunt on 19th January:

> I wrote my Brother a long letter a few days since which I desired him to communicate to You & that will inform you how affairs stand—*except* that Sir Ralph left his son John Executor, that *he* has refused to act or bury his Father—that on his refusing to act as Executor it was in Milbankes choice to take out Administration or not. He is *strongly* advised not to Act, and therefore could not interfere about the Funeral, as that would be construed into Acting and then any Creditor might have made him administer. His Will merely leaves the 5000£ he had a right to bequeath, to Mrs. Ridley and the Children—it could no way concern us as he had nothing else in his power.
>
> We shall be as poor as Job this year, for all *Arrears* of *Rent*, go to John Milbanke under the Deed of trust for the benefit of the Creditors of Sir Ralph. So that Milbanke will receive nothing till next November.
>
> As it is necessary to settle many things respecting Halnaby which can only be done on the Spot, we mean to go there the 1st of next Month for a short time. I daresay we shall find the House in a comfortless State. Mr. John has taken an House at Croft and Milbanke has suggested in a very pretty manner that it will save *both* some unpleasant Sensations if they do not meet for the first time on his taking possession. Every thing in the House is entailed, but I daresay we shall scarce find a pair of Sheets or a Towell . . . That Brute John Milbanke wants to seize the 5000£ left to Mrs Ridley & her *six Children*, as he fancies there is some flaw which enables him to do so, but I hope & believe it is safely theirs.
>
> Baker has been here some days, they left us this morning. You know how much he has Milbankes Interest at heart and he has been of *infinite use*, by his advice, and guarding Milbanke against doing any thing by which they could involve us in difficulties. My Brother wishes us to proceed on the best advice. He may safely rely on Baker and Hoar to prevent

any advantage being taken of Milbanke by any of his family, but the business we shall have is immense!

Though Sophy reported that Judith "found out many beauties" in the "*Family Mansion*" at Halnaby "that were *invisible* whilst the *Grapes were Sour*," "the *Angel* . . . does not like Halnaby so well as Seaham as she regrets the Sea and the Sands tho' she likes the Woods & the Garden here." Despite her foreboding of poverty, Judith spent most of the summer in lavish entertaining at Halnaby, culminating in a "brilliant Grand Gala" ball and supper for 187 people, including "a great deal of *Quality*—Carmarthens, Fauconbergs, Darlingtons, 10 Baronets besides squires innumerable." By September, through the agency of her aunt, she had taken a town house, No. 6 Lower Berkeley Street, for 300 guineas a year. As Annabella spent most of the summer at Seaham and was left at Halnaby while her parents went to London for three weeks before Christmas, Judith this year for the first time endured separation from her daughter for more than a few days.

While this change of habit was dictated by the novelty of her situation as a baronet's lady and chatelaine of Halnaby, Judith could not have left Annabella without confidence in her guardianship. During the summer the governess, Miss Walker, had been dismissed for neglect of her charge, and on hearing from Judith that her maid Clermont was with Annabella at Seaham, her aunt wrote on 7th August 1798:

> I was quite happy when inform'd by you that the darling was under the care of Mrs. Clermont, as I think, if any one in this world can be depended upon for taking care of her, she may, as she was always fond of her from her birth, & the child also of her. I therefore think, if you could prevail upon her to take the intire care of the dear Girl, by being her maid instead of yours, 'twould make you very easy, & in that case, as she would be her *Maid* not *Governess* she would dress & undress her, & sleep always in her room & be always with her when you were out.

The arrangement was the more readily adopted because Clermont's devotion and Annabella's confidence in her had been proved during her illness with scarlet fever the previous year. Nor might a governess to Annabella's liking have been easily found, for before Lord Wentworth's visit that summer, Judith wrote:

> I begin to be quite in a fuss for fear my Brother should be disappointed in his two Nieces. Sophy is certainly very *journaliere*, and as to *little* Madam, I do not feel sure whether he will like her very natural manners. She is excessivley talkative and entertaining if *she likes* people & very *coaxing* to her *favorites;* but she will judge for *herself* & cannot be *made* to *like* any body.

Mary Anne Clermont was to be bitterly satirised by Byron in the verses, "A Sketch from Private Life", published just before he finally left England in April 1816 and beginning,

> Born in the garret, in the kitchen bred,
> Promoted thence to deck her mistress' head;
> Next—for some gracious service unexpressed,
> And from its wages only to be guessed—
> Raised from the toilet to the table,—where
> Her wondering betters wait behind her chair.

She entered Judith's service in the autumn of 1789 when her personal maid, who had been with her for several years, left to be married. Recommending her as a friend of her own maid, Judith's aunt wrote on 1st September 1789:

> The greatest objection is her Age being only eighteen, & looks very young of that Age. She is Betty's acquaintance & was some time with the same millener . . . Betty thinks she is as *clever* as she was when she came to me & has had a better Education having been to school & can read & write well . . . She is plain & not tall but not awkward in her figure, but so extremely timid that she trembled so I could not get a word from her . . . Her Mother was Mrs. Lyells housekeeper seven years & the Girl is not poor but goes to Service more for improvement than necessity.

In a further letter, giving the girl's address as "Mrs. Claremont Princes Street Cavendish Square," Mary Noel added:

> Her father was a french man & she understands the language but does not pretend to speak it—I thought you should know that, that you might not talk secrets in that tongue before her.

At the time of Judith's pregnancy, when Clermont had been in her service nearly two years, her aunt was gratified that "you have so great a regard for Mrs. Clermont, & I am very happy to hear she is so deserving of your favor." A month later Mary Noel was so anxious about Judith's condition that she ordered her maid to inquire of Clermont:

> & I must say Clarmonts letter was one of the clearest, most sensible, & handsomest letters I ever read, in which she says that nothing upon earth but my Commands should have drawn the Secret from her, for . . . she knows her duty too well ever to betray one of yours . . . but I must beg of you not to mention this to her, as she was in agonies for fear of offending you & I promised not to tell.

When Annabella had "the Itch" in the summer of 1793, Clermont was "*Saucy*" in insisting that the trouble was not the Itch, but "I believe poor Soul she has suffered severely since, from knowing herself wrong & my being angry." At Christmas 1793 Clermont brought accusations of misconduct against Annabella's nurse which Judith found to be exaggerated; Judith further discovered that Clermont and the nurse had hated each other "*most inveterately* ever since the *Itch business*" and that Clermont had expressed herself "tired of Service, especially as I did not go to London & that she could not bring herself to be so long from her Mother & that she would leave me if I did not go to Town this Winter."

> There is a kind of *resolute* Sulkiness in her manner which is I think ungrateful & unpleasant, considering how very much her health & every thing else has been considered by me since she lived with me, and except that affair about *the Itch* I have never on any occasion said a cross word to her. I acknowledge I have a very high opinion of Clermonts principles & have always found her a very good and valuable Servant, but I believe her ill health makes her peevish & certainly nothing can be so dull as living in the Country to a Person who will never set their Foot out of the House & will never associate with any Servants either in this House or even when she goes from home . . . as either here or abroad she does not even attend the *common Meal-times* . . . I am sure she has never forgiven what happened about *the itch* . . . & I do believe she is *resolved to go* tho' I do not believe she will leave me in an unhandsome manner or till I have got another . . . pray tell me what *You* think about all this.

Having examined her own maid about her correspondence with Clermont, Mary Noel replied on 17th January 1794 that Clermont had never mentioned the possibility of leaving Judith's service before her mother's illness and "she loves you so" that, if she did have to leave, "it will almost break her heart, but her Mother is perpetually fretting about not seeing her again before she dies & I believe writes her terrible letters." Judith arranged for Clermont to go to London for a fortnight to see her mother and also to accompany Sophy to London instead of her own maid. There was no more talk of Clermont's leaving till Mary Noel suggested in August 1798 that she should be Annabella's maid instead of Judith's; she then informed Judith that, while she felt she should "return to live with her Mother," she "had no objection to devote herself to Annabella for *a Year or two*." In February 1799 the whole family "set forwards" to London "with Annabella, Clermont & the Cook in the Coach."

During this first visit of Annabella's to London her portrait was painted by Hoppner, the most fashionable portrait-painter between the death of Reynolds and the rise of Lawrence. It is a charming picture of an attractive child in a high-waisted summer frock, stepping round a rocky bluff with the sea behind her, as on the beach at Seaham; in her expression the painter conveys a suggestion of complacency. Early in this year, some months before her seventh birthday, Annabella was asked "if her Papa was not always in the right;" "Probably not (she reply'd), sometimes right, sometimes wrong, as *we all are*."

She delighted in her first visit to London, and in February 1800 Judith reported her "charmed with the thoughts of being in Town, as much as if she was Seventeen & was to begin her first London Campaign." In May 1801 Judith had to accompany her husband to Cheltenham, leaving Annabella in London with Mary Noel: "it was pain and grief to me to leave her, and I think to fetch her in about ten days." In reply to this the fond mother heard from her niece Sophy that "Annabella is very much annoy'd at the Idea of leaving Town, and says she is quite determin'd neither to *Eat*, *drink*, or *Sleep* if you are so cruel as to take her away," while Mary Noel reported her "quite well but very angry at the thoughts of leaving this place—several of my friends came yesterday under pretence of visitting me but really to see my dear Companion; she was in high Spirits & shew'd off in her best manner & sent them all away inchanted."

On 23rd August 1801 Judith wrote from Seaham, where "Annabella and I dip sociably together":

> Annabella is very happy and very *independent*, for her Papa has given her an allowance of £20 a Year, which she is to receive quarterly from Mr. Taylor and give her own Receipt. She was paid the first quarter the 17th inst. as it is to take place from her last Birthday, and she wrote the receipt herself . . . She says she shall save about all of it to spend in London.

In the following January, when Judith had deferred taking a house in town owing to financial troubles, she informed her aunt:

> Annabella is so impatient to be in London that she has some thoughts of writing to you, to know if you will take her and Clermont in to lodge & board, and to save travelling expenses, they are to go on the *Outside* of the Fly, which she thinks she can afford out of her allowance and the Money she can raise by the Sale of her Watch and Trinkets.

To which Mary Noel replied tactfully on 9th January 1802 in the last letter she wrote to her beloved niece:

> I should be very happy if dearest Annabella could be my lodger, but I fear I must wait for the pleasure of seeing her sweet face till you come, as this is not weather for flying or sailing, otherways I should recommend a Sea voyage as the more eligible of the two.

Though always in the spring Annabella was "all impatience to leave the Rural Scene for the Smoak of London," she went less frequently than she wished, for Judith's life was no longer as cloudless as formerly. At the time of her forty-eighth birthday she found herself again surprisingly pregnant, but miscarried in the fourth month. In February 1800 her niece Sophy reported that "considering the great disappointment she has had her Spirits are much better than could have been expected," but when she went to Tunbridge Wells to recuperate, she was worried by Annabella's contracting whooping cough, which remained troublesome throughout the summer while Judith was suffering anxiety over arrangements for Sophy's marriage.

In June 1798 Sophy had refused a proposal from the second Lord Grantley, a widower in his late fifties, as Judith related to her aunt:

> Yesterday we were surprised by the arrival of Mr. Jolliffe and yet more by his *Errand*. He came as Ambassador from Lord Grantley with a proposal in full form, and exerted all his Eloquence for his employer, sounding forth all his good qualities, his 8,000£ a year &c. But Sophy was obdurate to all he could say, to his great surprize, I believe, & he plagued Milbanke so much about it that at last he grew quite cross & told him Sophy was my Niece not *his* & he had nothing to do about it.

The following year Sophy met Lord Tamworth in a party of young officers at a ball. Three months older than Sophy and just of age, Tamworth was the only legitimate son of the seventh Earl Ferrers, who, long separated from his wife, had several children by his mistress, Betty Mundy, whom he married a fortnight after his first wife's death in 1799. Subsequently called the Erl-King by his daughter-in-law on account of his callously capricious behaviour, Lord Ferrers was not on good terms with his son, nor was he propitiated by an inordinately long letter from Judith, haughtily upbraiding him for offering "an allowance so entirely out of all proportion to your own Fortune, & to Your & Your Sons Situation & Rank, that it was almost an insult to offer it." Judith declared herself "quite worn to death" by the negotiations with Tamworth's "Devil of a Father", and a few weeks after the wedding on 5th August 1800, though then at Halnaby with Annabella, she felt "like *a lost thing* for want of Sophy."

In May 1802 Mary Noel died at her house in London, with Judith attending her. She was in her seventy-seventh year, but her death left both Judith and her brother with a deep sense of loss; in their youth she had been a second mother to them and they had continued always to confide everything to her, receiving habitually shrewd and tactful counsel.

In her last letter before being called to her aunt's bedside, Judith had explained how they could not afford "to be saddled with an expensive House" in town owing to "the almost total failure of the Coal-trade in the last Year." An election was also pending, with the prospect of an expensive contest. Milbanke's colleague, Rowland Burdon, had announced his retirement, and Sir Henry Vane-Tempest was standing, but the Bishop of Durham "has a personal enmity to Sir Henry & *I know* is endeavouring to persuade Burdon to come forwards again who very probably may now Peace is made, his *real* reason for retiring being, that he had got a Contract under Government to supply the Navy with Ropes, and which, had the War continued, would have been very profitable, but the Peace being made, is now not worth a *Ropes End.*"

From her aunt's funeral Judith had to hurry north to assist her husband in the election. By 18th August Wentworth was able to congratulate them "that your election had gone off so well," but Sir John Eden and Sir Thomas Liddell, who had both refused invitations to stand, seem to have been more deserving of congratulation on their prudence in declining the expensive luxury of assisting in their country's government. Liberalism was not a profitable profession during the Napoleonic wars; during the twenty-two years that Milbanke served as a member of Parliament—except for the brief life of Grenville's coalition ministry after Pitt's death in 1805—he sat on the Opposition back-benches and acquired nothing but out-of-pocket expenses. Moreover, as an Opposition member, he had to fight contested elections attended by heavy expenses.

Resumption of the war against Napoleon brought widespread economic distress. Prices rose, banks failed, and the "stock-jobbery" sponsored by Pitt's government converted such a Tory supporter as William Cobbett into a radical reformer. "The times are abominable," wrote Wentworth in November 1803, and in the following February he considered, "If Bonaparte ever means to put his threats [of invasion] in execution, he never could have a better opportunity." In August 1804 Milbanke tried vainly to raise a mortgage on his property; the banks were in a state of panic and "money transactions are chiefly confined to Stocks, Scrip, Loans, Omnium, &c." He was forced to sell his properties in Northumberland when land values were at their lowest, and Wentworth's old friend Bowater—now a lieutenant-general—wrote to Judith on 2nd January 1805 to "lament & regret that your Sale was so bad."

Under these anxieties Judith's temper suffered. In August 1804 she burst into a correspondence of voluble vituperation with her friend Mrs. Hoar over the services of a drawing master divided between Annabella and Mrs. Hoar's daughter Anne, each supposing that the other was demanding an unfair quota of his time. Though Sophy had troubles of her own with adjustments following her grandfather's death, her father's return to England with a large family by his second wife, her brother's ill health, and her father-in-law's habitual unhelpfulness, Judith accused her so bitterly of inconsiderate neglect that she wrote to "My dearest Aunt" on 3rd November 1804, "Let me entreat you not to accuse me of intending to drop a Correspondence from which I must ever derive so much comfort and happiness, nor think for one moment that I would have delay'd offering all the consolation in my power on the subject of your present uneasiness."

Her brother did not escape Judith's querulousness. Lady Wentworth was amiable and kindly, certainly generous to her illegitimate step-children and always attentive to her husband's old aunt. But she had suffered from the dominating characters of her sisters, Lady Bridget Tollemache and Lady Jane Aston, so she was prudently cautious towards her formidable sister-in-law. Small, delicate, and affectedly fashionable, she was irreverently described by Sophy at nineteen as "like a naked Doll in a toy shop"; the uxorious Wentworth usually mentioned her to his aunt as "your dear little Neice," and soon after Annabella's birth Judith remarked that her aunt now had "a little Great Niece" as well as "a Great little Niece." When the Wentworths seemed too often prevented from accepting invitations to the north or her brother lapsed in his correspondence, Judith frequently expressed displeasure to her aunt. "I very seldom hear from him, yet I believe he loves me dearly, if he was *permitted* to shew it," she wrote on 2nd March 1794, and on 25th August 1797, "It really hurts me very much that my Brother should have so little desire to see *my Child*." When she excused herself for not writing to Wentworth because "I have really suspected (& not without some appearance of foundation) that his affection for me was cooled," Mary Noel remonstrated from Kirkby on 2nd December 1797:

> I am very sure your Brother loves you as much as he can love anything but his dear Mary . . . ever since I have been here Ly W has always spoken of you in a very friendly manner, both before him & behind his back, & seem'd much hurt that you did not write, as she said he had a sincere affection for you . . . It is not now in any bodys power to do you & yours any Injury, as most of his estate was primarily settled upon you & your heirs by his Marriage Settlement after her . . . I am sure if he were to die, & you found he had done kindly by you, I know you so well that you would be very miserable. Now don't fly out & say you never did shew him any unkindness, for I don't *say* you have, but as they lay so much Stress upon writing, surely it is an easy matter to keep a trifling correspondence by letter . . . If you do not, you must pardon me if I say your affection must be as much cool'd as his, for his foolish tenderness for a certain person is more to be pittied than blamed, for she certainly does shew the greatest regard & love for him, & is very good to him in money matters,

& you know he was always a dupe to the female he lived with, & when all is said we have all our prejudices.

Judith accepted this rebuke; after the Wentworths enjoyed a happy visit to Halnaby in the summer of 1798, her correspondence with her brother continued with unruffled affection till the anxiety of her money worries caused her to think Wentworth showed too little concern. General Bowater was privileged as an old family friend to intervene on 22nd February 1805:

I would not have you think that your Brother is estranged from you. It is more his manner, which was allways particular in his Youthfull days. Age and Absence does not Improve that sort of Coolness, which is his habbit. And as he is Wedded almost to an Icycle you should make allowances, as I do, & his having lost & thrown away a Mint of Money, he is now becoming a Miser, buys Yearly into the Stocks, & was more rejoyced at Lord Scarsdale telling him he hoped soon to have it in his Power to repay him the twelve Hundred Pounds that he lent him on a Pressing Occasion than the Benefit which was arising to his Nephew Niece & other Connections.

But this is not the Man. We must lament that Nature makes such wretches of us, And that what we can enjoy for so short a period, we leave to those that who in a few Months will totally forget that we had a being.

It was to prove fortunate for Judith and Annabella that Wentworth in his declining years made an effort to relieve his estates of the encumbrances imposed by his earlier extravagance.

Meanwhile Judith accepted the General's remonstrance as she had accepted her aunt's, and Wentworth continued to write as if unaware of having caused her umbrage. "Tell Annabella," he wrote, "that altho' she is such a proficient in Latin & French, some good plain English in a letter to an Affectionate Uncle will be most acceptable," and little over a year later, "Annabella's letters are capital ones indeed, & I wish you would unknown to her send me a list of such Books as she will most like." He showed forbearance as well as affection when he wrote on 10th October 1807, "if you cannot write yourself, employ Annabella," for at no period of her life was Annabella's epistolary style as entertaining as her mother's.

One of the earliest of thousands of Annabella's letters preserved in the Lovelace Papers was written to her parents at the age of eleven. In November 1803 Judith addressed a political meeting in the north so successfully that her speech was reported in the London papers and the Bishop of Durham remarked to her brother, "What is it Lady Milbanke does not do well she has a mind to do?" Annabella was present at the meeting and recorded her impression of the speech:

You never forgot one word of your speech nor was any fear discernable in your speech, addressing a very numerous & in part a very respectable audience you never once forgot the proper action (for action is a very essential part in a good speaker).

Sir neither words, nor sentiments could be retrenched or added—they are just, precise, & elevated. The world Sir will speak more of the speech of your wife than of yours but I will engage not from *any* Idea of the inferiority of your speech but because it is more unusual for a woman to speak in public, if I have made more *praises* to your spouse than to you, it was because I could make compliments to her but to you they would be an affront.

Have I praised or have I flattered? let those who heard them judge—as it is I remain an impartial Tory—

A I

The pert self-assurance was the result of encouraging what Judith described in 1798 as Annabella's "very natural manners"; she was also encouraged to criticise, not only all she read and saw, but people she met, and as a young woman she recorded in her journals "Characters" of her acquaintance.

Her handwriting indicates rapid development from eleven to thirteen; the speech criticism is written in a normal eleven-year-old hand, with three blots and a smudge, but on 26th October 1805 she wrote to her mother from Seaham with a fine-pointed pen in elegant copperplate showing many characteristics of her always clearly legible adult hand:

Since you requested that some one would give you a scrawl today,—& as your *conjux* is occupied in playing at Backgammon with Mrs. Clermont, I have thought fit to take up a *mathematical* pen, to inform you that no limbs have been broken since your departure, & that we find each others' company so agreable, that *your name is seldom mentioned!*

You will of course know by this time the contents of Mrs. Chowles letter, which we received on Friday,—we are anxious to know the result of your journey.

I composed a few lines last night in Blank verse, imitating Young's most melancholy stile. I am doubtful whether I have succeeded, as I cannot say I was in a very gloomy humour. The subject I chose was a lamentation for a deceased friend. [There follow seventeen lines of blank verse]. I think line 15 is the best, & line 9 the worst—these things are humbly submitted to thy judgement, O Juditha. You will perceive the piece is not finished.

Mrs. Baker returned to Elemore on friday, her father is rather better, but not so much so as to afford hopes of his final recovery.

The weather (so essential in the composition of a letter) is in a very ill humour, so much so that I have not been able to get out, *ullo modo*, in any manner, & your spouse was for 2 days detained in the house.

The philosopher is as charming, the learned linguist as shy, & I make no doubt that the musician is as talkative, as ever, & I remain yours Affec.

A.I.M.[1]

The author of *Night Thoughts* was an unfortunate influence on Annabella's verse; five years later the great actress, Sarah Siddons, wrote to Judith on 11th July 1810:

I have the honour to call at your door before my departure to thank you for all your kind attentions & to return the paper you kindly indulged me with reading; I have read it very often and each time with encreased admiration and wonder. It breathes the Piety and Genius of Younge,—but God forbid the sweet mind of her who wrote it should ever partake also of his most pityable gloom and melancholy!

I really do think it is the most extraordinary production, *in any point of view*, that ever came under my observation. If it were possible for me to *express* my admiration of that Sweet Girl (even independently of her attainments and her Genius), you would at least call me an enthusiast, for you have too much knowledge & penetration to imagine it possible for me to be a mean *Adulator*, but there is something so above earthly, and so nearly resembling my idea of heavenly, in the divine illumination of that countenance of her's, that I who profess myself a physiognomist *never mistaken*, have associated with it, a Soul suited to it, and therefore it is that I am *what I am* with respect to her.

The Milbankes had been enthusiastic admirers of Mrs. Siddons ever since she achieved celebrity under Garrick's management at Drury Lane; after she was a guest at Halnaby in the summer of 1805, she corresponded regularly with both Judith and Annabella. On the evidence of her letters the greatest tragic actress of her time exhausted her genius on the stage, collapsing into a bathos of sanctimony and sentimentality in private life. In an early letter to Annabella she wrote:

I thank you over and above, my dear Miss Milbanke, for your kind letter. You will be not a little surprised when I tell you it cost me many tears, and led me into a train of thought, which fills my mind with the Sadly-pleasing images of long departed joys.

If you remember you had begun to Copy the Ode to the Poppy upon the paper on which you wrote to me. That Ode was written by the friend of my early youth, who found me in obscurity, and who, gifted herself with extraordinary Talents, cherishd and encouraged them in others, with a generous warmth of feeling, peculiar to her own aimiable mind and exalted understanding. She finishd that Lovely Poem in her Sick bed, while I sat by her anxiously watching every turn and change, of that countenance whose radient intelligence the united attacks of Sickness, pain, and Sorrow, could not diminish; in compliance with her desire I

[1] Five lines are added in Sir Ralph Milbanke's scrawl, including the date.

corrected some little mistakes, occasiond by the uneasy position in which she was obligd to write it: now you will no longer wonder.

If it is not arrogant to say so, She lovd me while She had life and while I live, her memory will be most dear and sacred to me. I cannot define the feeling that took possession of my mind, upon seeing the beginning of that Ode copied by your hand, or the comparison it led me to make between you. She was wonderfully endowd with mental power, She was young, and lovely, and belovd; here thank God the comparison ends! for She was unhappy. May God preserve you my sweet young friend from the errors and misfortunes of an exalted but misguided imagination! ! ! Remember me most kindly to dear Lady Milbanke and Miss Montgomery, my daughter and Miss W. desire their Compts, and I am, "Young budding virgin fresh and fair",

Your very affte:
S. Siddons

Mrs. Siddons gave her farewell performance as Lady Macbeth at Covent Garden in the summer of 1812; either then or in the previous year Annabella recorded the "Substance of Mrs. Siddons's opinions respecting the character of Lady Macbeth":

Lady M. is as much a *monster* as Caliban—as much a creature of Imagination, strange to Nature. Lady M's is a character of great feeling. With the assumption of guilty honours she loses all peace of mind—from that period it is Shakespeare's intention that a breaking heart should appear through the unyielding force which her self-command enables her to wear. After those solitary expressions of Misery—"Nought's had" &c—she resists her own remorseful despondency to rouse her husband from Despair. *She* never utters a complaint—her grief pent within, whispers the o'er-fraught heart, and bids it break. There cannot be a stronger proof of mutual affection than the fact that not a single reproach passes between Macbeth & her. He indeed relieves himself by lamentations, but is always considerately tender towards her. When he designs the murder of Banquo, he would spare her the anxiety of doubting its execution—"Be innocent of the knowledge" &c.

As early as 1805 Annabella's verse was not always shadowed by *Night Thoughts;* in the autumn of that year she accompanied her mother on a visit to the newly-installed Lord Scarsdale at Kedleston, and her cousin Sophy wrote on 1st November to ask for "Annabella's Verses on the *Kedleston Dogs*." This summer her uncle Wentworth sent her Boisgelin's *Ancient and Modern Malta* as a present, exciting the speculation that her interest in Malta may have been suggested by hearing from his Cambridge acquaintance Frend that Coleridge was living there.

William Frend (1757–1841), a clerical fellow of Jesus College who became a Unitarian, was banished from Cambridge in 1793 after trial by the Vice-Chancellor's court for publishing a pamphlet advocating peace. His victimisation for opposing the war recommended him to the Milbankes, and at fourteen Annabella opened with him a correspondence that continued intermittently till his death thirty-five years later. Amused by her precocity, Frend replied from 26 Portland Place on 25th November 1806:

> Mr Frend is very much concerned that a variety of occupations has prevented him from noticing the receipt of Miss Milbanke's communications but he wished to make some remarks upon them if this sort of vacation gave Miss M an opportunity of going over again the subjects on which she had been employed. He presumed, too, that the business of elections might engage some of her attention & he is very glad to congratulate Sir Ralph on his election, though the next parliament may present to the world very extraordinary scenes & will require the exertions of every honest man. From this time Miss M's exercises may be resumed & will in future suffer no interruptions.

After congratulating her on her "highly satisfactory" completion of the fourth book of Euclid and giving instructions for her study of the fifth book, he went on to the study of astronomy:

> The progress of the planets Venus & Jupiter with the Sun makes a plate of the evening's amusements for the next year & one plate is to be Chinese . . . About a month ago I received some Chinese books from Canton & among them one which I found to be on the same subject as mine on Tangible Arithmetick, published last year. I am not yet thoroughly versed in the characters though I can make out several propositions & it appears to me at present that the Chinese use more algebraical marks than we do & thus keep their ideas more distinct. When you return to town we will investigate this subject but I hope previously to obtain some information from a native of China. As soon as the plate is engraved I will send you a copy & you will require no assistance if you have my Tangible Arithmetick by you to make it out . . . I shall expect soon some Latin as well as Geomy. & Algebra & I think it may be time for you to begin Livy. You will of course send me some verses scan'd & let me know what is your present reading.

The humorous resort to pomposity in Frend's opening paragraph in the third person reflected the grandiloquence with which her parents playfully encouraged Annabella's precocity; pertly she retorted with grandiloquence amusing in a child, but having a literal and humourless understanding, she was unconscious of irony and gradually developed a pompous and pedantic style of expression.

She was always addicted to commonplace books, which indicate the scope of her reading. She read poetry and drama abundantly, being guided in the latter by her father, of whom she recalled, "Of

Shakespeare, Otway, Dryden, he was a devoted admirer, pointing out or reciting to me their finest passages, & he had the vice (?) of enjoying Darwin's melodious strains." One of her notebooks was devoted to "Traits of Character selected from different works with the view of applying them to *Real* Characters," with extracts from Shakespeare, Beaumont and Fletcher, Ben Jonson, and Massinger.

She had a book labelled "Philosophers", read Hartley, and confided to Frend in the autumn of 1807 her difficulties in writing an "essay on association." Frend's Unitarianism may have played a part in early persuading her to Coleridge's view that Christian doctrine was the supreme philosophy and the basis of all subsequent systems, but her mother's religious opinions impressed her with respect. After reading Gibbon, Judith had resorted to Bishop Watson to reassure her faith, and she sought the personal acquaintance of William Paley after he published his *Evidences of Christianity* in 1794. Annabella preferred Joseph Butler to Paley, but her mother's energy in good works convinced her "that the practical part of Christianity was of infinitely more importance than the doctrinal," an impression confirmed when "*Cowper's Poems* were introduced to me (at 14 years of age) by Lord Erskine, who read some passages . . . with enthusiastic admiration; they warmed my philanthropy, and closely united it with religious duty."

One of the first *protégés* she shared with her mother was the cobbler-poet, Joseph Blacket, of whom Byron wrote in *English Bards and Scotch Reviewers:*

> When some brisk youth, the tenant of a stall,
> Employs a pen less pointed than his awl,
> Leaves his snug shop, forsakes his store of shoes,
> St. Crispin quits, and cobbles for the Muse,
> Heavens! how the vulgar stare! how crowds applaud!
> How ladies read, and Literati laud!

Blacket died at the age of twenty-three in 1810 at a cottage in Seaham, where he had lived under what he called "your benevolent protection and patronage" in a letter to Judith of 23rd November 1809:

> Your Ladyship's generous zeal in contributing so largely to my happiness and welfare has been such as to render me incapable of thanking you as I ought, yet believe me Madam, the many liberal kindnesses you have shewn me, the hospitalities I have received from Sir Ralph, and the friendly countenance of the truly amiable Miss Milbanke shall ever be remembered with grateful respect. They are indelibly stampt on my heart. I recd. Twenty Pounds from the hands of Mrs. Claremont which your Ladyship and generous friends had presented me . . . I have been

> honoured with various copies of verses from the fair hand of Miss Milbanke, which I have perused and reperused with that delight which every admirer of Literature must experience while contemplating original matter. In Miss Milbanke's lines I find sublimity, and peculiar strength of thought, the sentences are compressed, and, for that reason, have double force. Her Ideas are wove in the finest Loom of Imagination—Classical, yet natural.

Two months earlier Annabella had written:

> If Mr. Blacket's verses (The dying Soldier to the Setting Sun) & Burns' verses on a similar subject had been shown to Miss Milbanke without the names of the authors, she would have had no hesitation in giving the preference to the former as containing the most original thoughts & most beautiful images . . .
>
> A gentleman with whom Miss Milbanke is acquainted has a drawing of the tree under which Charles Fox was in the habit of spending many of his leisure hours, & where he was accustomed to pursue his literary occupations. This Gentleman is desirous to have some verses appropriate to the subject, and which may be worthy to be transmitted to posterity with the memory of this great statesman & patriot. Will Mr. Blacket turn his attention to a composition on this theme?

The poet duly obliged; his "Lines Supposed to be found written on the tree under which the Celebrated Statesman Charles James Fox was in the habit of spending his leisure hours" were submitted in a manuscript dated "Seaham, Oct. 1809."

Most of Blacket's letters refer to his "continuing ill health." "'Man was born for society,'" he wrote to Annabella on 8th March 1810 when the Milbankes were in London, "and, by heaven! to be in perpetual Solitude must be to be miserable! . . . My lonely situation is painful! would that fine weather or the Family would return!" Two of his letters mention Miss Montgomery as Annabella's companion on her visits to him: he hopes that "the kind Miss Montgomery is much better" and laments that he has been unable to compose verses "for your fair friend Miss Montgomery's air."

Mary Millicent Montgomery's mother, a sister of the second Viscount Gosford, had died in 1799, leaving two sons and a daughter, who came under the guardianship of Judith's friend Lady Gosford. As a small child Annabella had preferred male playmates, especially older than herself; at six she was "doatingly fond" of her seventeen-year-old cousin Nat Curzon when he spent most of the summer at Seaham in 1798; in the autumn of 1801 Mrs. Bland left her son Godfrey behind for another week after she and the rest of her family departed, because he and Annabella were "happy together, and a Young Play-fellow does her good sometimes." As she grew older, she necessarily sought friends among her own sex. Mrs. Baker of Elemore had an only child Isabella, rather older than Annabella, but Annabella seems to have preferred the mother to the daughter. Lady Milner's younger daughter Emily was an intimate at least till Annabella's marriage, but through the Milners a more lasting friendship developed with Selina Doyle, whose brother was the husband of Lady Milner's elder daughter Diana. Elizabeth and Louisa Chaloner were daughters of another old friend of Judith's who remained Annabella's friends for many years.[1]

Mary Montgomery became Annabella's closest friend because, having no home ties, she was free to make prolonged visits to Seaham and Halnaby, and she won her protective affection as an habitual invalid. As she was the only one of Annabella's early friends to survive her, her invalidism was probably a neurotic withdrawal from life after being left parentless as a child. Annabella was convinced that her friend was doomed to an early death and accordingly concentrated on making her supposedly brief time on earth as happy as possible.

Her father was now in his sixties and frequently ailing; a life of indulgence in food and drink was taking its toll, and though his chief affliction was gout, Annabella's fears that she might soon be deprived of his uncritical affection must have been intensified by her concern for Mary Montgomery and Blacket. On 14th March 1809 she wrote:

> The fear of Death may arise from two causes which, as they are directly opposite, should, it seems, produce opposite effects—but it is not so. 1. *From want of belief in a future existence.* The idea of annihilation is terrible. 2. From a firm belief in a future existence, and a confidence in our being placed there according to our merits. On this subject Mrs. Carter speaks well (she has just mentioned Johnson's fear of Death): "You wonder that an undoubting believer & a man of piety should be afraid of Death, but it is such characters who have ever the deepest sense of their own imperfections, & deviations from the rule of duty, of which the very best must be conscious: and such a temper of mind as is struck with awe & humility at the prospect of the last solemn sentence, appears much better suited to the wretched deficiency of the best, human performance than the thoughtless security that rushes undisturbed into eternity."

She wrote this in London, recording on the other side of the page, "I have this day been to see Sowerby's Collection of Minerals &c. He gives me the idea of a remarkably happy man—his countenance denotes extreme good nature." Of this London visit there is no further record, but in 1810 she decided "from henceforth to keep a journal of my proceedings which will hereafter to *me* be very interesting."

[1] Isabella Baker married on 15th February 1816 her cousin, Henry Tower, but all these other friends of Annabella's never married.

3

THE LONDON SEASONS OF 1810 AND 1811

At forty Annabella recalled:

> Arrived at the age of 17, I was anxious to postpone my entrance into the world, of which I had formed no pleasing conception, and I was too happy in my pursuits—drawing, book-collecting, verse-making—to wish for any other appropriation of my time. But my "hour was come."

Her journal shows that she spent a full season in London with her mother from March to July 1810, beginning with a sombre note on 26th February:

> What is to become of me when the trials of affliction shall fall on me, with the terrible capacity I now feel of being miserable? If the miseries of others thus shake me, when such shall be *my* lot—ere they arrive, from Thee, Father of Pity, let me implore the only defence against the weakness of human nature that stands in the day of temptation. In the constant exercise of the duties of my Religion let me find firmness & resignation, in promoting the happiness of others let me seek the only source of pleasure that can hereafter be connected with Memory.

On 2nd March:

> This evening Lady Athlone[1] and Lady Milbanke argued respecting a person who undoubtedly behaved ungratefully to the latter. Lady A. blamed Lady M. for not resenting it. Upon this she, my mother, delivered her opinion on the Forgiveness of Injuries, from which none could dissent who professed the Christian tenets. I have seldom known truth declared in so rational and impressive a manner.
>
> "All the world may think me imposed on, flattered into blindness, but forgiveness of those who have wrong'd me rests between me & my God. Charity should teach me to attribute to *Z* the *best* motives; when conviction to the contrary shall be irresistible, Charity should also induce me to pardon him the *worst*. You say he should not escape with impunity; but vengeance is as little mine as judgment. You say too that I owe some consideration to myself,—I do, and for this reason I forgive as I would be

[1] Sir John Eden's second daughter Maria married in 1800 the sixth Earl of Athlone, who died 5th December 1810. She married secondly in 1821 Vice-Admiral Sir William Johnstone Hope and lived till 1851.

forgiven. I confess that I am sometimes too apt to censure hastily—to censure beyond what my cool reason justifies, and this may lead many to suppose me very deficient in Toleration; but I trust that when called upon to *act*, the principles of patience & long-suffering would direct me. At the same time in this instance I do not pretend to be solely governed by them. My inclination as well as my duty forbids me to manifest indignation. I could not do so without seriously distressing another person whose conduct has been to me as irreproachable as her attachment is sincere . . . If I devoted much of my time, of my comfort, to his welfare, 'twas done in obedience to the dictates of Conscience, and had I *not* done it, that same conscience would have disturbed my peace . . . If he has a heart he will deeply feel my present kindness—if he is insensible, my scorn would not cause him to repent his want of rectitude."

The next evening she recorded at midnight her "entrance into the world" after dining at the house of the Lord Chief Justice:

I have just returned from a small party at Lady Ellenborough's, where I saw some men of ability for the first time. Of these I immediately guessed Lord Ellenborough by his appearance. He has a most judge-like air of decision, and his face indicates strong powers of thinking. Lord Selkirk's appearance declares a man of deep study and reflection. The mildness of his deportment, and his unassuming mode of conversation particularly please me. He accompanies his words with gentle but expressive action, and when not speaking has the air of being lost in meditation. Lord Grey is in his exterior much more the man of importance. *His* seems to me the politeness of a gentleman, not the politeness resulting from a principle of benevolence. However, my opinion may perhaps be biassed by my having heard much of his *pride*.[1]

On 5th March at Lady Harcourt's she "saw the Persian Ambassador, the *marvel* of the present moment," with "his beautiful teeth and fine black beard"; she "also saw for the first time Sir Sidney Smith," the celebrated admiral, "and was much disappointed at not discovering the *Hero* either in his appearance or his manners." Sir Robert Wilson, just home from commanding a brigade at Talavera, was also there, but "he has not the air of ability." On 11th March she met "Sir John Sinclair, the famous agriculturist—he has by no means the appearance of ability, and his mouth has a very unpleasant expression."

Thereafter she found celebrities so disappointing that she rarely recorded impressions of them, confining her notes mainly to the arts.

[1] Ellenborough was the Lord Chief Justice to whom Shelley in 1812 addressed an open letter in protest against his sentencing a bookseller named Eaton for publishing part of Tom Paine's *Age of Reason;* later in the same year he sent Leigh Hunt to prison for libelling the Prince Regent, and Shelley considered his address "so barefaced a piece of time-servingness that I am sure his heart must have laughed at his lips as he pronounced it." The 5th Earl of Selkirk (1771–1820) was a Scottish lawyer and an early friend of Sir Walter Scott. Grey became the principal Whig leader after Fox's death and Prime Minister in 1830, his government negotiating the Reform Bill of 1832.

Seeing Kemble in the first part of *Henry IV*, she "was so little acquainted with the Play that I could not form a judgment at all satisfactory to myself of the manner in which it was acted," but a month later she "never saw Kemble act better" than in *Macbeth*—"it was Mrs. Siddons' first appearance since the riots, and on her entrance she was much agitated."[1] After hearing a concert by the celebrated singer, Samuel Harrison:

> I was not so much gratified as I expected, whether it was that my attention was diverted by the party with me, and my soul was not all in my ears, I cannot tell, but I was not once in the world of spirits. I most firmly believe that I have no love of Music—indeed I find it is repugnant to my nature, and sometimes quite terrible to me—I mean terrible from the sensation of extreme fatigue I experience in hearing *some* kinds of Music, or indeed *any* for a continuance.

Either because her mother—who was fond of music—insisted, or because music was an inevitable part of social entertainment, she attended numerous concerts and was at last moved to enthusiasm on 10th July:

> A most happifying party at Lady Ellenborough's. For the first time in my life I have heard a female singer that made me forget all but Heaven—Mrs. Bates. Oh, one could not imagine in hearing her that art was necessary to the command of music. She appeared to sing the dwelling feeling of her soul, and her expressive countenance confirmed the idea . . . She sung . . . several of Handel's songs.

During four and a half months Elizabeth Duchess of Devonshire, Lady Ellenborough, and Lady Cork—described by the memoirist Gronow as "the notorious lion-hunter of her age"—were her most frequent hostesses, and by July she felt "much respect" for Lady Ellenborough:

> She appears constantly actuated by a principle of disinterested universal benevolence. She says ill of none, indeed appears to judge not ill. I do not suppose her to be a person of superior abilities, but she certainly possesses understanding to regulate her conduct, and to make it more generally approved than that of most persons in the great world.

Several times she dined with the great advocate, Lord Erskine, a friend of her father's, "who was, as I always think him, very agreable." He told her that "he had done with politics and was turned Farmer," that "there are very few ends which may not be attained if they are kept constantly in view," that the Princess Charlotte "appeared to him

[1] The O.P. (old price) Riots followed Kemble's opening of the new Covent Garden Theatre in September 1809 with increased prices of admission. *The Times* declared "it was a noble sight to see so much indignation in the public mind," and the demonstrations continued for more than fifty nights till the management reduced the pit price from 4*s*. to 3*s*. 6*d*.

lively and clever," that in the House of Lords debate on the proposed alteration of the penal laws "Ellenborough talked a great quantity of nonsense, unworthy of him," that he had advised Napoleon, when first consul, on changes in the French legal system and "Bonaparte said he thought the French nation were not yet prepared for the trial by Jury after having so long been accustomed to a different mode of administering justice."

Seeing Mary Montgomery almost daily during these months in London, Annabella developed a new intimacy with Lady Gosford, the wife of her friend's cousin, the second Earl. The son of Judith's old friend, Lord Gosford succeeded to the title on the death of his father in 1807; he had married in 1805 Mary Sparrow, sister of his brother-in-law, Brigadier-General Robert Sparrow, who had married Lady Olivia Acheson in 1797. As Lady Gosford must have been about seven, and Lady Olivia fifteen years her senior, there was no little impertinence in Annabella's letter to her new friend after she had returned to Seaham in the autumn of 1810:

> I am glad you are so *much* disposed to like Lady Olivia. The observations I made in London on each of you lead me to believe she had more regard for you than you for her. I remember once signifying to you that there was something odd in your manner towards her. I suppose she did not perceive it, but if it had been exercised towards me, I much doubt whether I should now be writing to you. The only conclusion to be drawn from this is that she hath more humility than me—*much more* I believe, for I esteem this to be one of her principal virtues. Respecting your character she has always declared to me an opinion from which I am less inclined to dissent as I know you more. Of one point I think I can be certain, that she does not attach to you any faults which are not really to be found in your mental constitution.
>
> In my historical studies I have seen such fatal effects resulting from the want of that valuable privilege, freedom of speech, that I am determined not to relinquish it or let it become obsolete by neglecting to establish precedents. I shall therefore exercise it towards you even if you should erect yourself into a Court of Star-chamber . . . Did you ever notice the horrible deformity of your k— it is the ugliest letter I ever saw come from mortal's pen . . . What evil doth it denote?

So far from taking offence, Lady Gosford was soon a friend so intimate that Annabella differentiated between her two Marys by referring to her as MG and to Mary Montgomery as MM. In the following summer, when Judith felt the strain of the London season and went to Tunbridge Wells for the waters, Annabella was left as much under Lady Gosford's chaperonage as her father's.

Since he attended Annabella through her scarlet fever in 1797, the Durham physician Dr. Fenwick had become a close friend of the

Milbankes; "except your Parents," he wrote when admonishing Annabella on her behaviour to her mother, "there is not a friend of yours who loves you more sincerely than myself." In reply to her news to him from London soon after her arrival in April 1811, he wrote:

> I am glad you have found the most pleasant of your old acquaintances in Town . . . By your expressions I suppose Mr. Foster has in a great measure done away the unfavourable impression you had received of him in one point, & has considerably added to your general esteem. I am truly glad of it, & hope his public conduct will be equally honourable to him. He has, I fear, a difficult task to perform. The men from whom he receives his instructions are bigotted in their own plans, & the government which he has to treat with is one of the meanest that ever ruled a civilised nation. Indeed the People are not much better. Just emerged from a successful struggle for their independence, & governed by wise & just laws, they have shown no elevation of mind, no patriotism, no integrity. In short they contradict all political experience which in other instances has generally shown public & private virtue, as the result of Liberty & generous exertion . . . To treat with such a government & live with such a people is surely an arduous undertaking.

This was a Whig reformer's reaction to Annabella's news that Augustus Foster had been appointed Minister to the United States of America.

Born in 1780, the second son of Elizabeth Duchess of Devonshire's first marriage, Foster had gone from Oxford into the Guards and thence into the diplomatic service. His having served for a time as secretary of legation at Washington—which he described as an "absolute sepulchre"—was the only qualification of a young man in his thirty-first year to represent the interests of a nation at war in a country already hostile and soon to enter the war on the enemy's side, except that his mother was a duchess and the Prince Regent wished to oblige her. He was Annabella's first suitor; evidently his suit had not been favoured, but he may have hoped to make a formal proposal if he returned from his mission with improved prospects. On 20th September following, he wrote to Judith from Philadelphia a long letter of amiable gossip:

> I really do believe that in the Whole World there is no nation so barren of Curiosities . . . Some proofs of Genius, however, in a young Lad, a Native of this Town of the name of Leslie, may appear to you worth looking at, and I have sent you three little engravings from drawings of Cook in different attitudes. I beg of you to shew them to Miss Milbanke as she loves to encourage rising Merit. The lad is to be sent next Autumn to the Care of Mr. West[1] . . . I am doing what I can to get well acquainted with

[1] Charles Robert Leslie (1794–1859), born in London of American parentage, lived at Philadelphia from 1800 to 1811, when he returned to England to study at the Royal Academy under Benjamin West, P.R.A. He was elected R.A. in 1824. George Frederick Cooke, Kemble's chief rival on the London stage, died at New York during an American tour in September 1811.

this Country and to make myself popular here . . . It is, however, a sad Exile at best and I need not say how I long to be back . . . it makes me melancholy to see the List of Assemblies at which I have not been and where I would have given the World to have been . . . I hope I shall soon have the pleasure of hearing from you, my dear Madam . . . shall I add another most anxious wish—to know if the Season in London has been productive of no Change, if Things are as they were. This is all I can ask to know from this remote country & I trust you will understand me.

Foster had reason for anxiety if he heard of Annabella's activities. In April she resumed her habit of the previous season in listening demurely to such distinguished elders as Lord Erskine:

Lord E. spoke of the Duke of Gloucester in warm terms of approbation; he said no one better understood the constitution of England, or had more zeal to preserve its excellence . . . That the best thing that could happen to this Country would be the marriage of the Princess Charlotte with the Duke of Gloucester.

But with a season behind her, she was no longer regarded as an *ingénue*, and finding herself inundated with invitations, she forgot her religious preoccupations with illness and death in enjoyment of social pleasures natural in a girl of nineteen. Her journal became a crowded record of engagements—dinners, balls, assemblies, concerts, theatres. It was not surprising that her mother, now in her sixtieth year, retired to Tunbridge Wells at the end of June, though her father remained with her in London.

Annabella had now no dislike for music, at least if she heard it in good company, for she wrote to her mother of a visit to the Opera:

My neighbour in the box was Playfair the great Mathematician, whom Sir Ralph mistook for a man of the same name . . . who is the author of genealogical works, &c. Sir R. thought that Playfair was going to ask him, & *bother* him as he said, about his ancestors, and in consequence declined all conversation with the great man. I, who did not suffer from the same mistake, thought him very agreable . . . I heard Playfair say that he should go in a few days to Tunbridge, so if you meet him, you may ask him if I am not charming. I returned to Lady Gosfords after the first act of the Opera, and heard Mrs. Frere sing all kinds of Music, as beautifully as usual. Dr. Fenwick was extremely pleased with her singing.

Fenwick was in London for a brief visit to supervise a minor operation on Emily Milner; having observed Annabella's change of habit, he wrote after his departure to remind her of pleasure in "the beauties of Nature" with a warning against letting "your rational dissipation . . . hurt your health." Two days before, Annabella had assured her mother that she was "not at all tired with my two nights' dissipation," but on the third day, after attending a "breakfast" at Wanstead followed by a dance, she confessed on 11th July:

> I was very tired and wished much to come away at half past nine, but I could not get the carriage till after eleven. However Lady Gosford is a capital chaperon, and is never out of patience. We all (including Mr. Eden & Mr. Mackenzie) got away safe, after proving ourselves excellent philosophers. I like Mr. Mackenzie particularly, and danced with him the only country dance . . . The waltzing was most prevalent . . . I expect Miss Raine to dinner at six, and at ten Sir Ralph & I accompany Lady Gosford to Mrs. Frere's . . . Mrs. Lamb[1] leaves London tomorrow —I expect to meet her tonight at Mrs. Frere's . . . Farewell old Woman— make yourself very merry with thinking how merry I am. I shall write to you tomorrow on a subject which I have not now time to discuss. This I declare now because I like to excite your curiosity, and to delay gratifying it. I am a sweet chicken!!! You ought to think me the most barley-sugar daughter in the creation. I am tired of paying myself compliments but you may send me as many as you like.

Next day she did not mention the promised subject, but enumerated only her busy engagements. Looking forward to "some excellent music" at Mrs. Frere's, she had remarked, "if I like it, I shall not care about going to Lady Cork's, which is the same night, and will be a great squeeze without profit"; in the event, "I stayed at Mrs. Frere's till after twelve, and did not go afterwards to Lady Cork's, as Sir Ralph was rather tired . . . though he was very *willing* to chaperon." She explained how other engagements had prevented her from dining with Mrs. Gally Knight, an old friend of her mother's, and from accepting Lady Melbourne's invitation to the opera: "I believe a civil war will ensue because I cannot divide myself or be in two places at one moment. Don't publish my conceit." Ironically, in view of later developments, she showed no enthusiasm for the attentions of her influential aunt, writing on 16th July:

> Tonight I am going to the Opera with Lady Melbourne, which I would rather not do, as it is a considerable fatigue to me who do not take pleasure in flirting or listening to squalling, and I have never gone to bed rationally since you went away.

She was now "anxious to get to old Seaham," being concerned about Mary Montgomery's health:

> The evident daily decrease of life in MM makes me the more feel a separation from her. I think her case perfectly hopeless. Another of the Vertebrae has been discovered to be diseased since Fenwick went away,

[1]Mrs. George Lamb, wife of Lady Melbourne's fourth son, was to be one of Annabella's sympathisers when she separated from Byron.

and the benefit of the seaton is only partial, and cannot as the wise people say affect more than two of the Vertebrae, and those adjoining. Part of the Caustic is beginning to come out.

This confident knowingness about medicine and surgery was to become a tedious feature of her letters in later years and a source of affliction to her daughter.

If it was not the subject calculated to excite her mother's curiosity after the Wanstead excursion, a proposal of marriage from the Hon. George Eden was hastened by the imminence of Annabella's leaving London. The heir of Sir John Eden's brother who had been raised to the peerage as Lord Auckland for his services as ambassador in Spain and the Netherlands, George Eden was twenty-six, a practising barrister and a member of Parliament. Succeeding three years later to his father's title, he proceeded to a brilliant political career, being successively President of the Board of Trade, First Lord of the Admiralty, and Governor-General of India. On his death in 1849 the diarist Greville wrote of him:

> To his sisters he was as a husband, a brother, and a friend combined in one, and to them it is a bereavement full of sadness almost amounting to despair. He was a man without shining qualities or showy accomplishments, austere and almost forbidding in his manner, silent and reserved in society, unpretending both in public and in private life . . . Nevertheless he was universally popular, and his company more desired and welcome than that of many far more sprightly and brilliant men. His understanding was excellent, his temper placid, his taste and tact exquisite; his disposition, notwithstanding his apparent gravity, cheerful, and under his cold exterior there was a heart overflowing with human kindness, and with the deepest feelings of affection, charity, and benevolence.

Rejected by Annabella, he never married. Perhaps his cold exterior concealed a faithful heart; more probably his pride recoiled from possible repetition of the humiliating rebuff, which he accepted with dignity and grace:

> I dreamt a dream of happiness and presumptuously attempted to realise it . . . I will try to forget it all. Be a friend still to my Mother and to my sisters. I have taught them to love you & they need not unlearn it.

Lady Auckland also wrote on 26th July to Annabella, who had stayed more than once at Eden Farm, the Aucklands' home near Beckenham:

> From the time of your first visit, we had certainly blinded ourselves. And the conversations we had had together, during that short time, had convinced us that the family which might obtain you would possess a great blessing. As to our beloved George's sentiments, he has spoken for

himself. He must also judge for himself, whether he has strength of mind to accept of that friendship so kindly offered . . . His affectionate kindness to us all, endears him so much to his family, that there is no sacrifice we would not make to save him one pang. After our next interview our plan is never more to mention the subject to him . . . As to Lord Auckland and myself we so warmly admire what you have permitted us to know of a character so far beyond what any of your years possess, that it will be a real grief to us should our intercourse cease here . . . we flatter ourselves that at some future time . . . you will revisit Eden Farm, either with or without Sir Ralph & Lady Milbanke . . . you may depend upon no allusion of any kind being made by us to what has passed. My dear girls will enjoy your cheerful & improving society, & we will endeavour to forget that we had flattered ourselves with the possibility of a nearer connection.

Notably with Mary Dulcibella, the sixth of Lady Auckland's eight daughters, Annabella continued friendship and correspondence; curiously she accepted hospitality at Eden Farm in the autumn following her separation from Byron.

Lady Auckland supposed that Annabella's sense of duty and conscience fitted her as a mate for her high-minded son. But Annabella would have had to exert herself to live up to George Eden's expectations as a husband; she preferred always to condescend from a pedestal, as to the shoemaker Blacket and to the invalid orphan, Mary Montgomery. Even Dr. Fenwick, though privileged as an old family friend and her medical attendant from the nursery, was a social inferior and had to temper tentative advice with apologies for his presumption.

A poet of more substantial reputation than Blacket's, the Rev. James Grahame, became Annabella's friend and correspondent after coming as curate to Sedgefield, near Durham, in 1810. After practising as an advocate at Edinburgh, he published his poem, *The Sabbath*, in 1804, and some time afterwards took orders; his last work, *Poems on the Abolition of the Slave Trade*, appeared in 1810. Ralph Milbanke was one of William Wilberforce's supporters in parliament in demanding abolition of the slave trade, and when Annabella was going up to London in April 1811, Grahame wrote asking her to interest Wilberforce in the case of Forster Charlton, who had been committed to Morpeth Gaol for agitation against the slave trade.

Though she wrote with respect of both Grahame and his wife in her letters and notebooks, Annabella was able to condescend to them, for they were poor and Grahame was a very sick man. Soon after she went to London in April, Grahame returned to Edinburgh in the hope of improving his health. At first Mrs. Grahame announced that "my Goodman is better," though subject to "sleepy fits" on the slightest infringement of a strict diet; on returning to her children at Sedgefield, she wrote hopefully on 24th August, though Grahame was afflicted with "horror . . . at learning that some charitable persons have been pleased to ascribe the effects of his stomachic disease to intoxication or madness." He died on 14th September 1811, and on 18th October his widow wrote to remind Annabella of her "kind offer" to visit her, as she was now "able to meet you without either feeling or exciting any painful emotions."

During the winter of 1811–12 Annabella saw much of Mrs. Grahame, corresponded regularly with her throughout the following year, and recorded her "character" in her journal:

> Mrs. Grahame loves & practises truth of word & deed with an uncommon degree of disregard to the consequences on her worldly prosperity. This would be true magnanimity, were it not partly *supported* by pride, though *created* by the purest principles of Rectitude. She *glories* in being more independant of selfish interests than her fellow creatures. The influence of Pride is seldom confined to one part of a Character; in hers it has also produced too sensitive a suspicion of being slighted for the want of Fortune's gifts, and she haughtily despises those whom she imagines mean enough to regard the situation more than the person. From having experienced the selfish unkindness of the powerful, she is prejudiced in favour of the lower classes of society, and seems to think that the absence of refinement secures the absence of hypocrisy.

At least once Mrs. Grahame practised "truth of word" too frankly for Annabella's approval. Advising her "to keep free of the matrimonial noose till after your northern expedition," and considering "a clear head to be the best security for a good heart," she counselled Annabella to "secure your own happiness & that of some other person whose happiness may be dearer to you than your own . . . I am impertinent enough to beseech you to marry no one for whom you do not think you could submit, even if necessary, to beg; and through whom you might not gratify your darling passion with impunity." To this Annabella took exception, for Mrs. Grahame wrote on 18th February 1812:

> I deserved to be reproved, and I stand corrected, for having presumed to use the shadow of the semblance of the language of reproof to you. On the subject of heart and head, I find we have been playing at cross purposes. It appeared so clear to myself that Mr. Security could never appear in any more elevated character than that of second fiddle, until your letter undeceived me . . . My arguments on that subject were all, impertinently enough as I was conscious & told you at the time, directed to *a* particular case.

No sooner had she sent this letter than she feared having given further offence:

I do most solemnly declare that I had not any particular case in view, and that had I *ever heard of one*, I should have been the last person in the world who would have presumed to volunteer an opinion upon it, to you. Instead of "a particular case" I meant . . . "to a *supposed* particular case."

Mrs. Grahame seems to have recognised, partly from her own observation, partly from what she learned from Dr. Fenwick, that Mary Montgomery's elder brother Hugh was in love with Annabella, and that Annabella, though not in love with him, might drift into marriage with him through her devotion to his sister. Hence she advised her to make no decision till after a "northern expedition" which would presumably enable her to see more of Lord Seaforth's son, William Frederick Mackenzie, who had impressed her so favourably during the previous summer.

A journey to Scotland, if projected, was indefinitely postponed. Annabella spent Christmas of 1811 at Elemore with the Bakers, who accompanied her to Seaham for the new year. Judith's habits were unchanged; when she was at home, guests left only to be immediately replaced. Annabella described Captain Tower—Isabella Baker's future husband—as "a well-disposed young man with an inferior capacity"; unconscious of reflecting her own formidable coolness, she found his "best disposition" was "*gratitude*—He appears susceptible of the least kindness." Though disapproving his contempt for Campbell and Ossian, she preferred the older Captain Boothby, who impressed her with his appreciation of Milton and talked entertainingly of his experiences in Spain. Other guests were the poet Southey's brother Henry, a surgeon practising at Durham, and one of the Hutchinsons, the family to which Wordsworth's wife belonged. Their conversation inspired Annabella to consult Mrs. Grahame about the Lake Poets:

Robert Southey is an excellent man in private life. In society he deserves *admiration*, but does not appear so amiable, on account of a degree of self-confidence which tinctures his manner. He has rather an oracular way of delivering opinions. His eye seems animated with truly poetic fire. His voice is harsh . . . Mrs. Grahame thinks Wordsworth a more *pleasing* companion, because his manner is less assuming, & his voice not repugnant to the ear or the mind. She thinks him not free from self-importance in matters of opinion.

A week later, staying in Durham with the Hoars, she met Southey's naval brother and his wife, who expressed "great warmth in praise of Southey the Poet, for whom she says that all who are intimately acquainted with his character feel the greatest attachment."

> Of Coleridge she does not think so favourably. He at first deceived her by the enthusiasm he shewed for all that *deserved* admiration and reverence, but she now considers this as entirely a trick. He is intolerably self-sufficient and cannot bear to be *second* in the attention of the Company. Robert Southey is very partial to his society, & considers him as a "man of astonishing powers"—he acknowledges that he is "morally deranged", but regards this as *his* weak part, in which he is not more guilty than the rest of mortals. I have never heard any thing of Southey that displeased me so much as this anecdote.

Despite this ominous disapproval of Southey's tolerance towards moral weakness in genius, Annabella read his *Madoc*, and though "some passages are wearisome . . . it has perfectly convinced me that in genius he excels every living poet and that he *will* be ranked high among the more ancient ones."

By this time Judith was reaping something of her sowing in the spoiling of her daughter. Annabella had inherited her own self-importance and determination to get her own way without any of her charm, gaiety, and warm affection. While she could dominate her father with playful confidence, she resented her mother's authority and lost no chance of suggesting that she was old-fashioned. While Judith doated as devotedly as ever, she must have felt hurt by Annabella's mocking acceptance of her devotion while continually reminding her of her age, and her quick temper rose to retorts further alienating her daughter's sympathy. "Goodbye old Lady" was a characteristic ending of Annabella's letters at this period, and from Elemore that Christmas she wrote:

> The Elemorians are very good to me & I am very comfortable, only I sometimes give a sympathetic sigh for your dullness when you are *minus me*.

Her main concern in this letter was with Fenwick's opinion of MM's examination by the fashionable London doctor, Matthew Baillie—"I think he views it in too flattering a light." In her reply Judith reported of her own conversation with Fenwick that he was "very sanguine" about MM because a doctor of Baillie's reputation was unlikely to be mistaken in his diagnosis; in regard to Annabella's remark on Mrs. Hoar's report of a comment of Judith's she retorted, "I am aware, my dear Girl, that neither you nor I have much *philosophy in conversation*"—which can have been hardly gratifying to Annabella's self-esteem.

During January Judith evidently confided some of her worry about Annabella to her niece, for Sophy Tamworth wrote on 4th February:

> Sir Ralph and yourself are more than *commonly* blessed in your *treasure*, therefore no doubt your anxiety exceeds that which must naturally be experienced by parents in general. To know that Annabella was settled

to her own happiness, and consequently to your wishes, would indeed give real joy to all your true friends, but it is not every day that she is likely to meet with a *Mind* which ought to claim kindred with one so superior as hers. Therefore surely your first care ought to be directed to the preservation of your own health and Spirits that, whenever such a desirable event does occur, you may be fully able to participate in her happiness. I *will not believe* what you tell me of your having become an *Old Lady*—well remembering that you imagined yourself such, even at the time when I used to stand by your toilet at Richmond, *kneading* Powder and Pomatum.

Dining with Dr. Fenwick in Durham on 1st February, Annabella confided something of her friction with her mother, for he wrote:

I felt yesterday that you could not open your heart to me entirely on every subject, but I am confident I read your heart . . . *If* you have sought general admiration too much, check in future a desire which in excess is very injurious to a woman; & if you are conscious of any fault in your conduct to your Mother, delay not my dear Annabella to atone for it, & let me intreat you never to fall into a similar fault. I know you have a warm temper to struggle with; I have seen you subdue it & have been sensible of the effort it cost you. Should it have been too strong for you in any instance, your apology is in the firmness with which you in general express it, but in no case would that apology avail you so little as where your Mother is concerned. If she sometimes is mistaken as to the best method of securing your comfort, she is so truly affectionate, her confidence in you is so liberal, so entire & so honourable to both; in short her feelings as a Mother occupy so large a portion of her existence, that you cannot be too studious to make a suitable return.

Fenwick's advice conspired with Annabella's own conscience about leaving her parents while her father was ill to indulge her wish to be with MM in London, and she retired to her own room to write to her mother:

I express myself in writing not because I have any objection to speaking on a subject that cannot excite my irritability but because I want to *collect* my sentiments in order to make them known to you & my father.

I am perfectly aware of the great effort you make in sacrificing to me not only your wish for my presence, but your fears for my absence. I regard it as an extraordinary proof of *disinterested* affection,—and hope that the remembrance of it will prevent me from ever again indulging my irritable humours at the expence of your feelings.

I expected from your promise given last month that this offer would be made, and I had determined not to accept it, because I thought it would bring additional anxiety on you . . . It is also natural to me to be *less* disposed *to take*, in proportion as *more is given*, and it is really in opposition to this impulse that I do not refuse your offer.

My reasons are these—I find that you are always sensible of the unquiet state of my mind however the appearance of it is checked, and could I by long habit gain more perfect command of my manner & countenance, I regard it as *ultimately* an unkind thing to employ it in deceiving you about my feelings. When I am absent from a friend who is in such a state as MM, I cannot prevent myself from perpetually imagining *worse* than really is, and even when I do not yield to this kind of dread, the effort to subdue it interrupts my peace. I can truly say from experience that though I have often thought her dying *when she has been with me*, I never from that idea experienced anything so painful as the present total uncertainty with regard to the progress of her malady, and the propriety of the measures pursued. I have no idea that she is in any *near* danger—perhaps I may find her in less than when she was here, but from the accounts I receive I derive no satisfaction . . . Should I find myself happily undeceived from my apprehensions, I am sure that my journey will contribute as much to your peace as to mine.

But before I go I must be assured that my father's health is amending, else I should fly from one anxiety to suffer from another. I therefore propose not to be in London till this day fortnight, as the intermediate time will probably give me the certainty I desire of Sir Ralph's progress to good health. I shall also feel the separation from him & you less painful in proportion as I can hope that it will be shortened.

A.I.M.

I cannot express how calm & contented my mind has become since your kindness last night.

This epistle is indicative of the dominant emotion in Annabella's life—her passion for self-justification. Throughout her subsequent life she resorted to this practice of "collecting her sentiments" on paper, and having justified her conduct to her own satisfaction, she remained obdurate in her conviction of its rectitude.

Having in this instance indulged her orgasm of self-justification, she set out for London on 21st February, writing that night from Wetherby in accordance with a promise not to "forget my *patient Dad & Mam* whenever I can conveniently epistolize." She wrote from Doncaster on Saturday and Grantham on Sunday, before on Monday 24th February she recorded in her journal, "Arrived in London to be with MG." Next day she wrote to her mother:

I write this in bed, after the sound repose which is the consequence of being wearied with happiness. I have seen nothing but faces as smiling as my own, and MM's was light up with a degree of joy that for a time gave her the appearance of blooming health. She was however soon exhausted, and became pale & weak. I then saw how much more feeble she *is* than she was at Seaham. Her legs in particular are, as I understand, more habitually failing. I know nothing more at present, for I have not seen her spine . . . Lady Gosford . . . appears immoderately happy in the possession of me. Lord G. also seems very much pleased, and shews me every attention . . . I am a sufferer from Chilblains produced by the cold on my journey.

Her letter went on to relate inside information about the state of Sicily, how the Prince Regent had abused Lord Grey and the Whigs so violently that Princess Charlotte had "burst into tears, for I am told it is well known that she is a *sincere whig*," how Francis Doyle had secured a preferment under Lord Moira, and how Lady Gosford had invited Mrs. George Lamb "to come here on Thursday evening to see me—Ly G. was not acquainted with her before, but endeavoured to become so I doubt not for my gratification."

Though she assured her mother that MM "is my *first* object in coming here," clearly a close second was her appetite for social activity. With both objects was associated the taste for admiration against which Fenwick warned her—a weakness which she recognised to the extent of writing to her mother, "Your buttering speeches make me very happy. Remember that I am quite a Russian in my love for such grease."

Some friends of Judith's did not hesitate to express disapproval of Annabella's behaviour. To Judith on 27th February Annabella remarked, "Lady Athlone called here yesterday to enquire after Sir Ralph, whose illness she had heard magnified till she had become extremely anxious"; apparently she was more confidential to her friend Anne Hoar, from whom Dr. Fenwick "learn'd your apprehension that Lady Athlone blamed you for leaving your parents at the time you did."

4

THE BYRON SEASON OF 1812

Annabella sat to George Hayter for her portrait in March 1812. Hayter was commended to her by Ridley Colborne, a family friend whose taste in art she respected. "He is a young Artist just come to London and anxious to establish a reputation," she informed her mother on 8th March. His price was twenty guineas: "I cannot get myself done decently by any one for less." After the first sitting she decided, "Mr. Hayter is I think very clever, but it seems to me quite impossible that he should succeed in *me* for he has never seen *my* Countenance, because it is under the deforming influence of shyness in his presence." A fortnight later, when MM accompanied her to the sitting "to improve my countenance", she reported:

> He wishes very much to introduce some part of my hair hanging down, as he says that *formal arrangement* of dress is not consistent with the nature of my character. He seems so full of intelligence and taste that I am inclined to agree with what he recommends.

Hayter was only Annabella's own age, but he knew his business. He saw a small woman with a pretty figure and rich brown hair; he made the most of her figure and persuaded her to let down her hair, not only displaying its attraction but hiding the slightness of her shoulders and emphasising her neckline. Recognising her self-consciousness, he posed her to look away from him, but in pose and expression he succeeded in conveying, not merely her self-consciousness, but something of her complacency and condescension.

Undoubtedly she had attraction, though no beauty. She was also an heiress, for even if the Milbankes' financial embarrassment was known, they still entertained lavishly and she was an only child, with expectations from her childless uncle, Lord Wentworth. Hence she had no lack of suitors in succession to George Eden, though Mackenzie dropped out of the running. To her father on 14th March she wrote:

> Lady Gosford and I are very much amused by observing the nets prepared by Lady Seaforth to catch a daughter-in-law—O wondrous Fisher-

woman! . . . Mr. Mackenzie (the bait) is not yet in Town, and he intends visiting Seaham in his way. Pray shew him *paternal* tenderness.

After seeing Lady Seaforth frequently, she "saw Mr. Mackenzie the first time this year" at her house on 6th April; she danced with him at a ball two nights later, but on 13th April she informed her father, "I do not believe that Mac has any thoughts of me though I am sure Lady Seaforth has."

Three days after her arrival in London she met Lord Longford's brother, Edward Pakenham, a brilliant cavalry officer who was already a major-general at thirty-four. Evidently he was immediately attracted, for Annabella was continually in contact with members of his family during the next few weeks—with his mother, old Lady Longford, his elder brother and his sisters, Lady Wellington and Mrs. Henry Hamilton. She was entertained by his anecdotes of his brother-in-law Wellington, the national hero, but thought "his manners rather too *silken*," in "singular contrast with his military ardour which is very great." She disliked Lady Wellington, as "she is now so dreadfully under the sway of a ruling passion, *Bloodthirsty Ambition*," her husband's honours having "exalted her own pride till she will only notice people according to their rank or connection with herself." On 10th March she discovered that "Gen. Pakenham's opinions are not founded on the same principles as mine," and having heard that "all the Pakenhams have a strong family tendency to insanity," she rejected his proposal on St. Patrick's Day, writing to her mother on the 20th:

Gen. Pakenham has called here, as he requested that Lady Gosford would allow him to surmount the awkwardness of a first interview with me when there was no spectator but herself. He told her that he has now submitted to reason, and that he will never think again of his presumptuous hopes.

I met him with cordiality. He said, "I am grateful for your friendship—be assured you shall never repent it." I replied "I have perfect confidence in you"—& we then talked as if nothing of this nature had passed between us.

Being on leave—he shortly returned to Spain to distinguish himself at the battle of Salamanca—Pakenham may have been too impetuous in proposing. When Colonel Hervey-Bathurst—Wellington's "most favorite Aid de Camp," who impressed her with "a high idea of his ability and gentleness of disposition"—"spoke of Gen. Pakenham, whom he knows intimately, with very great approbation both as a soldier and a man," Annabella reflected that "the testimony of every body respecting him is to this effect," and felt the need for self-justification to her mother on 23rd March:

I received a letter from Lady Wellington which I enclose, as you will find that it takes all responsibility from me. I think that her expressions are very handsome in regard to me. I communicated the whole affair this morning to Lord G[osford], who perfectly approves both my actions and manner, & I think that *Men* are in these cases much the *best judges*.

Again on the 27th:

I have neither seen nor heard of Gen. P. since I sent the letter to Mrs. Hamilton which I copied for you. I therefore trust that it exactly answered my purpose, which was to prevent his encreasing his malady by a conduct that could only proceed from his unconsciously cherishing a remain of hope. I am quite satisfied with the part I have acted in regard to him. I meant it for his good, and I am sure that it has proved so.

On the day of Pakenham's dismissal she was already considering another possible suitor—Lord Jocelyn, the twenty-three-year-old heir of the second Earl of Roden. She understood that his engagement to the Duke of Richmond's daughter, Lady Mary Lennox, was "completely broken off":

So you see that I may still hope for this spouse, who in Lady G's opinion would suit me so well. Unfortunately she has lately discovered that his Mother was *a Bligh*, and that insanity is very strong in the family. Lord J. is ugly, not very unlike William Taylor in features, & extremely like in countenance, but he is dark. He is bandy-legged, very tall and ungraceful. He seems unaffected and ingenuous.

Four days later:

Lord Jocelyn improves very much on acquaintance. I should think he was *really honorable* (that is *honest*) without the *pride* which too often accompanies that character. There is much warm cheerfulness in his countenance, yet great capacity for reflection. He seems to think very little of himself in company.

On the 25th, after only a week's acquaintance:

Lord Jocelyn came to take leave of Ly Gosford previous to his departure for Ireland, whither he is going in consequence of his appointment of Treasurer of the Regent's household. His love appears at times in society to oppress his feelings, which however he commands in a manly manner.

A month later she recorded that "Lord Jocelyn's engagement is completely ended—he is not yet returned to England."

The coolness between the Milbankes and Lady Melbourne continued, but after meeting her aunt at a ball, Annabella paid a dutiful call on 2nd March and found Lady Melbourne had been "very unwell herself," which might be "some excuse" for her having expressed no concern about Sir Ralph—her "head was shaking this morning as if she had a paralytic affection." As a result she was "obliged to extend my chaperoning rule to *relations*" by "going to Lady Salisbury's tonight with Mrs. G. Lamb, whom I could not possibly refuse without offence." This was an example of her habit of making a virtue of inclination, as Mrs. George Lamb was the member of Lady Melbourne's family whom she liked.

Nearly seven years older than Annabella, Caroline St. Jules was nominally the "adopted daughter" of Elizabeth Duchess of Devonshire—actually her illegitimate daughter and half-sister to Annabella's suitor, Augustus Foster. When she married Lady Melbourne's fourth son in 1809, the Duke of Devonshire gave her a dowry of £30,000. Regarded as "amiable but impenetrable," she may have cultivated inscrutable demureness of manner and prudent conduct in reaction to her dubious birth and insecure childhood; despite the infidelity of an unsatisfactory husband, she seems to have been tempted only once and very briefly to trespass against convention, which self-abnegation was to render her the more susceptible to sympathy with Annabella in her separation from Byron.

Though she included Mrs. George Lamb among her "Characters", Annabella did not succeed in penetrating the armour of her reserve. She found her charm lay "in a graceful diffidence which obtains approbation from not exacting it," and while "she has not that romantic force of feeling which suggests extraordinary acts of disinterestedness . . . she regulates her conduct with a view to the welfare of others, as far as she *thinks* of the duty of doing good." Her "diffidence" enabled Annabella to feel at ease with her, by contrast with the wariness of her approach to Lady Melbourne and her other daughter-in-law, Lady Caroline, the wife of William Lamb.

Dining at Lady Melbourne's on 15th March, Annabella "was more pleased with Ly C. Lamb than before, because I thought that when she was silly, she was really *unmeaning*, not artificial."

> She seems clever in every thing that is not within the province of common sense. Julius Caesar, Lord Byron's new poem, and politics were the principal themes of conversation. William Lamb appeared to me self-sufficient.

After these notes in her journal, she expanded to her mother:

> Lady Caroline Lamb amused me very much by her *attempted* quotations from Julius Caesar which I imagine she knew nothing of till she saw it acted . . . I was not pleased with William Lamb's manners, which I think very consequential.

Ly Caroline has asked me to a party at her house on Thursday, not a very numerous one, and she told me with more consideration than I should have expected from her character that Lady Holland would be one of her company, and she thought it right to mention this, as you were absent, lest I might inadvertently be led to do what you would not approve . . . I replied that I was very much obliged to her for her kind considerations, but that I was sure you would not object to my being in the same party with any one whom she thought proper to receive as her guest. If I am asked to be introduced to Lady Holland's acquaintance, I shall certainly decline, but I think you will agree with me that no one will regard me as corrupted by being *in the room* with her.[1]

Lady Melbourne was *very* kind and seemed really anxious to promote my wishes, but nobody appears more *sincerely* friendly than Mrs. Lamb. Indeed I think her too kind-hearted to be *quite fashionable*.

At Lady Caroline's party she duly "saw" Lady Holland, whose "countenance says that she is capable of determined malice." On 22nd March, having heard everybody talking of it, she "began to read Lord Byron's poem entitled Childe Harold"; two days later she finished the poem, "which contains many passages in the best style of poetry."

He is rather too much a *mannerist*, that is, he wants variety in the turns of his expressions. He excels most in the delineation of deep feeling, and in reflections relative to human nature.

On 25th March—the day Lord Jocelyn called before leaving for Ireland—she went to "a morning party at Lady Caroline Lamb's" and "saw Lord Byron for the first time."

His mouth continually betrays the acrimony of his spirit. I should judge him sincere and independent—*Sincere* at least in society as far as he can be, whilst dissimulating the violence of his scorn. He very often hides his mouth with his hand when speaking. He professed himself very partial to Music, and said he could not understand how any one could be indifferent to it. It appeared to me that he tried to controul his natural sarcasm and vehemence as much as he could, in order not to offend, but at times his lips thickened with disdain, and his eyes rolled impatiently. Indeed the scene was calculated to shew human absurdities. There was the listless gaiety which so surely bespeaks the absence of enjoyment. Waltzing was in vain attempted to give animation. Music was listened to *as a duty*. *Thought* was engrossed by *self*. What a picture of the first-rate society of London! Of the company there I remember Lady Jersey, gentle & elegant as usual—Lord & Lady Kinnaird, She goodnatured, he

[1] Lady Holland, *née* Elizabeth Vassall, married in 1786 Sir Godfrey Webster, who divorced her by act of parliament in 1797, when she married Lord Holland. Mary Noel wrote to Judith Milbanke on 17th February 1797: "I have seen Ly Webster, who is so comfortably absurd about her daughter in Law that it is quite ridiculous. Sir G. is determined to be devorced that she may marry Ld. Holland, as he wd. not have it to answer for that she sd. be a common Woman."

superfine—Miss Mercer Elphinstone, incomprehensible. I suspect that she thinks it becoming to her situation to be assuming, and that the encouragement she unfortunately meets with, has encreased this disagreable habit, which *may* conceal a rightly disposed heart. She was very roughly obliging to me. Mrs. Lamb, sensible amidst this contagious folly. Lord Palmerston—in his element!

On the same day, after dining with MM, she called on her mother's old friend, Mrs. Gally Knight,[1] who "told me some authentic anecdotes of Lord Byron which gave me much concern, as they indicated feelings dreadfully perverted."

Next day she included some of Mrs. Knight's anecdotes in an account to her mother:

Yesterday I went to a *morning* party at Lady Caroline Lamb's, where my curiosity was much gratified by seeing Lord Byron, the object at present of universal attention.

Lady C. has of course seized on him, notwithstanding the reluctance he manifests to be shackled by her. What a shining situation she will have in his next satire!

He appears to be a very independent observer of mankind. His views of life participate that bitterness of Spirit which (as I hear) makes himself wretched. He quarrelled with all his family, and this was the cause of his foreign travels. Young Knight is acquainted with him, and was very much shocked by hearing him say "Thank Heaven! I have quarrelled with my mother *for ever*". He is so very proud that the shadow of advice even from the kindest motives, has excited his indignation to the highest degree and *for years,* which happened with regard to his sister. She had suggested that it would be better if he left his name with some common acquaintance. In consequence he would not speak to her for very long.

It is said that he is an infidel, and I think it probable from the general character of his mind. His poem sufficiently proves that he *can* feel nobly, but he has discouraged his own goodness. His features are well formed—his upper lip is drawn towards the nose with an expression of impatient disgust. His eye is restlessly thoughtful.

He talks much, and I heard some of his conversation, which is very able, and sounds like the *true* sentiments of the Speaker.

I did not seek an introduction to him, for all the women were absurdly courting him, and trying to *deserve* the lash of his Satire. I thought that *inoffensiveness* was the most secure conduct, as I am not desirous of a place in his lays. Besides I cannot worship talents that are unconnected with the love of man, nor be captivated by that Genius which is barren in blessings. So I made no offering at the shrine of Childe Harold, though I shall not refuse the acquaintance if it comes in my way.

[1] Selina, wife of Henry Gally Knight, of Langold, Notts., was the sister of Sir William FitzHerbert (1748–91) and Alleyne FitzHerbert (1753–1839), a distinguished diplomatist who was created Lord St. Helens in 1791. She was first cousin of Judith Milbanke's close friend, Mrs. Davison Bland. Her husband's estates near Mansfield were within a few miles of Byron's at Newstead Abbey. Her son, Henry Gally Knight (1786–1846), was at Cambridge with Byron and afterwards met him at Athens in 1810.

She enclosed some extracts from *Childe Harold*, on which her father commented on the 29th:

> I was entertained with your account of Lord Byron and the ladies yelping about him. I liked the parts of his work which you extracted, but was obliged to read them with attention two or three times. I think it is good poetry.

Nearly three weeks passed before Annabella saw Byron again. In the interval she attended the Lord Mayor's Ball, which prompted more reflections on the vanities of fashionable society, spent a week-end with the Aucklands at Eden Farm, George Eden being present, and stayed three days at Brocket Hall with Lady Melbourne:

> The party consisted of Lord & Ly Cowper, Mr. Lamb & Lady Caroline, the Duchess of Devonshire, Mrs. G. Lamb and Mr. Foster, who is a caricature of his brother Augustus . . . The Dss of Devonshire is a portrait of restless wretchedness. If vanity and dissimulation have been there, misery has chastened the soul from their influence. She has the spiritless look of penitential humility.
>
> Mrs. G. Lamb appeared to me more sensible than ever. I think her remarkably sincere in stating her own impressions on various subjects.
>
> Lady C. Lamb does not do justice to her own understanding. She conceals its power under the Childish manner which she either indulges or affects.

Caro George—as Mrs. George Lamb was called in the family for convenient distinction from Lady Caroline, who was Caro William—had a motive for engaging Annabella's confidence, having been instructed by her mother to ascertain whether Augustus Foster had any chance in his suit to Annabella. On 9th April Annabella wrote to her father:

> Mrs. Lamb on reconsideration thought it best to report to Foster the conversation that has passed respecting him. She found that even in his last letter his hopes were only checked, not abandoned. She therefore thought that the sooner they were extinguished the more peaceful his mind would become. Her only fear is that he will marry some American in the first impulse of his vexation. She says his feelings are very strong but not durable.

By this time she had attracted another admirer—William John Bankes, heir to the estate of Kingston Lacy in Dorset, who had been a Cambridge friend of Byron's—and continued to her father:

> Mrs. Bankes visited me the day before yesterday, in order to make an oration on the merits of her children, particularly William my suitor,

whom one of my smiles would encourage to propose, but I am very niggardly of my glances. The youth has £8000 per ann, independent of his father whose heir he must be. This information did not come from *Mrs. Bankes*, but from a more authentic quarter . . . I am *quite the fashion* this year. Mankind bow before me, and womankind think me *somebody*. But without jest I am certain that I am better liked in company, probably because I am stronger and more able to exert myself in the scenes of dissipation.

As Sir Ralph's health still prevented her parents' coming to open their house in Portland Place, her mother wondered if Annabella's prolonged stay was imposing on the Gosfords, but Annabella reassured her on 10th April that "there was not the least ground for your apprehensions," Lady Gosford having assured her, "*We* are most happy to have you."

Indeed yesterday she told me how precious she considered the time that was passed with me. I am convinced that you may rest satisfied on this point. Lord Gosford's conduct to me is marked by the most attentive kindness. You know I am not apt to intrude myself without reluctance, and you have often reproached me for being too ready to *take fancies* even about the sentiments of my best friends. Therefore you may believe that I am not in error when I am decidedly of opinion that I interfere with no one's comfort in this house, and that I give pleasure to the Inhabitants.

Three days later, to make some return of hospitality, she announced to her father, "I am going to open my house in Portland Place" for "a dinner of 14 persons":

The Wentworths will be arrived in Town, and I think that the admirable manner in which I shall do the honors of the House may procure me a *wing of the estate*. I hope Lady Mil will approve this *extravagance*. My party will consist of the Knights, Gosfords, Blands, Lord St. Helens, Lord Gambier (whom every body loves because he is the merriest of mortals), the Lambs & some men who cannot think that I am in love with them.

That evening, Monday 13th April, she saw Lord Byron for the second time—at Lady Gosford's assembly—and wrote the same night to her mother:

I have met with much evidence of his goodness. You know how easily the noblest heart may be perverted by unkindness—perhaps the most easily a *noble* heart, because it is more susceptible to ungenerous indignities.

On Tuesday she noted in her journal, "For the first time I conversed with Lord Byron—chiefly respecting Blacket, & was pleased with the humanity of his feelings on the subject." On Wednesday the 15th she expanded to her mother:

On Monday as I told you there was a party here, at which Lord Byron, the comet of this year, shone with his customary glory. He certainly is very shy, and in consequence our acquaintance did not proceed that night, as I had not leisure to concert an attack on him. Indeed I was tormented by that impudent Bankes who seems really to consider me as his property, and will not understand any rebuffs . . . Last night I went to a supper at Lady Cowper's of about fifty most agreable persons . . . Lord Byron and I had some very pleasing conversation—at least I thought it such. He begun to address me with great respect, saying that as he knew how kindly I had interested myself for Blacket, he wished to caution me against placing confidence in Pratt, of whose roguishness he had had personal experience.[1] His intention appeared to be a benevolent one, viz. to prevent the surviving child from being injured by the selfishness of Pratt.

Lord Byron is certainly very interesting, but he wants that calm benevolence which could only touch my heart. He is very handsome & his manners are in a superior degree such as one should attribute to Nature's Gentlemen . . .

I am just going to a morning party at Lady Caroline Lamb's. My Cousins cannot live without me.

Of Lady Caroline's party she noted:

I continued my acquaintance with Lord Byron, and was additionally convinced that he is sincerely repentant for the evil he has done, though he has not resolution (without aid) to adopt a new course of conduct & feeling.

The next day, the 16th, she expanded her impressions to her mother, omitting reference to the significant phrase "without aid":

Lord B. is without exception of young or old more agreable in conversation than any person I ever knew. Brilliant sense, in energetic & flowing language, softened at times by the more humane feelings. He really is most truly an object of compassion. All the tender ties have been torn from his heart, and in consequence of his satire, he meets everywhere with enemies whose malice rejoices in re-opening the wounds which are ever ready to bleed. I think of him that he is a very bad, very good man. Impulses of sublime goodness burst through his malevolent *habits*. In his Satirical poem he says "The time hath been when no harsh sound would fall" &c. I have no doubt that his character has been totally changed by the weight of misfortunes which fall with such tremendous violence on minds where principles of religious hope have not been implanted.

To her father she added on the 17th:

Do you know Lord Glenbervie? From what I hear I am inclined to respect his judgment and therefore to rely on his testimony in favor of Lord Byron, whom he knows intimately. He says that this extraordinary

[1] Samuel Jackson Pratt (1749–1814), a busy journeyman of letters, who edited Blacket's *Remains* in 1811 for the benefit of Blacket's child, with a dedication to "the Duchess of Leeds, Lady Milbanke and family."

man is deeply repentant for the sins of his youth, and sincerely desirous to be put in the right way.[1]

Though only a few weeks before she had been bored by the dutiful necessity of accepting her aunt's attentions, she now saw the Lambs almost daily, telling her mother on the 18th that Lady Melbourne "was as usual solicitously kind," that even her daughter Lady Cowper now seemed to "feel a non-natural degree of interest about me," and that "they seem quite at home with me, and have always so much to tell me & to ask me whenever we meet." Thus far, she cannot have suspected any impropriety between Byron and Lady Caroline, but she must have realised that Byron was frequently to be found at Lady Caroline's, and she now sought intimacy with the woman whose silliness she had despised only five weeks before.

On 18th April:

> Went to Lady C. Lamb's in the evening—met Lord Byron, Mr. Rogers, Mr. and Mrs. G. Lamb. The conversation was concerning the best English Novels. Lord Byron suggested Caleb Williams as a performance of wonderful strength. The Vicar of Wakefield was admitted nem. con. Miss Burney's novels were defended by Lord Byron, and justly attacked as I thought by William Lamb. The following interesting question was discussed in the course of conversation, "Must a poet have felt, in order to make his readers feel." Lord Byron asserted the negative.

On the 19th she accompanied Lady Caroline to supper at Lady Jersey's, where she met another poet of reputation, Thomas Campbell: "in some conversation with him" she "discovered the warmth of his Christian feelings," but "sorry was I to remark soon after in Campbell's manner that tenacious regard to his own dignity which debases his noble feelings by mixing with them." On the 20th she "went in the evening with Lady Melbourne to Lady Jersey's assembly"; both George Eden and Lord Byron were there, and next day she wrote in haste to her mother, "I wish I had time to narrate the conversation I had with Lord B. whose attention was so modest and respectful that it could not create mistrust, and deserved confidence."

During the next two days she went to the theatre with Mrs. George Lamb and to Campbell's first lecture on poetry at the Royal Institution. On 23rd April she dined at Mrs. George Lamb's and went with her and George Eden to the Lyceum; on the 24th she gave her promised dinner party at Portland Place;[2] on the 25th she met George Eden at

[1] Sylvester Douglas, Lord Glenbervie (1743–1823), then First Commissioner of Land Revenue and Woods and Forests. Byron was at his house on 2nd April and dined there with Hobhouse to meet Benjamin Constant on the 11th.

[2] She named her guests in her journal: "Ld & Ly Gosford, Ld Wentworth, Ld Gambier, Mr. & Mrs. G. Lamb, Mr. & Mrs. G. Knight, Mrs. Bland, Augusta Bland, MM, Mr. R. Colborne, Major Dickens, Col. Armstrong, Col. Bathurst, Dr. Wynn."

Mrs. George Lamb's, and after dining with MM, spent the evening "in perfect solitude" and "thought of poetical plans."

Though seven of Sir Ralph's letters to Annabella during this period have survived, none of Judith's—which were evidently more numerous—have been preserved. Her expressions of alarm compelled Annabella to defend her interest in Byron on 26th April:

> He is indeed persecuted to the greatest degree by those who know nothing of him except what they have learned from prejudice.
>
> On the other side he is as violently & unjustly exalted, but this affords him no gratification, for he has too much penetration not to perceive that his *talent* alone is considered, and that there is no *friendship* in all this *mouth-honour*. He has no comfort but in *confidence*, to soothe his deeply wounded mind. I consider it as an act of humanity and a Christian duty not to deny him any *temporary* satisfaction he can derive from my acquaintance, though I shall not seek to encrease it. He is not a dangerous person to me.

This passage was one of those she copied out and sent to Byron for his "amusement" more than two years later, on 17th October 1814, with the comment:

> So much for *self-knowledge!* but I was constantly afraid that my Mother should think me in danger of a hopeless attachment, and I therefore suppressed to her my kinder feelings as much as possible.

Apparently Judith had confided her alarm to Lady Melbourne, for after seeing nothing of the Lambs for the next three days, Annabella informed her mother on 29th April:

> I find that Lady Caroline has been very ill. She has desired to see me to-day, and I am going in consequence to Whitehall. I shall then exert my eloquence to prove to Lady Melbourne that there is no danger in my meeting Lord Byron.

Her journal records no visit to Lady Caroline that day, but in the evening she went "to Lady Heathcote's with Mrs. G. Lamb, & had there some conversation with Lord Byron."

> He spoke his surprise at my not being disgusted with scenes in which "there was scarcely one person who on returning home dared to look into themselves". Speaking of some character he said "The caprice natural to your sex" with the greatest gravity, as if it was an acknowledged truth which I had too much sense to deny.

Next day she dined at Mrs. Gally Knight's, the day after with the Aucklands; there is no further mention of the Lambs till the cryptic entry in her journal on Saturday 2nd May:

Went in the morning to Lady Caroline Lamb, and undeceived her by a painful acknowledgement.

Saw Mr. Sheridan there. He declared his opinion of the turbulence which was now *ready* to burst forth throughout this Country. What vigour is yet in his eye! Received Lord Byron's opinion of my verses. Dined at home.

What was the "painful acknowledgement"? Lately she had been seen frequently in George Eden's company: did Lady Caroline so embarrass her by inquiries about an engagement between them that Annabella "undeceived" her by revealing her rejection of Eden's proposal? If so, Lady Caroline did not likewise undeceive Byron, who wrote to Lady Melbourne on 28th September following:

I am not at all ashamed of my own bias towards your niece, nor should have the least objection to its being posted up in Charing Cross, though I should never wish to hazard a refusal. I certainly did wish to cultivate her acquaintance, but C—— told me she was engaged to Eden, so did several others. Mrs. L. [George Lamb] *her* great friend, was of opinion (& upon my honour I believed her) that she neither did could nor ought to *like* me, & was moreover certain that E—— would be the *best husband* in the world & I its *Antithesis* . . . was I to hazard my heart with a woman I was very much inclined to like, but at the same time sure could be nothing to me?—& then you know my unfortunate manner which always leads me to talk too much to some particular person or not at all.

Either at her own suggestion or at Lady Caroline's, Annabella had selected what she considered the best of her verses to be submitted to Byron for his opinion. He wrote on 1st May:

My dear Lady Caroline,

I have read over the few poems of Miss Milbanke with attention. They display fancy, feeling, & a little practise would very soon induce facility of expressions . . . The lines in the cave at Seaham have a turn of thought which I cannot sufficiently commend, & here I am at least candid as my own opinions differ upon such subjects. The first stanza is very good indeed & the others with a few slight alterations might be rendered equally excellent. The last are smooth & pretty. But these are all, has she no others? She certainly is a very extraordinary girl, who would imagine so much strength & variety of thought under that placid countenance? . . . I shall content myself with observing that they are better much better than anything of Miss M.'s protegee Blacket. You will say as much of this to Miss M. as you think proper. I say all this very sincerely. I have no desire to be better acquainted with Miss Milbank; she is too good for a fallen spirit to know, and I should like her more if she were less perfect.

By this time madly infatuated with Byron, Lady Caroline was eager to discourage any possible rival. It seems that she gave all the first part of the letter to Annabella, retaining only the conclusion, perhaps with intent to hold it against Byron.[1] While retaining the conclusion, she is unlikely to have refrained from reading to Annabella the passage so calculated to wound and rebuff her. Both impetuous and unscrupulous, she may have openly taxed Annabella with being interested in Byron, in spite of his being—as she alleged that she herself thought on her first sight of him—"mad—bad—and dangerous to know," thereby exciting Annabella to "undeceive" her by "a painful acknowledgement" that she was well aware of his character.

Three days before, Annabella had defiantly announced her intention of exerting "my eloquence to prove to Lady Melbourne that there is no danger in my meeting Lord Byron," but she records no such interview with Lady Melbourne. During the following week she accompanied Mrs. George Lamb to Lady Lansdowne's on the Wednesday, but otherwise saw nothing of the Lambs or of Byron. From her father she received a characteristic letter dated from Seaham, 6th May:

> Per varios Casus, per tot discrimina rerum,
> Tendimus, in Londonium tomorrow. Billy Eden has just been here and has dismissed me cured from the hospital, but with strong cautions and injunctions against late dinners, and late hours, so you must not depend upon me as a chaperon, nor shall I ever again encourage [*word illegible*], nor breakfast with *Jack* Thompson after a ball, at six o'clock in the morning—but as necessity has no Law I must submit for the remainder of my life to plain roast and boiled, and a minor quantity of wine—and so I shall live to a venerable old age.
>
> Your list of engagements is tremendous and makes my hair to stand on end which it has a great propensity to do from not having been cut for a length of time, I must be shorn before I appear in public . . . Adieu a revoir Sunday or Monday.
>
> Your most affte. Dad
> RA: MILBANKE

On the following Monday, 11th May, Annabella recorded:

> Sir Ralph & Ly Milbanke came to London. I went at night to a party at Mrs. George Lamb's with Lady Gosford & MM. Lord Byron was there with an improved countenance & milder manner.

Next day Lady Gosford and MM accompanied her to a ball at the Argyle Rooms:

> Lord Byron there. He spoke satirically of one of my best *friends* whom he did not know except by sight & report. This was evidently an effect of that irritability which renders him so wretched.

[1] The original letter, preserved in the Lovelace Papers, breaks off after the words "better much better." The rest of the text—presumably representing the last page which was retained by Lady Caroline—is taken from the version given in *Letters and Journals,* ii, 118–21.

Daily she fulfilled social engagements with either her mother or Lady Gosford, but these are now recorded perfunctorily in her journal, with lists of names and few comments—the zest and lively interest of March and April is lacking. On 20th May at Lady Oxford's "Waltzing Ball" she "had some conversation with Lord Byron—He called Campbell's valetudinarianism his 'Epic Airs'." Recording her daily round of entertainments, with lengthy comments on her weekly attendance at Campbell's lectures on poetry, her journal makes no reference to her receiving on 22nd May a long letter from Lady Caroline Lamb:

My dear Annabella—

I have faild in keeping my promise with you for you must be aware that when great duties are forgotten lesser ones are seldom remembered. Besides I once more repeat the advice I ventured to hint to you—shun friendships with those whose practise ill accords with your Principles. They may unfortunately be more amiable, more interesting than others, but they will by degrees do you harm. It is so difficult to blame those we love that we are always seeking to excuse their conduct, till at length we lose the horror we ought to feel at every deviation from right . . . Pitch defiles—of all evils avoid bad company—evil Communications corrupt good manners, a sentiment St. Paul thought fit to quote . . . it is so true that I cannot enough advise you to adhere to it for I do really believe more than three parts of the Faults of Women spring from the two dangerous opinions of being above Public censures setting at defiance the jurisdiction of their Fellow worms—& befriending & protecting those falling Angels, who are ever too happy to twine themselves round the young Saplings they can reach. But if they are falling you cannot save them—depend on that. No one was ever yet saved by such means . . . You must choose your course. If you are for a stormy voyage full of narrow escapes & difficulties, playing ever on the verge of a precipice & every one almost wishing you in it, so tired will they grow of prophecying your fall—if this is your desire, then act like me. It has its pleasures, & I have hitherto found but them, but if I live longer the bitter bitter pains will no doubt likewise be mine, & after all is it not a dream, a mere nothing this life unless we consider it in the higher view offered to a Christian, & if we do, where are such as I. No Annabella I will not wrong you so much as by offering you my Friendship. I know exactly how you feel towards me at this moment . . . you cannot now conceive how obliged to me you will be for avoiding you & refusing it. You seem to me like a Vanessa or a Jane de Montford, very superior to those I have the honour of associating with. It is the more pity that you are come to London, for everything that enters into this fair City is tainted more or less. Your danger will not arise from Balls, routs, Coxcombs & Gossips, but beware of what may come across you in the shapes of Genius, superior abilities, Heroic sentiments, affected innocence. Look to the conduct & do not attend to their prating. Avoid Friendships with Women—you are a little inclined to be taken in by a certain Frankness of manner . . . You are true—few at your age are—keep so—only cowards or the really depraved need be otherwise—leave your white lies & inuendoes & black deceits to them . . . God bless you my new & dear Cousin. I shall see you sometimes for my own sake, not often for yours—& that you may not fall in love with my Follies, let me end my advice by giving you one infallible rule of judging others . . . whenever you see a Man or a Woman & particularly the latter Galloping through the Parks as hard as horse can go, or what we term neck or nothing, set that Lady or Gentleman down immediately for a Fool, & ninety nine times out of a hundred you will not be wrong. Now when did you not see your most sagacious Cousin in that very predicament. Parrots can talk well—therefore as I said before in your friendships look ever—not to sentiments but to Conduct.

I am nevertheless most affectly

Yrs

CAR LAMB

Annabella's comment was limited to the endorsement: "A letter of Lady Caroline Lamb to me—1812—very remarkable."

The letter seems to indicate that, at their interview on 2nd May, Lady Caroline had broadly hinted her own attachment to Byron before advising Annabella to "shun friendships with those whose practise ill accords with your Principles," so stinging Annabella into "undeceiving" her with "a painful acknowledgement" that she was aware of Byron's reputation without need of Lady Caroline's warning. Hence Annabella abandoned her intention of convincing Lady Melbourne "that there is no danger in my meeting Lord Byron", and aware of an affair between him and Lady Caroline, became guarded and critical when she met him. Whatever Lady Caroline said to Byron of Annabella, it is likely that she informed him of Judith's confiding in Lady Melbourne her alarm at Annabella's interest in him; as her change of manner coincided with her mother's arrival in London, Byron conceived that "aversion" towards Judith of which he wrote afterwards to Lady Melbourne.

On her son's account Elizabeth Duchess of Devonshire was a watchful observer of Annabella's behaviour, on which she no doubt received regular bulletins from her daughter, Mrs. George Lamb. To Augustus Foster she wrote on 4th May:

She persists in saying that she never suspected your attachment to her, but she is so odd a girl that though she has for some time rather liked another, she has decidedly refused them, because she thinks she ought to marry a person with a good fortune, and this is partly, I believe, from generosity to her parents, and partly owning that fortune is an object to herself for happiness. In short, she is good, amiable, and sensible, but cold, prudent, and reflecting. . . . Lord Byron makes up to her a little; but she don't seem to admire him except as a poet, nor he her, except for a wife. Your little friend, Caro William, as usual, is doing all sorts of imprudent things for him and with him; he admires her very much, but is supposed by some to admire our Caroline more; he says she is like Thyrsa, and her singing is enchantment to him.

A week later, passing on a rumour that Byron was returning to his Mediterranean travels, she remarked, "I should not be surprized if Caro William were to go with him, she is so wild and imprudent." On 2nd June she decided:

Your Annabella is a mystery; liking, not liking; generous-minded, yet afraid of poverty; there is no making her out. I hope you don't make yourself unhappy about her; she is really an icicle.

After receiving Lady Caroline's letter of 22nd May, Annabella next saw Byron at Lady Cork's on the 31st: "Lord Byron was there, but we never spoke." On 4th June Byron left London for Newstead with his friend Hobhouse, who recorded on the 10th that "a page came from Lady Caroline Lamb, with letters for Byron"; on the 13th they returned to London after Hobhouse had enjoyed some sexual education from one of the Newstead housemaids. During Byron's absence Annabella had not repined; on 8th June she attended a ball with Mrs. George Lamb; both George Eden and Lord Jocelyn, back from Ireland, were there, and she "Stayed till Sunrise!!!" On the 16th she again "staid till sunrise" at a ball given by Mrs. Edward Ellice, wife of a Whig M.P.:

Lord Byron was there. I think he has a propensity to coquetry—there is certainly less simplicity in his manners towards women than towards men. Yet at times he appears to scorn himself for being influenced by female attentions.

On the 20th she attended the last of Campbell's series of lectures:

Lord Byron sat before me at this Lecture and when Campbell introduced the mention of Religion, he writhed himself into the strangest positions, perhaps embarassed by the consciousness that many eyes were fixed on him.

Regularly in Mrs. George Lamb's company, she decided on 15th June, "I have at last an opinion respecting the *defects* of Mrs. G. Lamb's excellent character":

She is too timid to disregard as much as she ought the inconsistencies of those around her, & is thus led to give more than a due share of feeling to passing trifles. Secondly, before she sees any thing morally good or evil in a character, she is too apt to estimate it by the consideration whether the possessor is *in* or *out of the world*, according to the fashionable phrase.

But if she discovers one mark of right feeling, her judgment rises above those shackles of *ton* by which she was not intended to be bound.

She was also frequently in the company of George Eden and Lord Jocelyn. On 23rd June she "discovered that Lord Jocelyn has a very delicate poetical taste, and a love for sublime nature." The next evening at a ball:

Both of them were with me during my stay there (which was till Sunrise), and I was particularly struck by the different character which pervaded their respective opinions on a variety of subjects discussed between them. GE's judgment of human nature was more just & wise, Lord J's more poetical & benevolent. GE seemed to have formed his opinions from experience, Lord Jocelyn from the visions of an enthusiastic imagination coloured by generous feelings. The former indulged no pleasing illusions, the latter yielded to the mild sway of Romance.

Lord Jocelyn was evidently the most favoured of Annabella's admirers, but there is no record that he ever actually made a proposal; he married a daughter of Lord Le Despencer the following January. Nor is there any record in Annabella's journal that William Bankes proposed, though he did so, for he confided to Byron the following December that she had rejected him.

After receiving her "very remarkable" letter, Annabella's next meeting with Lady Caroline seems to have been on 5th July, when she accompanied her parents to dine in a small family party with Lady Melbourne. The next day she went with her parents to a party given by Mrs. Siddons, the company including both Lady Caroline Lamb and Lord Byron, "who was very goodnatured to me." She saw Byron again at Lady Cork's on 14th July:

Lord Byron conversed with me about Miss Rawdon, whom he praised highly, saying she had no defect but that of *waltzing*. He seemed to have received an unpleasant impression from MM's countenance though he spoke of the cleverness it indicated.

Afterwards with Ly Melbourne to Ly Cowper's—wearied with want of tranquillity & found no pleasure!

Niece of Lord Moira (soon to become governor-general of India and Marquis of Hastings), Bessy Rawdon was an attractive girl more than a year younger than Annabella, who had herself written of her on 16th June: "Saw proofs that Miss Rawdon is free from envy, jealousy, or any illiberal feeling when she finds others preferred by those whom she wishes to please." Byron's praise of her evidently affected Annabella so much that she confided his opinion to her mother, who concluded that Byron had designs on Miss Rawdon, for on 28th September following Byron found it necessary to assure Lady Melbourne that, while "Miss R. has always been a mighty favorite with me . . . I never heard of the report Ly M[ilbanke] *starts* from, & I am sure you will do me the justice to believe I never dreamed of such a thing."

In this "want of tranquillity" Annabella discontinued her journal for three weeks after this entry, resuming on 4th August, when she left London for a few days to visit Tunbridge Wells, the Doyles at Ovington, and the Aucklands at Eden Farm. On her return to town she was almost daily under the chaperonage of Lady Melbourne, in whose company she went on 15th August "to Mr. Dick's supper"; both Lord Byron and Miss Rawdon were present, but Annabella made no comment on either and on 16th August again discontinued her journal.

Letters to her from Mrs. Grahame and Dr. Fenwick show that her parents remained in or near London throughout the following winter, partly because their health rendered inadvisable a return to the north, partly because a general election was pending. On 29th September Mrs. Grahame heard from Annabella of "Sir Ralph's determination not to offer himself a candidate for the County of Durham on the present occasion." The decision may have been dictated partly by his health, but principally by the financial strain of a contested election.[1]

Annabella confided her interest in Byron to both Dr. Fenwick and Mrs. Grahame, though the latter discouraged further confidences on 23rd April by austerely allowing that he might "be amiable, notwithstanding the indiscriminate virulence" of *English Bards and Scotch Reviewers*, from which her husband had suffered. After her removal from Sedgefield to Scotland during this summer, Mrs. Grahame heard less and less from Annabella; how far she had lost touch with Annabella's interests appeared when she wrote on 20th November to "congratulate you on your friend Mr. Mackenzie's success" in the general election—"It is desirable for the eldest son of a nobleman to be in Parliament."

Intimacy since her infancy had taught Dr. Fenwick the wisdom of engaging Annabella's confidence by endorsing her opinions in general so that he could offer advice when occasion demanded. Hence his letter of 8th June reflected something of Annabella's comments after her interview with Lady Caroline Lamb:

> With all his faults I cannot help feeling interested for Ld Byron . . . To me it seems that Ld B. is hardly more an object of censure than of compassion, & yet were it not for those strong sympathies of which (tho not without alloy) his writings furnish such abundant evidence, I should be inclined to own the justness of your comparison of his character with that of the Hero of Pandemonium. It is very strange that by a mistaken vanity

[1] Byron heard rumours at this time that Sir Ralph was "ruined" (see p. 148). Lord Lovelace wrote: "Sir Ralph Milbanke, Bart., M.P., retired after twenty-two years of silent and neglected whiggery, and the loss of all his property over elections" (*Astarte*, pp. 359–60).

he seems manifestly ashamed of those feelings, & no sooner has an expression of them escaped than he throws in some misanthropic remark in order as it were to redeem the weakness. His poetry has given me great delight.

Annabella's considered "Character of Lord Byron" was written on 8th October 1812, more than seven weeks after she discontinued her journal:

The passions have been his guide from childhood, and have exercised a tyrannical power over his very superior Intellect. They have often enveloped it in the obscurity of temporal delusion unenlightened by the *Faith* of an immortal existence. Yet amongst his dispositions are many which deserve to be associated with Christian principles. His love of goodness in its chastest form, and his abhorrence of all that degrades human nature, prove the uncorrupted purity of his moral sense. In one of his juvenile poems he says

"I love the virtues which I cannot claim"—

There is a chivalrous generosity in his ideas of love & friendship, and selfishness is totally absent from his character. In secret he is the zealous friend of all the human feelings, but from the strangest perversion that pride ever created, he endeavours to disguise the best points of his character. He has felt himself wronged, and he scorns to show regard to illiberality of opinion by condescending to a justification. He would shun ostentation, and he confounds it with that endeavour to prevent the misconception of our intentions, which is an essential duty of social intercourse. Sincerity is violated by every self-misrepresentation, whether favorable or unfavorable, whether prompted by vanity or pride. When indignation takes possession of his mind—and it is easily excited—his disposition becomes malevolent. He hates with the bitterest contempt. But as soon as he has indulged those feelings, he regains the humanity which he had lost—from the immediate impulse of provocation—and repents deeply. So that his mind is continually making the most sudden transitions—from good to evil, from evil to good. A state of such perpetual tumult must be attended with the misery of restless inconsistency. He laments his want of tranquillity and speaks of the power of application to composing studies, as a blessing placed beyond his attainment, which he regrets.

He is inclined to open his heart unreservedly to those whom he believes *good*, even without the preparation of much acquaintance. He is extremely humble towards persons whose characters he respects & to them he would penitently confess his errors.

Annabella wrote this "Character" in accordance with her usual practice of "collecting her sentiments" on paper preparatory to justification of her own conduct. For she had just received through Lady Melbourne a proposal of marriage from Byron.

5

BYRON BEFORE HE WAS FAMOUS

1788—1812

In spite of the colourful reputation credited by gossip, Byron had no very profound experience of dealings with women. His cynicism was an affectation assumed to conceal a lack of confidence deriving from earliest childhood. "I was not so young when my father died," Thomas Medwin reports him as saying, "but that I perfectly remember him; and had very early a horror of matrimony, from the sight of domestic broils." As his father died when he was three and a half years old and had left his mother a year earlier, Byron can hardly have remembered their domestic broils; having no doubt heard much about them from his mother, he professed to remember them as colouring for his habitual raillery against marriage.

His father, "Mad Jack" Byron, was a son of Admiral John Byron, younger brother of the fifth Lord. Born in 1756, he was a handsome spendthrift of twenty-two when he persuaded Lady Carmarthen to leave her husband and three children. She had wealth as well as beauty, being the only surviving child of the fourth Earl of Holdernesse and Baroness Conyers in her own right; he married her when she was divorced by act of parliament in 1779. When she died after a daughter, Augusta Mary, had been born on 26th January 1784, he married in the following year another heiress, Catherine Gordon of Gight, whose fortune was quickly dissipated to pay his debts. Their only child, George Gordon Byron, was born in a lodging-house at 16 Holles Street, London, on 22nd January 1788. In the following year Mrs. Byron took her baby to Aberdeen, where she could live economically on the meagre income salvaged by her trustees from her estate. There her husband left her in September 1790 on removing to the continent to escape his creditors; he died on 2nd August 1791 at Valenciennes, in a house belonging to his sister, Mrs. Charles Leigh.

An adoring wife to her unworthy husband, Mrs. Byron was a devoted mother, but she had a turbulent temper, which was not improved by unaccustomed poverty and consequent affronts to her pride. "Ah, you little dog, you are a Byron all over; you are as bad as your father!"

she would exclaim in a tantrum, but with equal energy she exhorted him to remember his pride of birth, less on account of the noble Byrons, who traced back to the Conquest, than of the Gordons—he recalled that his mother "was as haughty as Lucifer with her descent from the Stuarts, and her right line, from the *old Gordons*, *not* the *Seyton Gordons*, as she disdainfully termed the Ducal branch." While the boy imbibed from her this pride in ancestry, she also instilled into him the rudiments of his revolutionary sympathies, for she declared herself "quite a Democrat" at the time of the French Revolution, and did not think "the King, after his treachery and perjury, deserves to be restored."

Byron admitted that he "gave her cause enough" for her rages, being "rather lively—except in my sullen moods, and then I was always a Devil." His moody temper and tendency to self-conscious shyness were aggravated by sensitivity to his lameness, as he had been born with a deformity of the right foot, which had "a bend inwards towards the middle of its length," causing "a lack of ankle movement" and consequently a "sliding gait." This handicap was felt the more intensely because he was otherwise splendidly endowed physically. Besides his handsome head and features, he was deep-chested and strongly built, as if meant for an athlete; he had athletic tastes, too, being fond of boxing, wrestling, and shooting, and his feats as a swimmer became celebrated. Perhaps to lessen his sense of infirmity, as much as from her Scots superstition, his mother insisted in his childhood that his lameness was a sign of his destiny to become "a great man."

His upbringing by a Calvinist nurse coloured his religious teaching with a brooding sense of evil, later enhanced by the reading in boyhood of Gothic romances in the style of Mrs. Radcliffe, with their emphasis on predestination to malign fate. This inclination to melodramatic musing about his destiny was intensified by his removal at the age of ten from Aberdeen to the historic home of his ancestors at Newstead Abbey. He became heir-presumptive to the title when the fifth Lord Byron's grandson was killed in Corsica on active service in 1794, and succeeded on his great-uncle's death in May 1798.

The fifth Lord was known as "the Wicked Lord", mainly because in 1765 he had been tried by his peers for killing his neighbour, William Chaworth of Annesley, in a duel without witnesses over a dispute about preserving game; acquitted of murder, he was found guilty of manslaughter. In his youth he impoverished his estate by extravagance; he was a rake and figured unfavourably in the memoirs of the actress, George Anne Bellamy; separated from his wife, he lived latterly as a recluse, with a servant as his mistress. The sword with which he killed

Chaworth hung in the hall at Newstead; also his pistols, which particularly appealed to Byron, who became a practised shot and habitually carried small loaded pistols in his pockets, laying them close to his bedside at night.

The estate had fallen into neglect, and Mrs. Byron placed her affairs in the hands of John Hanson, a Chancery lawyer, who described "the Young Lord" as "a fine sharp Boy not a little spoilt by Indulgence but that is scarcely to be wondered at." Hanson made the boy a ward in Chancery and persuaded his distant kinsman, the fifth Earl of Carlisle, to act as his guardian. Unfortunately Lord Carlisle took little interest in his ward, thereby providing Byron with a lasting grievance; Hanson himself had to wean the boy away from his mother's possessive interference by placing him at a school at Dulwich and providing him with hospitality and the society of his own children during holidays.

From childhood Byron showed himself susceptible to romantic attachments. Before he left Aberdeen he met "my first of flames", Mary Duff, a child of his own age, and reflected in his journal in 1813, "How very odd that I should have been so utterly, devotedly fond of that girl, at an age when I could neither feel passion, nor know the meaning of the word." On hearing when he was sixteen that Mary Duff was married, his feelings "nearly threw me into convulsions." At the age of twelve he made his "first dash into poetry" in an infatuation for his first cousin, Margaret Parker, who died of consumption in adolescence; "my passion had its usual effects upon me: I could not sleep, could not eat; I could not rest."

"My passions were developed very early—so early that few would believe me, if I were to state the period," he wrote darkly in 1821; "Perhaps this was one of the reasons which caused the anticipated melancholy of my thoughts—having anticipated life." A note by Hobhouse has revealed that Byron confided how "a free Scotch girl used to come to bed to him" in his boyhood. This must have been his Scots nurse, May Gray, who was dismissed from Mrs. Byron's service in the autumn of 1799 after Hanson had reported Byron's complaints of her misconduct. Such wantonness in an apparently religious young woman may have helped, as Professor Marchand has suggested, to inspire Byron's contempt for cant and hypocrisy in devout people; more probably it left a legacy of fastidiousness amounting to prudery, such as inspired his dislike of women's waltzing—Lady Caroline Lamb said he "made me swear I was never to Waltz."

Before he was sixteen, during school holidays from Harrow, he fell romantically in love with Mary Chaworth, heiress to the Annesley and Wiverton estates of the Chaworth killed in the duel with the Wicked Lord. When he first met her, Hanson chaffed him that he "had better marry" such "a pretty young lady". Byron replied, "What, Mr. Hanson, *the Capulets and Montagues intermarry*?" The notion of himself as a Romeo, with a Juliet denied to him by family feud, appealed to his sense of melodrama; afterwards he wrote, "Our union would have healed feuds in which blood had been shed by our fathers,—it would have joined lands broad and rich, it would have joined at least *one* heart, and two persons not ill matched in years (she is two years my elder)." A boy not yet sixteen was hardly to be regarded as an eligible match for a young woman of eighteen, and in fact a marriage was already arranged for Mary Chaworth with John Musters, heir to neighbouring estates at Colwick. During six weeks of his school holidays he rode over to Annesley daily from Southwell, where his mother rented Burgage Manor while Newstead was let, till he devised a means of being invited to stay overnight by relating that he had seen "a *bogle*" while riding home at night—another instance of melodramatic fancy, as well as evidence of his Scots nurse's superstitious influence.

On his refusing to return to Harrow at the beginning of the school term, his mother complained to Hanson that "the Boy is distractedly in love with Miss Chaworth", asking him to find somewhere suitable for Byron to spend his next holidays away from Nottinghamshire. This was a step towards emancipation from his mother's influence that Byron eagerly desired. An early acquaintance of his mother's, Pryse Lockhart Gordon, described Byron at fourteen as "a fine, lively, restless lad, full of fire and energy," who, "though he was a spoiled child, and had too much of his own way, . . . never did any thing intentionally to disoblige or vex" his mother. But Hanson early contrived to discourage Mrs. Byron from visiting her son at Harrow; besides such habits as boxing his ears for biting his nails, she embarrassed him by rebukes in a loud voice within hearing of his schoolfellows and the servants. By the time he was sixteen, he was in adolescent revolt; his earliest letters to his half-sister Augusta contain complaints against his mother, who accused him of being "leagued with her bitter enemies"—meaning Hanson, Lord Carlisle, and Augusta herself.

Newstead was let to Lord Grey de Ruthyn, a young bachelor of twenty-three, who made Byron a welcome guest during school holidays for such sport as shooting sitting pheasants by moonlight, doubtless with pistols. But on 26th March 1804 Byron informed his sister:

> I am not reconciled to Lord Grey, *and I never will*. He was once my *Greatest Friend*, my reasons for ceasing that Friendship are such as I cannot explain, not even to you, my Dear Sister, (although were they to be made known to any body, you would be the first) . . . My mother disapproves of my quarrelling with him, but if she knew the cause (which she never will know), She would reproach me no more.

Of this broken friendship Hobhouse made a marginal note in his copy of Moore's *Life of Byron*: "A circumstance occurred during this intimacy which certainly had much effect upon his future morals." At least two of Byron's subsequent biographers have supposed that the "circumstance" was "some kind of sexual advance" by Lord Grey. Yet it seems more likely that the boy of sixteen, still dramatising his romantic passion for Mary Chaworth, was shocked by Grey's revelation of crude sensualities with servants and daughters of tenants on the estate. When he heard of Grey's marriage in 1809, Byron jeered, "So Lord G—— is married to a rustic. Well done!" Hobhouse, himself a prig, spent a week in June 1812 in "a delirium of sensuality" with a housemaid at Newstead,[1] and may well have understood that Byron practised such freedom with the Newstead servants according to his former tenant's example.

After eight months Mrs. Byron was still demanding her son's reconciliation with Grey when he confided to his sister in November 1804 that he "was half inclined to believe the dowager was in love with him."

> She has an excellent opinion of her personal attractions, sinks her age a good six years, avers that when I was born she was only eighteen, when you my dear Sister as well as I know that she was of age when she married my father, and that I was not born for three years afterwards.

The widow of forty naturally appraised her charms differently from her son, who would as naturally feel horror at the possibility of his mother's degradation by competition with servant girls.

Though Mrs. Byron may not have been above coquetry with her tenant, she must also have urged her son's reconciliation with Grey because she recognised his need for companions of his own quality. Byron was himself aware of this need, which is reflected in his seeking to establish intimacy with his half-sister. Soon after his birth his mother had transferred the four-year-old Augusta to her maternal grandmother, Lady Holdernesse, so that she was brought up with her half-brothers and her half-sister, Lady Mary Osborne. As she must have received some substantial provision from her mother's fortune, Augusta cannot have felt the humiliation of a poor relation, but as the child of their mother's scandalous second marriage, she had to win the regard of her half-brothers and sister by her own charm and affectionate nature. In 1801, when Lady Holdernesse died, Lady Mary Osborne married the second Earl of Chichester and was able to chaperon the seventeen-year-old girl.

Hence, when Byron opened a correspondence with her, her letters were always addressed from great houses, and while he genuinely

[1] See p. 116.

craved his sister's affection, he also showed pathetic anxiety to share her aristocratic connections. When she was staying with "my formal Guardy Lord Carlisle," he asked if Lady Gertrude Howard was handsome; he remembered one of her elder sisters, Lady Cawdor, as "a sweet, pretty woman," and had heard that the other, the Duchess of Rutland, "was handsome also." His particular friend at Harrow was Lord Delawarr—"do you know the family at all?"—though he had to admit "he is considerably younger than me"; being nearly four years his junior, Delawarr was probably his fag, as "by the rules of our Seminary he is under my power, but he is too goodnatured ever to offend me, and I like him too well ever to exert my authority over him."

Augusta's heart was touched by his expressions of affection towards herself as well as by his complaints against his mother. He assured her that his previous neglect of her was due, not "to a want of affection, but rather to a shyness naturally inherent to my Disposition"; she was "*the nearest relation* I have in *the world both by the ties of Blood* and *affection*":

> Ah, How unhappy I have hitherto been in being so long separated from so amiable a Sister! but fortune has now sufficiently atoned by discovering to me a relation whom I love, a Friend in whom I can confide. In both these lights, my Dear Augusta, I shall ever look upon you, and I hope you will never find your Brother unworthy of your affection and Friendship.

Augusta did her best for him by consulting Lord Carlisle about his complaints and writing to ask Hanson to arrange for Byron to spend his next holidays away from his mother, so that he could meet Lord Carlisle; she told Hanson that her brother's letters to her were "*quite perfect* and he does not express one sentiment or idea I should wish different." Byron obliged her by dining with Lord Carlisle, whom he thought "improves upon further acquaintance," though he was more interested in hearing about Augusta: "I return you, my dear Girl, a thousand thanks for hinting to Mr. H. and Lord C. my uncomfortable situation, I shall always remember it with gratitude, as a most *essential service*."

Whatever his earlier discomforts, he enjoyed his last year at Harrow in dispensing condescension and patronage to his juniors. He was always a generous patron; though in later years he drove keen bargains with his publisher, he grandly gave the proceeds from *Childe Harold* to a distant cousin, R. C. Dallas, then believing, like Landor, that a gentleman should not accept money from a bookseller. Hearing that an old servant of the Wicked Lord's wanted employment, he asked Augusta to "tell him we will see that something is to be done for him, for *while I live, he shall never be abandoned In his old Age*"; after Augusta had found the old man employment with the Duchess of Leeds for three years, Byron kept his word by taking him into his service and making handsome provision for him. When his first servant at Cambridge was accused of obtaining money by false pretences, he refused his mother's demands for the man's dismissal and stood by him till he was transported for felony.

On going up to Trinity College, Cambridge, in the autumn of 1805, he was soon in trouble for extravagance. "That Boy will be the death of me, and drive me mad!" wrote his mother to Hanson:

> I much fear he has fallen into bad hands, not only in regard to Money Matters, but in other respects. My idea is that he has inveigled himself with some woman that he wishes to get rid of and finds it difficult.

Enraged on hearing that he had given thirty guineas towards a statue of William Pitt, she added: "He has also bought a Carriage, which he says was intended for me, which I *refused* to accept of, being in hopes it would stop his having one." Byron had in fact resorted to moneylenders; when he asked Augusta to be "joint Security with me for a few Hundreds," she offered to lend him some money, but insisting that "I and I only will be injured by my own extravagance," he was so annoyed by her efforts to prevent his transaction with "these *sordid Bloodsuckers*" that he broke off his regular correspondence with her.

Despite Augusta's efforts, Byron still met few women of his own class; his Cambridge friends did not invite his intimacy with their families. He now followed Lord Grey's example in cultivating rustic amours. The heroine of the lines "To Mary, on receiving her picture," was "of a humble, if not equivocal, station in life"; she was probably the mistress whom Byron was credited by local gossip with keeping while he lived at Southwell. It was at Southwell, declared Hobhouse in his marginal notes on Moore's *Life*, "that he learnt . . . his first lessons in sensuality"; also, "one of the families mentioned winked at an intercourse between him and one of the daughters in hopes of entangling him into an unequal marriage." His correspondence with the lady's brother shows that her family considered him to have compromised Julia, daughter of W. S. Leacroft, who lived in the Westgate at Southwell; on 31st January 1807 he wrote "declining all future intercourse with those whom my acquaintance has unintentionally injured." The vicar-general of Southwell, the Rev. J. T. Becher, persuaded him to withdraw his first volume of poems on account of some erotic verses addressed to Mary; to another poem he appended a note to deny that Julia Leacroft was the "Lady who presented to the author a lock of hair braided with his own, and appointed a night in December to meet him in the garden."

The Leacroft scandal naturally troubled the youth of nineteen; to one of his Southwell friends, Elizabeth Bridget Pigot, he described the town as "your *cursed*, *detestable*, and *abhorred* abode of *scandal*." To the same correspondent he wrote from Cambridge on 5th July 1807 "with a bottle of claret in my *head* and *tears* in my *eyes*" after parting with "my *protégé*", Edleston—a Cambridge chorister, two years his junior, whom he had met by saving his life when swimming.

> His *voice* first attracted my attention, his *countenance* fixed it, and his *manners* attached me to him for ever. He departs for a *mercantile house* in *town* in October, and we shall probably not meet till the expiration of my minority, when I shall leave to his decision either entering as a *partner* through my interest, or residing with me altogether . . . I certainly love him more than any human being . . . In short, we shall put *Lady E. Butler* and *Miss Ponsonby* to the blush, *Pylades* and *Orestes* out of countenance . . . He certainly is perhaps more attached to *me* than even I am in return. During the whole of my residence at Cambridge we met every day, summer and winter, without passing *one* tiresome moment . . . He is the only being I esteem, though I *like* many.

Sophisticated modern critics have claimed that this reference to Edleston is indicative of Byron's bisexuality—that he turned from philandering with rustic mistresses to homosexual practices. Yet to suppose that, if he had indulged in homosexuality, he would have confided the fact to a feminine correspondent is surely to ignore contemporary conventions.

Recalling that, during his first year at Cambridge, his closest friend was Edward Noel Long, who had been with him at Harrow, he wrote in his diary of 12th January 1821, "*His* friendship, and a violent, though *pure*, love and passion—which held me at the same period—were the then romance of the most romantic period of my life." Despite his habit of self-dramatisation, Byron was never a hypocrite, and if the "love and passion" were for Edleston, he would not have emphasised that the emotion was *pure* if it was not so. Nor did the reference to the Ladies of Llangollen, Lady Eleanor Butler and Sarah Ponsonby, have the connotation conceived by modern critics; it was not speculation about their sexual peculiarity but, as De Quincey said, their "romantic retirement from the world at an early age" that "attracted for many years a general interest to their persons, habits, and opinions." As these two ladies had renounced the world in the heyday of their youth, so Byron now fancied himself retiring with a companion as suitably agreeable as this young man, who had the advantages of dependence on him as a "*Patron*" and of being "more attached to *me* than even I am in return."

The Wertherism that afflicted Southey at Oxford and Wordsworth in his *Lucy* poems and in "Lines composed a few miles above Tintern Abbey" was always strong in Byron. For him the time was always out of joint, the world a setting for his present mood. To his Cambridge friend, William Bankes, he described himself at this time as "a solitary animal, miserable enough, and so perfectly a citizen of the world, that whether I pass my days in Great Britain or Kamschatka, is to me a matter of perfect indifference." Cambridge was only tolerable by contrast with the "*Crater* of Dullness" at Southwell. "Improvement at an English University to a Man of Rank is, you know, impossible, and the very idea *ridiculous*," he informed his mother during his second term, repeating to Hanson nearly a year later, "a College life is neither conducive to my Improvement, nor suitable to my Inclination."

A good letter-writer suits his tone to his correspondent, and Byron was one of the greatest of English letter-writers. Miss Pigot was such an audience as he most favoured—a woman older than himself, sincerely and even tenderly concerned with his welfare, susceptible to the charm of a little gallantry yet too sensible to commit the indiscretion of taking it seriously—an audience of which he was to find in Lady Melbourne the perfect example. As she knew of his follies with Miss Leacroft and the "equivocal" Mary, he told Miss Pigot of his patronage of Edleston to show that he was capable of disinterested affection. But he was careful to keep her concerned about his waywardness: "My life here has been one continued routine of dissipation," he told her at the end of the Cambridge summer term of 1807, and having transferred himself to London eight days later, "I am here in a perpetual vortex of dissipation (very pleasant for all that)."

During his first term at Cambridge, describing himself as "the most steady Man in College," he had repudiated indignantly Hanson's "*indirect* charge of Dissipation": "the 'Metropolis' and the 'Cloisters' are alike unconscious of my Debauchery, and on the plains of *merry Sherwood* I have experienced *Misery* alone; in July I visited them for the last time." Seventeen months later, writing—ironically from Southwell—on 2nd April 1807, he confessed to Hanson, "*Wine* and *Women* have *dished* your *humble servant*, not a *Sou* to be *had*."

Of Edward Long, the friend of his first year, he recalled:

> We were rival swimmers—fond of riding—reading—and of conviviality . . . I was always cricketing—rebelling—fighting—*row*ing (from *row*, not *boat*-rowing, a different practice), and in all manner of mischiefs; while he was more sedate and polished.

Long left Cambridge after that year to join the Guards; being much occupied at Southwell, Byron made few friends in his second year, at the end of which he told Miss Pigot, "I am almost superannuated here." Such a *blasé* pose is usual in undergraduates at the end of their second year, and despite his Wertherism, Byron's Cambridge career was much like that of any other undergraduate with money, social standing, and sufficient talent to raise his personality above the commonplace.

As with any such undergraduate, his third year proved his most enjoyable. To Miss Pigot in October 1807 he described Cambridge as "wretched enough—a villainous chaos of din and drunkenness, nothing but hazard and burgundy, hunting, mathematics, and Newmarket, riot and racing," but looking back over the years in 1820, he recalled that it was during his first two years that he was "wretched" and "as unsocial as a wolf taken from the troop"; "it was not till 1807, after I had been upwards of a year away from Cambridge, to which I had returned again to *reside* for my degree," that he made enduring friendships and found himself accepted at something like his value. His volume of poems, *Hours of Idleness*, published earlier in the year, made him a man of mark among undergraduates and commended him to Hobhouse, "who, after hating me for two years, because I wore a *white hat*, and a *grey* coat, and rode a *grey* horse (as he says himself), took me into his good graces because I had written some poetry."

Eighteen months his senior, Hobhouse was an influential undergraduate: "he founded the Cambridge 'Whig Club' . . . and the 'Amicable Society', which was dissolved in consequence of the members constantly quarrelling, and made himself very popular with 'us youth', and no less formidable to all tutors, professors, and heads of Colleges." Hobhouse introduced him to several young dons who became close friends—Charles Skinner Matthews, Scrope Davies, and Francis Hodgson: "I had always lived a good deal, and got drunk occasionally, in their company—but now we became really friends in a morning."

Matthews was a ragger. When the Master of Trinity, William Lort Mansel, was disturbed at night by revellers, Matthews called from under his bedroom window, "We beseech thee to hear us, good *Lort!*" and "Good *Lort* deliver us!" Hobhouse, who took himself very seriously, was a favourite butt for Matthews: when both were guests at Newstead, Hobhouse was passing down the Long Gallery at night when he was startled by a groan from a stone coffin, out of which rose a cowled figure and blew out his candle. Doubtless under Matthews' influence, Byron cultivated a reputation for eccentricity becoming a poet by keeping a tame bear, which he proposed "should *sit for a fellowship*," and by entertaining a varied acquaintance including "a large assortment of jockeys, gamblers, boxers, authors, parsons, and poets."

While thus frivolously occupied, he wrote to Hanson on entering his twenty-first year, "I have neither spirits to enliven myself or others, or inclination to bring a gloomy face to spoil a group of happy ones." Hearing that Augusta, now married to her cousin George Leigh, was expecting her first baby, he wrote to her on 26th April 1808:

> Pray name my nephew after his uncle; it must be a nephew, (I *won't* have a *niece*,) I will make him my *heir*, for I shall never marry, unless I am ruined, and then his *inheritance* would not be great.[1]

Spending the Easter vacation at a London hotel, he confided to his Southwell friend, Becher:

> I am cursedly dipped; my debts, *every* thing inclusive, will be nine or ten thousand before I am twenty-one . . . Of Newstead I have little hope or care . . . I may *sell.*

Casually he informed his reverend correspondent:

> I am residing with a nymph who is now on the sofa *vis-à-vis* while I am scribbling. I have three females (attendants included) in my custody.

On leaving Cambridge in the summer, he went down to Newstead to entertain his friends. "I had got a famous cellar," he recalled in reminiscence, "and *Monks'* dresses from a masquerade warehouse."

> We were a company of some seven or eight, with an occasional neighbour or so for visiters, and used to sit up late in our friars' dresses, drinking burgundy, claret, champagne, and what not, out of the *skull-cup*, and all sorts of glasses, and buffooning all round the house, in our conventual garments. Matthews always denominated me "the Abbot".

The idea may have been conceived in mimicry of the Monks of Medmenham, or Hell Fire Club, of two generations earlier. Byron fancied himself as a macaroni of that period; when R. C. Dallas sought his acquaintance as author of *Hours of Idleness*, Byron warned him that he had few "pretensions to virtue" and had been "frequently compared" to the wicked Lord Lyttelton:

> The events of my short life have been of so singular a nature, that, though the pride commonly called honour has, and I trust ever will pre-

[1] Augusta's eldest child was a daughter. In her Bible she made the entry: "Georgiana Augusta Leigh born Novr. 4th. 1808 in Stratton Street & Christened there Jany 25th 1809—Sponsors The Pce. of Wales Countess of Carlisle Countess of Chichester." Augusta Leigh's Bible, an Oxford edition of 1782, is preserved in the Lovelace Papers. On the title-page is her signature, "Augusta Mary Byron," on the fly-leaf the inscription, "To Miss Byron from her affectionate Friend M. Elgin." Martha, widow of the 5th Earl of Elgin, though left a widow as early as 1771, survived till 21st June 1810 and "filled, with great credit to herself, the important station of governess to her royal highness the Princess Charlotte of Wales" (Burke's *Peerage*). On the blank leaves at the front and back of the Bible, Augusta entered the births, marriages, and deaths of her children; after her death some dates were added, apparently by her daughter Emily, after whose death the Bible was purchased by Lord Lovelace.

> vent me from disgracing my name by a mean or cowardly action, I have been already held up as the votary of licentiousness, and the disciple of infidelity.

Such was the character he claimed on the strength of a few rustic amours, undergraduate excesses, and local gossip at Southwell; many, like the humourless Hobhouse, accepted the character when professed by the handsome young peer who possessed an ancient abbey and a romantic ancestry—many more when he proved to be a poet of genius.

The pleasures of hospitality to the "monks" changed his attitude to Newstead. By November 1808, instructing Hanson about payment of his debts on his coming of age, he had decided, "If my resources are not adequate to the supply I must *sell*, but *not Newstead*." In the following April, seeking to raise money for his travels abroad, he repeated, "I can meet ruin, but I will never sell Newstead; the Abbey and I shall stand or fall together."

On hearing that *Hours of Idleness* was the subject of "a most violent attack" by the *Edinburgh Review*, he affected indifference—"it is nothing to be abused when Southey, Moore, Lauderdale, Strangford, and Payne Knight, share the same fate"—but understandably, after reading the mean gibes of the review at his youth and rank, he "was not easy till I had vented my wrath and my rhyme, in the same pages, against every thing and every body." He occupied the months at Newstead in extending and polishing *English Bards and Scotch Reviewers*, which was published through Dallas's agency in March 1809. Leaving Newstead for London in the new year of 1809, he instructed Hanson to make provision for a housemaid named Lucy, who was pregnant "(I need not tell you by whom)". After elaborate preparations, including a farewell party given by Matthews, Byron and Hobhouse left England with a retinue of servants on 2nd July.

As they travelled in the grand manner, they were everywhere entertained by the local dignitaries, and for the first time in his life Byron was occasionally meeting women of some social experience. In Spain he found nobody like Donna Julia in *Don Juan*, but at Malta he met Constance Spencer Smith, the Austrian wife of the British minister at Stuttgart, who seems to have made a habit of travel to avoid her husband's company and had been romantically rescued by a Sicilian nobleman when arrested at Venice on the French occupation of the city. Hobhouse described her as "a tall pretty woman with fat arms well made"; Byron wrote enthusiastically to his mother that she was "married unhappily, yet has never been impeached in point of character . . . not yet twenty-five . . . very pretty, very accomplished, and extremely eccentric."

John Galt, the Scots novelist, who had travelled from Gibraltar on the same boat, remarked that Byron "affected a passion" for Mrs. Spencer Smith, "but it was only Platonic. She, however, beguiled him of his valuable yellow diamond ring." Apparently she proposed to make arrangements to elope with Byron and they exchanged pledges—a seal in return for the valuable diamond ring. Unpractised in conducting an affair in polite society, Byron behaved so indiscreetly that his conduct became a subject of gossip and he had to challenge an officer of the garrison, who, after accepting the challenge, "agreed to a reconciliation." Though he paid tribute to Byron's "cool and manly courage" in the matter of the challenge, Hobhouse wrote caustically in his journal, "Lord Byron is, of course, very popular with all the ladies, as he is very handsome, amusing, and generous; but his attentions to all and singular generally end, as on this occasion, in *rixae femininae*."

This affair inspired Thomas Moore's just comment:

> In one so imaginative as Lord Byron, who, while he infused so much of his life into his poetry, mingled also not a little of poetry with his life, it is difficult, in unravelling the texture of his feelings, to distinguish at all times between the fanciful and the real.

At the time Byron was moved to write three sentimental lyrics—"To Florence", "Stanzas Composed during a Thunderstorm", and "Stanzas Written in Passing the Ambracian Gulf"—and the last stanza of the third probably indicated his feeling about Mrs. Spencer Smith at its date of composition, 14th December 1809:

> Though Fate forbids such things to be,
> Yet, by thine eyes and ringlets curled!
> I cannot *lose* a *world* for thee,
> But would not lose *thee* for a *World*.

By the following May he could relate casually how "I fell in love with a married woman" and "escaped murder and adultery," and he cynically dismissed the episode in seven stanzas (xxix–xxxv) of the second canto of *Childe Harold*. To Lady Melbourne on 15th September 1812 he related the episode as an example of how "three months have ever cured me" of such a passion as he felt for Lady Caroline Lamb:

> In the autumn of 1809 in the Mediterranean I was seized with an *everlasting* passion considerably more violent on my part than this has ever been . . . we were to meet next year at a certain time, though I told my amica there was no time like the present, & that I could not answer for the future. She trusted to her power, & I at the moment had certainly much greater doubts of her than myself.

In his diary of 12th January 1821 he recalled, "I was once *so desperately* in love with a German woman, Constance."

Travelling on with Hobhouse to Albania and Greece, he was inclined to forget his passion for Constance on arrival at Athens, where they lodged with the widow Macri, who had three attractive young daughters and also a shrewd sense of their value. When in March 1810 he and Hobhouse left Athens for Turkey, Theresa Macri inspired his charming song,

> Maid of Athens, ere we part,
> Give, oh give me back my heart!

It was a test of friendship for two young men to spend a year in daily companionship. Shrewdly Annabella observed "less simplicity in his manners towards women than towards men"; Byron was at ease only with those few friends, like Hobhouse, Hodgson, and—later—Douglas Kinnaird, who accepted his moods and poses because they loved him for his good fellowship, his generous impulses, and his basic kindliness. Sometimes he may have wished for the livelier company of Matthews, but he learned during this year of travel to value Hobhouse for his sound sense, sober judgment, and unquestioning loyalty. Sometimes he was irritated by his friend's assiduous note-takings and archaeological researches, the more so as he was himself disgusted by such plundering of Greek antiquities as Lord Elgin's removal of the Marbles. Still more he chafed under the restraint of Hobhouse's respectability. Discussing Byron's liking of solitude for contemplation, Moore remarked that "even the society of his fellow-traveller, though with pursuits so congenial to his own, grew at last to be a chain and a burden on him." Annoyed by the aspersion on his quality as a companion, Hobhouse pencilled the marginal comment on this passage, "He has not the remotest guess at the real reason which induced Lord B. at that time to prefer having no Englishman immediately or constantly near him."

News of his financial affairs from his mother and Hanson offered no encouragement for a return to England, and when Hobhouse started for home in July 1810, Byron revisited Athens, whence he wrote significantly to his mother on 27th July, "An usual custom here, as at Cadiz, is to part with wives, daughters, etc., for a trifling present of gold or English arms." On 23rd August he explained to Hobhouse why he was lodged at the Capuchin Convent instead of with the widow Macri: "the old woman, Theresa's mother, was mad enough to imagine I was going to marry the girl." On 4th October, using a code-word understood among his Cambridge friends as denoting "desirable and completely fulfilled occasions for sexual intercourse," he asked Hobhouse to tell Matthews that he had "obtained above two hundred" such occasions "and am almost tired of them."

Probably he exaggerated to impress Matthews with his exploits as a Casanova, according to his increasing habit of romancing about himself that was to precipitate the tragedy of his marriage and to provide material for speculative biographers. One romantic exploit he did undertake in rescuing a girl who, convicted of infidelity, had been condemned according to Mussulman custom to be sewn into a sack and thrown into the sea; Lord Sligo, a young man of exactly his own age, who was his companion for several weeks at Athens, testified to this incident, which supplied the subject of *The Giaour*. As his Cambridge acquaintance, Henry Gally Knight, also visited Athens at this time, some anecdotes of his conduct there may have been among those which caused Annabella "much concern, as they indicated feelings dreadfully perverted" (p. 106).

The only woman of his own social standing whom he seems to have met at Athens was William Pitt's eccentric niece, Lady Hester Stanhope, who disliked him for his moods: "one time he was mopish, and nobody was to speak to him; another, he was for being jocular with everybody." Years afterwards she amused the author of *Eothen* by mimicking Byron's affectations of speech. Byron equally disliked her; she had shown a "disposition to *argufy* with me, which I avoided by either laughing or yielding," he told Hobhouse; "I despise the sex too much to squabble with them."

To Hobhouse on 26th November, still two months short of his twenty-third birthday, he affected apotheosis in the last extremity of Wertherism:

> I have now seen the World, that is the most ancient of the ancient part. I have spent my little all, I have tasted of all sorts of pleasure (so tell the Citoyen [Matthews]); I have nothing more to hope, and may begin to consider of the most eligible way of walking out of it.

Disappointed in his designs on Theresa Macri—perhaps also in the charms of the girl rescued from the sack—apparently he did temporarily renounce the world to write his *Hints from Horace* and *The Curse of Minerva* in comfortable quarters at the Capuchin Convent, with "Hymettus before me, the Acropolis behind, the Temple of Jove to my right, the Stadium in front, the town to the left; eh, Sir, there's a situation, there's your picturesque!" So he wrote to Hodgson on 20th January 1811, and in his secondhand copy of a 1755 edition of Horace, inscribed on the flyleaf, "Byron—March 23rd 1811. Capuchin convt. Athens.", he wrote on a blank page at the end of the volume, "Mem. In the month of March 1811, I began & finished my Imitation of the

'De Arte Poetica' of Horace from this edition in the Frank Monastery Athens. Byron, March 23d. 1811."

As on 5th March he was suffering from "a cough and a catarrh and the piles," he was in no state for amorous excesses, but after leaving Athens in April, he wrote to Hobhouse on 15th May from Malta of "amours without number" and how he "was near bringing away" Theresa Macri, "but the mother asked 30,000 piastres!" Though in November he had ignored a reminder from Mrs. Spencer Smith of their tryst, he found her still waiting at Malta, and lingered a month before effecting his escape. As he related to Lady Melbourne:

> I had certes a good deal to contend against, for the Lady . . . had something to gain in a few points, & nothing to lose in *reputation*, and was a woman perfectly mistress of herself & every art of intrigue personal or political, not at all in love, but very able to persuade me she was so, & sure that I should make a most *convenient* & complaisant fellow traveller.

Tragedy greeted his return to England in July 1811 after an absence of almost exactly two years. His mother died suddenly at Newstead, where during his absence she had been practising business-like economies. On his arrival for her funeral, he heard that Matthews had been drowned while bathing at Cambridge, and wrote in affliction to Scrope Davies:

> Some curse hangs over me and mine. My mother lies a corpse in this house; one of my best friends is drowned in a ditch . . . I received a letter from him the day before yesterday. My dear Scrope, if you can spare a moment, do come down to me—I want a friend . . . In ability, who was like Matthews? . . . What will our poor Hobhouse feel? His letters breathe but of Matthews. Come to me, Scrope, I am almost desolate—left almost alone in the world—I had but you, and H., and M., and let me enjoy the survivors whilst I can.

Davies came, and "His gaiety (death cannot mar it) has done me service," Byron told Hodgson on 22nd August; "but, after all, ours was a hollow laughter."

To Augusta, in reply to her letter of condolence, he wrote, "I am losing my relatives & you are adding to the number of yours"; after inviting her to Newstead, he added, "By the bye, *I* shall marry, if I can find any thing inclined to barter money for rank within six months; after which I shall return to my friends the Turks." Augusta replied that the journey to Newstead from her home at Six Mile Bottom, near Newmarket, was too long for her to undertake with her two small children[1]—as to the elder, "Mr. Davies flattered me by saying she was exactly the sort of child *you* would delight in"; moreover, there had been "many *changes* in our situation since you left England; in a *pecuniary* point of view it is materially altered for ye worse." She concluded:

> Your letter (some parts of it at least) made me laugh. I am so very glad to hear you have sufficiently overcome your prejudices against the *fair sex* to have determined upon marrying.

Byron answered on 30th August:

> The embarrassments you mention in your last letter I never heard of before, but that disease is epidemic in our family . . . I don't know what Scrope Davies meant by telling you I liked Children, I abominate the sight of them so much that I have always had the greatest respect for the character of *Herod*. But as my house here is large enough for us all, we should go on very well, & I need not tell you that I long to see *you*. I really do not perceive any thing so formidable in a Journey hither of two days, but all this comes of Matrimony, you have a Nurse and all the &ca.s of a family. Well, I must marry to repair the ravages of myself & prodigal ancestry, but if I am so unfortunate as to be presented with an Heir, instead of a *Rattle*, he shall be provided with a *Gag*.

Next day he wrote again that he had heard of her husband's losing the Prince Regent's patronage and that "you have a brother in me, and a home here."

> You must excuse my being a little cynical, knowing how my *temper* was tried in my Non-age; the manner in which I was brought up must necessarily have broken a meek Spirit, or rendered a fiery one ungovernable; the effect it has had on mine I need not state . . . I only want to assure you that I love you, and that you must not think I am indifferent, because I don't shew my affection in the usual way.

Augusta replied that, if her husband had to travel to Yorkshire, she might contrive a visit to Newstead on the way; lest he supposed—as he had in fact—that she was hurt by his reference to Lord Carlisle in *English Bards and Scotch Reviewers*, she concluded delicately, "Are you going to amuse us with any more *Satires?* Oh, *English Bards!* I shall make you laugh (when we meet) about it." Thus early she knew that he liked companions to laugh with.

Apparently Augusta could not contrive a visit, and while Dallas was occupied in London with arranging for the publication of *Childe Harold*,

[1] Augusta entered in her Bible these details of her second child: "Augusta Charlotte Leigh born February 20th, 1811 at the Six-mile Bottom. Christened at Gogmagog Hills Feby. 21st, 1812 by ye Revd. R. Oram. Sponsors, The Dss of Leeds, Ly Gertrude Sloane & ye Honble Fredk. Howard. Died at Kensington March 4 1830. Buried Ma 10, at Willesden."

Byron settled to his former amusements at Newstead, informing Hodgson on 25th September:

> I am plucking up my spirits, and have begun to gather my little sensual comforts together. Lucy is extracted from Warwickshire . . . to be commander . . . of all the makers and unmakers of beds in the household.

News that his *protégé* Edleston had died earlier in the year again depressed his spirits; as he dated his elegy, "To Thyrza", 11th October 1811, his emotion on hearing of Edleston's death probably inspired the poem, though he led Annabella—and presumably Lady Caroline Lamb—to suppose that Thyrza was a girl he loved, who died untimely like his cousin Margaret Parker.[1]

At the end of October he went up to London, calling at Cambridge—and presumably at Newmarket—on his way. In London he became friendly with the poets, Moore, Rogers, and Campbell, and rescued Hodgson—who, though about to be ordained, was the most rakish of his friends—from a sordid affair with a trollop.

Returning to Newstead for three weeks over Christmas with Hodgson and an old Harrow friend, William Harness, he became interested in a young Welsh servant, Susan Vaughan, who apparently shared a bedroom with another maidservant named Bessy and some small children belonging to the family of his valet Fletcher. After he left for London on 11th January, Byron began writing daily to the girl, and she in reply. In response to his reproach that she was not upset at his departure, she protested, " 'Tis true, Bessy shed more tears than I did in your sight . . . but, oh Heavens . . . I was past crying . . . the real truth is my heart was ready to break." She received from him the present of a locket, which "is beautiful indeed," but "I have spent hours over it but cannot open it; therefore, I must leave it untill my dear Lord Byron comes to compleat it, for without him there is nothing right in my eyes." When she complained of the supplanted Lucy's unkindness to her, his gentle rebuke excited anguished appeal:

> Pray, pray, My dearest Friend, don't be angry with me, as I'm not in fault—Can I not percieve a coolness in this letter of yours that almost Breaks my heart . . . if you are angry with your poor little *Taffy* . . . I wish I was on one of the highest mountains in Wales, there to remain without seeing any body untill I dyed with grief and pain—the same as I now feel, and all for you.

Reminding him of "the night you come up to our room, when I was in bed—the time you locked the door," she reported one of the children's

[1] Writing in 1821 reminiscences of his boyish "passion" for Margaret Parker, Byron recalled that she died while he was at Harrow, and "Some years after, I made an attempt at an Elegy. A very dull one."

saying to her, "Don't you remember, Susan, me Lord putting his hand so nicely over your *bosom?*"

Her jealousy of Lucy unluckily inspired her to suggest that Lucy was having an affair with Robert Rushton, son of a Newstead tenant, who was a *protégé* of Byron's and being educated at his expense. On receiving a stern reprimand from his patron—"I see no occasion for any communication whatever between *you* and the *women*, and wish you to occupy yourself in preparing for the situation in which you will be placed"—Rushton apparently protested that it was he who had "something to complain of;" assured that if he made a full confession, "whatever it is, *you* shall be forgiven," he produced a letter of Susan's to prove her infidelity. The correspondence concluded with a letter from 8 St. James's Street, 28th January 1812:

> I write to bid you farewell, not to reproach you. The enclosed papers, *one* in *your own handwriting* will explain every thing. I will not deny that I have been attached to you, & I am now heartily ashamed of my weakness. You may also enjoy the satisfaction of having deceived me most completely, & rendered me for the present sufficiently wretched. From the first I told you that the continuance of our connection depended on your own conduct.
>
> All is over. I have little to condemn on my own part, but credulity; you threw yourself in my way, I received you, loved you, till you have become worthless, & now I part from you with some regret, & without resentment. I wish you well, do not forget that your own misconduct has bereaved you of a friend, of whom nothing else could have deprived you. Do not attempt explanation, it is useless, I am *determined*, you cannot deny your handwriting; return to your relations, you shall be furnished with the means, but *him*, who now addresses you for the last time, you will never see again.
>
> God bless you!
>
> BYRON

Byron wrote to Moore the next day: "I am in a state of ludicrous tribulation . . . I can think of nothing but damned, deceitful,—delightful woman." To Hobhouse he wrote on 10th February, "I have dismissed my Seraglio for squabbles and infidelities," and to Hodgson on the 16th:

> Last week I was very ill and confined to bed with stone in the kidney . . . The women are gone to their relatives, after many attempts to explain what was already too clear. If the stone had got into my heart instead of my kidneys, it would have been all the better. However, I have quite recovered *that* also, and only wonder at my folly in excepting my own strumpets from the general corruption,—albeit a two months' weakness is better than ten years. I have one request to make, which is, never mention a woman again in any letter to me, or even allude to the existence of the sex.

His distress at the infidelity of the servant-girl suggests that he sought sentiment in the most casual amours, deepening suspicion that his reported excesses at Athens were designed to impress Matthews and may have extended little beyond the girl rescued from the sack and such romanticising of Theresa Macri as of Susan Vaughan.

For those days *Childe Harold* was a long time in process of production, for Dallas had taken the manuscript to John Murray in August 1811 after rejection by Miller on account of its attack on Lord Elgin for removing the Marbles. Submitting the first proof sheets as early as 4th September, Murray tentatively suggested some alterations: there were "some expressions concerning Spain and Portugal which . . . do not harmonise with the now prevalent feeling" and "some religious sentiments which may deprive me of some customers amongst the Orthodox." Byron replied:

> With regard to the political and metaphysical parts, I am afraid I can alter nothing; but I have high authority for my Errors in that point, for even the Æneid was a *political* poem, and written for a *political* purpose; and as to my unlucky opinions on Subjects of more importance, I am too sincere in them for recantation . . . As for the "*Orthodox*," let us hope they will buy, on purpose to abuse—you will forgive the one, if they will do the other.

To Hodgson, about to take orders, he was at this time stating his religious views, much as he afterwards argued them with Annabella:

> I will have nothing to do with your immortality; we are miserable enough in this life, without the absurdity of speculating upon another. If men are to live, why die at all? and if they die, why disturb the sweet and sound sleep that "knows no waking"? . . . As to revealed religion, Christ came to save men; but a good Pagan will go to heaven, and a bad Nazarene to hell; "Argal" (I argue like the gravedigger) why are not all men Christians? or why are any? If mankind may be saved who never heard or dreamt . . . of Galilee and its Prophet, Christianity is of no avail: if they cannot be saved without, why are not all orthodox? . . . who will believe that God will damn men for not knowing what they were never taught? I hope I am sincere; I was so at least on a bed of sickness in a far-distant country . . . I looked to death as a relief from pain, without a wish for an after-life, but a confidence that the God who punishes in this existence had left that last asylum for the weary . . . I am no Platonist, I am nothing at all; but I would sooner be a Paulician, Manichean, Spinozist, Gentile, Pyrrhonian, Zoroastrian, than one of the seventy-two villainous sects who are tearing each other to pieces for the love of the Lord and hatred of each other . . . let me live, well if possible, and die without pain. The rest is with God.

When Hodgson argued for orthodoxy, he retorted:

I won't dispute with you on the Arcana of your new calling . . . You degrade the Creator, in the first place, by making Him a begetter of children; and in the next you convert Him into a Tyrant over an immaculate and injured Being, who is sent into existence to suffer death for the benefit of some millions of Scoundrels, who, after all, seem as likely to be damned as ever . . . I do not believe in any revealed religion, because no religion is revealed . . . Let us make the most of life, and leave dreams to Emanuel Swedenborg.

Eventually Murray advertised *Childe Harold* for publication on 1st March 1812, though he delayed putting copies on sale till the 10th. He chose his time shrewdly to follow Byron's speech in the House of Lords against the Government bill to impose the death penalty on Luddite rioters convicted of destroying the new machinery that was causing unemployment. Nottingham being one of the chief centres of the Luddite activities, Byron had first-hand knowledge of the subject, as he wrote to one of the leaders of the Whig opposition, Lord Holland:

My own motive for opposing the bill is founded on its palpable injustice, and its certain inefficacy. I have seen the state of these miserable men, and it is a disgrace to a civilized country. Their excesses may be condemned, but cannot be a subject of wonder. The effect of the present bill would be to drive them into actual rebellion.

His speech on 27th February was a success, as he told Hodgson:

Lords Holland and Grenville, particularly the latter, paid me some high compliments in the course of their speeches, as you may have seen in the papers, and Lords Eldon and Harrowby answered me . . . I spoke very violent sentences with a sort of modest impudence, abused every thing and every body, and put the Lord Chancellor very much out of humour.

The Radical leader, Sir Francis Burdett, who heard the speech from the gallery, described it as "the best speech by a *lord* since the '*Lord* knows when,' " and became thereafter a close personal friend.

As reflected in Annabella's journal, the publication of *Childe Harold* made Byron the lion of the season. "The subject of conversation, of curiosity, of enthusiasm almost, one might say, of the moment," wrote Elizabeth Duchess of Devonshire, "is not Spain or Portugal, Warriors or Patriots, but Lord Byron!" Samuel Rogers related how, "after Byron had become the *rage*, I was frequently amused at the manoeuvres of certain noble ladies to get acquainted with him . . . I would receive a note from Lady —— requesting the pleasure of my company . . . with a postscript, 'Pray, could you not contrive to bring Lord Byron with you?' " Lady Caroline Lamb disdained such contrivances; apparently she had secured an advance copy of the book, for she wrote to Byron on 9th March:[1]

Childe Harold

I have read your Book & I cannot refrain from telling you that I think it & that all those whom I live with & whose opinions are far more worth having—think it beautiful. You deserve to be and you shall be happy. Do not throw away such Talents as you possess in gloom & regrets for the past & above all live here in your own Country which will be proud of you—& which requires your exertions. Pray take no trouble to find out who now writes to you—it is one very little worth your notice & with whom you are unacquainted but who from the first has admired your great & promising Genius & who is now so delighted with what you have written that it would be difficult for me to refrain from telling you what I think.

As this is the first letter I ever wrote without my name & I could not well put it, will you promise to burn it immediately & never to mention it? If you take the trouble you may very easily find out who it is, but I shall think less well of Child Harold if he tries—though the greatest wish I have is one day to see him & be acquainted with him.

Within two days she wrote again, beginning in verse:

Oh that like thee Childe Harold I had power
With Master hand to strike the thrilling Lyre
To sing of Courts & Camps & Ladies Bower
And chear the sameness of each passing hour
With verse that breathes from heaven & *should* to heaven *aspire*

Then all confiding in my powerful art
With Friends attentions & expressions kind
Ev'n I might Hope some solace to impart
To sooth a Noble but a wounded heart
And pay the homage due to a superior mind

Nor think with prying eyes & Idle Jest
I'de wish to search the secrets of thy breast
or that a Womans Vanity should move
Me to affect—thy confidence & love—
ah no—I love nor will that word profane
Which those who know it not make light & vain
Strong love I feel for one I shall not name—
What I should feel for thee could never be the same—
But Admiration interest is free—
And that Childe Harold may receive from me

If you should think it worth while to releave my mind by assuring me you are not offended at this strange intrusion & have already destroyd my

[1] The date on the letter, "March 9th, 1812", is in Byron's handwriting. Lady Caroline told Lady Morgan that Rogers gave her the ms. of *Childe Harold* to read; more probably Rogers received an advance copy of the book which he lent to her.

letter which I do not ask as they say ladies always do—*to be refused*—but most seriously—write one line to say so & direct it to Mr Sidney Allison—& leave it at Hookhams Old Bond Street to remain there till it is calld for.

Let me also tell you that though my opinion as I said before is of much too little importance for you to care about, I hear all those whose approbation would most please you, express themselves, in the warmest & highest terms of Praise about yr new Poem—in a manner that I think could not fail to give you pleasure as they little suspect that I shall repeat it to you.

Byron showed both letters to Dallas on 11th March, wondering perhaps if he could suggest the correspondent's identity. He told Dallas that he would not answer the letters, but Dallas, who was seeing him almost daily as intermediary with his publishers, soon discovered that "he was not able to keep his resolution; and on finding his correspondent to be a fine young woman, and distinguished for eccentric notions, he became so enraptured, so intoxicated, that his time and thoughts were almost entirely devoted to reading her letters and answering them." Commenting on how far Byron's head was turned by finding that "his name was in every mouth, and his poem in every hand," Dallas remarked with justice, "He professedly despised the society of women, yet female adulation became the most captivating charm to his heart."

6

PROPOSAL AND REJECTION

July 1812—July 1813

That Lady Caroline Lamb did not lose her reputation long before she met Byron suggests that she might have been a better woman if she had married some other husband than William Lamb. If Lady Melbourne believed—as suggested in her friend Georgiana Duchess of Devonshire's novel—that a wife might do as she pleased after bearing an heir to her husband, she forgot that an heir might die childless, as did her eldest son Peniston Lamb in 1805. While her second son's paternity may not have been so "universally supposed" as Lord David Cecil has suggested, William Lamb himself must have realised that he was not Lord Melbourne's son, and the death of his elder brother created a situation as embarrassing to him as to Lord Melbourne, who showed his feeling by allowing William as his heir only £2,000 a year instead of the £5,000 allowed to Peniston.

Consciousness of his bastardy may have affected his character. Lady Holland thought him, as a young man fresh from Cambridge, "pleasant though supercilious," likely to "improve when he gets out of his love of singularity." He was thirty-three when he impressed his cousin Annabella as "self-sufficient"—well past fifty when the painter Haydon found him "arch" and "insincere". He seems to have affected indolence to mask ambition, self-sufficiency to screen uncertainty, cynicism to shelter wounded sensibility or self-esteem.

Apparently he was in love with Lady Caroline when he married her in 1805, he being twenty-six and she twenty. "I have loved you for four years, loved you deeply, dearly, faithfully," he wrote in proposing marriage. She told Lady Morgan that "he thought of me but as a child," yet he wrote her dull letters about proceedings in the House of Commons. Probably he alternated between the playful and the prosaic, but could not be natural for fear of exposing himself. "I adored him," she declared, and no doubt she did, for she was uncontrolled in her passions.

Trouble seems to have started even before the birth of her son in

1807, for her grandmother wrote to her mother in December 1806, "I do not like Caroline's still having these nervous attacks & I dread their becoming habitual." Her husband had neither tact nor tenderness in handling her hysterical outbursts: "ill tempers on both sides broke out together." In 1809 she had a dangerous flirtation with Sir Godfrey Webster, Lady Holland's son by her first marriage, who was barely twenty; disaster having been averted by Lady Holland and Lady Melbourne, she wrote to excuse herself to the latter with a simplicity carrying conviction:

> those principles which I came to William with—that horror of vice, of deceit, of any thing that was the least improper, that Religion which I believed in then, without a doubt & with what William pleased to call superstitious enthusiasm—merited praise, & ought to have been cherished —they were safeguards to a character like mine . . . William himself taught me to regard without horror all the forms & restraints I had laid so much stress on . . . he is superior to those passions & vanities which mislead weaker characters, & which, however I may be ashamed to own it, are continually misleading me.

Such principles she must have undoubtedly learned from her grandmother, Lady Spencer, a lady of character devoted to her family, but her own mother offered an example no more moral than Lady Melbourne's. Lady Bessborough bore at least two children by Lord Granville Leveson-Gower before he married her own niece; she seems to have merited Byron's nicknaming her Lady Blarney when she declared herself "quite frightened" on meeting after many years her distant cousin, Lord Bolingbroke, who in his youth had eloped with his half-sister, the daughter of Dr. Johnson's friend, Topham Beauclerk.

After the Webster affair Lady Caroline conducted a flirtatious correspondence with her cousin, Lord Hartington, another twenty-year-old, whose prudence or innocence prevented an outcome she would evidently have welcomed. In the early summer of 1811 her grandmother was vexed on hearing that "she had jumped over a couch at some assembly"—"Dear child, she does not know how much she lowers her character by such improprieties"—reflecting a few weeks later on "too probably the misery she is preparing for herself; & all this not from vice but vanity."

Vanity and appetite for adventure must have inspired her to write to Byron before she had even seen him. "The genius which the poem exhibited, the youth, the rank of the author, his romantic wanderings in Greece,—these," said Rogers, "combined to make the world stark mad about *Childe Harold* and Byron." Lady Caroline met Byron soon after he wrote to her at Hookham's bookshop, for it was at her morning party on 25th March 1812 that Annabella "Saw Lord Byron for the first time." She told Lady Morgan long afterwards that her first impression was that he was "mad—bad—and dangerous to know," but that was probably the impression she wished she had had and acted upon. More likely, she was enraptured on seeing that his handsome looks befitted the hero of his own romance, and excited on finding that he was socially unsophisticated and consequently a ready victim for her fascination.

Few men as handsome as Byron can have had so little amorous experience at twenty-four. As Dallas observed, "he had not admitted the ladies of his own family to any degree of intimacy; his aunts, his cousins, were kept at a distance, and even his sister had hitherto shared the like fate." Social inexperience conspired with self-consciousness in regard to his rank to make him readily vulnerable to Lady Caroline's advances. She was the daughter of Lord and Lady Bessborough; her mother was the sister of the late Georgiana, Duchess of Devonshire, the most celebrated society beauty of the last generation. She represented a dazzling conquest for the patron of housemaids and landladies' daughters.

Ironically he charmed her by a sentimental approach such as he had made to Susan Vaughan. It was refreshing for a married woman in fashionable society to have a lover jealous of her husband. "In his letters to me he is perpetually telling me I love him the best of the two," Lady Caroline told Medwin; "and my only charm, believe me, in his eyes, was, that I was innocent, affectionate, and enthusiastic." Lacking the experience to recognise that she was not behaving with the discretion customary among lovers in society, he encouraged her indiscretions to gratify his vanity. One day Dallas was with him when "the lady's page brought him a new letter . . . a fair-faced delicate boy of thirteen or fourteen years old, whom one might have taken for the lady herself . . . I could not but suspect at that time that it was a disguise." Rumours of such escapades had reached Elizabeth Duchess of Devonshire when she wrote to Augustus Foster on 4th May, "Your little friend, Caro William, as usual, is doing all sorts of imprudent things for him and with him."

By the middle of July Lady Bessborough was so distressed by the rising tide of gossip that she sought Hobhouse's mediation with Byron; when he called on her, Lady Caroline found them together and moved Hobhouse to indignation by suggesting that he and Lady Bessborough were "looking guilty." On 24th July Caroline and her husband were staying together "without a cloud" with her grandmother, but on the 29th Hobhouse was with Byron at his rooms in St. James's Street when Caroline arrived "in a most strange disguise" which she removed to reveal herself in a page's dress. When Hobhouse urged her to leave, she threatened melodramatically, "There will be blood spilt," and was held back by Byron from snatching up a court sword lying on the sofa. When she argued that she could not leave without changing her clothes lest she should be recognised in the page's costume, Hobhouse proposed that she should go to his lodgings to change, to which she eventually agreed on condition that Byron accompanied her in a hackney coach. When Hobhouse had finally disposed of her at the house of a woman friend after being compelled to promise that he would not prevent Byron from meeting her before she left London, he was troubled to learn from Byron that only his intervention had averted an elopement. On this same day Byron wrote to Miss Mercer Elphinstone, the most eligible heiress of her time, "London is very dull and I am still duller than London."

Byron may well have been in a mood for recklessness, for his financial affairs were going badly; Newstead was actually offered for sale by auction on 14th August, being withdrawn when bidding failed to reach the reserve of £120,000. On 9th August Lady Caroline sent him a gift of her pubic hair with an inscription:

Caroline Byron—
next to Thyrsa Dearest
& most faithful—God bless you
own love—ricordati di Biondetta
From your wild Antelope

Also a letter:

I askd you not to send blood but Yet do—because if it means love I like to have it. I cut the hair too close & bled much more than you need—do not you the same & pray put not scizzors points near where quei capelli grow—sooner take it from the arm or wrist—pray be careful—& Byron, tell me why a few conversations with the Queen Mothers always change you.

I think by the bye that you would make but a bad Minister a worse Ambassador. You would in the first case be always acting from pique—& resentment & in the latter soft words & pretty lips would make you another Duke of Buckingham. When you left me I must one night be in your arms—& now not even see you but in presence of a witness. Oh I could scold—but do as you think proper only this I assure you—se ti vedo ed il Principe e la ti Baccierò—dicendo Honi soit qui mal y pense.

Addio mio Bel & buono amico. Newstead A—that is a pity—why not have kept it & taken Biondetto there & have lived & died happy. Yet you give us both up no ties can bind but Newstead A bears your unkindness in sullen silence. I will kneel & be torn from your feet before I will give you up—or sooner be parted with.

The "Queen Mothers", Lady Bessborough and Lady Melbourne, prevailed only after another escapade by Caroline. When her mother called to persuade Caroline to accompany her to Ireland, Lord Melbourne entered to add his reproaches; Lady Bessborough went to fetch Lady Melbourne, and on their return, Caroline had fled. Lord Melbourne said she had "threaten'd him with going to Lord Byron, and he bid her go and be ——." Lady Bessborough hurried to Byron, who denied knowledge of Caroline but evidently had a good notion of where she was, for he elected to find her, did so, and "brought her away almost by force" to her mother's house, where Lady Bessborough was mortified to have to relate that "it was more by his persuasions than mine, and almost reproaches at her bearing to see me suffer so much," that she was induced to return to her own home with her mother.

Lord Melbourne complained of Byron's behaviour to the Prince Regent, who, declaring himself more shocked by Byron's confidences to the "Queen Mothers" than by his affair with Caroline, exclaimed loudly in company to Lady Bessborough, "I never heard of such a thing in my life—taking the Mothers for confidantes! What would you have thought of my going to talk to Ly. Spencer in former times!" Subsequently Lady Bessborough, under the stress of her anxiety, suffered a slight stroke, which Caroline sought vainly to turn to account as a means of postponing her removal to Ireland; contritely admitting that "I am the cause of my mama's illness, that my foolish and wrong conduct has caused it," she begged her father to postpone their departure for a month, as "it was madness to take mama on a journey of that sort, far from medical help, at such a time." As her mother's health was less likely to suffer if Caroline was removed from Byron's reach, her plea was disregarded, and Byron wrote to Lady Melbourne on 10th September:

> I presume you have heard & will not be sorry to hear *again* that they are safely deposited in Ireland and that the sea rolls between you and *one* of your torments; the other you see is still at your elbow. Now (if you are as sincere as I sometimes almost dream) you will not regret to hear that I wish this to end, & it certainly shall not be renewed on my part. It is not that I love another, but loving at all is quite out of my way; I am tired of being a fool, and when I look back on the waste of time, and the destruction of all my plans last winter by this last romance, I am—what I ought to have been long ago. It is true from early habit, one must make love mechanically as one swims. I was once very fond of both, but now as I never swim unless I tumble into the water, I don't make love till almost obliged.

With her reply Lady Melbourne enclosed a letter from Lady Bessborough, begging her not to lose her hold on Byron as, despite his professed wish to end the affair, he was still corresponding with Lady Caroline. Byron rejoined on the 13th:

> The end of Ly B's letter shall be the beginning of mine, "for Heaven's sake do not lose your hold on him". Pray don't, *I* repeat . . . Will you undertake me? If you are sincere (which I still a little hesitate in believing) give me but time, let *hers* retain her in Ireland—the "gayer" the better. I want her just to be sufficiently gay that I may have enough to bear me out on my own part. Grant me but till Decr. & if I do not disenchant the Dulcinea & Don *Quichotte* both,—then I must attack the Windmills, & leave the land in quest of adventures. In the mean time I must & do write the greatest absurdities to keep her "gay" & the more so because ye last epistle informed me that "8 guineas, a mail & a packet *could* soon bring her to London."

Having thus made a plausible excuse for continuing correspondence with Lady Caroline, he sought to convince Lady Melbourne that he was not in love with her. First, Lady Bessborough was partly to blame for the affair, as "at the commencement she piqued that 'vanity' (which it would be the vainest thing in the world to deny) by telling me she was certain I was not beloved," so inciting him to ascertain whether or not he was beloved. Then he assured Lady Melbourne that she was "all out as to my real sentiments."

> I was, am, & shall be I fear attached to another, one to whom I have never said much, but have never lost sight of, & the whole of this interlude has been the result of circumstances which it may be too late to regret . . . I told you in my two last, that I did not "like any other &c., &c." I deceived you & myself in saying so, there was & is one whom I wished to marry, had not this affair intervened, or had not some occurrances rather discouraged me . . . As I have said so much I may as well say all—the woman I mean is Miss Milbank. I know nothing of her fortune, & I am told that her father is ruined, but my own will, when my Rochdale arrangements are closed, be sufficient for both. My debts are not 25000 pds & the deuce is in it, if with R. & the surplus of N. I could not contrive to be as independent as half the peerage. I know little of her, & have not the most distant reason to suppose that I am at all a favorite in that quarter, but I never saw a woman whom I *esteemed* so much. But that chance is gone and there's an end.
>
> Now—my dear Ly M. I am completely in your power. I have not deceived you; as to —— [Lady Caroline] I hope you will not deem it vanity, when I solemnly say, that it would have been want of Gallantry, though the acme of virtue, if I had played the Scipio on this occasion. If through your means, or any means, I can be free, or at least change my fetters, my regard & admiration could not be increased, but my gratitude would.

Having now committed himself to the pose that he had allowed himself to drift into the affair with Caroline while his inclination was to an honourable suit to Annabella, Byron acted his self-appointed part with such conviction as quickly satisfied him of its truth. " 'Manage her'!" he exclaimed on 15th September when Lady Melbourne had approved of his policy of writing to Caroline to keep her "gay"; "it is impossible —& as to friendship, no—it must be broken off at once, & all I have left is to take some step which will make her hate me effectually for she must be in extremes." As evidence that "three months have ever cured me" of passion, he related his affair at Malta with Mrs. Spencer Smith.

As he proposed to break off at once only two days after explaining his policy of writing to Caroline to keep her gay, and declared that no passion lasted with him more than three months after confiding his love for Annabella, Lady Melbourne reasonably questioned his knowledge of himself. He replied on 18th September:

> You ask "am *I* sure of myself?" & I answer, no, but *you* are, which I take to be a much better thing. Miss M. I admire because she is a clever woman, an amiable woman & of high blood, for I have still a few Norman & Scotch inherited prejudices on the last score, were I to marry. As to *Love*, that is done in a week, (provided the Lady has a reasonable share) besides marriage goes on better with esteem & confidence than romance, and she is quite pretty enough to be loved by her husband, without being so glaringly beautiful as to attract too many rivals. She always reminds me of "Emma" in the modern Griselda, & whenever I may marry that is the woman I would wish to *have married*.[1]

On the 21st, announcing his intention to "write no more" to Caroline, as writing "would only lead to endless recapitulation, recriminations, botheration (take a Kilkenny phrase), accusation, & all-ations but *salvation*," he proceeded:

> Before I become candidate for the distinguished honour of *Nepotism* to your Ladyship, it will be as well for me to know that your Niece is not already disposed of to a better bidder; if not I should like it of all things, were it only for the pleasure of calling you *Aunt!* & soliciting your benediction. My only objection (supposing of course that ye Lady's was got over) would be to my *Mamma*, from whom I have already by instinct imbibed a mortal aversion. I am sadly out of practise in this sort of *suit*, & shall make some villainous blunder; but I will try, & if this fails, any thing else.

He added jocularly—though with a hint that Lady Melbourne should act promptly if she was so minded—that "If I marry, positively it must

[1] Emma, in Maria Edgeworth's tale, *The Modern Griselda*, is "neither a wit nor a beauty," but "*the pattern wife*." She "was capable of putting herself entirely out of the question, when the interest of others was at stake." Her "quick-sighted good-nature could discern the least portion of merit, where others could find only faults." She asks, "Does not a penitent cease to be a monster?" and counsels her emotional friend Griselda to "give her own excellent understanding time to act, and . . . not throw away the happiness of her life in a fit of passion."

be in three weeks," as he was already tempted to fall in love with one of several inamoratas he listed.

As Lady Melbourne was not sufficiently impressed, he exaggerated his pose of cynical indifference on the 25th. Caroline "must be left to Chance":

> As to Annabella she requires time & all the cardinal virtues, & in the interim I am a little verging towards one who demands neither, & saves me besides the trouble of marrying by being married already . . . she has black eyes & not a very white skin; & reminds me of many in the Archipalago I wished to forget, & makes me forget what I ought to remember.

Lest he seemed too flippant towards his correspondent's sex, he turned to gallantry:

> I have no very high opinion of your sex, but when I do see a woman superior not only to all her own but to most of ours I worship her in proportion as I despise the rest. And when I know that men of the first judgement & most distinguished abilities have entertained and do entertain an opinion which my own humble observation without any great effort of discernment has enabled me to confirm on the same subject you will not blame me for following the example of my elders & betters & admiring you certainly as much as you ever were admired.

Reverting to Caroline and quoting her boast that she "could make any one in love with her," he ended:

> any woman can *make* a man in *love* with her, shew me her who can *keep* him so! *You* perhaps *can* shew me such a woman but I have not seen her for these—*three weeks*.

Thus flattered by a man nearly young enough to be her grandson, the lady of sixty reasonably inquired, "What can you have in yr. Head?" She mocked him that "men of distinguish'd abilities" were "des Hommes comme les autres, & I am a Woman comme les autres":

> I may have been beloved—but Love is not admiration. Lovers admire of course without knowing why. Yours therefore is much *more flattering* . . . but you quite astonished me when I found your usual playfulness chang'd into such a formal tirade . . . Once you told me you did not understand Friendship. I told you I would teach it you, & so I will, if you do not allow C. to take you quite away . . . I admire you extremely for your resolutions respecting *her* but Dr. Ld. B. you deceive yourself—you never will be able to keep them.

Having made it plain that she did not blame him for his part in exposing Caroline to gossip, she remarked, "Poor Annabella, her innocent Eyes will have to contend with the Black & probably experienced ones of yr. Innamorata." Taunting him that he was a weathercock in his emotions and that he would find it impossible to manage another mistress as well as Caroline, she warned him wisely, "As a friend I say flirt as much as you please but do not get into a serious scrape before you are safe from the *present* one."

Her letter was written on 29th September before she received a further letter from Byron dated the 28th, in which he began by denying a rumour reported by Lady Milbanke that he was paying court to Bessy Rawdon before relating (in the passage quoted on p. 112) how he had been deterred from attentions to Annabella by the representations of Lady Caroline and Mrs. George Lamb that she was attached to George Eden.

After a flippant paragraph about his black-eyed inamorata, he wrote dramatically:

> *At this moment*, another *express* from Ireland!!! more Scenes! this woman will never rest till she has made us all—what she & I at least deserve. I must now write to her . . . I see nothing but marriage and a *speedy one* can save me; if your Niece is attainable I should prefer her—if not—the very first woman who does not look as if she would spit in my face . . . I do not care at all about Sir R's involvements, for I think that with the command of floating capital which my late R[ochdale] business has put in my power, some arrangements might be made with *him* that might be advantageous to both, supposing this marriage could be effected . . . Does Annabella *waltz!*—it is an odd question, but a very essential point with me. I wish somebody would say at once that I wish to propose to her—but I have great doubts of *her*, it rests with herself entirely.

Lady Melbourne's subsequent conduct has been condemned. One recent writer has likened her to Mistress Overdone, the bawd in *Measure for Measure*. Yet it is hard to see how she could reasonably have acted otherwise. Her reason for initiating a correspondence with Byron was to prevent renewal of his affair with her daughter-in-law; she was defending her son's interests, and was urged by Lady Bessborough to maintain her "hold" on Byron. She knew that Annabella was interested in Byron; evidently she had corresponded with her sister-in-law about this interest as long ago as the previous April, when Annabella had told her mother that she would "exert my eloquence to prove to Lady Melbourne that there is no danger in my meeting Lord Byron." Byron declared his intent to marry immediately and his preference for Annabella; it was reasonable for her aunt to inquire if she felt inclined to accept him.

The Milbankes left London on 8th October for a house they had taken at Richmond in Surrey. Two days before, on the 6th, William

Bankes called "to take his leave previous to his foreign travels," and Annabella noted caustically of this suitor:

> He either wants strength of mind to form decided principles, or courage to avow them. He equivocates in the declaration of his own sentiments when he is not certain that they will meet with approbation. In short he is a *feeble* character—a good heart without Judgment, Wit & ingenuity without common sense.

Apparently she was informed by Lady Melbourne of Byron's proposal before she left London for Richmond, as she dated her "Character" of Byron on the 8th.

Pique as well as prudence dictated her rejection of the proposal. Having seen both Lady Melbourne and Mrs. George Lamb almost daily in recent months, she must have known even more than common gossip about Lady Caroline's indiscretions. She had also noted Byron's admiration for Bessy Rawdon, and could hardly fail to regret that the hero of *Childe Harold* had not offered a more romantic approach than a proposal conveyed by an intermediary.

She went up to London to confer with Lady Melbourne, visiting Drury Lane to hear Byron's prize address for the re-opening of the theatre; the play was *Much Ado about Nothing*, Elliston as Benedick "neither good nor bad," but "he spoke Lord Byron's address vilely." Before returning to Richmond on 14th October, she wrote from Melbourne House to Lady Gosford:

> Lady M. shewed me yesterday all the letters relative to me which she had received from Lord B. They appear to me expressive not only of the sincerest but of the deepest attachment. In one that was written at the time of his having received the information of my positive engagement with GE, he says, that though he feels the blessing he had once thought of, beyond his reach, he is, and fears he shall ever remain attached to me, and that whoever else he may marry he shall always wish to have married me. At the same time he resolves as the case is hopeless, and as, even if there were a chance, he would not interfere with another's happiness, not to endanger his heart further, by entering much into my society. He speaks of my character as the only female one which could have secured his devoted respect and affection. Were there no other objection, his *theoretical* idea of my perfection which could not be fulfilled by the trial, would suffice to make me decline a connection that must end in his disappointment. I confess that this, and the Irreligious nature of his principles are my sole objections, but you know that I regard the latter too strongly to sacrifice it to the love of Man.

Ironically, in view of later events, she continued:

> I do not fear his passions, for they are united with that generous disinterestedness of character which I *now* think a better security against ill

conduct, than the *systematic* goodness of colder characters. I did not think any thing of Genius requisite for the man who would make me a good husband, but I am afraid that some genius *is* requisite to understand a fellow-creature, and a good heart is not the best proof of *penetration.* I think matrimonial unhappiness is often the consequence of one or both the persons having believed that they should be too easily contented. Had I married on the ideas which I entertained two years since, this would infallibly have been my case.

I must now tell you what most distresses me in this affair. I think Mrs Lamb's conduct has not been quite worthy of the confidence I placed in her. She talked to Lord B. of me & GE in a strain that gave him reason to believe the attachment mutual. Lady Caroline (from *worse* motives) *positively assured* him that it was so. Lady Melbourne was very sorry for all this, because she conceived it unfounded, but not being in my confidence she could not decidedly declare the contrary. I regret that I did not inform her of my situation relative to GE. I have now been obliged to do so, and surely I may be permitted to consult a relation on the subject, if GE's greatest friend makes no secret of it to an indifferent person . . . I do not think Mrs. L. ill-intentioned, but destitute of that strength of mind which is necessary for the perception of strict rectitude.

As usual, "collecting her sentiments" on paper induced a condition of self-complacency, enabling her to write a gracious rejection to Lady Melbourne:

I do not give my answer without that serious deliberation which is due to the honorable & disinterested nature of Lord B's Sentiments. I am convinced that he considers my happiness not less than his own in the wishes which he has expressed to you, and I think of them with the sincerest gratitude.

I endeavour not to yield to any decided preference till my Judgment has been Strengthened by longer observation, but I will not assign *that* as my only motive for declining the estimable & very uncommon advantages now offered. I should be totally unworthy of Lord B's esteem, if I were not to speak the truth without equivocation. Believing that he never will be the object of that strong affection which could make me happy in domestic life, I should wrong him by any measure that might, even indirectly, confirm his present impressions. From my limited observations of his conduct I was predisposed to believe your strong testimony in his favour, and I willingly attribute it more to the defects of my feelings than of his character that I am not inclined to return his attachment.

After this statement which I make with real sorrow from the idea of its giving pain, I must leave our future intercourse to his judgment.

I can have no reason for withdrawing from an acquaintance that does me honor, and is capable of imparting so much rational pleasure, except the fear of involuntarily deceiving him. I cannot appear insensible to kindness, and its influence on my manner might lead him erroneously to suppose that I had a stronger interest . . . Perhaps the most Satisfactory

Method of acquainting him with the contents of this letter would be to let him have it.

I have too much confidence in his liberality to think reserve or caution necessary in communicating my feelings . . .

Lady Melbourne forwarded to Byron this letter, together with a copy of the "Character" of him which Annabella had confided to her, but she must have taken much trouble over the composition of her covering letter, fearing the effect of the rebuff on Byron's vanity and pride. Apparently she expressed a hope that he would not punish Annabella by dropping her acquaintance, for Byron wrote from Cheltenham on 17th October:

"Cut her!" my dear Ly M. marry—Mahomet forbid! I am sure we shall be better friends than before & if I am not embarrassed by all this I cannot see for the soul of me why *she* should. Assure *her* con tutto rispetto that The subject shall never be renewed in any shape whatever, & assure yourself my carissima (not *Zia* what then shall it be? choose your *own* name) that were it not for this *embarras* with C. I would much rather remain as I am.

I have had so very little intercourse with the fair Philosopher that if when we meet I should endeavour to improve our acquaintance she must not *mistake* me, & assure her I shall never mistake her. I *never did* you will allow; & God knows whether I am right or not, but I do think I am not very apt to think myself encouraged.

She is perfectly right in every point of view, & during the slight suspense I felt something very like remorse for sundry reasons not at all connected with C. nor with any occurrences since I knew you or her or hers; finding I must marry however on *that* score, I should have preferred a woman of birth & talents, but such a woman was not at all to blame for not preferring me; my *heart* never had an opportunity of being much interested in the business, further than that I should have very much liked to be *your relation.*

And now to conclude like Ld. Foppington, "I have lost a thousand women in my time but never had the ill manners to quarrel with them for such a trifle." . . . I cannot sufficiently thank you for the trouble you have taken on my account, the interest with which you honour me would amply repay for fifty vexations even if I felt any & perhaps I do without knowing it . . . You talk of my "religion"—*that* rests between Man & his Maker & to Him only can my feelings be known, for A. it had been sufficient not to find me an "*infidel*" in any thing else . . .

Having received a second letter from Lady Melbourne, he wrote again the next day, remarking that Annabella's "Character" of him was "more favourable to her talents than her discernment, & much *too indulgent* to the subject she has chosen—in some points the resemblance is very exact; but you have not sent me the whole (I imagine) by the abruptness of both beginning & end."

Still there is something of the *woman* about her; her *proposing* that the letter to you should be sent forward to *me per esempio* appears as if though she would not encourage, she was not disgusted with being admired. I also may hazard a conjecture that an *answer* addressed to *herself* might not have been displeasing, but of this you are the best judge from actual observation. I cannot however see the necessity of its being forwarded unless I was either to admire the composition or reply to ye contents. *One* I certainly do, the other would merely lead to mutual compliments very sincere but somewhat tedious.

Having devoted most of his letter to discussion of Lady Caroline's latest communications, he concluded:

I thank you again for your efforts with my Princess of Parallelograms, who has puzzled you more than the Hypothenuse; in her character she has not forgotten "*Mathematics*" wherein I used to praise her cunning. Her proceedings are quite rectangular, or rather we are two parallel lines prolonged to infinity side by side but never to meet. *Say* what you please for or of me, & I will mean it.

He began a third letter on 20th October, "Tell A. that I am more proud of her *rejection* than I can ever be of *another's acceptance*—this sounds rather equivocal, but if she takes it in the sense I mean it & *you* don't blunder it in the delivery with one of your *wicked laughs*, it will do for want of something better." Making it clear that this was his dismissal of the subject, he proceeded to discussion of his immediate plans; his main objective at Cheltenham was pursuit of the charming Lady Oxford, whom he proposed "to play off" against Lady Caroline.

Having remarked of her "two famous letters" to him, "I never saw such traits of discernment, observation of character, knowledge of your *own sex*, & *sly concealment* of your *knowledge* of the *foibles* of ours," Byron might have equally admired Lady Melbourne's letter to Annabella of 21st October. She had waited three days in case he revised his immediate reaction to Annabella's rejection, and began by excusing the delay:

I have this day received an Answer from Lord Byron, who is much disturb'd at not having received my Letter as soon as he ought to have done, owing to his Servant not having forwarded it to him immediately. He desires me to say, how much oblid he is to you for the candour, & fairness, with which you have told him your Sentiments,—that altho unfavourable to his hopes, or more properly to his Wishes, for hopes he declares he had not, your conduct on this occasion has encreased the high opinion he had before entertain'd of your abilities, & excellent qualities, & encreases the regret he feels at your decision, as well as his admiration for your character.

After further skilful translation of Byron's phrases into terms of pomp such as the Misses Austen and Edgeworth attribute to characters in similar situations, she concluded:

He says to me, "I cannot sufficiently thank you for the trouble you have taken on my Account. The interest with which you honor me is very flattering, & I feel it with the sincerest gratitude. You may rely upon me, that I would not desire you to give any Message, or make any promise for me to Miss Milbanke, that should not be strictly true & fulfill'd with the utmost rigor. *I never will renew* a Subject which I am convinced would be *hateful* to *her*, & no *condescension* or *indulgence* from her, will ever lead me to suppose that I can be more to her than the most common Acquaintance to whom she shows civility when she meets them in Society."

I place the greatest reliance upon what he says, & I am sure he will trouble you no more. I therefore hope you may now meet without any awkwardness, there can be no reason for it on either side, & as to you I agree perfectly with him, that it must have raised you very highly not only in his opinion, but also in that of any other person acquainted with the transaction.

On receiving the letter, Annabella apparently went up to London to see her aunt, who asked to be informed what qualities she required in a husband. Returning to Richmond, Annabella indulged her favourite recreation of "collecting her sentiments." In addition to various subsidiary qualities, her husband "must have consistent principles of Duty governing strong & generous feelings, and reducing them under the command of Reason." Inviting her aunt's comments, she felt it fair to explain her own "defects of temper":

I am never irritated except when others are so, and then I am too apt to imitate them. This makes good temper in my companions very necessary for my peace . . . I am never sulky, but my spirits are easily depressed, particularly by seeing anybody unhappy . . . I can assure you *from experience* that I am very thankfully submissive to correction . . .

This confession provided an opening gambit for Lady Melbourne's long reply on 25th October:

. . . you mention what I think a quality that requires correction in the highest degree, & that is allowing yourself to be irritated when others are so. It is the very time when you should be cool & composed, & not allow yr Temper to be ruffled—& you who require that the Man of yr choice should have a perfect command over his feelings, & who say yt you from habit have learnt to controul yours, *own* yt when others are irritated, you imitate them: how does *this* agree? I really look upon it as . . . most necessary to yr happiness to learn to be cool & have entire possession of yourself, when you see others in a passion; otherwise you must be in the wrong, & aggravate the feelings of those with whom you live . . . if your Husband should be in ever so absurd a passion, you should not notice it at the time, no Man will bear it with patience; afterwards, if you have been good humour'd at the time he will listen to you with patience, & feel the obligations he has to you. Till you can attain this power over Yourself never boast of your command over yr passions,—& till you can practise it, you have no right to require it in others.

After commenting in detail on every quality Annabella required in a husband, she concluded:

On ye whole it appears to me that it is almost impossible while you remain on ye Stilts on which you are mounted, yt you should ever find a person worthy to be yr Husband. As you are determin'd to look only for Sterling worth, & make it a point to yield to no Amiable qualities, you will never yield at all, for the first without ye assistance of the second are not captivating. A Man possessed of such a Character as you have drawn would marry you from reason, & not from Love—which *you* will not say is what you would wish or like.

Annabella replied with a long essay in self-justification, concluding:

After so full an explanation you will perhaps take off my *stilts*, and allow that I am only *on tiptoe*. I quite agree with what you say, and I am trying to show you that it agrees more nearly with what *I* said than you seem to suppose.

Lady Melbourne was content to let her niece have the last word, for Byron had already written to her on 24th October:

As to A. that must take its chance—I mean the *acquaintance*, for it will never be anything more, depend upon it, even if she *revoked*. I have still the same opinion, but I never was *enamoured* & as I very soon shall be in some other quarter, cossi finiva.

Within a week afterwards he announced that he had taken Kinsham Court, on Lord Oxford's Herefordshire estate, for the purpose of living near Lady Oxford and therefore in some security from Lady Caroline's molestations.

Annabella continued to court her aunt's friendship. Resuming her journal on 8th December to review the past two months since coming to Richmond, she recorded: "We have made frequent excursions to London" and "dined several times with the Melbournes." Reviewing at forty events following her rejection of Byron, she recalled that her efforts "to alter the channel of my feelings" were discounted by her being "thrown amongst those who had received much more favorable impressions of the character than had at first been placed before me."

This recollection is at variance with the evidence of her own journal and letters. Nor did she want for warning against Lady Melbourne as Byron's principal partisan, for her old friend Fenwick, hearing of her intimacy with her aunt, wrote on 26th November 1812:

> Your Motives for cultivating the good will of *the Lady* are worthy of you, & deserve the success which has attended them, but much as the issue has contributed to your father's Comfort, I am not certain I could have rejoiced in it, had it been the means of your placing Your Confidence in her. She is in Many essential points unworthy of you, & tho She may in some instances exhibit the Appearance of Sincerity, You Must Not forget that she Can deceive, & has been in the habit of deceiving. I will not apologize for speaking so strongly of one so near to you, because I have promised at all times to speak without reserve to you when it seems for your advantage I should. Besides it appears to me that such a Character as the one alluded to is more calculated than almost any one to deceive a Young Mind however quick & attentive in observing. Those who are Naturally reserved & designing have usually in their manners such indications of their Character that the least wary are put upon their guard; but when those who are too indolent to practise art without some powerful motive, perhaps too bold & too little concerned about the opinion of others or for distant consequences to act from design, are led by Necessity to Concealment from having embraced a line of conduct they dare not avow, experience & even a previous knowledge of the General Character of the individual are hardly sufficient to preserve one from being misled. You are better able to judge than me whether the above resembles the situation & disposition of the Lady in question; What I heard of her many years ago induces me to think it is. I saw Lord Byron's Epitaph on his dog some months ago; the opening appears to me very beautiful; the remainder not less detestable & offensive. He will never improve much as a Writer, till he adopts better principles & is more estimable as a Man. At present something is perpetually falling from him which wounds our best feelings.

At Richmond MM was Annabella's companion for two months, still suffering from her vertebræ—concerning the treatment of which Annabella differed from the doctors—but undeterred from attending dinners and theatres. For the new year Annabella accompanied her parents to Kirkby for a fortnight and thence to stay with the Tamworths at Staunton Harold, where the most notable guest was Dr. Parr:

> I think his heart warm, & his conduct sincere . . . He is vain—of his *manners*, of his *wit*, but I think not of his *moral* qualities. His self-indulgence in some things is great, particularly in eating, in egotism, & in argument.

Going on to Kedleston, she was impressed by her cousin, Nat Curzon, whom she had not seen for thirteen years:

> An *age* of *Thought* is fixed on his countenance, when it does not regain the softness of youth in a playful smile . . . He appears to have all the finer sensibilities usually characteristic of Genius. His diffidence does not proceed from the humiliation of conscious deficiency, but from that apprehensive delicacy of a superior mind, which checks its powers for fear of displaying them. His mildness is evidently distinct from weakness. An independent judgement, and a constant spirit, appear through the tenderness of a benevolent heart.

She was also "very much pleased with Captain Clifford, the Dss. of Devonshire's *not acknowledged*, but *undoubted* son," though he was "more honest than wise."

Leaving Kedleston on 3rd February, she and her parents arrived in London on the 5th to be greeted the same evening by the inevitable MM. She now made "great progress" in her friendship with Selina Doyle, discovering "that she has sound & deep, though not strictly orthodox religious principles." She saw nothing of Lady Melbourne, who was evidently in the country, and continued to find her daughter unsympathetic, remarking of an evening at Lady Cowper's, "Oh the misery of being shy amongst those who are too impudent to sympathize with one's sufferings!" She soon attracted yet another eligible suitor —Frederick Douglas, only son and heir of Lord Glenbervie, who, though only twenty-one, had entered Parliament at the recent election and claimed attention later in the year with favourable notices of his *Essay on Certain Points of Resemblance between the Ancient and Modern Greeks*. Introduced to him at Miss Berry's on 15th March, Annabella found "he has the best parts of a foreign manner, & converses very agreably." Thereafter she attended few balls without noting that she "danced with F. N. S. Douglas."

She had been reading Cicero's letters and Southey's *Roderick*, but noted that *Pride and Prejudice* "is at present the fashionable novel"; having heard that "it is written by a sister of Charlotte Smith's, and contains more strength of character than most productions of this kind," she took a copy with her when she went to stay with her cousin Lady Tamworth, at Staunton Harold, late in April, writing to her mother on May Day:

> I have finished the Novel called Pride & Prejudice, which I think a very superior work. It depends not on any of the common resources of Novel writers, no drownings, nor conflagrations, nor runaway horses, nor lapdogs & parrots, nor chambermaids & milliners, nor rencontres and disguises. I really think it the *most probable* fiction I have ever read. It is not a crying book, but the interest is very strong, especially for Mr Darcy. The characters which are not amiable are diverting, and all of them are consistently supported. I wish much to know who is the author or *ess* as I am told.

If she had expected that Byron would behave like George Eden in courting her acquaintance after her rejection of his suit, she was disappointed. Lady Oxford was forty, but Byron declared "the autumn of a beauty like hers is preferable to the spring in others." A country parson's daughter, she had made what was considered a brilliant marriage with Edward Harley, fifth Earl of Oxford, but, according to Byron, Lord Oxford's "mind and body were equally contemptible in the scale of creation." "Had she been united to a man whom she had loved, esteemed, and respected," wrote her friend and Herefordshire neighbour, Uvedale Price, "she herself might have been generally respected and esteemed as well as loved; but in her situation, to keep clear of all misconduct required a strong mind or a cold heart; perhaps both, and she had neither." Price declared her "full of affectionate kindness to those she loved whether as friends or as lovers"; to Byron she seems to have given more than she received, and did much to protect him from Lady Caroline Lamb, who continued to alarm her family with her demonstrations. On receiving a letter from Byron bearing Lady Oxford's seal, Lady Caroline suffered a brainstorm, leaving her "in great prostration of mind and spirit." Later she employed village children at Brocket to dance round a bonfire in which she burned Byron's letters and miniature portrait—though it turned out that she burned only transcripts of the letters and a copy of the miniature, being not mad enough to destroy the originals, so valuable as armaments in her campaign.

Byron did not meet Annabella during his visit to London in February, though he wrote to Lady Melbourne on the 12th, "I shall be very happy to encounter A. in such a manner as to convince her that I feel no *pique*, nor diminution of the respect I have always felt for her." In her journal she noted that "Lord Byron makes no profit by his publications" and made a present of *Childe Harold* to "his friend Mr Dallas," who "was at that time in very distressed circumstances, owing to a failure of West India property, & he has a large family." She also heard that "Lord Byron never suffers the slightest hint in disrespect to Religion to *pass at* his table."

Significantly she cultivated the friendship of her rival for Byron's admiration, Bessy Rawdon, who repeated to her a remark describing "the style of Lord B's conversation so admirably that it deserves insertion—'He talks for Feeling, not for Fame.' "

Arriving in London from Staunton on 7th May, she "went to Lady Spencer's party where I saw Lord Byron at a distance for the first time this year." Three days later—on the same day as she first met Maria Edgeworth—at Mrs. Hope's assembly she "again saw Lord Byron, but without renewing my acquaintance with him." She was "introduced to Anacreon Moore & Sir James Mackintosh" at Miss Berry's on 19th May:

> Rogers the poet was there, and envy was never more strongly personified than in his countenance when Lord Byron was mentioned. I always thought Rogers mean, but I did not think him capable of such petty artifices as he used on this occasion to blast a rival's fame.

Daily attending fashionable functions, she must have been as often expecting to meet Byron. Instead she repeatedly encountered Maria Edgeworth, of whom she noted acidly, "Miss Edgeworth's countenance of *happiness* (and I have seen *no other*) does not reflect itself on me." She recorded "a painful confirmation to my physiognomical observations on Miss Edgeworth" on hearing at Mrs. Opie's that "her brother Henry Edgeworth died a few days after she came to London, but she & her companions agreed neither to mourn in raiment or spirit, as it would have injured their London campaign."

Annabella was still in London when she discontinued her journal on 26th June. Apparently Frederick Douglas made a proposal, for she wrote jocularly to her aunt, Lady Wentworth, on 4th September from Seaham, "As I have not married *M.P.* Douglas, my Uncle must work the harder." Though her journal records her daily doings from 6th May to 26th June, there is no mention of her meeting Byron during that time besides the glimpses of him on 7th and 10th May. Yet in her "Auto-description", written nearly twenty years later, having recalled how she "was thrown amongst those who had received much more favorable impressions" of Byron after her rejection of his proposal, she stated:

> We met the following Spring in London. I was extremely agitated on seeing him, and offered my hand for the first time. He turned pale as he pressed it. Perhaps, unconscious as I was, the engagement was then formed on my part. We met frequently, but every time I felt more pain, & at last I shunned the occasions.
>
> We went to Seaham, where I hoped for the peace I had lost in London. It might have returned, had it not been for a communication received from my Aunt Lady M——, authorized by him, previous to his sailing for the Levant. It tempted me to write him a farewell letter, and my parents sanctioned my doing so.

The meeting described was not in the spring, but after Byron's sister Augusta joined him in London at the end of June, for Annabella wrote of Augusta in March 1817:

> The only time I ever saw her before my marriage was one night at Lady Glenbervie's in the summer of 1813, with Lord B——. His playful

and affectionate manner towards her, as they sat together on the sofa, was favorable to both in my opinion; it seemed to prove that *he* had gentler qualities & she had the power of educing them.

When, after her engagement, she recalled to Augusta this sight of her, Augusta replied on 20th October 1814:

> I *was* at Ly Glenbervies on that well remembered night, & think even now that I can see the *Groupe* which excited so much *inward* interest, for I dared not speak on the subject & scarcely look towards it. I am not conscious of ever having seen you before that Night but it was quite sufficient to make me *know you* "*by Sight*" . . . How *much* I wish that I had known your intention of requesting to be introduced—how eagerly I should have met such a wish of yours! I will confess to you since you ask me whether I observed you—that I *did*, as much as I could *decorously* venture to do, *and* that I *fancied* I saw even thro' your "quiet manner" what I *then* wished to see—what I have *since* often despaired of seeing . . . I could not help at any rate feeling for you, for it struck me that *all things considered* you must have been rather uncomfortable, even if you thought of Byron with indifference & perhaps—I am not quite sure—that I did not think that must be impossible.

Annabella was evidently wrong in her recollection that "we met frequently." Nor did she recall that she had herself invited the "communication" from her aunt, Lady Melbourne.

7

ANNABELLA IN PURSUIT

July 1813—September 1814

Byron's affair with Lady Oxford ended on 28th June 1813, when she sailed for the Mediterranean with her husband and family. Probably she was unaware that the affair had ended, as he was talking of following her as soon as he could adjust his finances. Her health had begun to suffer from the stress of coping with the moods of Byron's Wertherism and with continual harassment by Lady Caroline Lamb; she could not show herself in London without fear "of being dragged herself into some scene, and put in peril by the scissors or bodkin of the enemy." His letters to Lady Melbourne contain hints that the serenity of his relationship with Lady Oxford was latterly no longer so unruffled as earlier; he told Medwin, "I knew she had been inconstant to me," and Annabella stated, "He told me that at the time of his connexion with Lady O she detected him one day in an attempt upon her daughter, then a Child of thirteen, & was enraged with him to the greatest degree."[1]

No sooner was he deprived of Lady Oxford's protection than Lady Caroline staged a melodramatic scene. His dislike of waltzing did not prevent his attending "a small Waltzing Party" at Lady Heathcote's on 5th July; Lady Caroline was there and melodramatically said to him, "I conclude I may waltz *now*." After she had danced, they met in the supper room; he remarked ironically, "I have been admiring your dexterity," and according to her own recollection:

> I clasped a knife, not intending anything. "Do, my dear," he said. "But if you mean to act a Roman's part, mind which way you strike with your knife—be it at your own heart, not mine—you have struck there already." "Byron," I said, and ran away with the knife. I never stabbed

[1] Lady Oxford's eldest daughter, Lady Jane Harley, born in March 1796, was described by Hobhouse as at sixteen "a delightful creature, but *un peu libre*." The second daughter, Lady Charlotte, was born in December 1801. To her, as "Ianthe", Byron addressed the dedicatory verses prefixed to the seventh edition of *Childe Harold*. On 5th April 1813 he told Lady Melbourne that he had given some of his jewellery retrieved from Caroline Lamb "to Charlotte Harley, whom I should love for ever if she could always be only eleven years old, and whom I shall probably marry when she is old enough, and bad enough to be made into a modern wife."

> myself. It is false. Lady Rancliffe & [Lady] Tankerville screamed and said I would; people pulled to get it from me; I was terrified; my hand got cut, & the blood came over my gown.

Doubtless she had no more intention of using the knife than of burning Byron's letters and portrait; her object was publicity, which she achieved, for, as she related, "It was in all the papers, and put not truly."

Evidently Annabella had left London before the *fracas*, as she wrote to Lady Melbourne, "Since I left London I have not heard anything of your proceedings, except such reports concerning Lady Caroline as I cannot credit." After inquiring how Lady Caroline was keeping "her good promises," she invited news of Byron by expressing the hope that "the *temptation* is far away." Having waited vainly during five months in London for Byron to continue their acquaintance, she had to resort to correspondence with her aunt as the only means of re-establishing contact, and hearing from her that "the temptation" was still in London, she tried to contrive an opening for direct correspondence by informing Lady Melbourne of a rumour that Byron had "behaved very unhandsomely to the young man who purchased Newstead—that the latter from the imprudent eagerness of youth bid much more for the property than it was worth and that, though almost ruined by the contract, Lord B. cruelly takes advantage of the Law to make him adhere to unfair terms."

> I should be very ungenerous if I did not put the most candid construction on all Lord Byron's actions and if I did not wish that others should do the same. As I shall not have an opportunity of seeing him again I should be glad if you would tell him that however long his absence may be, I shall always have pleasure in hearing that he is happy, and if my esteem can afford him any satisfaction, he may rely on my not adopting the opinions of those who wrong him.

She chose an unfortunate pretext for her overture. In the previous autumn Byron had accepted an offer of £140,000 for Newstead, but after paying a deposit of £25,000, the purchaser had failed to complete his bargain. The delay had prevented settlement of his debts, postponed his plans for going abroad, and compelled him into the expense of a chancery suit. So, on receiving Annabella's message, he replied to Lady Melbourne with a tart statement of the facts, adding that "the interesting *youth*" represented as the victim of his own "dreadful chicane & wily experience" was in fact "a *lawyer* of forty-five years." He dismissed Annabella in a postscript:

> You will make my best acknowledgements to Miss M—— & say what is most proper. I have not the skill—you are an adept—you may defend me if it amuses you—not else.

This rebuff is the only mention of Annabella in his letters to Lady Melbourne that can have inspired the "communication received from my Aunt Lady M——, authorized by him," which "tempted me to write him a farewell letter."

Doubtless Lady Melbourne expressed "what is most proper" in terms more soothing to Annabella's self-esteem than Byron would have been willing to "authorize." Lady Oxford's social experience had been some insurance against Byron's becoming involved in an open scandal; with this insurance removed, a revival of his interest in Annabella might be a desirable precaution against a possibly dangerous attachment.

In the previous March he had written to explain to his sister Augusta that the delayed sale of Newstead prevented his helping to relieve her own embarrassments:

> I am going abroad again in June, but should wish to see you before my departure. You have perhaps heard that I have been fooling away my time with different "*regnantes*" but what better can be expected from me? I have but one *relative* & her I never see. I have no connections to domesticate with, & for marriage I have neither the talent nor the inclination. I can not fortune-hunt nor afford to marry without a fortune . . . I am thus wasting the best part of life daily repenting & never amending.

When, on 26th June, he heard that she was tearing herself away from the claims of her improvident husband and three children,[1] he had to abandon a visit to the coast for a last farewell to Lady Oxford. On 1st July he asked Lady Melbourne to get him a ticket for a ball at Almack's the next day:

> It is for my Sister who I hope will go with me. I wish she were not married for (now that I have no home to keep) she would have been so good a housekeeper. Poor soul, she likes her husband.

He told Moore on the 8th, "my sister is in town, which is a great comfort,—for, never having been much together, we are naturally more attached to each other."

For the first time he and Augusta were daily together for a period of weeks. For nine years he had invited her affection; now he found her the companion most to his taste. Impulsively generous, tenderly affectionate, she was undemanding, confiding, amusing. She enjoyed the gift of laughter; though, with her three small children, she had graver reason than he for anxiety over financial embarrassment, she could abandon herself gaily to the pleasures of the moment. With

[1] Augusta thus entered her third child in her Bible: "George Henry John Leigh born at the S. Mile Bottom June 3d. 1812. Christened at Six Mile Bottom Jan. 2. 1813 by ye Revd. C. Wedge. Sponsors Duke of Leeds, Sir H. Fetherstonaugh Fenbroom."

engaging mockery she laughed him out of the morose moods of his Wertherism. Annabella wrote of her in the first months of their acquaintance, "She is much the best of the bad families with which she is connected in spirits, having a sanguine temperament that enables her to hope in the face of Despair," and recalling episodes of her married life a year after her separation:

> He told me he only wanted a woman to laugh, and *did not care what she was besides*. The peculiar charm of A[ugusta]'s society is a refined species of comic talent. Before she came to us in Novr. 1815, he was wondering what she would say to his "Mistresses", and conjecturing that she would begin to frown & lecture him, "but," he added, "I can make Augusta laugh *at any thing*"—it was a most melancholy truth!

"I cannot exist without some object of love," Byron had told Lady Melbourne in the previous November when announcing that, in Lady Oxford, "I have found one with whom I am perfectly satisfied." Now he learned to love Augusta with a lasting tenderness such as he discovered for no other woman. They were together in London for about three weeks before he travelled with her to Newmarket. When Lady Melbourne reproached him for having written to her only once in three weeks—and then only to write his tart answer to Annabella's inquiry about his Newstead chancery suit—he replied on 30th July:

> "I don't tell you any thing!"—very good. Every body rates me about my confidences with you. Augusta for example writes today & the last thing she says is "*this* must not go to Ly. Me."—& to punish you it *shant*.

Having thus recognised a dangerous rival as his confidante, Lady Melbourne took fright when Byron wrote after another visit to Newmarket on 5th August:

> My sister who is going abroad with me is now in town where she returned with me from New*ket*. Under the existing circumstances of her lord's embarrassments, she could not well do otherwise, & she appears to have still less reluctance at leaving this country than even myself.

So, having failed to draw Byron into correspondence by informing him through her aunt of her concern for his reputation, Annabella was encouraged to address him directly on 22nd August:

> I have received from Lady Melbourne an assurance of the satisfaction you feel in being remembered with interest by me. Let me then more fully explain this interest . . . You have remarked the serenity of my countenance, but mine is not the serenity of one who is a stranger to care, nor are the prospects of my future years untroubled. It is my nature to feel long,

deeply, & secretly, and the strongest affections of my heart are without hope. I disclose to you what I conceal even from those who have most claim to my confidence, because it will be the surest basis of that unreserved friendship which I wish to establish between us, because you will not reject my admonitions as the result of cold calculation, when you know that I *can* suffer as you have suffered.

Early in our acquaintance, when I was far from supposing myself prefered by you, I studied your character. I felt for you, and I often felt with you. You were, as I conceived, in a desolate situation, surrounded by admirers who could not value you, and by friends to whom you were not dear. You were either flattered or persecuted. How often have I wished that the state of Society would have allowed me to offer you my sentiments without restraint. As the language of Truth I was not too humble to think them more worthy of you than the worldly homage of persons who were my superiors in Talent. My regard for your welfare did not arise from blindness to your errors; I was interested by the strength & generosity of your feelings, and I honored you for that pure sense of moral rectitude, which could not be perverted, though perhaps tried by the practice of Vice. I would have sought to rouse your own virtues to a consistent plan of action, for so directed, they would guide you more surely than any mortal counsel.

In a letter to Ly Melbourne (after I had informed you of my sentiments) you expressed a determination to render your conduct as conformable to my wishes, as if your attachment had been returned. I now claim that promise . . . I have the right of a constant and considerate zeal for your happiness . . . I entreat you then to observe more consistently the principles of unwearied benevolence. No longer suffer yourself to be the slave of the moment, nor trust your noble impulses to the chances of Life. Have an object that will permanently occupy your feelings & exercise your reason. Do good . . . to benefit man you must love him, and you must bear with his infirmities . . . Feel benevolence and you will inspire it . . . imperfect as my practice is, I *have* enjoyed the happiness of giving peace & awakening virtue on occasions which only this habitual direction of my thoughts could have enabled me to seize . . . I request your secrecy as to this communication and its contents. Only my parents are aware of it. In particular I would not have it known to Ly Melbourne. I am indebted to her kindness, but we have little sympathy, and she is perhaps too much accustomed to look for design, to understand the plainness of my intentions . . .

Byron might have been warned by the complacent egoism, the want of humour preventing perception of her priggishness. But his egoism equalled hers. His vanity was piqued by the inference that she rejected him because her heart was hopelessly engaged—a fiction such as he might have himself affected; understandably he was irritated by the complacency of her condescension. He hastened on 25th August to deprive her of any illusion that he had languished in disappointment at her rejection of him:

It was however said that your heart was disengaged, & it was on that ground that Ly. M. undertook to ascertain how far I might be permitted to cultivate your acquaintance on the chance (a slender one I allow) of improving it into friendship and ultimately to a still kinder sentiment. In her zeal in my behalf, friendly and pardonable as it was, she in some degree exceeded my intentions when she made the more direct proposal, which yet I do not regret except as far as it appeared presumptuous on my part. That this is the truth you will allow when I tell you that it was not till lately I mentioned to her that I thought she had unwittingly committed me a little too far in the expectation that so abrupt an overture would be received, but I stated this casually in conversation & without the least feeling of irritation towards her or pique against yourself . . . We do not know ourselves, yet I do not think that my self love was much wounded by this event—on the contrary I feel a kind of pride even in *your rejection* . . .

All her impertinent admonitions were dismissed in a single sentence: "To the part of your letter regarding myself, I could say much, but I must be brief—if you hear ill of me it is probably not untrue though perhaps exaggerated." In conclusion:

I must be candid with you on the score of friendship. It is a feeling towards you with which I cannot trust myself. I doubt whether I could help loving you, but I trust I may appeal to my conduct since our eclaircissement for the proof, that whatever my feelings may be, they will exempt you from persecution, but I cannot yet profess indifference, and I fear that must be the first step—at least in some points—from what I feel to that which you wish me to feel. You must pardon me & recollect—that if anything displeases you in this letter—it is a difficult task for me to write to you at all. I have left many things unsaid, & have said others I did not mean to utter.

Though softened by its conclusion, the snub surprised Annabella into retreat and brevity:

I will trouble you no more—only this to express what I cannot withhold—my heartfelt thanks for your most kind, most indulgent answer. Nothing in your letter can displease me, the recollection of my own may. I ought more to have respected your sorrows, and I cannot forgive myself for having intruded on them from the impulse of an ill-judged kindness. That I may not increase the error, farewell. I will not regret the friendship which you deem impossible, for the loss is *mine*, as the comfort would have been *mine*.

God bless you.

Retreat was the surest course to encourage Byron. Besides, the note reflected genuine feeling, as well as providing a rare example of contrition by Annabella. He was therefore moved to write on 31st August a revised account of his proposal and rejection in more propitiatory terms. "I never did nor ever can deny that I aspired to the honour which I failed in obtaining"; to convince her that "I never even sought to conceal my ill success," he confided how he and William Bankes had compared notes and consoled each other in suffering the same disappointment. If she regretted any expression in her two letters, they should be destroyed or returned:

> Your friendship I did not reject, though in speaking of mine I expressed some doubts on the subject of my own feelings . . . I am too proud of the portion of regard you have bestowed upon me to hazard the loss of it by vain attempts to engage your affection. I am willing to obey you, and if you will mark out the limits of our future correspondence & intercourse they shall not be infringed.

Restored in self-complacency, Annabella replied on 3rd September:

> I shall wait with patience for as little or as much of your regard as you may be able to give. My esteem for you is confirmed by our recent intercourse and I shall always be gratified by any proof of your remembrance. Act then towards me as best accords with the state of your mind—there is no reason for constraint on our correspondence, which is sanctioned by the concurrence of my father & mother. I do not feel the slightest uneasiness respecting my letters, for I consider them as secure in your possession as in mine. Write therefore, if you think me deserving of so much confidence, whenever it is possible that you may find relief in the disclosure of your feelings, or of any events past or present, to one who promises you in return truth and kindness. I said the comfort would be *mine*, for the idea—is it a vain dream—of alleviating the bitterness of your despondency if only by the *wish* to do so, would give me real comfort. It is my happiness to feel that in some degree I live for others. For the purposes of consoling and calming the mind, I believe the friendship of women often better adapted than that of men, and I regret your general prejudice against the former. There are some whose wish to serve you might be of more avail than mine, but you must not look for them in the circle where I have met you.

She hoped to make him "acquainted with those whose characters would remove the unfavorable impression which has been created by an unfortunate knowledge of the worthless of the sex—with one in particular, whose age would prevent embarassment"—and she commended to him the elderly dramatist, Joanna Baillie, whose acquaintance she had cultivated since meeting her in March 1812 on Mrs. Grahame's introduction.[1]

[1] Annabella's Journal, 28 March 1812: "Went to Hampstead & introduced myself to the Miss Baillies. Miss Joanna pleased me very much by the character of simplicity & truth that appeared in her countenance & manner. Not a semblance of *display*—only the modest cheerfulness and unambitious sense of a mind untainted by vanity. She spoke of Mrs.

The idea of spending his evenings in the improving society of the Scottish sisters must have appealed to Byron's humour. He had ignored Annabella's request that he should not confide her correspondence to Lady Melbourne, who sent him Annabella's letter to her on her requirements in a husband, on which he commented on 5th September:

> I would rather have seen your answer. She seems to have been spoiled—not as children usually are—but systematically Clarissa Harlowed into an awkward kind of correctness, with a dependence upon her own infallibility which will or may lead her into some egregious blunder.

At this stage he recognised her self-righteousness too clearly to find her attractive, but she was Lady Melbourne's niece and both kindness and self-indulgence always inclined him to encourage the correspondence of female admirers.

"Agreed," he wrote on 6th September, "I will write to you occasionally & you shall answer at your leisure & discretion." He corrected her conception of his "*general despondency*":

> Now in common I believe with most of mankind, I have in the course of a very useless & ill regulated life encountered events which have left a deep *impression* . . . but I am not conscious of any habitual or at least long continued pressure on my spirits. On the contrary—with the exception of an occasional spasm—I look upon myself as a very facetious personage, & may safely appeal to most of my acquaintance (Ly. M. for instance) in proof of my assertion. Nobody laughs more . . . Your sweeping sentence "in the circles where we have met" amuses me much when I recollect some of those who constituted that society—after all bad as it is it has its agremens. The great object of life is Sensation—to feel that we exist, even though in pain . . .

The statement of hedonistic philosophy was a mischievous bait for which Annabella eagerly fell after waiting a demure interval till 16th September. Ironically, in regard to subsequent events, she began:

> "As your friend I will bear with your faults," and my patience for them is more than you will exhaust. Therefore I shall not be repelled by the irritable feelings of self-dissatisfaction which I imagine that you sometimes disguise under an appearance of levity. All these I will attribute to the *East wind* . . .

Grahame as possessing a very active mind, governed by a determined regard to what she judged *right*. Miss J. Baillie thinks Walter Scott a very agreable companion—he excels in narrating stories, yet never brings them unsuitably into conversation . . . *Miss Baillie* appeared more superficial than her sister in whose *solid* virtue I feel confidence. Her feelings seem to be of that composed nature which admits of permanency & depth."

"The world is slow to do you justice," she wrote oddly to a poet who had achieved celebrity at twenty-four, "you will be still slower to do justice to yourself, and I must anticipate the goodwill of both."

> Have you not defied or disdained general opinion—not reflecting, I am sure, on the mischief occasioned by such a disposition when associated with your mental endowments . . . Surely that craving for excitement,—the motive of thousands as restless as yourself,—is caused by the absence of a principle, which, if established in the mind, would prove a strong & constant, if not an impetuous source of feeling & action. But I shall disgust you by returning to my old theme—if my ideas respecting it are mixed with delusion, your superior penetration & experience may enlighten me, and I expect from you the same plain-spoken freedom as you permit me to use.
>
> You may be *gay*, but you have not convinced me that you are *content*. My reason for persisting in a different opinion is—though you are better than most of the righteous who stand high in public estimation, I do not think you good enough to possess the only real peace,—that of reflection . . . Once or twice I have fancied that I have detected in your countenance a laughter "false to the heart". Do you not sometimes laugh when you feel, because you are too proud to accept of sympathy? Remember that in regard to any parts of your character which I misconceive, your simple & serious assertion of the contrary is sufficient to convince me. I had unjustly concluded that you were prejudiced against women from a remark which you once made to me in conversation,—I thank you for undeceiving me.
>
> May I know your sentiments concerning Religion. Do not suppose I have a fancy to convert you—first, I do not believe you need conversion—secondly, I do not believe it in my power to convert from infidelity . . . I am not a bigot to Church Establishments, which in my opinion deviate widely from the purity of the Christian dispensation—and I am disposed to spare those who doubt, because I *have* doubted.

Byron was then too preoccupied with women to consider prejudices against them. Augusta had reconsidered her reckless decision to go abroad with him; though he conceded that she might take one of her children with her, she was loth to leave her husband to face their creditors alone. Byron declared hers an "abominable marriage," but Colonel George Leigh was her own choice, for whom she waited at least three years—apparently till he secured an appointment connected with the Prince Regent's racing interests. Associating with wealthy racing men, like Lord Darlington, Sir Harry Fetherstonhaugh, and Lord Frederick Bentinck, he lived far beyond his means, and creditors closed in when he lost the Regent's patronage. "She married a fool, but she *would* have him," wrote Byron. "They agreed, and agree very well, and I never heard a complaint but many vindications of him" a tribute to Augusta's loyalty of affection, a quality that Annabella was to find baffling in her.

In the second week of September Byron visited her at Six Mile Bottom; having again failed to persuade her to go abroad with him, he returned briefly to London before visiting James Wedderburn Webster at Aston Hall, near Rotherham. "Bold" Webster—as Byron ironically called him because he had quarrelled with Matthews in a party at Newstead in 1808 and left for London next morning, declaring that he could not challenge a fellow-guest under Byron's roof—had been three years married to Lady Frances Annesley, daughter of the Earl of Mountnorris; she was not well satisfied in her husband, and Byron went from Six Mile Bottom to Aston with intent "to vanquish my demon" by "*transferring* my regards to another." In planning the seduction of his host's wife, so far from feeling compunction at offending the conventions of hospitality, he seems rather to have found incentive in reflection that Aston Hall was a house in which his father had "adulterated" with Augusta's mother.

He was not too absorbed in Lady Frances to forget Annabella, to whom he wrote a note from Aston Hall on the 23rd lest "a letter from you may now be with my other epistles in London" and "my silence in that case should look like neglect, as I have not the plea of better avocations for delaying my reply." Back in London on the 26th, he replied at length:

> You don't like my "restless" doctrines. I should be very sorry if *you* did, but *I* can't *stagnate* nevertheless . . .
>
> "Gay" but not "content" very true.
>
> You say I never attempt to "justify" myself. You are right—at times I can't & occasionally I won't defend by explanations—life is not worth having on such terms . . . You have detected a laughter "false to the heart"—allowed—yet I have been tolerably sincere with you, & I fear sometimes troublesome. To the charge of Pride, I suspect I must plead guilty . . . it was however originally *de*fensive . . . I now come to a subject of your enquiry which you must have perceived I always hitherto avoided—an awful one—"Religion". I was bred in Scotland among Calvinists in the first part of my life, which gave me a dislike to that persuasion. Since that period I have visited the most bigotted & credulous of countries, Spain, Greece, Turkey. As a spectacle the Catholic is more fascinating than the Greek or ye Moslem, but the *last* is the only believer who practises the precepts of his Prophet to the last chapter of his creed. My opinions are quite undecided . . . I believe doubtless in God, & should be happy to be convinced of much more . . . the *moral* of Christianity is perfectly beautiful, & the very sublime of Virtue, yet even there we find some of its finer precepts in earlier axioms of the Greeks . . . I have sent you a long prose. I hope your answer will be equal in length. I am sure it will be more amusing . . .

Her answer of 1st October was more than equal in length, but amusing only if read with malice. Destitute of humour, she could never recognise the tedium of pedantry; accustomed to an assumption of intellectual superiority, she was unconscious of impertinence in presumption. She felt the necessity of pointing out "an error connected with your habitual propensity to suspect yourself the object of ill-will & ill-opinion *more* than in fact you are":

> I fear that the experience of your early years gave a melancholy ground for this disposition . . . It is true that by many you are thought of with a kind of vague horror but amongst my acquaintance almost all those for whose judgments I have the highest respect, believe your mind capable of excellence, & replete with the best feelings. They wish that your religious principles were more fixed . . .
>
> Nothing can be more satisfactory or more agreable to my wishes than your open & explicit manner of answering my enquiries. You are very liberal in not estimating Christian morality by the Professors who disgrace it. As I think that every one must principally be convinced by the suggestions of his own understanding, I am not desirous that you should study the arguments of the popular advocates for Religion. I have not a very high opinion of most Orthodox vindications . . . I believe, as you assert, that the maxims of the Gospel may be found *unconnectedly* in heathen writings, but were they ever united in a system so wonderfully & so wisely adapted for the good of mankind? In my moderate acquaintance with the Ethics of the Ancients, I have found only scattered lights amongst insufficient or impracticable doctrines . . . I will not expatiate further on this topic, being persuaded that I cannot offer you any idea which would not occur from your own attentive reflection . . .
>
> I do not insist on your following the same peaceful path in life, which I should choose. You possess great powers, and may require to be placed in scenes of stronger action . . .
>
> If you are fatigued by the too great seriousness of my thoughts, you must excuse it at this time as the unavoidable consequence of sorrow which I do not indulge. My most valued friend Miss Montgomery is going abroad by medical advice, in a state of health that renders her return extremely precarious. You will conceive that in these circumstances our approaching separation must be a severe trial . . . By attributing my depression to this cause, I do not seek to invalidate what I once hinted of another impression —subjected as it is to reason, I need not blush to own it. I *should* blush to be its slave . . .

There was much more in the style of a lecturer at a mission school. It was too much for Byron, who returned to Rotherham. He had invited Augusta to accompany him, thinking she would keep him out of trouble; when she excused herself, he was the more determined to find trouble so that he could reproach her for having failed him. While he had confessed his object to Lady Melbourne, he sought to excuse his conduct:

> If a man is not contented with a pretty woman & not only runs after any little country girl he meets with but absolutely boasts of it, he must not be surprised if others admire that which he knows not how to value.

"I am decidedly wrong," he admitted of his behaviour towards Webster, "yet—he almost provoked me into it—*he* loves other women, at least he follows them—she evidently did not love him even before." When the affair had progressed further, he protested:

> I am wrong—but you really *wrong* me too, if you do not suppose that I would sacrifice every thing for *Ph*—— [Lady Frances]. I hate sentiment, & in consequence my epistolary levity makes you believe me as hollow & heartless as my letters are light. Indeed it is not so . . .

Asked if he was prepared to go "all lengths":

> If you mean by "all lengths" any thing including duel or divorce, I answer *yes*—I love her.

Yet, when the Websters accompanied him to Newstead and Lady Frances offered herself, "I spared her. There was something so very peculiar in her manner . . . but still I know not what convinced me she was serious."

He had been prepared to play the game he had learned from Lady Caroline and Lady Oxford, but "poor thing, she is either the most *artful* or *artless* of her age (20) I ever encountered." He spared her because he could not match her in being serious; he had been playing a game to escape from preoccupation with a deeper emotion. So far from being a cad, he was—despite the experience learned in the past two years—still the sentimentalist who had been hurt by a housemaid's infidelity. Afterwards he grumbled that he had been "the fool of her whimsical romance," but his heart was never involved.

In the first week of October Annabella had written to tell her aunt how "very beautiful" she thought the additions in the enlarged fifth edition of *The Giaour:*

> The description of Love almost makes *me* in love. Certainly he excels in the language of Passion . . . I consider his acquaintance as so desirable that I would incur the risk of being called a Flirt for the sake of enjoying it, provided I may do so without detriment to himself—for you know that his welfare has been as much the object of my consideration as if it were connected with my own.

Byron commented to Lady Melbourne on 8th October:

> I have heard from *A*, but her letter to me is *melancholy*—about her old friend Miss My's departure &c. &c. I wonder who will have her at last.

> Her letter to you is *gay*, you say—that to me must have been written at the same time, the little demure Nonjuror!

Without owning that it was he who owed a letter, he wrote on the 23rd: "My Seaham correspondence has ceased on both sides, & I shall not renew it."

Annabella was incapable of suspecting that she might be considered a bore. After waiting a month, she wrote on 3rd November to explain that, in writing her previous letter, she had "thought it more attentive to answer immediately, but on reflection it appears that I should in reality have shown you more respect, had I postponed writing till I was capable of giving undivided consideration to what I wrote." She therefore composed a more elaborate discourse on the principle that "*By the improvement of the Reason & the affections*, Christian faith & good works must be attained," quoting Locke and Bacon as evidence that, "If you regard only what is philosophically good you cannot think it a misuse of Time thus *to improve the* Reason & the affections."

> I am not exacting an answer. I only request to be informed whenever my communications become unacceptable that I may discontinue them, & when you *partially* disapprove them pray tell me, that I may perceive my error.

Byron apologised on 10th November that he had been prevented from writing earlier by "a variety of circumstances & movements from place to place."

> Your opinion of my "reasoning powers" is so exactly my own, that you will not wonder if I avoid a controversy with so skilled a casuist, particularly on a subject where I am certain to get the worst of it in this world, and perhaps incur a warmer confutation in the next. But I shall be most happy to hear your observations on the subject . . . as by all accounts you are mistress of the practice as well as theory of that benevolent science (which I take to be better than even your *Mathematics*) . . .

Of his own mathematics he joked that he knew two and two made four, but wished he knew how to "convert 2 & 2 into *five*"; deprecating that "you are still a little inclined to believe me a very gloomy personage," he assured her "I look upon myself as a facetious companion" and "am happy so far in the intimate acquaintance of two or three men with whom for ten years of my life I have never had one word of difference—and what is rather strange, their opinions religious moral & political are diametrically opposite to mine." He had "been scribbling another poem as it is called—Turkish as before, for I can't empty my head of the East"; he proposed to send her a copy, though "there are some Mussulman words in it which I inflict upon you in revenge for your 'Mathematical' & other superiority."

When shall you be in town?—by the bye, you won't take *flight* when we meet will you? & imagine that I am about to add to your thousand and one pretendants? I have taken exquisite care to prevent the possibility of that, though less likely than ever to become a Benedick. Indeed I have not seen (with one exception) for many years a Beatrice—and she will not be troubled to assume the part.

I think we understand each other perfectly, & may talk to each other occasionally without exciting speculation. The worst that can be said, is, that I *would* & you *won't*, and in this respect *you* can hardly be the sufferer —and I am very sure I *shan't*. If I find my heart less philosophic on the subject than I at present believe it, I shall keep out of the way, but I *now* think it is well shielded—at least it has got a new suit of armour, and certainly it stood in need of it.

He referred in conclusion to her rejection of Frederick Douglas:

I have heard a rumour of another added to your list of unacceptables, and am sorry for him, as I know that he has talent, & his pedigree ensures him wit & good humour. You make sad havoc among "us youth". It is lucky that Md. de Stael has published her Anti-suicide at so killing a time—*November* too!

Deep in composition of *The Bride of Abydos*—"to wring my thoughts from reality," as he told Moore, "and take refuge in 'imaginings' "—he allowed this letter to lie a week in his desk before adding an apologetic postscript on 17th November.

Baffled by such unaccustomed flippancy, after a week's pondering, Annabella stepped down from her pedestal on the 27th to begin with the nearest approach to banter that she could muster:

Pray let me have your new composition. I have received more pleasure from your poetry than from all the Q.e.ds in Euclid. Though I think Mathematics eminently useful, they are by no means what I like or admire most, & I have not a friend more skilled in them than yourself.

She even conceded:

Perhaps I *have* occasionally forgotten the humility which should have regulated my opinions, and in giving advice I may have "taken occasion to show my own wisdom at my neighbour's expence,"—but . . . I never meant to engage with you in religious controversy—you will remember that I owned myself not qualified for converting—I would only persuade you to take the means of convincing yourself. If I should hereafter imagine it in my power to propose any beneficial consideration, I shall avail myself of your permission to do so.

Ambiguously she assured him, "I cannot now have the least fear of your entertaining a wish for more of my regard than you possess":

I look forward to meeting you next spring in London as one of the most agreable incidents which my residence there can produce. *I* shall not be distressed if the design to captivate should be imputed to *me* (which I think probable), but if my father & mother should be rendered uneasy by misrepresentation of my conduct, I shall try to avoid the occasions, & shall then frankly tell you why I do so, and what I wish . . . .

To this more feminine naturalness Byron responded by return of post on the 29th:

No one can *as*sume or *pre*sume less than you do though very few with whom I am acquainted possess half your claims to that "Superiority" which you are so fearful of affecting . . . My only reason for avoiding the discussion of *sacred* topics was the sense of my own ignorance & the fear of saying something that might displease—but I *have listened*, & will listen to you with not merely patience but pleasure.

When we meet—if we do meet—in Spring, you will find me ready to acquiesce in all your notions upon the point merely personal between ourselves . . . You wrong yourself very much in supposing that "the charm" has been broken by our nearer acquaintance. On ye contrary that very intercourse convinces me of the value of what I have lost—or rather never found—but I will not deny that circumstances have occurred to render it more supportable.

You will think me very capricious & apt at sudden fancies. It is true I could not exist without some object of attachment, but I have shewn that I am not quite a slave to impulse. No man of tolerable situation in life who was quite without self command could have reached the age of 26 (which I shall be—I grieve to speak it—in January) without marrying & in all probability foolishly. But however weak (it may merit a harder term) in my disposition to attach myself (and as society is now much the same in this as in all other European countries, it were difficult to avoid it) in my search for the "ideal"—the being to whom I would commit the whole happiness of my future life—I have never yet seen but two approaching to the likeness. The first I was too young to have a prospect of obtaining, & subsequent events have proved that my expectations might not have been fulfilled had I even proposed to & secured my early idol. The *second*—the *only* woman to whom I ever seriously pretended as a wife—had disposed of her heart already, and I think it too late to look for a third. I shall take ye world as I find it, & I have seen it much the same in most climates (a little more fiery perhaps in Greece & Asia, for there they are a strange mixture of languid habits & stormy passions) but I have no confidence & look for no constancy in affections founded in caprice, & preserved (if preserved) by accident, & lucky conformity of disposition without any fixed principles. How far this may be my case at present, I know not, & have not had time to ascertain. I can only say that I never was cured of loving any one but by the conduct, by the change, or the violence of the object herself, and till I see reason for distrust I shall flatter myself as heretofore & perhaps with as little cause as ever.

I owe you some apology for this disquisition, but the singularity of *our* situation led me to dwell on this topic . . . They say that a man never *forgives* a woman who stands in the relation which you do towards *me*, but to *forgive* we must first be offended, & I think I cannot recall, even a moment of pique at the past, to my memory. I have but 2 *friends* of your sex—yourself & Ly. Melbourne—as different in years as in disposition, & yet I do not know which I prefer. Believe me a better-*hearted* woman does not exist, and in talent I never saw her excelled & hardly equalled. Her kindness to me has been uniform, and I fear severely & ungratefully tried at times on my part—but as it cannot be so again, at least in the same manner, I shall make what atonement I can, if a regard which my own inclination leads me to cultivate can make any amends for my trespasses on her patience.

The word *patience* reminds me of ye book I am to send you—it shall be ordered to Seaham tomorrow . . .

This was as nearly a love-letter as contemporary conventions permitted. Apart from his boyish infatuation for Mary Chaworth, Annabella was "the *only* woman" of his choice, but her misguided vanity had induced the fiction that she "had disposed of her heart already." Further, with provocative mysteriousness, he repeated the hint that his heart had "got a new suit of armour"—"circumstances" had occurred to render his disappointment "more supportable". It was a situation to furnish the plot of a Jane Austen novel—indeed, the whole correspondence between Byron and Annabella reflects how faithfully the author of *Persuasion* portrayed the manners of their day—and like a Jane Austen heroine, Annabella resorted to a confidante in her dilemma.

Already she had confided to Lady Gosford something of her feeling for Byron, writing in pious mood on 26th November:

Surely the survey of Heaven-born genius without Heavenly grace must make a Christian clasp the blessing with greater reverence & love, mingled with a sorrow as Christian that it is not shared. Should it ever happen that he & I offer up a heartfelt worship together—I mean in a sacred spot —*my* worship will then be almost worthy of the Spirit to whom it ascends. It will glow with all the devout & grateful joy which mortal breast can contain. It is a thought too dear to be indulged—not dear for *his* sake but for the sake of *man*, my brother man, whosoever he be, & for any poor, unknown tenant of this earth I believe I should feel the same. It is not the poet—it is the immortal Soul lost or saved! Now I have written & thought till my tears flow . . .

Her self-esteem could not admit that she was suffering from anything so commonplace as being in love. She was incapable of the common sense that inspired her mother to permit the correspondence with Byron because she recognised that Annabella wanted him and would not be happy till she had him. Her sexual urge had to be disguised in vestments of spirituality; her object was to save Byron's soul, and after she had failed in her marriage, she reverted to this illusion for consolation.

The perceptions of the self-absorbed are slow, and her first reaction to Byron's "disquisition" was jealousy. Though she was professedly concerned with his soul and Byron had pointedly avoided "discussion of *sacred* topics" from "fear of saying something that might displease," she began her letter to Lady Gosford on 3rd December with the brief assurance, "He expresses every disposition which is desirable on the subject of Religion."

> There is much about himself & me, signifying, but in the handsomest manner, that the wishes which he once entertained of possessing me no longer exist tho' he is as sensible as ever of the value of my affection as ever, saying "It is true that I could not live without an object of attachment." At the same time he says there are only two women for whom he has a strong regard, & that of these he scarcely knows which to prefer—Myself & Ly Melbourne . . . His mode of speaking of his heart is very mysterious. I fear he has done something rash from a romantic motive. I *really* must take care of my own heart, since he so positively declares that it is out of his power to requite any attachment.
>
> Ly Athlone is here, as much interested as ever for MM. I am out of spirits, partly from apprehensions for your health, in consequence of part of your communication to-day, & for other reasons which I cannot bring myself to mention—Oh!

She added a postscript, "I did not write yesterday," and after pondering Byron's letter for two more days, she perceived the root of her dilemma and sought to devise a solution suitably garnished with fine sentiments:

> I want your advice most seriously. You know that in my first letter to B—— I signified the existence of an attachment in my mind, in order to destroy all his hopes, and in so doing I felt that I resigned some prudential considerations to a disinterested zeal for his welfare. I acted from enthusiasm. I would have devoted much more to his happiness had it been in my power. To this confession he has three times recurred & again in his last letter, where he declares he shall never marry, for it is now too late, since the only woman to whom he could trust the happiness of his life *has disposed of her heart to another.*
>
> Now certainly I am fully convinced that I never have done so. I have been in danger of it, in great danger—but that is past, & for ever.
>
> You will not suspect me of any selfish view. I am certain that my heart is purified from *self* in *this* concern, but I feel very uneasy at the idea of keeping up a deception, & especially with one who has undoubtedly practised no deception with me. Had the circumstance not been mentioned, I should not have felt it necessary or conscientious to allude to it in any way, but now a continuation of silence is an acquiescence in untruth.

She thought a detailed explanation "would be indelicate & improper," but "yet I think something might be done to alleviate the reproaches of my conscience for persevering in a fictitious character."

> It depresses me very much. Wisdom as well as Will is requisite to be perfectly true—the wisdom of Self-knowledge, in which I have failed.

For Lady Gosford's approval she drafted an evasive statement that she might send to Byron before concluding:

> I shall be unhappy till I can regain *truth*. Such are the unhappy effects of Imagination. He has never yet *suspected* me . . . Nothing can be more noble than the sentiments of his last letter.

In this preoccupation with casuistry she fell ill. Her depression was doubtless deepened by the false news that Byron had sailed for Holland with "wise and witty" Ward, the future Lord Dudley—one of his several discarded plans of travel. On 26th December she wrote briefly:

> Having heard that you are still in England—for very soon after I received your last welcome letter a report reached me that you & Mr Ward *had left* London to embark—another day shall not pass before I account for my silence, which without that excuse would have been ungrateful both for your verse & prose . . . If you should not return till summer I shall have one reason the less for regretting the postponement of our Journey to London, which on *my* account will not take place so early as I had expected. Though at present recovered from a severe illness, I remain more unequal than before to the labours of a London life . . .

To this she received no reply. Byron had failed "to vanquish my demon" by his attempt to fall in love with Lady Frances Webster, who for some time carried on a clandestine correspondence with him; if he had not "spared" her, she might well have repeated the behaviour of Lady Caroline Lamb. He anticipated some such trouble, writing on 8th November to reproach Augusta for not having accompanied him to Aston Hall, "You do not know what mischief your being with me might have prevented." To Lady Melbourne he declared himself "not very unwilling" for Lady Frances's conduct to "hasten a crisis of some kind or other"; even his death in a duel with Webster "would be so *dramatic* a conclusion—all the sex would be enamoured of my Memory, all the Wits would have their jest, & the Moralists their sermon," while Lady Caroline "would go wild with *grief* that—*it did not happen about her*."

Behind this usual self-dramatisation was more genuine emotional stress than ever before. Besides the unsatisfactory Lady Frances, the neurotic Lady Caroline continued to harass him, and he was cut off from Augusta, who, after withdrawing in August from his plan to take her abroad, had declined to be decoyed away from Newmarket. "I am much afraid that that perverse passion was my deepest after all," he confided to Lady Melbourne on 25th November.

He "began a comedy, and burnt it because the scene ran into *reality;* —a novel, for the same reason." Writing *The Bride of Abydos*, he felt that "in rhyme, I can keep more away from facts," but found that, even so, "the thought always runs through, through . . ." Against his own inclination—for "in composition I do not think *second* thoughts are the best, though *second* expressions may improve the first ideas"—he devised in the second canto that the lovers should turn out to be first cousins, instead of brother and sister, as the theme of incestuous love "is not adapted for this age, at least this country, though the finest works of the Greeks, one of Schiller's and Alfieri's in modern times, besides several of our *old* (and best) dramatists, have been grounded on incidents of a similar cast."

As one critic has remarked, since the heroine "believed throughout the action of the first canto that the nearer relation subsisted, this device to keep away from the facts does not affect the conclusion to be drawn from the published poem." Hence Lady Melbourne expressed alarm when, little more than a fortnight after *The Bride of Abydos* was published on 29th November, Augusta came to London.

After his visit to Six Mile Bottom in September, Byron had written to Augusta on 15th September in a tone of curt displeasure because she had declined to accompany him to Aston Hall. In reply to her protest, he assured her on 10th October that he was "not in the least angry"; on 8th November he apologised for his "long silence" and hinted at the "mischief" with Lady Frances Webster that Augusta's "being with me might have prevented." In his journal he noted on 16th November that *The Bride of Abydos* "was written in four nights to distract my dreams from * *"; on the 26th he reflected, "Oh how seldom we see those we love! yet we live ages in moments, *when met.*" Presumably he wrote to Augusta other letters which she prudently destroyed, for he noted on 24th November, "I am tremendously in arrear with my letters—except to * *, and to her my thoughts overpower me."

Augusta could hardly have failed to be deeply moved by the inference that she was the cause of Byron's entanglement with Lady Frances, and it may be assumed that she received an advance copy of *The Bride of Abydos*, for on 29th November she posted to Byron this message:

> Partager tous vos sentimens
> ne voir que par vos yeux
> n' agir que par vos conseils, ne
> vivre que pour vous, voila mes

voeux, mes projets, & le seul
destin qui peut me rendre
heureuse.

She enclosed a curl of her hair tied with white silk in a folded paper on which—under the hair—she wrote her signature, *Augusta*. On the outside of the folded paper Byron wrote:

La Chevelure of
the *one* whom I
most *loved* +

During Augusta's London visit Byron was so occupied that he discontinued his journal and did not find time to write even to Lady Melbourne—whom he esteemed as "the best friend I ever had in my life, and the cleverest of women"—till 8th January, when, apologising that "I have had too much in my head to write," he defended Augusta from gossip circulated by Lady Caroline Lamb: she was not separated from her husband, nor had she stayed under the same roof with Byron, but firstly with the Hansons at Bloomsbury Square and later with her friend, Mrs. George Villiers.

To distract Lady Melbourne from the subject of Augusta, he confided that "my old love of all loves," Mrs. Chaworth-Musters, "has written to me *twice*—no *love* but she wants to see me." John Musters was "the handsomest man of his day, of great assurance and very imposing address"; according to Squire Osbaldeston, "as a sportsman and Master of Hounds he was less successful" than as "a great favourite with the ladies." Having now temporarily left him, his wife had taken refuge with a relative, Miss Radford, at a house on the Musters estate at Edwalton, about ten miles from Newstead. The romantic appeal of an approach from the heroine of his boyish love was naturally not lost upon Byron, who made the most of it in his letters to Lady Melbourne. But, as a disaffected wife, Mrs. Chaworth-Musters was in a situation dangerously like Lady Frances Webster's; she even, like Lady Frances, invited him to write to her through a third person. It is unlikely that Byron, armed with the experience of the past two years, ever seriously contemplated the possibility of returning to his old flame; on 11th January he admitted to Lady Melbourne:

It is impossible I should now feel any thing beyond friendship for her or any one else in present circumstances, and the kind of feeling which has lately absorbed me has a mixture of the *terrible* which renders all other, even passion (pour les autres) insipid to a degree.

Though he spent three weeks at Newstead from 17th January to 6th February, he did not call on Mrs. Chaworth-Musters.

It is true that he was snowbound during most of his stay at Newstead, but Augusta was with him. He had at last persuaded her to visit the home of her father's family, which she had never seen. Though cut off by snow from visits and visitors, they enjoyed their own company, "as we never yawn or disagree, and laugh much more than is suitable to so solid a mansion; and the family shyness makes us more amusing companions to each other than we could be to any one else."

Rebuking him for absorption in that "kind of feeling" with its "mixture of the terrible", Lady Melbourne blamed Augusta for encouraging him, but while he allowed that she could not "well have said less" of his own "folly", he defended Augusta:

> You are quite mistaken however as to *her*, and it must be from some misrepresentation of mine that you throw the blame so completely on the side least deserving and least able to bear it. I dare say I made the best of my own story as one always does from natural selfishness without intending it, but it was not her fault, but my own folly (give it what name may suit it better) and her weakness—for the intentions of both were very different and for some time adhered to—& when *not* it was certainly my own—in short I know no name for my own conduct. Pray do not speak so harshly of her to me—the cause of all.

Facts endorse the sincerity of this statement. When Mrs. Gally Knight described Augusta to Judith as "a very *weak* woman," though Annabella was by then building a case against Augusta as having caused the failure of her marriage, she wrote to her mother, "Mrs Knight touches on the true cause of all ——'s deviations, when she speaks of weakness—she is not bad-hearted I am convinced." Augusta never disguised her devotion to "my beloved B.", as she called him in letters to Annabella as well as to Hodgson. Her romantic feeling for her husband had been long since eroded by domestic friction; harassed by his debts and by the problems of a household inadequate for the upbringing of a family of young children, she found in Byron her only source of tender consideration and in his promises of assistance her only insurance for the future security of herself and her children. With her warmth and generosity of temperament, it would be hard for her to refuse anything to Byron.

Annabella had for many years nourished a vendetta of hostility against Augusta when she ascribed to her "a kind of Moral Idiotcy from birth" and derided her religion as "the Chichester Gospel." Augusta and her half-sister, Lady Chichester, had received a strictly religious upbringing from their grandmother; if, by comparison with Annabella's own brand of nonconformity, theirs was a conventional religion, its very conventionality must have afflicted Augusta with compunction for any offence against decreed morality. Her social background was also conventional. The family of her half-brother, the Duke of Leeds, moved in the stuffy court circle surrounding old Queen Charlotte; her husband, a cavalry officer and a racing man, mixed with sportsmen of the first fashion who, like Lord Darlington, paid for their pleasures with actresses and chambermaids while depending on their wives' correct deportment in social and domestic functions.

After retracting her reckless impulse to go abroad with him in August, Augusta resisted all Byron's persuasions to leave Newmarket before she came up to London in mid-December. Though he reproached her for having failed to avert his involvement with Lady Frances Webster by accompanying him to Aston Hall, tenderness for her feelings may have deterred him from dramatising his emotions to her as to other correspondents. That he felt remorse on her account appears in his journal, in his letters to Lady Melbourne, in the anguish of Selim for Zuleika in *The Bride of Abydos*, in the haunted broodings of Conrad—finding comfort only in his love for Medora—in *The Corsair*, which was written in three weeks from 18th December and inspired his publisher to write on 3rd February 1814:

> Never, in my recollection, has any work . . . excited such a ferment . . . I sold, on the day of publication,—a thing perfectly unprecedented—10,000 copies . . . You have no notion of the sensation which the publication has occasioned; and my only regret is that you were not present to witness it.[1]

The heavy snow provided an excuse for staying so long as three weeks at Newstead; he wrote to Hanson, "Mrs. L. is with me, and being in the family way renders it doubly necessary to remain till the roads are quite safe." On his return to London he found that the success of *The Corsair* was attended by attacks in the press. With *The Corsair* were published the "Lines to a Lady Weeping," which had been first published anonymously two years before, when Princess Charlotte had burst into tears at the Regent's displeasure with the Whig lords, Grey and Grenville, for refusing to join Lord Liverpool's administration. The Tory papers were "in a sad commotion" over the avowal of authorship, the *Morning Post* inferring "that I am a sort of R[ichar]d III—deformed in mind and *body*"—which "*last* piece of information," said Byron, "is not very new to a man who has passed five years at a public school."

On 18th February he had a note from Lady Melbourne in the country, concerned with hearing that he was "much out of spirits."

[1] On 17th January 1816—two days after Annabella had left Byron and was debating whether he was mentally unbalanced—Augusta reported of an interview with John Murray, "He confessed to me that he thought B very odd the 2 last times he had seen him & that while he was writing the Corsair he thought him in a compleat phrenzy."

I wonder if I really am or not? I have certainly enough of "that perilous stuff that weighs upon the heart," and it is better they should believe it to be the result of these attacks than of the real cause; but—ay, ay, always *but*, to the end of the chapter.

So he wrote in his journal, and to Lady Melbourne:

You seem to think I am in some scrape at present by my unequal spirits. Perhaps I am, but you shan't be shocked, so you shan't.

Apparently she replied by attributing his depression to Augusta's having forbidden his visiting her at Newmarket, for he wrote on the 21st:

I am not "forbidden" by —— though it is very odd that like *every one*, she seemed more assured (and not very well pleased) of your influence than of any other, but—I suppose being pretty certain of her own power—always said "do as you please, & go where you like," and I really know no reason for my not having been where I ought, unless it were to punish myself, or—I really do not know why exactly.

You will easily suppose that, twined as she is round my heart in every possible manner, dearest & deepest in my hope & my memory, still I am not easy. It is *this*, if any thing, my own—in short I cannot write about it.

Still I have not lost all self command. For instance, I *could* at this moment be where I have been, where I would rather be than any where else, and yet from some motive or other—but certainly not indifference—I am here, & here I will remain, but it costs me some struggles. It is the misery of my situation—to see it as *you* see it, & to *feel* it as *I* feel it, on *her* account, & that of others. As for myself, it is of much less, & may soon be of no consequence. But—I will drop ye subject.

Already he had agreed with Lady Melbourne that a wife might be his "salvation." Without enthusiasm he considered the possibility of Lady Frances Webster's younger sister, "who is very pretty, but fearfully young, and I think a *fool;*" he thought he "might manage this easily with" her father, Lord Mountnorris, "but I don't admire the connection."

I do believe that to marry would be my wisest step . . . But all wives would be much the same. I have no *heart* to spare,—& expect none in return; but, as Moore says, "A pretty wife is something for the fastidious vanity of a *roué* to retire upon." And mine might do as she pleased so that she had a fair temper & a *quiet* way of conducting herself, leaving me the same liberty of conscience.

What I want is a companion—a friend rather than a sentimentalist.

The timing seemed thus opportune when Annabella resumed their correspondence on 10th February:

I cannot, without serious disappointment, inform you that our hope of meeting is deferred. My strength will not yet enable me to enter into the general society of London, & my father & mother think that I shall receive more benefit from a residence in the Country during this year. Do not however suppose that my health is at all alarmingly impaired . . .

Reminding him that he had "kindly done away every supposed objection to my wish, early formed & since more strongly felt, of conversing with you on terms of mutual confidence," she led up to the evasive statement designed "to alleviate the reproaches" of her conscience which she had discussed with Lady Gosford in December:

You have thought we perfectly understood each other. I hope I shall not give you reason to retract that opinion by any *future* false estimates of your character. Those which wronged you no longer exist . . . You have understood *me* at least as well as I understood myself. Both may have been partly deceived, though unwittingly by me, but I have found that Wisdom (often the most difficult Wisdom, Self-knowledge) is not less necessary than Will for an absolute adherence to Veracity. * How I may in a degree have forsaken *that*—and under the influence of an ardent zeal for Sincerity—is an explanation that cannot benefit either of us. Should any disadvantage arise from the original fault, it must be only where it is deserved. Let this then suffice—for I cannot by total silence acquiesce in that, which, if supported when its delusion is known to myself, would become deception.*

I was sensible of many excellencies in Lady Melbourne. Your opinion will incline me to look for more . . . You know her much better than I do, since I have seldom been with her except in mixed company, for a few hours . . .

She had been "deeply interested" in *The Corsair* and had argued "with some of your *moral* censors, who perceive an immoral tendency in the imposing grandeur with which you clothe the Victims of Remorse & Despair," forgetting that they admired without censure in Milton's Satan "the noble broken fragments of an immortal mind in ruins." Her assurance that "the prejudices against you are subsiding" was followed by commendation of Locke's *Reasonableness of Christianity*.

Replying on the 12th that he was "just returned to London after a month's absence" with regret that her own would "be so much longer," Byron quoted a passage from her letter that he could not understand (the passage between asterisks above):

I do not see in what you have deceived yourself, & you have certainly never been otherwise than candid with me—and I have endeavoured to act accordingly. In regard to your kind observations on my adoption of my conduct to your wishes, I trust I should have been able to do so even without your suggestion. The moment I sunk into your friend, I tried to regard you in no other light. Our affections are not in our power, but it would seem strange indeed because you could not like me that I should repine at the better fortune of another. If I had ever possessed a preference, the case would have been altered, and I might not have been so patient in resigning my pretensions. But you never did, never for an instant trifle with me nor amuse me with what is called encouragement.

He gave her a long account of his boyish romance with Mary Chaworth and of her subsequent history, ending with the assurance that these circumstances "bear no relation whatever to what I hinted at in a former letter as having occurred to prevent my reviving the topic discussed between us—at least with a view to renewal." He added a postscript in praise of that "*supreme* woman," Lady Melbourne—"I do love that woman (*filially* or *fraternally*) better than any being on earth."

Apparently reflecting that he had snubbed her too sharply, he wrote again on the 15th to say that he had omitted to reply to her recommendation of Locke's treatise: "I have redde it formerly though I fear to little purpose since it is forgotten." Briefly he referred to the press attacks caused by "Lines to a Lady Weeping" as evidence that "your kind congratulation on the subject of certain prejudices against me having subsided is a little premature," and ended with courteous concern for her health.

So far from feeling snubbed, Annabella replied by return on the 17th to his first letter:

I will comment as explicitly as I can on the passage which you wish me to elucidate.

I have twice implied that I suffered from Disappointment. It was an effort to make such a disclosure . . . I resolved to overcome a reluctance that seemed so ungenerous . . . In this fever of Sincerity I first made & afterwards repeated the allusion to my attachment, yet even then I had doubts which prevented me from expressing it more fully & distinctly. I had certainly felt greater interest for the character I attributed to one man (with whom my personal acquaintance was comparatively slight) than for any other within my knowledge. In believing him deserving of happiness, I earnestly wished he might enjoy it . . . I indulged no hope, & had hope been offered, should have rejected it from regard to the views & wishes of others. Circumstances have since made it impossible for me even to dream of Hope. If an inclination which so far prevailed without support, had been encouraged either by myself or its object, and the esteem on which it was solely founded, *confirmed* by habits of intimacy, I imagine it might have gained an ascendancy over the obstacles that *actually* checked its progress. As it is, I have sometimes deeply regretted that lost chance of domestic happiness . . .

As plainly as she could, she was telling him that he himself had been the only object of her attachment; she felt no snub in his letter because, with her self-esteem, she conceived that he had only succeeded in being "so patient in resigning my pretensions" through having so few opportunities of meeting her. As to his confidence about Mary Chaworth:

> You may feel secure that your secret rests with me alone. My father & mother being perfectly satisfied as to the general nature of our communication, with their usual generous confidence, enquire no further.

She wrote again on the 18th, as "Your letter of the 12th must have been delayed on the road—it only reached me the day before that of the 15th"; again she urged him to call on Joanna Baillie, from whom she had just heard "her opinion of the Corsair," ending:

> I showed your last letter to my father & mother. I have not formed any friendship on which they reflect with more satisfaction than on ours, and they wish to assure you that they are not insensible of its value to me.

Deliberately Byron chose to be obtuse:

> I had no right to interrogate you on such a subject, & had I been at all aware that my question would have led to any explanation of feelings to which you do not like to recur, of course I should have remained in silence & in darkness.
>
> Still it is not to be regretted in one point of view even on your own account, as it sets all apprehension of the revival of a subject already discussed long ago between us—at rest;—it is true that it was not in any great peril of revival before, but it is now more completely "numbered with the things that were" and never can be again.
>
> Ignorant as I am of the person & the circumstances to whom & which you allude, I can form no opinion, except—that if he has put it out of his power to avail himself of such a disposition in his favour, he is fortunate in not knowing that it ever existed.

To add to this freezing of her hopes, he declared his sympathy with Bankes and Douglas, "both very clever & excellent men, & attached to you . . . I should have been glad to have seen one of them in a fair way for happiness," and concluded on a note of Byronic melodrama:

> I am at present a little feverish—I mean mentally—and as usual, on the brink of something or other, which will probably crush me at last, & cut our correspondence short with every thing else.

As he wrote this to Annabella on 19th February, remarking, "I am told also that I am 'out of spirits'" and "Ly. M. I have not yet seen, but I believe she is well, & I hope to find her so shortly," presumably he wrote the same day to Lady Melbourne a letter of which the last page only survives, beginning:

> . . . prospect) I never shall. One of my great inducements to that brilliant negotiation with the Princess of Parallelograms, was the vision of

our *family party*, and the quantity of domestic lectures I should faithfully detail, with our mutual comments thereupon.

Two days later he confided to Lady Melbourne his "struggles" about Augusta.

On the 24th Annabella chose to ignore that part of his letter relating to herself, concentrating on an attempt "to withdraw your thoughts from the afflicting contemplations with which they appear to be occupied."

Ere now I hope Lady M. has assisted you to recover a happier and a *better* state of mind. I should not fulfil my duty towards you were I not to reprove the temper of feeling which you suffered to prevail when you wrote on the 19th. "The heart knoweth its own bitterness"—the heart and One besides, by whom alone it can be removed, to whom it should *first* be offered. Had you more humbly bowed before the Chastener, that fever of spirit would have been calmed . . . To signify some calamity impending over you, yet to leave me in painful suspense as to its nature and the possibility of averting it, is not quite considerate towards one who so anxiously desires your welfare. You can *only* wrong me by doubting *that*—by refusing me a participation in your cares. It might possibly a little decrease their burden to you, & could not grieve me more than the vague conjectures which I am left to form.

She then attempted to match him in self-dramatisation:

My prospects are full of uncertainty, and inspire me with doubts respecting my future peace. On the whole I think myself formed for domestic ties, but I cannot seek them on the principle of Self-love or Expediency. Could my choice have been regulated by such views, perhaps it might not have been deceived in either of your friends.

Again she urged him to visit Joanna Baillie, "for our intimacy will seem to be strengthened—particularly in absence—by a mutual friend, from whom I may know of you."

Vainly hoping for enlightenment on the cause of his foreboding, she wrote to their only mutual friend, Lady Melbourne, who forwarded the letter to Byron. He commented briefly:

I return A's letter with many thanks. I have had *one* too.

To Annabella he wrote almost as briefly on the 25th to explain that he had not introduced himself to Miss Baillie, partly because he hoped the time might come when "you will do it in person," partly because "I have a strange awkwardness & repugnance in making new acquaintances, & have had ever since I was a child."

He wrote again on 3rd March, addressing her for the first time as

"My dear Friend" and expressing regret for "having perhaps alarmed you by something I said, writing hastily in one of my late letters."

> I do not recollect exactly what I said—it was the "hectic of a moment" probably, occasioned by a variety of unpleasant circumstances pressing upon me at the time, and arising from follies (or worse) into which I betray myself—& escape I cannot tell how . . .
>
> I thank you very much for your suggestion on Religion, but I must tell you at the hazard of losing whatever good opinion your gentleness may have bestowed upon me, that it is a source from which I never did, & I believe never can derive comfort. If I ever feel what is called devout, it is when I have met with some good of which I did not conceive myself deserving—and then I am apt to thank any thing but mankind. On the other hand when I am ill or unlucky, I philosophize as well as I can, & wish it over one way or the other without many glimpses at the future. Why I came here, I know not—where I shall go it is useless to enquire. In the midst of myriads of the living & the dead-worlds—stars, systems, infinity—why should I be anxious about an atom?

Having thus disposed of her worry about "calamity impending" and declared his position towards religion, he added a postscript offering an opening for her to clarify the real issue between them:

> I was told today that you had refused me "a *second* time" so that you see I am supposed to be the most permanent of your plagues & persevering of Suitors . . . If this multiplication table of negatives don't embarrass you, I can assure you it don't disturb me . . .

Annabella was not thus to be drawn so soon after he had ignored her advance. Besides, she never in her life neglected an opportunity to assert the infallibility of her own opinions, so her letter of 12th March was mainly a dissertation on religion:

> In regard to the despicable opinion you hold of man, & of yourself as man—true, we are atoms in the universal scale, but is an atom nothing or worthless to the *Infinite* Being? . . . Man must be endeared and exalted to man, by the conviction that *man* is an object of benevolent interest to the Supreme Being.

She quoted the incident of the Samaritan woman in the fourth chapter of St. John as assurance that "He who looks up to a 'Father in Heaven' will take a kind interest in his own existence."

> I always touch the sacred subject with reverential fear. My interest for you will not be altered because at present you *cannot* be convinced—or by me. Despair not of yourself—I still hope the best for you, and whence soever it may come, though not through *my* means, it will add to *my* happiness . . .

As for the report, it is absurd enough to excite a smile—false in *name* as well as *number*. In avoiding the possibility of being in a situation to refuse, I cannot consider myself as having refused. They who credit such tales must know little of you.

The semblance of steadfastness, her confidence in his character, and her concern for his welfare impressed Byron so favourably that he wrote in his journal, "A letter from *Bella*, which I answered. I shall be in love with her again if I don't take care"—the "again" suggesting that he was now prepared to assume a pose of having in fact been in love with her when she rejected him. Replying by return on the 15th, he evaded sober discussion of religion by giving a lively account of an *Anti-Byron* satire which his publisher had just sent to him in manuscript, before concluding with flattering warmth:

You do not know how much I wish to see you—for there are so many things *said* in a moment, but tedious upon the tablets. Not that I should ever intrude upon your confidence any thing (at least I hope not) you should *not* hear—yet there are several opinions of yours I want to request, & though I have two or three able & I believe very sincere male friends there is something preferable to me in ye delicacy of a woman's perceptions. Of this at least I am sure—that I am more liable to be convinced by their arguments. As for ye *report* I mentioned, *I* care not how often it is repeated—it would plague me much more to hear that I was *accepted* by any body else than rejected by you.

He wanted to see her, and she herself believed that his "inclination" to her required only to be "*confirmed* by habits of intimacy." Annabella's problem was how to contrive their meeting. As she had told him, "My health improves daily," but plans had already been made for her to miss a fifth London season. The only solution was to persuade her parents to invite Byron to Seaham, but her father could do nothing without consulting her mother, who had gone to London the week before, travelling with Selina Doyle, who had been invited to Seaham as Annabella's companion after MM's departure abroad and had "been a great comfort to us all this winter." She had to wait nearly four weeks before her parents could be persuaded to enable her to write on 13th April:

I have been prevented once or twice when I was going to write to you. Am I mistaken in imagining that you are disposed to visit us? Perhaps you think of repeating your journey to Yorkshire and would extend it. My father & mother desire me to say, in case you should have any intention of doing them that favour, that they shall have most sincere pleasure in seeing you as their guest. I agree with you that the pen is unsatisfactory in discussing interesting topics, and I could not object to converse with you on *any*, even Religion which I am in the habit of declining sometimes because I do not like the practice of familiarizing it . . .

I still do not wish to inform my Aunt of all the circumstances of our intercourse, yet I must account to her for your visit, if purposed. Do you think it necessary to say more than that you have been invited to Seaham whenever you again travel northwards? My father will himself express to you that invitation, if you give us reason to hope it will be accepted. Perhaps these are idle speculations, and then think of them no more.

Having vainly sought an opportunity for consulting Lady Melbourne personally, Byron wrote to her on 18th April:

Though I think *that chance* off the cards, and have no paramount inclination to try a fresh deal, yet as what I may resolve to-day may be unresolved to-morrow, I should be not only unwilling but unable to make the experiment without your acquiescence.

Circumstances which I need not recapitulate may have changed *Aunt's* mind. I do not say that *Niece's* is changed, but I *should* laugh if their judgements had changed places and exactly reversed upon that point. In putting this question to you, my motive is all due selfishness, as a word from you could and would put an end to that or any similar possibility, without my being able to say any thing but "thank you."

While awaiting the aunt's acquiescence, he replied tentatively to the niece on the 20th:

If I could flatter myself that my visit would not be disagreeable to you or yours I should very willingly avail myself of Sir Ralph's possible invitation. Distance is no object with me, and time can hardly be misspent in your society—besides a good deal of mine is generally passed in my own company, so that I could almost hope that I should not be found an intruder upon your studies or amusements. You will do as you please—only let it be *as you* please, & not to gratify any supposed or real wish of mine that you make this sacrifice at the shrine of Hospitality.

He had good reason to suppose that Lady Melbourne might no longer consider him an eligible suitor for her niece, as he had confided to her much of his absorption in Augusta. On 22nd March he had noted in his journal the possibility of marrying Lady Stafford's eldest daughter, Lady Charlotte Leveson-Gower, because "she is a friend of Augusta's, and whatever she loves I can't help liking." Six days later he noted that Augusta wanted him to make up his old quarrel with Lord Carlisle: "I have refused *every* body else, but I can't deny her any thing." On Good Friday, 8th April, he informed Lady Melbourne that he was just returned from spending six days at Newmarket with Augusta while her husband was absent in Yorkshire. On 15th April

Augusta gave birth to a daughter, to which event[1] Lady Melbourne evidently referred in replying to Byron's request for her "acquiescence" in his accepting Annabella's invitation, for he wrote to her on 25th April:

Oh! but it is "worth while"—I can't tell you why—and it is *not* an "*Ape*" and if it is, that must be my fault. However I will positively reform. You must however allow that it is utterly impossible I can ever be half so well liked elsewhere, and I have been all my life trying to make some one love me, and never got the sort I preferred before. But positively she & I will grow good & all that—& so we are *now* and shall be these three weeks & more too.

Meanwhile Annabella had written on the 23rd from Durham:

I *wish* to see you, and am happy to think I shall not wish in vain. I promise you that neither on this or any future occasion will I make any sacrifice for your sake, because the neglect of my comfort or advantage could not, in my estimation, be friendly towards you, and when I consult my own well-being I believe you would thank me for regarding it. Will you adopt the same principle towards me? I am from home, but shall return to Seaham tomorrow or the day after, & shall then know what time my father can propose for your visit—not when we expect an influx of company, for you shall not be made a *Lion.*

On her return to Seaham she wrote again:

I have written by this post to Lady Melbourne informing her of my father's invitation to you, which *I think she will be glad to learn.*[2]

After discussing criticism of *The Corsair*, she enclosed eight lines of her own verse addressed "to a friend who wished to correct me of a habit of frowning."

This letter Byron enclosed when writing to Lady Melbourne on 29th April:

I don't know what to say or do about going. Sometimes I wish it, at other times I think it foolish, as assuredly my design will be imputed to a motive, which by the bye if once fairly there is very likely to come into my head—and *failing*, to put me into no very good humour with myself. I

[1] Of her fourth child Augusta entered in her Bible: "Elizabeth Medora Leigh born at the Six Mile Bottom April 15th 1814. Christened there, May 20th 1814 by the Revd. C. Wedge. Sponsors—The Dss. of Rutland Mrs. Wilmot & Lord Byron". Lord Lovelace (*Astarte*, p. 37n.) stated that the godmothers were Lady Francis Osborne (Elizabeth) and Mrs. Wilmot, but Lady Francis (wife of Augusta's half-brother and one of the many sisters of Annabella's suitor, George Eden) was probably substituted on the death in 1825 of the Duchess of Rutland, who, before her marriage in 1799, was Lady Elizabeth Howard, Lord Carlisle's second daughter.

[2] The italicised words were underlined by Byron, with the comment, "*Will she?* credo di *No.*"

am not now in love with her, but I can't at all foresee that I should not be so if it come "a warm June" (as Falstaff observes) and seriously, I do admire her as a very superior woman a little encumbered with Virtue . . .

I am quite irresolute—and undecided. If I were sure of *myself* (not of her) I would go, but I am not & never can be, and what is still worse I have no judgement & less common sense than an infant. This is *not affected humility*—with *you* I have no affectation . . .

The next day Lady Melbourne stung him into a further defence of Augusta:

You, or rather, *I* have done *my A—* much injustice . . . really & truly—as I hope mercy & happiness for her, by that God who made me for my own misery, & not much for the good of others—*she* was not to blame, one thousandth part in comparison. She was not aware of her own peril till it was too late, and I can only account for her subsequent "*abandon*" by an observation which I think is not unjust—that women are much more *attached* than men, if they are treated with any thing like fairness or tenderness.

As for *your* A, I don't know what to make of her. I enclose her last but one—and *my* A's last but one—from which you may form your own conclusions on *both* . . .

As for my A, my feelings towards her are a mixture of good & diabolical. I hardly know one passion which has not some share in them . . .

Your Niece has committed herself perhaps, but it can be of no consequence. If I pursued & succeeded in that quarter, of course I must give up all other pursuits, and the fact is that my wife if she had common sense would have more power over me than any other whatsoever, for my heart always alights upon the nearest *perch* . . .

The same night he continued to defend Augusta:

She surely is very clever, and not only so, but in some things of good judgment. Her expressions about A[nnabell]a are exactly your *own*—and these most certainly without being aware of the coincidence—and excepting our one *tremendous* fault, I know her to be in point of temper & goodness of heart almost unequalled. Now grant me this—that she is in truth a very *loveable* woman—and I will try and *not* love any longer . . . It is indeed a very triste and extraordinary business, & what is to become of us I know not—and won't think just now.

Did you observe that she says "*if* la tante approved she should?" She is little aware how much "la tante" has to *dis*approve . . .

The information that Augusta was prepared to approve his suit to Annabella was likely to incline Lady Melbourne further towards disapproval. For the moment she withheld her "acquiescence" and Byron did not write to Annabella. But events during the next three weeks caused Lady Melbourne to change her attitude.

On 4th May, in reply to Moore's request for a song to be set to music, Byron sent him the celebrated "Stanzas for Music":

I speak not, I trace not, I breathe not thy name—
There is Grief in the sound, there is Guilt in the fame—
But the tear which now burns on my cheek may impart
The deep thoughts that dwell in that silence of heart.

Too brief for our passion, too long for our peace,
Was that hour—can its hope, can its memory cease?
We repent, we abjure, we will break from our chain—
We must part, we must fly to—unite it again!

Oh! thine be the Gladness, and mine be the Guilt—
Forgive me, adored one—forsake, if thou wilt—
But the heart which is thine shall expire undebased
And Man shall not break it whatever thou may'st.

And stern to the haughty, but humble to thee,
This soul in its bitterest moment shall be—
And our days seem as swift, and our moments more sweet
With thee at my side, than the world at my feet.

One sigh of thy sorrow, one look of thy love,
Shall turn me or fix, shall reward or reprove—
And the heartless may wonder at all I resign—
Thy lip shall reply—not to them—but to mine.

The same week he made arrangements for Augusta to receive £3,000 towards payment of her husband's debts, bidding her, "Now, don't 'affront' me by any more scruples." On 14th May he began to write *Lara*, the sequel to *The Corsair*, the opening lines of which were suppressed, including:

Let none complain how faithless and how brief
The brain's remembrance, or the bosom's grief—
Or e'er they thus forbid us to forget,
Let Mercy strip the memory of regret,—
Yet, selfish still, we would not be forgot—
What lip dare say, "my Love, remember not,"—
Oh best, and dearest, thou whose thrilling name
My heart adores too deeply to proclaim,
My memory almost ceasing to repine
Would mount to Hope if once secure of thine.

On 19th May, after accompanying Byron to see Kean in *Othello*, Hobhouse and Douglas Kinnaird "made mutual confessions of frightful suspicions."

On 17th May Annabella wrote to say that she was going for a week to Halnaby: "the welcome of a friend must always await you here whether you claim it sooner or later," but she reminded him, "You are deep in epistolary debts." Still he did not reply, but on the 25th Lady Melbourne wrote to her niece a long letter of society gossip containing only this brief and guarded reference to Byron:

> I was very glad to hear of my Brs. invitation to Ld. B—— as should he accept it, I am sure you will be highly delighted with his Society, & I have no doubt you will all think me justified in the Character I have always given you of him.

Living in rooms in Albany, Byron was keeping a busy round of social engagements. Following the first Peace of Paris and Napoleon's retirement to Elba, London was a scene of revelry while the Prince Regent entertained the allied sovereigns, and Byron recalled eight years later how *Lara* "was written amidst balls and fooleries, and after coming home from masquerades and routs, in the summer of the sovereigns." Unfortunately at these festivities he had too many opportunities of meeting Lady Caroline Lamb, who resumed her impetuous pursuit of him. At the end of May she was writing to complain of his "barbarous usage" and of his contemplating "immediate *marriage*" to escape from her. Byron chose to suppose that she was referring to Lady Rancliffe's sister, Lady Adelaide Forbes, whom he had considered briefly as a possible wife in the previous year, but Lady Caroline evidently knew more of his affairs than he suspected. About the end of the first week in June she wrote to him:

> I go to the 'squerade—shall you—tell your sister to try & not dislike me. I am very unworthy of her I know it & feel it but as I may not love you nor see you, let her not judge me harshly—let her not pass me by as Lady Gertrude Sloane does, & Lady Rancliffe. Tell her, I feel my faults my crime sooner—but try & make her forgive me, if you can, for I love that Augusta with my heart because she is yours and is dear to you.

To this letter Byron referred in writing to Lady Melbourne on 10th June:

> She seems puzzled about me, & not at all near the truth. The Devil who ought to be civil on such occasions will probably keep her from it still, & if he should not, I must invent some flirtation to lead her from approaching it.

Lady Caroline may have formed suspicions on much the same data as Hobhouse and Kinnaird; certainly she was more likely to take note of Byron's indiscretions than Mrs. George Villiers, who remembered two years later that "he had advanced at Holland House the most extraordinary theory upon such subjects" as his relationship with Augusta. But nearly two years before she had been forced to protest to Lady Melbourne that "I never opened or intentionally read any letter of yours," though she had "found a part of one on the floor;" she was now even less likely to scruple if offered an opportunity of prying into her mother-in-law's correspondence.

Byron received warning from a most unlikely quarter when, after more than a month's silence, Annabella wrote on 19th June:

> I have been charged with this correspondence. The directions of letters were, I know, observed once or twice. If you should hear of it, do not suffer yourself to be embarrassed by my injunction of Secrecy. Not wishing to attract observations of *any* kind, I should have preferred silence . . . but I should acknowledge without a blush that I have *sought* your friendship and find in it an over-payment for the censure of superficial judges.

Her letter began on a note of pathetic appeal: "Pray write to me—for I have been rendered uneasy by your long silence, and you cannot wish to make me so."

Finding this letter "prim & pretty as usual," Byron forwarded it to Lady Melbourne with the remark, "Somebody or other has been seized with a fit of amazement at her correspondence with so naught a personage, and this has naturally given a fillip of contradiction in my favour which was much wanted." On the same day, the 21st, he replied to Annabella:

> I wished to fix a time when I might have the pleasure of availing myself of Sir Ralph's very welcome invitation. You may be assured that "my kindness" as you are pleased to call it, *is* "undiminished." You have much more cause to apprehend its troublesome progress, than conjecture its decay . . . I shall wait your answer and your convenience before I pretend to name any period when I can hope to see you . . . You have been "charged with this correspondence"—might I ask by whom? It is no great matter—unless with those very discerning persons who think that between people of our time of life and in our situation there can be but one topic of discussion.

For the first time he signed his letter "very affectly. & truly yrs."

Before receiving his reply, Annabella wrote again on 23rd June to say that her mother had left that morning for Kirkby "on account of Lady Wentworth's hopeless illness."

> . . . in these melancholy circumstances Lord Wentworth looks only to his Sister for support and consolation. Expecting by every post to hear of Lady Wentworth's death,[1] & uncertain how long my Mother will be

[1] She died 29th June 1814.

absent, you will perceive that we cannot with propriety receive any visitors for a *short* time, and you may perhaps be spared some ineffectual arrangements by knowing this as soon as I can inform you. I feel much for my Mother as well as my Uncle in that sad scene, & should have accompanied her had she not wished me to stay with my father.

The next day she was "made very happy by your letter and the certainty which it affords of your intention to visit us."

> The charge which I mentioned was not made directly to me, but to Mrs Baker, a neighbour of ours & sincere well-wisher, in a manner that called for a defence of my proceedings . . . She was unwilling to name the persons by whom the misrepresentation was made . . .
>
> The formality and coldness which are, I know, sometimes observable in my manners as well as in my writing, have a source that is painful to myself—therefore pray do not allow me to seem, what to you I can never mean to appear. After each time that I met you the last year in London, I was vexed by the idea of having been repulsively cold towards you . . . I was as anxious then as since, to make my real feelings known to you . . .

For the first time she began a letter "Dear Lord Byron"—a form of address then more intimate than it became with the creation of the Victorian middle class—and ended "Ever affectionately yours."

Whether inspired by the blended sadism and masochism that impelled him to play with fire, or by a notion that he might protect Augusta from her malicious gossip, Byron seems now to have encouraged Lady Caroline in her excesses. After more than two years of tantrums she had learned how to play upon his better feelings as well as his vanity. In one of her apparently half-crazy notes she wrote:

> If I had followed you, you would have made me make the Bed for your new favourites—you are just a Man to exact it & with all my violence you would have made me do it. I have done all but that already, have I not—& really that night I expected the handkerchief would have been thrown every moment. I saw you lift the vail up twice. It was a strange adventure, but you were not kind that night as formerly. You thought of others *even while with me*—of that I am sure—+ The remembrance of that night & your accusation of coldness are disagreable to me. God Bless my friend—or sooner my hearts enemy. God Bless & preserve thee this night & make even thy dreams blest.

Though he could ask Lady Melbourne to imagine "how *demure* I must have been," Byron confessed to her a state of mind conducive to recklessness:

> I am as mad as C.—on a different topic and in a different way, for I never break out into scenes—but am not a whit more in my senses. I will

however not persuade *her* into any *fugitive* piece of absurdity, but more I can't promise. I love no one else (in a proper manner) and whatever you may imagine, I can not or at least do not put myself in the way of—let me see—Annabella is the most prudish & correct person I know . . .

He may have encouraged Lady Caroline in the hope that her scandalous behaviour with him would exclude gossip in another connection, but she soon plagued him more than he could tolerate. Though "all bolts, bars, and silence can do to keep her away are done daily and hourly," he could not keep her out of his rooms; "she comes at all times, at any time, and the moment the door is open in she walks." He lamented that he was "almost a prisoner; she has no shame, no feeling, no one estimable or redeemable quality." On 1st July she "played off the most extraordinary tricks" at a masquerade which Hobhouse attended with Byron; "not all I could say could prevent her from displaying her green *pantaloons* every now and then," and though she was "closely masked," she was "always trying to *indicate* who she was, not to me so much as to every body." Two days later he escaped to Augusta at Newmarket.

He persuaded Augusta to spend a holiday with him at Hastings in a house which Francis Hodgson engaged for a month from 13th July. He returned to London on the 7th, and Augusta stayed a few days at an Albemarle Street hotel before accompanying him to Hastings on the 20th. During these few days in London he presumably had his last clandestine meetings with Lady Caroline. Whether or not Lady Caroline's use of the symbol + — which Byron and Augusta used to symbolise love—may be taken as indicating that she had seen some of Augusta's letters, events proved that Byron made indiscreet confidences to her about Augusta. In her recollections to Medwin she asserted:

. . . he pressed his lips on mine (it was in the Albany) . . . & I said, "yes, I *am* changed, & shall come near you no more."—For then he showed me letters, & told me things I cannot repeat, & all my attachment went. This was our last parting scene . . .

On 19th July, the day before Byron left for Hastings with Augusta, Annabella persuaded her father to write a formal letter of invitation:

I have the pleasure to acquaint your Lordship with the certainty of Lady Milbanke's return this week, and hope the delay occasioned by her journey will not have rendered it inconvenient to you, to favour us with your Company at as early a period after this, as you are disposed to fix.

This she enclosed with a long letter of her own:

Before we meet all uncertainty and obscurity should be removed, and this object is too essential to be sacrificed by either to false delicacy. There is one expression in your last letter which on recollection appears ambiguous . . . You spoke of circumstances that "*might* encrease a regret which is *now* useless". I was sensible of an allusion to myself in *that* regret, . . . and I rejoiced . . . To speak as openly as I always do with you, I believe it is not in my power to withdraw a regard which after two years of active and progressive exercise . . . may be termed affection . . . I thought this affection, imperfect as it is, might be to you a bond of peace with yourself, with your God—and of late, so far from apprehending to have it returned too largely, I have evinced some fear of a decrease so great as to prevent my advances towards that end. If I have been mistaken, God forbid I should aggravate a regret which I cannot remove! . . . I would only use it as the guide to your peace. If you love me, make it your first object as it is the first object to me . . . You are responsible for a part of my peace in consulting your own. Above all, do not conceal any thing from reluctance to give me pain . . . I have now only to ask that if I am in any respect mysterious to you, if you desire any explanation of the past or present, you will believe that I shall give it most willingly . . .

Aware of her incoherence, she was asking him to recognise her difficulty. Between 12th February and 15th March he had written six letters to her and encouraged her to believe that he wished to see her; since she had proposed his visit, he had written only twice in three months—on 20th April and 21st June. She had implied her regret for having rejected his proposal, but did he still regret the rejection?

Byron well understood her meaning, but felt no urge to persevere in a pursuit for which "I must give up all other pursuits." He was now again persuaded that he must marry to escape more dangerous involvements, but Annabella was not even his first choice for matrimony. During June he had several times met Lady Charlotte Leveson-Gower; finding her "shy as an Antelope, and unluckily as pretty," he asked Augusta to "do something to improve our acquaintance." He declared himself "disposed to do any thing reasonable or unreasonable" towards "making it up with Lord Carlisle," whose wife was Lady Charlotte's aunt. Hence he replied evasively to Annabella from Hastings on 1st August:

Your letter has only reached me this day from London . . . *this* is my second answer to your letter—the first I have destroyed—because on considering yours more attentively, it appeared to me that I had misunderstood you and that my reply would in that case only produce perplexity. Pray then write to me openly and *harshly* if you please. If there is anything you wish to know or to say, I am ready to answer or to listen—but whether present or absent, in enmity or in charity you are the last person I would wish to misunderstand.

My best thanks are due to Sir R. for the invitation which accompanied your letter . . .

After signing himself "Ever most affectionately yours," he added in a postscript:

. . . whatever my regrets or my regard might have been—or may be—I have not so far lost all self-command as to betray either to an extent that would render them troublesome to you; and my memory is still retentive enough not to require the repetition that you are attached to another.

Lame as well as evasive, the letter threw Annabella back to her situation in the previous December, when she had consulted Lady Gosford about her statement of "truth."

Yet the letter was the result of some deliberation. During their three weeks at Hastings, Byron and Augusta were visited for some days by his first cousin, Captain George Byron, a naval officer about a year his junior and the heir to his title, and Annabella wrote in March 1817:

G. Byron—who was at Hastings with B & A in 1814, when it was in debate whether the proposal to me should be renewed—says that she then decidedly influenced him in favour of that measure. But she had for some time contemplated another matrimonial scheme for him, which they have often discussed in my presence, and it was in the Autumn of 1814 instantly upon its failure, that he wrote the letter which gained my consent.

Informing Lady Melbourne that Augusta "wished me much to marry, because it was the only chance of redemption for two persons," Byron asserted, "The other was undoubtedly her *favourite*." But his letters to Augusta show that Lady Charlotte Leveson-Gower was also his favourite; while Augusta might well have preferred Lady Carlisle's niece to Lady Melbourne's as a sister-in-law, she may have advised Byron to take the bird in hand, as his chances with the Carlisle connection were unpromising. He fancied Lady Charlotte not merely because, like Lady Caroline Lamb, she had the look of a "wild antelope," but because she was Augusta's friend, "and whatever she loves I can't help liking."

Annabella wrote humbly and patiently on 6th August:

I thank you for the forbearance which made you pause and suspend a judgment of my meaning till it should be elucidated, as I hope it now will, beyond doubt. When I find ambiguities in your expressions I am certain that they are created by myself, since you evidently desire at all times to be simple & perspicuous.

When I last wrote I feared from some reconsiderations that you might still be in danger of feeling more than friendship towards me . . . I have not entertained the least apprehension that your self-command would fail in any way that could affect me disadvantageously or disagreably. On the contrary I feared the silence more than the confession of those sentiments, should they arise, because to the owner silence is the most dangerous. I must have smiled, had I not been almost vexed, at your reiterated and most kindly intended assurances to destroy my supposed dread of a renewal, when after your first assurance I should never have doubted that your determination was irremoveable. The rest, you may think, was not my concern, but what can touch *your* happiness has been always much more my concern than the trivial inconveniences to which *I* could be exposed. Exemption from them, if you should suffer, would not be consolation to me. Instead of fancying you likely to conceive my regard greater than it is, I have invariably observed that you did not understand how great it was . . .

My doubt then is—and I ask a solution—whether you are in *any* danger of that attachment to me which might interfere with your peace of mind. . . . Next, on the supposition of a reply unfavourable to my wishes, I would ask you to consider by what course the danger may be avoided . . .

Sometime ago I had meant to acknowledge clearly, knowing that you would not mistake the motives of my acknowledgement, that I had been deceived . . . in thinking I had ever formed a decided attachment. The reasons which led me to believe the character of one person suited to my own, have disappeared with opportunities of fuller investigation, and though I am far from being indifferent to him, and shall probably always continue the very sincere & unembarassed kindness of which he is the deserving object, nothing could now induce me to marry him . . .

While a reading of the contemporary novels of Jane Austen and Maria Edgeworth reveal the constraint imposed by convention on an unmarried woman's correspondence, Byron might have taken warning from such an aptitude for sophistry. Her letter was addressed to Albany, whence he replied on the 10th after his return from Hastings:

I will answer your question as openly as I can. I did, do, and always shall love you, and as this feeling is not exactly an act of will, I have no remedy and at all events should never find one in the sacrifice of your comfort. When our acquaintance commenced, it appeared to me from all that I saw and heard—that you were the woman most adapted to render any man (who was neither inveterately foolish nor wicked) happy. But I was informed that you were attached if not engaged—and very luckily—to a person for whose success all the females of the family, where I received my intelligence, were much interested. Before such powerful interest, and your supposed inclinations, I had too much humility and pride to hazard importunity or even attention, till I at last learned, almost by accident, that I was misinformed—as to the engagement. The rest you know . . .

What your own feelings and objections were and are I have not the right and scarcely the wish to enquire. It is enough for me that they exist . . . It would be a very hard case if a woman were obliged to account for her repugnance. You would probably like me if you could . . . You ask me how far my peace is, or may be affected by these feelings towards you?

I do not know—not quite enough to invade yours, or request from your pity what I cannot owe to your affection.

Annabella's rejoinder on 13th August was, to say the least, charmless and obtuse:

I shall not doubt on the same subject again, and I regret that my recent doubts should have compelled me to extort from you the profession of sentiments to which you would have wished me rather to comprehend in your silence. Before a certain stage, our affections *are* I believe under our command, at least I have had some cause to think so, and I hoped that yours were checked *in time*. The determination that mine towards you shall remain at that stage, is founded, if you care at all to know why, on a very simple yet well-considered reason—which would always have been presented by a comparative view of your character and my own—that they are ill adapted to each other. Not believe me, that I depreciate your capacity for the domestic virtues . . . Nevertheless you do not appear to be the person whom *I* ought to select as my guide, my support, my example on earth, with a view still to Immortality.

From Lady M—— I learned that the present Lord Auckland[1] was unjustifiably named as the object of my attachment. Never having imagined *him* to be so, I could not have to persuade any one that he was . . . I must add in exculpation of him, since he deserves from me the highest tribute of esteem, that I am persuaded he would have felt as much indignation as any one at the busy zeal of his unauthorized advocates. They had heard from myself, what I sincerely believed, that my heart was unengaged, though I was afterwards led, by a combination of ill understood feelings, to deviate from this opinion—but not in regard to Lord Auckland.

To conclude this topic of discussion—You are the only man with whom I should not scruple to continue our intimacy in these relative circumstances, but as my father and mother trust equally to my discretion and to your honour, I will only request you to use or discontinue my intercourse, now and always, as it may be found to give pleasure or pain . . .

Byron would have been more than human to forget the assumption of his unfitness to be her guide, support, and example. He replied tersely on the 16th:

Very well—now we can talk of something else. Though I do not think an intimacy which does not extend beyond a few letters and still fewer interviews in the course of a year could be particularly injurious to either party, yet—as, if I recollect rightly, you told me that some remarks had been made upon the subject—it is perhaps as well that even that should end. This is a point upon which yourself can best determine, and in which I have nothing to do but to acquiesce. I shall leave London in a few days, but any letter addressed to me here will be forwarded, should you deem it proper to answer this.

You have not said anything of your health lately from which I infer that it is improved . . .

[1] George Eden's father, Lord Auckland, had died on 28th May 1814.

With Augusta and her children Byron left London for Newstead on Sunday 21st August; Annabella's letter written that day from Seaham was redirected from Albany:

> In one case only should I willingly relinquish the pleasure of your correspondence—if its exercise were become disagreable to you. I shall now try to make a better use of it than of late, since I infer from your silence that my dream of seeing you soon is to end . . . What are your principal occupations? your projects? How is your health? In giving you so often the example of Egotism I wish it to be followed. I continue well, with prudence, but any approach towards the ways of the fashionable world occasions a return of complaints which originated there. Without so good a reason, a fashionable life must always be slavery to me, though I endured it as patiently & cheerfully as possible because my Mother was made unhappy by my repugnance to scenes where she deemed it advantageous for me to appear. I entered them at the age of seventeen with a caricatured opinion of their follies and vices, and looked on them with coldness and indifference . . . Of these faults you have perhaps not suspected me. After leaving London that year in disgust, I spent the months of seclusion in salutary reflection, and returned with a little more charity. I had become sensible that it was pride in mortals to be offended at what God beholds and suffers . . . This then became my task—to perceive the loveliness of human character through all the incumbent shades of error . . . I do not study much. My constitution requires many hours of sleep and exercise, & besides I do not enjoy the general acquisition of knowledge for its own sake. Books of *poetry* & *philosophy* are the only ones I *wish* to read . . . Yet on some subjects I desire to be less ignorant. Will you tell me what books of modern history you think I might peruse with most advantage & pleasure? I am now engaged with Sismondi's Italian republics . . .
>
> I have read Lara. In the last Edinburgh Review I find an opinion which I had formed before it prevailed as it does at present—That Shakespeare alone possessed the same power as you have shown, of diving into the great deep of the human heart . . .

Of "that exultation of Despair, that exhiliration of Misery" in *Lara* she remarked, "In some early essays of mine, I could show you these and other conceptions, feebly similar to yours."

Byron replied from Newstead on the 25th with a library list enlivened by entertaining comment; briefly he answered the questions about himself—occupations "nothing," projects "I have none," health "very well"; he agreed with her views on fashionable life while reminding her that "even mischief is remotely productive of advantage to some one or something in this best of all possible worlds"; it would give him "much gratification some day or other" to see her "early essays," and he added in a postscript, "I regret it will not be in my power to proceed to Seaham during the present year."

However deeply she felt disappointment of the hopes encouraged by his letters in the spring, Annabella wrote in a tone of unruffled composure on 2nd September:

My father & mother sincerely regret the change of plan which deprives us of your visit—and I, but I need not speak of what should be as well known to you as to myself. We had avoided every engagement which might interfere with that more welcome one. Now, we shall probably remain here some time longer, expecting to be joined by Lord Wentworth . . . I fear again to rest my hope of seeing you on any determinate period . . .

Tenaciously she reverted to religion:

I do not quite like your ridicule of "this best of all possible worlds." Without subscribing to all the assumptions of Optimism in admitting *this not* to be the best of all possible worlds, we should have the consolatory idea of a better, and from experience that all present is vanity and vexation of spirit, should spring the hope that Disappointment is of a temporal, not of an eternal nature. Is it a proof of reverence for the Governor of all worlds to mock his government in this? . . .

She had "not read the whole of Gibbon" but would resume her reading on his advice, and her father was ordering Sismondi for her. It was as if she had written a model letter for her parents' approval; before sealing it, she impetuously added a postscript the following morning:

I should like to burn this letter—for the same reason as I have burned others—"but let it go." If we could have met, all my apparent inconsistencies would have been dispelled. I must now find comfort in reflecting that the burden of them rests solely with me, and *ought* therefore to be supported chearfully.

If it be not very irksome to you—as I sometimes fear it is—pray write soon. I have no right to ask it, but—I *do* ask it, and if I can be justified, *you* will justify me.

By this appeal from the heart Byron was unmoved when he replied from Newstead on 7th September. He discussed Porson on Gibbon; informed her that negotiations for the sale of Newstead had broken down, the intending purchaser having forfeited his deposit on failure to complete the purchase; taunted her that her religious preference for the contemplative life was "the very essence of the Epicurean philosophy", commented thus coolly on her postscript:

You accuse yourself of "apparent inconsistencies." To me they have not appeared—on the contrary, your consistency has been the most formidable apparition I have encountered. There seem to me no grounds for complaint on one side nor vindication on the other, and as to explanations, *they* are always a puzzle. After one or two letters which lately passed between us, and to which I must request your pardon for recurring, we—at least *I* (to speak for myself) could hardly have met without some embarrassment, possibly on both sides, certainly on one. This has been avoided, and so far is a subject of congratulation.

Your letters are generally answered on the day of their arrival so that it can't be very "irksome to me to write soon."

Replying on 13th September, Annabella showed no consciousness of rebuff and sought to suit her style to his:

The "apparition" of my Consistency ought not to be "formidable" to you, since like other apparitions, it may owe its effect chiefly to the Imagination of the spectator, and might vanish with the light of day . . . after much reflection it is *my* opinion that you could not have suffered by our meeting . . . Though our meeting must at first be attended with some mutual embarassment, I hoped *that* would soon have been removed. Explanations on paper I shall, according to your advice, not attempt again . . .

She went on to defend Porson from the charge of habitual drunkenness on the authority of her friend, Elizabeth Raine: "notwithstanding their great intimacy, it is a fact that to her he never appeared in that disgraceful state."

The day after writing this letter she received another from Byron. Augusta had been corresponding with Lady Charlotte Leveson-Gower, whose "frequent epistles and excessive attachment to +[Augusta]" contained "sentences which were *not* to be answered, or if answered, replied to in a *particular* manner, &c., with a hundred little things" which convinced Augusta that her correspondent was well disposed to Byron's suit. But suddenly—evidently on 8th or 9th September—came a letter from Lady Charlotte "full of alarms" about "some family scheme . . . of a *compact elsewhere;*" she had been "so foolish" and "was in such a dilemma," as the intended suitor was even then about to visit her family for the purpose of making the proposal—"what was she to do?" Realising, as he told Lady Melbourne, that "the little girl had no will of her own, and might not be aware of what she had been doing," Byron "made + write a kind but satisfactory answer, taking it *all* on herself, and getting the other out of it completely."

From Byron and Augusta, Annabella later learned that "before this" Byron's maiden aunt Sophia Byron, his father's sister, had visited them at Newstead,

& the question was whether Lady Surrey[1] or myself should be the object of his matrimonial addresses. Mrs S.B—, who did not then know

[1] Lady Charlotte Leveson-Gower married on 27th December 1814 Henry Charles Howard, who become Earl of Surrey in 1815 and 13th Duke of Norfolk in 1842.

me, spoke in my favour, from the impression given her of me by a mutual friend [Selina Doyle].

According to Moore's recollection of what he read in Byron's destroyed memoirs, after Lady Charlotte's alarmed letter had ended that project, Byron said to Augusta, "You see that, after all, Miss Milbanke is to be the person;—I will write to her." The rest of Moore's account is endorsed by Annabella's:

> He showed that letter to A[ugusta]. She desired him to reflect upon the seriousness of such a step & to consider thoroughly if I should suit him, for—as she has told me—she at that time feared I might not, from having heard him repeat the prejudicial opinions Ly Melbourne had given of my character, particularly of my self-willed dispositions & over-strained notions of propriety. He put the letter into his desk—took it out again before post hour—& she made the observation, "It is a very well written letter." Upon which he determined it should go—rang the bell, sealed it with the greatest haste, & dispatched it, as if anxious to deprive himself of the power of retracting.

In fact, Byron may have deliberated overnight, for his letter, though dated from Newstead Abbey on 9th September, was postmarked from Mansfield on the 10th:

> . . . There is something I wish to say, and as I may not see you for some —perhaps for a long time—I will endeavour to say it at once. A few weeks ago you asked me a question, which I answered. I have now one to propose, to which if improper, I need not add that your declining to reply to it will be sufficient reproof. It is this. Are the "objections"—to which you alluded—insuperable?—or is there any line or change of conduct which could possibly remove them? I am well aware that all such changes are more easy in theory than practice, but at the same time there are few things I would not attempt to obtain your good opinion—at all events I would willingly know the worst. Still I neither wish you to promise or pledge yourself to anything, but merely to learn a *possibility* which would not leave you the less a free agent.
>
> When I believed you attached, I had nothing to urge. Indeed I have little now, except that having heard from yourself that your affections are not engaged, my importunities may appear not quite so selfish however unsuccessful. It is not without a struggle that I address you once more on this subject. Yet I am not very consistent, for it was to avoid troubling you upon it that I finally determined to remain an absent friend rather than become a tiresome guest—if I offend it is better at a distance.
>
> With the rest of my sentiments you are already acquainted. If I do not repeat them it is to avoid—or at least not increase your displeasure.

Annabella stated that she was told by Augusta:

Till my answer arrived his agitation was excessive, and though he told her he was sure I should refuse him again, he was often speculating upon the consequences of an affirmative, saying he must then go immediately to Seaham. He used to sit upon the steps before Newstead watching for the post two or three days before my letter came.

She replied on the 14th, immediately on receiving his letter:

I have your second letter, and am almost too agitated to write—but you will understand. It would be absurd to suppress any thing. I am and have long been pledged to myself to make your happiness my first object in life. *If I can* make you happy, I have no other consideration. I will *trust* to you for all I should look up to—all I can love. The fear of not realizing your expectations is the only one I now feel. Convince me—it is all I wish—that my affection may supply what is wanting in my character to form your happiness. This is a moment of joy which I have too much despaired of ever experiencing. I *dared* not believe it possible, and I have painfully supported a determination founded in fact on the belief that you did not wish it removed—that its removal would not be for your good. There has in reality been scarcely a change in my sentiments. More of this I will defer. I wrote by last post—with what different feelings! Let me be grateful for those with which I now acknowledge myself

Most affectly. yours

A.I.M.

Like her three previous letters, this was addressed to Albany and re-directed to Newstead, but by the same post she sent a note to Newstead:

I have written a letter in answer to your second, directing it to the Albany, and accompanied by a few lines from my father[1]—but, on the chance of sparing you a moment's suspense, I write also directly to Newstead, to say that I hope you will find in my other letter *all you wish.*

A.I.M.

She recorded what she heard of her letter's arrival:

He received it at dinner—the Apothecary was the only person present besides A—. B— described the effects to me himself, & she has confirmed the account.

Seaham Sepbr. 14th 1814.

[1] My dear Lord

My Daughter has communicated to me and Lady Milbanke the letter which she received from you this day, and to which she replies by the same post that takes this.

Her happiness is the point nearest our hearts, and I trust she will find it in the esteem and affection which you bestow on her, and which I will venture to say she merits. I will only add that whenever you favor us with a visit, you will be most cordially received by me and her Mother as one dear to us for her sake.

I wish to assure your Lordship at the same time of my personal regard and esteem and that I am

My Dear Lord

Very truly yours

RA. MILBANKE

His remark to her as he handed the letter across the table, looking so pale that she thought he was going to faint away, was—"It never rains but it pours." It happened singularly that before they left the dining room, his Mother's wedding-ring, the same I now wear—which had been lost since her death—was brought to him. The circumstance was very impressive to his superstitious Imagination.

A— has always spoken of his temper during the two days he remained at Newstead with her, as better than she had ever seen it. No triumphant levity, but a deep & serious gratitude appeared to her the predominant feeling. He would say, "Well, after all, Heaven has been kinder to me than I deserve." His intentions seemed to be in every respect disinterested and honorable. He expressed a total—and as she thought a "romantic" disregard of fortune, which she has mentioned as strangely contrasted with the subsequent absorption of his feelings in avaricious hopes and fears.

Sobriety rather than exultation was certainly the tone of Byron's first response on the 18th:

Your letter has given me a new existence. It was unexpected, I need not say welcome—but *that* is a poor word to express my present feelings, and yet equal to any other, for express them adequately I cannot. I have ever regarded you as one of the first of human beings—not merely from my own observation but that of others—as one whom it was as difficult *not* to love, as scarcely possible to deserve:—I know your worth, & revere your virtues as I love yourself and if every proof in my power of my full sense of what is due to you will contribute to *your* happiness, I shall have secured my own. It *is* in your power to render me happy—you have made me so already.

He found himself in such difficulty that he took a cue from her being "too agitated to write": "I wish to answer your letter immediately, but am at present scarcely collected enough to do it rationally." Tentatively he felt his way into the pose to be assumed for her benefit:

I was upon the point of leaving England without hope without fear—almost without feeling . . . from the moment I became acquainted my attachment has been increasing, & the very follies—give them a harsher name—with which I was beset & bewildered, the conduct to which I had recourse for forgetfulness only made recollection more lively & bitter by the comparisons it forced upon me in spite of Pride—and of Passions, which might have destroyed but never deceived me.

Feeling this effort unequal to the occasion, he wrote again on the 19th:

I wrote to you yesterday—not very intelligibly I fear—and to your father in a more embarrassed manner than I could have wished. But the fact is that I am even now apprehensive of having misunderstood you and of appearing presumptuous when I am only happy—in the hope that you will not repent having made me more so than I ever thought to have been again.

Perhaps in some points our dispositions are not so contrasted as at times you have supposed . . .

Whereupon he felt himself upon the safe ground of self-exposition:

Our *pursuits* at least I think are not unlike. You have no great passion for the *world* as it is called, and both have those intellectual resources which are the best . . . *My* habits I trust are not very anti-domestic. I have no pleasure in what is named Conviviality . . . and with regard to other and perhaps far more objectionable faults & levities of former conduct . . . yet there have been circumstances which would prove that although "sinning" I have also been "sinned against." I have long stood alone in life . . .

Declaring himself "more tremblingly alive" to their meeting "than I quite like to own to myself," he added the tactful postscript, "Do not forget me to your father & mother, whom I hope to call mine."

Yet again he wrote on the 20th:

There is one point on which—though you have not lately pressed it—I am sure you feel anxious on my behalf . . . Religion. When I tell you that I am so convinced of its importance in fixing the principles, that I could never have had perfect confidence in any woman who was slightly impressed with its truth, you will hardly believe that I can exact more tolerance than I am willing to grant. I will not deny that my own impressions are by no means settled, but that they are perverted to the extent which has been imputed to them on the ground of a few passages in works of fiction, I cannot admit to those whose esteem I would secure . . . I am rather bewildered by the variety of tenets than inclined to dispute their foundation—in a word, I will read what books you please, hear what arguments you please, and in leaving the choice to your judgment, let it be a proof that my confidence in your understanding & your virtues is equal. You shall be "my Guide, Philosopher and friend" my whole heart is yours, and if possible let me make it not unworthy of her to whom it is bound, & from whom but one event can divide it.

After remarking, "I proceed on my way to London tomorrow," he ended:

With every sentiment of respect and—may I add the word?—Love,
Ever yours
BYRON.

Significantly his correspondence with Lady Melbourne had lapsed since he announced on 2nd July that he was joining Augusta at Newmarket. During his eleven days in London between arriving from Hastings and leaving for Newstead, he had written a brief note in sending her a present of grouse, but presumably she had declined to continue correspondence while Augusta was with him. Immediately on hearing from Annabella, he wrote to ask her aunt's approval:

> Miss Milbanke has accepted me—and her answer was accompanied by a very kind letter from your brother. May I hope for your consent too? . . . I lose no time in telling you how things are at present. Many circumstances may doubtless occur in this as in other cases to prevent its completion—but I will hope otherwise.

He added the assurance:

> In course I mean to reform most thoroughly & become "a good man and true" in all the various senses of these respective & respectable appellations—seriously. I will endeavour to make your niece happy not by "my deserts but what I will deserve." Of my deportment you may reasonably doubt—of her merits you can have none. I need not say that this must be a *secret*.

On the last day before he left Newstead, he and Augusta carved their names in the bark of an elm behind the Abbey, with the date, 20th September 1814.

8

FOUR MONTHS' ENGAGEMENT

September—December 1814

Annabella was as much in love with Byron as her self-complacency could have allowed her to be in love with any man. Events proved that she did not love him—at least not enough to tolerate his failings as a husband. Having talked with him briefly and infrequently at crowded social functions, she did not know him well enough to love him; she was only in love with her own idea of him. She coveted possession of him not merely from vanity—from the knowledge that she would be envied by most of her contemporaries in London society. Preoccupation with her own importance had decided her that this admired romantic genius was the man most worthy of her missionary zeal; as she told him, "I am and have long been pledged to myself to make your happiness my first object in life." A woman who loved might have felt disappointment at the absence of passion in Byron's three letters greeting her acceptance of him; Annabella could feel only gratification at his assurance that she should be his "Guide, Philosopher and friend"—that he placed his confidence in her understanding and her virtues. Secure on her stilts, she could graciously condescend.

Even in her "moment of joy which I have too much despaired of ever experiencing," her self-absorption demanded immediate explanation of those "reproaches of my conscience" confided—partially—to Lady Gosford in the previous December. Receiving on 22nd September Byron's letters of the 18th and 19th, she wrote on the 22nd:

> It is indeed a pleasure to me to write when I need no longer measure, not my words, but my feelings. When conscious that the latter *would* exceed the bounds which I had imposed on them, I was silent—You little suspected *why*. Since I made myself yours, I have had a happiness, deep as it promises to be durable—not a moment of doubt. Nothing but gratitude for all this—so unexpected, and which from some strange principle in human nature or in mine, I have sought to avert, and to bring despair on myself as well as you. Had I *known* that you suffered, the baseless fabric would sooner have fallen. It seemed almost selfish to seek

what—notwithstanding my desire to find objections—I *felt* would be so much for my own happiness that I forgot it could be as much for yours. God grant it may! I have been very foolish, and if you had not been wiser, we might both still have been without hope.

Eagerness for self-justification in "collecting her sentiments" on paper prevented her observing that confession of her concern with her own emotions contradicted the illusion of her being "pledged to myself" to consider only Byron's happiness. Speculation on reasons for his evasions and silences did not occur to her as she continued:

On *your* part every thing seems explained. I cannot at least remember those accusations which, whilst I made, I answered as well as you could. On mine something shall be said for your satisfaction or your amusement, of that *phantom* of an attachment. A "horrible shadow" to me, since it stood between us—though I should have some obligation to it, for had I not conjured it into being, my impulse to write to you would probably not have prevailed against principles that forbad the measure. Till the time of my acquaintance with you I had never been in danger of an attachment. Placed by Lady Melbourne's precipitancy in a situation where I thought decision a duty, I feared to risk a disappointment to you, and though aware that you could excite affection, I doubted if your character, as I then misconceived it from false accounts, could *support* that affection in one who *loves* only where she can *honour*. I resolved then to resign—irrevocably I thought—all power over your affections. Lest mine should become engaged to you I sought an object for them, and fixed on—Mr Montgomery, the brother of my friend, and who so far from showing affection to me, had bestowed it elsewhere. On the foundation of cold esteem for a person whom when present I had never thought agreable, my imagination elevated in his absence that visionary attachment by which I deemed myself justified in being *your friend*. Yet it was almost intolerably painful to me that you should think my heart devoted to another. Nevertheless I *would not* be conscious of the true cause. Some time after I commenced my correspondence with you, he came here. The illusion could not withstand the presence of its object—for I had not seen him since its creation—and he was no more to me than he had always been. Then ensued my long silence to you. Having lost this only defence against my feelings I tried to write, but could not without disclosing them. At last I *did* write, still determined not to know myself, and when you asked an explanation on this particular subject, I was more inclined to revive than to remove the error. A sort of quiet despair possessed me, for you had assumed an *impossibility* of renewal on your part, and you repeated it more strongly in the answer to that very letter. It haunted me till I heard from you last week, and forced me into those *hopeless* determinations. Mr M—— was here for a fortnight some time ago, and we were very good friends, though I could not quite forgive him for having *innocently* been your rival. It is natural that you should suppose his sister had a share in misleading me, but she never even *wished* for the connection. The folly was *all* mine—you cannot condemn it more severely than I do, since it pained you as much as myself. Do not apprehend from these proofs of my potent imagination *in absence*, that it has been acting in your case. No, I remember too well what I last felt in your presence, under that coldness—my only resource and at the same time my vexation. What I may seem to feel when we meet again I cannot guess—I could shrink from it too, yet let it be as soon as possible . . .

The naïveté and egoism were natural in a woman of twenty-two, but the distortion of fact was symptomatic of the self-deception that created tragedy for herself, and for her daughter, her son-in-law, and her grandchildren.

That same day, 22nd September, she wrote to Hugh Montgomery:

My dear friend,

I am released from obligations of secrecy by this post—therefore you see that I do not long delay my promised communication to you. The "Thane" is found—I am engaged to marry Lord Byron. If his character had not been greatly misconceived in the world (as you know characters sometimes are both for better and worse) he would never have been the object of a choice in which I feel *myself* honoured. Convinced that he deserves my highest esteem as he certainly possesses my strongest attachment, I look forward to the most rational happiness, and in those views I have the satisfaction of finding that my father and mother fully and confidently join. You do not know *him*, but you know *me*, and if you estimate his principles and character by mine you will certainly not form too favourable an opinion. I therefore hope, my dear brother Hugo, for your sanction. I am sure I shall have Poll's [MM's] if *Jealousy* will permit.

. . . As I know not if my future will approve of a correspondence with *handsome young Batchelors* I must here relinquish it, hoping at the same time very often to hear *of* you and I shall expect an answer to *this* with some impatience. Afterwards my Mother will gladly receive from you any communications concerning Poll's affairs . . .

Montgomery's response was not so soothing to her conscience as she had hoped, for, on receiving his letter, she wrote to Lady Gosford:

He seems as much disinclined to epistolary as to personal intercourse. I wish it were otherwise . . . Assure him, as you now may with equal safety and truth, of *my* unalterable friendship and grateful sense of *his* . . .

There are grounds for suspicion that Annabella had used Hugh Montgomery as an insurance against spinsterhood. Since women's emancipation they are thought to retain youth's freshness at twenty-two, and Annabella had still some years before she reached the situation of the Elliot sisters in *Persuasion*. But she had weathered four London seasons and achieved a formidable, if not forbidding, reputation. She had discouraged if she had not formally rejected Augustus Foster; she had certainly rejected George Eden, General Pakenham, Byron, Bankes, and Douglas. General opinion must have inclined to the Duchess of Devonshire's assessment of her as "odd" and "an icicle."

Her mother evidently realised that Montgomery was deserving of sympathy, for she wrote to him with warm affection on 1st October:

> My dear Hugh,
>
> As You are turned over to me for a Correspondent, *I* will begin it, and request *you* will not decline it, tho' it is I confess a miserable exchange for You—but take pity on me and recollect how much I shall want the comfort of my friends; therefore let me often hear of You and Mary. My love and anxiety for her is nearly *maternal*, and was it not for her welfare I should regret She is not in England to be my Companion and Comforter—for what is to become of me when I lose my Darling I know not! It seems to me at this moment that every hour of my life will seem a desolate blank—and Mil and I shall be looking at each other, as if seeking something we could not find.
>
> With Annabellas future prospects I am well pleased, having every reason to believe that *his* attachment to *her* is deep and sincere, founded on the best basis, *Esteem*. His Relations and dependants all adore him—therefore trust he is calculated for *domestic happiness*, and that he looks forwards to *that* I think is shewn by his resuming Newstead Abbey (which was about to be sold) on being accepted. I know your Sister has been long partial to him, therefore hope She will have pleasure in hearing of the Event. My Brother also gives his *kindest Sanction*, which has gratified me much. My brother is to be here tomorrow, and I imagine Ld Byron will be here in the course of the week. I wish the meeting was over—he is now in London on *Law business*, as he writes, & I conclude preparatory to seeing Sir Ra: . . .

After much about MM's travels, she ended by inviting Montgomery to "write to me, as if to a Mother you *loved*, but did not *fear*."

Her performance in getting her own way about going to London in February 1812 suggests that Annabella may not have been easy to live with during the months occupied with her reproaches of conscience. Her mother suffered reaction in release from the long anxiety; she herself described her disorder as "a violent bilious attack," but Annabella informed Byron on 28th September:

> My Mother has been ill . . ., partly I believe from agitation. You will conceive that she must experience it in these circumstances, though they are "to her heart's desire." It is rarely that so fond a mother is so little selfish. Her indulgence is for my sake—not her own. Are you not afraid that such a spoiled child will prove a Xantippe?

Judith showed her old vitality and common sense in writing to Lady Melbourne on the 25th:

Knowing the Sincere interest you feel for Annabellas happiness, it would be ungrateful in me not to give you the satisfaction of knowing that I believe her to be very much so at present—and that Your Brother and myself partake in it, and give a free and unqualified Consent to the engagement She has made. Lord Byron has proved that his attachment is steady and sincere, and I trust founded on a knowledge of her Character, which I am persuaded will not sink in his estimation by being more intimately acquainted with it. You once *scolded* me for wishing Your Daughter married—I now feel you had reason, for my agitation is great and I dread the thought of parting from her, tho' not so selfish as to wish it otherwise . . . I was much gratified by a letter Annabella received yesterday from my Brother . . . he gives his cordial Sanction . . . and adds "I shall only speak laconically of Your noble Lover, in the words of his own Motto, *Crede Byron.*" He always speaks of her as his *Heir*, and decidedly told me so when I was last at Kirkby—but do not name this, as people do not like to have these intentions declared, except by themselves. If it proves so, the Succession will be *very considerable*, as well as a good House and respectable Residence—but what I write on this Subject is to go no farther—I depend on your Secresy. Annabella says You *quiz* her most unmercifully, but that She will endure it, and perhaps She deserves it—but like You I do not understand these Lovers, who seem to have delighted in perplexing themselves and each other. I have *always* thought Ld Byron was the only Man who ever interested her—and I was right . . .

Judith was not slow to remind her daughter that her predilection dated from the spring of 1812, for Annabella wrote to Byron on 29th September:

My letters to my Mother at that time, for she gave them to me lately to read, show how much you had occupied my attention—my interest. Though I tried to see in you what I had heard of you, mystery & mischief, your character appeared to me very simple. Of your truth, of your deep and disinterested feelings, I never doubted.

Yet I do not claim a perfect superiority to the contagion of Prejudice. In some points I deferred too much to the authority of others. My friend Grahame once warned me most earnestly to beware of this disrespect for my own judgment, entreating me to consult, and confide in it, even if opposed by opinions of seeming validity. He added "If you do not, *you will suffer*"—and the words would have been prophetic, if *at last* I had not trusted to myself. During the last part of the season you ceased to notice me at all. I had not attributed your notice to any serious motive, and I did not seriously account for its discontinuance. My interest for you had not depended on your attention—was not altered by the loss of it. At one supper party, where you sat between Lady Melbourne and me, but conversed only with her, I heard you say, "Thank God, I have not a friend in the world." You knew not the pang which you inflicted on a friend so near. Those words of bitterness chilled me. When I returned home to solitude I wept over the recollection of them, and prayed that you might receive consolation from a friend below, as well as from a friend above.

Thus she valued herself on her own judgment in refusing to listen to rumours of "mystery & mischief", though after a lapse of years she convinced herself that she had been influenced by "those who had received much more favorable impressions of the character than had at first been placed before me."

After leaving Newstead for London on 21st September, Byron wrote twice to Annabella on the 26th. The first letter declared that her explanations had "removed a weight from my heart, and a restlessness from my brain that would have made me—I know not what," but after the assurance that "now I am yours," dissolved into a eulogy of Lady Melbourne. He wrote again the same day for the same reason as he had written on three successive days from Newstead: "My letters always leave me dissatisfied—something, so much is unsaid." His second letter followed her example in constructing conceptions of emotions inspired by their previous meetings, but while her motive was self-justification, his was to devise a pose for himself to act in their future relationship:

> I thought you attached & engaged. Regret was useless, but how much would have been spared to me had I been aware that your heart was your own—that it could ever be exchanged for mine. In very truth, from my heart of hearts, dearest Annabella, I can now tell you that then—at the very time when I became unworthy of being yours—it was to you my attachment had turned, it was you from whom it was wrenched. Those feelings cannot be quelled, only removed, and my sole resource was to suppose that I felt for another the love which you would not accept.

Unluckily for them both, he encountered in Annabella an egoism more formidable than his own in being unmitigated by imaginative sensibility. Subtlety and innuendo were wasted on her self-absorption; instead of returning the ball for his rally, she was concerned with practising her own service:

> The situation of an only child, exposed from my birth to extreme partiality, has made me study to repress the vanity of thinking myself a treasure. I should have had less hesitation in giving myself to you if I had thought the gift of more value . . . My powers are, I hope, in every thing superior to my actual attainments . . .

Those "feelings" which could not be quelled were dismissed as "faults" since she conceived them to be unrelated to herself:

> I *will* see your faults though more disposed to see my own. I *have* given you proofs that I am not blindly attached—if I were, a change might be feared. In respect to the past errors for which you "cannot forgive" yourself, I would not extenuate them—I would only be your peacemaker. As I have thought of them "more in sorrow than in anger," do you the same . . .

After his two letters on 26th September Byron was silent for a week till, on 3rd October, he wrote what he described apologetically as "more like a *factor's* letter than anything else" to explain that he was still awaiting his agent's arrival in London, that he was advised to sell Newstead rather than Rochdale, where the mineral rights were likely to increase in value, and that he must "take the proper steps for making any settlement in my power upon you . . . and determine these points before I join you at Seaham." On the same day Annabella wrote to him:

> I know why you do not write—you think you have nothing to say that is worth saying, and I am in the same predicament, but I do as I would be done by, and hope that *anything* from me will give you the same pleasure as I have in *anything* from you.

She was finding excuses for him not merely to himself, for the news of her engagement was producing letters of not unmixed congratulation. In the light of her later conduct Selina Doyle's ecstasy of 24th September is of interest:

> God bless my Annabella! the big tears fall, but they are not tears of sorrow. I am hopeful for thy happiness thank God, my Child—yes, ever my loved Child. Oh it does me good to shed these tears . . . My zealous prayer shall be, is, that he whom you have chosen may appreciate the Treasure he will possess, & render himself worthy of you by being Happy! I was prepared for this decisive communication . . . yet the certainty that your fate was fix'd awed me. However I feel no alarm. My confidence is built on your sense of religion, which will enable you to find Peace & Consolation in the fulfilment of your Duties, even should my hopes, my prayers for your Worldly Happiness prove vain! But I am sanguine for I know the motives of your acceptance—they are pure . . .

Joanna Baillie wrote with some acidity, for Annabella had apparently confided indiscreetly something of her feelings as well as her vain attempts to persuade Byron to make her acquaintance:

> I wish you most heartily every good thing that can be bestowed upon you in this world, and infinitely more than all this hereafter. As to the very extraordinary man to whom you are to be united, tho' I have never had the honour to see him, I should still have wished him well, from the admiration I have of his genius, had he married a person perfectly unknown or indifferent to me; as it is, I hope his married state will be a state of happiness in the highest sense of the word—of steady improving happiness. As to being introduced to him, my only reason for ever shrinking from this honour was the fear of being intruded on his Lordship's notice without his really desiring it. What you have formerly written to me upon this subject, I have never read nor shewn to any creature breathing, and I have always had the precaution to burn the letters . . .

A third unmarried lady was Francis Doyle's sister-in-law, Emily Milner:

. . . *Your* approbation of Lord Byron at once destroys in my opinion all that an envious world has said to his disadvantage. I know you too well to fear your having been dazzled & captivated by the mere brilliancy of genius or that you have fixed your expectations of future happiness on so frail a foundation; in taste & talents I believe you to be similar & I trust to God in heart disposition & principles you are equally so. Such communications where there is so fair a prospect of happiness usually excite only pleasurable feelings in the bosom of a friend, but you are too dear to me for *mine* to be totally unaccompanied by those of nervous anxiety on first hearing of the awful change about to take place in your situation. When I was first told of your engagement I began to meditate on all I had heard of Ld Byron & could call to mind nothing unfavorable to the happiness of his wife but a certain gloominess & despondency of disposition which has been attributed to him. His attachment having existed for two years however accounts most satisfactorily for this tendency, for when once he knew the Heart to which he has aspired I can well imagine he cd not know happiness till he had gained it . . .[1]

Remarking that Miss Baillie wrote "with I think rather more of doubt—though not expressed—than is just," Annabella complained with some reason to Lady Gosford, "Nothing affronts me so much as a doleful *hope* that I shall be happy," before proceeding to such a defence of Byron as she was writing to other correspondents:

I had a letter from him yesterday—quite mathematical—about his affairs, which he is staying to arrange with as much discretion and good sense as if he had never arranged verses in his life. Nothing can be more rational and considerate—it pleases me much more than if in the impetuosity of love he were to yield to his first impulse, and visit me without regard to anything but his wishes. His great anxiety is to be free from *debts*, and of that object he seems to be quite secure without assistance from my fortune, respecting which he says he has "neither conjecture nor anxiety," and this I can readily believe from his extreme disinterestedness. My ready money is £16,000. I should think his annual income between 5 & 6 thousand, so we shall do very well, as I am not of an extravagant disposition.

Next day she added to the same correspondent:

In *his* life . . . I should venture to establish the *visible* truth of a supreme benevolence. In the school of misfortune he learned a degree of reflexion without which his happiness could never have been of a stable nature. The woman for whom his early years were "in phantom-chace mispent" has since proved herself totally unworthy of his devotion. (Do not men-

[1] Annabella had written to Emily Milner on 23rd September, "It is no precipitate step. The attachment has been progressive for two years." Replying to Miss Milner, she remarked complacently, "For his despondency I fear I am but too answerable for the last two years."

tion this fact again). Happy then that he escaped! The persecution of which he has been publicly the object, has taught him the nothingness of popular opinion, and secured him from the temptations of Vanity. After the second disappointment of his hopes he tried & found the inefficacy of all pleasures, of all ways of abstraction from self, which were not founded on virtue. In short by a stern & cruel experience he has acquired that *Wisdom* which can alone cope with his strength of *passions*, and now he looks forward to a brighter prospect, and depends on one who will never deceive, and I pray to God may not disappoint him. He will, I trust—

Find something dear to rest upon
That pays him for the loss of all.

With regard to myself, though my perils have not been equally evident to common eyes, I have had "hair-breadth scapes." After having had nearly "the world before me where to choose," I have fixed with mature judgment on the person most calculated to support me in the journey to immortality—one by whom my powers & virtues must be exalted, not depressed—one to whom I cannot give my heart too perfectly. For all this —for the blessings we have both received—for the ills we have both escaped, we will offer our gratitude to Heaven *together*, during as many years as may be spared to us . . .

Only sixteen months after writing this epithalamium she was to be marshalling all the resources of the law to preserve her from living with the husband chosen "with mature judgment"!

Even before he learned her conception of his character, Byron found difficulty in communicating with Annabella. He was indeed delayed by lawyers, who, as he remarked, "are never in a hurry," and Hanson was the more dilatory from being preoccupied with the affairs of his son-in-law, Lord Portsmouth, whose relatives were seeking to prove that he was mentally deranged when he married Hanson's daughter. The progress of legal business supplied him with a subject for his letters; he found another in a newspaper paragraph contradicting the announcement of their engagement—which he ascribed to the malicious inspiration, firstly of Lady Caroline Lamb, then of Claughton, the defaulting purchaser of Newstead.

His first worry was allayed when Lady Melbourne gave her approval to the engagement; she could not have done otherwise without not merely betraying Byron's confidence, but making charges against Augusta which he must have denied and which Annabella would not have believed in her present state of infatuation. As he ingratiated himself again into her favour, Byron was soon writing with greater ease to the aunt than to her niece. His second worry was removed when Lady Caroline—as he informed Annabella on 9th October in explaining how "to me she has been the cause of much wretchedness not unattended with self reproach—& yet I did try to preserve her"—was "quiet and rational enough" on hearing of the engagement. His chief concern was with defending Augusta from Lady Melbourne's condemnation.

To Lady Melbourne on 25th September Judith had written, "I expect my Brother next Wednesday (September 28) and conclude it will not be long before we see Ld Byron." Possibly she wrote again to express impatience for Byron's arrival while Lord Wentworth was at Seaham, for Lady Melbourne rebuked Byron for delay and blamed Augusta's influence. Byron assured her on 4th October:

> + never threw any obstacles in the way—on the contrary she has been more urgent than even you that I should go to S[eaham]., and wished me to set out from N[ewstead]. instead of London.

He was also able to tell her that Augusta had written to Annabella, as she had with tact and charm on 1st October:

> I am afraid I have no better excuse to offer for this *self-introduction* than that of feeling unable any longer to reconcile myself to the idea of being *quite* a *stranger* to one whom I hope *soon* to call *my Sister*, and one—may I be allowed to add—whom I already love as such. If I could possibly express how deservedly dear my Brother is to me, you might in some degree imagine the joy I have felt in the anticipation of an event which promises to secure his happiness.
>
> Grateful as I am, I feel that I never can be sufficiently so for the blessing bestowed upon him in the possession of esteem and affection such as yours, for which I justly consider him (as he does himself) the most fortunate of human Beings.
>
> I have been most anxious to write to you for the last fortnight, but delayed it from day to day in the hope that my Brother would be at Seaham to *chaperon* the arrival of my letter & make excuses for the writer who is but too sensible of her inability to express her feelings on this occasion. But, on finding he is still provokingly detained in Town by business, & unable to fix a day for his departure, I have resolved not to wait any longer, and trust entirely to your indulgence for forgiveness.

Annabella wrote to Byron on the 3rd that she had been "disappointed by the last post," which brought no letter from him:

> I received some compensation in a letter from your Sister—*mine*—so cordially kind that I cannot say how much I thank her. I have replied—but not much to my own satisfaction, for I can't find expressions when I want them most. I confidently trust to the kindness which prompted her to write, for a goodnatured opinion of my answer.

This provided Byron with a paragraph for his letter on the 7th:

> It gives me much pleasure to hear that Augusta has written to you. She is the least selfish & gentlest creature in being, & more attached to me than any one in existence can be. She was particularly desirous that

I should marry and only regretted—what I must regret a little too—that she had not earlier the pleasure of your acquaintance.

On the same day he was writing to Lady Melbourne, "+ is the least selfish person in the world . . . you don't know what a being she is—her only error has been my fault entirely, & for this I can plead no excuse—except passion, which is none."

Lady Melbourne was less than usually tactful in urging Byron to hasten to Seaham; by this time she should have known him well enough to realise that, forced upon the defensive, he would develop doubts of himself in gloomy brooding. On 12th October he protested:

Well, but I *am* going, am I not? What would mine aunt have? You forget that I shall not be a whit nearer marriage when I get there, and really without being more impatient than other people, you must allow that it is rather a trying situation to be placed near, and with one's intended, and still to be limited to intentions only.

With experience only in irregular amours, he mistrusted his approach to Annabella's primness; as he told Hobhouse on the 17th, "I confess that the character of wooer in this regular way does not sit easy upon me." By that date, though he had previously protested that "you very much mistake me if you think I am lukewarm upon it," he confessed to Lady Melbourne that he was "horribly low-spirited."

Augusta sought to relieve the burden of his correspondence with Annabella. There was no reason for her to write again, and she had difficulty in finding an excuse for doing so. Probably Byron asked her to write as a refutation of Lady Melbourne's suspicion that her influence was delaying his visit to Seaham. She wrote on the 15th from Six Mile Bottom:

. . . the very kind reception you gave my first letter encourages me to hope you will not be less indulgent to my motive for writing again . . . I wish sincerely that we could *speak* instead of *write*, & I console myself for the *present* impossibility by hoping it will not be of long duration. In the mean time, pray think of me as of one most desirous to *deserve* your future friendship & affection, & believe me when I assure you that so far from standing in need of any of *my* "*candid indulgence*" for what you term yr "*apparent insensibility*," I can most fully appretiate the motives for your *doubts* & *fears* of being able to make my dear Brother happy.

He writes me word that he hopes *very* soon to see you. It is most provoking that his departure to Seaham should have hitherto met with so many impediments . . .

Annabella announced to Byron on the 17th, "Mrs Leigh has written to me again with such confiding goodnature as prevents my *pen* from being shy, and I have answered as comfortably as if we *had* been sisters." In fact she invited Augusta to accompany Byron to Seaham, and Augusta replied on the 20th:

> . . . I am not only grateful for yr kind & immediate answer to my letter but gratified very much by your having wished & intended to write even before you received it. You cannot imagine how very sensible I am of yours & Sr Ralph & Ly Milbanke's kind wish of seeing me at Seaham, or how much—*very much*—I should like to go there. I almost fear it is more than difficult for me to leave home at present. I am *a Nurse* to my Baby, Governess to my eldest Girl & something between both to my two intermediate Babes . . .

After recalling her glimpse of Annabella at Lady Glenbervie's in the summer of 1813 and her belief then that she could not have regarded Byron "with indifference," she went on:

> This is betraying *all* my partiality, but I am *now* not afraid to let it appear to *you*. Every-body who knew him a *little* would agree with me in thinking him clever agreable & good-natured, but to you who will soon love him for qualities much more *love-able*, I may venture to speak as I think. You would not be surprised at my attachment surpassing that of Sisters *in general* if you knew all his kindness to *me* & *mine*. It is indeed beyond all praise. I hope you will soon see him my dear Miss Milbanke. It seems as if I were as impatient as he is for his joining you, but I am so anxious for you to know him better, being convinced he will gain by it in your estimation—and I am anxious *too* for his sake & that of the *family shyness* that his first arrival at Seaham should be over. I am sure you will be amused at his having expressed a wish that *I* would endeavour to describe *his* portion of this fatal shyness to you, & a great many other of what he terms the peculiarities of his disposition . . .

Already, in reporting to Byron on the 19th her invitation to Augusta, Annabella had remarked, "Is she not shy and timid? Her letters look so," and Byron commented on the 22nd:

> You ask me if Augusta is not "shy". To excess—she is as I tell her, like a frightened hare with new acquaintances, but I suppose has made a grand effort to overcome it in this instance. She is now nursing, which will I fear prevent her accepting your father's very kind invitation—I wish with all my heart she could.

Daily aware that her laggard lover was incurring criticism from her parents and her uncle, Annabella bore up very well during the weeks of waiting. "I have something like a fear to know the day of *your* arrival," she wrote on 2nd October:

> I should be unhappy if I did not expect it, yet when fixed, I shall perhaps wish that we *had* met, rather than *were* to meet. I must be thoughtless if I could be *simply glad to see you.*

When he wrote that he was delayed by "arrangements which must be completed before we can meet free from all anxiety," she replied on the 10th:

> If you were here *what* "Anxiety" would remain? Till you are here we shall all feel *some*.

Reporting her father's opinion that legal difficulties were "*as* likely to be obviated by your presence here as in London," she added, "He and my Uncle are both *impatient* to see you."

To keep the pot of their correspondence boiling, she selected from her letters of congratulation to send him a typically unctuous epistle from Mrs. Siddons, on which Byron commented, "her style to be sure is vastly poetical, and her epithets would be no worse for weeding than her periods for pruning, but then with her dramatic habits all this is but natural and you ought to be very thankful it was not in blank verse." When she sent him selections from her letters to her mother in the spring of 1812 containing her impressions of him, both were enabled to renew interpretations of their emotions.

With the passage of time hints increased that her patience was no longer unstrained. On 17th October:

> No letter—and none can come tomorrow. Wednesday will perhaps repay me by news of your *approach*.

On the 18th:

> I am thinking and feeling *in the next week*—and so are you perhaps.

On the 19th:

> I think this will be the last letter you receive from me. If you are so much alone and not always busy, why have I not had more of your thoughts?

When she heard on the 22nd that he was still waiting for Hanson to set out for Seaham before him, she introduced a peremptory note of urgency:

> My Uncle is obliged to leave us next week, and is in despair lest you should not arrive before he *must* go. It is odd enough that my task should be to pacify the old ones, and teach *them* patience. They are growing quite ungovernable, and I must have your assistance to manage them.

To soften the goad she wrote next day:

> I do trust that this letter will return to visit you here . . .
> Of our meeting—I have no doubt that we shall prove admirable

philosophers on that as well as former occasions . . . I never like to MAKE *scenes* even on the most favourable opportunities . . .

I cannot say how kind Mrs Leigh has been to me—it will not be forgotten.

O for tomorrow's post! I walk to meet it every day, and sit in the Blacksmith's cottage till it arrives . . .

Byron responded immediately to the spur on the 25th:

It is with great regret that I shall miss meeting Lord Wentworth at Seaham, but so it is. I could till now fix no precise day, and whatever appearance or consequences these delays may have or create, I must bear them. Hanson whom I have been expecting & urging from day to day, now writes that he is ill, but will send his son. This will not do—it was his duty & is to be present and to meet Mr Hoar in person, and he shall do so, or it shall be our last difference. Whether the man is mad, or only wishes to make me so, I know not. I have been acquainted with him since I was ten years old, which gives him a kind of claim upon what good-nature I possess, which he is pushing a little too far. However, let that rest. I will set off on *Saturday*, and leave out Newstead & Newmarket on my way which I had at first intended to visit. If I can get away a day before, it shall not be lost, but I fear that I cannot remain at Seaham under the present circumstances above a few days . . .

The same day—Tuesday the 25th—he wrote harshly to Hanson: "What to say to them I know not," with a warning that, if the marriage was broken off, he would "never look upon any one again as my friend, who has even been the innocent cause of destroying my happiness." He wrote also to Augusta, who wrote immediately to Annabella on the 26th:

. . . I have just received a letter from Byron written in such evident agitation & lowness of spirits, as would make me quite unhappy if he left me ignorant of the cause, but he tells me he has heard from you that Ld Wentworth is about to leave Seaham & in despair lest B: should not arrive there before he must quit it. At the same time he encloses a letter from Mr. Hanson assigning illness as the cause of delay in *his* movements. It being VERY *material* that they should meet Byron appears & expresses himself perplexed & distressed to the greatest degree, & wishes *me* to write to you to explain those *contre temps* & account for the apparent strange delay on his part. The eagerness I must always feel to comply with any request of his will *I hope* appear a sufficient excuse to you my dear Miss Milbanke for thus tormenting you, when his own letters will plead for him so much better than mine can. At all events I hope it will only convince you more forcibly that he is most anxious you should attribute his prolonged absence to no cause but the true one.

I cannot help *taking it upon myself* to enclose Mr. Hanson's Epistle . . . *What* my Brother will determine upon, I cannot exactly guess from his letter, but of course *you* will be better informed. He says he has scarcely time to write to me "having exhausted himself in a very angry letter to Mr. H——" fm. which he gives me a short quotation—which (to say the truth) I wish may not encrease the evil. I am lamenting I cannot go to him, to afford him at least the consolation of *talking over* all this *worry* . . .

She wrote again on the 27th:

. . . I have in the first place to acknowledge & thank you for your very kind letter of the 23d, & next, I have so much pleasure in telling you that I have had a line from B—— *in better spirits*, for he has received a letter from Mr. Hanson assuring him of his speedy arrival, & enabling him to fix Saturday as the period of his departure to Seaham. I fear I shall not have my promised *glimpse*—which I had anticipated with so much pleasure—but if he travels quicker the other road, I am but too well satisfied to resign this hope. I would not be the means of detaining him even one moment from you.

I cannot exactly at this distance explain to you *how* qualified I am by *experience* to enter into *every particle* of *your* feelings at this most unfortunate "procrastination". You cannot think how much I have felt on the subject for *you* as well as for Byron. It is indeed most vexatious that he should not have been able to reach S—— before Ld. W——s departure from it, and you are most kind and considerate in concealing from him the extent of *your* regrets, & those of others, that you may not encrease his. I flatter myself nothing more will now arise to occasion delay—it will gladden my heart to hear from you of his arrival as a termination of all present anxieties.

Thank you a thousand times my dear Miss M—— for the confidence you kindly repose in me on the Subject of Newstead & others connected with the disposal of it. I cannot help feeling sorry for its loss—if indeed it must go—but no joy can be *perfect* in *this* world, & it would be ungrateful indeed in me to repine when I have so much cause to rejoice. I must persist in my opinion that "*he* is the most fortunate of human beings". I am more & more confirmed in it, & that *I* can never be sufficiently grateful for the blessing of thinking of him as such. It is a circumstance which surpasses all the hopes I had ever in my most sanguine moments dared to form. I own I thought it so improbable he ever would be loved for those "more loveable" qualities *we have agreed* in thinking him possessed of. You know—or you *will* know how much pains he has taken to conceal them from at least *general* observation. In short I always end by wishing we could *speak* instead of *write*—the latter is very unsatisfactory, where so much is to be said . . . I only want to hear that *B* is with you to be a very happy person . . .

These two letters were written by Byron's expressed wish to "account for the apparent strange delay on his part" when he had suggested to Augusta, as to Hanson, that the marriage might be "broken off" as a result of the delay. According to Annabella, they succeeded completely in their object, for when in 1817 she drafted her "Narrative of Circumstances connected with AL," she asserted, "Her correspondence naturally influenced my opinions of his motives, and softened away excentricities that would otherwise have suggested unfavorable doubts more strongly." Believing that these two letters "were exactly calculated to remove every apprehension I entertained, and to account for the strangeness of his behaviour by the vexatious circumstances of the moment," she sent them in the spring of 1817 to Francis Doyle with the query, "What do you think of her character as displayed in these ingenious compositions?" As he was one of Annabella's active partisan's, Doyle's reply must have disappointed her:

> They have all the internal evidence of sincerity at the time they were written. Her desire of *marrying* him at that period seems to have been uppermost—whether in a moment of romantic feeling about him she really thought his welfare might be promoted by it, or that it might silence any other reports then beginning to be prevalent. There are one or two passages in which her manner of speaking of him, tho no warmer than what an affectionate Sister might employ, yet evidently seems to herself as if she thought it might be so considered & she proceeds to qualify and account for it. Whatever was her object she had no hesitation in exposing her future sister to every risk in attaining it. Not that she put it to herself in so many words, & deliberately resolved to sacrifice her—I should not think that was the case. But she viewed her immediate object as necessary, & became zealous & eager in prosecuting it, without reflecting on the consequences . . .

Byron duly left London on Saturday 29th October, but he stayed that night and "till late on Sunday" at Six Mile Bottom. Staying the Sunday night at the inn at Wansford and hearing that Lady Rosebery had recently stayed there when eloping with her brother-in-law, Sir Henry Mildmay, he wrote to Lady Melbourne from Newark on the 31st:

> Don't you think they are not much better than some people you may have heard of + who had half a mind to *anticipate* their example—& don't yet know whether to be glad or sorry they have not!

He remarked that Augusta's husband "knows that I have made + my heiress"; he was "proceeding very slowly" to Seaham, and grumbling that "it was very foolish dragging me out of town before my lawyer had arrived," declared, "I shall not stay above a week if I can help it."

Annabella recalled his arrival at Seaham late on Tuesday, 1st November:

> He had been expected for the two preceding days. My Mother was impatient & dissatisfied at the delay. I remained calm, with that perfect self-possession which had not suffered any interruption since the time that I accepted the offer of marriage. I was sitting in my own room reading,

when I heard the Carriage. I put out the Candles, deliberated what should be done, resolved to meet him first alone. It was so arranged. He was in the drawing room standing by the side of the Chimney-piece. He did not move forwards as I approached towards him, but took my extended hand & kissed it. I stood on the opposite side of the fireplace. There was a silence. He broke it. "It is a long time since we have met"—in an undertone. My reply was hardly articulate. I felt overpowered by the situation, and asking if he had seen my parents, I made an excuse to leave the room, in order to call them—but they had met him at the door.

They returned with me to the drawing room. I sat by him. The conversation became general. I think he talked of Kean, and with an animation of manner that seemed to proceed from agitated spirits. When we were to retire he asked me what time I generally appeared in the morning. I said we assembled about ten. We shook hands & parted. I went to bed, my imagination coloured by hope, but tranquil, & feeling obedient to the Disposer of the future. I rose early and went to the Library, thinking that a lover's feelings might anticipate the hour. But I waited till near twelve, and then finding that I had symptoms of head-ache, I determined to take a walk, supposing that B. must have left his room by the time of my return.

Afterwards she added the comment:

I had been struck by an appearance of personal vanity in him the first night, and by the air with which he played with his large watch-chain. But these impressions were overpowered by my prepossessions.

Besides her own prepossessions, she might surely have recalled the "family shyness" which both he and Augusta had so recently mentioned to her, as well as the agitation she herself noticed.

After more than forty years, writing of herself in the third person, she thus recalled her impressions:

No sooner did she see him than she felt most distinctly, "he is coarser, sullied, since we last met"—it was like a death-chill. In the animation with which he conversed, & in the sentiments shewn towards herself, she however lost that impression. Still there was a mysterious shadow, to which he made frequent & self-reproachful allusions.

Such statements, made at the end of a lifetime dedicated to self-justification, were inevitably distorted by retrospective brooding, especially as by that time she had deluded herself into a conception of Byron's feelings towards herself contradictory to that of which she was convinced at the time of their separation. But there was a factual basis for the retrospective distortion.

When she asked him if it was true that he had quarrelled with Augusta "for three years on occasion of some frivolous offence,"

He acknowledged its truth, and with apparently deep condemnation of his conduct towards her, said, "You might have heard worse than *that*." After a minute's pause he added, "But I have done all in my power since to make her amends for it"—as if "the flattering unction" he laid to his soul was the pecuniary assistance he had afforded her.

She declared that, naturally enough, she "sought to be prepossessed in my Sister's favour, & everything conspired to make me form the resolution that I would be her zealous friend, and rise above the little jealousy of her perhaps superior influence."

He spoke of her with an air of sorrowful tenderness . . . He told me . . . that no one would ever possess "so much of his confidence & affection as Augusta." I felt an instant's pain—it was perceptible only to myself—and was succeeded by a more cordial friendliness towards her. He told me she always treated him as a child, and spoiled him—that I sometimes reminded him of her when I was playful.

He also made a mysterious remark which he repeated during the first few days after their marriage:

"Had you married me two years ago, you would have saved me *that* for which I never can forgive myself." I asked for an explanation—he passed it off lightly.

After two days Byron wrote his own impressions to Lady Melbourne on 4th November:

Your brother pleases me much—to be sure his stories are long, but I believe he has told most of them, & he is to my mind the perfect gentleman. But I don't like Lady Mil. at all. I can't tell why, for we don't differ, but so it is. She seems to be every thing here, which is all very well, and I am & mean to be very conformable & dutiful but nevertheless I wish she & mine aunt could change places as far as regards me & mine. A's meeting & mine made a kind of scene, though there was no acting nor even speaking, but the pantomime was very expressive. She seems to have more feeling than we imagined, but is the most *silent* woman I ever encountered, which perplexes me extremely. I like them to talk, because then they *think* less . . . I am studying her but I can't boast of my progress in getting at her disposition, and if the conversation is to be all on one side, I fear committing myself, & those who only listen must have their thoughts so much about them as to seize any weak point at once . . . I can't yet tell whether we are to be happy or not. I have every disposition to do her all possible justice, but I fear she won't govern me, & if she don't it will not do at all . . .

I have always thought—first that she did not like me at all—& next, that her supposed after liking was *imagination*. This last I conceive that my presence would—perhaps has removed. If so, I shall soon discover it, but mean to take it with great philosophy, and to behave attentively

> & well, though I never could love but that which *loves*—& this I must say for myself, that my attachment always increases in due proportion to the return it meets with . . .

Which last sentence perhaps uncovers the root of their tragedy: by contrast with Augusta's use of the word "love", Annabella insistently offered "affection" and "esteem" while "thinking a reciprocation of Passion highly culpable and absurd."

Also on 4th November Judith wrote to Hugh Montgomery:

> Ld. B. arrived here on tuesday. I am relieved that the first interview is over. Every thing so far is satisfactory to my feelings both in his manner and conduct, but I am in a state of agitation You would pity.

On the 6th Byron cheerfully assured Lady Melbourne that "Annabella and I go on extremely well":

> She is, as you know, a perfectly good person, but I think not only her feelings and affections but her *passions* stronger than we supposed . . . I hope she will be happy. I am sure she can make and keep me so if she likes.

His opinion changed completely during the following week, as he wrote to Lady Melbourne on the 13th:

> Do you know I have grave doubts if this will be a marriage now:—her disposition is the very reverse of *our* imaginings. She is overrun with fine feelings—scruples about herself & her disposition (I suppose in fact she means mine) and to crown all is taken ill every 3 days with I know not what. But the day before and the day after she seems well, looks & eats well & is cheerful & confiding & in short like any other person in good health & spirits.
>
> A few days ago she made one *scene*, not altogether out of C's style—it was too long & too trifling in fact for me to transcribe, but it did me no good. In the article of conversation however she has improved with a vengeance, but I don't much admire those same agitations upon slight occasions . . . I hear of nothing but "feeling" from morning till night—except from Sir Ralph with whom I go on to admiration. Ly. M. too is pretty well, but I am never sure of A. for a moment. The least word—and you know I rattle on through thick & thin (always however avoiding anything I think can offend her favourite notions) if only to prevent one from yawning—the least word, or alteration of tone, has some inference drawn from it . . . I have lately had recourse to the eloquence of *action* . . . & find it succeeds very well & makes her very quiet which gives me some hopes of the efficacy of the "calming process" so renowned in "our philosophy." In fact and *entre nous*, it is really amusing—she is like a child in that respect, and quite *caressable* into kindness and good humour. Though I don't think her temper *bad* at any time, but very *self*-tormenting, and anxious, and romantic.

In short, it is impossible to foresee how this will end *now*, any more than 2 years ago—if there is a break, it shall be *her* doing not mine.

The "scene" was recalled by Annabella during the last decade of her life. Concluding that "his strange words & ways" derived from "a mind ill at ease with itself, & probably from an over-excited imagination," she consulted with her mother and "a very intelligent old friend, Dr. Fenwick of Durham":

Both of them urged me to regard it only as the result of highly wrought feelings & irritating circumstances.

After resting on that opinion for a few days, the evidences of something beyond it became more & more conclusive to me, & I determined to have an éclaircissement before it was too late to save him from a fate which I could not but suspect that he dreaded.

One Evening, when alone with him, I asked him gently and affectionately to *trust* me—to tell me openly whether there was not some reason which made him look forward to our Marriage with altered feelings—that I should never seek to know what that reason was, my only wish being to act as his true friend and to take upon myself the rupture of the Engagement. He became quite livid whilst I was saying those words, staggered, and fell back upon the Sofa fainting.

Minutes must have elapsed before he could recover himself. He murmured indistinct words of anger & reproach—"you don't know what you've done." I implored pardon at his feet, but he remained inflexible, petrified. I could not put any other construction on such a frenzy of despair, than that he thought I had meant to break with him, so I determined never to renew that train of feelings in his mind.

But from that time he lost the confiding manner he had had towards me, & continued to refer to the Past as involving some fearful mysteries. A burthened conscience or an overwrought imagination were the only causes I could conceive. There was too much unequivocal mental excitement to make it possible for those expressions to be from the mere love of producing effect. I walked on firmly to the Goal, but with the conviction that I had linked myself to Misery if not Guilt.

The last sentence alone suggests that, while the facts were truthfully related, the deductions and emotions were developed and distorted in retrospective brooding. Byron had already noted that "the least word, or alteration of tone, has some inference drawn from it," and in recalling continually over the years every detail of her life with him, Annabella came to fancy significance in every shadow; consequently, in subsequent reflection she attributed motives and emotions to herself and to Byron that neither may have recognised at the time.

According to Harriet Beecher Stowe's account of what she was told by Annabella in 1856, Annabella's first reaction to the "scene" was, "*Then* I was *sure* he must love me"; only later did she recognise that

Byron's emotion may have been caused by "fear of detection." She also recalled:

> One day *before* my marriage, & after some affectionate expressions on my part, he said in a low voice with a look of the most fixed malevolence, "I will be even with you yet." When I asked what he meant, he turned it off, and expressed every feeling of tenderness.

After her marriage she had reason to suppose that he cherished resentment against her for her refusal of his first proposal, and in making out her case against Augusta, she sought evidence that his "vindictive feelings" towards her had been known to Augusta, who replied to her inquiry on 22nd March 1817:

> I will look over the letters I have, but I cannot recollect a single expression of the "vindictive feelings" *after* your acceptance. *You* first told me of their existence. I had heard *before* that something of the kind, which at *the time* I really thought any thing but *serious*. The change after we parted & he was in Town appeared to me to be owing to *pecuniary embarrassments*, & I am more & more confirmed in that opinion, which I can explain to you. I'm afraid I've burnt many letters of his which I wish you could have read during his 1st visit to Seaham—they make my opinions differ in many points from yours of his feelings towards *you*.

If Byron had told Augusta that he would "be even with" Annabella for her rejection of him, she would have laughed and mocked him for his vanity; Annabella could never dismiss a remark as "any thing but *serious*."

Byron left Seaham to return to London on 16th November. Annabella wrote to him the same evening:

> Dearest *B*, If I do repent you shall not have the satisfaction of knowing it. If our present and I hope last separation should spare you the anxiety which my troubled visage has sometimes communicated it is enough. When you return my troubles will be ended—or very nearly. The Elders are not in very good humour with me as accessory to your departure, which they regret for their own sake at least.
>
> Are you quite sure that I love you? Why did you doubt it? It is *your* only trespass. As for *my* trespasses I must not think of them. I wish we were married, and then I should do my best, and not quarrel with myself for a thousand things that you would not mind. I expect that you will write me a *lecture*—it shall be studied *con amore*. I must write to our Sister—plead for me with her, and plead for me too with my Lord & master, beseeching him still to "love and cherish" his undutiful wife
>
> AIM

Byron too wrote the same evening from the first stage of his journey at Boroughbridge; he began, "My Heart," and ended "ever thine", but included no protestations or endearments and three sentences were charged with sarcasm:

> If it will give you any satisfaction, I am as comfortless as a pilgrim with peas in his shoes, and as cold as Charity, Chastity or any other virtue. On my way to Castle Eden I waylaid the Post, & found letters from Hanson, which I annex for the amusement of Lady Milbanke who having a passion for business will be glad to see any thing that looks like it. I expect to reach Newstead tomorrow & Augusta the day after. Present to our parents as much of my love as you like to part with, & dispose of the rest as you please.

He added a cryptic postscript: "I will begin my next with what I meant to be the postscript of this."

It would appear that he had carried "the eloquence of *action*" further than Annabella's modesty was willing to allow, and dreading the effects of repeatedly repelling his advances—perhaps doubting her ability to repel them—she had suggested his going away till they could be married. He departed in umbrage, and in building her case against Augusta in 1817, Annabella recalled of "his visit at Six Mile on his way from Seaham to London":

> His unaccountable conduct had nearly determined me to relinquish the engagement. As soon as he arrived at her house he wrote a letter to me declining it on his own part. She dissuaded him from sending it. This she has acknowledged before me upon his recalling it to her mind, and saying, as he continually did, "It is all your fault"—"it was all your doing, Augusta."

Comfortless and cold at Boroughbridge, he had perhaps thought of adding a postscript to suggest breaking off the engagement, and then decided that he would first consult Augusta.

All the propitiation came from her side. On receiving his Boroughbridge note, she wrote on the 17th:

> Your scrawl is—no, nothing but yourself can really be welcome to me now. My own dearest there is not a moment when I would not give my foolish head to see you. I knew it would be so, and think it a salutary chastisement for all my misdemeanours. I *am* in my most sober senses I assure you. What says our Sister? . . .
>
> Dad & Mam are quite disconsolate without you . . . I am in "dim eclipse". Even Billy Hoar told his wife you were "fascinating" . . .
>
> Wilt thou take me to thy heart? my home "till Death do us part"—and don't turn me out of doors in revenge as you threatened.
>
> Ever thine
>
> AIM

On Saturday the 19th:

My own Byron, I must say goodnight before I go to rest. It is my comfort to think of that kind promise that you would make yourself as happy as possible.

The spirit of Self-denial which has always strangely possessed me, must have tyrannized over me when I agreed to your departure . . . my *feeling* is that I would rather share distress *with* you than escape it without you. My fear was that I should *create* it by disappointing you . . . I certainly was not myself during your stay. "Now being gone, I am a—what—again."

Before you pass sentence on me finally, wait to see *me myself*. *Myself* is by no means the grave didactic, deplorable person that I have appeared to you. I am only sage under some visitation of anxiety—this I wanted you to understand and to help me out of that atmosphere of sober sadness in which I was almost suffocated. Those who have seen me *quite* as a domestic animal have had more reason to complain of my nonsense than my sense. It has however always been a long time before I could recover my natural temperament with a new inmate . . .

She ended, "Remember me as Thy wife."

Her mother also wrote on the 19th:

Dear Lord Byron

I return you the letters which you desired Annabella to shew me, as perhaps You and Mr. Hanson may wish to refer to them. It seems probable that Mr. Claughton will purchase. You think I have a passion for business—if You knew me better, You would discover that I am the most idle of mortals and always escape it when I can.

The arrival of Your letter from Borobridge was most acceptable, for Annabellas Spirits sank as Your chariot wheels receded and I believe she had exerted her self-denial to allow You to leave her. Yet I am persuaded it was better for *both* that it should be so. She was becoming apprehensive and agitated, and required a few quiet days to calm her mind and collect her thoughts. Your kindness has reassured her and She is as happy as She can be in your absence, for which She consoles herself by speaking only of You.

If Sir Ralph and myself looked forwards with pleasure to this Union before we had the satisfaction of seeing You here, believe that pleasure is now without alloy, except the losing our dear Child's Society, which has been the source of our happiness for many Years. Do not be angry with me, if You see me very foolish and very low—but I am sure *You* will feel for me.

I conclude Mr. Hanson will inform You when *he* expects to be at Seaham—within a Month from this time probably every thing may [be] concluded.

I wrote to Mr. Noel yesterday to inform him about the time his attendance might be required. In respect to a Special Licence or not please yourself, but the Church is so near and may be so perfectly private that perhaps it is unnecessary.

As I am sure Annabella tells You all her feelings I shall say nothing of her, except that She looks much better than for some days past and is in excellent Spirits, delighted and happy with her future prospects.

believe me Dear Lord Byron

Yours truly and *affecly.*

JU: MILBANKE

On the 20th Annabella wrote a brief note:

> I hope for a line from you to-day. I want it very much—not so much as yourself—yet I still think, perhaps only for obstinacy's sake, that just now we are better apart . . . I have nothing to tell you, and only wish that you knew—I will leave you to guess what . . .

Also on the 20th, from Newmarket, Byron wrote his second letter since leaving her. Her two letters had "been received with those to Augusta, who tells me that she has answered them"; he spoke of the business of the marriage settlement; begged her not to tax herself by writing "more frequently or at length than is perfectly agreeable"; asked if her health and her spirits were better, adding satirically, "I trust that your prescription for the reestablishment of the last has not failed in its effect"; and signed himself "most entirely & unalterably your attached B." Perhaps Augusta protested that the letter was too cool, so he added a postscript, "I don't ask you to consider this as a letter, but merely a memorandum that I am thinking of you now—& loving you ever—my wife."

Two days later he wrote from Cambridge to explain that he was there detained "to vote for a friend who is candidate for a vacant medical professorship." He was at an inn with his friend Hodgson, who was then "in the very act of writing to *his* spouse-elect," and concluded:

> Don't scold *yourself* any more. I told you before there was no occasion—you have not offended me. I am as happy as Hope can make me, and as gay as Love will allow me to be till we meet and ever my Heart—thine
>
> B.

On the 23rd he wrote again to enclose an enthusiastic account by Hodgson of his reception by undergraduates at the Senate house—"a piece of information that will come better from him than me."

Meanwhile Annabella had written briefly during a visit to Durham on the 22nd: "I had a letter yesterday not from thee, dearest, but our Sister, with welcome contents—but I cannot write till I am inspired by a line from you." She added a postscript:

> Remember your promise to tell me faithfully all your feelings & reflections concerning *us.* Mine are at this moment—not *quite* such as I wish to communicate. I am not very well, but shall be before you receive this—therefore don't think of it.

She wrote again from Durham on receiving his Newmarket letter:

> I received your no letter just after mine with the *naughty* postscript was snatched from my hands to the post—before I had time to reconsider it, or it would probably have been withheld. Such are the evils of absence. I am always thinking after I have written that I have not written what I wished—and then it is irremediable . . .

Clearly she was in an emotional state of sexual frustration, which she did not choose to remember when recalling how she "walked on firmly to the Goal," conscious of self-sacrifice in linking herself "to Misery if not Guilt." She wrote to Lady Gosford on 23rd November:

> I am in a very happy temper, with every reason to be so which a situation like mine can offer. It is impossible to be exempt from many anxieties—mine are of such a nature as to prove that there are no important causes. I wish I was married. I am sure we shall be more agreeable after the *courtship* is ended. His ideas are consonant to mine on many more subjects than I had imagined, and we shall assimilate more and more. Every one who has seen him here *loves* more even than *admires*, Dr. Fenwick particularly. There are abominable stories in circulation concerning me. We don't care for all the attempts to make us appear wrong or ridiculous. The world will be obliged to recant . . .

She added a postscript after receiving Hodgson's letter from Cambridge:

> After post, I have just received an account that the world *has* recanted. When Ld B—— being near Cambridge went to vote there for his friend Dr. Clarke, and walked up the Senate house, the young men recognised him from the Galleries, and broke out into the most enthusiastic applause, and the same hearty tribute was repeated on his return. Yet the young men had been *forbidden* to testify their approbation by any such tokens—their disobedience in this one instance was not only pardoned but approved by their elders after it was manifested.

To Byron she began a letter on the night of Thursday the 24th:

> Your letters of somethings or nothings always make me as glad now as they used to make me sorry. Seaham is no longer home to me without you. Make it home when you will—too soon for my wishes it cannot be. Do not regard my up and down spirits—if I am high and low, I am never hot and cold. You are more likely to be wearied with the constant temperature of my affection than disturbed by its inequalities. Perhaps it is not possible for any thinking person to be in my situation without some anxieties—mine were of such a nature as to prove that I cannot find a *good* reason for apprehension. I am not preparing you for a second representation of my dismay—if possible, I will make you forget the first . . .

As to Lady Gosford, she continued her letter after receiving Hodgson's on the 25th:

. . . A letter from Newmarket has given me scarcely less pleasure than yours. I shall be too happy—*there will be no reverse*[1]—whilst you love me there cannot. Remember, I have done with doubts—since I saw you none have occurred on the subject of our happiness. I *was* indeed a *little* unhappy one day that I wrote from Durham. The cause, in which you had not a share, I have *partly* told you—it is all over . . . My Mother does not see any necessity for Hanson's return . . . In a fortnight or very little more I hope to be yours. Do not stay away from your home. Your return will bring joy to us all.

If she had doubts, she was so urgent in her appeals for his disregard of them that she seemed rather to be pleading for dismissal of doubts on his side. On 26th November she wrote:

I wish for you, want you Byron mine, more every hour. All my confidence has returned—never to sink again, I believe. A confidence in the power of my affection to make me anything, every thing that you wish and I wish. Do I understand you? you asked. Surely I do, for I would not understand you otherwise. I should fear to love you less were you different from what has made me love you I won't say "not wisely, but too well" . . .

On the 27th she began, "My dearest—husband, shall I call you so, to persuade myself that you are." On the 30th she was undismayed on hearing from him that Lord Portsmouth's house at Farleigh would not be available for their honeymoon, as Portsmouth's brother was bringing a suit "to lunatize him, or stultify him"; assuring him that "our residence at Halnaby may be prolonged without inconvenience," she urged:

Tell me the latest not the earliest day that you think to arrive here, for my Philosophy likes not "hope deferred." It did me no good before, though *during* those weeks of suspense and renewed disappointments, I would not yield to anxiety for a moment, the *consequences* have made it felt. Now they are surmounted, and I am in every respect well . . .

On 4th December:

. . . I shall be making a visit to Albany some day, if you stay there much longer. I do all I can to be as patient as you wish I should during this last Separation . . . At least I have learned that I cannot enjoy anything without you—these long blank days! . . .

On the 5th:

. . . I don't like to have my love but half believed, since, being wholly yours, it is to me my first *virtue*—that of which I am proudest. What else

[1] The five italicised words were underlined by Byron, with the comment, "Prediction fulfilled February, 1816," when returning the letter to Annabella on 3rd April 1816.

> can I do for you but love you? I have never questioned *your* attachment judging from myself that you would be pained by any thing like mistrust of it, and were it not to exceed half what mine has been, I should not require nor think I deserved more. You have not understood me in this, but *do* understand me, and though I may have exaggerated the principle of not professing, you must not therefore conclude that "nothing can come of nothing." Oh if you could know—well, I won't despair, as I have done, that you *will* know, and shall wait in patience not in pride. I believe you are the only man who ever really loved one that had not flattered him—on the contrary, one that has censured with the tongue when she approved with the heart. A very common practice of mine.
>
> I was at Sunderland this morning, suffering the extraction of a tooth, the loss of which contributes much to my comfort . . .

Perhaps toothache accentuated her physical discomfort, but surely these plaints reflect none of the generosity of a woman in love, but rather an egocentric's resentment at the discovery that she was afflicted with the indignity of sensual appetite? She wrote again on the 6th:

> Ever since our correspondence began, a long time, I have had to contend against an inclination to say or signify "I love you," and to go in quest of foreign subjects . . . And when you were here I so often appeared "the most silent woman in the world" because I could not think of any thing else. At least I have taught you to interpret my silence—or if resolved to talk, I could more easily have pronounced a philippic, than have said indifferent things. It must be my comfort to think that I succeeded wonderfully well in my desired object—not to appear to more advantage before than after matrimony . . . I think I have now secured myself against a relapse. Will you prove your confidence in this assurance by returning before the papers are completed—they do not want an escort, and you have not mentioned any other business to detain you. Take away a few of these wearisome, restless days to *me*, if not to *you*, and let me *see* that you love me. Trust me you will not have to regret the indulgence if you grant it to my petition . . . *Wish* at least to return, if you do not . . .

Did she fear that he might withdraw from their engagement? Did she afterwards prefer to forget that she had ever written these repeated appeals, on realising the humiliation that he had never loved her? Without doubt her subsequent relentlessness in building up her case against Augusta derived inspiration from the reflection that her appeals would have been impotent without the support of Augusta's persuasion.

From Byron she received little encouragement in her course of erotic protestations. "Your letters are very kind, my Love, as to the doubts," he wrote on 29th November; "Never mind—you see I have said nothing about them." Plainly he had no taste for inviting further exposition of her "fine feelings." His letters were brief and factual, relating Hanson's preoccupation with the Portsmouth family wrangle, progress of negotiations with the Lancashire lawyer Claughton for the sale of Newstead, an exchange of calls with her uncle Wentworth, his views on Kean's Macbeth and Southey's *Roderick*. He wrote no letters to Lady Melbourne because he was seeing her with regular frequency at least till 3rd December, when "that family firebrand, Ly. C." returned to Whitehall. On 5th December he wrote:

> I wont tell you all the conjectures &c. my journey has given rise to. Ly. M. says it has set all the talkers in tattle, and all is contradiction and mystery. *She* did not half like my coming away—that was no fault of mine, but we will make up for the past.

Lady Melbourne had already expressed her disapproval to Annabella on 1st December in a letter franked by her former lover, Lord Egremont:

> I have seen Ld. Byron who is grumbling at having so much business upon his hands which will probably prevent his returning so soon as he wishes. I told him I supposed his leaving you was unavoidable, otherwise I should have scolded you for allowing him to come away, as I am far from agreeing with you when you say "I dont think that a short separation will be disadvantageous." To you two personally it certainly will not—but there are disadvantages attending it to ye World, & it puts me out of humour to be ask'd by every person I meet, what is the reason of this delay? Why is he come to Town? as it is a proof that all sorts of reports are current—& you see also things have occur'd to delay his return which was to be expected at such a distance . . . I am talking to you about these things, as I hope you intend to descend to ye common details, tho' that expression of Yours strikes me as if you were still a little in ye Clouds of Romance, & above the feelings of common hum drum beings, who would not have affected to be indifferent to a seperation just at this time, which he laments, & says he wishes most sincerely he had not been forced to leave you . . .
>
> I was very happy to find by yr Letter that yr Sentiments concerning Ld. Byron were exactly the same as what he had express'd to me in a Letter from Seaham about You. You say he has every thing that can make me the happiest Woman in ye World—& he says I am convinced that your Neice can make me extremely happy & has the power of keeping me so. Nothing surely can be better, & must be so pleasing & comfortable to your Mutual Friends, amongst whom I trust & hope you assign me a distinguish'd place . . .

In reply to Byron's letter of the 5th, Annabella wrote on the 7th:

> Dearest—"*I* will make up for the past." Talk and tattle are very harmless, and would not depend on your *locality*. The good people will be tired of conjectures in time . . .

She assured him that, in accordance with his wish to dispense with "white ribbon knots & fooleries," their marriage ceremony should be "as obscure and ignoble as possible," but on the 9th she informed him:

> ... I trust to *you* not to keep us asunder longer than needful ... It was reported three days ago in Sunderland that our wedding had just taken place, and so much credited, that all the bells were jingling in our honour. This mistake I rather enjoy ...

When she came to blame Augusta for her praises of her brother, she did not refer to her own letters to which Augusta's were responses. Augusta did not hesitate to reveal that Byron had confided to her the details of his "scene" with Annabella, for she wrote on 30th November:

> Our B's return will I trust not be long delayed, & I am relieved at hearing that the ceremony will take place sooner than I expected when I saw him here, & he confided to me what Ly Milbanke had written him on the subject. I assure you, there is not any one who can so entirely enter into & understand all your *late* feelings as I can. I may add that I *shared* them, previous to B's first arrival.

Annabella replied on 2nd December:

> B. has not said any thing of his return—he may think it necessary to find a substitute for Farleigh before he leaves the South. I hope our abode will not be *more* distant at least from yours. I don't think we should be very bad neighbours, and to the very disinterested satisfaction which you derive from our prospects will I trust be added the gratification of seeing him even with more facility than before. We shall form a very amiable trio I am certain. Shall I take away your share of the compliment by saying that I am afraid I might be captivated by the Devil, if he were cousin german in kindness as well as kin to my *better* half—so I must call him, as I think him, in defiance of matrimonial etiquette. There is no reason, unless Mr. Hanson's delay should create one, why the ceremony should not take place early in the week after next.

She wrote again to Augusta on the 9th:

> ... Mr. Hanson's procrastination is indeed made too evident in this business. I know from good authority that he has taken an unreasonable and unnecessary time for the completion of the settlements, particularly as he had only to give them into other hands to be engrossed, and to read them over. He is I suppose too much *engrossed* himself (will you pardon a pun?) with the troubles of his own family. When he was in this Country he generally said "Lord Portsmouth" when he meant "Lord Byron", which showed what was uppermost in his mind. I am informed that the writings are not to be in readiness for their journey in less than a week ...
>
> As you like to hear of the hearts that B. has won, I might give you a list

of all who met him here. I am as jealous as possible, and begin to fear that even my father and mother will soon prefer their son to their daughter. I am sure he does not know how much they like him—that *incurable diffidence!* Every body who approaches him must think he is made to be loved, but he will not know it himself. Do you think he will ever find it out?

Augusta replied on 12th December:

. . . B. does not tell me when he goes. You have of course heard that Mr. Claughton's proposals were inadmissible about poor dear Newstead, which may have detained him longer than he intended. I fear another Purchaser must now be looked for—but this is one of my prohibited subjects while we are asunder, & perhaps when we meet it may be too late to discuss it . . .

I am delighted with your account of B's *conquests*, but above all it does my heart good to read what *you* think of him. From living so little in *the great world*, I have seen but few of his *intimate* friends. You know how those who are not that *may* mistake his character, & it has been my fate *often* when speaking of him & feeling quite animated by the subject to witness looks of surprise & compassion in my Listeners—as if to say, "poor Thing! it is natural *she* should think him all perfection"—& you may imagine the happiness after this of communicating with one who loves him quite in my own way, & after my own heart . . .

Byron had written to Annabella on the 8th that Claughton's "proposition is inadmissible as it not only involves reduction of price but delay in payment," remarking, "Now dearest, I will not add one word as from myself or my own wishes, but leave it to you and yours to determine how far this may, will, or ought to cause any further delay in our marriage." Annabella replied immediately on the 10th:

Byron, my own, there shall not be any delay to our marriage on account of these circumstances if you are sure that you can reconcile yourself to the privations necessarily attendant on so limited an income. *I* can be as happy with little as with much, provided that little be not exceeded, and debt incurred. Of debt I have so great a horror that I should cheerfully make any exertions to avoid it . . . We can only keep one carriage, & one house—if it be within a day's journey from London we may in a great degree unite the advantages of Town & Country. We may receive that quiet kind of society which I think we both prefer. I have never mixed with crowds but on principle—I *love* retirement—how much more shall I love it with the person who is dearest to me and the few associates whom he may select or approve. All this we may have with ease, if we resign the *ostentation* of a fashionable career, in which *your* wife, unless very unworthy to be so, must be secure of the highest place *whenever* you choose that she should assert the claim . . . If your opinions differ, tell me—you know I *will* look to you as the guide . . . It is certainly the extreme of perverseness in a woman not to take her own way when offered.

. . . If Hanson should not fulfil within the promised ten days, I shall begin to think he means to keep you for another Miss Hanson . . .

Again, on the 11th:

Dearest—If you give your consent to our immediate marriage, we have only to gain Hanson's. All my discomposures have arisen from the uncertainty of our situation—it is trying to me, I own. I should be a different being, if it were at an end. Of this I meant to say no more till I should have your answer to my last letter. You have my thoughts as they rise, and if ever they appear other than you wish, I do believe the fault is in their expression. I hope I have not any that would disagree with yours in reality. I should not keep them long most probably, if they did. I am not now so engrossed by selfish considerations as to forget how long this time is to thee, my dearest B . . . *I* never wished to escape from time, as time, before . . .

On the 12th she was able to quote her father's attorney, William Hoar:

. . . He says "I rejoice to think that I have prepared the Drafts of the Marriage Settlements on the cautious plan which I have adopted. I have done them *without any reference* to the projected sale to Mr. Claughton, which I was well aware might end in talk, and I have therefore vested the Newstead Estates in the Trustees for the purpose of Sale *generally*, and *so they must stand*. In consequence of this plan there need not be the least delay in the marriage as you have made up your mind to submit to the difference of yearly income until a Sale actually takes place."

So she concluded, "Everything rests with you."

Byron was himself writing on the 12th in petulant comment on the premature bell-ringing at Sunderland:

I must needs say that your Bells are in a pestilent hurry, a little like their prototypes of Bow—"turn again Whittington, Lord-Mayor of London." I am very glad however that I was out of hearing—deuce take them.

The papers will I suppose be finished in this week or the next—undoubtedly my remaining in London will tend to hasten Hans[on].

Perhaps pique at the comment on the bells stimulated Annabella now to apply the spur, as before his first visit to Seaham; she wrote on the 14th:

. . . Thine came to-day, saying "this week *or the next*." I don't wish to encrease *your* vexation of spirit, made manifest in the hideous d's, but the continuation of these *unnecessary* delays creates vexation of spirit to my father and mother, who have been throughout so indulgently anxious to adopt my views & wishes instead of imposing on me any of their own, that I am sorry they should have even temporary cause of dissatisfaction in the proceeding. The time which Mr. Hanson has taken must be considered unreasonable by every person conversant with the business . . .

She then echoed Lady Melbourne's rebuke to herself, "You and I do not mind appearances much, but we must allow them to have more weight with those who are not under the influence of our particular feelings," before concluding:

I must borrow an appropriate quotation from you—"I am a little anxious to have your answer and must conclude this."
Wife or not—always
Thine
*AI*M

On the same day Byron was writing:

Dearest—I waited an entire day and night in the hope or rather intention of sending thee a most heroic answer, but it won't do. The truth is my Love, you have made me vain enough to believe that you would marry me if I had not a "denier"—and I am very sure I would *you*, if you never *were* to have one.

The sale of N. would have liquidated all my debts and left us an immediate surplus sufficient for most of our present exigencies and even wishes. As it is "I am cabined—cribbed"—at least for the present. I should not have cared for the limitation of income, so much as the *debts* . . .

. . . Things must come round in the end, for even if N. & R. are one or both sold at a loss, they will at least leave us clear, and your settlement secured into the bargain. Well, "to marry or not" that's the question—or will you wait? Perhaps the clouds may disperse in a month or two. Do as you please . . .

Each received the other's letter of the 14th on the 16th, but Byron also received one from Augusta:

My dearest B+

As usual I have but a short allowance of time to reply to your tendresses + but a few lines I know will be better than none—at least *I* find them so + It was very + very + good of you to think of me admidst all the visitors &c &c. I have scarcely recovered *mine* of yesterday. La Dame did talk so, oh my stars! but at least it saved me a world of trouble. Oh, but she found out a likeness in your picture to Mignonne[1] who is of course very good humoured in consequence + I want to know dearest B + your plans —when you come + when you go—umph! when the writings travel, when ye Cake is to be cut, when the Bells are to ring, &c. &c. &c. By the bye

[1] Sending this letter to Mrs. Villiers on 6th March 1817, Annabella wrote: "I shall enclose a long promised letter from A. to Ld B. which I will trouble you to return. It is nothing without the key. You probably know that *Mignon* was another name for her who has lately *changed her name*." Augusta's daughter, Elizabeth Medora, was called Medora till she was about three years old, but subsequently became Elizabeth or Libby.

my visitors are acquainted with *A* & did praise her to the skies. They say her health has been hurt by studying &c &c &c.

I have not a moment more my dearest + except to say

ever thine

Byron made no attempt at argument. He told Annabella that the parchments were ready, though he had not known that "till yesterday"; he was applying for a special licence, so that they could be "married at any hour in any place without fuss or publicity," and as soon as the licence was received, he would fix a day for his arrival at Seaham; he thought it would have been better to have had the sale of Newstead arranged before marriage, but "be it as it is." He did not in fact wait for the licence before fixing a date, writing again on Sunday the 18th to say he hoped "to set off on Saturday next."

Annabella wrote on the 16th:

Dearest—Let us marry then as soon as the writings are done, and we will disperse "the clouds." I feel nothing but sunshine in the thought of being thine—thy wife. You have made me most happy. If you had sent the "heroic" reply which you meditated, I won't tell you what mischief you might have done, so I do hope that without more *ifs* and *heroics* you will end this questionable state forthwith. You still leave your own wishes in sublime mystery—to try my powers of Divination?

We have gone on too long with the magnanimity-s that might keep us at a distance for ever, and if you won't I must take the responsibility of speaking plain, only—Don't let me marry you against your will. If assured that I shall not, I desire with all my heart to give myself to you.

We can have Halnaby as long as we like . . .

On the 17th:

Dearest—My only anxiety is to learn that you are coming. Then I am sure we should not find any of these obstacles. If difficulties should continue for a short time they will be very pretty amusement after we are *one* —till we are, the molehills are mountains . . .

. . . What can I say to hasten your journey? I am scolded every day for your absence feeling it *most* myself . . .

She had been consulting Hoar again—she was to become a great addict to lawyers—and wondered if Byron was aware of "a power being given of raising £20,000 on the Estate by a temporary Mortgage."

On the 20th, after she had heard that he had applied for the marriage licence, she wrote a letter which she afterwards valued as evidence that she had offered to release Byron from their engagement:

Dearest B—If *you* think there would have been some convenience in having Newstead sold before our marriage I wish it had been so, but as it must be a long business, and the settlements are adapted to that contingency, it really appears to me that the previous sale is of little importance compared with other considerations—but I feel that these *pros* & *cons* have been already too much discussed between *us*. I have entered on topics so repugnant to me in the belief that what was to be said respecting them would be less disagreable to you from me than from others, whose sentiments I have therefore conveyed with my own. I have one request to make from *myself*. If you conceive or feel there is *any* cause which can render you dissatisfied, or less satisfied with your intended return next week—that you will prefer it to all I have said in favour of that measure. Your letters leave something for conjecture. We shall have the more to talk of, and—if I don't forget it all as usual in your presence, I have many things to ask and hear. But it is useless to think of them before, so I will try to go sleep.

She added a postscript:

Why should I not own to you some conjectures which, if the mere workings of imagination I am not too proud to submit to censure—if not, it is for *my* good they should be confirmed. I will then ask—Are you less confident than you were in the happiness of our marriage? *You will never deceive me*—to that promise I trust, entirely and exclusively.

Next morning, the 21st, she apologised for her overnight mood:

Was I not a little in the heroics yesterday? I cannot play that part two days together. If we do not marry under circumstances that might afterwards cause you to wish it had been delayed, I care little what they are . . . I shall accede to whatever is thought best, and propose nothing myself. You won't think me better versed in self-knowledge than I am in the knowledge of others, when I tell you that I am a perfect Tory in my natural disposition to passive obedience. Opposition of every sort has always been an exertion to me, and made from principle solely, whether right or wrong. Very unfeminine!

. . . Forgive my heroics in consideration that they are first cousins to yours—their best apology to myself . . .

Later the same day, after receiving his of the 18th:

"Saturday." The hope though not quite expectation rejoices me . . . Feel no "anxieties on my account." I cannot imagine any circumstances in which *for my own sake* I would not be your wife . . . Dearest, you and happiness will come together . . .

For five weeks she had been appealing to him almost daily to return and marry her, with repeated protestations of yearning. Could she have seriously supposed that, having secured settlements and licence, on the eve of setting out, he might take advantage of that single expression of doubt to recant? It seems almost as if she wrote that letter of

20th December with a litigious instinct for the saving clause. Fourteen months later, all her other letters were forgotten and this one only remembered when she wrote to her father on 5th February 1816:

> . . . if pecuniary considerations occasioned his evident intention of forcing me to a separation, why did he marry me? Since he must remember (as you do my father) the letter in which I previously requested & strongly urged that "if his embarrassments were such as would interfere with *his* comfort in marriage, he would not consider himself bound to fulfil the engagement, but the contrary."

9

THE HONEYMOON

2nd to 21st January 1815

Byron wrote to Annabella on 23rd December 1814:

> Dearest A—If we meet let it be to marry. Had I remained at S. it had probably been over by this time. With regard to our being under the same roof and *not* married, I think past experience has shewn us the awkwardness of that situation . . .

Next day he set off, as promised, with Hobhouse, who wrote in his journal under the date of Christmas Eve:

> I rode up to London, and at twelve set off with Lord Byron on his matrimonial scheme. At Chesterford we parted, he for Six Mile Bottom, and I for Cambridge.

On Christmas Day Byron wrote briefly, enclosing a briefer note from Augusta, who excused her brevity because "I feel in no very good humour at the impossibility of accompanying B to Seaham"—she had been invited, but explained the domestic difficulties of leaving her four young children, while Byron remarked in his letter, "Col. L. is opposite to me making so many complaints of illness and calls for medicine that my attention is called off and the rest of my letter will be like a prescription if I don't leave off."

On Monday the 26th Hobhouse noted:

> Byron did not arrive until three, when we set off and went three stages to Wansford . . . never was lover less in haste.

They reached Newark on Tuesday, with Hobhouse enjoying the new edition of Gibbon's autobiography, but "The bridegroom more and more *less* impatient." At Thirsk on Thursday Hobhouse noted, "Indifference—almost aversion." They arrived at Seaham on Friday the 30th at eight in the evening:

> Miss Milbanke came to me when alone in the library, and with great frankness took me by the hand at once. Presently in tottered her father.

Miss M. is rather dowdy looking, and wears a long and high dress (as Byron had observed) though she has excellent feet and ancles. The lower part of her face is bad, the upper expressive but not handsome—yet she gains by inspection.

She heard Byron coming out of his room, ran to meet him, threw her arms round his neck and burst into tears. She did this *not before us*. Lady Milbanke was so much agitated that she had gone to her room—our delay the cause. Indeed I looked foolish in finding out an excuse for our want of expedition.

Miss M., before us, was silent and modest, but very sensible and quiet, and inspiring an interest which it is easy to mistake for love.

With me, she was frank and open, without little airs and affectations. Of my friend she seemed doatingly fond, gazing with delight on his bold and animated face—this regulated however with the most entire decorum. Byron loves her personally, when present, as it is easy for those used to such indications to observe.

Their fellow guests were William Hoar and his family "and the Revd. Thomas Noel, Rector of Kirkby Mallory, and illegitimate son of Ld Wentworth (Miss M's uncle maternal), a buck parson of the better sort . . . Byron won his heart by his kindness & open manners." On Saturday the 31st there was "a little jollity upon the signing the settlements which was done in the morning." As a result of "some private talk . . . on Lord B's affairs" with Hoar and Annabella, Hobhouse "began to entertain doubts of Hanson's probity," but decided, "The young lady is most attractive." After dinner at six, Sir Ralph told some of his stories good enough for Hobhouse to note, as of Archbishop Moore's telling him that he "changed the archiepiscopal signature from Cant to Cantuar: because he wished to avoid the mistakes which the bad writing of his predecessor Cornwallis has caused the readers of his processes to commit." The evening "concluded jollily with a mock marriage," Hobhouse as bride being given away by Hoar, and they "shook hands for new year."

The Hoars left on New Year's Day, and "we had not quite so jolly a dinner as yesterday . . . Byron at night said, Well, H. this is our last night—Tomorrow I shall be Annabella's—(absit omen!!)." On Monday 2nd January 1815:

I dressed in full dress with white gloves, and found Byron up and dressed, with Noel in canonicals.

Lady M. and Sir R. soon came, also dressed. Her Ladyship could not make tea—her hand shook.

Miss Milbanke did not appear. The Revd. Wallace came in, also in canonicals. At half past ten we parted company—Byron and I went into his room, the others up stairs. In ten minutes we walked up into the drawing room, and found kneeling mats disposed for the couple and others. The two clergymen, the father and mother, and myself were in waiting, when Miss Milbanke came in, attended by her governess, the respectable Mrs. Clermont.

She was dressed in a muslin gown trimmed with lace at the bottom, with a white muslin *curricle* jacket—very plain indeed, with nothing on her head.

Noel was decent and grave. He put them, Byron, and Miss M. on the cushions, Lady M. placed Sir R. next to his daughter, I stood next to Sir R. My lady and Mrs. Clermont were rather opposite in the corner. Wallace read the responses.

Miss M. was as firm as a rock, and during the whole ceremony looked steadily at Byron. She repeated the words audibly and well. Byron hitched at first when he said "I, George Gordon" and when he came to the words "With all my worldly goods I thee endow" looked at me with a half smile.

They were married at eleven.

I shook Lady Byron by the hand after the parson, and embraced my friend with unfeigned delight. He was kissed by my Lady Milbanke. Lady M. and Mrs. Clermont were much affected. Lady Byron went out of the room, but soon returned to sign the register which Wallace and I witnessed.[1]

She again retired hastily, her eyes full of tears when she looked at her father and mother, and completed her conquest—her innocent conquest.

She came in her travelling dress soon after—a slate coloured satin pelisse trimmed with white fur—and sat quietly in the drawing room. Byron was calm, and as usual. I felt as if I had buried a friend.

I put a complete collection of Byron's Poems in yellow morocco into the carriage for Lady Byron as a wedding gift . . . At a little before 12 I handed Lady Byron down stairs and into her carriage.

When I wished her many years of happiness, she said "If I am not happy it will be my own fault." Of my dearest friend I took a melancholy leave. He was unwilling to leave my hand, and I had hold of his out of the window when the carriage drove off.[2]

Of the drive of the bridal pair from Seaham to Halnaby, Medwin represented Byron as declaring himself "somewhat out of humour to

[1] The entry in Seaham parish register shows that the witnesses were John Cam Hobhouse, of Chauntry House, Wilts., and Richard Wallis, Vicar of Seaham.

[2] Thomas Noel's daughter, Mary G. Noel, wrote to her friend Henrietta Jervis from Kirkby Mallory on 10th January 1815: "Papa is at length returned from the North, he has been absent much longer than was expected owing to the many delays the Lawyers occasioned in drawing up the settlements &c. &c. However he passed a very pleasant month at Seaham. With Lord Byron he is quite charmed, he found him so different to all the representations he had heard of him; he is very engaging in his manners, exceedingly goodhumoured, and has great spirits. Lord B. brought a friend (Mr. Hobhouse) with him to be present at the ceremony, this gentleman Papa found to be very entertaining, he has been a great traveller, and has a fund of good sense and information and so goodhumoured that he is never so happy as when he can amuse others with the description of his travels which he clothes in such pleasing language that Papa says he could never be tired of listening to him. Mr. Hobhouse gave Papa the highest character of Lord Byron, he told him he was generous, had great sensibility, and had the most noble and exalted sentiments, and he related many instances of the goodness of his heart. With such a man, I should think Lady Byron cannot fail to meet with the happiness she deserves. After the ceremony Lord Byron took a handsome ring from his finger, and presenting it to Papa, begged him to wear it as a token of remembrance; however, Papa expects something more *substantial* for the service he has rendered Lord Byron, Lady Milbanke at least gave him reason to think so."

find a lady's-maid stuck between me and my bride." This unlikely story was denied by Hobhouse, Mrs. Clermont, and Annabella herself, who, remarking that "Sir John Hobhouse handed me in, & closed the door upon Lord Byron & me," added, "My Servants, Thomas & Jane Minns, still living in Durham, went all the way on the Box." About fourteen months later Annabella recalled:

> As soon as we got into the carriage his countenance changed to gloom & defiance. He began singing in a wild manner as he usually does when angry and scarcely spoke to me till we came near Durham, when he said amongst other things calculated to excite mistrust, "You had better have married —— [? Eden], he would have made you a better husband." On hearing the Joy-bells of Durham ringing for us, he appeared to be struck with horror, and said something very bitter about "our happiness."
>
> On this journey he also told me that one of his great objects in marrying me "though I said nothing of this before" was to triumph over those who had pretended to my hand, adding that there was no glory in gaining a mere woman of the world, but "to *outwit* such a woman as you is something." He called me to account in a revengeful manner for having so long withheld my consent to marry him, signifying I should suffer for it, and had better not have married him at all.
>
> At the Inn at Rushyford he turned to me with a bitter look & said, "I wonder how much longer I shall be able to keep up *the part I have been* playing"—or some equivalent expression, decidedly expressing that he had worn a mask which he now intended to throw aside. Before we reached Halnaby he began to reveal his hatred of my Mother, and told me some unfavorable things which Lady Melbourne had asserted of her character.

Of their arrival at Halnaby two accounts were given long afterwards. Harriet Martineau reported an interview with a servant described as "the old butler" at Halnaby:

> The bridegroom jumped out of the carriage and walked away. The bride alighted, and came up the steps alone, with a countenance and frame agonized and listless with evident horror and despair. The old servant longed to offer his arm to the young, lonely creature, as an assurance of sympathy and protection.

Though Annabella might well have worn such a demeanour after the journey she described, the impression too aptly suits the partisanship of a militant feminist acquainted with Annabella's character in widowhood. Annabella's maid, Jane Minns—a young married woman who returned to her service for the period of the honeymoon—told a newspaper reporter in 1869:

> she was buoyant and cheerful, as a bride should be, and kindly and gaily responded to the greetings of welcome which poured upon her from the

pretty numerous group of servants and tenants of the Milbanke family, who had assembled about the entrance to the mansion.

Whatever her feelings, Annabella must have assumed an appearance of gaiety to meet the greetings of servants and tenants who had known her since childhood, while Byron, afflicted by his usual shyness and feeling that the warmth of welcome was addressed to her, may well have found an excuse soon to withdraw from the scene.

Annabella recalled that, "After dinner, he said in a mysterious & alarming manner, 'Now I have you in my power, and I could make you feel it.' " Speaking of William Lamb, he said:

> "Caroline Lamb must be to her husband's heart like a perpetually-falling drop of water—it wears & petrifies"—and added malignantly that I should find *I* "had got much such a partner."
>
> I attributed part of his irritability to his pecuniary embarrassments & anxiety about Newstead; hoped there was a latent and generous feeling *for me* in his despair on these subjects, and made to myself every excuse for his extraordinary solicitude about my prospects of fortune.
>
> He was, even on the day of our marriage, calculatingly curious as to the state of my father's & uncle's property, and their dispositions to bequeath it, looking forward to their decease with an unfeeling eagerness, which, at a subsequent period, was more shamelessly displayed . . . I experienced an indistinct & painful impression; but this was the man of whom I believed that Generosity & Disinterestedness were the strongest impulses; the atoning virtues of his too ungoverned career!

Late in the evening:

> He asked me with an appearance of aversion, if I meant to sleep in the same bed with him—said that he hated sleeping with any woman, but I might do as I chose. He told me insultingly that "one animal of the kind was as good to him as another," provided she was young—and that with men, this was not any proof of attachment.

Of what followed Annabella understandably omitted to record an incident that Samuel Rogers remembered from his reading of Byron's destroyed memoirs:

> on his marriage-night, Byron suddenly started out of his first sleep: a taper, which burned in the room, was casting a ruddy glare through the crimson curtains of the bed; and he could not help exclaiming, in a voice so loud that he wakened Lady B., "Good God, I am surely in hell!"

Annabella resumes:

> Perhaps the deadliest chill that ever fell on my heart was on the morning after my wedding day; he was late in appearing, but as soon as he came

downstairs I went to him in the Library. With the most forbidding aspect, and in a tone of cold sarcasm, he said, "It's too late now—it's done—you should have thought of it sooner." I told him I did not repent, and tried to inspire a hope which was almost extinguished in my breast.[1]

According to her various recollections, this first day after their wedding was full of menace and foreboding:

The day after my marriage he said, "You were determined not to marry a man in whose family there was insanity" (He had heard this from Lady Melbourne)—"You have done very well indeed," or some ironical expression to that effect, followed by the information that his maternal grandfather had committed suicide, and a Cousin—a Gordon also—had been mad, & set fire to a house.

He was superstitious to excess. The day after my marriage, my wedding-ring being too large, I had tied some black silk round it. This was an omen of the most alarming nature to him. To relieve him I took it off, and as we were standing before the fire in my dressing-room, in warming my hand, the ring fell into the grate. It was another shock to him, and occasioned some expression of foreboding which I do not recollect.

He endeavoured to make me believe him guilty of atrocious crimes, & seemed to have a strange satisfaction in suggesting such painful ideas.

The day after we married, when he had said he was "more accursed in marriage than any other act of his life," he also said, "I am a villain—I could convince you of it in three words."

This last recollection, written in March 1816, became thus embellished in compiling the case against Augusta in March 1817:

On the first day, and continually in the first week of our marriage, he gave way to the remorse which was preying upon his mind, but the word *remorse* I do not remember that he named. His style of expression was this —"I have done that for which I never can forgive myself"[2]—"I was a villain to marry you"—"I am more accursed in that than any act of my life"—"Hobhouse knows I am a villain"—and in particular he said, "Had you married me two years ago you would have saved me from that which I never can get over," implying a dreadful load of criminality he had incurred in that interval. I answered that I would then consider the

[1] She wrote two other versions of this incident. Firstly:

The morning of the day after my marriage, he met me repulsively, and said in a cold & cutting manner, "It is too late now—you know *it is done* (or *cannot be undone*, I forget which)."

Again:

The first Morning, when I went down to him in the Library, he uttered words of blighting irony. On my turning away to conceal tears, he said coldly "It is too late now—I hate scenes." I could not but think he was, for some hidden reason, doing violence to his better nature in treating me thus, & I acted as if he were better than he seemed. I tried with all the power of affection to "smile the clouds away" to call out his higher & more generous feelings.

[2] So in the first draft, called "Narrative Q" by Lord Lovelace, but this sentence was deleted in the revised draft, Narrative F.

burden as mine, whatever it might be—that I only asked to bear it for him here & hereafter . . . The temper was always that of vindictive bitterness towards me, and he accused me of all his misery because I had married him—"What a fool you were to marry a man of whom you knew so little."

In reading Annabella's various statements, it is important to note the dates of their composition. Those of January and February 1816 were written to provide lawyers with ammunition for forcing Byron to agree to a deed of separation; those of March 1816 were written at the request of her chief legal adviser, Lushington, for possible use if the case had to be taken to court; those of March 1817 were devised to assemble all possible evidence against both Byron and Augusta as improper persons to have the custody of Annabella's child; everything of later date was directed towards persecution of Augusta and justification of her own conduct in deserting her husband. The later statements must be regarded with caution as evidence of fact, not merely because her memory became dimmed by time—"I often am surprised when talking with you to find how much that was said and done in that 1815 you seem to have forgot," Mrs. Clermont wrote to her on 30th March 1830—but because the skeletons of fact became hidden under the constructions she built upon them.

Even the earliest and freshest recollections must be read with reservations. Not only were her statements devised as memoranda for her lawyers, as material for a prosecuting counsel; her impressions became distorted from the moment of their conception by the ponderous machinery of her analysis. As Byron remarked to Lady Melbourne during his first visit to Seaham, "the least word, or alteration of tone, has some inference drawn from it"—she was always "squaring her notions to the Devil knows what," and Byron's personality presented a problem in subtlety beyond her pedantic understanding.

Finally, she was devastatingly humourless. When he mocked her prudent determination to avoid a husband with insanity in his family, there was surely no more than a schoolboy's mischief in telling her that his grandfather committed suicide and he had a cousin who set fire to a house. The "mysterious & alarming manner" must have been almost certainly assumed in playful mockery when he told her, "Now I have you in my power, and I could make you feel it." His practice of acting a pose and his schoolboy sense of fun were alike encouraged by her literal and humourless understanding, so that he must have piled extravagance upon extravagance, marvelling at her limitless credulity. On the other hand, he must have been irritated by her smugness, as when she sought with wan endurance to "smile the clouds away" in a self-conscious effort "to call out his higher & more generous feelings."

When, in the best manner of his Wertherism, he implied the "dreadful load of criminality he had incurred" since her rejection of his first proposal, she saw nothing insulting or incongruous either in her ready credulity or in her pious proposal to bear the burden of his sins. Augusta would have laughed gaily that he sustained his dreadful load too easily for her to conceive his criminality as very formidable, and soon had him laughing with her at his own histrionics. She did her best to warn Annabella of the attitude to take towards Byron's moods: "*I* have no *doubts* of YOUR success AGAINST *Magician* (this is quite a *Newmarket* phrase excuse it)—how happy I shall be if I am right!" she wrote on Wednesday 4th January:

> I wrote you some very imperfect congratulations on Monday, & am not a little impatient to receive the next account from Seaham which will *confirm* you my Sister . . . I never can express how much I wish you & my dearEST B—— all possible happiness . . . God bless you my dear *Annabella.* I have set the example, & beg for the future to be your
>
> most affecte *Augusta*[1]

Annabella recalled that Byron received a letter from Augusta on that eventful "day after my marriage":

> It affected him strangely, & excited a kind of fierce & exulting transport. He read to me the expression, "Dearest, first & best of human beings," and then said with suspicious inquisitiveness, "There, what do you think of that?" My answers on all such occasions appeared to convince him of my unsuspecting goodwill towards her. Another expression in one of her letters at that time, and I think in the same, was to represent her sympathy with his agitation during the marriage ceremony—"as the sea trembles when the earth quakes." He admired it as poetical. Yet he generally spoke of her as "a fool," with equal contempt for her understanding and principles.[2] He was however continually lamenting her absence, saying no one loved him as she did—no one understood how to make him happy but her. I therefore wrote to her from Halnaby to entreat she would visit us there. Two or three days after my marriage suspicions had indeed crossed my brain, if transient as lightning, not less blasting. Their first occasion was this—I accidentally alluded to an incestuous union of brother & sister through ignorance of their parentage (I had recently been reading Dryden's Don Sebastian). His terror & rage were excessive. He said, "where did you ever hear of that?" with an air of frantic distraction. I quietly explained. He took up his dagger, which with his pistols, lay on the table, and left the room. I heard him violently close the door of his

[1] All her letters before Annabella's marriage were begun, "My dear Miss Milbanke."

[2] He also called Annabella a fool in writing to Augusta: "She's a fool, and when you have said that, it is the most that can be said for her" (25 Feb. 1817). Of himself to Augusta: "What a fool was I to marry—and *you* not very wise, my dear—we might have lived so single and so happy, as old maids and bachelors. I shall never find any one like you—nor you (vain as it may seem) like me" (17 Sept. 1816).

own room in the long gallery, and, I thought, lock it. My apprehensions for the immediate consequences left me at the moment without power to reflect upon the cause, but when I looked back upon this incident I could not doubt that he feared a personal application of my inadvertent expression. My first idea was that he might have had a connection with some girl whom he afterwards discovered to be a natural Sister. This was rendered more probable by his father's libertine character. He returned to me in the sitting room within half an hour, having assumed that appearance of cold tranquillity so well described in Lara.[1]

She did in fact write as early as 4th January to invite Augusta to Halnaby, for Augusta replied on the 8th:

My dear Sister,

"*Would*" that I COULD go to you! but I'm sure you will understand ye difficulties attending such a removal, & that ye power not the *will* or *wish* is wanting. I feel not a little grateful for all the kindness you express on the subject & hope that we shall meet & *soon, somehow* & *somewhere.*

Your kind letter of the 4th & B's only reached me this morning. I mention this for fear you should be *marvelling* at my tardy reply to the first from my "Sister *in*deed," & one so very gratifying from all ye kindness it contains—"poor Gussey" thanks you from her heart & hopes to deserve it more than she can as yet. Col. L. desires me to say a great deal from him as well as myself in return for your message, & would be too happy *to be able* to remove the difficulties in ye way of moving from hence . . . B will tell you what a *helpless* person I am, which you will think Somewhat excusable considering MY YOUNG FAMILY . . .

Augusta wrote again the next day, beginning "My dearest Annabella":

Your letter my dear Sister makes me both glad & sorry. The latter sensation is the consequence of not being able to *set out immediately*, as my inclination would lead me to do, to see you & *our* B. I wish the distance was not so formidable in short I wish a great deal—& am in very bad humour when I reflect upon all the difficulties in my way, & which I fear are *insurmountable* . . . I am amusing myself with ye thoughts of what B's countenance must have expressed during ye continuance of the DURHAM PEAL. I am going to *scold* him so Adieu My dear Sister . . .

From which it appears that Annabella read in Byron's reaction to "the Joy-bells of Durham" no such alarming significance at the time as she afterwards discovered. She was evidently reporting his moods as harmless eccentricities, for Augusta wrote again on the 11th:

[1] For Lara's brow upon the moment grew
Almost to blackness in its demon hue . . .
Yet looked he on him still with eye intent,
As if he loathed the ineffectual strife
That left a foe, howe'er o'erthrown, with life;
As if to search how far the wound he gave
Had sent its victim onward to his grave.
—Canto II, iv.

What a *super-excellent* Sister you are! I am only afraid you have adopted B's spoiling system, for you must have discovered that I am thoroughly *his* Enfant gaté—but I try & *will* try *not* to be *spoilt* by your very great kindness.

I think you may guess what will be my reply to your questions . . . oh yes, I will indeed be your "ONLY *friend*," but how can I thank you for considering me so kindly, all unknown as I am except by B's partial report . . . Your letters received this Morng. have been read and I know not how many times, & cannot be too often as they tell me of your happiness & dearest B's. I am more & more convinced of his good fortune *respecting you* & your fixed determination on ye subject of confidence & friendships is particularly adapted to his taste & his comfort, as far as *I* understand both . . . I can easily believe that B. is not "blue-deviled" in his present abode . . . I am quite prepared to laugh with you at the "*comical proceedings*" of which I have some idea already. I agree with you that *you alone* (or at least such another "DETERMINED" person as you) would have been proof against them. Thank Heaven! that the present rewards you for those little trials of the past, which none can fully understand who have not experienced similar ones . . .

Annabella thus recalled some of the "comical proceedings" little more than a year later:

One night in bed he said he would tell me to what he alluded as preying upon his mind, if it were not another person's secret. I asked if Augusta knew it. He replied with the greatest horror "O for God's sake don't ask *her*." He said he never ought to have married me, on account of *former circumstances*, and would not, if he had known before how deserving I was, but that people told him I was methodistical and every thing that was disagreable.

He said that since he had fulfilled the Engagement like a man of Honor, he was now at liberty to express his hatred of marriage, & discontent with every part of the business. Spoke of the Settlements as if I were a Beggar, and with anger of my Father's circumstances as being so much involved. Enquired eagerly into my Expectations from my Uncle, and seemed disgusted with their uncertainty.

He absented himself from me during the greater part of the day at Halnaby—frequently went into one sitting room when I entered the other. Often sent me out of the room as appearing to hate my presence, with some expression of this kind, "I don't want you," or, "I hope we are not to be always together—that won't do for me, I assure you." When I returned he has been angry either that I staid too long, or too short a time.

He used to get up almost every night, and walk up & down the long Gallery in a state of horror & agitation which led me to apprehend he would realize his repeated threats of Suicide, and he has alluded to mysterious & dreadful causes of this restlessness.

When he has seen me depressed by his unhappy state of mind, he would say "Don't be sentimental," and treat my affection for him sarcastically as very troublesome.

He desired me to write to Mr. Hoar to make his Will, for the purpose of leaving every thing he could devise to Mrs. Leigh, and as I was not mortified, but said I thought he was very right, he seemed disappointed. He also told me he had two natural children whom he should provide for. At this & many other times he has told me he had another Wife—one of his expressions was "I have another wife *somewhere*." When I laughed at this, he has said, "You may find it true," or other words to impress the belief.

He continually endeavoured to make me jealous of his Sister, lamenting my presence and her absence, saying "Nobody understands me but Augusta"—"I shall never love anybody as well as her."

In this statement of March 1816 her frequent lapses from the preterite to the perfect tense indicate its composition for a lawyer's consideration. A year later, when she was endeavouring "to retrace the course of my impressions concerning A L," her recollections became more detailed:

I know not if it was on the same night that after he had been walking up & down the long gallery at Halnaby like a Maniac, & he returned to bed, I laid my head upon his shoulder ("where thy head so oft hath lain") and he said "You should have a softer pillow than my heart." I uttered almost the only expression of despair which ever broke from me in his presence "I wonder which will break first—yours or mine." He expressed that sort of *unrelenting pity*, if I may so call it, which has so often made me feel the *hopelessness* of my situation more than his most unkind & insulting expressions . . . He would continually say "poor thing" to me, and sometimes add "you should have married a better man," and the tears would even suffuse his eyes, and freezing there, give the appearance of more icy hardness.

Here she seems to be only reflecting a conflict between egocentrics, each feeling self-pity without sympathy to spare for the other. But she had a psychiatrist's preoccupation with interpretations fitting a case-history:

Again one night at Halnaby, I tried to make him consider the past as reparable, and solicited him to make me the sharer of his griefs, assuring him that I had been too conversant with the strong passions of human nature not to pardon the excesses to which they might have led him. He said I could know nothing of the things to which he alluded—good women could know nothing—that he would tell me one of them, but that it was another person's secret. He spoke of it as a seduction—far worse than what he had confessed to me of Ly F[rances] W[ebster].

I asked—without any suspicion concerning A—— —if *she* knew of it. His alarm was extreme & he said "Oh, for God's sake don't ask her!"—and made me promise not. He then said he would go to sleep—evidently an excuse for discontinuing the conversation—but that if I would ask him after breakfast in the morning he would disclose to me what he meant.

After breakfast I reminded him of the conversation. He at first attempted to evade. I pressed him to trust me unreservedly. He seemed torn by conflicting passions, and as my tenderness encreased his eyes filled with tears, but none overflowed. He resisted my affection, and rising from the sofa where he had been stretched in agony, he stood before the fire, and with that terrible blackness of countenance which he has described in Lara, & which I [have] ever seen associated with remorseful recollections, he told me I might know his secret if I would—but he bade me remember Caleb Williams and threatened me I should be miserable for life, and the victim of another Falkland. I must observe that from the allusions he made it did not appear to me that he was then chiefly thinking of the circumstance on which this narrative is founded. *Murder* was the idea suggested to my mind. He said another time at Halnaby that many a man who had committed murder walked about unsuspected, & added with trembling horror & mystery, "I know some"—but the very frequency of his allusions to this crime as well as to the melancholy subject now before me, inclined me to scepticism in regard to both, and together with his intimations of hereditary madness, I even then conceived the *hope* (for such it was to me) that the madness was not of the *heart but head.*

"His madness was not of the head but heart."—Lara.

Annabella's narrative has indeed the overcharged melodrama of Godwin's then popular novel, *Caleb Williams*; like Falkland in the novel, Byron was "the fool of fame," and Annabella seemed cast for the part of Caleb Williams in suffering his persecution and yet pursuing him to his doom. On the other hand, Annabella seems to have developed an attitude to Byron much like the mood in which Catherine Morland became General Tilney's guest at Northanger Abbey; from everything she observed, she deduced some diabolical inference. Unlike Catherine, she never awakened from her illusions to recognise ruefully that her conceptions were her own interpretations, though, with her reading of *Caleb Williams*, *The Monk* of M. G. Lewis, and the romances of Mrs. Radcliffe, she might have realised their influence on Byron's pose. Remarking that the villain in Mrs. Radcliffe's novel, *The Italian*, set the pattern for Byron's Lara, Walter Raleigh shrewdly pointed out that "The man Lord Byron tried to be was the invention of Mrs. Radcliffe."

Byron afterwards confessed to Hobhouse that, on the first night of his marriage, "he had been seized with a sudden fit of melancholy, and had left his bed, and that this oppression had lasted during the first week of his residence with Lady Byron, at Halnaby." His mood cannot have been improved by his having caught a cold: "I am sorry to hear he has a cold and know how to pity him," wrote Judith to Annabella on 8th January, "as I have suffered a good deal during the last week from the same cause." Having drifted into marriage against his inclination, he must have felt dismay at the reflection that he was trapped into sharing his life with a young woman of whom he knew little. Her own recollections indicate that she irritated him by amply endorsing his unfavourable impression of her habit of drawing inferences from "the least word, or alteration of tone." He could not but feel further irritation at her troubled anxiety to please, at her pious determination to share his burdens without thought of lightening them by making light of them. "He told me he only wanted a woman to laugh," she noted, and instead of accepting this as a hint to herself, she underlined as a reflection on Augusta's character his addition to the remark—"and *did not care what she was besides.*"

> My affection was sanguine, and under its influence besides other conjectures formed in a wilderness of doubt, I sometimes fancied that he had taken up the part of Petruchio from the idea of my being a Katherine and I *would* not believe him worse than the actor of a most unkind part. I suspected a foreign influence stimulating him to correct me as a spoiled child, and I thought he must see the error of such advice as he became better acquainted with my character.

The "foreign influence" was of course Lady Melbourne, and Annabella recollected after two years that Byron "was rather piqued . . . by her writing to me since my marriage, as the first person to be considered, instead of to him." Byron had written to her on the day after the wedding and again on the 7th, but Lady Melbourne tactfully acknowledged his first letter by writing to her niece on the 8th:

> My dear Ly. Byron,
>
> I was very much delighted on receiving Ld. B's letter yesterday . . . I know yt. in proper form I ought to answer Ld. B's letter, but he must expect to see you have the preference on most occasions, & therefore it is best to accustom him early to what he must learn to bear patiently in future, so you may tell him I will write soon & in the mean time that I wish him joy with all my heart & soul—& if you are not too modest, or too shy you may add that *he* has drawn a prize—& that *I believe* you have too, only I make that reservation, as I never speak so confidently of a man as I do of a woman—but even as it is, I feel the greatest obligation to you for having given me a Nephew whom I like so much . . .

Still without answering Byron's letters, she wrote again on the 16th:

> Dear Annabella,
>
> You see how soon I profit by yr permission, & pray believe yt my addressing you by yr present name was no proof of want of affection as I have it much at heart to be on ye most cordial & affectionate terms with you and your caro Sposo & I hope to see you as much as possible.

Having explained that she had just left her daughter's home at Panshanger to be at Brocket for a week before going to London:

> I am sorry I have not a chance of seeing you there as soon as I had hoped, but your reasons are very good, & I hope a little patience will conquer all difficulties. I am more & more convinced every day of ye efficacy of that receipt, & at Home I have so much occasion for it myself & so many occasions for preaching it that I go about repeating it habitually.

After thus applauding the virtue of patience, this mistress of innuendo related the latest gossip about another young bride, Harriet Pearce, who had been married only a few weeks to George Germain, second son of the unfortunate soldier and statesman, Lord Sackville of Drayton, and had been warned to "subdue him at first for if she gave way to him she would find it impossible to live with him—he was of such a Sulky bad Temper":

> her Spirits seem likely to carry her thro' what Ly Asgill says is ye real test of a Womans cleverness—that is managing her Husband. She says it is what every Woman ought to study for her own happiness & her Husbands too, & she never can think any one can have any pretensions to cleverness who does not do so, by some means or other. Dont let Ld. Byron see this, for he'll abuse Ly Asgill who has always had ye greatest wish to know him, & he'll say I am preaching up rebellion—which by ye bye I'm always accused of in every sense of ye word.
>
> But really & truly that would be a very unjust construction to put upon what I have said for I do not believe there will be any necessity for such advice. I have a totally different opinion of him & am convinced yt I shall have an opportunity of retorting an expression of his upon himself, & shall call him the Conjugal Baron, as he used to call Emily the Conjugal Countess.
>
> Of one thing I am persuaded—yt nothing ever will have any effect upon him but ye greatest kindness & affection & that in no one thing does he resemble Mr. Germain, or indeed any other Man . . .

On this pregnant letter Byron commented on 22nd January:

> I cannot sufficiently admire your cautious style since I became chicken-pecked, but I love thee, *ma Tante*, and therefore forgive you your doubts *implied* but not expressed, which will last—till the next scrape I get into, and then we shall wax confidential again, and I shall have good advice—I look upon you as my Good Genius.

Lady Melbourne offered wise advice in exhorting her niece to demonstrate her reputed "cleverness" in managing her husband. In two and a half years of close correspondence she had learned to know Byron very well. She knew that he responded to kindness and affection, that he was easily wounded and susceptible to moods of sulkiness and gloom, that he was quickly corrected by cajolery and loyal in his attachments if for no better reason than a sentimental sense of obligation. "What I want is a companion—a friend rather than a sentimentalist," he had told her, and "my attachment always increases in due proportion to the return it meets with." He had confided his fears of Annabella's "fine feelings" and "agitations on slight occasions"—his fear that "she won't govern me, & if she don't it will not do at all." She was reminded by his letter of 7th January:

> Bell & I go on extremely well so far without any other company than our own selves as yet. I got a wife and a cold on the same day, but have got rid of the last pretty speedily. I don't dislike this place—it is just the spot for a Moon, there is my only want a *library*, and thus I can always amuse myself, even if alone. I have great hopes this match will turn out well. I have found nothing as yet that I could wish changed for the better —but Time does wonders, so I won't be too hasty in my happiness.

If hardly befitting an infatuated bridegroom, these sentiments do not suggest the psychopath described in Annabella's recollections. "He made it a point that I should write to every one of my happiness," she recalled with litigious intent to discount any possible evidence that she had not seemed to suffer at the time so desperately as she afterwards attested, adding, "I did to some." Hearing from her mother that Lord Wentworth's letters "speak only of joy and gladness about You and Lord Byron," she assured "My dearest Uncle" that "I am still more happy that my happiness can extend itself so effectually to you," and ended with "every kind wish to *our* Uncle."

After staying in Durham during the week following the wedding, her mother wrote from Seaham on 8th January:

> . . . it seemed very odd to me when I came here yesterday to see Your place unoccupied. Yet I endeavor to get the better of these useless thoughts and hope in a little time I shall do so. I ought to be happy, that You are so . . .

The Milbankes' wedding anniversary was 9th January, and Sir Ralph wrote on the 12th:

> Dear Lord Byron,
>
> Accept my best thanks for your kind recollection of the 9th of this month —38 years ago—and for turning our old age into youth, and in the true Ovidian Style . . . I will indulge the pleasing illusion. I am young in imagination and will be so, and would kill any man who should venture to tell me, I had lived 67 years, this evening, though when I awake to-morrow, I shall feel the cruel wrinkles on my brow and see the *damnable grey* hairs when I look in the glass. But on the principle of your Metamorphose I am convinced that you and Lady Byron are old married People almost verging on Baucis and Philemon . . . but no, it must not be, whatever moral and philosophical writers say of old age, *Curse* it, I hate it . . .

On the same day Judith wrote to Annabella:

> I wish you had seen how Dad chuckled over Ld Byron's letter. *You know* how it would please him. Bless You and *My Son* . . .

Since 1813 Annabella had kept no regular journal, but she noted down some "Reflections," dated "Halnaby—Jan. 13, 1815." She was reading Baron Trenck's *Autobiography* and Conyers Middleton's *Free Inquiry*, and copied out extracts from both, but also noted three sayings by Byron followed by the initial "B":

> There is more vitality in the beings of Fiction than those of History—in Falstaff than in Julius Caesar.
>
> Moore said of Campbell that "he bathed in the waters of Helicon—but was sometimes seized with the cramp."
>
> C. must be to her husband's heart like a perpetually falling drop of water—it wears & petrifies.

Here there is no comment to suggest the malignant significance attached when quoting the epigram on Caroline Lamb in her recollections, and the other two remarks indicate that Byron's conversation was not so unremittingly intimidating as she afterwards recalled.

Among her reflections she remarked:

> Amongst the weakest arguments adduced in favour of Christianity is that of its extensive acceptance with mankind. The principle of *credulity* must have exercise, and is in itself no proof of *credibility* . . . I never read a work *for*, without a disposition to infidelity, nor a work *against* without a disposition to belief. We feel the strength of answers which we conceive ourselves, much more than any arguments supplied by others.
>
> Religion in my opinion is *Gratitude*—not *Interest*, as it is preached by those who would "make Godliness great gain" . . . The highest virtues of which we have any conception could not exist without the existence of obstacles, and "the gold" of human nature must be "tried" in "the furnace of adversity."

The terse clarity, the antitheses, the occasional picturesque phrase—so unlike Annabella's usual laboured pedantry—suggest that she was either quoting Byron's remarks or her own arguments interpreted by his comments. Here there is no hint of the resentment expressed in her subsequent statements against "his attempts . . . to subvert my principles," as in 1817:

> Soon after we got to H[alnaby] he told me to read "Middleton Free Enquiry" as the work which had undermined the very foundations of Christianity. I read it with great attention, and formed a different opinion—as I told him. Most of his infidel arguments seemed to have less originality than his thoughts on any other subject—to be repeated from

what he had heard & not derived from what he had examined. Some of them assumed a positive falsehood, as that no mathematician could believe in Xtianity.

Her persistent inquiries into his religion before their engagement and his proposal to accept her as his "Guide, Philosopher and friend" were forgotten when she wrote:

A day or two after Marriage, after he had renewed, as he perpetually did, contrary to my wishes, different topics of religious controversy, he said to me with an air of defiance "Now—sit down and convert me."

Was his air "of defiance," or merely of mischief?

I declined the argument as usual, telling him that if he needed to be convinced, his own dispassionate reflection and lengthened experience were more likely to produce that effect than any discussions between us. I endeavored on all these occasions to make him sensible, by a temperate firmness, that my essential principles were not affected by his attacks, whilst I disclaimed every thing that had the character of bigotry, and made religion consist in ceremonials and "the traditions of men." I had to contend against the imputation of methodism of which I understood from Lord B. that Hobhouse had been the author to him. I wished to make my religion "more felt than seen" as evidenced in my forbearance & forgiveness—my resignation and disinterestedness—as "casting out fear" and bestowing peace & cheerfulness, even in an atmosphere of darkness & doubt, in opposition to his tenets of the universal *Necessity* of wretchedness. He told me that I was "pitied half over England," and named Hobhouse as the authority.[1] His Imagination dwelt so much upon the idea that he was *a fallen angel* that I thought it amounted nearly to derangement, and the tradition that Angels, having fallen from Heaven, had become enamoured of mortal women, struck him particularly, and he said he should compose upon it, and that *I* should be the woman, who was all perfection.

He told me, at the moment when a silent enthusiasm perhaps animated my countenance, that its expression was to him an argument for Immortality. Such exaggerated admiration was the language of love, and yet how could I believe myself beloved by him, who continually told me that we must separate, and he should only live with me, *if he could*, long enough to have an heir?

Could Byron have failed sometimes to feel depression at continual reminders that Annabella's reputation for "cleverness" was a myth and that he had married an intellectual prig of impregnable self-complacency? Must not his mischief have been tempted to test how far her humourlessness could carry her credulity? Confronted by her

[1] She was writing this in March 1817, a year after Hobhouse had loyally and actively supported Byron through the Separation. As will be seen from her own confession, she felt no hostility towards Hobhouse during the first months of her marriage.

pious expression of concentration on "forbearance & forgiveness" towards an errant inferior, may not a mood of mischief have been irritated into impatience and vituperation?

That her own behaviour might have contributed to his never occurred to her, for humility was absent from her character as from her conception of religion. Besides her suspicion that Lady Melbourne's influence inspired him "to correct me as a spoiled child," she "attributed part of his irritability to his pecuniary embarrassments & anxiety about Newstead":

> He himself endeavoured to impress on my mind at H[alnaby] two or three times that the business of Newstead was what made him so distracted—probably from a wish to remove the effect of his other intimations, a motive that actuated him also to say "If you won't mind my *words* we shall go on very well together," & he expatiated on his random way of talking. Not seeing through his motive at that time, I determined as much as possible to avoid reasoning from words that might be idle, however strange.
>
> He told me several times at Halnaby that he should leave to Augusta all the property in his power, seeming to wish I should feel this as an insult and desired I would write to William Hoar Esqre. of Durham to make his Will accordingly. I did so, but Mr. Hoar replied that it was necessary for him "to see Lord B." He appeared very anxious to know what I thought of the measure. I told him I considered it perfectly right, and I urged its final execution. He mentioned the intention again when we returned to Seaham before others, but did not take the trouble of consulting with Mr. Hoar in person.
>
> Suffering as I did at Halnaby from a conduct of which the causes were then so vague to my apprehension, I thought the kindest & most prudent part was that of concealing my misery from A. I was not sufficiently sure of her discretion or her interest for me to trust her with any thing that could have made mischief between him and me if communicated. He had also appeared wretched at the idea of her knowing his state of mind—so much so that he objected when I wished to send her his gloomy compositions, one of which was "O Mariamne."[1] I therefore employed the transient visits of Hope in making my correspondence with her as cheerful as possible, yet I believe my letters would show many of those half-jests which spring from dissembled anxiety.

Her letters have not survived, but Augusta's replies indicate that Annabella was more confidential than she remembered. She confided Byron's concern about Newstead, for Augusta wrote on 15th January:

> I cannot but feel that it is all *my* fault that *you* are distressed & uncomfortable about Newstead. Nevertheless I must own that I am more

[1] "Herod's Lament for Mariamne," the manuscript of which is dated "Halnaby, Jan. 13, 1815." The manuscript of "We sate down and wept by the waters" bears the same date, and a third of the *Hebrew Melodies*, "From the last hill that looks o'er thy once holy dome," was finally corrected and dated "Halnaby, Jan. 18, 1815."

than puzzled by what you tell me of B—— on that subject—half inclined to believe I am mistaken, or rather that HE is mistaken in thinking I know his "comical ways" better than most people.

Be this as it may, of course his happiness must be the first object. The "associations" are I conclude (& HOPE) connected with circumstances & events of a period when alas! he & I were seperated—perhaps you don't know that such was the case from the *end* of the *first* to about the twelfth year of his life, & for many after that we were little better than strangers. But I wander from my original subject—dear Newstead. My only comfort is that you have *heard* Mr. Hobhouse's (who is not *a Byron*) opinion too, which may perhaps just prevent your thinking me *une Insensée*. I cannot describe my feelings & affection for it, except by comparing them a little to what one feels for one's native land. I wish you had seen it which would have justified me a little more, but my regrets are of no consequence & when it is gone, I *will* "ever after hold my peace." This resolution has been made & broken thro' repeatedly already *because* the dear Abbey has been as often preserved almost miraculously . . . I am afraid my dear Sis I have interrupted your happiness & *that* vexes me—however the *motive* must be my consolation, & was to save you & B—— FUTURE REGRETS . . . I will quit this subject which makes me very melancholy for a more cheering one. How happy I shall be to see you both! if (as you throw out a hope) it is possible & probable you may come this way.

I can laugh at this distance even at the continuation of the "comical proceedings"—it is so like him to *try* & *persuade* people that *he is disagreable* & *all that*. Oh dear!!

Two years later Annabella commented:

He was always enraged by any attempts she made to dissuade him from selling Newstead, calling her "a fool." He said once, "*She* ought to know better." When he was disappointed about the sale of it—in London—he exclaimed "My intellect, my existence depend upon the sale of that place" with the pallid countenance of fixed despair. He told me it was a judgment upon him that he could not sell it—that the very reason which made him love it before he married, made him hate it now. This surely pointed to what had passed there between him & her. How strange she should not have apprehended it!

This was surely an instance of Annabella's over-reaching herself in her habit of drawing inferences. She seems to have supposed that Newstead was the scene of Augusta's seduction and subsequently a regular rendezvous for guilty meetings. In fact Augusta had visited Newstead only twice—in January 1814, when she was snowed up there with Byron, and for a month between 21st August and 20th September following—and both occasions were long after negotiations for its sale had begun. Byron's affection for Newstead dated from long before Augusta's visits—from the autumn and winter of 1808–9, when he and his Cambridge friends had imitated the monks of Medmenham and he had told Hanson, "I will never sell Newstead." Augusta knew more of his feelings than Annabella ever allowed herself to discover, as appears from her next letter of 18th January:

> When in the act of opening your letter this Morng., I made a most philosophical determination to read with becoming fortitude *the last dying speech & confession* of poor dear Newstead. You may therefore imagine a little of my hearts content at the *reprieve*. *My* head was also in a puzzle when I last wrote to you on this subject, but the more I reflect & remember, ye stronger is my conviction that Newstead was ONCE *most* dear to B—— & would be so again could he UNmake up his mind to the necessity of disposing it—it has really been *torn* from his heart & affections. If not prejudicial to *your* comfort & *his*, I bless Heaven for the delay that must take place in the sale . . . By the by, I hope the fit of *grumps* was not in consequence of any of *my* Sayings about it . . .

Augusta was right in thinking that Newstead was once dear to Byron and that he did not wish to sell it, but she was not at this time aware that Annabella's marriage settlement provided no ready money for the settlement of his debts and that the sale of Newstead was the only alternative to harassment by his creditors. It was because the sale was forced upon him by necessity against his inclination that he was irritated by arguments against it.

Annabella had also confided something about his *grumps*, for Augusta wrote in the same letter of the 18th:

> You cannot *Seriously* entertain a single doubt *I hope* about the IMPERTINENCE of writing "as if you had known me from your cradle." I wish I could convince you of the happiness your letters confer upon me . . . indeed My dear Sister I *feel* how much cause I have to be grateful for such a friend in My B's Wife—& such a Wife for him. "*What think'st thou*"—why I think & with *joy* that you are a most sagacious person, & have in one fortnight made yourself as completely Mistress of "the art of making B happy" as some others would in 20 years. To be sure, when that is understood the task is not difficult—*what think'st thou?* I will own to you my dear Sis *all my folly*, as it now is proved to have been—which was that you might *not* understand all his "comical ways," "façons de parler" & "grumps," and that such a *misunderstanding* would have made *you* unhappy, which he would soon have discovered & his own candid representations of his qualifications for domestic life would have had *beau Jeu*. But now I give my fears to the Wind, & I am sure you do right "to laugh away" "all anxieties" for not even *I* can know him better . . .

This shows subtlety as well as perception, especially as the correspondents had never met. Virtually echoing Byron's own warning that she should not "mind my *words*" and "his random way of talking," Augusta advised her plainly that laughter was the balm for his moods. This letter, like many others subsequently, endorsed Byron's opinion that "Nobody understands me but Augusta"—a remark which Annabella had evidently reported in the letter acknowledged by Augusta on the 15th.

In a third letter within a week she presumably reported Byron's further remark, "I shall never love anybody as well as her," for Augusta replied on 20th January:

All you say of Newstead is consolatory to me . . . I can perfectly understand all you tell me of B's *fits of vexation*. I am always grieved to think he is vexed. In this case however I can't help hoping all will ultimately be well. His *superstitions* are very amusing—if I was inclined to indulge them mine would be of a *contrary* nature . . .

My dear Sis, I wish I deserved half the kindness he feels & expresses towards me. I may think myself most fortunate that he has a Wife who is *not* "*affronted*" at such declarations as ye one you tell me of—for without disparagement to my two other *belle Sœurs*,[1] I should like (or rather I should *not* like) so see ye effect of such a one from *their* Spouses!!! . . . No Brother can ever consider me as B—— does, & you may imagine better than I can describe how he is loved in return—& his dear kind Wife who is so indulgent to "Guss" . . .

If Byron's behaviour was extraordinary—as, according to Annabella, it was—surely it was more than matched by her own in discussing it, during the course of a three weeks' honeymoon, with a woman she had never met! Impossible to a woman in love, her conduct was that of a spoilt child, accustomed to her parents' pampering and to the flattery of social inferiors. Like a spoilt child, if afflicted or mystified, she besought explanation and reassurance.

When Fanny Kemble spoke of "Lady Byron's beautiful power of silence," she did not know how many people had received Annabella's intimate confidence. During her pursuit of Byron she had confided in Lady Gosford, Selina Doyle, and possibly MM; when he first came to Seaham, she had consulted her mother and Dr. Fenwick about "his strange words & ways." Now, alone with her husband in a housefull of servants, while writing about him to a woman of whom she was already nourishing "suspicions," she forgot dignity and loyalty by confiding those suspicions to her maid:

The person who attended upon me at Halnaby was not the maid that was in my service during the whole time after I returned to Seaham till the conclusion of my separation—but a farmer's daughter, Jane Minns, then married, whom I had known from childhood, & whose faithful attachment & good sense had been sufficiently proved. One day when feelings of hopeless misery quite overpowered me, I expressed them to her, yet with

[1] The Duchess of Leeds and Lady Francis Osborne, wives of her elder half-brothers.

every possible reserve as to B's intentional cruelty towards me—but I told her I was sure there had been something most dreadful between him & his Sister which he never could recover. I imposed a silence which has been strictly kept.[1] Yet I afterwards bitterly reproached myself for having departed in this single instance from the duty of concealing a husband's misconduct.

Annabella thus recorded how she formed the suspicion about Byron and Augusta that she confided to her maid:

A few evenings after our marriage he took out some of my letters to him, previous to my engagement, when we corresponded on friendly terms—& showed me with rage & threats of revenge an expression in one of them which was in reply to his mention of sclf-condemning recollections—that I wished I could be the means of reconciling him to *his conscience*. He asked me what I had meant in a sort of frenzy, and reproached me bitterly for the pain I had inflicted upon him by refusing my consent for so long a time (This was a curious inconsistency, for he also bitterly reproached me for having married him!). I thought he would have proceeded to personal violence, and my first impulse was to disarm him by affection. He was sitting before the fire, and had his red portfolio by him. I found myself on my knees with my arms round his neck & said, "You forget we *are* married, I believe." This calmed him, and he said he had worked himself up to the feelings of that past time.

From the same portfolio he took out a letter of Lady M[elbourne]'s, expressing his admiration of her for having written it, and his sense of her friendliness . . . The letter in question was evidently written before his engagement, & its contents will now fix the date pretty nearly. He read me parts of it then, and parts of it again in London in the interval between A's first & second visit to us. I cannot now discriminate what passages I heard at these times respectively and from the partial communication at H[alnaby] I did not draw any conclusion as to the circumstances, though impressed with the vague idea of something horrible, but of the following contents I am certain.

Lady M. endeavours to dissuade him from the commission of some "atrocious crime," saying it was worse than any thing she had ever heard or known of. "It is a crime for which there is no salvation in this world

[1] Jane Minns's husband, a footman, was also present at Halnaby during the honeymoon. The *Newcastle Daily Chronicle* reported of an interview with her at the time of Harriet Beecher Stowe's revelations in 1869:

"Mrs. Minns was her constant companion and *confidante* through this painful period, and she does not believe that her ladyship concealed a thought from her. With laudable reticence, the old lady absolutely refuses to disclose the particulars of Lord Byron's misconduct at this time; she gave Lady Byron a solemn promise not to do so; but language would be wanting to express the indignation with which she repudiates the gross explanation which Mrs. Stowe has given of the matter. So serious, however, did Mrs. Minns consider the conduct of Lord Byron, that she recommended her mistress to confide all the circumstances to her father, Sir Ralph Milbanke, a calm, kind, and most excellent parent, and take his advice as to her future course. At one time Mrs. Minns thinks Lady Byron had resolved to follow her counsel and impart her wrongs to Sir Ralph, but on arriving at Seaham Hall, her ladyship strictly enjoined Mrs. Minns to preserve absolute silence on the subject, a course which she followed herself."

whatever there may be in the next." She tells him that whatever he may affect she knows how susceptible he is to opinion, and will he do that which must utterly destroy his character? She remonstrates with him on the cruelty of depriving of all future peace or happiness a woman who had hitherto, whether deservedly or not, preserved a good reputation—that he must always consider himself as the cause of her misery, and even if their distresses, after he had taken this fatal step, should arise from external causes, they would always reproach themselves for their reciprocal unhappiness—that he was "on the brink of a precipice, and if you do not retreat, you are lost for ever."

The occasion of the letter, as was proved by a context I cannot exactly remember, was a scheme he entertained of going away with the person in question (I know from him & her, and her friends were at the time acquainted with the circumstances that he thought of taking A—— with him to Sicily, and she had consented).

His comment on this letter of Lady M's when he read it to me the last time was "She is a good woman after all, for there are things she will stop at." He said that he had followed her advice *in part*, but not *altogether*—"Ah, I wish I had," with a look of anguish & horror. He told me Lady M. then encouraged his intrigue with Lady F[rances] W[ebster] because she was afraid he would get into this *worse* business.

Previously she had applauded his dislike of society as according with her own, but how far her habit of inference had distracted her from justice is suggested by her comment in this context:

He had before accounted for his dislike to society from an extreme susceptibility to what was said in conversation—that there was always something which jarred with his feelings—for which *conscience* may I believe be substituted justly.

Recollections of her honeymoon at Halnaby were renewed at intervals till the last year of her life, but the later her recollections, the more her memory of facts became clouded by her inferences.

Especially she developed in later years her own theories of Byron's religious opinions, as her grandson Lovelace observed:

After Lord Byron's death, Lady Byron became more and more inclined to think he had believed in the God of the Bible and to exaggerate some rather uncertain indications that he had been what Shelley called "hardly better than a Christian."

While the statements made during the last thirty years of her life reflect "the growth of theories insufficiently supported by facts," Lovelace justly remarked that "nevertheless they contain personal recollections worth recording and some impressions striking enough in spite of more or less distortion of the medium of transmission." One useful feature of her later recollections is in offering qualifying comment on her earlier statements, which, though factually more reliable, were written as indictments for possible use by lawyers.

In a rough draft written in 1816 she referred to Byron's self-consciousness of his deformed foot:

> With the dark predestinarianism, which early Calvinistic impressions, and later Oriental observations, had tended to infix in his mind, I perceived, immediately after my marriage, that a proudly mortifying consciousness of his personal defect was associated. He told me afterwards—in London—that he had once been reproached with it by his Mother, and that a remark which Mrs. C[haworth] had made upon it and which had been repeated to him, was the real cause of his abrupt manner of leaving her (This he has since described in "The Dream"), and he has said that he thought some allowance for it would be made to him at the Day of Judgment . . .
>
> At Halnaby, as at many times subsequently, he expressed a wish to revenge himself on Heaven for this malformation, & to consider himself justified in doing so by every kind of impiety. Together with his own insinuations (artful ones I *have* much reason to believe) of hereditary & constitutional derangement, this notion impressed me with some doubts of his Sanity. At least I supposed it *might* amount to one of the hallucinations which are described by Darwin in his chapter on Diseased Volition . . .
>
> I thought it desirable to break through the morbid reserve which, tho' he constantly *alluded* to the subject, prevented him from ever naming it directly, or suffering me to apprehend it openly, and by degrees I effected my object so that he would at one time talk familiarly of his "little foot," & tell me of the sensations of bodily uneasiness it habitually occasioned him.

Doubtless as showing Byron in too sympathetic a light, she omitted this passage from the draft prepared for the lawyers:

> The nature of his impious language at Halnaby was this—& it was always uttered under a visible influence of superstitious terror, which acted, as fear always did upon him, to inflame his fury—That God was a malignant spirit, delighting in the sufferings of his creatures . . . that he was himself created only to exist in torture, and foredoomed to evil. In this fatalism concerning himself personally, he was most anxious to believe—
>
> "And half mistook for fate, the acts of will."
>
> But he lamented to me once in London that he *could* not resign himself implicitly to that tenet as the Turks did. His gloomy creed of predestination had however an earlier origin in the Calvinistic doctrine of Election amongst the Scotch, and his was the pernicious bigotry which—by depriving God of his best attributes, those of a Benevolent Being—creates the wish to annul & the resolution to deny his existence . . .
>
> He often spoke of a mysterious necessity for his return to the East, and vindicated the Turks with a spirit of Nationality, admiring above all their

complete predestinarianism. He would say "The East—ah, there it is," . . . and he has two or three times intimated to me that he abjured his religion there. In the autumn in London, he said with a shudder of conscious remembrance, "I was very *near* becoming a Mussulman." He preferred the Turkish opinions, manners & dress in all respects to ours. This idea of his conversion to their faith having occurred to me at Halnaby, derived some confirmation from his composing at Seaham that part of the Siege of Corinth which relates to Alp's assumption of the Turban, and also from a paper which he then wrote as the commencement of a Critique upon Leake's work, afterwards reviewed in the Edinr. by Hobhouse.[1]

Reading this revised draft in 1836, she forgot what she had written in the rough draft twenty years before, and commented:

In looking over these pages, to see how far they would give to a Stranger the true colour of our life at Halnaby, I find that I have not spoken of the morbidly tenacious feeling he had as to his lameness. There was a connection in his Imagination between that & his Predestination to Evil, or his being an Exiled Angel.

These ideas were not suggested to his mind by chance-circumstances, but appeared to be deeply rooted there. There was a bitter feeling towards his Mother in regard to his Foot—I could not understand why, & did not like to ask questions. Some boys had early tormented him about his deformity.

On the other hand, she asserted categorically in 1850, "He was no Sceptic," though she had written in 1816:

His theories of Scepticism were various according to the state of his spirits—after drinking brandy, even in a small quantity, he was outrageously profane. To this I do not remember any exception, but he did not drink any thing but wine at H[alnaby] except twice I think. I was not then aware of his propensity to intoxication, & one evening when he expressed a wish for some brandy, I went to fetch some French B[randy] that was in my Dressing Case. He seemed pleased, & said it was like a good wife—or words to that effect—desiring me with a sort of jesting malice to tell A[ugusta] that I gave him Brandy, from which I inferred that she had objected to his having it, and was led to be more cautious in future. The idea was not long after confirmed to me by himself when he told me that he had been for the last two years in the habit of this pernicious indulgence—that the Corsair was written in about ten days, or rather nights, during which he sat up drinking brandy & water till four or five in the morning, and the last night was reduced to such a state of nervous debility that he cried like a child—which perhaps suggested the passage,

"His Mother's weakness crept
To those wild eyes which, like an infant's, wept."

[1] The manuscript of the beginning of this review of Leake's *Researches in Greece* was among the Byron mss. delivered by Annabella's trustees to her grandson. Hobhouse's article appeared in the *Edinburgh Review* of February 1815.

Adapting this statement in her "Narrative" of March 1817, she substituted "inebriation, either convivial or solitary," for "this pernicious indulgence," and added:

> Unlike Cassio, who, in a passage Lord B. was fond of repeating, is made to pray when he is drunk, *his* violence on all subjects, but particularly Religion, was always encreased by Brandy.

Yet, even so soon as eighteen months after the events, her memory of facts seems open to suspicion, for events suggest that it was not at Halnaby, but subsequently at Seaham, where she discovered Byron's weakness for brandy.

10

SEAHAM AND SIX MILE BOTTOM

21st January—28th March 1815

"We shall be most happy to see you & Lady B. on the day you have fixed," wrote Sir Ralph to Byron on 12th January. Byron tried to escape the visit to Seaham, probably on the pretext of looking for a house in London for them to live in, and Annabella recorded:

> He fixed the day for leaving Halnaby himself—the 20th of Janry, that his birth-day, the 22nd, might be kept at Seaham. But as the day approached he declared he would not go, and wanted me to go alone, or to remain at Halnaby whilst he went to London. To these proposals I resolutely objected, and after trying to move him by every argument to his better feelings, which I found ineffectual, I represented to him how strange it would appear to every one on his part. This succeeded, but he insisted on postponing his journey till Saturday the 21st, because it was unlucky to travel on a Friday. I appeared a little amused by the superstition, and he assumed greater earnestness on the subject, alleging as one reason that it was the Mahomedan Sabbath.

This difficulty she had immediately reported to Augusta, who wrote on the 20th:

> I do not wonder at your unwillingness to part with B. I am sure I should feel ye same, were I his wife, & it appears to me that he would only be still more plagued (as you say) in Town & without *his Rib* to comfort him.

Annabella recalled that, on leaving Halnaby, Byron "said in the carriage":

> "I think you now know pretty well what subjects to avoid touching upon," and expressed an opinion that we *might* "go on together."

At Seaham Mary Anne Clermont was with Annabella's parents to greet them and long afterwards recalled the bride's changed appearance after her honeymoon: she had gone to Halnaby "looking like a flower," but "returned so changed in three weeks, lookd as if she cared for nothing."

Mrs. Clermont had left the Milbankes' service after nearly twenty-two years in the early summer of 1811, presumably because long familiarity had given her an authority which Annabella at nineteen found embarrassing and unseemly. As she herself related, "I had been for several years in possession of a sufficient independence fallen to me by the lamented death of my only brother"; the legacies received on the deaths of both her mother and her brother she gave to Sir Ralph Milbanke in return for an annuity which was continued by Annabella after her father's death. She had since visited Lady Milbanke "every year for some months, as her Companion, to play at Chess, read &c.," and impressed Byron favourably when he met her for the first time at Seaham before the wedding, as Annabella recorded:

> When I first mentioned Mrs. C. to Lord B. I said that I thought myself indebted to her for always speaking the truth to me. He replied—then he had rather she should be my friend than his. . . . He invariably expressed a favourable opinion of her, and *earnestly pressed me* to take her with us when we married. This I declined, as I should have done *any* third person.

Remarking that she was "honoured with the friendship" of Annabella's parents, Mrs. Clermont stated when Moore's biography of Byron was published:

> I was treated by Lord Byron with more than the ordinary degree of politeness I might have expected from any gentleman whom their daughter had married. I never had at any time personal cause for dislike to Lord Byron quite the reverse, from the hour of his marriage when he pressed me to go with them to Halnaby until after Lady Byron was at Kirkby.

Byron was always kind to servants and social inferiors—a quality that would commend him to Judith Milbanke—and there is no reason to doubt Mrs. Clermont's statements of fact, which find frequent endorsement in the evidence of others. With a touchiness inevitable in her socially equivocal position, she was subsequently wounded and resentful when Annabella, having admitted her to too familiar confidence, excluded her from further intimacy, but she remained always devoted. Her devotion, together with the social position that enabled her to listen to conversations in which she could take no part, intensified her observation, as she remarked to Annabella on 30th March 1830:

> I often am surprised when talking with you to find how much that was said and done in that 1815 you seem to have forgot, it seems to have made a much stronger impression upon my brain for it seems to have erased most that had before passed and also to have filled it so that it can contain no more.
>
> I had before a retentive memory and a pretty quick comprehension, but since that time I know not half what I knew before . . . while I

could repeat every Word and relate every circumstance connected with you at any moment.

In the presence of her parents Byron usually behaved with what Annabella called "his company-kindness"; he explained his changed demeanour when alone with her by asserting "that he always loved me better when any one was present, because *then* he might not *seem* to love me so well"—

> of this I was so completely the dupe that till a very late period I was rather gratified than estranged by his company-kindness, as if it were the proof of some latently existing feeling which he would not disown to others, though so often to me.

Augusta's replies indicate that Annabella reported progress to her every two or three days. "You cannot be more *delighted* than I am that he is 'delightful' & *at home* at Seaham," wrote Augusta on 26th January, and hearing that Byron had snatched Judith's wig from her head in an after-dinner game, she wrote on the 28th:

> I have scarcely recovered the fit of laughing I was seized with on reading the account of your *frolic*—oh dear! I only wish some people whom I know & many others whom I *don't* know could have peeped in at the door —to have been convinced that *Owls* can frolic sometimes, & moreover that *B* can play the fool.
>
> But pray how is Lady Milbanke—I fully expect to hear that she has at least a very bad cold in her *head!*

In her statements Annabella was prudently decorous, following Pepys's example in resorting to shorthand when recording remarks or incidents which she regarded as "indelicate," but at this early stage of her married life she did not hesitate to mention her sensual inclinations, as Augusta remarked in this letter of 28th January:

> I am glad B's spirits do not decrease with THE *Moon.* I rather suspect he rejoices at the discovery of your "ruling passion for mischief in private".

She wrote again on 30th January:

> I am so glad to hear B—— is *Spoilt* at S—— because he would have it nobody could spoil him but me—& (alas!) I never could half enough, or as much as he deserved. God bless you my dear, kind, Sister.

Recalling events in the following year, Annabella wrote:

> At Seaham I do not remember having felt any strong suspicions respecting A—— except once. It was after we had been making bout-rimés

together in the drawing room with that sort of mirth which seeks to jest away bitter truths.[1] The accidental coincidences were very singular & he desired me to send the verses to A——. I said I would distinguish his lines & mine by crosses. He turned pale—and entreated me not, for I should "frighten her to death." I had before casually remarked these crosses in their letters, and in one of his to her when he was at Seaham first, which he took out to read me one passage . . . He then told me he never wrote anything to A—— about *love*. I did not much consider the reason.

In a statement of March 1816 on Byron's relationship with Augusta, asserting "That he has intimated a dreadful secret, and a cause of Remorse between them," she recorded, "He has signified that the crosses + + in their letters referred to this dreadful mystery," and after relating the incident at Seaham, she added:

He wore a broach of her hair on which were three of these crosses, and she had a similar one of his. These have been often alluded to by him with the same intimations of their nature—and a letter of hers to him, written before my marriage, contains such marks in very questionable situations.[2]

On 2nd February Augusta wrote, "you have not yet heard *all* MY woes," but there broke off because "they have just called for my letter." In reply to Annabella's inquiry about this cryptic remark, she wrote on 5th February:

Oh! my "anxieties" are not about B's happiness for on that score thank Heaven they are at rest—he has all the *essentials* to make him happy & tho I do so love him that all his little uneasinesses disturb me almost more than they do him, yet I feel & know that from some no one can be exempt —& I hope these minor calamities will soon cease.

The "minor calamities" were the necessity for selling Newstead, the pressing demands of creditors if Newstead continued unsold, and the problem of finding somewhere to live—for Byron declined the Milbankes' offer of Halnaby as a temporary residence and was presumably as reluctant to confine himself at Newstead without distractions from Annabella's company. Augusta's reactions contrasted with those of

[1] Presumably Annabella sent the best of the verses to Augusta, who acknowledged receipt of some bout-rimés on 30th January, but a few were preserved and endorsed by Annabella, "Bout-rimés Nonsense at Seaham 1815." In this example the first and last lines are in Byron's hand, the middle two in Annabella's:

My wife's a vixen spoilt by her Mamma
Oh how I pity poor hen-pecked Papa
The Lord defend us from a Honey Moon
Our cares commence our comforts end so soon.

[2] Presumably the letter postmarked 15 Dec. 1814, given on pp. 243–4. On 15th October 1816 Byron wrote to Augusta of "original love-letters and verses of Lucretia de Borgia & Cardinal Bembo" he had examined at Milan:

And pray what do you think is one of her *signatures?*—why this + a Cross—which she says "is to stand for her name &c." Is not this amusing? (*Astarte*, p. 275).

Lady Melbourne, who wrote on 7th February in reply to Annabella's attempt to discover if Byron had confided more to her than to herself:

> You are wrong when You Suppose that he has given me any information respecting yr future intentions, or about Newstead. I am in a total state of ignorance, & dont guess who you are in treaty with, or with whom the contract is to be signed of which you talk . . . His Letters to me are extremely merry & gay, but as to business, I dont think it is a Subject he is ever inclined to enter upon.

Apparently Annabella had commented adversely on the confidences by George Germain's bride to Lady Asgill, for Lady Melbourne rebuked her:

> I think you are a little hard upon Mrs. Germain, if she feels happy why should she not say so. Because it may not last in its full brightness—I think that, "sufficient for ye day is the evil thereof" & it is quite time enough to think of any calamity when it happens instead of foreseeing it. Besides you are more interested than you are aware of in this discussion—for I presume You will not condemn Ld B—— when he expresses his happiness in his Letters to his Friends, which I have heard from Chatsworth, where Mr. Moore was who had received them.[1] Therefore do have more toleration for Mrs. Germain, she certainly must feel great contentment at not being tormented by her Mother who used her very ill. I have just been interrupted by a Bride who is something in ye same Situation as Mrs. Germain, & shews it in her Looks & appearance. This is Ly Charlotte Howard—it is ye common opinion that her Mother was severe & unkind to her—& she certainly does not appear Shy & alarm'd as she did when following her into an Assembly but seems very pleasant & conversible.

The reference to Lady Charlotte Howard, *née* Leveson-Gower, who had been Byron's choice for a wife before his engagement to Annabella, lent a feline barb to the rebuke which was a little smoothed by reference to Sir Ralph's speech at Durham "agst ye renewal of the property Tax", with the comment:

> You must now begin to think of these things—no Young Lady before marriage knows what a World of trouble she entails upon herself by accept-

[1] Byron had written to Moore at Chatsworth on 19th January:

So, you want to know about milady and me? But let me not, as Roderick Random says, "profane the chaste mysteries of Hymen"—damn the word, I had nearly spelt it with a small *h*. I like Bell as well as you do (or did, you villain!) Bessy—and that is (or was) saying a great deal.

He wrote again on 2nd February after hearing that Moore had left Chatsworth:

Since I wrote last, I have been transferred to my father-in-law's, with my lady and my lady's maid, etc., etc., etc., and the treacle-moon is over, and I am awake, and find myself married. My spouse and I agree to—and in—admiration. Swift says "no *wise* man ever married;" but, for a fool, I think it the most ambrosial of all possible future states. I still think one ought to marry upon *lease*; but am very sure I should renew mine at the expiration, though next term were for ninety and nine years.

—*Letters and Journals*, iii, 172, 175–6.

> ing a Husband, & yr determination to be the best of Wives will make you feel it in all its force.

Apparently Annabella concluded that the tart tone of admonition was inspired by her aunt's pique at being left "in a total state of ignorance" about their plans, so she invited her assistance in finding them a suitable home in London.

This was her expedient to avoid Byron's going himself in search of a house, as she related:

> He wished to leave me at Seaham, and go to the South alone—a project he had also entertained at Halnaby. I resisted it, because I was convinced that our only mutual hope was in the constant exercise of my watchful affection, and I had flattered myself at that time that he was becoming more kind—at least that he felt I was a comfort to him in some respects, if merely from habit, of which he is so much the creature. He was not content if I was away from him, except on the "black days" (Vide a subsequent letter of A's [22nd February]) when he would shut himself up in frenzied gloom.

Besides his financial worries, Byron was bored, in spite of his denial to Lady Melbourne on 2nd February:

> The *Moon* is over—but Bell & I are as lunatic as heretofore. She does as she likes, and don't bore me—and we may win the Dunmow flitch of bacon for any thing I know. Mamma and Sir Ralph are also very good, but I wish the last would not speak his speech at the Durham meeting above once a week after its first delivery. I won't betray you if you will only write me something worth betraying.

To Moore he wrote on the same day:

> Upon this dreary coast, we have nothing but county meetings and ship-wrecks . . . My papa, Sir Ralpho, hath recently made a speech at a Durham tax-meeting; and not only at Durham, but here, several times since after dinner. He is now, I believe, speaking it to himself (I left him in the middle) over various decanters, which can neither interrupt him nor fall asleep.

He added a significant postscript:

> I must go to tea—damn tea. I wish it was Kinnaird's brandy, and with you to lecture me about it.

On 10th February he informed Moore, "I have a plan of travel into Italy . . . If I take my wife, you can take yours; and if I leave mine, you may do the same."

With Annabella reporting his moods and pedantically requesting their explanation, Augusta must have read between the lines. Fearing perhaps that he might rebel against Annabella's possessiveness and take flight to her, thereby giving her reason to nourish grievance against herself, she dropped a hint on 26th January that they might together visit her in remarking that her husband was away:

> I am still in a *widowed* state, which makes our habitation one degree more capacious. B. will have described its dimensions and I hoped you would have arrived during this period—whenever you do, I need not say how welcome you will be.

Annabella recalled that she "Proposed to B—— that we should occupy one of the houses to be let near Newmarket for a time as S[ix] M[ile] B[ottom] was so small, and the owners so poor that we could not be received without inconvenience." Augusta discussed on 2nd February the possibilities of finding a "Castle" for them, adding,

> Don't imagine from my discussing this part of the plan first that *my "hospitality"* would be easily or soon tired of such guests—but ye truth is that your patience or B's would incur some risk of being so from the inconveniences & small dimensions of this dwelling . . . We have *one small* spare bedroom which I would occupy myself resigning my own for the sake of its size & quiet to you and B, & *if* my Sposo was absent his dressing room wd be devoted to yr Abigail, & B should have a *drawing room* (not in general used) to dress in.

On 8th February Augusta wrote:

> I can easily believe all you tell me of the melancholy state of *female hearts* where ever B—— makes his appearance. I think I see him behaving VERY PRETTILY—it *is* well indeed! you are not given to Jealousy. Above all I am pleased that your Father & Mother *approve*. Oh! I have had a letter to day from ye North (besides yours) telling me so much of the charms of my too "charming Brother."
>
> There is nothing on earth so delightful to me, as to hear of or read praises of him.

She added in a postscript:

> I am so glad he allows himself to dine—*improvement* the first!
> I am sure *you* will effect all you wish.
> I shall expect shortly to hear of his *rising with ye Lark*.

The improvements had been halted by the incident on the night of the 5th described next day by Byron to Lady Melbourne:

> last night was nearly *my* last—as thus. Thanks to my father in law & your worshipful brother's collieries & coals, my dressing room fire was so diabolically pregnant with charcoal that I was taken almost to Ladylike

fainting—& if Bell had not in the nick of time postponed old Nick for the present and sluiced me with Eau de Cologne and all sorts of waters besides, you might now have been repairing your latest suit of black to look like new for your loving nephew . . . Bell herself has not been quite well since with her exertions. . . it was in bed that I was overwhelmed (though the Charcoal was in the next—my dressing room) and how her lungs withstood it I can't tell, but so it is—she is alive, and thanks to her so am I.

Lady Melbourne replied on the 11th with sober admonitions about the dangers of vapour from sea-coal, but Augusta had already replied on the 10th to Annabella's account of the accident:

What could possess B. to put out his Fire? It is astonishing how active the Lords of the Creation are in doing *Mischief*. I think you must have been frightened at his *Stupor*. Oh! yes his own account of this exploit would I daresay be comic, but dearest Annabella don't allow him to play the fool any more in this way, & do hide YOUR *Brandy Bottle*—I suspect he had stolen it again! But to be serious—I am unhappy at your hint about his health. You must have discovered that his ways of treating it are not what one could exactly desire—at least they used to fidgit me sadly tho' as I found remonstrances ineffectual I ceased to remonstrate. You must not mind all his ideas about his "*predestined*" Misfortunes. I must tell you that it is a family failing in ye *Bs* to have *uneven* spirits. I have even remarked it in a much stronger degree in some of us than in B—— and when the *glooms* prevail I too well know the effects.

Dearest Sis, tell me soon how B—— is—& his cold & your cold—& *all about you both.*

Augusta's reactions to Annabella's account of the incident indicate that its effects on Byron were more serious than he suggested in his letter to Lady Melbourne, and the account related in one of her statements seems to reflect what Annabella must have written at the time to Augusta:

His anxiety about his health approached to valetudinarianism, yet was perhaps exceeded by the alarms of his personal vanity, and I have seen him seriously affected by the idea of his hair going grey, or a single tooth becoming blemished. When he thought himself unwell, or in danger of two or three complaints which terrified him, he always had recourse to me for support & cheering—and after feeling his pulse gravely, I used to laugh away his apprehensions, unless I thought that they might be instrumental in deterring him from injurious excesses. The occasion on which I saw him most alarmed was at S[eaham]. He had thrown water upon his dressing-room fire, in a rage at its burning too fiercely, and sat there for some time afterwards before he came to bed. After he had lain down a few minutes he appeared very oppressed—fainting & suffocated. He said he was sure he was going to have his Patras fever again—that he had had such a fever three times I think—at an interval of years which had now elapsed since the last attack. He then talked of futurity with frantic terror, but at the same time with "impenitent Remorse"—said he would defy Heaven & earth to the last—that as he had lived, so he died—that he asked no mercy &c—with many blasphemous expressions. I persuaded him to get up, & led him to a chair where he turned quite giddy, and his head dropped on his chest apparently without recollection. By the application of Eau de Cologne he was recovered, and in the morning seemed unusually sobered by the recollection of his apprehended danger—and asked with a mixture of real earnestness & assumed levity about the strange feelings he had manifested.

Augusta recognised the symptoms of which Annabella had evidently been unaware till she was warned to hide her brandy bottle.

As a result of this incident both Byron and Annabella had colds, and Mrs. Clermont recalled:

Lady Byrons whole attention was evidently employed in endeavouring to keep him from shewing ill humour and although he sometimes appeared personally fond of her he never seemed to consider her wishes or comfort in any respect. In consequence of having caught a violent cold by attending upon him when he had been nearly suffocated from throwing water upon the fire in his dressing room after she was in bed, she was so ill as to go to bed about four o'clock having told me she would get Lord B to make her excuse for not dining with the company. I was soon after surprized by finding her again up although looking very Ill. She said Lord B was so angry at my being in bed & said he would not go to dinner that I was obliged to get up & must go down & bear it as well as I can. She went every day into the room where he breakfasted & frequently left it in tears & evident unhappiness indeed I hardly ever saw her after they had been together that she was not in that state.

Annabella soon forgot how much of her troubles she had reported to Augusta, for, reading over Augusta's letters of this time for the purpose of making out her case against her, she noted, "It appears that I had not perfectly observed my rule of not writing to A—— in moments of depression." On 13th February Augusta wrote:

"Alas!" indeed! "Naughty B"! as the children used to say when he affronted them. I am not many degrees removed from a fit of despair at his *untoward* ways.

After relating the progress of her efforts to find them a house near Newmarket, she continued:

I am so glad to hear my dearest B—— is better & that he has been persuaded to breathe the fresh air. You could not give me a stronger proof of *your influence* than this. I have long thought air & exercise would be of use to him. I wish you would by & bye persuade him to ride. I wonder my dearest A—— that you don't think me (but perhaps you *do*) the most troublesome creature on earth! forget all I have said if it torments you, & attribute it to my anxiety & love for him, & then I think you will also forgive me.

Again on the 15th:

My dearest Annabella—You are only too good to indulge me by granting all my requests. I am afraid to reflect whether they are always reasonable ones. 100,000,000 thanks for your account of dearest B. Your opinion is exactly what mine has been this year & half. I am quite convinced that if he would condescend to eat & drink & sleep *like other people* he would feel ye good effects—but you know his way is to fast till he is famished & then *devour* more than his stomach in that *weak* state can bear—& *so on*—but I really do hope your wise & judicious endeavors will bring about a reformation on those points. I can fancy the Conjugal race—& only hope for *your* sake that you have not Such *Hills* as there are at Hastings—I never shall forget his *tearing* up them & my vain & weak endeavors to follow![1]

Apparently it was of the period while the "glooms" prevailed and they were both suffering from colds after the incident of the dressing-room fire that Annabella recalled:

The first time I remember his mentioning Thyrza by name was at Seaham. When he was talking over the names he had given to the personages of his poems, he said, "I took the name of Thyrza from Gessner—She was Abel's wife"—and his tone of mysterious agitation precluded further enquiry, for I never had the disposition of Caleb Williams to kindle a consuming flame in the visible darkness of Suspicion. Another night (for he was always more open then than in the day) he said—after some expressions of affection which I hoped were genuine, though I felt all the misery by which they were overwhelmed—

"I think I love you—better even than Thyrza"—

but he lamented that he could not feel as he had once felt—and about the same time composed at midnight after drinking brandy & water the lines,

[1] Byron's spells of drastic dieting were inspired by his tendency rapidly to put on weight when he was not taking regular vigorous exercise. Samuel Rogers told a story of how Byron dined with him for the first time:

When we sat down to dinner, I asked Byron if he would take soup? "No; he never took soup."—Would he take some fish? "No; he never took fish."—Presently I asked if he would eat some mutton? "No; he never ate mutton."—I then asked if he would take a glass of wine? "No; he never tasted wine."—It was now necessary to inquire what he *did* eat and drink; and the answer was, "Nothing but hard biscuits and soda-water." Unfortunately, neither hard biscuits nor soda-water were at hand; and he dined upon potatoes bruised down on his plate and drenched with vinegar . . . Some days after, meeting Hobhouse, I said to him, "How long will Lord Byron persevere in his present diet?" He replied, "Just as long as you continue to notice it."—I did not then know, what I now know to be a fact,—that Byron, after leaving my house, had gone to a Club in St. James's Street, and eaten a hearty meat-supper.

Rogers had a reputation to sustain as a raconteur. There is in fact abundant evidence that Byron frequently indulged in spells of drastic dieting on dry biscuits and soda-water, and such irregularities of diet must have accentuated the effects when he resorted to brandy.

"O there's not a joy"[1] &c. After that kind assurance which gave me the hope of some future good from my own devotion to his welfare, he added that if he could get rid of the past he would be good—that he believed there was some pleasure in it after all, but he never could be a free agent again. And I think he *then* quoted—as he has since done more than once—the words of Lord Littleton, "I have been too bad ever to be good." "If I had known you since I was 5 years old, I might have been happy." When I endeavoured to represent to him the redeemability of all the past, my arguments & persuasions seemed to have no effect because he thought me incapable of conceiving the oppression of his conscience—"What can *you* know (or what can a *good woman* know) of strong passions &c."—and yet he was often on the brink of trying the effect of confession upon me.

In the same statement, and apparently of the same period, Annabella recalled:

He told me he had never read over the last Stanzas of C[hilde] H[arold] since they were written. He alluded to those which have the character of despair, occasioned I believe by the death of Thyrza, & some remorseful recollections (from what causes I cannot tell, but they were plainly such) embittered & perpetuated his grief . . . He mentioned Thyrza to me but two or three times, but I felt that several associations recalled that being to his mind—& always with the deepest emotion. The mention of *consumption* of its delusive bloom—"yes, I have seen that"—would he say in a tone that "echoed to the heart as from its own." Of fair hair—I thought that in a large collection of hair which he once showed me, there was a beautiful tress of Thyrza's by the feeling with which he regarded it. He then said he never loved but two women personally, and added that Mrs C[haworth] was *not* one—in a tone of some bitterness.

In another part of the same statement:

To return to Thyrza—He talked to me of her another time in London—at the period when A[ugusta] was absent, for I wrote it to her, said that he believed now she was gone, his breast was the sole depositary of that secret—that he had never mentioned her name. He described *her* beauty as he has described beauty in the abstract—told me of the emotion with which he used to expect the hour of meeting, when he would walk up & down till he almost fainted, & said he was sure that such a state of excitation, if circumstances had not put an end to it, must have destroyed him. He spoke of the encreasing induration of his feelings—that he could not

[1] There's not a joy the world can give like that it takes away,
When the glow of early thought declines in Feeling's dull decay;
'Tis not on Youth's smooth cheek the blush alone, which fades so fast,
But the tender bloom of heart is gone, ere Youth itself be past.

Sending these "Stanzas for Music" to Moore on 2nd March 1815, Byron wrote, "I feel merry enough to send you a sad song." A Harrow friend, the fourth Duke of Dorset, was killed by a fall from his horse on 14th February, and Byron told Moore on 8th March that these stanzas were inspired by "the death of poor Dorset—and the recollection of what I once felt, and ought to have felt now, but could not." A year later, in the midst of the Separation proceedings, on 8th March 1816, he reminded Moore of these stanzas "as being the truest, though the most melancholy, I ever wrote."

now feel even for her as he had done. He had heard of her being well at Malta on his return from Greece, and at his arrival in England he learned her death. Whether he saw her corpse I never ascertained—his descriptions of death have inclined me to imagine so, but yet I think the fact would have been mentioned to me, or would have appeared more decidedly in the poems at the end of C[hilde] H[arold].

In the hour of partial tenderness which I have described as passing between us at Seaham, when he named Thyrza, he said—as in reference to myself—that to him one of the most convincing reasons for believing in Eternity was that we never *could* LOVE *enough* in this state of being—that we could not mingle "soul in soul." This is beautifully expressed in the Hebrew Melody. He had written it out for me, before I married—with this comment, made evidently as an experiment upon my feelings, "*perhaps* I was thinking of you when I wrote that."

The Hebrew Melody to which she referred was "Oh! snatched away in beauty's bloom," the manuscript of which she endorsed, "Given me at Seaham before my Marriage." But another of the *Hebrew Melodies*, a manuscript which she endorsed "Seaham 1815," seems to have been inspired by the state of mind in which Byron confided to her these reflections on Thyrza:

Were my bosom as false as thou deem'st it to be,
I need not have wandered from far Galilee;
It was but abjuring my creed to efface
The curse which, thou say'st, is the crime of my race.

If the bad never triumph, then God is with thee!
If the slave only sin—thou art spotless and free!
If the Exile on earth is an Outcast on high,
Live on in thy faith—but in mine I will die.

I have lost for that faith more than thou canst bestow,
As the God who permits thee to prosper doth know;
In his hand is my heart and my hope—and in thine
The land and the life which for him I resign.

Seeking an excuse for being unable to feel for his wife the tenderness or passion which she expected and which he himself wished to feel, "he lamented that he could not feel as he had once felt," and drawing on his fancy to devise the story of a lost love about the effigy of Thyrza, he worked himself into such a state of Wertherish self-pity as he had expressed when news of Edleston's death followed closely upon the deaths of his mother and Matthews. Such a woman as Augusta would have recalled him from the past to the present, reminding him in tenderness and laughter that he had only just passed his twenty-seventh birthday and might still expect to experience more joys and sorrows than those he lamented of the past. But Annabella had never loved

Byron, because she had had no means of getting to know him. She was in love with her own conception of the author of *Childe Harold* and pedantically intent on diagnosing his troubles so that she could reform his character and restore him to the path of righteousness. The spoilt child had never before suffered rebuff, and finding herself baffled, herself resorted to self-pity, while Byron, realising that she accepted all he said with unimaginative seriousness, piled on the agony in striking attitudes before the distorting mirror of her limited perception.

Mrs. Clermont asserted that, during their stay at Seaham, "it was then impossible that I should not have seen and heard enough to make fear for the happiness of Lady Byron."

> Her parents must have felt the same, but there are sometimes apprehensions of so fearful a nature that we dare not communicate them even to our most intimate friends, and this was probably the case with them, at least I know they did not speak upon the subject. Once only Sir Ralph Milbanke did express to me his doubts of Lord Byron's affection for his Daughter—(Lady Milbanke was not present).

In 1846 Mrs. Clermont enlarged on this statement to Dr. Bence-Jones, who recorded:

> Her father during their stay saw what he did not like & one day said to Mrs. C., He persecuted her to marry him & I believe he only married her to persecute her—if it is so he shall have my dying curse.

In her earlier statement Mrs. Clermont continued:

> No remark was at any time made upon what he [Byron] said by her parents, and Lady Milbanke shewed the most unremitting and kind attention to what is termed his excentricities,—not only during the time of their stay in her house, but also during the whole time of their connection, as I could shew by many instances within my knowledge and that of others indeed.
>
> I am persuaded that Lady Milbanke liked Lord Byron, and would have had for him the affection of a mother, had he not made it impossible. Sir Ralph Milbanke I think very soon did not like him, but that was only to be discovered by those who were well acquainted with his usual manner.

She reported to Bence-Jones:

> He could live on nothing but fish & two grooms were constantly looking for it. He said he was starved. One time when with her parents & Mrs C she received a note which she gave him to read. It was from a lawyer [Hoar] to say he must see him before he made his will. He then abused her asking if he had not told the lawyer plainly what he wanted—to give all he had in the world to his sister.

Yet the "glooms" seem to have been much relieved when Byron recovered from his cold, for, after her reference to "the Conjugal race" on 15th February, Augusta wrote on the 19th:

> I am but just recovering from one of *B*'s fits of laughing at the account of "Duck & Devil"—Oh Dear!!! I am so glad to hear of his continuance in "well-doing", & cannot sufficiently praise you for having brought about such improvements. After having been so liberal of my approbation I cannot resist saying that I am also glad poor "Guss" is not quite forgotten —altho' it must be confessed that she is introduced sometimes very mal-à-propos[1]—or rather that she *would* be—to any less indulgent *Rib* & *Sis* than you are. Oh! that I *could* see him "jumping & squeaking on the sands"!

Revisiting Seaham in 1818, Annabella wrote:

> I mount on the craggy brow where he stood. Are the shadows of my young days flitting around in the sea-spray?

Many years later she added:

> and *his*, who was sometimes a wild mirthful boy when climbing the rugged rocks & defying me to follow him in scrambling.

Later still, in 1853:

> There was a Crag, called the "Featherbed", on which I have stood, with more than one, long since gone:— Sir Samuel Romilly had planted his foot on that very same jutting out, & at high tide insulated rock (sketch made by Mrs. Jameson), from which Byron afterwards looked upon a solitude shared only by myself. He became a boy sometimes, in scenes so remote from all painful associations, & would defy me to follow him in scrambling. The sight of a human being was always a check to his lighter mood, & brought on a gloomy and suspicious temper.

This eccentricity of Byron's, suggesting painful self-consciousness but surely no symptom of insanity, provides an example of Annabella's inclination to magnify trifles into portents, for she included it among Byron's "principal insane ideas" in a statement to Dr. Baillie when doubting his sanity the following January:

> He has a horror of being observed by any eye to which he is not accustomed, and in the Country when I forced him to walk with me, he would turn pale & tremble if he were to pass any one on the road—and hide himself if possible—if not he would stand still till the person were gone, or run past him.

[1] Appending this and others of Augusta's letters to her Narrative of 1817, Annabella noted: "I had told her in the letter to which this is an answer of the preference he so often expressed of herself to me—a strong proof that I at that time hoped it was innocent, for otherwise I could not have named it."

Augusta's letter of 21st February reveals that Annabella had reported further outdoor exploits, as well as Byron's condescending to play parlour games in the evenings:

> Your "ramble-scramble tumble-cum-jumble" must have been delightful & I wish I could have been of the party, to have helped you out of the Bog or stuck there with you . . . Only think! of B playing at Drafts! I never should have suspected him of such a thing tho' I don't exactly know why—is it at that Game that he wins so much *Silver*.

To acknowledge "Yours of Monday" on Wednesday the 22nd:

> Dearest Annabella—No one, I do believe, can feel for & with you on the subject of the *black days*, as I can. It is in vain that I scold & reason with myself, when such occur, & we all know they must be in every body's "Calendar". No one occurrence upon earth except the *illness* of those I love is such a trial to me—but I hope we may be able to discuss these "*Comicalities*"[1] (a new word I believe) very soon de vive voix.

On the 24th:

> Dearest Annabella—I scribbled to B. yesterday—to you the day before —and I must Scribble again today, if only to thank you for your kindness —indeed you *do* spoil me. As for B he *is* certainly *very* lazy—but don't Scold him for it, poor dear B! he must have So many occupations, *walking*, *dining* playing at Drafts with "Mama" &c. &c. &c. & no time to scribble to "Guss". I am vain enough to think he does not forget her—& so— never mind.

Of this letter Annabella noted in 1817, "He would not write to her, & during the whole time of my marriage scarcely ever did, seeming to feel angry & ashamed when I urged him to it." Of the reference to playing draughts she noted, "He was sometimes diverted from his glooms in the Evening by playing at this game or commerce, which we accordingly contrived for him."

On 27th February Hobhouse wrote to Annabella from Whitton Park:

> When at Seaham I promised your Ladyship an autograph of the Prince de Ligne and I now take the liberty of inclosing it.

The rest of his letter described his acquaintance with the Prince de Ligne, whom he had met at Vienna in November 1813. Of this letter Annabella recorded:

> At S[eaham] when H[obhouse] sent me some autographs, he [Byron] would not suffer me to send him even a formal acknowledgement, telling

[1] At this word, when including the letter in her Narrative of 1817, Annabella noted: "This is one instance of the levity with which I endeavored to treat my then sources of unhappiness."

me he was not a man whom I ought ever to write to. H was at that time corresponding with him on the business of Newstead, and I thought with friendly zeal for the arrangement of his affairs. In one of the letters H—— recommended him to commit them entirely to me. H—— frequently dictated measures to him as to a child—"Now Byron you must do so & so"—or phrases of that kind—nor do I ever recollect that he disobeyed, or delayed to comply.

In the same reminiscence she asserted:

I showed every disposition to cultivate the acquaintance of *his* friends. He said at H[alnaby] and repeated the same thing once, if not oftener, in London—that the only thing he had gained by marriage was to get rid of his friends, whom he seemed to consider very burdensome. When I mentioned—upon the supposition of our prolonged stay at H[alnaby]—that Hob. would perhaps come to visit us, he said with an air of dread, "No—God forbid." He spoke of him with Suspicion at that time—told me that their *friendship* had begun by H's *hatred* of him, when he B used to ride about at Cambridge in a white hat, and that H—— never found out there was any thing in him till he had published his first poems. He said H was disappointed himself as an Author, and attributed to him a certain degree of envy under the mask of friendship. He told me that once when they were in a boat together, I think in the Archipelago—and in danger —Hobhouse began to upbraid him in the bitterest manner. He produced this not as an instance of the individual but of the natural depravity of the human heart—that the greatest friends, when the dread of death overcame the usual restraints of manner, should indulge the passion of hatred. He had himself remained sullen & moody under the tempest of H's invective.

This statement is a revelation of Annabella's reading of portents in remarks intended to be interpreted humorously. Readers of Byron's letter to Murray can hardly suppose that malice was intended in telling of Hobhouse's "hating me for two years, because I wore a *white hat*,"[1] and presumably the boat incident was that described in Byron's letter to his mother of 12th November 1809 with humorous reference to the behaviour of his valet Fletcher. Byron may have felt reluctant to encourage friendliness between his wife and his former intimates lest they should furnish too much food for her inferences; if so, he had reason to dread exchanges between such literal and humourless understandings as Hobhouse's and Annabella's. In a paper headed "Reflections, &c. Seaham, Feb. 1815" Annabella noted among Byron's sayings: "The virtues of some Characters, like the words of Cassandra, are fated not to be believed till *too late*, when we have to deplore that they *were*—in vain!"

Without any word directly from Byron, Augusta seems to have been in doubt as to where he wished to go, while at the same time she was

[1] *cf.* p. 129.

fearful of offending Annabella. After emphasising the limited accommodation at Six Mile Bottom, she spent a fortnight in fruitless search for a suitable house to let near Newmarket, while deferring any possible descent upon herself with the excuse that she did not know whether a visit from her Aunt Sophia Byron was imminent or not. Apparently Byron suggested that, though Augusta's accommodation might be strained by their going together with their servants, it would not be so by only one of them, for Annabella stated:

> When, after great reluctance, he had consented that I should accompany him to the South, he still would have gone to S.M.B. alone—& have sent me on to London—this point was also yielded.

When first assembling for the lawyers her case against Augusta in March 1816, she stated:

> His horror & confusion when we first went to S.M.B. were indescribable. He several times told me I was a fool for going—wanted me to go on to London, and wait for him there, letting him visit her alone.

"We leave this place to-morrow," wrote Byron to Moore on 8th March, "and shall stop on our way to town (in the interval of taking a house there) at Col. Leigh's, near Newmarket." They left Seaham before receiving Lady Melbourne's letter of 7th March, beginning:

> Dst. Annabella
>
> I have just taken the Dss. of Devonshire's House from next Sunday the 12th for one Year at 700£. As Ld B wants Space I hope it will suit him—but after that, I am rather in a fright at what I have done—but all I can say is, that I have not done it hastily—for at first I would not take it—& have this morning been with all ye great House brokers—& on seeing what they ask for very indifferent Houses & how few are to be let furnish'd I went back to this, & concluded the bargain.

In 1851 Annabella stated:

> At Lady Melbourne's suggestion, Lord Byron took inconsiderately at a high rent, the Duchess of Devonshire's house in Piccadilly Terrace—far too large,—it has since been altered.

Yet it appears that it was Annabella who asked her aunt to find a house for them and passed on to her Byron's desire for "Space," while she evidently failed to urge upon Byron the advice offered in Augusta's letter of 19th February:

> Could not B—— content himself with a *small* house in Town. Oh no—I know his *soaring* spirit—but why not—*till* he *could* have a *great* one! Don't you like *my* pretending to settle your affairs!—but dearest Annabella

> the real truth is that B—dearest B—had already *all but* spoilt me, & *you* have compleated it—by your indulgence & understanding all my "*words*", "silences" & ways—you are a *great deal* too good to me.

Despite her record of persecution, Annabella's habit of getting her own way was still so far prevailing: she had refused to be left at Seaham while Byron went alone to London, refused herself to go alone to London while he visited Six Mile Bottom, "forced him" to take walks with her—it is unlikely that she had nothing to say in the choice of their London house.

On the morning of Friday 10th March Judith wrote to Annabella, "No letters for You or Lord Byron came yesterday, tho' the Newspapers did"; the next morning she wrote again:

> Your letter to *Dad* afforded us much pleasure, as it reported progress so far as Boroughbridge and also that You have secured a House in London, which I hope You and Lord B. will approve—at all Events the *Situation* is pleasant.[1]
>
> I return *five* letters to Ld B. by this Post—tell him, I think too much of him and too kindly, to neglect his commissions, therefore the caution about letters being sent was unnecessary.
>
> . . . Mrs. Dickens has lost her third son, who was in the Navy . . . We wait for this days Post with some anxiety, for the accounts from London are alarming, and matters will not be mended by the bad news from America.
>
> Our fine Weather continues and wish Ld B. and You were here to take Your Sea-side *Runs* . . .

Sir Ralph acknowledged Annabella's letter in verse the same day:

> My Dear Lady B, your Letter I've got—
> And hope you'll proceed, in a very brisk trot,
> And gaily, and merrily, hold on your Course,
> Unimpeded by dècadence, of a post horse,
> So that this very day, before it is dark yet
> You will both arrive safe, at the place near Newmarket—
> To my Lord of Bўrōn, my remembrance give,
> Your affectionate Dad, me ever believe,
> And I beg you'll present, if it is not too free,
> My Compliments best to dear Mrs. Leigh.

Lady Melbourne also wrote on Saturday 11th March:

> Dr. Annabella—
>
> Not having any idea of yr leaving Seaham so soon, there are some Letters upon ye road, but they are of no signification.

[1] Objecting to Medwin's reporting Byron's describing himself as having been "shut up in a dark street in London," Hobhouse noted, "Lord Byron lived at No. 13 Piccadilly, looking into the Green Park."

I have just been at the House, to tell ye Servants that your Housemaid was on her way . . . if I can be of any use, employ me *sans ceremonie.* Tell Ld B. I wrote him a Letter Yesterday being in a gracious humour—otherwise I should have taken no more notice of him than he has of me lately—but I wanted to send him This extraordinary News & also an Acct of Kean in Rd ye 2d.

She wrote at greater length to Annabella the next day, with a lively account of demonstrations by rioters in London against the Government's levying new taxes to renew the war on Napoleon's escape from Elba, and enclosing a plan of the ground floor of the Duchess of Devonshire's house. Writing on "Tuesday Morn: from my Pillow," Judith also mentioned the London riots and expressed satisfaction that "Your House will be ready for You," after beginning:

Oh! You lazy Travellers!!—at Wansford the third days journey. *I* should have *dined* at Six mile bottom that day.

On Thursday 16th March she wrote again to Annabella:

Yesterday I heard of your being established at Mrs. Leighs. You will miss the *Riots* which I am not sorry for. You are very good to write so often, which gives pleasure and comfort to us poor old Folks, who are always thinking of You. I dreamed last night of Ld. B and I think my dream will not come true—it was that we were at *dinner* and that he eat voraciously of a Roasted Leg of Mutton, and said it was *excellent. Joseph himself* would be perplexed to expound this dream.

According to Annabella's account, she and Byron did not dawdle on the road for pleasure:

As soon as we were in the carriage, he re-assumed the same ferocity of manner which had been disguised at Seaham to a great degree, but which I recognised too well from my experience at Halnaby, and on the journey the day of my marriage. It was a vindictive exultation over my defenceless state—"the unleavened *Hatred* of the heart." He spoke with the language of that passion & towards my parents also—and some words of my Mother's, as if confiding me to his protection, were a subject of his bitterest invective, as well as my slight emotion in parting with her—("What did she mean by that?—Are you not more fit to take care of yourself than I am to take care of you?"). However by means of cheering, & the assumption of a gaiety I did not feel, he became in a few hours less violent—what Augusta would have called "less disagreable." I used to find a good reason for these verbal extenuations on her part whilst I remained with him—because I thought it her duty, as a friend to our united welfare, not to render my impressions more deep—and her constant endeavours to prevent disunion formed another argument against the imputation of any Self-interest to her motives.

On the road the second day he talked of her as "a fool." I said something in her favour that she was a fool only in being disinterested—he added more emphatically, "She IS a fool indeed."

We slept at Wandsford the night before we reached S.M.B. In the beginning of the evening—for we arrived I think rather early—he was capriciously strange to me, but at night he said to me the kindest words I could even have wished to hear—"You married me to make me happy, didn't you?"—I answered with some expression of attachment. "Well then, you *do* make me happy!"—with passionate affection, I fancied. I was silent, and he saw not, but felt the tears of joy which rose from my heart. Then again he seemed to pity me for some impending, inevitable misery.

The stage before we reached SMB he was in the most agitated state of spirits, & said, when within two or three miles of the house, "I feel as if I was just going to be married." My maid was in the carriage, & I know not if she heard these words, but he seemed immediately apprehensive of an inference from them, for he began caressing me, & wanted me to kiss him. I did not draw the inference at the time.

We arrived. He wished me to remain in the carriage whilst he went in "to prepare Guss". However she was not below stairs, and we went into the room together. His perturbation was great, but he found a letter about the sale of Newstead, by which he endeavored to account for it.[1] She came down, shook hands with me, & received him affectionately. He had dwelt much upon her shyness. She took me to see the rooms above—and when alone with her, I expressed my happiness in being under her roof, and kissed her. She went down to him again & mentioned what had passed, and he afterwards rallied her in my presence maliciously, for not having greeted my arrival more warmly.[2] Her manners were sedate yet timid & guarded.

I thought that he & she, after so eventful an absence on his side, would have much to impart to each other, and I left them for some time together. After I returned he showed me undisguised preference of her society, and by his hints, sent me upstairs early. This was the case every night[3]—sometimes he more openly desired my absence—("We can amuse ourselves without you, my dear" or "my *charmer*" sarcastically—Such was his general style of treating me there)—& treated me with such aversion & insult that I sometimes could not have remained without bursting into tears, which on A's account, believing as I did of her tender-heartedness, I should have regretted. He used to make himself more furious by drinking Brandy.

[1] In another statement Annabella wrote, "The blackness of his Countenance was dreadful . . . he put it upon a letter he had received respecting the N. Sale."

[2] In another statement: "On our arrival at S M B, Augusta did not kiss me, & he reproached her for it that evening—mysteriously, & as if to vex her."

[3] In his notes of "Conversations with Ly B", January 1851, the Rev. F. W. Robertson wrote:

> After 9 weeks at Seaham, they went to Six Mile. There Ly B. was turned out of the room every night at 9 p.m. with an avowed purpose—wh. she wd. not believe.
>
> He used to taunt his sister scornfully till she seemed as if she wd. sink
>
> We must fly—We must part to unite it again.
>
> "You remember when I wrote those lines to you?"
>
> "You know that is my Child!" but this was equivocal, for Medora was his *God*child. Then he wd. calculate the time of Col. Leigh's absence & prove that it cd. not be his child.

When he came to my room the first night he was in a state of frenzy—black & enraged—manifesting his loathing of me in every possible way—& he said to me "Now I have *her*, you will find I can do without *you*"—"I told you you had better not come here, and you will find it so." He gave me to understand that he had been indulging in a criminal passion for her—but never that she had indulged him in it . . .[1] In the morning, her calm & unconcerned manner of embracing him again lulled my suspicions. In the course of that day he asked her ironically, alluding to hopes which it appears that she had expressed of his reform from marriage—"Well, Guss, I'm a reformed man, a'nt I?"—It was plain from this that his conduct must have been very bad, but his blasphemous manner of *talking* might account for it sufficiently. She looked disconcerted by the question, and said "she *had* observed some improvements already." I *hoped* his conduct was but another cruel experiment on my feelings, and if his only offence were towards me, I could not hesitate to pardon,—whilst I yet hoped to save.

He talked with her in my presence of the intrigues he was carrying on during the time of his correspondence with me, & of which she had been the confidante. She produced some of his letters at his desire. In one of them which was written I think within the year after his return from abroad, he said he should "never marry now but *for money*."[2] Many of his letters during the time of his engagement to me were by his account—which she did not deny—in a tone of aversion to the marriage. In one of them which she showed me were these words, "What would the woman be at now?"—enclosing a letter of mine. He derided my delusion, saying, "All that time you thought I was dying for you."

His earliest letters to A—— from school were romantic & open-hearted—by no means sensible, but their affectionate character was highly interesting. It changed between the age of 16 & 17, and she has often dwelt upon this change both to him—& to me in his absence—and he has acknowledged it with mysterious horror. It took place in the interval of a parting and meeting between them, and the first letter in that altered style is short mysterious & cold, with a tinge of malignity. He says—in another, I think, for it appeared to answer some remarks of hers upon the change—that it was not owing to *love*—of this he solemnly assures her.[3]

[1] In a later statement Annabella wrote:

She has since confessed to me the truth of what when he came to my room the first night he gave me to understand that he had been attempting to renew his criminality with her. He said to me—"Now I have her, you will find I can do without you"—and seemed to regard me with loathing. Yet when we three met in the morning, her calm & unconcerned manner of kissing him & me shook my belief. *He* seemed at that time only to see with her eyes—he was in tolerable good humour with me once because *she* had said I was pretty. Her kindness to me at this time was all I could wish—she appeared to sympathize with my feelings & my sufferings, and to have no view but that of mitigating his cruelty towards me. I talked to her about him, & one day when we were out told her that he had desired I should ask her as to some circumstances of his conduct *relating* to amours before marriage. She looked perfectly unconscious of his allusion.

[2] See pages 135–6.

[3] During his first year at Cambridge, he wrote histrionically to Augusta on 7th January 1806, "I will not however pretend to say I possess that *Gaieté de Coeur* which formerly distinguished me, but as the diminution of it arises from what you could not alleviate, and might possibly be painful, you will excuse the Disclosure . . . You know me too well to think it is *Love*."

From that time he was only a cause of misery to her. She showed me his picture, and has since promised it to me, taken when he was at Harrow. It was delineated before "Conrad's day was dim," and the sanguine hectic of Hope was still over the Countenance. Hence arose a conversation about his portraits, and what was the *best* view of his face. I said *I* should like to have him painted when he was looking at Medora (A's youngest child)—the tenderness of expression at those moments I had thought quite lovely. This affected him incomprehensibly to me at that time. I don't remember what was his remark to her about it, but a mystery was implied in it.

A & I walked out together sometimes, and I talked to her one day of his feelings towards me. She usually gave me little encouragement to think he loved me, but when I said that his conduct immediately after my marriage had convinced me he did not care for me, she replied that she hoped I was now of a contrary opinion—or perhaps she said "undeceived"—but the import of the phrase was not such as could justify me in believing *her* of opinion that he married me *for love*. I expressed a hope that my persevering affection would gradually awaken a return, and she spoke of *habit* as of great power over him. I consulted her about my future conduct in avoiding *occasions* of jealousy, for at Seaham he had made some objections to my shaking hands with men. She advised me not to regard those fancies, and told me that when she was with him at Newstead, & G[eorge] B[yron] also, he had been excessively jealous at her treating her cousin with that degree of familiarity. One day also when I was walking with her, I asked her, as he had once desired me to do, and mentioned that reason, to tell me some circumstances relating to his amours before my marriage. She said, without embarrassment, that she did not know what he meant.

At S.M.B. he used to say significantly, "Aunt M—— does not like my being here," and I observed—for I then corresponded with her—that she never said a favorable word of A. He has told me Lady Melbourne thought her very clever & very wicked.

A day or two after we got to S.M.B. he received from a Jeweller—Love & Kelly, I think—two gold broaches, on one an A on the other a B with their hair respectively, & 3 X X X on each. They wore them from that time almost constantly till he laid his aside before A came to Town in Novr. & about the period when he burnt her picture. His observation at the time to A—— was—in my presence—"She does not know what these mean"—or "if she knew what these meant" for I cannot remember the particular turn of phrase, but with the tone of voice, it expressed an allusion to some shocking signification—& a contempt for my ignorance & blindness.

He would often say at S.M.B. "A you're my only friend"—"you're my best friend"—to which she once replied, "I fear I've been your *worst*" in a tone of suppressed wretchedness.

His delight was—what I shall describe in his own words applied (sometime afterwards) to me & another person—*to work us both well*. [He kept her in a state of misery beyond mine I thought][1]—that she was in his power from

[1] This sentence within square brackets was deleted.

some cause I could not often doubt—with all my endeavors to do so—and that he made the most cruel use of that power. I pitied her from my heart if Guilt had brought her thus low, and would not have aggravated her oppression of mind by a single look.

Some of his expressions convey too indelicate a sense to offend the eye of the reader, yet I fear it may be necessary to preserve what will give an idea of my trials—if absolutely necessary—and of those words of Guilt & Insult which fell like drops of fire upon my heart and without kindling a flame almost consumed it. I shall use Beeby's Short-hand, without abbreviations.[1]

[He would draw personal comparisons] between [us, in the most vicious manner.] And he has said twice (perhaps oftener) once at S.M.B. and once in London, [in speaking of womens dress], "A *I know* [you wear drawers]"—or to me, "*I know* A [wears them]," with an *emphasis* perfectly unequivocal. It was his pleasure to torture me as it were by an instrument so evanescent that I could not produce it to convince others, & I might even suspect it to be the phantom of my own Imagination, whilst I was writhing under its wounds.

Another time at S M B he said, remarking that A did not look well, "I know [what makes you look black round the] eyes, [since] I've [been here], don't I?"—His [personal intercourse with me was less at] S.M.B. than [ever before, but] towards [the end of our visit there it was renewed], yet without any appearance of affection for me, and he signified some reason which did not make the alteration very flattering to me during those three or four days. [I heard from] A—— herself, [that she was in a particular way during those days.] He said once, I *think* oftener, to her in the morning alluding, apparently, to the night before—"So you wouldn't Guss"—mischievously. His insinuations of the passion he felt for her were continual—I never would appear to understand them.[2]

These are my only reasons for having suspected a renewal subsequently to my marriage—except one at the last, which I shall speak of hereafter. I have after mature consideration resolved to banish that suspicion—Vide my correspondence with A. Had it been confirmed I should cast her off as the basest of human beings . . .

In her company one evening he said à propos, I think, to the resemblance of character between her & him, "You know, A, you're of an inflammable constitution"—most significantly. He would lie down on the sofa, and oblige her and me to kiss him by turns, but I was sensible that he was more warm towards her than me. One evening after talking of his transgressions during the time he had deceived me into a belief of his attachment to me only, he said to me before her, "Ask A. if I have been a virtuous man." She said she was afraid there was no such thing as a virtuous man in these days. But a degree of constraint on these occasions would have confirmed my worst suspicions, if I had not thought it might be caused by her fear of exasperating him more against me to which she

[1] Annabella's shorthand passages in the two following paragraphs are given within square brackets; the words within the brackets are Lord Lovelace's transcription.

[2] Giving the substance of the two foregoing paragraphs in another statement, Annabella further reports Byron as saying:

"I may SAY or DO anything with Guss you know—mayn't I"—childishly.

has herself often attributed her leniency towards him on various occasions.[1]

I was so miserable at night that I could not go to restless bed till near the time of his leaving A. and I trembled as I heard his terrible step. He swore at Fletcher whilst he was undressing with a degree of rage that seemed to threaten his life, and every night he came to my room in the same mood, except once or twice, when I heard the freezing sound of heartless professions. He never spent a moment with me that could be avoided & even got up early in the morning (contrary to his general habit) to leave me, and to go to her. Yet on one of the occasions I speak of he told me that he liked the night so much better than the day, & wished it longer, because he was with me!—I replied with calm & indignation, "Spare your professions"—they were more intolerable to me than his moroseness or uncontrolled abhorrence. He appeared alarmed at this. I never got to sleep till four in the morning, and was often waked by these words—with which I was afterwards familiarized—"Don't touch me"—in a voice of raging detestation. One night I could not bear it, and got up—he asked with a more subdued tone, where was I going? I replied without anger—"to my own room"—there I wept myself into that peace which even my friendless & fearful prospects could never entirely banish.

Here Annabella's narrative, designated "Narrative R" by Lovelace, ends, but another, designated by Lovelace "Narrative S" as evidently supplementary, this begins:

I could scarcely touch any victuals whilst at S.M.B., though I had constantly the sensation of being famished. "My heart is withered away, so that I forget to eat my bread." A—— was most kindly anxious about me, and when I turned from his barbarity to her affectionate care, could I have repaid it with the ingratitude of believing her actually his accomplice? I said—"it is impossible—there is internal evidence it cannot be—I will not visit his sins upon her—I will spare her feelings"—& I loved her better, as is natural, because I sacrificed something of my selfish passions to these wishes. I yet could not so far divest myself of suspicion concerning the past mingled with pity, as not to speak to her then sometimes, and I have often done so since, as if there were a tacit understanding between us . . .

Besides she was trampled upon even whilst she was the object of a personal & disgraceful preference, and was I to embitter those insults to which she submitted as if she hoped an earthly retribution might half-exhaust the vial of wrath poured upon her guilty head. His malice towards her, on occasions of perpetual recurrence, was "poorly veiled in the affected carelessness of mirth."

[1] Repeating the substance of this paragraph in another statement, Annabella added:

Her constraint on all these occasions would have confirmed my worst impressions, if I had not thought she was constrained by the fear of exasperating him more against me. He was anxious to send me to bed, and sat up with her an hour or two afterwards, drinking brandy. He came to me always in the most savage state, & got up early in the morning to go down to her. His insinuations of the passion he entertained for her were continual—I never would appear to understand them. There have been moments when I could have plunged a dagger into her heart but she never saw them. They remain in my memory to make me more thankful that I never yielded to revenge, & resisted suspicion to the utmost.

He said to her one day—in my presence—"She (myself) gives me leave to be unfaithful—*mind that*, Goose"—as if it concerned her personally. I explained what he had chosen to interpret in this manner—I had once expressed the opinion that a single transgression of this nature might be forgiven.

At S.M.B. he inveighed with bitterness against his marriage as the cause of all his wretchedness—"Cursed fool that I was"—looking at me with an expression of hatred—sometimes adding a sarcastic apology that he meant nothing personal.

Another time when he was kissing her upon the sofa, he said, "do you remember our signs at Newstead?"—and he also reminded her of the presence of mind he had shown there, on some occasion which I now conceive to have been an interruption—but I don't know what I then surmised.

He was in the habit of quarrelling with her about Lord Carlisle—whose part she took—& he threatened to publish more satire upon him. His violence on this & all other topics, but particularly Religion, was always encreased by Brandy—unlike Cassio, who (in a passage he was fond of quoting) begins to *pray* when he is drunk . . .

He was talking of me in my presence to A at S.M.B. and said he thought I should *do* for him, for I was "malleable." I reminded her of this when we were left alone, & observed that he was mistaken if he thought my character unformed at present.

He made me read "The Italian" [Mrs. Radcliffe's novel] at S.M.B. and observe the character of Schedoni—mysteriously, & as if for my information respecting himself. I showed him a passage which was the closest prose version of some lines in Lara, but I have now forgotten it. He acknowledged it in these remarkable words—spoken in a tone of horror—"I take it—it is only pouring out of the same phial."

I watched A's manner narrowly, and never did I detect in it the slightest emotion of too warm a nature towards him. She submitted to his affection, but never appeared gratified by it . . .

Her parents' letters indicate that Annabella confided to them nothing of her state of mind. They were much concerned with the international situation following Napoleon's escape from Elba, and Sir Ralph wrote on 20th March:

In regard to Nap: and the *ould gentleman* now on the throne in France, I am little solicitous who succeeds, save and excepting, that Nap: is possessed with an unquiet Spirit, "seeking the bubble reputation even in the Cannons mouth." He is a kind of Raw head & bloody bones, to keep the world in continual alarm . . . but the poor *ould* gentleman will be *a*sy and quiet happy in the enjoyment of his soup and bouilli and a *remove* of a fricassèe of Frogs.

Besides I do not wish to have my Slumbers on the Couch after dinner disturbed by damnable drums and Fifes, nor my grey and unoffending locks *Porcupinized* by the Clang and Din of war . . . let me end my days in Peace . . .

On the 22nd Judith described how Sunderland rioters had been "imitating the Mob of the Capital," and remarked of Napoleon, "he is a gloriously daring Madman, but *mad* this Enterprise always appeared to me." On the 25th she wrote "to answer your questions about returning visits" on their arrival in London:

> In former days, when people were presented at Court—which is now uncertain from there being no regular Drawing Rooms—*Brides* did not return *visits* or appear in public, till this Ceremony was gone thro'.
>
> I imagine *now*, that it will [be] necessary for *Charles* to return Cards, to all such as *leave* or *Send* Cards for You—and this tolerably soon—and I think You may trust to him to make out the *List*—and to get a Book to put the names and abodes in.
>
> I remember Lady Melbourne's saying how frequently people gave offence and got abused by being *covetous* of little bits of Cards and I believe it is very true—as to people who *call on You*, in course they will expect a Call in return.

Expressing anxiety about her brother Wentworth's health, she begged, "do encourage him to see Baillie," and went on:

> Is it true that Mrs. Leigh is appointed to the Situation that Mrs. Feilding had? viz. Bedchamber Woman? I heard this from London—I am anxious to hear of your arrival there.

Augusta was newly appointed as lady-in-waiting to Queen Charlotte, a post that secured her rooms in St. James's Palace, and for the purpose of taking up her appointment, she made a prolonged stay with the Byrons.

Annabella related:

> We left S.M.B. after a fortnight's visit—very reluctantly on his part—but she evidently did not wish to detain us. As we drove from the door he waved his handkerchief to her in the most passionate manner—& when he had ceased "to after-eye" her, he began talking of her to me, appearing very anxious to know what impression she had made upon me. I said I thought her more clever than he had described her to be. He was delighted with this commendation and seemed to pique himself as he has often done, on making us friends!
>
> As I left the scene of such deep horrors, I endeavored to shake off its associations. I persuaded myself it was his morbid desire of creating a sensation which had instigated him to torture me with groundless suspicions, and that the object of this assumed part had escaped her penetration. She had appeared to sympathize with my feelings, and to have no view but that of mitigating his cruelty. He told me she liked me, and he was kind again—kinder for about ten days (the interval which elapsed before she visited us) than I had almost ever seen him. I tried to believe this happy change a consequence of her influence in my favour, which,

though it might exasperate him at the time, took effect afterwards. It was necessary for her to be in London on account of her recent appointment about the Queen. He had proposed to her in my presence that she should visit us—and I renewed that offer of accommodation.

It seemed impracticable for me to pursue any other line of conduct—for these reasons. If I had refused to admit her, I must have assigned a cause to him. False excuses would have been seen through & over-ruled, even if I could have reconciled myself to such a departure from simplicity of conduct. Consider the consequences of telling him the true reason at that juncture. I was not sure of its foundation, *but* supposing it to have been true that a criminality *had* existed before my marriage (for this was my impression, and I thought less of systematic guilt than of some fatal & unrepeated *hour*) I should have fixed his malignant temper, which imputed the knowledge of his crimes, as the greatest crime, into a rooted hatred towards me, and have made myself too much the object of suspicious dread to be regarded as a friend—or admitted either to influence or to console, at any future period. I should thus have thrown him & her more decidedly together against myself—his self willed & revengeful impetuosity would (probably) have overcome even prudential considerations, and have necessitated an extension of this communication for my own personal Security. This would at once have closed all my hopes of united welfare, and the ruinous consequences to A, and her children, of exposing my reasons, were also, I remember, amongst the strong deterring motives of an experiment which I *now* think would have been unpardonable, considering the existing circumstances.

Secondly upon the supposition that no such cause of Remorse had existed, and that it was either the vision of a disordered brain, or assumed to work upon me, my acknowledged perception of it would have been most injudicious—in the former case as confirming the malady, in the last as indulging a temper of cruelty, which was likely to be thus encouraged.

It was hopeless then to keep them apart—it was not hopeless, in my opinion, to keep them innocent. My Duty allowed me no resource but to constitute myself the Guardian of these two beings, who seemed indeed on "the brink of a precipice"—in the study of their welfare, I sought to forget my own miserable, and under an earthly aspect, most humiliating condition.

II

MARRIED LIFE IN PICCADILLY

April—December 1815

Byron and Annabella left Six Mile Bottom on 28th March, and Augusta wrote on the 30th:

Dearest Annabella—I need not say that your letter is most acceptable to poor forlorn *me*. The contents (some of them at least) might have been more agreable, but your kindness is not the less felt. You understand by this time how ill I can *express* my feelings on this & many other Subjects —& that this *dumb stupidity* is all in your favor—for the more I love a person the less I can *Say* about them.

I am glad to hear of the comfort & CONVENIENCE of your house . . . I am inclined to suspect you are a better judge of "Uncle's" BLOOM than B, who had only seen him once before. His intelligence about Court is very consoling to weak minds who like to put off the evil day. Dearest Sis I do not require your account of the view from yr Windows as an inducement to pay you a visit. You will perhaps be a better judge by & bye whether I shall not be a plague—& you must tell me *truly* if I am likely to prove so —you know I should not be "affronted". *Never* think about a frank for *me;* I have very few correspondents who do *not* frank, which will I hope remove yr scruples should you feel any.[1] I am in a little agony about one of Bs, for *Aunt Sophs* letter of yesterday—*how* & *when* obtained &cc &cc. I wish she would not be so stupid as to ask *him* to frank . . .

I have this Morng received a congratulatory Epistle from Lady Harcourt upon this appointment of mine, in which she says many fine things about the Queen's pleasure in appointing me (for the sake of my Grandmother & Mother) but one which surprises me about the Prince, that she believes "what determined the Q—— most upon this occasion was its being the Regent's wish"!!!!!!!

My *youngsters* do not forget "Aunt Bella" & "Uncle B". Georgie looked at the Chair B used to sit in last night & very piteously exclaimed, "Nobody in that chair NOW"! God bless you dearest Annabella—kiss "*Duckey*"! for Sis & if possible give me a favorable report of the "Wind & the Weathercock"—Ever yr most affecte

Guss

[1] As a peer, Byron could frank letters for free postage. Augusta was warning Annabella not to refrain from writing from fear of Byron's inquiring why she was writing.

Judith wrote to Annabella on 6th April, "thank You for sending Mrs. L's letter, it causes me to *love her*, because She seems to *love You*." She wrote again on the 9th:

> my being in Town for thursday's Drawing Room is out of the question—it is indeed a *great mortification* to me that I cannot attend You—so *great a one* that I do not like to write about it . . . I shall be figuring You to myself in your *white Sattin* and Blond and wishing you well thro' the Ceremony—of which I shall expect a full account.
>
> Is the Mr. Wilmot you name a Son of Sir Robert Wilmots? and did he marry a Miss *Horton? She* is a distant relation of mine . . .
>
> *Dad* is very much delighted with the idea of pacing up and down in Ld B's Spacious Box. I long to know how *You* like *Kean* . . .[1]
>
> The account you give of Your proceedings gratify me much. It reminds me of Frends prediction that You & B. will not be "a vulgar fashionable pair." The idea that You found it *more comfortable* to return home after the Play, instead of going to a Party and Ball, is very unfashionable . . .
>
> Give my Love to Ld B.—tell him I am recollecting all the *old* Scandal I can for his *edification* . . .

On the 12th Sir Ralph wrote to Annabella:

> In consequence of your letter received by this days post giving *so alarming* an account of Lord Wentworths health, Lady Mil determined to set out immediately for London, which she did between two & three oclock—and probably will be in Town, unless she meets any impediments on the road, before you receive this. I greatly fear by your letter he will not recover.

The second Viscount Wentworth died at his London house on 17th April 1815, and was buried at Kirkby Mallory on the 28th. As he left no legitimate children, his viscounty expired and the barony of Wentworth fell into abeyance among the children of his two sisters, Judith Milbanke and Sophia Curzon, and eventually devolved upon Annabella on the death of her cousin Natty Curzon, Lord Scarsdale, in 1856. Thanks to his economies during his latter years, his property—as Byron wrote to Lady Melbourne on the 22nd—was "more considerable" than had been expected; the entailed estate of Kirkby Mallory, together with half his personalty, went to his surviving sister Judith, and her husband was authorised by royal licence on 20th May following to assume the name and arms of Noel.

Annabella had been called to her uncle's bedside when he was taken ill, but as soon as her mother arrived in London, Byron sent round a note to her:

[1] She and Sir Ralph had visited Newcastle in Easter week to see Edmund Kean in *Richard III* and *Othello*.

Dearest—

Now your mother is come I won't have you worried any longer—more particularly in your present situation which is rendered very precarious by what you have already gone through—

Pray—come home—

ever thine

The signature was the monogram of twirls habitually used by Byron and Augusta in writing to each other. Byron had some reason for concern, as Annabella was now pregnant—her father wrote to her on 21st April that he was "highly rejoiced at the *news* in your last, which had indeed peeped out before."

By this time Augusta had arrived for a stay of over two months at Piccadilly Terrace, as Annabella related:

She wrote to me desiring that I would have no hesitation in preventing her visit if *I* saw any reason to think it would be inadvisable . . . Her willingness to come—if I did not—was to me the most convincing proof that *she* was unconscious of any secret reasons against it, & only had the scruples which a S-in-law might feel. I removed them. She came. He went out of the house purposely when she was expected to arrive—& met her on his return with the same black agitation as I have described & not kindly. After some minutes however he grew very fond of her—& then told me *I was a fool for letting her come & I should find it so—that it would make a great difference to me in* ALL *ways.*[1] Indeed it did. His preference of her society to mine during all this visit was marked, & his treatment of me most savage. So much so that when my Uncle was dying (He died 17th April 1815) & I went to his house for 3 nights, I felt that death-bed scene a relief from the horrors of an incestuous home—for my suspicions were then at the height, & I declared them explicitly to ——— who can corroborate this account. I was almost mad, & to prevent myself from indulging the passion of Revenge I was obliged in that tumultuous state of mind to substitute another—that of a romantic forgiveness. Besides I still thought—though my impressions were so strong—that their sensible causes did not justify me in acting upon a supposition thus unconfirmed. I was to endure & to pardon. I attached myself to my little Niece, & thought to touch her Mother's heart by having her picture taken, & giving it to her.

In another statement:

His treatment of me was generally that of hatred & loathing. He sat up with her almost every night for an hour after I went to bed—that hour to me was madness. My mind was in a degree affected by illness arising

[1] In a memorandum evidently written in reply to queries by Dr. Lushington during the separation proceedings in March 1816, she wrote:

The Evg. she came to Town in particular—he said to me before her—"You were a fool to let her come—You will find it will make a good deal of difference to you *in all ways*"—in a manner which could not leave a doubt as to the meaning—particularly connected with circumstances.

from my pregnancy, and I used to lay awake watching for that footstep by which my hopes & fears were decided—it was always expressive of the mood that had the ascendancy. It was either the stride of passion which seemed to print its traces on the ground with terrific energy, or it was the irregular pace of animal spirits, rousing up "flashes of merriment," & then he would laugh with A—— as he came up the staircase. For some days I was so ill as to keep my room, & there were apprehensions of miscarriage—and though he was usually desirous of an heir, he marked his neglect of me at this time more inhumanly, and when he came up for half an hour to my room it seemed only in order to continue the exercise of his hatred over my solitary hours—for he would give me such intimations as to the nature of his own character, as must leave a rankling anxiety. In particular he brought me the German's tale to peruse, with a reference to Conrad's character as his own, and identifying most pointedly the keystone of the narrative. He constantly alluded to that Tale, and was beginning to compose a Tragedy upon it in the end of 1815. He read me some passages, but I believe he burnt it afterwards.

Recalling in another statement how "He & A—— would then laugh together as they came up the Staircase," she continued:

One night when they were later than usual & my Imagination was on the rack, I could not lay still any longer, but got up & walked about. They heard me below, and he sent her upstairs to see what was the matter. I was in an agony of tears, & tried to conceal them as I heard her approach—but the thought of his dagger lying in the next room, for I was in the adjoining room (then the library), crossed my mind—I wished it in her heart. It was an instant of revenge, and her voice of kindness extinguished it—yet if I should ever go mad perhaps these remembrances would be prevailing ideas, & to a principle of Forgiveness I feel indebted for the possession of my intellects under circumstances that made my brain burn. If I have seemed to carry this principle too far, it is from the consciousness of its being *necessary*—in its utmost extent *to myself.*

On her own showing, Annabella had worked herself into an overwrought state of neurosis, and her recollections must be read with due regard to her state of mind. If Byron was out of humour, she thought he was menacing; if he laughed, she was jealous because he laughed with Augusta.

Nor do her recollections indicate much attempt on her part to share his preoccupations. As soon as he settled in Piccadilly, he became absorbed in his duties as a member of management committee of Drury Lane theatre on the one hand, and in dealing with dunning creditors on the other. His published letters abundantly show how actively he engaged in the management of the theatre, but Annabella—despite her former interest in the theatre displayed in her journals—seems to have taken little interest beyond securing Byron's box for her father's use while he was in town. Perhaps she remained aloof from his theatrical interests through interpreting literally a remark that may have been intended only in a spirit of mischief:

> When he first became one of the Drury Lane Committee he informed me of his profligate intentions in regard to the actresses & for sometime before his connection with Miss —— [Boyce] has said "I am looking out to see who will suit me best."

Denying to Annabella that Byron had ever expressed "vindictive feelings" towards her in the period between their engagement and marriage, Augusta wrote on 22nd March 1817, "the change after we parted & he was in Town appeared to me to be owing to *pecuniary embarrassments*." From Seaham on 26th January Byron had written to Hobhouse, enumerating his liabilities and concluding that "My debts can hardly be less than thirty thousand." In a statement on finance to the lawyers in January 1816 Judith remarked, "It appears to me that Lord Byron has *now* no Income at all or very little—except the Interest of the £20,000 which Sir Ralph gave her." This interest was only enough to cover the rental of the Piccadilly house—though the rent appears to have been still outstanding nearly two years after the end of their tenancy.

Byron thus was harrowed by financial anxiety, but the spoilt child, having been always protected by her fond parents from such anxieties, construed his worry only as an offence against herself:

> He was, even on the day of our marriage, calculatingly curious as to the state of my father's & uncle's property—and their dispositions to bequeath it—looking forward to their decease with an unfeeling eagerness, which, at a subsequent period, was more shamelessly displayed . . . I experienced an indistinct & painful impression; but this was the man of whom I believed that Generosity & Disinterestedness were the strongest impulses: the atoning virtues of his too ungoverned career!

Lady Melbourne may have supposed that a pretentious residence might have inspired creditors with confidence to await settlement. The reverse seems to have happened; the creditors concluded that Byron was in funds and that this was therefore the time to press for payment. Lord Wentworth's death probably stimulated the pressure, though litigation long delayed implementation of his will and Sir Ralph's embarrassments were as harassing as Byron's.

As Augusta stayed with them till the last week of June and Annabella's parents were in London from the end of April till the beginning of August, there is little correspondence to reflect what happened to the Byrons during the early summer. Annabella wrote to her old friend

Dr. Fenwick about her meeting Walter Scott, for he replied on 29th May:

> I recollect Mrs. Wilmot giving a description of Walter Scott which very much agrees with Yours. She described him as having the countenance of an acute sensible man, without any marks of strong feeling & imagination untill he began to read the Works of his countryman Burns, when his eye lighted up, & the tones of his voice changed in a wonderful manner. She added that he marked the beauties with so much feeling & commented on different passages with so much interest & taste that She was delighted with him. The broken sentence which fell from W. Scott in conversation with Lord B. leaves no longer any doubt of his being the Author of Waverley.

The young American traveller, George Ticknor, was susceptibly impressed by Annabella when he called to see Byron on 20th June:

> She is pretty, not beautiful—for the prevalent expression of her countenance is that of ingenuousness. "Report speaks goldenly of her." She is a baroness in her own right, has a large fortune, is rich in intellectual endowments, is a mathematician, possesses common accomplishments in an uncommon degree, and adds to all this a sweet temper. She was dressed to go and drive, and, after stopping a few moments, went to her carriage. Lord Byron's manner to her was affectionate; he followed her to the door, and shook hands with her, as if he were not to see her for a month.

Three days later he "went by appointment to see Lord Byron" and "found Lady Byron alone."

> She did not seem so pretty to me as she did the other day; but what she may have lost in regular beauty she made up in variety and expression of countenance during the conversation. She is diffident,—she is very young, not more, I think, than nineteen,—but is obviously possessed of talent, and did not talk at all for display. For the quarter of an hour during which I was with her, she talked upon a considerable variety of subjects—America, of which she seemed to know considerable; of France, and Greece, with something of her husband's visit there,—and spoke of all with a justness and a light good-humour.

He then had with Byron "an extremely pleasant and instructive conversation of above an hour . . . of his own works he talks with modesty, and of those of his rivals, or rather contemporaries, with justice, generosity, and discriminating praise." He found him "in everything . . . unlike the characters of his own 'Childe Harold' and 'Giaour'." On 26th June Ticknor "passed the greater part of this morning" with Byron and again met Annabella, having "a very pleasant conversation with her until her carriage came, when her husband bade her the same affectionate farewell that struck me the other day." He was unable to think "either of his early follies or his present eccentricities; for his manners are so gentle, and his whole character so natural and unaffected, that I have come from him with nothing but an indistinct, though lively impression of the goodness and vivacity of his disposition." On the 27th he had a seat in Byron's box at Drury Lane:

> There was nobody there . . . but Lord and Lady Byron, and her father and mother . . . Lord Byron was pleasant, and Lady Byron more interesting than I have yet seen her . . . Lady Milbank, Lady Byron's mother, is a good-natured old lady,—a little fashionable, however, I fear,—and her husband, a plain, respectable Englishman, who loves politics, and hates the French above everything . . . I think I have received more kindness from Lord Byron than from any person in England on whom I had not the regular claim of a letter of introduction.

The ingenuous Ticknor may have been a scarcely percipient observer, but Annabella evidently betrayed no more in her demeanour than in her correspondence the tortured emotions of her recollections. Augusta had presumably left Piccadilly just before Ticknor's arrival, and Annabella related:

> there seemed no probable termination of her visit—I then conceived it a duty to my husband to remove a guest who whatever the cause might be, seemed to encrease his ill dispositions. I was the occasion of her fixing a time to go—and I would not retract the measure, but as soon as she had left us, though for a few days I experienced the benefits I had expected from her absence, my heart reproached me for these suspicions & I again resolved to consider the gratification of her feelings instead of my own—to atone in every possible manner.

Most of Byron's biographers have assumed that Augusta was a silly woman, but Lovelace arrived at a juster assessment from the evidence of her letters:

> often very lovable . . . vague about facts, unconscious of duties, impulsive in conduct . . . she was of a sanguine and buoyant disposition, childishly fond and playful, ready to laugh at anything, loving to talk nonsense . . . She did not feel that there was much harm in anything which made no one unhappy . . . On the side of virtue she was weak, but the character was not altogether weak, rather incomplete. She was shy and timid, and there was great apparent facility and yieldingness, but in emergencies she could be steadfast and act with considerable courage. She had a sort of good feeling that led her to risk her own skin for some who needed it, and for whom she cared more or less. But there was always a blend of artificial sentiment. She excelled in simulation; herself she could persuade of almost anything. She feigned without thinking, perhaps felt what she feigned, unmindful of tangible truths at unsuitable seasons.

While she admitted jealousy of Augusta's ability to laugh Byron out of his "glooms," Annabella acknowledged Augusta's considerate conduct towards herself:

> when I was kind to her she would say *it was because I did not know her*—and when we were together in the carriage, & she was mentioning her fear that he should think her interested in a pecuniary point of view, I replied that I did not believe he ever felt *those* suspicions, but that he sometimes suspected her of *not being a virtuous woman*—those were my words. Her gesture at first expressed humiliation & consciousness. Then she vindicated herself from an imputed attachment to F—— H——.[1] She was always devotedly kind to me, & consulted my wishes on every occasion—I cannot now think how feelingly without emotions of gratitude.

Elsewhere she recalls instances of Augusta's kindness to her during this visit:

> During Mrs. L's former visit to Piccadilly, Lord B's conduct towards me was such that she told him she would not stay in the house to see me so badly treated. He would not speak to *me* for four days, and demonstrated the most violent aversion. No perceptible cause. I was then very ill—it was just after my Uncle's death.

Possibly Byron was impatient with Annabella's frequent indispositions; her letters show that, even as a young woman, she was much of a hypochondriac, and Byron had expressed alarm, when visiting Seaham during their engagement, at her being "taken ill every 3 days with I know not what." Having witnessed Augusta's behaviour during pregnancy, he may have suspected Annabella—in the Nottinghamshire vernacular—of being "mardy," *i.e.* of making a fuss about nothing.

Annabella further recorded:

> one of the circumstances which excited my gratitude towards A. was her always taking the part of my parents against his most cruel & insulting system of conduct towards them. On my birthday the 17th of May 1815 They had sent us an invitation to dine with them alone . . . then, as on many occasions, he spoke with disrespect & dislike of my parents. He has at different times spoken of their deaths as the most desirable Event, and dwelt upon the expectations depending upon it. Soon after my marriage he expressed his determination to estrange me from them & all my friends more & more—and not to show them any attention himself. Consistently with this last determination he never called upon them in London, & would not accept their invitations.

After relating this instance of her gratitude to Augusta, she continued:

[1] Lovelace identified this as a reference, not—as most students of Byron might suspect—to Francis Hodgson, but to Lord Carlisle's third son, Frederick Howard, who was killed at Waterloo in his thirtieth year. Nearly two years younger than Augusta, he was one of the sponsors for her second child, Augusta Charlotte.

He said to her "Ly M[elbourne] does not like you Guss." She expressed something to this effect—that she was ignorant of any offence she had committed against her. He replied very significantly he would tell her why, and went up to whisper something, after which she looked embarrassed. He would sometimes threaten her—half jesting, half serious—"I'll tell Augusta"—to which she one day replied (desperately I thought) "I don't care." He said, "Well if I ever heard any thing like the impudence of the woman."

Among Annabella's friends who survived her was Sophia, wife of Augustus De Morgan, mother of William De Morgan the novelist, and daughter of Annabella's tutor, William Frend. Consulting her when first examining his grandmother's papers, Lovelace related in his notes:

A singular, (to me) incredible story was at one time believed in—and with perfect good faith—by some of Lady Byron's friends—who had very likely misunderstood some veiled allusions of hers.

Mrs. De Morgan said she had understood things to have happened thus: "Once Lady Byron had been sent out of the room by Lord Byron early in the evening and told to take care of her health and go to bed, as he and Mrs. Leigh did not want her. For some reason she came down stairs again later, and surprised them in what appeared to her to be certain guilt, and there and then charged them to their faces with *incest*—using the word. For the moment they seemed terror-struck and submissive to any condition that might be imposed."

Lovelace justly regarded this story as incredible, as it would make nonsense of all Annabella's painstaking explanations of her conduct towards Augusta. About the same time as he heard it from Mrs. De Morgan, he obtained a decisive contradiction from an even older surviving friend of Annabella's, Lady Wilmot Horton, whose husband had acted as an intermediary in the separation negotiations:

As to the question respecting Mrs. Leigh I have only the fact of *her great friend* Mrs. G. Villiers having been *convinced* that Ly. N.B's [Noel Byron's] suspicions were well founded, and I *fully believe* having received Mrs. L——'s confession as to the *previous* connection—any subsequent to Ly. B's Marriage being *stoutly denied.*

Augusta's letters to Annabella immediately after leaving London in June have not been preserved, but she wrote to Hobhouse from Six Mile Bottom on 5th July:

I am aware of your being very anxious to hear from my brother; and knowing him to be just now very lazy, I think the next best thing to hearing *from* him must be to hear *of* him . . . I returned home ten days ago, after more than two months séjour in Piccadilly, during which time

B. was much delighted by several kind and interesting letters from you. *I* heard him sometimes declare an intention of answering, *then* vow that he did and would not write to anybody! and so on . . . All which you, I am sure, can easily imagine him to say. He is looking particularly well, eats very heartily of *meat*, bread, and biscuit, allows himself half-a-pint of claret at dinner, when at home (and he seldom dines out), has abjured brandy and other spirituous liquors. Lady B. is *not* looking well or feeling so, but there is a very good reason for this temporary indisposition.

What a blessing it is that he has such a Lady B! for indeed I do think her the most perfect person I ever saw, heard of, or read of . . . The only drawbacks to their present happiness and comfort are *pecuniary* concerns, and I grieve to say the remedy is to be the sale of Rochdale and Newstead, on the 28th of this month. Alas! for the dear old Abbey! . . .

The sale was a measure hastily determined upon in a moment of despair, and I can't help fearing that, at least as far as poor Newstead is concerned, will be repented of if it takes place; but nothing can be urged successfully against it, and I have left off urging almost upon principle. I really believe that Lady B's father and mother are most kindly and generously disposed; but their power is very limited at present, owing to difficulties of their own, and the want of ready money which till all the different bequests of Lord Wentworth's are disposed of and arranged cannot be forthcoming. Lady B. is, of course, most anxious B. should be convinced of their good will, and whatever may be wanting on hers on this and other points just now, I feel sanguine that a little time and patience will set all right and enlighten his *now* prejudiced mind as to who are his *real* friends. They go out but little, I think (and Lady B. thinks) almost *too* little, but you know B. can't do any [thing] moderately, and that being the case, it is perhaps the best extreme of the two, particularly as her health is not such as could bear hot rooms and late hours . . . I am glad to hear that they propose going to Seaham, which Sir R.N. offers for as long as they please. B. is well pleased at the thought of it, and they intend remaining there until after Lady B.'s confinement . . . Lady B. is most anxious you should not attribute B's silence to her. Really and truly laziness is the whole and only cause . . . I am a fellow sufferer, for he does not write to me.

Augusta was aware of difficulties about Lord Wentworth's will that prevented Annabella's parents from helping Byron for the present, but she also recognised that Annabella was a little "wanting" in sympathy with Byron's worries. She noted significantly that Annabella thought they stayed at home too much; Annabella may have been right indeed in concluding that Byron stayed at home to avoid accepting invitations from her friends. Though she had claimed in their correspondence before her engagement that she disliked "a fashionable life," it will be remembered that she had eagerly sought social pleasure when she persuaded her parents to let her stay with the Gosfords in the spring of 1812. Though her recollections refer to her being continually ill, she was not too ill to go out, and Hobhouse recorded "the fear of some friends that his Lordship confined himself too much with Lady Byron, and that occasional separation—for they were never seen apart—might be more conducive to their comfort." It seems that Annabella persevered in her habit of getting her own way and must have irritated Byron by her insistence on accompanying him wherever he went, so that he stayed at home as a reprisal.

Hobhouse returned from abroad on 24th July, and "saw Lord & Lady Byron—for the first time since the marriage" on the 27th. The next day he accompanied Byron to Garraway's, where Newstead was bought in at 95,000 guineas and Rochdale at 16,000, and afterwards "called on Lady Noel who wants Byron to sell hugely." On 31st July he "saw Byron, who is not more happy than before marriage." On 4th August he "passed night with Douglas Kinnaird and Byron who tells me he and she have begun a little snubbing on money matters—marry not, says he." On 8th August he "dined with Kinnaird, Burdett, Byron, Knight—no great things this—they all grumbled at life." He then left London—according to Lovelace's examination of his unpublished journals—and did not see Byron again till 25th November. Thus in the space of a fortnight Byron saw his old friend five times, including dining out with him twice, and these were their only meetings in eleven months—yet Annabella recorded:

> Sometime after she [Augusta] went H[obhouse] returned from abroad. B—— told me it was upon business—to him, of the most friendly nature—but the effect was that of making him adopt a system of estranging himself from me & pursuing every vice, less from inclination, as it appeared, than from a principle of destroying every better feeling—Drinking brandy.

During July Annabella wrote the first letter in a correspondence that was to continue—apart from two lapses of several years—for thirty-six years with the Hon. Mrs. George Villiers, who was the sister of the second Lord Boringdon, created Earl of Morley in 1815, and wife of the third son of the first Earl of Clarendon; her own eldest son, a distinguished statesman, succeeded his uncle as fourth Earl of Clarendon. Born in 1775, she married in 1798 and survived till 1856. Nearly nine years older than Augusta, she was generally regarded as her "great friend," and was so considered by Annabella. In fact she does seem to have maintained an affectionate regard for Augusta, and the first lapse of several years in her correspondence with Annabella was due to her view that Annabella was treating Augusta unfairly. Yet the part she was to play as confidante in Annabella's long and relentless persecution of Augusta presents an aspect of friendship chilling to the heart.

Since his early connection with the Prince of Wales's racing interests, Augusta's husband had seen military service in Spain, but with the end of hostilities at Waterloo, he was in search of employment. Having presumably met Mrs. Villiers during Augusta's stay at Piccadilly, Annabella wrote to her as Augusta's friend:

Col. Leigh returned here after the Royal audience . . . The P.R. [Prince Regent] was very gracious, though not familiar, (Co. Thornton being present) and promised to give some place or appointment. For what is the Petitioner qualified?—A puzzling question, which his R.H. may *fairly* take some time to consider—unless any particular situation can be pointed out by application from Col. Leigh's friends . . . He is himself so much elated by the favour of an interview, that he thinks no further exertion necessary . . . I feel so much obliged to you, my dear Mrs. Villiers, for your kind opinion of me, and particularly during an acquaintance when I certainly have not appeared to the best advantage . . .

In the following year, on 17th September 1816, Byron wrote bitterly to Augusta of her being "so admirably yoked—and necessary as a housekeeper—and a letter writer—& a place-hunter to that very helpless gentleman your Cousin." Half a century later Augusta's nephew, the third Earl of Chichester, told Lovelace "that Colonel Leigh abominated Lord Byron, but absolutely and totally denied and disbelieved in Mrs. Leigh's guilt."

Sir Ralph and Lady Noel—as Annabella's parents were named after 20th May 1815—left London on 11th August, when Judith wrote:

Dear Lord Byron,

I am very Sorry I did not see You last night, to take my leave of You before I leave London, particularly as I wished to prevail on You to visit us at Kirkby, where we shall be very *quiet* not being *blessed* with a *Neighbourhood*, and the journey is *Short*,—it is not ten miles out of your way when You go North—and an excellent Library for [you] to *tumble about*, which I know You like.

Annabella I am sure requires Country Air, her looks shew it, and it will do You both good. In her Situation She manifestly requires it—and *that* is the first thing to be considered at present. How delighted Sir Ralph and I should be to see You and her is a secondary consideration but wh. would give us the greatest pleasure.

We are just setting out—so Adieu!

Yours very truly & affecly.

JU: NOEL

On the 15th Annabella wrote to her father:

B. has just found out an Etymology for Blucher's name which is quite in your way.

The Prussian regimental being *blue*, and the disposition of that General meriting the canine epithet, people were wont to say as he passed "There goes the *Blue Cur*"!

She concluded, "I have recovered from my indisposition."

To her mother she wrote on the 16th:

> Lady Melbourne called on me yesterday (she goes on Friday) and told me what she had heard of Bonaparte from Mr. Lyttleton, who was on board the Northumberland, as you saw in the papers. Bonaparte conversed in a very dignified rational manner on several topics which were suggested by the curiosity of those present with respect to his opinions—of Fox, Pitt, & Windham. Of the first he said he, B, would have made peace with him as the Minister here—"Car c'etait un homme sincère". Windham, he said, was so "acharné" against him (B) that he could not have trusted him. Of Pitt he gave no opinion. On a sudden Bonaparte shivered & said, "Il fait un peu frais ici," turned round, & decamped to his cabin, taking some paces in a pas de quadrille, to the astonishment of the Spectators. Mr. L—— seemed to think him a little mad—but I interpret the gesture to be much the same as snapping his fingers at the fools he had been talking to.
>
> B—— desires me to say, with his love, that if you have not game enough at Kirkby, you can have as much as you please from Newstead.[1]

Under the date of 16th August she jotted down some "Miscellanea":

> B. gave W. Scott a vase containing some skull bones that were dug up near Athens. This circumstance was told with the addition of the following story—that the skull was that of Demosthenes, and in proof a *pebble* was found in the Jaw bone!

Among Byron's sayings recorded was one of Miss Mercer Elphinstone: "We were talking of Miss M.E.'s long withstood attacks on the D[uke] of D[evonshire]—Nil desperandum—*te duce*." Of another she did not record the context: "Those who *tell* lies do not *believe* them—(i.e. those they hear from others)." On the 17th she wrote again to her mother:

> B. & I called on the Hollands yesterday, but they were not at home. Is it my good or evil Genius that prevents our meeting? I cannot conclude without praising my abstinence which could not be greater if I lived at the Pulteney Hotel—No Green-gages nor fruit pies . . . By the bye, we saw *Dad* scribbled on the walls of Piccadilly yesterday, & B. said it was a memento left us by our honored parent.

To her father on the 20th she wrote of a call on Lady Jersey—"I found her at home, eating her dinner during her morning levee—and so many fine men that I nearly ran away." She added, "Tout va bien—except the pocket which is in a confirmed atrophy."

Judith's letters told of how she was taking possession of affairs at

[1] When Napoleon left the *Northumberland*, in which he was deported from Europe for his voyage to St. Helena, the crew expressed the opinion, "He is a fine fellow, who does not deserve his fate."

Kirkby with her usual vigour, despite the hindrance of the estate bailiff, Lynes, but she spoke also of financial affairs. On 18th August:

The intelligence from the North is most melancholy. *We* shall suffer very severely from Mowbrays business, and so will *Baker*. *Stobart* is *done up*, Davison loses 500£—the Tenants have not a Shilling at Halnaby—fortunately those at Seaham are not more injured than what must be from the general depreciation of every article throughout the County. Seaham is quite ready for You—and the Whole House has been cleaned and white-washed and looks exceedingly nice, the people from there tell me.

On the 22nd:

Clermont will tell You what a situation we are placed in by the failure of the Durham Bank—which is very disagreable, and if Sir James[1] does not soon return and listen to reason I know not what we shall do—for Government Extorts are *the Devil*, and also Sir Ra: has 1500£ to pay to the Bishop, as his half of Mowbrays defalcation in the Bishops Rents for which Sir Ra: and Mr. Baker (who has the like sum to pay) were *Mowbrays Security*. It is a strange thing that Baker, who has for some time known pretty well the Situation of the Durham Bank, should *forget this Security*, and neglect to have it withdrawn for himself & Sir Ra: he is now ready to hang himself about it . . . I think *Money matters* are destined to torment us, and at least at *present* to interfere with all our comforts and happiness—tho' if we can parry the *present evils*, better prospects present for future days. I am told here that there is no money in this Country, Cattle, Horses, &c go to the Markets and return *unsold*—every body in dispair, but the great *Capitalists* . . .

Now I am *old* and You are *Young*, and may look forward I hope and pray to a long life—and will profit by the *amazing* advance in these Estates—which I have reason to believe may be *more than doubled*. Every day something comes out to that effect—and I am anxious to investigate the truth, because if so, it will enable us to *assist* those we most love—during my life and afterwards it will be their own.

The situation of the Country has much to do with the inconveniences we all suffer—and I do not see that the Nation has greatly profited by *Waterloo*, the *Bourbons* or *Napoleons Captivity*.

By the terms of their marriage settlement Byron was to share equally with Annabella in the income from the Noel estates after Judith's death; hence her assurance that she was doing her utmost "to *assist* those we most love" during her life. She wrote again on the 28th:

If Sir James does not return soon and act as he ought to do, the inconvenience and loss to me will be dreadful! I find I cannot give notices to the Tenants to quit, without the Signature of the Trustees—and that

[1] The executors of Lord Wentworth's will were Sir James Bland Burges and the first Lord Henley, whose wife was the late Lady Wentworth's youngest sister.

Some of them who hold Land at one pound an Acre which is worth three or four, will avail themselves of any legal Error to *hold over* at the old Rent.

On the 30th:

I asked General Ross about the Pension and he says Mrs. Leigh must apply to the *Secretary at War*, when in course it will be granted. I am very truly grieved that the Leigh Affairs turn out so ill—but every thing is unfortunate with *us all* at present—too much so to write about, without pain.

If difficulties delay the *longer* journey, surely You and Ld. B. could come *here*, for a short time at least, as the journey is easily done in two half days. It would do You *both* good I am sure—and if *quiet* is desired, We have none here to interrupt it. Pray tell Ld B. this, and how delighted Dad and Mam would be to see You both.

Annabella wrote to her mother on 30th August:

I have been making enquiries of every person who was likely to know, both for Dad & Lord B, if Mortgages were to be had—and amongst others of Col: Doyle, who has a good deal of intercourse with people of business. I enclose his answer. It seems that it is quite hopeless to raise the £10,000 by the *common* Mortgage, and any other would not I suppose be consistent with the provisions of the Settlement.

. . . Do you know I am a Widow for a day or two? Byron is just gone to Augusta, which I am glad of. It is possible there may be an exchange of husbands (Heaven forbid it should be in *reality*) and that Col: Leigh, who is not now at home may come here on business.

I am going to Hanson myself this morning.

Again on the 31st:

I have got your letter. You must see how impossible it is for us to say where we can best go—though a very short time will probably give grounds for a decision. I saw Hanson yesterday. He was very civil, and is going to Newstead to-day to do what he can, but has not any favorable expectations. The fact is that the Tenants all *wish* to be broken up, and to relinquish their Leases which are so much higher than the Farms could now be let for. Claughton still corresponds—and desires to purchase, but acknowledges that he can pay nothing at present, which would not answer . . .

I have heard from B—— to-day from Epping. I think the change will do him good, for he was worried to death here by business in which no exertions could avail. Hanson told me last night that "Lord Byron was *very flat* indeed," but that he had told him he must not suffer himself to be concerned about these matters. Very easy to prescribe—but what few can practise as well as I can. I had a good night and am well to-day—going to dine with the Doyles . . . Sir J. Burges is come back.

Apparently Byron's chief motive for going to Six Mile Bottom was a crisis in Colonel Leigh's affairs. One of his relatives had died, but a

Mrs. Longe was disputing the right of George Leigh and his mother to a bequest. Having achieved the favour of an audience from the Prince Regent, George Leigh—"that very helpless gentleman"—thought "no further exertion necessary" and "from the same cause he is grown quite indifferent to the chance of his inheritance." It was even left to Augusta to seek the military pension to which he was entitled.

Byron's note to Annabella from Epping on the 31st was to ask her to send on to him at Augusta's "*two phials labelled 'drops'*", which his valet Fletcher had forgotten to pack. He signed it "ever most lovingly thine B (not *Frac.*)," meaning that he was not feeling in what she called his "fractious" mood. She had already written to Byron the same day:

Darling duck—

I feel as if B—— loved *himself*, which does me more good than any thing else, and makes young Pip jump.

You would laugh to see and still more to hear the effects of your absence in the house—Tearing up carpets, deluging staircases, knocking, rubbing, brushing!—By all these I was early awakened, for Mrs. Mew seems convinced that my ears and other senses have departed with you. She no longer flies like a sylph on tip-toe, but like a troop of dragoons at full gallop. The old proverb—

"When the Cat's away, the Mice will play"—

They shall have their holiday, but I can't fancy it mine. Indeed, indeed *nau* B—— is a thousand times better than *no* B.

I dare not write any more for fear you should be frightened at the length, and not read at all. So I shall give the rest to Goose.

I hope you call out "Pip, pip, pip"—now & then. I think I hear you —but I won't grow lemoncholy—— A——da!

She added a postscript:

I have just got Post—with dear good B's mandate which shall be obeyed, and *I* am rather obliged to Fletcher for his forgetfulness.

Sir J. Burges returned.

Augusta wrote on 1st September:

My dearest A——

I've just got yr letter & thank you from my heart for all your kindness. I hear from G—— that he has sent Mrs. Longe's paper to Lord Chichester . . . I think Mrs. Longe *a Devil* & THE Devil! oh fie! but never mind I can't help it . . . I'm sorry for Hanson's opinion of my Mother in Law's concerns. She seems well disposed not to resign her *right* of administering . . .

B. was quite well yesterday—he is as yet invisible this Morng—but I will obey you de bon coêur . . . we had a little *Sparring* about *Brandy* last night—but I came off victorious—I'm not sure however that the contest may not be renewed. After I wrote yesterday, *Hob* was mentioned apropos of Newstead & Mam—& I had probably ye same account of their conversation that you had.[1] I did not say much, but defended Mam *gently*—& said H—— must have mistaken her meaning, & that even if *she had* said *so* & *so* no TRUE friend of *his ought* or *would* have repeated it to him. He has confessed almost all his *naughty fits* & *sayings* but without seeming to have an idea that I might have heard them, & of course I did not betray that I had. Upon ye whole I am pleased with him as far as relates to Pip—of whose merits he seems convinced as he ought to be, & of whom he talks quite pathetically as the "best little Wife" in ye World . . . Georgey's eyes sparkle more than ever at Unc—poor Guss is better—*Do* [Medora] very pale but well.

B. is writing for himself & his own acct. will be much more agreable than all I can write—so God bless you dearest Sis—

Ever thine Guss

or *Goose*

Byron wrote thus:

Dearest Pip—

I am very glad that Sir James has at last found his way back—he may now transfer his attention from his son's leg to your Mother's *leg*-acy—which seemed in some peril of amputation also in his absence.

Goose left a mousetrap in the apartment allotted to me the consequence of which is that from the very convenient place of its application I have nearly lost a toe.

The parcel came & contained also a billet from Roody[2] to my Valet—from which I infer that she is better in one sense & worse in another. All the children here look shockingly—quite *green*—& Goose being as *red* as ever you have no idea what a piece of patchwork might be made of the family faces.

Has Hanson marched for N[ewstead]?—Goose is taking a quill from her wing to scribble to you—so—yrs. alway

most conjugally

B.

A——da——

Judith also wrote to Annabella on 1st September: "I very much fear that the Settlements both of Halnaby and Newstead are entire Bars to raising Money in the way Doyles Note mentions." She suggested that Doyle should be asked, "Will the Lender agree to furnish the Money on an *entailed Estate*," adding, "I say *this of Noel—You* and *I* agreeing to it;" it seemed that "an Annuity at 10 pr. Cent, Secured on Land, is not an unreasonable demand, more especially *if redeemable*," though General Ross "told me it was *impossible* to raise Money on Mortgage at present . . . also, that there was little prospect of selling Land." She continued:

[1] Hobhouse presumably reported to Byron the conversation he had after the abortive sale on 28th July when he "called on Lady Noel who wants Byron to sell hugely."

[2] Ann Rood had become Annabella's maid at Seaham in the previous February; she afterwards married the valet Fletcher. "Rood is rather better," wrote Annabella to her mother on 30th August; "I believe I saved her life by a timely dose of Castor Oil when she was in danger of an inflammation in her bowels."

I fear Ld B. would find his Sister very much distressed, God send us all a good deliverance!

Selina [Doyle] too writes in bad Spirits, nothing is chearful but the *Sky*, and that is clear and bright—an East Wind would cause dispair.

Seldom losing an opportunity to be pert in condescension to her mother, Annabella replied on 2nd September:

I have every thing I could wish in letters from B. and Augusta. She is much the best of the bad families with which she is connected in spirits, having a sanguine temperament that enables her to hope in the face of Despair. Do ask her to give you some lessons.

Doyle had gone out of town, but she thought of consulting William Frend, and "I am now expecting Sir James Burges."

From all these letters written within four days between 30th August and 2nd September, it appears that Annabella had at last awakened to some sympathy with Byron's financial worry, probably because her parents and the Leighs had similar affliction; she was "glad of" Byron's visiting Augusta, as he was "*very flat* indeed"; sleeping and feeling well, she was very busy, seeing Doyle and Hanson on business, dining out with the Doyles, and receiving a call from Sir James Burges. The contemporary evidence thus affords a startling contrast with her recollections, written after the lapse of only a few months:

He went to S M B Aug . . . after having been perfectly ferocious towards me for 4 days—the nights he ordered a bed apart. Then, just before he set out, he asked my forgiveness half in earnest & half in jest—but a kind word from him was then too precious to me to be rigorously examined. I was very ill—he had kept me awake almost all the preceding night to exercise his cruelty upon my feelings, & notwithstanding the self-command I could generally maintain, my convulsive sobs at last forced me to get up & leave the room. When I returned somewhat more composed, he accosted me with a cold & sneering expression. My parents & almost all my friends were out of Town. I was left without any human being to take care of me in my then very precarious situation except Mrs. C[lermont] whose constant devotion to my welfare had kept her in Town—but she was not in the house, and after he left it, it seemed to be inhabited only by the remembrances of his Misery. I did not then, though I did afterwards explain to A[ugusta] the sufferings he had inflicted upon me. A fear of the post principally deterred me—I did not suspect her of then yielding to his criminal wishes. She had wished to prevent his coming—& assigned as the reason to me that in the case of his being enriched by the probable sale of N[ewstead] she feared his generous dispositions towards her would be worked upon by her husband to make some present inconsistent with his own circumstances, & not so advantageous to them as assistance in a more judicious form.

I liked the disinterestedness apparent in the first reason.

> He returned after 5 days absence—most kind towards me, but offended with her. She had written to me of her taking the part of my parents against his false & malignant abuse of them. I attributed this gleam of hope to her—& the more regretted my former & not totally extinguished suspicions on one point. Something he told me of her saying towards him alone revived the suspicion that she wished to flutter him into a guilty passion for her—I can scarcely repeat it from its indelicacy, but it did not afford evidence enough to have any lasting effect. He was very affectionate towards me for 4 days after his return from S.M.B. After 4 days his manner towards me changed—he spoke of her with vindictive feelings almost as strong as influenced him towards me and it was about this time I think that he said to me one day in the carriage—in the midst too of a lighter strain—"I shall break your heart & A's after all"—as if it were a fate which he was doomed to fulfil.

While she could thus express appreciation of Augusta's "disinterestedness" in fearing lest her husband might trespass upon Byron's "generous dispositions," Annabella could also write of Byron's conduct at this period, "His absorbing passion for money might arise from its being indispensably necessary to his plans of concealment."

"B—— comes back to-day, and Augusta writes that he has been very disconsolate without me," Annabella told her mother on 4th September; "I am marvellous happy at the expiration of my Widowhood." He was no sooner with her than she became critical of his occupations, informing her father on the 5th:

> Drury Lane opens on Saturday—I don't much like the concern, and I believe it is the general sentiment, as far as regards B's share of it. Lady Hardwicke told me it was only fit for *a six and eight penny man*, and it seems to involve a species of business & attendance which I did not at all foresee. In short it is the vocation of an *Acting* Manager—to superintend candle-snuffers, lecture the performers, &c &c.
>
> It is no easy matter to get rid of it now, but I think it will produce unpleasant consequences, in opinion at least. It is one reason for which I think it would be advantageous to leave Town. Of that I know nothing.

Perhaps she would have felt more interest in the theatre if her friend Mrs. Siddons had been employed there, but Mrs. Siddons had declined Byron's invitation to an engagement owing to her commitments at Edinburgh. Byron took a deep interest in his duties, as his published correspondence shows; he encouraged contemporary dramatists, like Coleridge and William Sotheby, personally supervised the casting of plays, and tried to assemble a company of the best quality available. Annabella was surely tactless in opposing an interest that served as a distraction from brooding over money worries.

Nor can Byron have been in the best of moods to brook opposition. "B—— has got a bad cold in his head, and a swelled nose!—but I have not caught it yet," wrote Annabella on 6th September, with another item of news unlikely to have pleased him, "Lady Melbourne is returned to Town—and called on me to-day—but was not admitted." To her mother's query, "Seaham is ready for You, or if You cannot go *there*, Why not come *here?*" she replied on 8th September:

I wish I could see the practicability of our going to Kirkby, but I do not. The moment B—— were to leave Town, for a permanency, some measures that are now suspended would immediately ensue. He is in great anxiety about me, and would have me go by myself—which I *will not*. As long as I am with him I am comparatively comfortable, and the anxiety of absence under such circumstances would far overbalance any little good that a change of air might do. In short it is my *summum malum* at present—and of these things I think no one can judge for another.

Tactfully her mother offered no comment on this emphatic decision, confining her next letter to the progress of financial negotiations, but by 21st September she was reconciled to its being "finally settled that You are to be confined in Town," and approved of Annabella's choice of a medical attendant, Francis Le Mann, "in preference to any of the fashionable Accoucheurs." Annabella's recollections seven months later may be compared with her pronouncement to her mother:

When I was strongly advised in the Summer to leave Town for my health I could not persuade him to accompany me though he said he should be very glad to be left by himself, in the most unkind manner, & when I represented that I was not in a situation to take the long journey (to Seaham alone) he was not induced to attend in any degree to my health or comfort.

He said that if I went to Seaham he should not stay with me there nor be with me at the time of my confinement.

I replied—if that were the case I should remain with him—unless he commanded me to go.

Upon this he appeared apprehensive and gave me leave to stay.

In contempt of Byron's occupation at the theatre, she referred to him as "the Manager." "*The Manager* is as flourishing as the *Magpie* whereof Renown is rife," she told her father on 24th September, and after herself seeing Dowton as Shylock on 5th October, she wrote to her mother next day, "I asked Lady Melbourne to go with me—for as the Manager is always trotting about behind the Scenes, I should not much like to be alone, unless I had an amant to interrupt my solitude." Yet she testified to Byron's conscientious attitude to his work when informing her father:

Byron was this morning at a Drury-Lane Committee, where I fancy he acquired great credit by the propriety and temperance of his conduct when Mr Kinnaird flew into passion because he could not make B—— and the other members quite subservient to his wishes & opinions. *To revenge himself* he gave in his resignation, which was *gladly* accepted by the proprietors, though it was a very unhandsome step towards those whom he had induced to become Committee-men, and now deserted on this sudden pique. B—— addressed the meeting to this effect—that whatever difficulties he might at present apprehend in the concern, he did not conceive it honorable to relinquish his share in them this year, when it was too late for the proprietors to select other managers—and when these had already undertaken the responsibility of measures that could not now be changed. As far as he was qualified to support them, his services were at the command of the Proprietors. So they were all mightily pleased.

Her parents were doing their best to assist in money matters. Sir Ralph had sold some of the farms on the Seaham estate to a Colonel Dalbiac for £7,350, but as in the case of Byron's former sale of Newstead to Claughton, the purchase money was not forthcoming and a bill in Chancery had to be filed. He had now transferred his affairs from William Hoar to Gerard Blisson Wharton, senior partner in Wharton & Ford, a firm of attorneys which was to act for him, for Annabella, and for her grandson over a period of seventy-two years. On 9th October Annabella heard from her mother: "Colonel Dalbiac has taken alarm at the order to file a Bill against him, and will complete the bargain as soon as the Deeds can be drawn, and the proper signatures obtained." To this she replied ominously on the 11th:

It seems from Wharton's Statement that the Execution & Col. D[albiac]'s payment will run a race—and it would be a sad thing if the latter were to lose it by a few days. For positively the Execution cannot be suspended beyond the 6th of Nover:—I fear that Wharton meant only the *finishing* of the deeds which are now Ingrosing, not their *Signing* (a business of some days at least) when he named the 1st week in Novr. for their conclusion. Do you know of any means by which a week might be gained? Perhaps you may be in Town about that time. I should very much lament the seizure of the books. I believe the sum is now £1600.

When B—— has any hope of avoiding this last extremity, he is quite a different man—for he feels it dreadfully, and distracts himself with the idea of Bailiffs in the House at the same time with the Midwife. For my part, it would probably be the time when I should care least for them—but I care very much to see him in an agony.

On the 13th she reported a plan by which "Claughton is to have the furniture of Newstead for £1200—and to take the house off our hands for a certain rent till he can compleat the purchase, which he would be able to do by the sale of one of his own Estates." The lawyers also launched a complicated transaction by which Sir James Bland Burges and Lord Henley, as the Noel trustees, were to borrow £6,000 on mortgage from Lord Melbourne and advance it to Byron on account of the £20,000 devised by Sir Ralph to Annabella in her marriage settlement. But the difficulty of raising a mortgage on an entailed estate, which had occurred to Judith's lay mind on 1st September, only penetrated to the lawyers' perceptions in October, whereupon five firms of attorneys—respectively representing the interests of Sir Ralph Noel, the trustees of the Byrons' marriage settlement, the Noel trustees, Byron, and Lord Melbourne—began an interchange of correspondence towards obtaining the necessary consents and endorsements.

On Friday 13th October Annabella wrote to her mother, "I suppose you see in the Papers that ma Chère Cousine is returned, having imported I believe several improvements in iniquity." The same day she received the following:

> My Dear Lady Byron—I was most sorry to be out when you had the kindness to call here. Will you accept a Lyonese scarf it is made of such thin materials that I have torn it & nearly spoild it—as they made me wear it on Landing—to prevent the Sharks from siezing it. I am going to Brighton to see my Boy, but I hope to return soon. Will you do me the favour of reading the 2 MSS, which I was urg'd to present to one of the Managers at Drury Lane—& if they are worth any thing will you shew them to your husband. I know nothing of their Author except his having made me this request. George[1] is out of Town—are you offended that I thus venture to torment you—
>
> believe me ever sincerely
> & gratefully yours
> CAROLINE LAMB
>
> Melbourne House
> Friday Morng
> will you have the kindness to deliver these mss to Lady Melbourne when you have lookd at them . . . would your husband like to have a Book—belonging to Napoleon—with the Eagle on it.

Annabella informed her father on the 14th:

> Mrs. Leigh expresses just the same satisfaction in the idea of attending me *with Mam*, as I am happy to find is reciprocal. I daresay we shall all be very agreable.
>
> We had rather a satisfactory notice from Mr. Wharton yesterday, in consequence of which I have written to Mr. Bland requesting to know when his Signature may be obtained.[2]
>
> Then I had a present yesterday from Lady C. Lamb!—"Timeo Danaos et dona ferentes"--and with this French Scarf, & Ly Holland's

[1] Her brother-in-law, George Lamb, was one of Byron's colleagues on the Drury Lane Committee.

[2] Thomas Davison Bland, of Kippax Park, was one of the trustees of the Byrons' marriage settlement, along with Douglas Kinnaird, George Baker, Cuthbert Ellison, William Hoar, Charles Hanson, Sir Thomas Henry Liddell, and John Cam Hobhouse.

Necklace, of which I think I told you, my livery will be quite complete.

I am very well.

"I have a *very bad* Cold in my head . . . can scarce see to Write," wrote Judith next day, and on the 21st Sir Ralph reported "that our *Mam* . . . has had an attack of Rheumatism from taking Cold," so she was unable to accompany him to London towards the end of the month. Annabella wrote to her on the 31st:

I never heard of any thing so comical as my danger of being a Sister—it certainly shows the *caution* of the Executors.

Dad dines to-day at Whitehall, and is to go afterwards, as he calls it, to the *opposition* box—Lady M's is vis-a-vis to ours, and above that is Lady Besborough's . . . A person very well acquainted with their contents says he would match the iniquity of those two boxes against that of *all* the rest of the House.

Lady C L—— is there every night, making herself conspicuously ridiculous, with William, as well as the House, to witness her frantic follies . . .

Everybody said I was looking better yesterday than for a long time—and I have recovered my grace & agility, which are only impaired when my Stomach is disordered. I entertain daily a higher opinion of Mr. LeMann's judgment . . .

On 1st November she was feeling no resentment against Byron, for under that date she wrote some memoranda which she afterwards endorsed "Reflections on Lord B's character written under a delusive feeling in its favor":

Whatever may be the appearances to the contrary, his sense of Religion is strong, and ineffaceable—but from early superstitions & Calvinistic impressions, as well as from various circumstances in later life, his views of Divine Government here, and Judgment hereafter, are unhappily discoloured with gloom and despair. From such ideas he naturally desires to take refuge, and imagines it is to be found in the total disbelief of their fundamental principles, not in the removal of a painful and mistaken association. Thus he feels towards Religion in general the irritation which its *perversion* has excited . . .

He has very vague ideas of Virtue, having never studied even practical morality as distinct from religion—nor known to do its duties except from the instinctive goodness of his heart. His neglect of them is also connected with the *misdirection of his Imagination*—

1st—It is too exalted—and when he cannot do good on the vast scale which it presents, he does not descend to perceive the lesser opportunities of common existence.

2ndly—It is too absent from the present—too much busied in the past or speculating on the future, and therefore throws no light on those daily duties which it ought to illustrate . . .

He has for some time past been striving to make a worldly wisdom, which is foreign to his nature, the governing principle of his conduct—from an erroneous belief that the more disinterested impulses of his heart can only be repaid with disappointment (as they have been under a *romantic* direction) and that *they* are the happiest who live for themselves, whilst he regrets & depreciates in himself the finer qualities that oppose his imitating them, and that still raise his thoughts to the "wisdom from above." It is necessary to show him . . . the fallacy & misery of this selfish system . . . Hypocrisy has been called the homage of Vice to Virtue. In him it is the homage of Virtue to Vice. It is better never to *give credit* to what is false in feeling or opinion, & unworthy of his nature. Wicked people have, for a time, induced him to act on wrong motives, by discrediting his right ones. And, on the contrary, by insisting on the right ones we may rouse *him* to do them justice.

Amongst other appearances that are *out of the natural character* we may sometimes observe, particularly under disappointment & mortification, those of a worldly vanity. Such casual motives are *borrowed* from the false measures of little minds. Let their incompatibility with real dignity or happiness be pointed out—from obvious instances—and how poor & insufficient their objects are found in possession. All errors of *judgment* (I scarcely know of any others) ought to meet with opposition to the best of our abilities . . . I think it very dangerous to attempt even a desirable end by working on a weakness—since Error strengthens in action . . . He is the worse for all indulgence of foibles beyond the Christian temper of forbearance & forgiveness.

She was still in this mood when she wrote to Augusta:

My head is better—and I wish to make a few observations respecting the nature of my greatest fears for B, and I think I daily understand the case better. His misfortune is an habitual *passion for Excitement*, which is always found in ardent temperaments, where the pursuits are not in some degree organized. It is the Ennui of a monotonous existence that drives the best hearted people of this description to the most dangerous paths, and makes them often seem to act from bad motives when in fact they are only flying from internal suffering by any external stimulus. The love of tormenting arises chiefly from this Source. Drinking, Gaming &c. are all of the same origin. How far *it* may depend on body or mind it is difficult to ascertain. I am inclined to think that a vitiated stomach, particularly if arising from habits of Excess, is a chief cause of the sensation of Ennui—and that change of Scene, air & exercise are more efficient to its removal than any efforts of Reason. As for seeking a cure in worldly dissipation, it is adding to the evil—and for that reason I so much dread B's entering into those pursuits of Fashion, whose votaries are always the victims of this misery, in the intervals of their mischief-making occupations. At the same time I would have his mind diverted from itself by every possible means that would not lead to an accession of the Disease—and so far from considering my own tastes, if I find that the disease is making a progress I will court Lady M[elbourne]'s Society for him, or any thing in the world to arrest its *fatal* course. I know in what it must end if it encrease—and with such apprehensions will you wonder if I am sometimes almost heart broken before my time. My dear, dear A, do give me every opinion of yours on this, & don't mistrust your own judgment. I will not blindly adopt it. Such were my waking reflections last night.

The lawyers' delays had resulted in the threatened execution when she wrote to Augusta on 9th November:

Everything is explained by a Bailiff sleeping last night in the house. From the old quarter—all this occasioned by a delay between Mr. Hoar & Hanson (as Dalbiac's money has been ready above 3 weeks and my father waiting to sign) who did not choose to commence the legal part till it ought to have been done.

God knows what I suffered yesterday & am suffering from B's distraction, which is of the *very worst* kind. He leaves the House telling me he will at once abandon himself to every sort of desperation—speaks to me only to upbraid me with having married him when he wished not—and says he is therefore acquitted of all principle towards me, and I must consider myself *only* to be answerable for the vicious courses to which his despair will drive him—and is driving him. The going out of the house & the drinking are the most fatal. He was really quite frantic yesterday—said he did not care for any consequences to me, & it seemed impossible to tell if his feelings towards you or me were the most completely reversed—for as I have told you, he loves or hates us together. God knows what he will do. I find in a religious trust the only comfort & peace I can experience. Things never were so serious—I don't mean the circumstances, for they *must* mend, but his feelings.

You shall hear again tomorrow but I hope for no better. It is only fair to Hanson to state that Mr. Hoar is most to blame, in having allowed Mrs. Hoar's dangerous illness to prevent him from drawing the deed.

Don't be unhappy about *me*—and perhaps you will see less cause than I do to be so about *him*.

Later the same day she added:

I have waited to the last in hopes of some change—but all is inexorable pride & hardness. O Augusta, will it ever change for me—I scarcely know what I say. Tho' I have been making the best of things till yesterday, when self-deception became impossible, I have thought that since last Saturday (on which night he sat drinking with Kinnaird's party till ½ past four in the morning) his *head* has never been right—and he will add I fear more & more to the cause.

Again to Augusta on the 10th:

B. relented last night—for he returned earlier from the play, and I took the opportunity of attacking him, which I had scarcely had before, as he had never been in my company throughout the day for much more than an hour. He was kind to me again, but still rather odd. However I am very thankful, after my fit of despair imparted to you—cruelly I fear.

He does not think I know the circumstances of our unwelcome guest. I wish George B[yron] or some man friend of common sense were in the way to laugh B—— out of his excessive horrors on this subject which he seems to regard as if no mortal had ever experienced any thing so shocking, and *we* can do less, because he thinks that women don't enter into those sublime grievances. They are quite the subject of his *romance* at present.

After post—

I say so little to you of your own concerns because I cannot speak very fully on paper, but there are none of which I think more, or wish more to talk to you.

I must tell you that you are "Augusta" again to B—for you were "Mrs. Leigh" during the paroxysm, & I expected you would soon be "The Honorable." I ought to have laughed at this—but I took it as another misery, fancying that *I* was in some way the cause of such an alteration. And now for my peace & comfort, dearest A, let me express my earnest desire that whatever you may see or hear towards me, you will never think it an act of friendship for me to risk B's displeasure. I suspect you of any *disinterested folly* of this kind. But in the first place under any circumstances I should be *more* grieved if he & you were to differ—and in the second (which may have more weight with you) I don't think it could do *me* any good to have *my part taken*. So remember.

I am afraid *this* Bailiff is a sad brute, & will proceed to very great inconvenience. I have written to my Mother on the subject, who if she can will certainly send me some money—but my father has been as nearly in Gaol as possible.

Her letter to her mother is not preserved, but she had already informed Augusta that, despite her illness, her mother was "to be in Town the end of next week, which is a great satisfaction to me, as I am pretty sure she won't fidget at this juncture." She also wrote to the lawyer Wharton's partner Ford on the 11th:

Lady Byron having understood that Mr. G. Wharton has put Mr. Ford in possession of all the necessary information respecting the deeds by which £6000 of her Fortune is to be transferred by her Trustees to Lord Byron, wishes to enquire if those writings which were to be completed under Mr. G. Wharton's direction for the signature of the different persons in that trust, have been accordingly presented, or are ready for that purpose, as the deed of *Mortgage* which Mr. Hoar was to prepare is now ingrosing by Mr. Hanson. It is desirable that all delay should be avoided, and Lady Byron trusts that Mr. Ford will have the goodness to provide against it as far as may be in his power.

The same day to Augusta:

Don't be afraid for my Carcase—it will do very well. Of the rest I scarcely know what to think—I have many fears.

Let me see you the middle of next week—at latest.

Hobhouse is come—I have great reason to think to arrange a plan for going abroad. My heart aches—it has been severely tried—but I won't say more on paper.

You will do good I think—if any can be done.

My dearest A, I feel all your kindness.

The same day, Saturday, 11th November, Hobhouse noted in his journal:

Called on Kinnaird—hear Douglas is doing very well, but that he & Byron tussle abominably—called on Byron, saw him and her Ladyship—he is unaltered in any respect, dear creature, but owns that marriage makes him selfish—"I have not written to you, you see"—I forgive him—He does not dine with his wife—Well, he says—don't marry.

Byron afterwards told Medwin, "I have prejudices about women: I do not like to see them eat,"[1] adding:

I do not like to be interrupted when I am writing. Lady Byron did not attend to these whims of mine. The only harsh thing I ever remember saying to her was one evening shortly before our parting. I was standing before the fire, ruminating upon the embarrassment of my affairs, and other annoyances, when Lady Byron came up to me and said, 'Byron, am I in your way?' to which I replied, 'Damnably!' I was afterwards sorry, and reproached myself for the expression: but it escaped me unconsciously—involuntarily; I hardly knew what I said.

Annabella paid heavily for her determination that he was "the worse for all indulgence of foibles," and so little regard had she for his idiosyncrasies that she included in her first statement of reasons for the separation:

For four or five months before my confinement, he objected unkindly to dine with me, though I was willing to conform to his hours, and once when his dinner was accidentally served at the same table with mine, he desired his dish to be taken into another room (in my presence, & the servants attending) with an expression of rage. For the last six weeks before my confinement he hardly ever addressed me except in the most harsh & unkind manner.

After months of sullen resentment at her possessiveness and determination to reform him according to her own conception of what he should be, the bailiff's invasion precipitated a brainstorm. Annabella did not exaggerate the "agony" that this indignity inflicted on Byron though she considered his "horrors" were "excessive" because she

[1] Beside this passage in Medwin's *Conversations* Annabella noted in January 1851, "Lord Byron was in the habit of dining *alone*—in his own house, & sometimes when at Seaham Lady *Noel* having always made arrangements which left it option with him to do so, & never taking it amiss."

had never appreciated how deeply and for how long he had been harrowed by awareness of his embarrassments. He had wished to postpone their marriage till he was assured of some measure of security; after the marriage he was continually oppressed by consciousness of dunning creditors and by forebodings of possibilities if financial relief was not forthcoming. He had done all he could to avert the dreaded indignity by again offering Newstead and Rochdale for auction, and he had reason for grievance that Sir Ralph had been unable to fulfil his obligation—urging the London agent of Lord Melbourne's attorney to expedite payment of the £6000 advance, Wharton wrote on 12th October: "Lord Byron ought to have had this Money last May and has been and will continue to be put to the greatest Inconvenience till it is pd." Doubtless he did not allow that Sir Ralph might have pride equalling his own in hiding the extent of his embarrassments; Judith stated that "unavoidable and heavy losses from Bankruptcies of those who rented Collieries and also the recent failures of the Durham and Sunderland Banks have swept away *many thousands*."

While abundant records of Annabella's emotions at this crisis survive, there are none of Byron's except in the distorting mirror of hers. Moore quoted from a lost journal in which Byron related with his usual humour an interview with the bailiff, who endorsed Annabella's view that there was nothing "shocking" in the situation by remarking, "I have been in Sheridan's house a twelvemonth at a time—a civil gentleman—knows how to deal with *us*." Without doubt Byron was equally civil, keeping him in concealment by attending to his comfort; Annabella suggests that he tried to conceal the man's presence from her, and evidently Hobhouse had no suspicion of it when he called. He ordered the sale of his books—though this was proved unnecessary by events—and the only letter he seems to have written during these troubled weeks was on 14th November, when he declined with dignity and grace his publisher's offer of an advance of £1500 to meet the emergency.

Justly Moore emphasised the agitating effect on Byron of this embarrassment, though he seems to have exaggerated the visitations by bailiffs in stating, "his door was almost daily beset by duns, and his house nine times during that year in possession of bailiffs." Too easily he assumed that the "defects" of genius rendered Byron "unfitted for domestic happiness," nor did he indicate that the separation was invoked by Byron's seeking escape from despair like many lesser men of no genius—in getting drunk.

The resort to drunkenness involved him in another offence, which must have seemed to him afterwards contemptibly trivial by comparison with its consequences, as Annabella recorded little more than two months later:

He had for many months professed his intention of giving himself up either to women or drinking, and had asked me to sanction these courses, adding however that he should pursue them whether I gave him leave or not. Accordingly for about three months before my confinement he was accustomed to drink Brandy & other liquors to intoxication, which caused him to commit many outrageous acts, as breaking & burning several valuable articles, and brought on paroxysms of rage or frenzy—not only terrifying but dangerous to me in my then situation—and of this he was so well aware that he has asked me on occasions of extreme ill-usage, if the Child was dead.[1] About two months before my confinement he took a Mistress, of which Circumstance I was ignorant till informed by himself. He had given many hints of it, to which I deemed it prudent to appear blind, till he forced the knowledge upon me in the grossest and most insulting manner—saying, he could not take the trouble of acting the Hypocrite, therefore thought it best to tell me, declaring that he should not give up the connection. He studiously & maliciously informed me of the times of his visits to this woman, & seemed to have a pleasure in alluding to the subject before me & others. He has at various times declared to me that he should have no scruple in connecting himself with any woman that came in his way, and told me that if I were dissatisfied with his conduct in that respect I was perfectly at liberty to do the same—as it was a matter of indifference to him, & perhaps the easiest way to get rid of me would be by a Divorce.

Following up this statement immediately after receiving it from Annabella's mother, the lawyer Lushington assembled the following evidence:

Lord B: has admitted the fact to Lady B: to Mrs. L[eigh]: to Capt. B [George Byron]: & it is apprehended to Mr. K[innaird]:

Lord B: frequently visited Miss B[oyce]: at her Lodgings. This can be proved by Miss B's servants—& Lord B's. Correspondence by letter between them (Mrs. L: & Fletcher).

Lord B: took her home frequently in his carriage from the theatre, & staid a considerable time with her at her Lodgings—Coachman & Footmen certainly—Miss B's servants—NB. Lord B: often took Miss B: from the theatre after the Play.

Once Lord B: found that Miss B: had left a broach in his carriage[2] & he next morning sent his footman to search the carriage—he informed Mrs. L: of this fact & expressed great anxiety to have it found.

Lord B: has declared to Mrs. L: that Miss B: had cost him considerable sums of money & also he ordered Jewels of some value at Love & Kelly's

[1] On this part of the statement the lawyer Lushington noted: "Ld. B: was in habit of getting intoxicated with Brandy—Fletcher & his wife both can prove the breaking &c—& his conduct was particularly outrageous to Lady B: has confessed the breaking &c to Mr. Le Mann."

[2] This was on 15th November, according to Susan Boyce's published letters to Byron: "I lost my brooch in the carriage last night. If you receive this before anything is said about it you will then be on your guard and can say what you think proper."—"*To Lord Byron,*" by George Paston and Peter Quennell, 1939, p. 181.

Jewellers of Bond St. which jewels were carried to Miss B: it is believed by Fletcher. Lord B: has told this to Mrs. L: & to Lady B:

Lord B: used to permit Miss B: to come to the private Box at the theatre—(Box keepers)

There must be witnesses to prove great intimacy Mr. Rae probably, & Mr. K: & others about the Green Room.

Miss B: has made many demands for money upon Lord B: & he has declared he has broken off intercourse with her on that account—Mrs. L: & also to Lady B:

The connection has been acknowledged to Capt. B:

In recalling his experiences in the management of Drury Lane, Byron wrote:

> Players are said to be an impracticable people. They are so; but I managed to steer clear of any disputes with them, and excepting one debate with the elder Byrne about Miss Smith's *pas de*—(something—I forget the technicals)—I do not remember any litigation of my own. I used to protect Miss Smith, because she was like Lady Jane Harley in the face, and likenesses go a great way with me. Indeed, in general, I left such things to my more bustling colleagues.

Doubtless observing his kindness to Miss Smith, one of the minor actresses, Susan Boyce, drew Byron's attention to herself by writing to complain of having been "attacked last night in a most cruel manner by Mrs. Scott who by the way was *much elevated*—I don't know whether it was the *smell* or *taste* of gin." The date of the complaint does not appear, but she was courting his attentions when the bailiff's invasion drove him "quite frantic," and he seems to have drifted into an association with her when he was too drunk to consider either his emotions or his actions. He remembered her after six years as "a transient piece of mine, but I owe her little on that score, having been myself, at the short period I knew her, in such a state of mind and body, that all carnal connection was quite mechanical, and almost as senseless to my senses, as to my feelings of imagination."

Hobhouse recorded on 12th March following, "Byron owned to Scroope Davies and me, at last, that he may have been *bereaved of reason* during his paroxysms with his wife." Evidently he was too drunk to remember what he said to Annabella, for he also told Hobhouse "that except with Miss B he had never been guilty of any infidelity towards her—& that she could not guess this." Annabella was therefore recording ramblings under the influence of brandy:

> The first time that he obliged me to know that he had a mistress, he asked me if I meant to forgive him.
>
> I said that no one was more indulgent towards a *transgression* than myself,

however I might object to the *principle* & *practice* & I cordially forgave him for *this*—on which he said with a sneer "Generous Woman!" & declared his intention of pursuing the same course.

In a statement written within a few days of her first on 18th January:

I did not mention that for a considerable time before my confinement he would not see me himself for above an hour—or two—if so much throughout the day & left me therefore alone all the evening till Mrs. L—— came, for he had always objected to my having *any* society at home. When he did stay at home himself, it was to drink Brandy—& he would then dismiss me to my room in the most unkind manner. He told me he must either have *his Brandy or his Mistress.*

A few weeks later when beginning to assemble her case against Augusta, she added:

He told me to write to her of his vicious courses at the theatre, as if his taking a mistress was out of revenge *towards her*—& a greater injury to her than to me! I would not be the medium of such communications, and used quietly to decline them. He desired me to send her some very unkind messages—and when she was come to Town said he did not want her then as he had formerly done. The encrease of dispositions which were not less threatening to his own existence & welfare than to mine was the motive which at this time made me look to A. as my only efficient friend—& I confess I had at that time so far lost the suspicions in which he was concerned from the apprehension of crimes on his part yet more dreadful, that my only scruple in requesting her to come was lest she should suffer in any way from her interest for *me*—& particularly as to the pecuniary prospects of her children. This will appear from some letters written to her at that time which she has returned to me [the letters quoted on pages 323–6].

The reference to her "apprehension of crimes on his part yet more dreadful" may be adduced as evidence in support of Professor Wilson Knight's thesis that homosexual practices were a cause of the separation, but Annabella's habit of drawing inferences was now being nourished upon alcoholic ramblings intended to shock her. More difficult of explanation is Annabella's eagerness for Augusta's company during her confinement. As Augusta protested six months later, when catechised by her friend Mrs. Villiers at the time scandalous gossip was busy with rumours, "if Ly. B had ever heard such reports or if she had not treated them with the contempt they deserved, would she have invited me to come?" Annabella's reply to Mrs. Villiers on 12th May 1816 was on the lines elaborated in her recollections:

It must be remembered that my *Conviction* was progressively formed, and not till lately fixed—and though my suspicion had been awakened very early, it was not at the period you allude to, sufficiently corroborated to have been made a principle of conduct without risking a cruel injury to one who professed herself most affectionately & disinterestedly devoted to my welfare. There was no medium—I must either have treated her as guilty or innocent—My *Instinct* too strongly dictated the former, but the *evidence then* rested chiefly on his words & manners, & her *otherwise* unaccountable assent & submission to both . . . Besides at the time of her return to Piccadilly, I conceived there was no danger to her from him, as his inclinations were most averse from her, & absorbed in another direction.

Of Byron's behaviour before Augusta's arrival Annabella further recalled:

One night when he came to bed after having been with his Mistress, he said *you* appear to me very respectable from the comparison I have just been making (sarcastically).

When Mrs. Leigh was expected in town he having before confessed to me the fact of adultery said he should communicate *all* the particulars of the connexion to her & I might ask her if I wanted to know them always expressing his intention of continuing the Intercourse . . .

On his return from the Theatre he has minutely & insultingly described his familiarities with those women—and particularly Miss Smith—with whom he desired me to report by letter to Mrs. Leigh the particular liberties he had taken, asking me maliciously on these occasions, "How do you like *that*"—Sometimes "I would not give any thing for a woman who would not be jealous." When provoked by the unconsciousness I wished to affect in regard to Miss —— [Boyce], he at last said "Well then—*I tell you*—I *have* been *nau*"—which is his word for criminality.

He has threatened me with his intention of bringing his Mistress home with him at night,—if I should displease him in any thing—This I think in Mrs. Leigh's presence.

Before I left Town he threatened an intention of admitting her into the House.

Though she does not seem to have lived regularly at the house, Mrs. Clermont had been in London since April and daily in communication with Annabella. In one of her statements of March 1816 she related:

Lady Byron has several times since her marriage said to me that she believed she should be compelled to separate from her husband—saying "I will try all that is possible but I fear it will come to that at last."

Early in November she said "I cannot continue to live with him I must desire my father to take a house in town for me to lay in as I can not travel at this time and I am sure I shall not be safe here—but I fear it will kill my Mother when she knows how things are & I am sure she would be distracted if I were remaining in his House after she knew of his conduct. I must think of it a little more"—She afterwards determined to stay untill after her confinement & to keep it a secret from Lady Noel untill she could get to Kirkby again repeating her conviction that she could not continue to live with Lord B:

Judith herself stated in a memorandum on 23rd January 1816:

> To explain why *I* was *so long* kept ignorant of these Circumstances and *why* so little fell under my own observation after I came to London on November 16th to attend my Daughter in her Lying-in—I must state, that I was ill when I came, and principally confined to the House, that my Daughter was apprehensive that the *Shock* of being *then* informed of it, might *seriously* injure my health, so far as to prevent my recovery—and that Mrs. Clermont *fluctuated* between her fears for me and Lady Byron. Two days before She was brought to Bed, I took *to mine*, with Fever, Erysipelas and Asthma combined, and the very day the Child was born, I was in the opinion of Sir Henry Halford *seriously ill*.

Situated as she was, Annabella seems to have been satisfied to set aside her suspicions for the benefit of Augusta's society and support. When establishing her case against Augusta, she could recall in March 1817 that Byron's behaviour had not been uniformly vindictive:

> He told me at as late a period as Novr. 1815—whilst the Bailiff was in the House—that I was "the most uniformly cheerful person" he had ever known: and when I appeared gladdened by the scarce hours of his society bestowed upon me, he said "Well—poor thing—you are easily pleased to be sure"—& again "Never was any woman pleased with so little." He seemed to appreciate this as an effort of my affection (though without being moved by it from the stern & deliberate purpose of his soul) for he once said that if I had complained & been irritated "like most wives," he "should not have felt half so wretched." Another time . . . when I showed pleasure in the prospect of his company for a few hours, he told me he believed I felt towards him as a Mother does towards her child "happy when it is in her sight, because then she knows it is not in mischief." He would now & then accept with a smile my little attentions to his comfort or wishes—would say I was "a good kind thing"—"a good-natured Pip"—"the best wife in the world" and when one of these trifling circumstances occurred, he said, between jest & earnest, that he should remember it when he wrote "Pip's life," because it showed character so much more than events of greater consequence. Such kindly appearances were never indeed followed up by the conduct, but to me they afforded moments of consolation . . .
>
> In the autumn of 1815, when he was systematically endeavoring to drive me from him, or to sink me into the accomplice of his vices, he used to disguise the latter object under this specious phrase—"I meant to marry a woman who would be *my friend*—I want you to be *my friend*." I once replied—that I would renounce all personal feeling as his wife, and be his friend *only*—but that as such I never would sanction the vicious & self-destructive courses which he declared he was resolved to pursue.

Augusta arrived on the day when Miss Boyce was worried about losing her brooch in Byron's carriage. Annabella related:

When she came—Nov. 15—his reception was most ungracious—but he soon returned to his former habits of familiar confidence towards her—not however apparently with any of those inclinations which could alarm me for the present state of their intercourse—though with a thousand intimations which corroborated my belief in their criminality before my marriage.

It was however to receive its strong & I may say final confirmation (for her explicit confession has hardly strengthened it) from her expressions of self-accusing despair during his supposed insanity.

She appeared joyful to believe in it—thankful (I imagined) that he was exonerated by malady from so awful a responsibility, yet more deeply sensible of its recoil upon herself.

But her horror was evidently fixed upon a period antecedent to my marriage (when he *began Lara*, as she once signified) and her consolation appeared to be that towards me she had been innocent. We were left many evenings alone together when he went out professedly to indulge his most depraved propensities. I was wretched—but I thought her more so—and was I to visit upon her the cause—guilty as it was—of her broken-heartedness. One evening, when I said if he had had a friend of firm principle he might perhaps have been saved from such depravity, her remorseful feeling almost overpowered her. She said "Ah—you don't know *what* a fool I have been about him"—!—

The bitterness of her look as she threw her hair back from her forehead with a trembling hand, wrung my heart. I kissed that forehead where I saw penitential anguish, and left the room. Will you condemn me, reader?

During my sufferings till I quitted the house she was devoted to me. To defend me from his threatened violence & cruelty she seemed to acquire a fortitude inconsistent with her timid nature—& her accounts of his angry outrages towards her prevented my suspicions of worse during the midnight hours she passed with him to prevent in some degree his wilful disturbance of my rest.

One thing only, of a very indelicate nature which he said to her in my room about a fortnight after my confinement, & which she took with necessary indifference, made me suspect the return of his wicked purposes. I soon after wrote a note to her, for I was then too weak to venture upon agitating discussions, desiring that she would *only* consider what was eligible for herself as to remaining with us—that I would not *ask* her to stay one moment longer—at the same time I expressed & truly the consolations I felt in her society.

She required in return that I should tell her if I thought there was any reason for supposing her presence detrimental to *us*. I knew none (*if she did not*) & her exertions seemed necessary to secure me from the utmost excesses of Lord B's malevolence—she had said she *dared not leave me* with him—that she should be more miserable away & with the exception of that single speech I saw nothing that could create suspicions of guilt which I believed she would sooner die than submit to renew.

Mrs. Clermont stated on 22nd January following:

> The first time I ever had any conversation with Mrs. Leigh . . . was about the twentieth of November. She expressed herself as being excessively shocked at the Conduct of her Brother and acknowledged that the violence of his temper was so great as to cause the same apprehensions to be entertained by her for Lady Byron as by myself. A few days after Mrs. Leigh intreated me to come and sleep in the House at the time of Lady Byrons confinement after saying if he continues in this way God knows what he may do. She said he then appeared to feel the greatest hatred towards his Wife and the unborn Child that he sometimes said he hoped they would both die and then he should be at Liberty that he never would see the Child or her after she was brought to bed but should go abroad immediately.
>
> The impression that these and other circumstances made upon my mind was that he was likely to put her to Death at any moment if he could do it privately. I told Mrs. Leigh such was my opinion. She replied I will never leave him alone with her untill she is brought to bed, and then you must stay always with her.
>
> The only cause I heard that Lord Byron alledged for this ill-treatment of his Wife was that their marriage settlement prevented him selling his Estate for any thing he could get which he would otherwise do and go abroad with the money.

Annabella herself stated on 19th January:

> For several weeks previous to this period [of her confinement], his conduct had been such as led me & others in the house to believe my safety would be endangered by his violence during my confinement—and indeed throughout the whole of my pregnancy he had never shown me the least consideration or tenderness in conduct. . . I can bring 3 witnesses, if not more, who will swear to their belief that I was not safe in his house for some time before I quitted it.

Assessing the evidence on this point of Annabella's statement, the lawyer Lushington noted:

> His conduct towards Lady B: was so violent that strong apprehensions for her personal safety were entertained by Mrs. L. & Capt. B [George Byron]:
>
> Fletcher his valet has declared that he was so much alarmed for Lady B's safety that he several times watched Lord B: when he was preparing to go to bed until he was in bed, lest he sh'd go up to Lady B: & use personal violence. Lord B: was in the habit of having pistols with him & Fletcher was afraid he might use them.
>
> Lady B: bg. apprehensive of violence desired Mrs. L: to tell Fletcher to be upon the watch; Mrs. L: entertained the same apprehensions & told Fletcher. Fletcher said he had before taken care to do so, & continued to watch afterwards.

Annabella herself commented for Lushington's information:

I suspect that threats of violence towards me have been used to Fletcher —and that this testimony will be very important, particularly as he is quite incapable of suppressing or disguising the truth on cross-examination—being of a timid & simple disposition—much attached to his master, but interested also for me.

Mrs. Byron [Byron's Aunt Sophia] was in London for some time before my confinement—and till within a few days of my departure. Mrs. Leigh confided to her the general tenor of Lord B's conduct towards me—as of the most harsh & alarming nature—and I believe also most of the particular facts. I spoke latterly to Mrs. Byron of the measures proper to be taken on the supposition of Insanity. Mrs. B. knew that Mrs. Leigh was afraid to leave me alone with Lord B. &c &c—nearly as deposed by Mrs. Clermont. Mrs. B. was convinced—and is still—that Insanity must be the cause—and *she* chiefly instigated the consultation with Dr. Baillie. I can depend upon Mrs. Byron for a true & decided testimony—and have written proofs of her entire satisfaction with my conduct.

On 25th November Hobhouse called on Byron for the first time since his visit on the 11th, and noted, "In that quarter things do not go well—strong advices against marriage—talking of going abroad—&c." On the following Saturday, 2nd December, he was again in London—"saw Kinnaird & Byron—each as usual." He did not notice that Byron was drinking too much, but on both occasions they met in Kinnaird's company, and as Kinnaird was a hard drinker, over-indulgence in his company was no matter for remark.

On 5th February following, the day the demand for the separation was received, Hobhouse recorded, "Byron confessed he had been often out of temper with her (Lady B.) refused to live with her friends—told her she was in his way—but then he had a liver complaint and from one to four executions in his house at a time." Bailiffs must have been in occupation from early November till close on Christmas—perhaps later—for Hanson wrote to Wharton & Ford on Saturday 16th December "to acquaint them the different Deeds in Ld. Byrons Business have been executed and Mr. Hanson wishes to know whether the Mortge Money will be ready to be paid over to his Lordship on Monday night." Whether the money was then forthcoming does not appear from the several lawyers' correspondence, which was mainly concerned for many weeks with wrangling over their own costs, but on 22nd December Wharton & Ford sent to Hanson Colonel Dalbiac's promissory note for a thousand pounds, endorsed in Byron's favour by Sir Ralph Noel.

Hence it appears that Byron's fears were realised of having the bailiffs in the house at the time of the child's birth. Annabella began her statement of 18th January:

> On Decr. 9, the day before the child was born, when I had informed him that my labour was commencing, he asked me (without any previous disagreement) with the strongest expression of aversion & disgust, if I chose to live with him any more—& when I endeavoured to turn off the question in jest, said he had particular reasons for wishing to know, with an air of deep revenge—he seemed gratified when at length he brought me to tears. He then went out to the Theatre, & after his return at night told a person[1] who was staying in the house of the question he had proposed to me, asking how my spirits were. When that person reproved him for agitating me at such a moment, he said carelessly, "Yes, I am a fool—I always *mis-time* my questions."

Of this incident Mrs. Clermont recalled:

> The ninth of December being the evening before the birth of the Child Lady Byron having been ill all day went to the drawing-room where Lord Byron was. She soon after returned up stairs in excessive agitation and grief saying that he had been using the most insulting Language accompanied by gestures of menace and every appearance of the most malignant feelings towards her.

Byron's question was doubtless "mis-timed" but understandable if he was aware of the subject Annabella had been discussing that day with her parents' old friend, Serjeant Heywood, for she afterwards wrote to Lushington:

> Sergt. Heywood can witness that I consulted him on the subject *the day before my delivery*—and proposed the question if I should not then leave the house—This too by the desire, or at least full concurrence of Mrs. Leigh—which of course I would not unnecessarily reveal to commit her with her brother.

According to Hobhouse, Annabella complained next morning to her physician Le Mann that Byron spent the night "throwing up soda-water bottles against the ceiling of the room above which she slept as to deprive her of her sleep." Hobhouse afterwards examined the ceiling and found "no mark of blows," concluding that Byron's habit "of knocking off the heads of the bottles with a poker, sufficiently accounted for the noise." Annabella related of this:

> During my confinement, one night when I was in Bed, Ld B's violence below stairs was such that Mrs. L. who had likewise gone to rest (up two pair of Stairs) came out of her room to listen (by her own account) in the greatest alarm, fearing that he intended to come up to me in a fury.
>
> The Nurse on this & other occasions was very much alarmed by the strange noises made below me, as I afterwards found, though nothing had then been said to her on the subject.

[1] Mrs. Leigh, Lord Byrons Sister. [Note by Lady Noel].

Fletcher had remarked some additional preparations on Ld B's part to use his pistols, which combined with the evident rage against me, probably suggested stronger ideas of personal danger. I understood from Mrs. L. that Fletcher said to her—"I *hope* my Lord won't do you or my Lady *any harm.*"

The reason Mrs. Leigh assigned for sitting up late with Lord B. during my confinement was to prevent him as much as possible from making noises in the room below mine. In this she has said she could not always succeed—for he would break Soda water bottles—or throw them about the room—though told of the danger of disturbing me.

Annabella was delivered of a daughter at one o'clock on Sunday afternoon, 10th December; Augusta reported the next day to Francis Hodgson, "both Mother and Daughter have been, and are, as well as possible in every respect." Annabella recalled of Byron's behaviour:

After the birth of my child, he was saying he wondered [where it was begotten],[1] "if it was at Newmarket, no wonder if it should be like A[ugusta]"—with a horrid & vicious expression of countenance.

The other incident after my confinement was—What he said to her.

Hobhouse related what he called "a horrid story of Lord Byron having asked his wife when in labour whether the child was dead." It would indeed have been "horrid" if Byron had addressed such a remark to his wife during her labour, but it is highly improbable that he was present during her labour. Annabella's statement suggests that Byron asked the question of Augusta—as he might well have done while waiting downstairs in anxiety, particularly as in such a situation he was likely to be tormenting himself with gloomy forebodings.

Lady Anne Barnard related in reminiscences published by her great-nephew, Lord Lindsay:

When her lovely little child was born, and it was laid beside its mother on the bed, and he was informed 'he might see his daughter,' after gazing at it with an exulting smile, this was the ejaculation that broke from him, 'Oh! what an implement of torture have I acquired in you!' Such he rendered it by his eyes and manner, keeping her in a perpetual alarm for its safety when in his presence. All this reads madder than I believe he was; but she had not then made up her mind to disbelieve his pretended insanity.

Whether this is true or not, it is too often forgotten that Annabella was henceforth continually haunted by the possibility that Byron might demand custody of the child, and her subsequent elaborate preparation of her case against Augusta was inspired by that fear. That the fear

[1] The four words within square brackets were written in Beeby's shorthand, and are thus transcribed by Lovelace.

was in her mind during the rest of her time at Piccadilly Terrace appears in one of her statements:

> Lord B: declared to Mrs. L. before I left the house that he should take the child from me & she was so convinced of his intention to do so that she consulted Mrs. Clermont as to the answer she should make to Lord B: if he proposed to give her the care of it. He also declared to Mrs. Leigh that he had still hopes of getting rid of me by a divorce.

To this statement Mrs. Clermont added:

> Above a week after Lady B: was at Kirkby Lord B: told Mrs. Leigh he should write to propose a separation but that he was not decided whether to write to his Wife or to her Father upon the subject that he would do it coolly & with consideration. Mrs. Leigh asked what he would do about the child. He replied O I shall give that up intirely to her to prove to the World I have no fault to find with her.

12

THE SEPARATION—ANNABELLA AT PICCADILLY AND KIRKBY

December 1815—20th February, 1816

Hobhouse came up to London from the country on Thursday 21st December 1815, went to the play, and "passed evening afterwards with Byron." Next day:

> Called on Lady Noel, who seems very ill!!—called on Byron—saw his child Augusta *Ada*—the latter a name of some one who married into his family in the reign of King John.

On Friday of the following week, 29th December, Hobhouse recorded, "Generals Sebastiani and Flahault, Byron & Kinnaird dined with me at Wattier's—when Flahault & Kinnaird went away, Sebastiani, Byron & I talked Italian and Sebastiani was very entertaining . . . separated at twelve."

In his subsequent account of "The Byron Separation," Hobhouse wrote:

> It was about the end of November that Lord Byron had begun to talk vaguely with one friend of the absolute necessity of his breaking up his establishment after Lady Byron should have been confined. After her confinement, which took place on December 11 [in fact, the 10th], his Lordship renewed this conversation with his friend, and owned that his pecuniary embarrassments were such as to *drive him half-mad*. He said "he should think lightly of them *were he not married*"—he wished "he could go abroad." This he said once or twice, but afterwards dropped that expression and talked of going down into the country. He said "that no one could know what he had gone through"; that no man should marry—it doubled all his misfortunes, and diminished all his comforts. "My wife," he always added, "is perfection itself—the best creature breathing; but, mind what I say—*don't marry*." Such was his talk with one of his friends, and only one.

Perhaps, when drunk, Byron informed Annabella that he had talked of his domestic affairs to Hobhouse, but certainly by this time the annoyance created by Hobhouse's making mischief about her mother's eagerness for the sale of Newstead had deepened into animosity. In her statement to Dr. Baillie on Byron's mental condition, she wrote on 8th January 1816:

> He believes himself to be guilty of a dreadful crime, to which he never hears or reads an allusion without the deepest agitation, & violent struggles to suppress it—and he identifies himself with every character of the sort which comes under his knowledge—either in books or life. This remorse does not change like other feelings & seems to absorb them daily more & more.
>
> It is in my opinion doubtful if it be the *effect* or the *cause* of Insanity (for I have some corroborating evidence of such a *fact*). I have reason to think there is a person who possesses the key, & whose visits always *evidently* produced the diseased associations, till we seemed to notice them. Since then Lord B. has studiously disguised them, & appeared confused & guilty at the mention of that friend. He has repeatedly tried to find out if I have suspicions of this real or imaginary crime, & I am certain that my life depends on my seeming unconscious for once, when (from the hope that his mind would be relieved by confession) I touched but distantly on the subject, he grew terrible—quoting some words from Caleb Williams, that if I once knew his secret I was miserable for life, & he would persecute me for ever.
>
> A word or look more from me would have brought on immediate violence.

The application of the reference to *Caleb Williams* in her recollections of her honeymoon at Halnaby at first suggests that she is referring to Augusta as the "person who possesses the key." But she would hardly have referred to Augusta as "that friend," and who but Augusta was associated with herself in noticing Byron's recent behaviour? Reference to her Halnaby recollections (page 258) shows that she was not referring to Augusta in this statement to Dr. Baillie, for there she declares:

> I must observe that from the allusions he made it did not appear to me that he was then chiefly thinking of the circumstance on which this narrative is founded. *Murder* was the idea suggested to my mind.

That she was referring to Hobhouse in the statement to Dr. Baillie appears in her letter to Lushington, her chief legal adviser, on 11th February 1816:

> I was the more disposed to be severe on Mr. Hobhouse's letter from having long had reason to think that under the mask of friendship he was endeavouring Lord Byron's ruin, and had instigated, *more* than any one else, the conduct which has disunited us. Ever since his return to England in the Summer, there has been a decided change for the worse in Lord B. towards me—and Lord B. did then signify some important communica-

tion from Hobhouse on the Subject of our marriage; with a revengeful & mysterious air. I *know* that Mr. H. has always represented my parents in an invidious light. His flattery to myself has been so gross & disgusting that it was evidently a *disguise*.

From this emerges the appalling revelation that, throughout the year of their married life, Annabella suspected Byron of having committed murder—doubtless during his Mediterranean travels with Hobhouse. More than ever it appears that she entered upon married life with Byron in a state of mind as susceptible to "horrid mysteries" as that of Catherine Morland on her visit to Northanger Abbey! In a statement presumably written within a week or two of the above-quoted letter to Lushington, she declared:

Lord Byron has never *expressly* declared himself guilty of any *specific* crime—but his insinuations to that effect have been much more convincing than the most direct assertion.

At Halnaby he did several times declare that he was guilty of *some* heinous crime, which he said he would tell me when I had a child—for any woman might be bound by that tie.

I forgot however that he has positively declared at various times that he had another wife living—that he has mentioned such a fact to Mrs. L. in my presence.[1]

Of Mrs. Leigh he has always spoken to me as his *Mistress*—and when he began the connection with Miss B[oyce] seemed to regard it as a greater injury to Mrs. L. than to me. He has told me that she was not a virtuous woman, and that *he knew it*—significantly, & sneering at my ignorance . . .

He has shown me various similarities in the characters of Murderers—and in his own—with a manner to impress their truth.

While Annabella consulted Serjeant Heywood on the day before her delivery about leaving Byron's house, she soon found reason to suspect that Byron was himself considering the prospect of a separation:

In speaking of his intention to go away from me (after my delivery) he said that a woman always loved her husband less than her child—or less when she had a child. I answered with agony at such misconception of my feelings—"You will make me hate My child if you say so."

Again:

He used to ask me repeatedly after my confinement in a mysterious manner—if I loved him—to which I used generally to reply by some

[1] In another statement, which seems also to have been written in March 1816, Annabella recalls that Byron made this assertion, not in Augusta's presence, but during the honeymoon at Halnaby, when he added that "he had two natural children whom he should provide for" (see p. 257). Byron seems to have acknowledged no natural children before his marriage, apart from his hint to Hanson that the Newstead housemaid Lucy owed her pregnancy to him (p. 131).

expression of this kind—Surely you have had proofs enough of my affection—I cannot deny that I love you. On which he would smile maliciously & cunningly—and say "you don't know me—you don't know why I ask." Nor could I then comprehend, but I have now every reason to believe that during all that time he was cross-questioning me with a view to this event. For after particular things tending to such a purpose I perfectly remember that he would say significantly—"*mind* I have said this"—"remember I did so and so out of regard to your wishes"—when I knew they arose from other motives, & I had not expressed any wish. Whenever he did not like to go any where, he told others & tried to make me believe that it was out of regard to my desire—which never influenced him in any point.

During the time of the confinement Judith had continued seriously ill, as she recorded on 23rd January:

Mrs. Clermont the day before Lady Byron was delivered, was deterred from following the impulse of her feelings under the conviction that Something dreadful might occur to Lady B. by the apprehension that I might sink under Sudden knowledge, and that Such Event might be fatal to my Daughter, or She would have *insisted* on Lady Byrons ordering a Carriage and coming *here* (to her father and me at Mivarts Hotel) for the *Completion* of her Labor. For Mrs. Clermont not having left Lady B. for two or three days—*indeed not daring to leave her*—was ignorant that that day I was in a degree of incapacity from fever. This complaint prevented my going to Lord B's till the 8th day and then I was carried by two Men up and down Stairs, being too weak to walk. Other visits I repeated whenever I was able—but Sir Henry H[alford] expressing great anxiety about me, and the necessity of getting into the Country as soon as I could travel, my Daughter's filial tenderness induced her again to postpone the disclosure and to *insist* on others being equally secret and I was *studiously deceived*—notwithstanding which, I had many suspicions *but in my turn* dreaded agitating Lady B. by questions.

On 28th December, before leaving for Kirkby, she wrote to Annabella:

Dearest—I *never have* nor *ever can* for a moment doubt Your Love, duty & attention to me and Your Father—therefore never Suffer yourself to believe that any thing You do will be so interpreted by us.

That You and the Dear Babe should come to Kirkby will be the greatest delight to us. I also think it would be of the greatest Service to *both* in regard to health, especially if You come with a *quiet Mind.* I hope Ld B. will *also come* and have written a letter to ask it—*which Mrs. Leigh* approves. You may talk to *her* about it, as I will leave it *with her*, to deliver or not as She and You judge best. It is simply a kind invitation with assurance that We hope he will not consider himself under any restraint there but do exactly as he likes.

You can therefore act as You think best. I believe the Lease of Your House is out at Lady-day—Why not continue as long as You like at Kirkby? I have no inducement to come to London after Easter, but to See You, and if You are in the Country with us, I shall be happy there.

I *rather* think I must be in London for three or four days the first Week in Febry. but Sir Ra: will not—therefore he will remain to take care of You.

To Byron she wrote on the same day:

Dear Lord Byron,

I am so shaken by my recent illness, that I am too nervous to enter into any Subject that interests me, without being more agitated than is good for me or pleasant to those I speak to. Let me therefore tell you in writing that Sir Ra: and myself have set our hearts on seeing *You*, our *Daughter* and *Grand-daughter* at Kirkby. I think You would see them both benefit by Country Air. We have no Neighbours to molest us, the place is quiet and we can give You all much more *Spacious* accommodation than Seaham allowed us to do—and surely I trust *You* would not think yourself under any constraint but to do exactly what You like, when at Kirkby.

Reflect on the happiness it will afford *me* in particular, to watch the growth and improvement of the lovely Child, and the mortification I have already endured by seeing so little of her and Annabella, from my long illness. Take compassion on poor Grand-mama & believe me Dear Lord Byron

Yours ever most truly and affecly.

JU: NOEL

Though this letter remained in Annabella's possession, there seems no reason to suppose that she and Augusta decided to withhold it from Byron; indeed according to her statements it might have been considered likely to contribute to her purpose.

Yet this invitation to Kirkby seems to have provided the impulse to the separation. In her first Statement of 18th January Annabella related:

During the first three weeks of my confinement, when Mrs. Leigh had used every means to restrain his violence, he came up to me for a short time every day, in better temper than he had been in for two months before, yet generally seemed impatient & constrained, & frequently gave hints of some suppressed & bitter determination concerning me—particularly after he had drawn from me any expressions of affection & tenderness. He said more than once, "As soon as you & the Child can travel I shall pack you off to Kirkby or Seaham" and signified his intention of living in London as a single man—or going abroad—the latter intention seems to have been constantly in his mind since our marriage. In the summer when he expected the payment of part of my Fortune, he declared that he should reserve the greater part of it to go & live abroad without me, & from that time he has continued preparations for that purpose. The day after my marriage he told me it must come to a separation—talked of this foreign project, but said he should stay with me if he could till he had an heir. If it be necessary to recur to the early part of the time since our marriage (Jan. 2, 1815), I can state that his conduct during the three weeks of our stay at Halnaby was so alarming & cruel as disposed me several times to make my escape. He then had his loaded pistols & dagger (which are always by his bedside at night) on the table through the day, and frequently intimated a design of Suicide.[1] Once he seized the dagger, & ran with it to his own room, the door of which I heard him lock. Not being myself of a timid disposition, these weapons would not have frightened me, if his menacing deportment & countenance had not suggested the idea of danger, either to himself or others.

These appearances have of late encreased so as to alarm almost every person in the House . . . On Wednesday, Jan 3, he came to my room, and after a short time grew very quarrelsome—talked of his Mistress, & his intention to continue those courses, though tired of her personally, with other marked determinations to *do every thing wicked*—such as he has repeatedly expressed. I being then weak, could not controul my tears. After much unkind & violent language (the tones of which were heard by a person in the next room), he left me with a threatening aspect.

To this she added:

Amongst other unkind things said to me on Jan. 3rd was this declaration "A woman has no right to complain if her husband does not beat or confine her—and you will *remember* I have neither *beaten* nor *confined* you. I have never done an act that would bring me under the Law—at least on this side of the Water."

The person in the next room was the nurse, as appears both from Lushington's Notes and from Annabella's statement assessing what evidence the nurse could supply:

She overheard his violent tones of voice on Jan. 3rd . . . She knows that he would not see me for some days after.

She saw me during that time under the deepest grief, and full of apprehension. I told her he was deranged. She knew and saw the terror which I felt from that time whenever I expected to see him . . .

Without orders from me, her own sense of danger to me was such, that she locked the doors leading to my room at night . . .

She left me on Jan.—[*sic*] entreating Mrs. Clermont to persuade me to leave the house, as not being *safe* with Lord B. It was decidedly her opinion that my life was in danger.

On the other hand she would probably say that she has seen Lord B. appear personally fond of me during the few minutes she has seen us together.

There was nothing in her correspondence to indicate a state of crisis. On New Year's Day she wrote to her mother while suckling her baby, referred to as "Augusta Junr.", remarking, "I was churched this morning, by the Revd. Tom [Noel]." On the 4th she told her

[1] Lushington noted: "Lord B: has repeatedly threatened to commit suicide to Lady B: & often to Mrs. L: but it is doubtful if he has done so when both were present."

father, "I have had another airing to-day," and the baby was to be vaccinated next day. Also on the 4th she wrote to Lady Melbourne, "My confinement has been rendered so comfortable by Mrs. Leigh's kindness and attention, which I never can forget, that I feel no inclination to break loose"; she announced the coming publication of "two new poems":

> The subjects are founded on historical facts—"The Siege of Corinth" and "Parasina". There is more description in the former and more passion in the latter—which will be preferred on the whole I know not.

After the scene on the 3rd, she recorded, "He did not come any more to see me or the Child, but on Janry. 6th sent up a note," as follows:

> January 6th 1816.
>
> When you are disposed to leave London, it would be convenient that a day should be fixed—& (if possible) not a very remote one for that purpose. Of my opinion upon that subject you are sufficiently in possession—& of the circumstances which have led to it—as also to my plans—or rather intentions—for the future. When in the country I will write to you more fully. As Lady Noel has asked you to Kirkby, there you can be for the present—unless you prefer Seaham.
>
> As the dismissal of the present establishment is of importance to me, the sooner you can fix on the day the better—though of course your convenience & inclination shall be first consulted.
>
> The child will of course accompany you—there is a more easy and safer carriage than the chariot (unless you prefer it) which I mentioned before—on that you can do as you please.

Annabella stated, "The next day I replied in writing as follows":

> I shall obey your wishes, and fix the earliest day that circumstances will admit for leaving London.

Mrs. Clermont recalled of Annabella's reception of Byron's letter:

> Lord B: not having seen Lady B: for [left blank] sent a note by Mrs. Leigh desiring her to go from his house she cryed & said although I expected it I cannot help feeling *this—to think* that I have lived to be hated by my husband.

From this it appears that Byron ordered Annabella to leave his house for Kirkby and that she was distressed by the dismissal, but her own statements suggest that she had been planning to escape from considerations of her own safety and her child's. Suspicion arises that she must have said on 3rd January something unrecorded that induced Byron, after three days' consideration, to dismiss her to Kirkby as she desired. In one of her statements about Augusta later in the year she wrote:

From all I have said it will appear that it was not the positive evidence of any one crime of which he had been guilty—nor the malignity of his conduct towards me that formed my motives at the time—but the conviction derived from an experience persevered in to the utmost extent of duty, that his mind was thoroughly depraved, and that his object was as he so often told me before I would believe it—to execute all the wickedness his Imagination could devise. I could not have remained with him except on the terms of becoming his accomplice, and the attempt to make me so, if carried any further, would only have added to his guilt & future remorse.

Having written on Sunday the 7th her acceptance of her dismissal she wrote the statement of Byron's supposed insanity on which she consulted Dr. Baillie:

The principal insane ideas are—that he *must* be wicked—is foredoomed to evil—and compelled by some irresistible power to follow this destiny, doing violence all the time to his feelings. Under the influence of this imagined fatalism he will be most unkind to those whom he loves best, suffering agonies at the same time for the pain he gives them. He then believes the world to be governed by a Malignant Spirit, & at one time conceived himself to be a fallen angel, though he was half-ashamed of the idea, & grew cunning & mysterious about it after I seemed to detect it. This is the case with all his hallucinations—he keeps them sacred whilst they are in force—the only way to check & change them for a time is by diverting his thoughts to some jest or nonsense—and making him see himself in a ridiculous light. Then he will become childish & playful—I have hardly ever known him free enough from morbid feelings to endure to be considered seriously . . .[1]

Undoubtedly I am more than any one the subject of his irritation, because he deems himself (as he has said) a villain for marrying me on account of former circumstances—adding that the more I love him, & the better I am, the more accursed he is. When he uses me worst he seems most sensible that I do not deserve it—and speaks of me as the most perfect of human beings, with passionate affection—at times—at others he expresses loathing & hatred—and there is no sort of injury or outrage within the Law which he has not *studied* to inflict, against his feelings, & from what I conceive to be an insane principle. I am convinced that my removal will compose him for a time—and I wish to defer any attempt at restraint till its effects are seen—but should they be such, ought I to suffer him to fulfil his intention of going abroad to the spot with which I know his most maddening feelings to be connected, without restraint, if I can impose it?

Dr. Baillie's advice seems to have been discreetly verbal; events indicate that he recommended Annabella to persuade Byron to be examined by her own medical attendant, Le Mann.

[1] Here follow the passages already quoted on pages 286 and 340.

Annabella also sought an interview with Byron's attorney Hanson, whom she visited at his house, as Hobhouse related on Hanson's information:

At that meeting she stated her apprehensions, and stated them so strongly that Mr. Hanson *actually thought it possible* her Ladyship might have a design of *resorting to personal restraint.* Consequently he took the liberty of warning her most seriously against such a desperate, and, as he thought, mistaken measure, which might produce even the very mischief which she dreaded, or perhaps a more terrible catastrophe. Lady Byron mentioned to Mr. Hanson many particulars on which she founded her opinion, and showed him at the same time her *marked* volume of the "Medical Journal", on which Mr. H. could not help remarking that he could account for all his Lordship's eccentricities in a more simple manner than by supposing him afflicted with hydrocephalus.

Lady Byron told Mr. Hanson the story of the laudanum bottle, which, Mr. H. remarked, he understood his Lordship had for many years carried about him. She mentioned his practise of keeping loaded pistols in his bedroom; to which Mr. Hanson replied that Lord Byron from his childhood had been exceedingly apprehensive at night; that it had been his practise from that period upwards to examine his room carefully before he went to bed, to order his servant to look under the bed; and that once he was in the habit of having a ladder of ropes in his room, fearing the chance of fire. Lady Byron mentioned several of Lord Byron's strong expressions, and was otherwise so detailed on this subject that Mr. Hanson thought it his duty to ask her "what were her actual apprehensions, and *whether she laboured under any personal fear for herself?*" To which Lady Byron answered, without the least hesitation, "Oh, no, not in the least; my eye can always put down his!!!" and then added that her suspicions were that Lord Byron might make an attempt upon his own life.

Mr. Hanson, who has known Lord Byron and had him in his family since he was eleven years of age, told Lady Byron, that in all that close intimacy he had never seen the least sign of insanity; that his Lordship was liable to irritation, and, perhaps, sudden bursts of violence and passion; that he had long been in the habit of indulging in a conversation which was not to be taken "to the letter"; and that during his late great pecuniary embarrassments and his ill-health he might have suffered himself to commit and speak extravagancies, of which his return to comfort and good health would probably prevent the recurrence. He repeated his deprecation of all violent measures, and her Ladyship left him apparently more satisfied than she had entered his house. At parting she begged Mr. Hanson to use his efforts to induce Lord Byron to follow her as soon as possible to Kirkby, and on getting into her carriage said, "If I am wanted in London, pray let me know; I will come down at a minute's warning," alluding to the chance of Lord Byron's increasing malady requiring her presence in Piccadilly.

This interview happened a few days before Lady Byron left London for Kirkby.

On the 7th or 8th Annabella wrote to her father:

> . . . do not be surprised if we should reply to your Invitation in the Improvisatore style, and come upon you some day unawares. B. was very much pleased with your epistle and you'll be affronted when I tell you that he called you "the good old man" . . . Le Mann is very anxious for my departure.

On Saturday the 13th Sir Ralph replied that her letter received "on Wednesday last" had given them "the pleasing hope of seeing you all here in a Moment . . . but alas since . . . three long days have elapsed without a line either from yourself, Mrs. Leigh or Clermont," though the Kirkby steward Milward "had a letter from his wife with the intelligence of the marriage of Mr. Fletcher & Mrs. Rude to whom (pray make her smile) by giving her my Congratulations." Besides delaying for consultations with Baillie, Hanson, and Le Mann, and for the wedding of her maid to Fletcher, Annabella was also insuring that Augusta would not be left alone in the house with Byron, as she stated:

> When I had determined to go she positively & repeatedly declared her intention of removing immediately also.
>
> I mentioned at that time to Mrs. B. her Aunt [Sophia Byron], that Lord B. had intimated criminal dispositions towards her, & I gave it in charge to Mrs. B. to take care that she should not be left in an unprotected Situation. Mrs. B. was anxious on this subject (vide her letters[1]). G[eorge] B[yron] came to reside in the House, which diminished the danger & A. gave me such strong reasons for thinking her stay necessary to Lord B's safety, for it must be recollected that the idea of Insanity was then very strong in my mind, and that Suicide had been repeatedly threatened, that I should have thought I incurred the most fearful responsibility, if I had refused my sanction to her guardian endeavours. I heard so much too of his addiction to other amours—besides the worse practices I suspected—that there was no ground for alarm on her account (vide her letters), & her remaining in Town really afforded me comfort during the early time after I left it.

Perhaps Byron was irritated by her delaying her departure, perhaps suspicious of her motives—he may have heard from Hanson of her visit to him. Annabella gives no reason for his behaviour in stating, "on Jan. 13, he called me out of the room where Capt. Byron & Mrs. Leigh were, with such looks as made them both, by their own confession, remain in a state of the greatest apprehension for my safety." In her "Desultory" statement written a few weeks later, she asserted:

> I never apprehended *immediate* danger to my life till the 13th Jany.—having always before relied on my prudence or firmness to avert or check

[1] See pages 420, 530.

his violence—and from such prudential motives I have made divers concessions to which I felt objections at the time—though I do not think I have ever deviated from Truth in any serious answer.

She offers no explanation for Byron's exceptional rage, but relates in the same "Desultory" statement:

In his endeavours to corrupt my mind he has sought to make me smile first at Vice, and with regard to others has revealed this system of corrupting by degrees—saying, "There is nothing to which a woman may not be reconciled by repetition, or familiarity." There is *no* Vice with which he has not endeavoured in this manner to familiarize me—attributing the condemnation of such practices merely to the manners of different Countries, & seeking either to ridicule or reason me out of *all* principle. He has said that a wife was only culpable towards her husband if her infidelity were practised openly—that the right or wrong consisted merely in its being known—that he should not dis-approve of any secret proceedings of this kind in me.[1] He has said that any woman might be driven to Vice by her husband's ill conduct, and he should teach me "a few things"—though he has expressed doubts if I were not the only exception to this rule, and once just before I left Town he said, "Yes, *you* are an exception—yet unexceptionable in every thing."

He has frequently united Blasphemy with Indecency by Jests about the Virgin Mary &c.

He has always expressed his aversion to this Country, and has acknowledged that it arose from his dislike to *controul*—either of Law or Morals. To this cause I attribute his desire to go abroad, with some additional but inferior motives.

He has said that his great desire to sell Newstead was to go & live abroad, & has talked of plans to avail himself of his privileges in order to defraud his Creditors.

The only time that he has appeared to think of any provision for me was a day or two before I left Town—he said, decidedly alluding to his intention of living with me no more, "Whilst I live, half of what is mine shall be yours—God knows it is little enough."

Among the additions to her Statement of 18th January she noted:

I have never been provoked to utter one hasty or intemperate word in conversation with him. He said the night before I left London that my temper was the most trying in the world, because it was impossible to overcome it.

Some time before he said, "I believe you will go on loving me till I beat you."

In further additions to the same Statement, written probably within a few days after the 18th:

[1] Annabella gives no contexts, but here Byron may well have been explaining the fashionable attitude to adultery, as expounded by "Lady Besford" (supposedly Lady Melbourne) in Georgiana Duchess of Devonshire's novel, *The Sylph*, and pointing out how Lady Caroline Lamb offended against convention by advertising her infidelity.

He has taken all possible pains to convince me that I was an object of indifference to him before his accepted proposal, & of aversion & disgust since—seeming always to feel my presence oppressive, even in the kindest moods. He has told me, & did so the night before I left Town, that if he was in love at all when he married me, it was with another woman, naming her. Amongst other things said that evening were these "You know I *could* prevent your going if I chose, but luckily I don't wish for your stay." When I urged him to go with me to my father & mother—"No—I have had enough of them."

Then again this contradicatory speech—"You are very much mistaken if you think I don't love you."

When I seemed affected by these words, he said, "I wanted to make a philosophical observation on your tears." He did not reject my kindness —neither on this nor the other days when I had come down since his command that I should go—but his own was strangely mixed with a secret bitterness . . .

I cannot tell how often, but very often indeed, he has told me that marriage had made him more wretched than any thing—and there was no appearance of jest in these declarations, for when I wished to take them so he *compelled* me to believe him serious. It is to be observed that the worst treatment has not been confined to moments of intoxication.

A statement by Mrs. Clermont gives the last glimpse of Annabella at Piccadilly Terrace:

she was after her confinement persuaded that Lord B. was insane. She then said if he is insane I will do every thing possible to alleviate his dissease but if he is not in a state to be put under care I will never return to his roof again.

The evening before she left London she said "if ever I should be fool enough to be persuaded to return I shall never leave his house alive."

She left with her maid and baby on the morning of Monday 15th January and wrote the same evening from "Wooburn" to Mrs. Clermont:

My dear Mrs. C—

I and the Child are safe—and considering all things I am very well—rather fatigued by the carriage.

I have been endeavouring to write such a letter as may accord with the medical advice I have received for Lord B——, and with the wishes of those relations who concurred in deeming it necessary. I therefore wrote cheerfully & kindly, without taking any notice of what might revive diseased associations. You will conceive with what feelings & expectations I shall reach Kirkby—but don't be sick from sympathy—I am more in my senses to-night than this morning.

AIB.

To Byron she wrote:

Dearest B—

The Child is quite well, and the best of Travellers. I hope you are *good*, and remember my medical prayers & injunctions. Don't give yourself up to the abominable trade of versifying—nor to brandy—nor to any thing or any body that is not *lawful* & *right*.

[2]Let me hear of *your* obedience at Kirkby—[1]though *I* disobey [you] in writing to you [instead of to Augusta—My love to her].[1]

Ada's love to you with mine—

Pip.

Jan. 15, 1816
Wooburn

Reaching Kirkby Mallory on Tuesday the 16th, she wrote to Byron next day:

Dearest Duck

We got here quite well last night, and were ushered into the kitchen instead of drawing-room, by a mistake that might have been agreable enough to hungry people. Of this and other incidents Dad wants to write you a jocose account, & both he & Mam long to have the family party completed. Such a W.C.! and such a *sitting*-room or *sulking*-room all to yourself. If I were not always looking about for B, I should be a great deal better already for country air. *Miss* finds her provisions increased, & fattens thereon. It is a good thing she can't understand all the flattery bestowed upon her, "Little Angel". Love to the good goose, & every body's love to you both from hence.

Ever thy most loving

Pippin . . . Pip——ip.

From Woburn on the evening of the 15th she wrote also to Selina Doyle:

The facts that have taken place since I saw you will have been communicated. Though there is still a doubt as to what must be the *future* ground of conduct, the *present* seems simple enough after the confirmation of a further opinion from Dr. Baillie. To avenge disease on its victim would be as inhuman as disgraceful, and if we cannot relieve others we must preserve ourselves to the best of our power without adding to *their* sufferings. On this ground (the future sufficiency of which remains to be tried) I act—and a moral decision must be suspended from such physical causes. If these should not become *more* convincing, they *have* been *so* apparent, that I might hereafter adduce them to justify the intermediate measures, if it were necessary to take a different line of conduct on different grounds—and I think it could only be attributed to a patient & persevering affection that I did not immediately sieze the advantage, when the only reward of delay must be the privilege of a melancholy attendance on hopeless suffering. How can such conduct be interpreted to my disadvan-

[1] This was a first draft of the letter, retained by Annabella. The words in square brackets were deleted in the fair copy, as sent, and the clauses 2 and 1 transposed.

tage? But were I now to take the final step, whilst the relations are possessed with this idea, they would desert me—and were the unhappy consequences which they apprehend to Ensue, what should I feel? Deeper regrets than under any other Circumstances.

I was desired to write from hence—and pursuing the plan thus laid down I have done so—a few lines in the usual form without any notice of serious subjects—nor shall I ever commit myself on them. As for my own opinion of Causes, it does coincide with the opinions of others, but under such restrictions as make me fear that I must still undertake the responsibility of that Measure, which Duty, not Timidity now determines me to postpone for a short time.

Impart the contents of this to the kind friend with whom you consulted for me.

Significantly, she kept a copy of this letter; it marks the beginning of the elaborate labour of self-justification that so largely occupied the remaining forty-four years of her life.

Augusta wrote daily bulletins of Byron's behaviour, beginning her first letter on the afternoon following Annabella's departure "in a real agony of nerves waiting for Le Mann." She had been with George Byron to see Hanson, who was "very zealous & kind":

Speaking very kindly of you & very rationally on *the* subject, he said when he heard of yr departure "Well perhaps it is as well" & that ye only thing is to enforce medical advice. I told him of course all you desired & that Le Mann was to see him today—which he thought all right *but* wishes Le M. to call on him after, merely to give him a pretence to speak on ye subject to B—— which he means to do most openly as to the danger he is incurring by his habits & not having advice when it is evident he so much wants it. Now Le M. must judge for himself on this subject & I think may object after what he expressed about H. ye other day. H. seemed so positive *I* ought *not* to go for a day or two that I really think I cannot—tho I had packed up & am certain I ought to go home *if possible* —but *can I* after this. My poor dear A I fear you are not more happy than I am—or I would not mind any perplexity at least feel your being free from it a comfort.

B. rose early—seems quiet, but complains of languor & feeling ill—asked how you were. I said pretty well & spoke as you desired *lightly* of yr feelings. He has not said much & that little in good humour. He talks of fasting today.

Just before the postal collection at five o'clock she added:

Le Mann has been with B. who was confused at first but afterwards talked openly rationally & goodhumouredly *avoiding always ye main point.* Le M. of course turned all on ye score of health—proposed Calomel, which at last was agreed to, or any other medicine advised. He begged Le M. to call again tomorrow. All was said that *could* with prudence & policy for a 1st visit. He was asked if he wished to have a Physician—

answered no . . . Le Mann votes for my staying a few days so I certainly must & shall . . . Le M. objects to H's proposal as I thought.

Thus it appears that Annabella curiously timed her departure on the day when Byron was persuaded to have his first medical consultation, and that she was not then expecting—as she afterwards recalled—Augusta to remain long at Piccadilly after her own departure.

That evening—Monday the 15th—Augusta accompanied Byron, their cousin George, and Scrope Davies to Drury Lane, as she related to Annabella the following afternoon:

I've not yet seen B., but he is at dinner, so Dieu merci does *not dine out.* I heard from Fletcher that his pills from Le Mann met with a *miss for tin*[1] & were crushed, so he did not take them last night. I hear Le M. has been with him "some *time*" today . . . The Play last night affected him much even to tears, but G[eorge] said it was nothing to ye last time. He appeared very odd all the time there & I am perfectly sure that Scrope D remarked it from his looks & manner. B. set him down in our way home & proposed a *supper at Wattier's* which made me *shake*, but ye other scarcely answered & most determinedly *held off* from every thing of the sort. The Miss Cookes as usual was the principal theme. Very little has been said of your departure & I always treat the subject lightly—but I really was annoyed at all the *folly* displayed last night & defy any body not to discover *something is amiss.* Mrs. Clermont call'd this morning, & we had a confab: it is a comfort to me her being at hand I feel so deplorably responsible now you are gone. He went to Bed earli*er* last night & drank wine instead of Brandy . . . Mrs. Clermont agrees with me as to ye probability of his following you. Le Mann's plan is to gain his confidence before he hints at *ye main point* which I think very sensible . . . His manner of mentioning having seen L.M. to me was curious—perfectly unsuspecting & only childishly talking of being *torpid*, tho one saw much real apprehension & fidgets under it.

She added in conclusion:

I've seen B one moment. He told me he had seen Le M. who said his liver was very bad—shewed me yr letter and desires me to tell you *the misfortin* of the pills & that therefore his life is still in *abeyance.*

Also on Tuesday the 16th Mrs. Clermont reported to Annabella:

I have seen Mrs. Leigh this morning. She says she feels most forlorn without you—but means to stay a few days longer. She is every thing that is affectionate towards you. From her you will hear the particulars of what passed with Hanson. I find he was not displeased at your going as he said he believed your stay was not safe & that upon the whole it was better you should leave him for the present. The day passed without any

[1] It was as characteristic of Augusta that, despite her anxieties, she could still be amused by the idiosyncrasies of Fletcher's Nottinghamshire dialect, as of Annabella that she transcribed the phrase as "misfortune" when making her copies of Augusta's letters.

Irritation a good deal of the usual Nonsense was talked at the Theatre about Miss Cooke & mar[r]ying Miss Mercer if he could get rid of his present connection—would not drink Brandy at night on account of his Liver—says he will take any thing Le Man gives him but Flecher says the pills were crush'd & so he would not take them last night.

I have received your letter from Woburn & seen that which came to Miss Doyle.

On Wednesday Augusta wrote:

> I'm sorry to say the pills are still *untaken* & that Perry's dinner is *today*. He is going but with a resolution to be "*moderate* on account of his Liver" of which he talks to every one. No Brandy last night or the night before. In ye course of the Eveg. George & I were quite struck with his ill looks—so much so we cd not help asking if he felt ill—he said yes, *very*. Went at 9 to the Play with S. Davies—I really think ye only inducement was the *Cookes* & that there seems no promise of success *there*. He came home early but sat up late & upon desiring me to give him his watch off the chimney piece, added "don't touch that Pistol instead." I own I was not quite happy at perceiving one there & asked carelessly *why*. He said he had observed a man lurking about the street door & did not like it! However he proceeded quietly to bed, saying he should not take ye pills because of his dinner today . . . You are mentioned by him with great kindness. I always long to write down at ye moment for *my Liver* does not admit of much *memorv* at present—but one thing was, "Tell her as I told Murray that she is the only woman I could have lived 6 months with." Your letter was read many times but with what reflections I could not exactly discover. "Why does Pip object to my *versifying*"—"What a letter nothing in it but what I'm to do or *not* to do"—& so on.

She concluded with her usual addition just before posting time:

> Just seen Le M. who has been an hour with B—*very favorable* as far as it goes—he has promised him not to drink much to-day, & is very tractable.

Unfortunately for this resolution, as Hobhouse recorded in his journal, they dined together that evening with James Perry, editor of the *Morning Chronicle*, and afterwards Hobhouse "came home with Byron sat with him till two in the morning—Lady Byron gone into the country—Byron won't go!!!" Augusta wrote a lively account to Annabella next morning:

> I write very much in the dumps. B returned between 12 & 1 this Mng with Hobhouse—both drunk—sent me & George to bed, & call'd for Brandy! Fletcher says H. drank none but B replied to his declarations to that effect "So much the better—there will be the more for me"—& drank two glasses—would not take his Calomel & in short so far so bad! One comfort is *H* looks really dying—God forgive me, I hope He will take him to a better world—but however B. frown'd to such a degree at me to

go away that this dear friend (I mean fiend) either was or pretended to be quite shock'd—said he wd go—& when B pursued me out of the room to apologise for his frowns (when by the bye he tumbled flat on his face up the staircase) H said to George all sorts of *tendresses* of course to be repeated to me—I was *all the Angels* in ye world & fortunate for him I was married! Fletcher has just informed me he left the house door open at 3 o clock in ye morng. & "lucky we had not all our throats cut!"

At this point in her letter the post arrived, with letters from Annabella to herself and to George Byron. In the latter Annabella wrote:

My father & mother unite with me in opinion that it would be most desirable for the Patient to be removed to this place, where he might pursue a medical regimen according to the London advice—with the additional advantages of air and exercise, which he cannot be induced to take in Town. They will devote their whole care & attention to the alleviation of his Malady . . . I wish you or Augusta to communicate with Mr. Le Mann as to the time & manner of effecting this measure, which if not considered injurious to the object of our endeavours, must be more consolatory to me than any other . . . *I* deem the change of scene of the greatest consequence—and this place particularly eligible . . .

I request you to acquaint Mr. H[anso]n with the contents of this letter.

Self-absorption always limited Annabella's perception. She had herself failed to induce Byron to visit Kirkby; even though Le Mann was daily attending herself and Augusta's daughter Georgey—who had been seriously ill—it was only after her departure that Byron had admitted him to consultation. Yet within two days of escape from his domination, she was deputing Augusta and her cousin to accomplish what she had been unable to achieve herself.

As George Byron was preoccupied with his plans for marriage—"he is gone to *pop* to *M*[ary] *P*[ole] this morning, in a troubled state of nerves"—Augusta hurried off to see Hanson, resuming her letter on her return:

Just come home from Hanson, to whom I shewed yr letter to G. & communicated what I thought right of the contents of mine, such as the plan in case of need of Sr R[alph] & G[eorge Byron] speaking to Hob [house]. Hanson says not only to him but to the Father, Sir Benjamin, who is a very respectable person & has his Son completely in his power & wd. not under the present circumstances allow him to accompany B. Hanson is in despair about last night & is confident such practices will kill him & that no medicine can do good whilst they are continued. He desires me to consult Le M. upon yr letter to G. & the going into the Country—both he & Mrs. Clermont think it might not be prudent to press that measure *too soon* for fear of creating suspicions.

She further reassured Annabella:

I can't discover from Fletcher that any thing of abroad was mentiond last night. Whatever was the subject of conversation I could have heard it & so could George from the top of the house—so loud! B's head is very bad this morning Fletcher says. I really have told you as nearly as possible all that has passed about you since yr departure. Le Mann thinks he is so far aware of his malady that he feels yr absence a relief—fancies he is less observed & under less restraint. He was *an hour* with him yesterday & told me as far as he had been able to observe quite rational—tho what we had told him proved sufficiently he was occasionally the contrary. I talked to him of the lameness & the Hip. He does not apprehend any thing to the Spine, but says it is quite possible *that side* may have received a *shock*, tho not absolutely palsy, & that may account for ye small eye looking now so much smaller. I really think my dear A, ye more ill he is today the better.

She added her last-minute bulletin before posting time:

Just seen Le M. who has been with B.—a promise to take ye pills to-night. Le M. talked *very* seriously of the drinking which he owned to—but thinks it most judicious not to recommend ye Country *too hastily*—in which I agree.

Late the same night she wrote even more reassuringly:

A few calm lines before I sleep to say that when I went down to dinner B. shewed me yr letter with which he seemed *quite* pleased & in ye best of humours. He has continued so with very little variation all ye Eveg—staid at home—not taken Brandy & swallowed the Calomel Pills. I asked him if he had written to you today—"No, but that is my laziness—tell Pip I'm longing to write to her." He seems quite delighted with your mention of *little Pip* & it strikes me *the Heir* & *Bosworth Field* will take him to Kirkby. I have been trying to detect bad effects from *Hob's* visit but could not. I fancy he (H) is absorbed in his *new Book* by what I can learn. I got into a fright once, that ye pills would not be taken & Le M. a *humbug*, but I really believe it was only the thoughts of *something new* & the aversion to Calomel. Le Mann . . . spoke very strongly to B about the *drinking* & its effects, but as I believe I told you is afraid of going to work too precipitately about the Country. B told him he had two more dinners in view but they were *quiet* ones. More will come into my head dear A by & bye. He looked very ill & his face swelled, which [he] remarked himself tonight. Le Mann says the pains in his loins &c are all Liver. His memory has failed him this Eveg to such a degree he exclaimed at it himself.

She resumed this letter on Friday afternoon:

Just seen Le Mann who says all is going on quite well. B is to take ye pills again to-night. All has been said that could by L.M. today & even the Country mentioned to which he did not object nor to *Horse exercise*—is very gracious to Le Mann. I've seen him B for a moment—he complained of the pills &c having made him *very bad* but not acted so *very* much. However he laughed & I told him he *looked* better & I thought him much more so than I expected to find him . . . Nothing has been said of you today. I saw [him] but for a few minutes when he sent for me to settle with Holmes the Painter when I wd *sit for my picture!!!* & now he is gone to eat mutton broth for dinner. I forgot to say that the amusement last night was reading a very *nau* paper about a business which is to come on before the H. of Lords.

Also on Friday the 19th, Augusta found time to write tactfully to Annabella's mother, assuring her that she and her cousin George "shall both do our best to comply with every wish of yours & Sr Ralph's":

At the same time we can't help requesting you to suspend any *positive determinations* for the present. The case is ye most difficult that could be imagined. That *malady does exist* can't be doubted but it is not such as yet as to admit of controul. Mr. Le Mann thinks much good might be done by a perseverance in medicines & regular habits—but who can enforce them!

The obvious inference was that an affectionate and devoted wife might have enforced the regimen. As the wife had decamped, both Hanson and Le Mann seem to have been well satisfied of Augusta's beneficial influence, since both urged her to prolong her stay. As she informed Annabella, it was not easy for her to arrange a prolonged stay. Her daughter Georgey, who was with her, was just recovered from illness and would have been better in the country; with two of her younger children down with colds at Newmarket, her husband wrote to require her return, and when she put him off, proposed to come up to town to see her. Despite his dislike of George Leigh, Byron was prepared to receive him as a guest for the sake of retaining Augusta, who informed Annabella:

my Spouse talks of coming Thursday or Friday next, & I mentioned such an intention to B. yesterday when he desired he wd. on no account think of lodging any where but here. So that is settled & my mind & *conscience* more at ease about staying till then. He (Sposo) has been seized with such a comical fright of B. following me if I go home that he now entreats me to stay.

Augusta was glad to find a distraction for Byron in their cousin George's affairs. Having been accepted by Mary Chandos-Pole, George Byron thought of going to Leicestershire to consider Bosworth House as a residence, but was temporarily cast down by his prospective mother-in-law's objections, as Augusta informed Annabella:

Poor G.B. is in sad consternation, tribulation, &c at Mrs. *Fool's* objections, which only regard his want of *monies*. She wants them to have £600 a yr. more! & to wait a year or 3 years in hopes I suppose of finding a

> *mine*—& he swears he won't wait—& the young lady that she will never marry another—& so on, quite en regle—but worst of all they want to see *ME!* to talk it over. Heavens & earth! as if I had not enough to do without such an addition! My dear A I shall look like a fool & talk like one. GB. still wishes to know if *Bosworth House* is vacant—will you enquire for him without saying exactly *why*. B. is in a fuss about it all & I rather like his having such a subject to fuss upon.

On the evening of Friday the 19th she wrote to Annabella:

> B & G. are gone to the Play, and I will scribble to *thee*. B is in very good sorts—complains a little of the pills being *inactive*, but has promised to take them again tonight. He has a cold & soreness of his face & head which I have remarked before after a fit of tip. He dined on mutton broth—has talked of you & *Miss*—& says he is sure *you want him terribly* and that *Miss* will be spoilt even without him to help. I have not—nor has Fletcher heard one word of *abroad* & I can't help suspecting the scheme is at a stand still or as *torpid* as the *Liver*. It is strange it never occurs to him that Le Mann talks to me of him, & he takes special care not to repeat certain parts of the conversation. I am in hope Hob. has disappeared again for I've not heard of him to-day. B. has not mentioned any intention of *Kirkby* today at least to me. I believe I told you Le Mann had so far introduced the subject as this—that he recommended exercise especially riding—upon which B. said he could not ride in Town, & ye other asked if he thought of going into ye Country. "Oh yes—he should have gone sooner but for laziness." I hope dearest you are not tormenting yourself with repentance & scruples—for I do think your having gone will somehow be of use, & so does Le M. B. asked him yesterday what effects *ye Liver* had on people—if it did not make some *hypochondriac*. This is ye most he has said on *the main point*, & Le M's conduct appears to me most judicious. I wish I could but see you for I am afraid you are in a very uncomfortable state, & suspect Ly N. may not continue so calm as at first. I really think if ye present system is persevered in it may produce good, & that is all that can be done at present.

Her fears of Lady Noel were very soon to be justified, and in the same letter Augusta made another prophetic remark:

> I am to sit to this ugly Painter tomorrow, who will report to Ly *C. L.* & the *Round House*—a fine affair in their imagination your absence—& my stay!

Immediately after posting her letter to George Byron on Wednesday the 17th, Annabella wrote to Le Mann, having "received from Mrs. Leigh some further information as to the plan you intend to pursue":

> I had written before the last post came, requesting that my decided opinion in favour of removing the Patient should be communicated to you—but from the particulars I have since learned, I conceive that some time must be allowed for you to acquire the necessary ascendancy . . . I remain ignorant of the bodily disease which you are now led to suppose.

Mrs. Clermont wrote on the evening of Thursday, the day after Byron and Hobhouse had attended Perry's dinner:

> As to his coming to Kirkby I have no doubt he will do so after a little time but not immediately nor do I think it desirable until he is either better or the case more decided. At present *you* could not prevail on him to follow medical Advice nor even to abstain from Brandy as you will hear that after all his fears of his Liver he last night drank to excess & you know he will not bear the least restraint nor will he ever unless it becomes positive controul & it is not yet a case in which that can be used. I would to Heaven his excess would make him Ill very seriously so I mean but that does not seem likely to be the case . . .
>
> Mrs. Leigh is scolded a little sometimes—he has not yet taken any Medecines.

Thus, by 18th January, Annabella was concerned with Byron's medical treatment and not yet considering a separation. But Le Mann indicated that he was treating Byron for "bodily disease"—the "liver complaint," as Byron himself described it—without reference to insanity, and Annabella now heard from Selina Doyle:

> On the whole I feel satisfied at the temper of Mind in which You wrote from Woburn & more so at the idea of this Experiment than I expected to be, from all I have collected of his yesterday's conduct, which will be communicated to you . . . The Friend I consulted on the subject seems no less interested than Myself about you. He thinks this ought to lead to a *final* Step & that you ought to communicate on the Subject with your legal adviser—but he does not know *you* as well as I do. I think it should lead to that *final step* if things remain as they are—but if the disorder comes to a crisis I know that the "Melancholy attendance on hopeless sufferings" wd alone satisfy your Heart—Is it not so?
>
> My Friend attributes the conduct I have depicted to him in a gt degree to the effect of Jealous Love worked up to a morbid passion & acted upon by a distempered imagination which has by degrees led to the outrages committed one after another with a view to make you Love the Man as it were for his Essence in spite of his qualities & of your Sense of virtue —in spite of ill treatment & every thing calculated to inspire hatred. That is a species of insanity certainly & such as should particularly lead to the final Step, for your presence must aggravate the Complaint instead of soothing. Still he is inclined to think he may in other respects keep as he has done for many Years it seems within the bounds of reason (of the head). We have both (you & me) at times talked of His treatment of you as an experiment but I think my F followed up the point better than either of us ever had so I have put it down. He thus accounted for the pains he has ever taken to persuade you he is the most guilty of human beings & perhaps with an imagination like his his desire to persuade others of this has made him believe it falsely of himself. Perhaps you are not the first on whom he may have tried his powers thus—but would he love you were he to conquer your strong sense of virtue? I do not believe therefore even

though you could sacrifice your real God to an Idol (which I think you incapable of however) still you would not win your game. I doubt whether this is intelligible but I have gone over the same ground so often with you that you will be able to fill up the chasms.

Events proved that the "friend" consulted by Selina Doyle was her brother, Colonel Francis Hastings Doyle, a professional soldier considered to be an arbiter of correct conduct, besides having experience in dealing with men of business; he was to play an active part in the burning of Byron's memoirs and still later to act as an intermediary in the separation of Edward Bulwer and his wife Rosina.

Selina Doyle was a friend of Judith's as well as of Annabella's; seeing a letter from her and knowing that she was in Annabella's confidence, Judith must have inquired for news and been given the letter to read. Hysterically Annabella explained what was meant by "outrages" and "ill treatment," whereupon Judith decided immediately to go up to London for legal advice and Annabella retired to her room to compose the "Statement given to my Mother."

On her mother's departure Annabella wrote to Mrs. Clermont:

I hope you will find my Mother reasonable & temperate. If the few days in London should not injure her materially, I think her presence there may much advantage our cause, and her absence from me may not do harm—I have had but one wild fit. What I think must be best for my character as well as for my feelings, is to forbear every harsh measure that is not absolutely necessary for my safety & justification—and to leave others as much as possible to take the responsibility on themselves. And what I would desire of all my advisers is to maintain my cause with least injury to him. It can never prove in a Wife's favour with the world to seek to make the worst appear of her husband whilst there is a possibility of avoiding that extremity. Wrongs should only be declared when rights cannot otherwise be obtained. Keep my Mother to these views as much as possible in all the counsel she is empowered to seek—and for which purpose, painful as it is, I have thought it my duty to furnish her with the strongest statement that I could swear to. We shall then know what such grounds will authorize without being thereby compelled to act upon them, if there be any eligible means of avoiding that cruel alternative.

I am sure you will allow for the dread I feel of being obliged to *publish* what must damn him, believing him more *suffering* than *sinning*. *But I certainly can do him no good*—therefore have not even a disinterested motive for wishing to live with him—and I promise you that I won't sacrifice myself for nothing. Read over the paper I have given my Mother—and if you see any thing very objectionable, and she should agree in that opinion, I empower you together to blot it out—but of course nothing must be added—tho' perhaps I have omitted material facts.

She was already herself making additions, as well as following her old practice of "collecting her sentiments" on paper:

By indecisive measures we allow him to unit the privileges of Disease with the powers of Free-Agency. If it be Malady, I having been its decided object for a length of time, am of all persons the most improper to be with him, on account of those associations which in such cases it is of great importance not to revive.

If it be Malevolence peculiarly directed against me, I can have no reason to hesitate.

If it be prejudice inspired by evil counsellors, & which the experience of my good conduct has not been able to overcome—what security can I have against similar misery in future?

There is another consideration which the nature of his character presents—He knows he has injured me too deeply ever to forgive me.

The last premise had an obvious corollary—was she aware that already she had too widely betrayed her husband's confidence to hope for forgiveness? Was not the whole memorandum an attempt to appease conscience for having deserted her husband when, by her own account, he needed the care which a wife might have been expected to give? "It is my happiness to feel that in some degree I live for others," she had told him on 3rd September 1813: "You can *only* wrong me by . . . refusing me a participation in your cares" (24th February 1814): "I am and have long been pledged to myself to make your happiness my first object in life" (14th September 1814). For one so confident in the powers of her beneficent influence, her abdication was surely precipitant.

Mrs. Clermont informed her on 19th January:

. . . that there is Disease I cannot doubt, but I am equally sure that you never should go under *his* roof again unless it is so decided as that he is positively under controul and that may *never* be the case. Capt. B: & Mrs. Leigh say that his memory was yesterday quite gone at times [this was the day after he had sat up with Hobhouse drinking brandy till 2 a.m.] that he told the servant to let in Capt Byron if he called & when she said why he is living in the House with you he did not seem for some time to understand her. That might be only a fit of abscence. He was much delighted with your Letter which was I understand the second you had sent. I think it is unnecessary that you should write again until he does, or why not ask for the Epistle of consequence that he said he should write.

So far from feeling pleasure that her letter had "delighted" Byron, Annabella was already regretting that she had written it. Her reply reflects agitation:

You & I are quite agreed by your last letter. Heaven knows I am desirous enough never to see him again if it could be *decently effected.* My agony is about that second letter of Jan. 16. I must have been mad to write so, for it contained an expression of regret to be away from him—and compromised my parents by the mention of Kind wishes on their part towards him. But I was distracted between Law & Medecine, & followed the prescriptions of the latter—I fear to the neglect of the former.

However, what can it appear but as another proof of my tenderness? though by the bye it may seem like hypocrisy in conjunction with subsequent proceedings, & invalidate the evidence of preceding facts. On this point I am most anxious to be relieved.

If there were no probability of his coming here I don't know whether or no the lapse of a little time before the finale would be advantageous—perhaps to quiet these *malady people*—who mean to think me a brute if I am not a slave—for nothing.

I have had one of my very bad heads to-day—worse than since my confinement—and want physic, but have no idea what to take. Do ask Le Mann to send me a prescription for some opening medecine.

She added a postscript:

I never must see him again—I shall wish otherwise when I am less sane—but let me be preserved from it by every means.

To her mother she wrote:

My dearest Mother—

Pray remember your assurance to me that you would take *advice* but not *measures*—but don't let Mrs. Leigh or GB. know of the papers I have committed to your care. It certainly is best (if an interval can safely be allowed for the elucidation of *Malady*) that he should during that period remain in London—and it does appear to me that the act of admitting him here would cancel all former grounds of complaint or justification—?? I hear he was much pleased with my second letter—I conceive because it gratified his pride—and perhaps he thought it would answer some purpose of his, which I hope it will not. Take care of me amongst you in this most difficult & delicate case. I would willingly resign my judgment into anybody's hands, and be found non compos myself.

State the purport of the letters we have written from hence, to the advisers—[and make them enter into that *tenderness* of my Conscience which would make me irreparably miserable if I were to take a harsh measure that was not positively inevitable. I wish I had no conscience, for it is more plague than profit.][1]

Now do take care of yourself, for if you wear out your brain what is to become of mine?

You & I can see through a milestone—all our neighbours are as dull as posts. My only fear of coming off *second best* arises from the extreme policy with which he has conducted himself towards me, and on which he has avowedly piqued himself—As never having *beaten*, or *confined* me, or used *abusive* language.

But surely if there be protection in law I must not sink the Victim of such diabolical cunning. Enquire of C[lermont] to what she can depose, as having known from Mrs. L. during her stay in the house.

I perceive that he is playing a deep game to gain over Augusta.

[1] The passage within square brackets was deleted.

Half-measures won't do with him. I think he may be *awed* by decided ones. Communicate all my opinions to S[elina] D[oyle].

It is also to be remembered that he is more jealous than any one of his character in the World. How far he may thereby be brought to terms?

Don't be taken in by hearing of his tender speeches about me. We have had too much of them—& the kindest words have often preceded the most malevolent behaviour. The bairn is quite well.

Again she added a postscript:

It is to be observed that I cannot swear to having been put in fear of my life at any one time—but only to my general conviction of Danger.

In regard to my unfortunate letter from hence, I can produce one sent by the same post which will plainly prove that I wrote on the presumption of Malady—and the letters which I had recd. by the preceding post will prove that I had all the grounds for such a presumption which could be given by the opinion of others. You will learn from C. all the strongest facts. I wish you not to mention to Sir S[amuel] R[omilly] or any one what has only passed in conversation between us, as it was very much discoloured by my feelings—Sometimes one way, sometimes another.

Probably on the same day she wrote this "addition" to her statement:

My Motive for writing the two letters in question (of 15th & 16th Jany. 1816) was the conviction that I had left him in a state of Derangement, to which I still believe him to be *partially* subject—and I had consulted Mr. Le Mann on that point before my departure, (who had recommended my absence on medical grounds) and he said that if the Patient's mind were left in a state of irritation by any appearance of neglect on my part, the beneficial effect of my removal would be frustrated.

During one of those periods of Derangement soon after our marriage he pointed out Zeluco as a character resembling his own, and dwelt on the circumstance of his *strangling the Child* as prophetic of what he might do if he had one.

Of Dr. John Moore's novel, *Zeluco*, Walter Raleigh wrote, "Zeluco, the Byronic villain, and Laura, his amiable and suffering wife, are highly conventional types of evil and of good." Probably Byron, in a Wertherish mood, drew a general parallel between himself and Zeluco, but he himself indicated the grounds of the comparison in the preface to *Childe Harold:*

. . . it had been more agreeable, and certainly more easy, to have drawn an amiable character . . . but he never was intended as an example, further than to show, that early perversion of mind and morals leads to satiety of past pleasures and disappointment in new ones . . . the outline which I once meant to fill up for him was, with some exceptions, the sketch of a modern Timon, perhaps a poetical Zeluco.

In her own "Notes on Childe Harold" Annabella remarked at the words "and certainly more easy":

> B. has often told me he *could not* draw any other kind of character—and it is to be accounted for from the fact that almost all his reflections on human nature are derived from self-inspection, and that his feelings & sympathy are only kindled by what he can identify with himself. In all the characters on which he has had any inclination to dwell, there have been, at least in his imagination, strong resemblances to himself—as Rousseau, Bonaparte, &c. In fiction Conrad—Zeluco—Falkland—Vivian (Miss E[dgeworth]'s)—The Armenian—Richard 3, &c.

To Mrs. Clermont she wrote again on the night of Sunday the 21st under the heading "*Private*":

> By all I hear there is no prospect of an immediate journey hither—and therefore if I could but have a little time for *composing* my resolutions, I know myself, and know that the more deliberately I proceed, the less I shall repent.
>
> I hope you will keep my Mother sober. She will break my heart if she takes up the thing in *bitterness* against him. The more I think of the whole conduct on his part, the more unaccountable it is. I cannot believe him *all bad*—though the case is quite as hopeless as if he were. I see a change in Mrs. L's last letter.
>
> Her sanguine disposition leads her to suppose that because the liver is a little better, all must be couleur de rose. Alas! that can never be for me—and I know my duty to be most opposite to my feelings—but I have ever followed the former, and it must guide me to peace here & the hope of happiness hereafter.
>
> Tell my Mother that from facts which I have recollected I have reason to think myself mistaken in regard to any *existing* security on Newstead and that it was paid off out of Claughton's forfeiture. I fear that in my wild fit I dropped some hints of another transaction connected with that place. For God's sake do away the idea from her mind. I did not know what I said—really I was frantic—she had agonized me about the Child. I am very low to-night—and have been trying to cure myself with a dose—a bad head again.
>
> My father is deeply indignant—& will never forgive. I really am afraid he will have a fit of illness from the state of his spirits.
>
> I have closed the letter to my Mother. Suggest to her therefore that if she has not yet seen Sir S. R[omilly] and the advice of Heywood & F D[oyle] should prove satisfactory, there may not be a *necessity* for carrying the affair any further—unless it were necessary to retain a Counsel immediately—which of course cannot be done without my concurrence. Then Sir S. R—— certainly—but one would not wish to extend the confidence at this moment. Many are my cares. You & Selina (by what I have heard from her to-day) must have lost some of my letters—for I have written daily to one or the other.

Before she could post this letter on Monday the 22nd, she must have received Augusta's cheering letter of Friday evening, concluded on Saturday with the usual last-minute postscript:

> Le Mann is sanguine still . . . B came home very well last night—no brandy—& he took ye Calomel again & I have ordered a Fowl for his dinner.

The warmth of this reassurance so far penetrated the overcharged melodrama of her self-pity that Annabella added a postscript to Mrs. Clermont:

> Monday—I am so sure that a little *Time* would do a great deal—and relieve me from that responsibility which I have suffered so much with a view to avoid—that it would be a pity if after all I incurred it without absolute necessity. Urge this against any immediate measure.

By the same post she lamented in a misdated letter to Augusta, "Indeed, I don't think you do know what I am feeling, nor all the causes I have to feel," but concluded, "O that I were in London, if in the coal-hole." The same day she wrote to her mother:

> For Heaven's sake don't let a whisper of my wrongs get abroad . . . Legal measures ought certainly to be *subsequent* to some direct application to him—and from his regard to appearances, as well as from a strange, though uncertain, generosity of character, *I am convinced* that, if he had no reason to suppose harsher measures were in preparation (which would drive him to fury) he would make every requisite acknowledgement of my unexceptionable conduct, and give every security for the Child, & a due provision. It would be a death-blow to me to be obliged to come forward publicly—and depend upon it the public will take my part warmly enough under any circumstances. I should *die* of such a measure if I *could* carry it through—which I doubt—and it would be better to avoid an enterprize for which I doubt my strength. If you love me, impose silence on all whom we consult.
>
> To enter a little into philosophical causes (as not supposing derangement) I think that a despondent & remorseful conviction of his unworthiness may account for a great deal—if, as I still believe, he loves me distractedly—and particularly for his revengeful dispositions towards me, on whom he would visit the sufferings of wounded pride—& the higher I am esteemed, the worse for me in regard to his feelings. Then again Remorse for ill-using me—irritating to further ill-usage—This must go on to madness if the object were not removed. So *for him* it is best, and after all, that belief will go furthest to reconcile me to what is best *for me*. I do not see that it can advantage me in the world to deny these feelings. The more I love, the stronger causes must be supposed for such a measure. I have never yet been *untrue* and why should I begin with dissimulating that which, if my misfortune, is not my guilt. A spirit of animosity on my part cannot tend to my justification. The temperate are always believed.

Present these considerations to F [Doyle]. I trust in him more than any one to save me from a cruel extremity . . .

I wish very much to have altered part of my Statement particularly the last paper. That "unintermitting principle of Revenge" was not a justifiable assertion—it is impossible to divine the principle. Nor can I think there has been any *design* or *cunning* in the business—far too much incoherency.

Despite its vanity and self-complacency, this letter shows a perception and freedom from prejudice in marked contrast with most of her statements, suggesting that, if Augusta had been her only coadjutor, she might soon have inclined to reconciliation.

Unfortunately she was to hear the next day from Selina Doyle:

Your Mother has seen & talked to F [Doyle], & he has read the Copy of your statement, on the consideration of which, together with that of your feelings, he thinks the first & immediate object should be to effect a legal separation of Bed & board; & that, if *possible* by mutual arrangement without the intervention of public proceedings, in a court of Law—but so as to secure you *effectually* from any resumption of authority on the part of your Husband. However attempting such a negociation precludes the acting in the business as if you had at present reason to believe the malady confirmed, & therefore if the arrangement is not acceeded to which your Father may propose, he thinks as Matters now stand that you should resort to legal Measures for to obtain that object. Should the Malady encrease to such a degree as to satisfy all his Family & the world in General that he is a lunatic F does not conceive that your having proceeded in, & effected either of the above Measures can preclude your stepping forward under those circumstances & claiming the privilege of guardianship nor does he doubt but that the Chancellor or whoever is to decide, will admit your Claims to be just & yield to them when brought forward (as they may be) with the force of truth. In consequence of these opinions he thinks that Ldy. N's first object should be the best legal opinion (Sir S Romilly's for instance) on these three questions. Is not the Case one which wd entitle you to a legal seperation? whether that seperation can be effected by an arrangement between the parties without the intervention of any public proceedings in a Court of Law so as to secure you from any resumption on the part of Ld B——? If the Husband object to a seperation, which are the legal steps to be taken to effect that object? He thinks it better thus to feel your way before you begin the negociation. If Ld B's Friends as well as his Legal & Medical advisers do not think him in a fit state of Mind to enter into such a negociation they ought to proceed to take out a statute of Lunacy. But F doubts, notwithstanding all he hears that as it stands at present, the case is sufficiently decided to obtain it & thinks it a most perplexing one . . . as to the Child F thinks if the seperation is by mutual agreement your keeping it should be insisted on . . . tomorrow Morg. I shall see the paper that Mrs. Clermont is to communicate.[1]

[1] This was Mrs. Clermont's Statement of 22nd January, designated *Γ* by Lovelace, which has been quoted on pages 334 and 336.

Her mother also wrote to her on the 22nd:

I arrived at Clermonts about 3 o'clock yesterday. I must begin by telling You, that there is no present intention of a Leicestershire journey—as some business in the House of Lords is professedly waited for. Nor do I find from Clermont that any particular irritability has taken place, tho' extreme *oddity*, for it perplexes every one to say whether it is *Malady* or not.

In the Afternoon I had Heywood with me for two hours, and I was after that more than two hours at Selinas with her and Frank . . .

Heywood and Doyle both concur in one opinion, which is that Your Father must be the Person to *act*—taking upon himself the authority which both nature and Custom allow to a Parent, in any case of a Child suffering injury or being distressed. They also concur in another point, that it is extremely difficult to decide whether to take it up as a Case of *Malady* or wickedness. If any proposal is made to B. to agree to separation, settlement &cc it precludes the person who makes that application from future Plea of Malady—but I have this moment received a letter from Romilly appointing me to go to his Chambers at a quarter past three o'clock . . .

She added later in the day:

I am just come from Sir Samuel . . . he says it is one of the most distressing Cases which ever came before him.

He thinks Sir Ra: ought by no means to suffer him to enter the House at Kirkby and also that Sir Ralph must take the business up for You, not You for Yourself. But Romilly says no delay should take place in *determining*—and I believe he will wish me to consult a *Civilian* as it must come into the *Ecclesiastical* Court—if carried on by Law, but he advises that a negociation should be commenced by a letter from Sir Ra: to B. But Romilly is going to recur to the business of *Lady Ferrers* before I see him tomorrow.[1]

Mrs. Leigh said that a few days since he declared he would go and stay six months at Kirkby. Last night he took a *savage* fit with her—and when G.B. talked of looking at the House at Bosworth when they went down, B. said, he would never go into Leicestershire, and that G.B. need not look out for a House for HE *would lend him Seaham as long as he* liked.

Mrs. Clermont wrote the same day:

I have this Morning seen the Capt & Mrs. Leigh & had much talk with them, all as satisfactory as possible as to their feelings towards you. I told *them as my Opinion* that Sir Ralph having drawn from you the history of the past would never allow you to live with or see him again if he could prevent it which they seemed to think quite right. The Capt signified that had he known you before the marriage he should have endeavoured to save you from it as knowing him unfit for domestic life. Mrs. Leigh has since been with your Mother an hour they were perfectly agreed on

[1] Presumably the wife of the fourth Earl Ferrers, who obtained a separation from her husband some time before he was hanged at Tyburn in 1760 for murdering his steward in a fit of rage.

all points he has been very quiet till last night when he was very cross & inclined to be savage abused her Children offered the Capt Seaham as if it had been his own said he should live in a Lodging wished he had kept those at the Albany & such like strange talk. I do not think they are at all inclined to think you a brute but continually express their astonishment how you could have borne what you have.

Empowered to act on Annabella's statement, Judith could hardly have done other than she did. As to Mrs. Clermont, she had been receiving Annabella's confidences for the past two months and had been led to suppose that Annabella's life was not safe under Byron's roof. In justice to Selina Doyle it must be admitted that she also had received similar confidences.

The effect of these letters on Annabella was to convince her that she had gone too far to retract. If she now behaved with the generosity of love, she would face a charge of weakness in preferring inclination to duty. Augusta was now fighting a losing battle. On Sunday the 21st she had maintained her tone of reassurance to Annabella:

all went on very well yesterday and it appeared to me B. was particularly well last night. He complained of pain from his pills &c but upon my telling him that was *quite right* seemed satisfied & said he thought he was better—staid at home—no brandy—& said very seriously he should go to Kirkby in Feby. & that "they must *keep* us for 6 months." Of course I said nothing to discourage such a plan. I have seen him but a moment today when he was eating a stewed knuckle of Veal with broth & rice.

Thus far the picture of Byron in Augusta's daily reports bears no resemblance to the menacing neurotic of Annabella's statements. Only the pistol on the mantelpiece indicates the eccentricities that had intimidated her, which incident—so carelessly noticed by Augusta—was credited with sinister significance by Annabella: "The fact of the Pistol is striking, such apprehensions are on the *very verge* of derangement; and there is but little difference between such an *intention* and its *execution*."

The arrival of Lady Noel in London may have suggested to Augusta that only a conviction of Byron's mental illness would deter Annabella from legal proceedings, for the serenity of her optimism becomes for the first time clouded in her letter of Monday the 22nd:

B. staid at home yesterday Eveg—no brandy—& took his medicines . . . B. was well ye beginning of the Eveg, but towards ye end grew *frac*tious & in reply to a question from George apropos of his own wish to see Bosworth House of *when* he thought of going down to Kirkby, he said after a vacant stare "I go there! not at all—I have no thought of it if I can help it"—& from that moment talk'd all sorts of strange things, fell on *me* as usual, abused my Spouse, my children, in short all as you know & have heard before—talked of you quite *coolly*, of his intention of going into lodging by himself—with that total absence of feeling that it wd *look strange* or *be so*—which is my greatest horror being so totally unlike himself—in short looked black & gloomy, nobody could tell why or wherefore ye rest of the night.

Today I've not seen him yet, but have been with yr Mother & had both your letters my dearest Sis. How well, *too* well I know all your feelings—alas! I can not mend them I fear. I mean to shew the two intended for inspection to B. as I judge it best or not—for no one can judge that *does* NOT *see* . . . Ly N. seems to think *his* relations can't let him go on in this state, *yet* what *is* to be—what *can* be done! One of the things he did & said last night was desiring George to go & live at Seaham exactly as if it were his own! & even before our dinner he said he considered himself *the greatest man existing*. G. said laughing "Except Buonaparte!" Ye answer was "God! I don't know that I do except even him!" . . .

He has lent the Box to the *Poles* tonight & I really am in terror of some mal a propos speech for in *that* he is worse than ever! Not a word has dropt of *abroad* & I can't help thinking ye scheme at an end . . . There was *wildness* & *incoherency* to the greatest degree in all he said last night. GB. was *astonished* never having seen him so bad.

On Tuesday the 23rd Augusta continued:

last night he was pretty much ye same as I described ye night before—*excessively* horrified by Ly N's coming, asking *why*. Of course I said business of her own—shewed yr two *ostensible* letters, which he read & smiled *good*naturedly at ye mention of the untaken pills & *your* Liver—asked if that was *all* from you, He seemed harping on Ly N's coming all the Evg & came out with it repeatedly said once "by the bye Augusta she is I suppose (or I fear) in a devil of a pucker with me." I answered "Why?" —"Oh! because I've not written or gone there." I turned it off *lightly* & pretended to know nothing which must be ye case without ye thunder is to crush him at once.

He lent the Box to the Poles & made his appearance—behaved civilly, but very shy & grave, & did not remain long. He came home before us & answered a careless question of mine on the subject that Ly Holland had set him down. It was I think *true*—tho till I heard that I suspected otherwise as *nau* had been determined on before he went out. I really think he will be in a most serious scrape with the *Cookes* as the Father is respectable . . . I write so openly both as a duty & feeling *in yr case* it wd be what I wished. If you go on feeling ill & so wretched, I really wish you *would* come to Town—or decide on any positive line of conduct which you consider best. He asked me yesterday if I had given his love to you. I said "No, you did not tell me." "Oh but you might say something civil to keep up the look of the thing"—to which I answered "I could not invent *civil speeches*" or something to that effect & why did he not write—how *lazy* he was! The reply was the usual *malicious sarcastic* look & smile.

While she thus conveyed the impression that Byron was behaving abnormally owing to illness, Augusta said nothing to endorse a charge of insanity, and reported that Le Mann "assures me *nothing* can be done by *us* (his family) without medical opinions to authorize restraint & controul & that *he* (tho convinced of derangement on certain points) could not take on himself to say it was sufficient for that."

If Annabella had loved Byron, she could not have read Augusta's letters without feeling tender concern for him and jealousy of Augusta's devotion and deftness in managing his difficult moods. Making the mistake of supposing that Annabella loved him as she herself loved him, Augusta now sought to awaken her tenderness by describing his ailments and her jealousy by reporting his attentions to other women. On Wednesday the 24th:

I found B. very bad with ye pain in his head when he sent for me yesterday before my dinner & after his . . . it seems now first over one eye then ye other, then between & over the nose & at times spasmodic. I shall talk to Le Mann about it . . . Hanson call'd yesterday morning, & B sent him word from his bed he wd call on him in the Eveg. He did *not*, & made me go to the Play with him before which I had an opportunity of saying what I have long thought of & considered—that I had heard & from various quarters that his conduct at the Theatre was much observed & talked of—*Miss Boyce* even mentioned, & others hinted at. He tried to laugh at first wanted to know my authority which of course I did *not* give & took ye opportunity of mentioning also his want of discretion. He seemed very evidently *much* struck by my intelligence & to be sure he had not *flirted* (owing to it) when he returned to the Box, & Mr. Holmes has I find been desired *not* to go to paint Miss Cooke.

George last night spoke to him very sensibly & seriously of *you* & what he was bringing on himself—ye same arguments *I* have gone over a thousand times & with ye same effects.

I've seen him just now—ye same pain in his head which he attributes to ye mercury, I've persuaded him is *rheumatic* . . . His temper good, but he is much perplexed by a letter from Ly F. Webster again! & I'm to copy it for you & send it *for yr opinion* & *advice* if possible!!!

I told him yesterday & today *I* had *not* heard in answer to his enquiries —from you, but of you from Mrs. Clermont that you were unwell. He seemed quite unhappy & said "Poor thing! she worries herself about *it* all—I had better write to her." Today he asked again after you, & *if you wanted* HIM.

Late the same night:

B. has been at home this Eveg, & *very* well. When I first saw him he had much of the pain in his head, but Le Mann set him at rest about it, I fancy, & I sent for some Aromatic Vinegar which gave him ease. This letter from Paris [from Lady Frances Webster] has set his brain into a sad ferment. He has begun an answer which is civil & cool enough, but whether he will send it or not I don't know. In ye present state of things I think it rather desirable he *should*, because any change respecting *you* may induce him to do some mad thing or other on that subject. He has already mentioned going with Hobhouse to Paris *to see* what she *means.* Is it not (hers) the most *barefaced* impudence you ever heard of? I had not time to tell you the handwriting this time is *her own* I mean *not* disguised & the seal the Dove returning to the Ark with ye Olive leaf motto, "La Fidelité merite la Confiance." B's first idea was "had she heard you had left Town?" or any reports about you & him—in short his poor head is quite off on this subject & *I* should like to knock *hers* agst the wall! . . .

. . . during George's conversation with him last night, upon his (B's) appealing to me about something I told him that I had said 1000 times most of what George was then saying & had really desisted lately finding him *quite* IRRATIONAL on *that* subject. I said it very quietly & of course fearlessly with G present, in hopes of its being dwelt on afterwards in his reflections—& I believe it was for today in speaking very good humouredly of last night's discussions, he said, "You think me *mad* on *that* subject." I replied you certainly dont speak rationally upon it.

Surely if *controul* is out of the question, ye next best thing is to try to make him aware *Malady does exist.* He has not been near Hanson—has said I think nothing particular about you tonight—asked after the Child —told Le Mann you were not at all well, & that Kirkby was a damp, swampy place & disagreed with you.

Each day during this week Augusta was seeing Judith, to whom she referred tactfully in her letters to Annabella without comment on the conversations she had with her or on her activities with lawyers. Each of her letters contained affectionate expressions of sympathy with Annabella's wretchedness—for Annabella wrote of little but her own feelings. She uttered no word of reproach to Annabella, though sometimes a hint of sarcasm may be suspected. When Annabella told her, "You cannot think how severe my father is—much more than my mother," Augusta replied, "I am sorry for what you say of yr Father because it will add to *your worry,*" and remarking, "I foresee nothing but wretchedness for us all," she added, "Happy those! who can feel they don't deserve it—& that must ever be *your* comfort."

On the morning of Thursday the 25th Augusta was annoyed that Byron allowed his barber to cut his hair—"a wise thing to do with cold in his head!"—and more so to "find Hobhouse is here." Hobhouse recorded in his journal:

In London—went in the evening to the Royal Society where met Byron who was inaugurated by my father—then Drury Lane—behind the scenes &c.

After spending the evening with George Byron and the Poles, Augusta wrote to Annabella:

B. went *with Hobhouse* to the *Royal Society* & then to the Play, & came home soon after us in the worst of humours & more mad than I've seen him since you been gone. *Paris* is ye favorite theme. "H. is going abroad & will be his companion if he goes but does not wish or ask him to go"—& then H says I look as if I did not like him & thought he made B drink Brandy! and a great deal more in this style apropos of *nothing!* I was summoned as usual to attend him to his room when ye subject was renewed in a stronger manner by B. & at last I begged to know why there was this wonderful defence of H. when nobody had accused him? that as far as related to *my* opinion of him & the subject of going abroad I was quite ready & willing to give my objections *to himself* & repeat all I had said on the subject whenever he liked to hear. This produced no slight consternation. "I'll be *d——d* if you shall speak to him in my presence or out of it"—a great deal more in ye same way which it is useless to repeat—all to defend H. from any thing to do with his conduct about you & yours—that he (H) pitied you & said "poor thing!" In short my dear A I was quite in an *internal* rage & calmly to all outward appearance looked steadfastly at B & asked him whether "HE thought well of H?" You never saw such confusion—he is certainly VERY unpleasant tonight—says he will go off with ye first woman who will go with him—& constant allusions to Ly F[rances Webster], to whom he has written a most improper answer. I don't know if it is actually gone, but it must do mischief if it does go & if by chance her Spouse gets hold of it I think will cause an uproar. I am sent to Hanson tomorrow upon all sorts of business—it is strange he won't go himself! & he has been FLIRTING if not worse at the Theatre tonight. To say the truth I think flirting is ye *worst* for everybody talks & stares of course.

All Augusta's efforts to excite feminine reactions were wasted on Annabella. To Augusta's concern lest "ye thunder is to crush him at once," she replied:

"The thunder" to which you allude would not be so terrible. If it be disease any strong shock will for a time restore reason, though in the end it can make no difference . . . I cannot regret the report of *derangement.*

Apparently perceiving Augusta's attempts to awaken her jealousy, she thought "he had better not know, or be encouraged to believe the power he may have over my feelings, as the desire to *work upon them* might lead him to measures more hurtful to himself." As to Lady Frances Webster, she remarked, "The Paris scheme was *very near* executed in the Summer."

Self-absorption prevented any stirring of her imagination even by Augusta's vivid picture of happenings in Piccadilly. In the change of mood created by the letters received from her mother, Selina Doyle, and Mrs. Clermont, her vanity was most likely to have been stung by the sentence in Augusta's letter of the 23rd, "If you go on feeling ill & so wretched, I really wish you *would* come to Town—or decide on any positive line of conduct which you consider best." For, on the same day as she received this letter from Augusta, the necessity of preserving her reputation for strength in rectitude was endorsed by a further letter from her mother of 23rd January:

My dearest Child,

It appears to me by your letters that the first thing to be attended to in the present instant is the State of *your own mind*, for I too plainly perceive that Your agitation and unhappiness (which I do not wonder at) bring on apprehensions of evils which bad as things are, *do not* or *ever can exist*. Let me entreat You therefore by the duty and affection I so well know exist in your heart towards me, to endeavour to *calm* your mind, and not see *imaginary Bugbears*, when so many *real* Ones exist.

Be sure of this that nothing worse can happen than what has taken place, and it is great comfort to me to find Sir Samuel, Heywood and Doyle, all unanimous as to the *first Step* to be taken, namely Sir Ralph writing to Lord B.—of which letter I am to form a Copy and then subject it to Sir Samuels correction, which he will give it—in whatever may be *wrong* or *indiscreet*. Now as this letter can only be written when I get back, and is the *first thing to be done*, You perceive no *measures* can be taken till we have met. Also the *Trio* agree that should Lord B. attempt to visit Kirkby, he must ON NO ACCOUNT be admitted—but Sir Ra: must state as *his* reason, that things have *recently* come to his knowledge, which make it impossible for him consistently with his *Duty* as a *Father* and his *principles* as a *Man*, to allow that Ld B. should be an inmate of his House, or allowing You to return to Lord B's. If violence is attempted it must [be] repelled by force —but I do not believe there is any chance of his going down.

I have been with Romilly first and then with Heywood for an hour each and am just returned. They *both* have their *Hearts* in the business especially Heywood who is quite earnest in the Cause. I am to see *Lushington*, a Civilian, that I may know before I leave London, what Measures to take Should B. not accede to *treaty*—that we may not be laid helpless.

Heywood has kindly undertaken to procure an interview with Lushington for me, without the intervention of a *Proctor*—which in the *civil Court* answers to a *Solicitor* in the other Courts.

I was an hour with Le Mann last night, who has seen B. most days . . . he says he thinks B's *general health* improving, but remains perfectly persuaded of his *Malady*, from circumstances which have come to his knowledge, but that if examined if he individually had witnessed any *derangement*, he could only say, that unless talking very foolishly sometimes he never had. But as Le Mann was walking in the Street yesterday, he met a Gentleman of his acquaintance who stopped him, saying, "I am sorry to hear Your friend Lord B. is mad." Le Mann in course put on an Air of Surprise—on which the Gentleman added, "why it is very well known at the Theatre, he acts so oddly that everybody perceives it."

As to Your fears that *I* should be cajoled by *Sweet Words*, I can only say "old Birds are not caught by Chaff"—and in respect to Mrs. Leigh She has so committed herself before me and Clermont that *She cannot retract*, nor do I now believe She is inclined to do so—but it [is] I believe the wish of her heart that it should prove *Lunacy* not *depravity* without that excuse.

I never had such an idea as to shew *her* or *G.B.* that paper.

Clermont has committed to paper what You wished & R[omilly]. and H[eywood]. have both seen it this morning and think it *essential* . . .

I assure You *I am very Sane*, my Brains are particularly clear—like B. I can collect myself on *great occasions* . . .

Sir Samuel has a very bad opinion of H[anso]n, but this you must not repeat publickly. He also thinks Lady M[elbourn]e as infamous and wicked a Woman as ever existed—he means thro' a common acquaintance to find out if G. L[am]b has ever observed or said any thing about B's being *odd* in his manner at the Theatre. As soon as I have had this conference with Lushington I shall leave London, as my Stay here is of no use.

This moment I have your letter of Monday—to-day You will have one *from me* which I hope will allay the terrible irritation of Your Spirits—recollect that You will see me before any thing is done. I have had Mrs. Leigh [&] G.B. both with me—*both right*. Lord B. sent yesterday to *dun* Murray for the 1000£ for his Poem, giving as a reason that he wanted to give the greatest part of it to *Godwin*[1]—in course Murray would not send the money, and on refusal B wrote as Augusta and GB *suppose* a very *violent letter*. B is still eager about Miss Coke and also about Miss Boyce, and talks in such an obscene Stile before Miss Leigh,[2] that her Mother is obliged to keep her out of the Room.

He still declares he will take a Lodging and live as a Batchelor & declares he will never go to Kirkby—nor to *Seaham*, tho' he once thought of *living there* by *himself*—and again offered it G.B.

Yet he went to the Play last night, and was introduced to the *Pooles* and behaved very well . . .

Both GB. and Augusta declare Your life would not be safe with him, and have so pledged themselves to *this declaration* that they cannot be off. Colonel Leigh is expected on thursday.

I forgot to say B. was very struck when he heard I was in Town, and asked what I came about! they told him business of the *Executorship*—he then asked if I was come to take him to Kirkby? and whether I meant to visit him. I have heard of no soft Words about *You*, therefore suppose none are used.

Annabella's self-esteem could not tolerate the suggestion that her mother surpassed herself in composure, judgment, and resolution, so she retorted promptly on 24th January:

I being in a sound state of mind & body do give my authority for such measures as may be necessary to effect a separation—of the propriety of which none of the advisers seem to doubt. I therefore no longer consider that person as connected with me, or as the subject of consideration in any

[1] Byron had at first declined to accept the thousand guineas offered by John Murray for *The Siege of Corinth* and *Parasina*, but, at the suggestion of Sir James Mackintosh and Samuel Rogers, he proposed to give £600 to William Godwin and to divide the rest between Coleridge and Maturin, the author of *Bertram*. When Murray protested that it was "heartbreaking to throw away my earnings on others," Byron not unnaturally replied with asperity on 22nd January, even demanding the immediate return of his manuscripts.

[2] Augusta's eldest daughter Georgiana, then aged seven.

way but that of business. My last letter to you was written in a wavering temper & contained some folly I believe—but no more of that.

The *last* accounts seem to me to tend more strongly towards Insanity than any other—but in my opinion *that* ground will not do. Even *I* could not swear to a positive belief in it. That excessive pride which would defy God & Man to the utmost is very characteristic however of the Malady.

The great thing to be dwelt on with the world is the *aversion* he has manifested towards me. For as to *character*, people may say I should have known that sooner, but no one can suppose he gave me reason to think he hated me. His conduct towards me has certainly been *malevolent*.

I shall await further directions tomorrow, and conform to the best of my power, if by any exertion I can atone to you & my father for this unhappy connection.

She was now assured of Byron's "aversion," though only two days before she had declared her belief that "he loves me distractedly." Annabella's was the misfortune of the egocentric; she was the victim of her own vanity, the winds of which made a weathercock of her emotions. Despite a year spent daily in his company, she really knew little of Byron; her self-love had prevented her loving him and getting to know him through love. She was to write of him a few months later:

His character was a labyrinth, but no clue would ever find the way to his *heart*—

"It cannot feel for other's woes"—

applicable to a certain state of selfish absorption, in which the victim may not be conscious of the very sufferings he inflicts.

Meanwhile Judith had enjoyed her first interview with Dr. Stephen Lushington, and from the moment of his taking charge of negotiations there was no chance of reconciliation. A smooth, shrewd careerist, Lushington became a Whig M.P., figured prominently with Brougham as an advocate of Queen Caroline's cause, and acquired sundry profitable posts in his progress to a civilian judgeship of the Admiralty. At this time only thirty-four, he survived to complete his ninety-first year, and after Annabella's death interposed every possible obstruction to delay her grandson's securing her papers—doubtless fearing a revelation of the decisive part he had played in the separation and of the handsome remuneration he had received over many years for his advisory services.

Judith wrote on 24th January:

I would not but have seen Lushington for the World—he seems the most *gentlemanlike*, clear headed and clever Man I ever met with—and agrees with all others that a proposal should be sent by Your Father for a *quiet adjustment* . . .

BUT OBSERVE—that he insists on Lord B's not being allowed to remain *an instant* at Kirkby should he go there—and he says YOU must not see him on ANY ACCOUNT—and that Your father should remain in the Room *with You.* If you see him voluntarily or he is suffered to remain, You are wholly in his power, and he may apply to the Spiritual Court for a restoration of Conjugal Rights & oblige you to return as they term it—neither must You answer any letter he writes. He was surprised to find *I* had given this advice before I left Kirkby—he said it was the best possible.

I have a great persuasion that Ld. B. will not oppose *the arrangement* & I hope he will not—but if he does, Lushington thinks that the Spiritual Court will grant a Separation on the ground of *cruelty* and *temper*.

He thinks also there is sufficient and ample ground to Swear the Peace against him, either as a Person *occasionally deranged* on particular subjects or from what he has already done. He also is of opinion that You will not be interrupted in retaining the Child—and is happy You have now possession of it. Ld. B. may move for a Writ that the Child should be brought into Court, but he does *not* think that in this Case it would [be] granted, at all Events the Lord Chief Justice of the Kings Bench could *not decree*, without hearing the Situations of the respective Parties—which in this case would be highly advantageous to the Mother—as his habits of life & acknowledged *partial* derangement at least, would be proved even by *his* nearest Connections, also the extreme indecency of his language, before even Georgina—which obliges her Mother to keep her out of the Room...

Now I hope Ld B. did not write by to-day's Post—or if he did that You have not answered it—for God-sake do not.

Consider of Some one to be appointed by Sir Ralph to meet the Person who Lord B. may fix on, to confer on Articles of Separation. I daresay *he* will appoint *Hanson*, tho' at present he will not see him . . .

I have reason to believe that the conduct of Ld B. is pretty well known in London, and that the Story runs that he has sent You away & is mad himself. His connection with Miss Boyce and *others* also, is well known to all who have any connection with the Theatre.

Lushington observed to-day, that from Miss B's *Character* which *he* well knew, Your *health* was not safe if You continued with Ld B.

He still continues his pursuit of the Cookes and talks of it openly to his Sister and others.

I find that Murray says the letter B. wrote to him was as if he was writing to the greatest *Scoundrel* and *Blackguard*—but Murray passes it over from consideration of *insanity* . . .

Lushington *intimated* having a very bad opinion of *H*[*anso*]*n*.

She did not tell Annabella "what passed last night in Piccadilly", as she found Mrs. Clermont had already written:

Mrs. Leigh & the Capt have both been here.

Last night Capt B: told him of the ill conduct he was & had been pursuing of his ill treatment of you &c at which he seemed very much astonished, at least that it had been observed, first said he had not ill used you, had not told you to leave his house.

When the other said I know you have & as to the turning her out there is a written proof of it he said but I asked her to stay *after*. The other replied that will not do—can you suppose that she could go to her parents in that way without their becoming acquainted with your conduct as well as that they must have heard it from different Quarters. His Answers were in his usual strain[:] he did not care if her & her friends chose a separation [—] let them have it [—] was violent but not inclined to Quarrel with Capt B:

Your Mother told them that she thought the proposal of a separation which your Father would think it right to make if acceded to appeared to be the best plan. They both agreed in the necessity of it upon your account & that *your feelings only* should be considered. Nothing can exceed their kindness towards you & I am only distressed when your Mother becomes harsh in speaking of *him* to Mrs. Leigh although she has upon the whole behaved very well. I mention this that you may in writing to her speak kindly of Mrs. Leigh or rather as She *has deserv'd* from you & do not suffer any wild fancies to make you unjust. Miss Doyle was here during the conversation & did great service.

By her own account, in a letter of the 25th, Miss Doyle hardly shared Mrs. Clermont's consideration of Augusta's feelings: "I felt for her but as I could not pretend ignorance I thought by speaking my real feelings before her, I should spare hers more than by Silence which would have left more than the truth to imagine." Miss Doyle had therefore asserted:

That you would willingly sacrifice the daily comfort of your Life for to be of use to Ld. B—that for one year you had made the experiment that so far from being of use to him or having encreased his Happiness his habits were as bad, his misery in consequence greater as the wrongs you suffered from him engendered hatred with remorse—that you remained till all in the House considered your Life in danger—that your Duty towards him as well as that towards your Parents & your Child & yourself urged your seperation from him—that to say he was a rational being that could thus fly in the face of his own welfare was absurd—that he was to a certain degree insane there could exist no doubt. I appealed to both Mrs. L. & Capt. B—whether they did not agree with me—they did—& they also agreed in my opinion that notwithstanding this perversion of reason on his part he is not in a state of confirmed Lunacy such as wd justify their taking his affairs out of his hands & subjecting him to Coercion. They agreed also in thinking that he was as incapable of receiving Happiness from you as of imparting it—therefore is not a seperation desirable for both parties? they agreed. I pleaded the necessity of his Friends joining with yours to bring about this seperation by negociation . . .

An adept stoker in adding fuel to a fire, Miss Doyle then digressed at length in her own analysis of "the madness of His conduct," which "Courses . . . make him to my Satisfaction an irrational being," before finally concluding: "I expect you will have occasional returns of despondency but conscious rectitude of intention should still support you."

That evening her brother conferred with Lushington, so next day Miss Doyle composed another long epistle, full of the dire possibilities "should the negociation fail," emphasising the point most calculated to disturb—"the question of the retaining the child is the least clear"—and embellishing reports with picturesque suppositions:

> I sometimes think the Love of Excitement would make him Glory in bringing upon himself the odium of the world. It broke out when G.B. threaten'd him with Your Parents taking up your defence—he interrupted him with the most animated Expression of Exultation & said, "Let them Come forward I'll Glory in it". . . Moderation in any thing is intolerable to his Nature—he has Courage to rush upon perdition but not that which is necessary to pursue the rugged path of repentance which he feels must be his road to Virtue—"I cannot be positively good—but what prevents me from being positively bad?—Nothing—Well I'll shew the World Im fit for Great things"! Should some such insane purpose seize on his wild imagination he may spurn the negociation on purpose to force you to an Exposure of his Conduct. . . . As a real wife you were Contemn'd but when you become again the beau Ideal of his Imagination between the possession of which & him there is an insuperable Barrier You will be a second Thersa perhaps surplant her totally . . . I have as little doubt that had he Married Thersa he would have been to Thersa what he has been to You—She could not better have "Ministered to a mind diseased" than you did when living with him than You do in leaving him.

Annabella did not reply to Miss Doyle, who accompanied Judith and Mrs. Clermont to Kirkby, leaving London on the morning of Saturday, 27th January, and arriving at Kirkby on the Sunday evening. To her mother she wrote a brief note as Mrs. Clermont had suggested:

> I have been comforted & confirmed as usual by one of Mrs. Leigh's kind letters. She has been the truest of friends to me—and I hope you regard her, & *seem* to regard her as such, for I very much fear that She may be supposed the cause of Separation by many, and it would be a cruel injustice.
>
> I have nothing to say or to do but what I am bid—and shall be very obedient.

This crossed a letter from Judith, enclosing a draft of the letter prepared by Lushington for Sir Ralph to write to Byron:

> . . . both Doyle and Lushington are of opinion not *one Word* must be changed—that an accurate Copy must be kept in Sir Ralphs own handwriting and that the sooner it is *sent by the Post*, the better. Therefore Sir Ralph must set to Work, and get it done for Monday's Post—as delay is detrimental. I shall be at Kirkby on Sunday certainly.

She was full of praise for Lushington:

> *Lushington* has *most kindly condescended* to be the professional Person on our side. I say *condescended*, because it is quite out of *Etiquette* for him to meet a *Solicitor*, and I told him I believed Hanson would probably be fixed on by Ld. B.
>
> I wish you knew Lushington—he is the most rising Man in the Spiritual Court and the Man most looked up to—added to this, his Character as *a Man* stands high—and he appears to me to have as much delicacy of feeling for You, as Doyle or I can have. He is *jointly* recommended to me, by Doyle and Heywood . . .
>
> A very short time since, a Lunacy Cause came under Lushingtons inspection, and the Fact was quoted in the Argument, that *Tasso* was decidedly mad on one Subject *only*—viz. that he was fully persuaded that he had intercourse with a *Spirit*—*partial* disease, as the case with B— would to God it had been on as mild a Topic.

That same evening Lushington wrote a lengthy epistle to say little beyond asking permission to wait on Lady Noel next morning at Mivart's Hotel before her departure, and she had no sooner gone than he wrote again to her at Kirkby about possible contingencies, as "It is my duty to look forward to all possibilities, & guard against them in due time."

Annabella had meanwhile reverted to her "low" mood, thus "collecting her sentiments" for her own satisfaction:

> Under the circumstances of this awful & afflicting change I cannot yet think the last year of my life to have been *thrown away* on the person to whom it was devoted. He is habitually more impressed by objects in the past than the present—and his Imagination dwells more with Memory than Observation. If then I have been deserving of Love it will be awakened or produced when I am contemplated through the softening & yet deepening medium of Time—and the good which irritated when in action, will attach in retrospect. It may even excite better thoughts, if a *despairing pride* should no longer check them. The Images of Tenderness in the past have hitherto been on the side of Vice. If I should be the means of creating one virtuous association, I rejoice to have suffered, & only wish I had left still better traces on Memory. Yet this has been the least erring of my years. Had my trials been those of Happiness, I might have fallen—but Sorrow is not less a Guardian than a Chastiser.

As she was doubtless fully aware, there is pathos in this attitude of a young woman of twenty-three, resigned to abdication from the life of her own self-dedication after only a year's experiment. But such an attitude could be assumed only by an egocentric; only a few days before she had implied that she had made a mistake in her choice of a husband when proposing to her mother to "atone to you & my father for this unhappy connection," and vanity was already devising self-justification.

The same day she wrote a long letter of self-explanation to Augusta:

It is not my intention to discontinue my considerations of B's welfare (which have hitherto guided me in *every* thing) if they can be of the least comfort to you. Consult me therefore on this subject whenever you please, excepting only—that I must request to be left wholly ignorant of his thoughts or feelings *concerning myself*, and should they be such as it is desirable for my parents to know you can communicate to Mrs. Clermont. Though I have been from particular causes incapacitated from executing my own plans for his benefit, I cannot think myself mistaken in my views concerning it, and therefore wish to give you some opinions.

It is *most desirable* to impress him with the sense of his Malady, as having existed at times for years—*during which times he would not be considered an accountable Agent.* Seem not to suspect that he *did* any thing under its influence, but leave him to draw the only inference which can be consolatory to his conscience—and could he once be led to this, *it would do more good than any thing.*

In regard to any strange step he may meditate, the same idea must be employed. Let it be signified that the *strangeness* of his conduct has already been so observed, that any thing more of the same kind may lead some person to *take a strong measure.* He will understand—even if he pretends ignorance, as the idea of being lunatized has never been wholly absent from his mind.

In regard to myself—when he shall know that I am no longer his—let the ground of my conduct be represented, as it truly is—the impossibility I found of making him happy—on the contrary that I had made him more unhappy—that I have no resentment for any part of his conduct—and I *think* it would be better for him to suppress what you know of my feelings, and to represent me as more of the "cold & calculating" person I *was* believed. Gratifying as it would still be to me to think he knew how dear he *is*—it is better he should not, for it would only excite more remorse which always leads him to desperate courses. Let him then suppose me to have provided *for my own* happiness—with a prospect of enjoying it——!

You may if you please subject the contents of this paper to Mr. Le Mann's inspection . . .

There is another reason why it is desirable that he should not know his influence over my feelings—because the desire to pique them might lead him to extravagances. Don't let him think I can be *worked upon* in any way—yet let him not believe that I give up *the hope of his salvation* (an idea which may hereafter occur in the strange mixture of *Methodism* & Pride) for I would be (as I have been at times) connected in his Imagination with a future world, where, he twice told me, *he thought my prayers would avail for him*—God knows they shall never be wanting. Even now I do not think that the year I have lived with him may have been quite thrown away with regard to any hope that may yet remain of his recovering a better or sounder state of mind. You must have observed that the strongest existing impressions on his mind are from objects in the past rather than the present—and that *Memory* seems to have the greatest power over his feelings.

The day may come, though distant when I shall be remembered to some good, perhaps—at least let me think so—it may soften the bitterness of what is *torn* from me. If I had lost the most perfect felicity of the world, I could not be more afflicted than by the duty of resigning those prospects of wretchedness. Strange!—but *you* will not wonder.

Saturday Nt.

You must not let him know that I had communicated this intention to you before—it would prejudice me & mine, if he chose to take advantage of it. What you have already told him will give you reason not to appear *surprised.* You will also at present give as *your opinions* of my motives what I *tell* you of them—& in all this, you only can judge what will suit or not with the actual feeling.

Pardon me if I seem to dictate—I write to *a friend.*

At the time of writing this letter on Saturday 27th January—nearly a fortnight after she left Piccadilly—she still thought of Augusta as a sister, supplying the same place in her affections as her cousin Sophy Tamworth had supplied in her childhood, as she had expressed in verses entitled "A Sister's Sentiments," apparently written about September 1815:

A sister's love! best soother once to me—
Friendship herself must yield the palm to thee.
They whom one bosom warm'd, the same arms prest,
Whom the same soft endearments lull'd to rest,
Must, when of souls that would unite by choice,
Feel double sympathy from Nature's voice;
Each truly imaging the other's heart
In thoughts where none beside can claim a part!

In this letter she was in fact resigning to Augusta her own charge of caring for Byron's welfare.

But the next day—the day of her mother's arrival from London—she was reminded of Lushington's injunction that she must not communicate with Byron, and realised that her instructions to Augusta, on how far her feelings might be imparted to him, could be construed as indirect communication with him. So she did not send the letter, but wrote instead a brief warning that Augusta might expect the arrival of Sir Ralph's letter: "It must not be known that I had anticipated to you my father's communication, as it would be prejudicial to me and mine."

After dispatching her decisive letter to her mother on the 24th, she had written:

My dearest Augusta,—Shall I still be your sister? I must resign my *rights* to be so considered; but I don't think that will make any difference in the kindness I have so uniformly experienced from you.

Augusta replied on Saturday the 27th:

> You will ever be my own dearest Sis! How can you be otherwise—*indeed, indeed* every day makes you if possible dear*er*, & gives you additional claims on me. But I can't say half enough you know I'm always dumb when I feel most & *you* understand it.

She continued her narrative of events at Piccadilly:

> I've not seen B. today. He is at dinner but he staid at home last night & was tolerably quiet, tho singing wildly & irritable. He gave me an opportunity of saying much more of *derangement*, & took it very quietly. He said "Oh don't say so or talk of it because of my Will"—told me about Grandfather's end & his Mother always perceiving a resemblance between them—talked quietly & rationally abt it, but seemed rather alarmed at the thought. I am more & more inclined to impress this idea, as nothing else CAN be done. George went to *M*[ary] *Po*[le], so we had a tête-a-tête of you. He talked as if in expectation of what is going to happen—said, "I think things can't go on as they are, don't you?" that he only wished you wd take some step, & so on. *Paris* is uppermost certainly. He said jestingly I should be in such a fuss if he went there, to which I calmly replied, "No, my fusses can't be increased or diminished"—which seemed to strike him & he pressed me to say more. I declined, giving as a reason that it made no impression & therefore I had better be silent. I'm sometimes inclined to differ with you as to the effect of the approaching event, but most likely I am wrong. I have been quite silent to him of the determination yr F[ather]. & M[other]. have taken. By the bye I saw Hanson yesterday on business for B. Of course there was some conversation on *this* subject also, but I pretended total ignorance of ye intentions on your part & said *I* had & did feel it quite impossible to offer advice or opinions. H. wants me to talk to Hobhouse, which I shall *not* do—I think CERTAINLY NOT. He means *to hint ye malady* which H. would turn into ridicule & tell B.

This was Augusta's last communication before the arrival of Sir Ralph's letter to Byron, drafted by Lushington:

> *Very recently* Circumstances have Come to my knowledge which Convince me, that with your opinions it cannot tend to your happiness to continue to live with Lady Byron, and I am yet more forcibly Convinced that her return to you after her dismissal from your house and the treatment she experienced whilst in it is not consistent either with her Comfort, or, I regret to add, personal safety.

He therefore proposed "that a *professional friend* should be fixed on by you, to Confer with a person of the same description appointed by me, that they may discuss and Settle such terms of Separation as may be mutually approved." Dated and posted from Kirkby on 28th January, this letter arrived at 13 Piccadilly Terrace on Monday the 29th—to be intercepted and returned unopened by Augusta.

Augusta acted as she might have been expected to act if she had received Annabella's long letter explaining her feelings towards Byron. She knew that, for all Annabella's conception of herself as a strong and independent personality, she was easily influenced by environment and would always convince herself of the rectitude of her own conduct. Augusta also knew how Byron's pride would react on finding himself threatened by lawyers, as she knew how his generosity would respond to a gesture of conciliation. If Sir Ralph's letter was delivered, the fat would be in the fire; she therefore sought to keep the pan's balance a little longer in the hope that the fry of the marriage might yet be salvaged, writing on the 29th to Annabella:

For once in my life I have ventured to act according to my own judgement—not without 10000 fears I assure you. But I do it *for the best* & I do hope at least it will not be productive of evil, as I only wish *a few days delay*, & that you would hear all that I have to say before you send the enclosed.

It appears to me of the VERY *utmost* consequence for *you* & *your child* (for you must believe *that* to be my first consideration) that you should *pause*. See Ly Noel—hear what passed between Le Mann Sr H. Halford & her. The former was with me too late for me to write by Saturdays post & [is] so very strongly *of my own opinion* upon this subject that I begin to think it can't be a foolish one . . . you must my dear A—— believe that I can only wish *your good* in venturing to act as I have. Pray *assure* Sr Ralph of this & obtain my forgiveness if possible.

George goes tomorrow (if nothing very urgent prevents him) to Bosworth, & will write from thence to know if yr Father & Mother will see him. I very much wish it as writing is so unsatisfactory compared with speaking.

I must now tell you that while Le Mann was with me talking over B & his conversation with Ly Noel on Saturday, B received a note from Ly Melbourne desiring him to go to her yesterday. It put him in a fine fidget & me in a fine humour anticipating all manner of *evil*. However *he went* & came home in very good sorts & had as I could perceive a pretty good scolding for his behaviour to you & yrs. Some part of it was repeated to me but I'm sure only the *mildest* part. Don't suppose me fool enough dear A—— to think ye impression will be *lasting*, but at least I wish you to be apprised of this *renewed intercourse* before THE letter is sent. It *may* or *may not* make a difference—in the effects on him—you will judge best. . . . He is to go to her again today. She discourages also all *Paris* correspondence. In short I never was so pleased with her as from what I gleaned of yesterday's conversation. It has just occurred to me you may fear a visit from him by the delay but, I'm sure you need not as *Parliament* will prevent that which is one of the present hobbies . . . I suppose Ly N. will tell you Le Mann's opinion & Sr H.H.'s of the danger of precipitation in this business. . . . *My own* feelings & wishes (as I have told you I believe repeatedly) are, that *the whole blame* should rest on him, & if ever a shade of it *rested on you* it would break my heart QUITE. Do see George or beg yr Parents or Mrs. Clermont to do so. I will write more fully by him for I'm now in such agitation at what I've ventured to do that I CAN'T write rationally . . .

Having failed in her efforts to excite emotions of tenderness and jealousy, Augusta now sought to deter Annabella by warning her of the possible consequences of her action, writing on Tuesday evening (30th January) the letter which George Byron carried with him to Kirkby:

I shall tell George in few words what I wish which is nearly as I expressed myself yesterday—that you would *pause* a few days, consider the *probable* & *possible* consequences of this letter from ye effects on B—for they *must* affect *you* & *your child.* I am very strongly of opinion *revenge* will be uppermost & this from my late observations. What revenge could he take so effectual as depriving you of the child! & *who* could prevent him. Can *we* all say that a man who is not deranged *sufficiently* to admit of being *controuled* is unfit to have the care of his own child! & what would be the consequences to that child & your own feelings! Don't fancy I mean you to follow my advice, only to consider of these things. I too well know & feel all you have suffered, but my dread is yr suffering *more*, & my knowledge of your disposition only adds to this fear.

. . . Then there is Ly M[elbourne]. who has spoken only from ye information she gleaned from common report, & talks to him as to a *rational* man—without she is informed of the truth she will, *I* think, do harm at the crisis judging from *his representations* of the business, which is all she will have on which to ground an opinion mixed up with her own *immoral* & *worldly* notions. *As yet* her whole aim has been evidently to be a peace maker, at least to induce B. by all she *dares* urge to behave well to YOU—talks of your merits & attachment to him in ye VERY strongest manner. Of Sr R. she has said nothing bad but with respect to Ly N. does harm—for which we must be *so far* considerate as to remember she hates her & that B is more *irrational* on *that* than *any* thing & consequently gives her a fair opportunity of launching out in invective & repeating past occurrences in her own way. *But*, she always ends thus—"However much you may dislike them or however ill you may be used, you ought for Annabella's sake to behave well to them."

I hear she talks of calling on me—is there any thing you can suggest for *me* to *say* should she *begin*, or in any case that wd be right or could avert ill effects. I'm a coward with *bad* people. I daresay my dearest A I've omitted 1000 things but George must fill ye chasm . . . Le M. is of opinion that he will take some very wild step in the fit of irritation *the* letter may occasion . . .

Augusta's impulse served no useful purpose, as Sir Ralph, accompanied by Mrs. Clermont, immediately left for London, so that his letter could be delivered by hand to Byron. He carried with him a brief statement from Annabella:

I object to the expression of "personal safety" as particularly calculated to exasperate, and therefore likely to prevent all dispositions to an amicable adjustment . . . surely it is most desirable to effect the conciliatory views. I deem the omission of that phrase to be *essential* to their success.

He consulted Lushington, who deleted the reference to Annabella's comfort and personal safety, substituting, "those on whose protection she has the strongest natural claims would not feel themselves justified in permitting her return thither."

Ironically Augusta's action was damaging to herself, as thenceforth she was regarded by Annabella's partisans as exclusively devoted to her brother's interest. Both Judith and Annabella—for different reasons—became highly agitated on hearing of the intervention, and Judith began a letter to Augusta on 30th January:

Annabella has just received Your letter. I believe that not much longer will any care for her in this World be necessary. She is in a dreadful State and agitated in a degree that is become *terryfying*.

Your *cruel wicked* Brother has broken her heart.

As to what Le Mann says, *he can form no judgment*—because he is as yet unacquainted with the greatest Enormities Ld B. has been guilty of . . .

She quoted Sir Henry Halford's opinion "that there is a *degree* of insanity—but a naturally malevolent disposition," before continuing:

I cannot think You had a right to Stop the letter, or to prevent any Steps Sir Ralph found it necessary and proper to adopt—*You were not to judge for him* . . . The reasons for stopping the letter will be the same next Week, next Month and next Year and so on—Would You wish my poor miserable Daughter to be exposed to the attempts of either a Madman, or a cruel Savage? for one of the two he is—that She must continue to live terrifyed at what he may next do? . . . if You apprehend Violence to *himself*, You have a good and *more reason* to apprehend violence or mischief to her . . . You have done infinite mischief, which if You really love and pity Annabella You will regret and lament—and for what reason do you imagine that a few days will *change his nature?*—or Why favor him at her Expense?

Apparently Annabella prevented her sending this letter, and likewise another outpouring next day:

Your barbarous and hard hearted Brother has I am too firmly persuaded broken the heart that was devoted to him—and I doubt not will have pleasure in the Deed. *She* will not long exist, so he may glory in the Success of his endeavors. She is dreadfully ill and was last night and this day in a State which terrifys me—tell Lord Byron this if you please.

His plans of *Revenge* will soon be satiated I fear—and he will *regain that liberty* he so regrets having lost. If he has not the heart of a Tyger he will cease to molest her, in her present sufferings . . .

No imputation *can* take place on my Daughters Conduct . . .

Wonder not that I write *Strongly*, who could see that Suffering Angel Sinking under such *unmanly* and *despicable* treatment, and not feel? Ld Byron is sending her Parents also with Sorrow to the Grave—let him *glory* also in *that*—and that he has three Lives to answer for at the great account, as much as if he had plunged his Dagger in our hearts—indeed *that* would have been a short suffering compared to a *broken* Heart—Oh! my God! how has my poor Child been sacrificed! not only to a *wicked*, but *unmanly* Creature! *her* only Error, too strong an attachment to him, and how has he rewarded it!

Restrained from posting her letters to Augusta, Judith wrote to Mrs. Clermont on 31st January:

Captain B. has named to-day that Lord B. said in conversation with him, "that the Sooner *we* took measures for a *separation* the better"—and that if this declaration will be of any use, he is ready to come forwards to prove it. Name this to Dr. Lushington.

Captain B. would tell You all that had occurred since I left London, & that it was not from fear of *self*-violence that She Mrs. Leigh witheld the letter—Capt. B. treats all fears on *that account* as I do.

I suppose he would tell You that the business is now very publickly talked of—and what the Dowr. Dss of Leeds said to Mrs. Leigh—that She *ought* to *quit* Ld B's House—and *so She ought*, but She is a fool—and perhaps her Brothers having left *her* all he has to dispose of may make her shy of offending him.

A second interview has taken place between Ld B. and Lady Melbourne. She knows only what is so commonly observed, his conduct at the Theatre & his connections there. She told him he was losing his Character, and that he ought to go down here—his reply was, is there any thing extraordinary in my Staying to attend Parliament?

She continued her letter next morning with the confession that she was "*wretched*—and apprehensive of what the manner may be in which Ld B. will act":

Sir Ralph should consult Doyle and Lushington on the manner in which he should act about Lady Melbourne, You or Sir Ra: telling *Lushington* (Doyle already knows it) her *dangerous* and plotting Character, and her *concealed Enmity* to *us*—and her total want of Principle—that She would sacrifice Annabella in every respect to serve Ld B.—tho' She *dare not appear* to do so.

Sir Ralph was to be warned not to trust "Annabellas deposition and Yours out of his hands, except to *Lushington*," and she ended:

Annabella bids me say She is now *better* than when she sealed the letter She wrote.

The enclosed must be given to Sir R.—tell him to shew it You.

The enclosure was a startling revelation which presumably Byron had intimated to Annabella when seeking to shock her during one of his brandy bouts:

Ld —— has told his Wife that in 1813 he had *absolute criminal* Connection with an *old Lady*, at the same time as with her Daughter in Law—that *She* absolutely *proposed it to him*—and that he said "She [was] *so old* he hardly knew how to set about it." Ld *B.* has told this also to his *Sister*—*this explains much*, which was before *inexplicable*. Do not notice this in your letters, as I dare not withhold them from the *Lady here*—and dare not tell her I have disclosed *this*—but D[oyle] and L[ushington] ought to know it. You *must* shew them this—it has been *said* and believed in that *diabolical Set* the Lady lives in—but with *that Set* it is *not reprobated*—can too great caution be used to such a Woman?

To Sir Ralph she wrote on 2nd February, after referring to the "Paper for You in my letter to Clermont":

I have further to add that Lady B. saw—Ld B. shewed it her—a letter from the Viscountess written to the Lord, in which are these Words, after speaking well of Lady B. She adds—"but She has always been used to have her own way and has been flattered into a high opinion of herself—but *You* must break her of *this and subdue her*."

I request You will let Doyle and Lushington see this account . . .

What an infamous Woman She is—if *the Lord* is to be believed, She sent for him to the House in W[hiteha]ll, *expressly* to visit Ldy C[aroline] L[amb] and each Lady *knew* the conduct of the other.

I request You will *buy* and *read* the Book entitled, Les Liaisons dangereuses . . . You will *there* find *the Viscountess* depicted exactly in *La Marquise* . . .

Quere? as the Viscountess must be exposed if it comes to *publicity* can any use be made of that apprehension? by hints that She will be implicated?—I only mean in case Ld B. is refractory.

For Godsake do not let any *consideration* for *her* influence You—for it is owing in a great degree to the *settled hatred* She has long born to *You* and *Yours* . . . the Viscountess never forgave Annabella the involuntary Act of coming into the World—which injur'd her dearly beloved Brother & Nephew[1]—and it has been a regular Wish to *injure* ever since.

So far as Judith was concerned, the gloves were off and she was prepared to fight for her daughter and grandchild with tooth and claw. The contagion of her attitude was conveyed to Mrs. Clermont, whose daily letters for the next few days were designed to fortify

[1] John Milbanke, only brother of Sir Ralph Milbanke and Lady Melbourne, died in 1800; his son, John Peniston Milbanke (1776–1850), succeeded to the baronetcy on the death of his uncle, Sir Ralph Noel, in 1825.

Annabella's determination on a separation. To Judith she wrote on 1st February:

> Dr. Lushington and Colonel Doyle have just left us. Dr. Lushington did not think the objectionable sentence material he has therefore altered it which he did most willingly not only on account of Lady Byrons feelings but because he is very desirous of avoiding any expression that was calculated to Irritate Lord B:

To Annabella on the same date:

> Dr. Lushington & Colonel D: are perfectly decided that the Letter should be sent. I told them that I had seen Mrs. Leigh who says he has been for this two days past talking in a very quiet way of proposing a separation that he could not live with you he must be at Liberty and so forth.

Again:

> I am sure you would feel satisfied that it could not be in better hands than those of Dr. Lushington if you saw him he is both mild & temperate —speaking of Lord B: he said he must be judged by his actions as to sanity or insanity the opinions of medical men are so vague and often contradictory that they are not to be acted upon—now from all I have been able to collect ever since your departure it does not appear he has had any desire that you should return which I confess when you left I thought he would . . . I have not the smallest doubt his real wish is that a separation should take place at the same time he would chuse that you should remain attached to him.
>
> Talking of it the other night he said what will they give me I wonder nothing can be given him that will do him any good in his present temper that is very clear. I wish he may ever be in a state to receive benefit from your affection it is possible that may be the case hereafter but he must feel himself a free man again and he will do it by some means or other even though he should break your heart & have that upon his conscience ever after. Now if you can never be of use to him you must not give yourself up to despair and leave undone the good you must do to others great powers have been given you by God and you will be criminal in allowing them to be destroyed (which had you continued with him they soon would have been) or in sinking under the disappointment of your hopes.

On Saturday 3rd February:

> C: Doyle quite laughs at the Idea of Lady M: as either having the power or daring to make the attempt of influencing any Opinion in favour of B: against you he says when you are in *a rational state of mind* that is *as* when you wrote last you think justly & that your distractions will go off.
>
> I am sure they will *in time* as I think you only *deranged now* & *then* & can not believe you to be quite a *Goose*.

From which it appears that Annabella, during her hysteria earlier in the week—when her maid Mrs. Fletcher reported to her husband that "she was rolling on the floor in a paroxysm of grief at having *promised* to separate from Lord Byron"—had excited her mother's fears of Lady Melbourne's talent for subtle intrigue.

But she needed no reinforcement from Mrs. Clermont's cajolery. George Byron had reported on 31st January that Byron was himself disposed to a separation, and Judith informed Sir Ralph on 3rd February.

> Annabella's mind has been more relieved than you can imagine, by finding that Lord Byron had thoughts of proposing a separation, for with her Angelic Mind, the great doubt was, that she was inflicting pain on him. She has been *infinitely* more composed since She heard this, and her Countenance is quite changed for the better.

Truly Annabella had been formerly concerned with Byron's feelings, and henceforth she paid little regard to them, but the change and its cause suggest wounded vanity; it was very well that she, self-righteous as the injured party, should contemplate a separation, but insult was added to injury by Byron's doing so. She had already written to Mrs. Clermont:

> Pray don't let Sir R. stir a step or write a line without the legal counsels. I hope this thing will be done soon.
>
> A bold countenance will go a great way with those who are conscious of not having a good conscience—and decision may save many difficulties & delays . . .
>
> If Ld B. demands explanation from Sir R. of further reasons, it will only be a trick for time—and must not be attended to—but a reference given to the professional friend.
>
> I cannot help thinking that when once he has given his consent to an arrangement, my presence will be necessary and satisfactory to myself.
>
> Take care that Ld B. is not *admitted* if he should try to surprise Sir R. into a conversation. I have some fears of his being led to commit himself by some artful people. His answer to *all* must be—that he cannot discuss the subject at present. Pray beware of all such visitors. He had better sit in one room & have those who call shown into the next—because then he is not obliged to see every one who may gain admission.
>
> I was distract when I last wrote—and hope I did not influence any measure except the *personal safety*—against which my opinion is uniform. . .
>
> I do not now wish for any delay, & think I should be better if it were over.

Thus it appears that Augusta's intervention had an effect opposite to her intention. If Byron had received Sir Ralph's letter on 29th January, an immediate reply would have found Annabella still in her "low" mood and hesitant to take the "final step." As it was, he received Sir Ralph's letter on Friday 2nd February, when Augusta wrote at his direction:

My dearest Annabella
I am desired by B. to write you a line and ask whether the separation between you (proposed this day by your Father) is *your* wish—and if so, he will acquiesce, & that you need not be under any apprehension of intemperate feelings or conduct on his part towards those belonging to you.
I need not say with what grief I write on this subject. God bless you & dear little Guss
Every yr most affec Sis
AL

This she enclosed with a note headed "*private*":

I am desired to send ye enclosed, & have to add that he is *quiet*, & that a *temperate* answer is *begun*. To Sr R's letter he objects that it is *exaggerated*, tho he admits his conduct not to have been good. But all this I expected. He particularly dwells in his defence to *me* on the effect of pecuniary embarrassments on his mind, & ("if he is to believe Le Mann") that he has "been labouring for some time past under illness which occasions fits of PARTICULAR IRRITATION." Remember this is for *you alone*—at least I should not wish it to be repeated as it was said to me *in confidence*. Towards you there is no feeling but of kindness & much annoyance at the grief he sees he occasions me. Poor dear Soul! But I can't dwell on or bear to think of *you* my dearest dear Sis & all yr sufferings . . .

She wrote again on Saturday afternoon:

Things are *I know not how*. No answer has yet been *sent*, tho' one was *written* last night & with fewer objectionable points in it than I expected. George came this morning & is now with B. & must answer as his own discretion & good sense dictates for the best . . . B—— alarmed me much last night by his looks. He said himself he was very ill & felt exactly as before he began with his fevers—a chilliness & headache. Fletcher was as much frightened as I am. This morning he *looks* still very ill. He sent me to Hanson to shew yr Father's letter. H. is not in Town & may not be till Monday. B. can't believe the wish of separation is *yours*, & said when he heard you were unwell & suffering he *never could* forgive himself if any thing happened to you. In short he has been for days in a greatly agitated state about you & had settled to go to Kirkby on Sunday had this letter not come. God only knows what is best—from my heart I wish I did & *could* give either you or yours comfort . . . Le Mann is indeed a great comfort to me. Whatever his *visionary* ideas may be my dear A surely there is *good sense* in thinking a person in the state of mind & body *he is convinced* his Patient *is* in, ought not to be treated as one *sane* & *sound*. . . . He has pressed him in vain to have other advice, & very pointedly alluded to *the* malady & ye responsibility he felt in acting *alone*.

Byron replied to Sir Ralph with dignity and frankness:

To the vague & general charge . . . I must naturally be at a loss how to answer . . . Lady Byron received no "dismissal" from my house in the sense you have attached to the word—she left London by medical advice—she parted from me in apparent—and on my part—real harmony—though at that particular time rather against my inclination for I begged her to remain with the intention of myself accompanying her—when some business necessary to be arranged permitted my departure. It is true that previous to this period I had suggested to her the expediency of a temporary residence with her parents:—my reason for this was very simple & shortly stated—viz. the embarrassment of my circumstances & my inability to maintain our present establishment. The truth of what is thus stated may be easily ascertained by reference to Lady B. who is Truth itself—if she denies it, I abide by that denial. My intention of going abroad originated in the same painful motive—& was postponed from a regard to her supposed feelings on that subject. During the last year I have had to contend with distress without, & disease within:—upon the former I have little to say—except that I have endeavoured to remove it by every sacrifice in my power—& the latter I should not mention if I had not recent & professional authority for saying that the disorder which I have to combat—without much impairing my apparent health—is such as to induce a morbid irritability of temper, which, without recurring to external causes, may have rendered me little less disagreeable to others than I am to myself. I am however ignorant of any particular ill treatment which your daughter has encountered:—she may have seen me gloomy, & at times violent, but she knows the causes too well to attribute such inequalities of disposition to herself—or even to me—if all things be fairly considered.

And now Sir—not for your satisfaction, for I owe you none—but for my own, & in justice to Lady Byron, it is my duty to say that there is no part of her conduct, character, temper, talents, or disposition, which could in my opinion have been changed for the better—neither in word nor deed—nor (as far as thought can be dived into) thought—can I bring to recollection a fault on her part, & hardly even a failing. She has ever appeared to me as one of the most amiable of beings—& nearer to Perfection than I had conceived could belong to Humanity in its present existence.

Having said thus much—though more in words, less in substance, than I wished to express—I come to the point, on which subject I must for a few days decline giving a decisive answer. I will not however detain you longer than I can help—and as it is of some importance to your family as well as mine—and a step which cannot be recalled, when taken—you will not attribute my pause to any wish to inflict pain or vexation on you & yours—although there are parts of your letter, which—I must be permitted to say—arrogate a right which you do not now possess. For the present at least, your daughter is my wife;—she is the mother of my child—& till I have her express sanction of your proceedings, I shall take leave to doubt the propriety of your interference. This will soon be ascertained—& when it is, I will submit to you my determination—which will depend very materially on hers.

On Saturday he wrote to Annabella:

I have received a letter from your father proposing a separation between us—to which I cannot give an answer without being more acquainted with your own thoughts & wishes—& from *yourself*:—to vague and general charges & exaggerated statements from others I can give no reply:—it is to *you* that I look—& with *you* that I can communicate on this subject. When I permit the interference of relatives—it will be as a courtesy to them—& not the admission of a right.

I feel naturally at a loss how to address you, ignorant as I am how far the letter I have received has received your sanction—& in the circumstances into which this precipitation has forced me, whatever I might say would be liable to misconstruction. I am really ignorant to what part of Sir Ralph's letter alludes—will you explain?

To conclude—I shall eventually abide by your decision—but I request you most earnestly to weigh well the probable consequences, & to pause before you pronounce.

Whatever may occur, it is but justice to you to say that you are exempt from all fault whatever—& that neither now nor at any time have I the slightest imputation of any description to charge upon you.

I cannot sign myself otherwise than
yours ever
most affectionately
Bn.

On the same day, Saturday the 3rd, Annabella was writing to Augusta:

You are desired by your brother to ask if my father has acted with my concurrence in proposing a separation. He has.

Abstaining from reasons, she recalled only Byron's "avowed and insurmountable aversion to the married state" and how he had "too painfully convinced me that all those attempts to contribute towards his happiness were wholely useless & most unwelcome to him." She sent this letter to her father for submission to Lushington before it was forwarded, and next day wrote a note to Augusta asking that she should "on no account withhold from your brother the letter which I sent yesterday in answer to yours written by his desire."

From an unlikely source she was offered a last opportunity for retraction, Mrs. Clermont writing to Judith:

I send you the Copy of Lord Byrons letter & have sent the Copy of one to Annabella which has been agreed upon by Dr. Lushington & Colonel Doyle to be sent by her to Lord Byron if she determines to persevere but

Colonel Doyle is most anxious that she should not be pressed to pursue the course *legally* pointed out if she is not quite certain of having sufficient strength to persevere in it if she chuses rather to run the risque of a negociation with Lord Byron *which* might leave it more open to reconciliation at a future period he thinks she should not be forced into the other measure as although it would probably be for her future comfort that the separation should be finally concluded he is doubtful wether self reproach for having carried it into effect might not kill her before her reason had recovered sufficient power to sustain her.

The doubts of her strength and recovery of reason were unfortunate; throughout her life Annabella always valued herself on her powers of determination, reason, and judgment.

Before receiving the intimation of Doyle's concern for her weakness, she had been moved on Sunday the 4th by Augusta's description of Byron's agitation on receiving Sir Ralph's letter, writing to Mrs. Clermont:

I received a letter by the last post from Lord B.—temperate, but of so ambiguous a character that it is impossible to tell whether it is dictated by Love, or Pride, or Cunning. I have enclosed a Copy of it to Lushington.

Mrs. Leigh writes me a most alarming account of the agitation which ensued on the *night* before last and of its evident effect on the *health.* Pray don't let me have his death to answer for—if there should be *danger* things must not be pursued too hastily. You *must* consult Le Mann on this. This idea is painful to me—but on the whole I was less affected by to-day's post than the nature of its contents might have occasioned.

The conviction of Insanity returns more strongly to my mind from some effects of this business—whilst other facts tend to invalidate it. It is a misery not to have a fixed opinion.

I hope you don't deceive me, and represent things in a *harder* manner than is just. How does Sir Ralph feel? . . .

I enclose a note for Mrs. Leigh, which *observe*—is only to be delivered *in case* Lushington deemed it prudent to send her *the longer letter* yesterday. . . .

Mrs. Leigh's letter was very weak to-day—and full of things to *move my tender feelings.* Don't tell her of this—but it was foolish.

Also on Sunday the 4th she wrote to Lushington:

I enclose the copy of a letter which I received this day from Lord Byron. I know not how to reply—and perhaps, if you have sent the one I wrote yesterday, to Mrs. Leigh, its contents may be a sufficient answer. It would relieve me very much to have your opinion by return of post.

The last account from Mrs. Leigh of Lord Byron's health in consequence of *this* agitation was alarming—and if the causes of alarm should encrease, I trust to your humanity to consider his welfare as much as possible without compromising me in the measures I am unhappily obliged to take.

Next morning, having received Mrs. Clermont's letter reporting Doyle's concern for her weakness, she added a postscript to Lushington:

> Lord B. particularly piques himself on a talent for equivocation which renders it impossible to discover the real sense of his words—of this I have had many proofs in his letters, and I think the enclosed is another—for, according to the disposition of the reader, Love, Pride, or Cunning may be supposed the predominant motive. You will be better able to form an opinion than I am.

Thereupon she settled down to a long screed to her father, analysing Byron's letter addressed to him. She acknowledged that "medical opinions were in favour of my going into the Country," but "I left his house under the persuasion that his health was alarmingly affected . . . & Mr. Le Mann . . . recommended my absence very strongly." She objected that "*He* did *not* part from me in apparent harmony. There was no demonstration of tenderness unmixed with bitterness—and he more than once *intimated* in a threatening manner that I should not see him again." Her remark on Byron's reference to his financial embarrassments reveals how little she had sympathised with his anxieties:

> Whenever he had mentioned his intention of sending me away, he implied, & frequently expressed, as the motive, *a desire to be away from me.* I did not then, nor can I now understand that there were any economical views of mutual comfort. But this desire he has not concealed from the first day of our marriage and if pecuniary considerations occasioned his evident intention of forcing me to a separation, why did he marry me? . . . He did not postpone his intention of going abroad from "*a regard to my supposed feelings*"—for to those he had paid no attention, & told me himself after my confinement that he should have gone abroad *at that time,* but his friends told him "*it would make a hue & cry*"—lamenting that he had *by that means* been influenced to stay, and accusing me of having instigated those remonstrances. The payment of part of my Fortune had then relieved him from the particular difficulties to which he had before at times attributed his cruelty towards me.
>
> But in regard to causes, it does not appear to me *necessary* to enquire whether they be, as he states, *medical* & *pecuniary,* since the effects are such as render it impossible for me to live with him without sinking under his tyrannical & cruel treatment.

She concluded:

> My ultimate & deliberate decision is this—I desire to be finally & securely separated. If the Security be as good without a legal process, I earnestly wish to avoid one—even with the sacrifice of some advantages in terms. But if my Counsel is convinced that the grounds are such as not to endanger my failure in a Court of Law, I would have recourse to it, *rather than remain in any degree in Lord B's power.* At the same time I would not have

a process rashly commenced, on account of some *perhaps transient* refractoriness on his part.

I fear he will strive for *delay*—and it must be obviated by every possible means. Amongst others I propose my going to Town—?

I send you an authority on the opposite page, which may be necessary should he suddenly prepare to go abroad—In which case I desire the process to be served immediately.

The words of the enclosed authority were addressed to her father:

I authorize you to pursue such measures as may be necessary to effect a secure & final separation between Lord Byron & myself.

No sooner had she committed herself thus decisively than every letter she received seemed calculated to shake her decision. Mrs. Clermont wrote to Judith on the 5th:

Capt. Byron called this morning he says Lord B: declares himself quite astonished that he believes he has for sometime past not always known what he did but that he never meant to use her ill &c complains of feeling Ill and looks so but is very quiet.

She wrote to Annabella the same day:

Capt. B: says he professes himself quite ignorant of any ill treatment you have received from him talks of his Vile temper & that he is told his head is not right which he believes may be the case says his Stomach is in a Bad way. I have no doubt that although he has been always wishing and endeavouring to drive you to a separation his Pride at least will suffer dreadfully but he is a being whose whole talents seem to be employed in bringing unhappiness upon himself & it is not in the power of any mortal to prevent him from doing so.

Byron himself also wrote that day:

Dearest Bell—No answer from you yet—perhaps it is as well—but do recollect—that all is at stake—the present—the future—& even the colouring of the past. The whole of my errors—or what harsher name you choose to give them—you know—but I loved you—& will not part from you without your *own* most express & *expressed* refusal to return to or receive me. Only say the word—that you are still mine in your heart—and "Kate!—I will buckler thee against a million"—

ever yours dearest
most

The signature was the monogram of twirls used in his correspondence with Augusta. Perhaps the quotation from *The Taming of the Shrew* was ill chosen, as likely to recall his associations with the theatre, but he committed a worse error of tact—on Hobhouse's advice—in addressing his letter to Annabella's maid with the instruction, "Mrs. Fletcher is requested to deliver the enclosed with her *own hands* to Lady Byron."

Nor was Annabella favourably impressed by Hobhouse's intervention at this stage, in view of her suspicions and dislike of him. During January he had seen Byron only twice, but on Monday 5th February he rode up to London and found him "very low indeed." Having been told of the proposal for the separation, he was shown the "Dearest Duck" letter, which he "thought inexplicable."

> George Byron had been down at Kirkby, and found Lady Noel like a fury. Byron confessed he had been often out of temper with her (Lady B.) refused to live with her friends—told her she was in his way—but then he had a liver complaint and from one to four executions in his house at a time. I never saw him so much affected in my life.

He then went home to Whitton Park and wrote an appeal to Annabella:

> I feel secure that five minutes conversation with you would convince you that the extremity meditated is not the treatment that either the former or present feelings of your husband can be said to deserve . . . suffer me to come down & speak to you at Kirkby—this dreadful thing must not be done—the whole must be misunderstanding.

He wrote a much too long letter of expostulation and appeal the next day, but Annabella had already replied tersely and promptly to his first letter:

> You must be ignorant of the long *series of circumstances* which have necessitated this afflicting step. If *my* determination were not formed on such grounds as render it *irrevocable*, its adoption would be perfectly inexcusable. I must therefore decline your visit, and all discussion on this subject, though obliged by the friendly intentions expressed in your offer.

Lushington had already supplied her with the draft of a letter to Byron, so he wrote to her on the 6th:

> On reading the copy you have sent this morning both Mrs. Clermont & myself are apprehensive that Lord B: will not rest satisfied with the communication made to him through Mrs. Leigh . . . I suggest therefore that in reply to Lord Byron's letter you should write a letter of a similar tenor to that copy sent to you on Sunday evening, only premising that you hoped the letter to Mrs. Leigh would have been sufficient . . . Let this letter be forwarded either to me or to Sir Ralph.

She accordingly wrote to Byron on the 7th:

> If I had not written to Mrs. Leigh what I deemed a sufficient answer to the contents of your first letter, I should not have deferred the still more

painful task of addressing yourself. Your second letter, received yesterday seems to require from me this exertion. I am surprised at the manner in which that letter was delivered to me, since my correspondence, as well as my determination, is free. I have indeed placed myself under the protection of my parents, but I act on my own conviction—independently—as they do on theirs.

You know what I have suffered, and would have sacrificed to avoid this extremity—and the strong proofs of duty & attachment I have given by a persevering endurance of the most trying inflictions. After seriously & dispassionately reviewing the misery that I have experienced almost without interval from the day of my marriage, I have finally determined on the measure of a Separation—which my father was authorized to communicate to you—and to carry into effect.

It is unhappily your disposition to consider what you *have* as worthless—what you have *lost* as invaluable. But remember that you declared yourself *most miserable* when I was yours.

Every expression of feeling, sincerely as it might be made, would here be misplaced.

A I: BYRON

Byron had already written on the 7th a second letter to Sir Ralph. Citing the two affectionate letters written immediately after her leaving Piccadilly as evidence that Annabella had then no thought of separation, he declared himself "reduced to the melancholy alternative of either believing her capable of a duplicity very foreign to my opinion of her character—or that she has lately sunk under influence, the admission of which—however respected & respectable heretofore—is not recognized in her vows at the Altar."

I cannot suspect Lady B. of making the grounds stated—the pretext for dissolving our connection—with a view to escape from my shattered fortunes, although the time chosen for this proposition, & the manner in which it was made—without enquiry—without appeal—without even a doubt—or an attempt at conciliation might almost excuse such a supposition . . . I may not debase myself to implore as a suppliant the restoration of a reluctant wife, but I will not compromise my rights as a husband—& a father. I invite Lady Byron's return. . . .

Next day, on receiving her letter, he wrote directly to her:

All I can say seems useless—and all I could say might be no less unavailing—yet I still cling to the wreck of my hopes, before they sink for ever. Were you then *never* happy with me?—did you never at any time or times express yourself so?—have no marks of affection—of the warmest & most reciprocal attachment passed between us?—or did in fact hardly a day go down without some such on one side and generally on both?—do not mistake me.

I have not denied my state of mind, but you know its causes—& were these deviations from calmness never followed by acknowledgement &

repentance?—was not the last which occurred more particularly so?—& had I not—had we not—the days before & on the day when we parted, every reason to believe that we loved each other—that we were to meet again—were not your letters kind?—had I not acknowledged to you all my faults & follies—& assured you that some had not & would not be repeated?—I do not require these questions to be answered to me, but to your own heart. . . .

Will you see me? . . . I will say & do nothing to agitate either—it is torture to correspond thus . . .

You say "it is my disposition to deem what I *have worthless*"—did I deem *you* so?—did I ever so express myself to you—or of you to others?—You are much changed within these twenty days or you would never have thus poisoned your own better feelings—and trampled upon mine.

There was doubtless an error of tact in suggesting that Annabella, always so confident of her independent judgment, was susceptible to influence. But the appeal was moving, and it was supported by a letter on the same day from Augusta, who had been silent for six days since the day after Sir Ralph's letter was received:

My silence will not have been misinterpreted by *you*, but all I could have said within ye last few days would only have added to what I know you are suffering. You have better advisers than *I* can be, tho none more anxious for yr peace & happiness. *I am on the spot* however & feel it a duty to say that I am apprehensive of the most serious consequences from the manner in which *he* has taken this *sad* business to heart. He writes today to ask you to see him—*pause* ere you refuse *for God's sake.* Heaven direct & bless you! my dearest Sis. I feel *dying* to say a great deal to you, but I know not I am right—I think perhaps *wrong.* Then, when I think of you & your dear child & another VERY dear to me, I am distracted with the prospect, which offers nothing but *ruin, destruction & wretchedness* in the most alarming forms. B. has desired me to say many things—I know not what—except that *his Picture*[1] was sent *down* BEFORE he heard from yr Father, & that he hopes you have had copies of the letters to Sr R. from him—that he enclosed ye last to yr Maid because he had reasons to suspect his letters might not be given you.

I must beg that this from me may be considered *private* . . . I wish—— a great deal I can't accomplish. . . .

Two days later—on Sunday the 11th—Augusta wrote a brief note to enclose copies of Byron's letters to Sir Ralph:

I send the enclosed by B's desire, as he thinks in fairness to all parties you ought to read them, & from the last letter he received from yr Father he has reason to suppose you may *not* have seen them.

I am also requested by B—— to say that he understands from Fletcher that he has written to his Wife to desire she will quit your service, & B——

[1] The miniature by Holmes, reproduced here.

is *particularly* anxious you should know it was without his concurrence or even his knowledge of the circumstance.

Annabella had received Hobhouse's second letter on Thursday the 8th; despite its length, she made a copy of it for Lushington, as it "throws some light on the business, impertinent & absurd as it is in itself. Nothing can be more ungentlemanly." She thought Mrs. Clermont "very much mistaken in Supposing that the arrangement will be made easily, quietly--or speedily." Her impression was confirmed by Byron's letter. "I received a letter from Lord B. yesterday written evidently from Self-delusion not Deception," she wrote on Sunday the 11th in asking Mrs. Clermont to seek an interview with Byron, "which if you will execute with temper & firmness, telling *truths*, and hearing his answers, you will probably secure an addition to my future peace."

For I wish to know every thing now that I might hereafter know. Pray do this.

If you see Dr. Lushington tell him he shall have a copy of Lord B's last letter to me tomorrow. I have not time to Copy it to-day. It is distracting to me and I am not able to write to any body else.

If Lord B. should absolutely decline a negociation, as it were to-day, wait to see if he will not change in a day or two, which is most probable. My horrors of the Law are great—though Dr. Lushington would reconcile me if any one could. . . .

I have written to Mrs. Leigh to request that she will explain some intimations which she has given. . . .

Tell Lushington I am decidedly of opinion that my letters to Lord B. of Jan. 15 & 16 ought to be explained as they *must* appear like duplicity—or extreme irresolution . . . Such an explanation must also tend to convince him of the present firmness of my decision.

She then settled to compose her "Remarks on Lord B's letter of Feb. 8":

"Were you then *never* happy with me?" &c.

I have not denied that there were intervals of relief, which *comparatively* were happiness. During these, when I have appeared in good spirits, he has sometimes said with surprise, "Well, there never was a woman so easily pleased"—or—"who could be content with so little." When I partly attributed to pecuniary distresses the strange state of his temper, I was anxious not to aggravate it by any appearance of depression myself. He *might* have suspected, if I had, that his "shattered fortunes" could alienate me. But for a considerable time before I left his house I gave him no reason to think me happy. Before my confinement I had very strongly warned him, though with respect & tenderness, of the unhappy & irreparable consequences which must ensue, both to himself & me, from his conduct. To these representations he replied by the most hardened determination to *do every thing wicked*, though it should break my heart—he did not care for that or any thing in the world, but his own selfish gratification.

This was not the result of passion, but appeared to be a fixed intention. The last of my remonstrances was on Jan. 3 (Wednesday) when he had repeated his wicked declarations (as I have stated) and I sought to awaken some sense of duty in his mind. The effects were so alarming, though I spoke very mildly, as would have prevented me from risking them again even if I had not afterwards been deterred by the encreased persuasion of Insanity. When I say *alarming* I do not allude to any *distinct* apprehension, but to every expectation of Revenge that looks & significations could convey. He desired me in that conversation to *remember* that he had neither *beaten* nor *confined* me, adding "I have not done an act *that would bring me under the power of the Law*—at least on this side the water."

"A day never *did* go down," except when he would not see me, without some affectionate attention on *my* part—and I think the style of his letter proves his conviction of my deep & tender attachment, to which it is an appeal. Is *that* then to be made my crime? and every kind expression alledged as duplicity?

I did not act with a view to Separation, as long as there was a possibility of Union—but I have now reason to think, from comparing times & circumstances, that *he did*—and has drawn answers from me for that end. I could mention many, after which—or after his own replies he has said—"*Mind* this"—and particularly after he has insisted on my owning that I loved him, which I cannot deny, has looked cunning & malicious, saying "You don't know me"—& implying some motive for the enquiry which I could not then understand.

In making my love for him the instrument of my misery, did he prove any corresponding feelings on his part?

"Acknowledgement & repentance"—I have before stated his candour in speaking of my conduct & occasionally of his own. Of the *feeling* of repentance it may be presumptuous to judge—but certainly *no disposition to amendment* was evinced. In regard to his last admission of having ill-treated me, in less than half an hour after it was made, the former irritation which had appeared to me only *suppressed*, was breaking forth again, and he desired me to leave the room.

These "Remarks" she enclosed to Mrs. Clermont on Tuesday the 13th for transmission to Lushington, adding:

I should have been *more* deceived than I was by his letters, if he had not pointed out to me in similar ones addressed to others, the deepest design in words that appeared to have none. On this he piques himself—and also on being able to write such letters as will convey different, or even opposite sentiments to the person who receives them & to a stranger. I fear this ambiguity of Language will avail him in the Law to which he has always had a view. Yet I think he is *afraid* of it. . . .

Every day proves deeper art. Is this human nature? Such confidence in guilt—It reminds me of these lines in *Lara*—

"Can this mean peace? the calmness of the good?
Or Guilt grown old in desperate hardihood—
Alas!—*too like in confidence are each*
For Man to trust to mortal look or SPEECH—
From *deeds*, & *deeds alone*, may he discern
Truths which it wrings the unpractised heart to learn."

It is extraordinary what an effect those *words*, from former associations, still convey. My softness is much against me, for one tender remembrance sweeps away accumulated injuries. I have a good Memory—but it is sad to employ it in recollecting wrongs . . .

The Child is weaned *necessarily* & without difficulty.

Meanwhile Judith continued to fulminate against Lady Melbourne. Sir Ralph was never an assiduous letter-writer, and now prudence combined with inclination in allowing Mrs. Clermont to act as his secretary. Judith complained on the 6th:

I have to lament that You never answer the *purport* of my letters and under this miserable and anxious State we are in, you will not inform me of many things I wish to know. You have never told me whether Lushington has seen *all I wrote* about Lady M. I can hardly conceive it possible that You would sacrifice Your Daughters welfare to *Such a Woman*, and trusted the influence She many Years since exercised so much to Your disadvantage had ceased.

She quoted passages from Lady Melbourne's letters to Byron at the time of his first proposal, Annabella having remembered very accurately the references to herself:

If Lord B. is to be believed, he was at *that time* carrying on a criminal connection with Lady M. as well as with Lady C.L.—at least *so* he has told his Wife. . . .

Let it be considered that She is now *plotting with him* . . . did She know of his *Atrocious* behaviour . . . might it alarm her? and induce her to wish accommodation privately? At all events Lushington *ought to know* the Character he has to deal with—but I can get no information from You . . . and am rather inclined to believe You have *shrunk* from exposing *this Wretch*. . . .

I have had a return of Erisupilus, but . . . I have dined at Table every day tho' in my Night-Cap—my head being too large and too Sore to admit of my Wig. . . .

God bless You! my Dear. I shall only add—that from the time we married, the only unhappiness You have occasioned me, has been from seeing *the Sway* Lady M. has at times had over You—and that before *I was able to oppose it*, or had courage to do so. She has pillaged You of *tens of thousands*—recollect this—and *now despise her*.

Later the same day, after Annabella had received Byron's second letter by Mrs. Fletcher's hand, Judith wrote by express to Sir Ralph:

I see that Ld B. is playing a deep Game, that he is supported in his schemes by the advice of Lady M. and that Mrs. Leigh will *decidedly* do all She can for him—and from the *basest motives—profit*. I think as ill of *her* as possible. . . .

Ld B. has been *for sometime* I am convinced *acting* the part of derrangement to shield his iniquity—he is no more *Mad* than I am—but if that pretence is held out, does it follow that his Wife is to be committed to the custody of a Madman, and dangerous and brutal in his madness!

Or is that Madman to have the care of the Child?

I am convinced that it is plotted for Mrs. Leigh to take it with an allowance which will be of assistance to her *poverty*. . . .

The Way in which this letter was sent proves that he either believes, or chuses to *imply* he believes, that You and I have urged her to Separation . . .

If his *revenge* was so deep and bitter for *the first refusal*, what would it *now become*, for what has passed?—was She daring enough to risk it? but thank God! She is not.

She has just shewn me a Copy of her Answer . . .

Mrs. Clermont replied by return:

Will you never be satisfied that Dr. Lushington and Colonel D have both been made acquainted with all that you have said about Lady Mel & everything else. I have just returned from Dr. Lushington. I read him your letter of this Day he says as to Lady M: I am well acquainted with her character and from circumstances that have come under my knowledge in other cases I have no doubt that she has plotted this Business, but I think it would be highly injudicious at present at least to give her notice of our knowledge that she has acted in so wicked a manner. . . . As to Mrs. Leigh he said it is a pity she should write letters that distress Lady Byrons feelings but Lady Noel goes *too fast* in attributing to her any wrong intentions. . . .

I have always thought Mrs. Leigh weak about her Brother particularly but I do believe her intentions good. I have seen her once & her great fear then seemed to be that he would from malice take away the Child if the proposal of separation came from Annabella that if it came from himself he would give it up intirely to her.

Judith had reason for her suspicions of Lady Melbourne, who had written to Byron on the 5th:

There is a report about you, so much believed in Town, that I think you should be informed of it. They say you and Annabella are parted . . . I am still confined, but ye first time I go out I will call upon Mrs. L. I should like to see You then, & tell you several things which I do not like to write, & I can not see you at Home.

Hobhouse noted on the 9th:

Douglas Kinnaird told me this morning that the Melbournes are in arms against Lady Byron. George Lambe called her a d——d fool, but added that Caroline Lambe accused Byron of ———.[1] Poor fellow, the plot thickens against him. He is depressed most dreadfully, yet still laughs as usual, and says he shall "go to Court to be presented on his separation."

On Saturday 10th February Hanson called at Mivart's Hotel and met Lushington with Sir Ralph, as Mrs. Clermont reported next day to Judith:

. . . he began by saying he did not come from Lord Byron but of himself signifying his sorrow at the state of things & hoped that there might yet be some means of reconciliation . . . Sir Ralph replied Lady Byron has determined upon a separation for which she has the most ample reasons. . . . Hanson then said he knew from Lord Byron himself that his conduct had been blameable in many respects but could not as yet make up his mind to advise him to own himself guilty which he would do by acceding to the separation unless there were stronger reasons than he was acquainted with . . . Lushington said I would advise that you Mr. Hanson should question Lord B: himself. Hanson said he had but that Lord Bs memory was very treacherous. Dr. L [:] I think you will get from him sufficient to satisfy your mind. Hanson still pressed for specific facts which the other declined giving . . . Dr. L: said suppose threats had been used what should you think of that [?] Hanson repeated the word threats then talked of the letter of the 16th. Dr. Lushington said an explanation can be given of that. He then again expressed his hopes that a reconciliation was not impossible. Sir Ralph said it *was* that the separation must be effected & it was his wish that it should be done in as amicable a way as the nature of the circumstances would admit . . . [Hanson] then talked of Lord B: being a Man whose spirits were more easily depressed than others & that he was at this time under such agitation as made him hardly fit to decide that he had become so violent the evening before he was obliged to leave him but that he would talk with him again upon the subject & that Sir Ralph should hear from him.

Of this conference Mrs. Clermont reported to Annabella:

I cannot help thinking Hanson will persuade Lord B: to agree to the arrangement.

His object seemed to be in great part to plead that your Father would allow a little time.

This impression was confirmed by Hobhouse, who noted on the 12th, "Hanson has got Sir R. Noel to suspend proceedings."

Of Annabella's suggestion that she should seek an interview with Byron, Mrs. Clermont wrote:

I shall see Dr. Lushington tomorrow & have his opinion as to the interview you propose if it should be practicable but I do not think *he* would talk with *me*.

[1] This is the earliest mention of the charge of ———, usually represented by a prolonged and thickened dash, which has been assumed to mean homosexual practices.

Already Annabella had had second thoughts on this idea in a letter that crossed Mrs. Clermont's:

> Of course you will consult Lushington as to the expediency of your interview with Lord B. in which perhaps it would be very difficult with his art for you not to commit us.
>
> Besides *you* might have a return of *Love*. You see I am not at this moment under that visitation—but this last letter has had a dreadful effect on me . . . I shall be persecuted with correspondence. How can I stop it? . . . You have not spoken of Le Mann lately. Is not Lord B. very ill?

To this inquiry Mrs. Clermont replied on Tuesday the 13th:

> I should hear if *he* was particularly Ill by Milward who goes there almost every day. I asked him this morning about Lord B's health he said he was there last night that Fletcher said his master was low but that he did not hear a word of his being Ill that Hobhouse is there a great deal & Lord B stays at home. There is little danger of my being in love again I think his present conduct confirms all the bad principle that I before sometimes doubted of—he knows that he made you unhappy *either* intentionally or because he could not help it . . .
>
> That he wished for a separation I am convinced but like every thing else would have it in his own way namely that he should live as he liked & where he liked upon the money he has & is to receive upon your account that you should live with your parents & at their expence crying & sighing for his return . . .
>
> Sir Ralph last night received a letter from Lady Melbourne saying she had but just heard he was in London & begging to see him as it was very awkward for her to hear you continually talked of without knowing what she might or might not say—the letter is expressive of much affection for you and her sorrow for your parents who must have felt your sufferings severely. I do not think Lord B: & her have met since he received your Father's first letter. Dr. Lushington told me that some very scandalous Annecdotes of Lord B: had been told him a few days ago & that he knew they had been imported from Brocket. Sir Ralph is going to Lady Melbourne & I to Dr. Lushington . . . your letter is sent to piccadilly. Dr. Lushington says he wishes to get you out of the corespondence if possible but that he can not see any means of doing so at present, but that no interview must be allowed to take place.

The letter sent to Piccadilly was a brief note from Annabella to Byron, written on the 11th: "I have determined, *if possible*, not to indulge the language of feeling in addressing you . . . By means of our authorized friends, those points which require conversational discussion can be settled—and whatever may now appear to you inconsistent, satisfactorily explained." On the day this was written she heard from Lushington, who dealt with Hobhouse's long letter of expostulation:

No plea of friendship for Lord B: can I think justify the stile which Mr. H: has thought proper to assume in addressing you; I apprehend the scope of his arguments (if false conclusions from false premises are so to be called) is to excite intimidation; for no mind, however distorted, could suppose that conciliatory feelings could be called forth by such a composition . . .

Mr. Hobhouse is perfectly correct in his surmise that the world, should these circumstances become public, would throw all the blame upon Lord B:—That would certainly be the case & no exertions of Mr. H's could prevent it. He is much mistaken if he thinks any statement of his would obtain credence in opposition to the real facts; & you may rest perfectly assured that no blame whatever will or can attach upon Sir Ralph or Lady Noel, much less upon yourself.

But he referred to the matter much on Annabella's mind:

With respect to the letters you addressed to Lord B: after your departure from London, which contained kind & affectionate Sentiments, it would certainly have been desireable that no such letters should have been written, because the production of such letters unexplained would naturally lead to an inference that the mind, which dictated kind expressions, could not be suffering from a succession of unmerited injuries. But I do not conceive that circumstance could deprive You of your right to legal redress. It could only produce an effect until the explanation was given & as you have the power of proving the motives which actuated the writing in such terms that they did not arise from a light consideration, or oblivion of past illtreatment, but from a humane & laudable anxiety not to aggravate the personal maladies of Lord B:, I trust, that if he should venture to ground his defence on such a basis, the explanation would not only overthrow it, but place your character as undoubtedly it deserves, in a still more favorable light.

He had already delivered himself, in a letter received by Annabella the day before, of his opinion on Byron's second letter to Sir Ralph:

The motive which induced you to write the letters alluded to in the first paragraph acquits you of the duplicity that is insinuated.

You will excuse my saying that I can feel nothing but indignation at what follows. The remotest hint that his pecuniary embarrassments could form the slightest motive for your recent conduct is so repugnant to all my notions of truth justice & liberal feeling, that I forbear further comment . . . If anything were wanting to confirm you in the propriety of the step You have taken the recollection of this insinuation must remove even the shadow of a doubt. It is really ludicrous to talk of receiving a person to his heart, whom he could for one instant suspect of abandoning him because of his embarrassments.

As a lawyer, Lushington was concerned, not with truth, but with making his case; he did not allow himself to consider that Byron's suffering under his embarrassments might have been the primary inspiration of his moods and conduct. A loyal wife might have resented such aspersions on her husband by a stranger, but Annabella's conception of loyalty had allowed her to confide in a stranger even during her honeymoon. She now told Lushington that she "received great satisfaction from your kind letters of yesterday & to-day—and the privilege you allow me of considering you as a friend contributes essentially to my relief," before embarking on a further analysis of Byron's letter of the 8th:

> It is the most forcible appeal to every tender recollection—and was perhaps written in that State of Self-delusion to which he has an extraordinary power of working up his imagination. In *this* letter I do not observe any *art*—but strong passion, principally, I conceive, *wounded Pride* . . .[1]
>
> I am too well acquainted with the sudden & dreadful transitions of his mind from Tenderness to Revenge . . .
>
> There is certainly nothing in his words, even if they could counterbalance his actions, to be *depended upon*. He is a most unhappy being, & suffers, I believe still more than he inflicts . . .

Her little understanding of Byron and her infinite capacity for inference were alike illustrated in her postscript: "If Lord B's letter enclosed is *art*—how deep!"

Though Augusta expected that "My silence will not have been misinterpreted by you," Annabella began to have doubts of her fidelity when her daily reports from Piccadilly ceased with the announcement of the separation proceedings. In her resentment at Byron's sending his letter of the 5th through Mrs. Fletcher, she had written to Lushington, "I consider Mrs. Leigh to have forsaken me," though next day she wrote again, "I wish to retract a doubt which I expressed yesterday too hastily of Mrs. Leigh—though it never occurred to me to suspect her *sincerity*." She recognised that Augusta was placed in an appalling position as her own chief confidante and protectress, while bound to Byron by her devotion: "I cannot say how much I feel for you," she told Augusta on 12th February; "*Myself* is a lesser grief."

Yet even as she thus recognised the anguish of Augusta's feelings, she was ruthlessly sacrificing them to her own interest, writing to Lushington on the 11th that, with Byron's letter of the 8th:

> I recd. one from Mrs. Leigh—not endeavouring to induce my return, but stating his distracted state, and implying that she had some material communications to make to me—but knew not if it was *right*. I have written to desire that she will (as far as I am concerned in the scruple) make them.

[1] This letter proceeds to the comments on Hobhouse, already quoted on pp. 340–41.

To Augusta she wrote on the same day, "I must desire that you will write to me in the MOST EXPLICIT MANNER—and represent every thing that you allude to as suppressed."

Augusta received this demand on 12th February, when Hobhouse called at Piccadilly:

> there saw Mrs. Leigh & George Byron—and from them learnt what I fear is the real truth that Byron has been guilty of very great tyranny—menaces—furies—neglects, and even real injuries—such as telling his wife he was *living with another woman*—& actually in *fact* turning her out of the house.
>
> George Byron suspected she would leave him & told him so, a month before she went—but she had no intention of doing it when she went from London.
>
> Locking doors, showing pistols, pouring reproaches at her in bed—everything he seems, to believe them, to have been guilty of! and they acquit him—how? by saying that he is mad—certainly—and that Mr. Le Mann says it is the consequence of a torpid liver—which has already affected his eyes—made one smaller than the other & made him squint . . .
>
> Whilst I heard these things Mrs. Leigh went out & brought word that her brother was crying bitterly in his bedroom—poor, poor fellow.

Later the same day Hobhouse returned to Byron's:

> met Lady Melbourne—who abused Lady Noel violently—Byron was tranquil and jesting—but when I told him what I had heard *in the streets* that day he was astounded indeed—!—and after Lady Melbourne went questioned me.
>
> He had heard he was to be accused of cruelty drunkeness & *infidelity*.
>
> I got him to own much of what I had been told in the morning—he was dreadfully agitated—said he was ruined, & would blow out his brains—he is indignant but yet terrified—sometimes says "and yet she loved me once" and at other times that he is glad to be quit of such a woman. He said if I would go abroad he would separate at once.

After her talk with Hobhouse that morning, Augusta was "*so* harrassed . . . that I really fear my nerves are scarcely equal to allowing me to write *clearly*," but she began to answer Annabella's request for an explanation of "some intimations":

> You desire me to state *explicitly* every thing I allude to as suppressed. B—— is in the deepest grief & has been so ever since he received Sr Ralph's first letter. He seems DETERMINED *never willingly* to resign you. What is the alternative my dear A? That as YOUR Friends ARE *determined* upon a separation this sad business must come before the Public. *Supposing* even that nothing is LEGALLY PROVED against him which can procure you this separation, what will the *world think!* won't his character be blasted for ever! He is convinced of this, & *I* am convinced not only will his

reputation be sacrificed to this exposure but *his* LIFE. My dear A, don't suppose I judge from any declarations to put an end to his existence in the usual strain of such—no, those who make them are in general ye last to execute them. But he has at different times but constantly expressed in very mysterious terms a *deep* & *dreadful* tho *vague* intention—to more than me, to those who know him better, who have stronger minds, better judgements—NOT to SURVIVE such disgrace. Remember most of HIS predeterminations have become *actions*. What would be your feelings SHOULD *this* be the consequence—or even his eternal disgrace in *this* world—he is in *every* way in *any* way a ruined man.

I am called away . . . pray don't decide hastily in driving him to desperation . . .

She resumed next day, Tuesday the 13th:

I had I believe mentioned to you what wd be the consequences of this sad business being brought before a public court . . . I must now say I can't at least be mistaken in what *are* the consequences *already*. The whole Town is full of reports of the *worst* kind. B. is quite aware of it, but *still* determined never to give you up, without he is compelled.

. . . B is this morning in such a dreadful agitated state that I don't know *what* to do. I attribute it in a great measure to some *pecuniary* concerns. He is disappointed you do not write, *tho* he was so nervous with ye expectation of a letter that he desired me last night *to open it* if one came, as he *could not* . . . He says however that he is still *most* anxious for an *interview*, which would not bind you to anything . . . There is one thing my dearest A, you should be prepared for (if worse don't occur) which is about the Child. He seems determined to have it, & I understand *the Law* wd allow it to him when a year old. I see in short such a *host of evils in perspective* & not ye least of all what your feelings would be if *any one* was the consequence of yr separating from him. You will think perhaps *I* of all people ought not to dissuade you from it.

I've just been down. He is more quiet . . . I must just say that yesterday George B: & I *together* found it necessary to be explicit with Hobhouse & *he* has made a communication to *George* which must keep him in order respecting ours. George says he cannot tell *me* or any one but it is something which wd prevent his going abroad. Be QUITE silent on this dear A to EVERY living thing. Our joint opinions of H—— are much improved since this conversation, & his advice to B was immediately reversed . . .

B. has just got yr letter—Alas!

He desires me to say they refuse him all explanation whatever—that is yr Father &c.

On the 13th Annabella was writing again to Byron. Lushington's comment on the two affectionate letters having increased her anxiety about them, she explained that she had written the two letters because "I left your house under the persuasion of your having a complaint of so dangerous a nature, that any agitation might bring on a fatal crisis."

For the same reason "I did not remonstrate at the time of leaving your house," though "I had before warned you, earnestly and affectionately, of the unhappy and irreparable consequences which must ensue from your conduct, both to yourself and me." She concluded:

> I cannot attribute your "state of mind" to any cause so much as to that *total* dereliction of principle, which, *since* our marriage, you have professed and gloried in. Your acknowledgements have not been accompanied by any intentions of Amendment.
>
> I have *consistently* fulfilled my duty as your wife. It was too dear to be abandoned till it became hopeless. Now my resolution cannot be changed.

Next morning she enclosed this letter to Lushington for him to forward "unless you think it objectionable," adding:

> I am more & more convinced of the necessity of my determination. I hear that a delay is proposed—if it *cannot* do harm to the cause, let it be granted—but no reliance must be placed even on the *word of honour* . . .
>
> I could add many facts to my written statement in which I do not find any exaggeration on the calmest reperusal—but I hope it will not be *necessary* to record them . . .

Thereupon she occupied herself by dictating to her mother a further statement of facts, beginning:

> A day or two before I left London, he asked me to return to him his own letters which he had addressed to me before marriage; I declined and asked him his reason—he said after a moments pause—"because I shall perhaps say now, what will contradict things I said then."
>
> The night before I left London, in Mrs. Leighs presence, he said, very significantly—"*When Shall we three meet again?*"—to which I replied "*in Heaven I hope*". I parted from him that night in a violent agony of Tears and went into the Room where Mrs. Leigh and Mrs. Clermont were—in that State having quite lost the self-command I could in general assume.

Enclosing this statement to Lushington on the 15th, she wrote:

> I wait to know if you have sent my letter of explanation to Lord B. If not, I should deem it advisable, in order to destroy the hopes which in my opinion induce him to propose delay, that I should address him in very decided terms as to the impossibility of an Interview, he having again proposed it by Mrs. Leigh. I have reason to think that advantage is taken of the delay by his advocates, to give the first impression in his favour by accusing me of having acted from pique & precipitancy. He has been assuming the character of an injured & affectionate husband with great success to some. These acts estrange me more than the most unkind treatment, and make me less reluctant to expose facts. I enclose a paper of memorandums tending to prove the existence of a *long design* . . .
>
> I understand that your kind solicitude to save me from the legal process

has led you to think of Lord Holland as a Mediator. I am inclined to fear that he would be imposed upon by Lord B's superiority of intellect, and powers of persuasion. But Mr. Brougham is personally acquainted with Lord B. and if fully possessed of the circumstances (which could not I presume be objectionable) would perhaps endeavour to effect the desired object by a conference . . . Lord B's great art is his candour—or rather pretensions to candour. He confesses so much, with such an ingenuous air, that it is impossible to suspect any reserve. Of this I have known many dupes, and have been one myself . . .

Meanwhile Byron replied on the 15th:

I know not what to say—every step taken appears to bear you further from me . . .

How far your conduct is reconcileable to your duties & affections as a wife and a mother, must be a question for your own reflection—the trial has not been very long—a year, I grant you, of distress, distemper, and misfortune—but these fell chiefly on me, & bitter as the recollection is to me of what I have felt, it is much more so to have made you a partaker of my desolation.

On the charges to be preferred against me, I have *twice* been refused any information by your father & his advisers:—it is now a fortnight—which has been passed in suspense, in humiliation, in obliquy—exposed to the most black & blighting calumnies of every kind:—without even the power of contradicting conjecture & vulgar assertion as to the accusations, because I am denied the knowledge of all or any particulars, from the only quarter that can afford them. In the meantime I hope your ears are gratified by the general rumours.

I have invited your return—it has been refused—I have entreated to see you—it is refused—I have requested to know with what I am charged—it is refused. Is this mercy—or justice?

We shall see.

And now, Bell—dearest Bell—whatever may be the event of this calamitous difference—whether you are restored to, or torn from me, I can only say in the truth of affliction, & without hope, motive, or end in again saying what I have lately but vainly repeated—that I love you, & shall do to the dregs of my memory & existence. If I can feel thus for you now—under every possible aggravation & exasperating circumstance that can corrode the heart, & inflame the brain—perhaps you may one day know, or think at least, that I was not all you have persuaded yourself to believe me—but that's nothing—nothing can touch me further.

I have hitherto avoided naming my child, but as this was a feeling you never doubted in me, I must ask of it's welfare. I have heard of it's beauty, & it's playfulness, and I request, not from you, but through any other channel—Augusta's, if you please—some occasional news of it's well being.

Augusta explained her position to Francis Hodgson on the 15th:

These legal measures sound most horrible—& I fear there is nothing but *open war* to be expected . . .

It is a *sad, sad* business dear Mr. H. B. deceives himself & deceives others, but his conscience will occasionally speak. Heaven grant Your prayers that it may end better than we expect, but I dare not hope it. I am glad you have written to Ly B.—so have *I*—all that I see hanging over us—in every shape—some of it *certain*—ye rest but too much to be dreaded —but *I* CAN *not* urge her to return, & expose herself to a repetition of all I have witnessed—& heard of. She must decide for herself.

She had invited Hodgson to come to town to see Byron on the 10th; he had interviewed both Byron and Hanson, and ventured on the 13th to address Annabella with more tact and wisdom than Hobhouse had shown. Avoiding any impertinent inquiry into the causes of difference, he appealed to her "goodness" and "indulgence" to save Byron from the possibility of "absolute and utter destruction" so that they might "both yet be, what God intended you for, the support, the watchful correction and improvement of each other."

On the same day as she replied to Hodgson, the 15th, Annabella wrote to her father:

I enclose you a letter which I received to-day from a very excellent man, and the only one of Lord B's friends who is of that description—Mr. Hodgson, the Translator of Juvenal—whom I have never seen. His letter is a perfect contrast to Hobhouse's—and nothing could be better adapted to my feelings. As it however makes no impression on my *opinion*, I regard it as an additional proof of the sound reasons on which it has been formed. In proportion as my mind gains strength, I am more convinced of the escape I have had, and the impossibility of ever regretting the step I have taken—whilst the wicked & artful principles that are daily more & more developed, must estrange affection more even than the most unkind treatment. Of course I feel less dread of the Law as my consideration for *him* diminishes. *All* I have suffered can never be known . . .

I have answered Mr. H. very kindly. He deserves it. Show his letter to Col: Doyle . . . and keep it for me . . .

Hodgson is an Enthusiast—and *has* just the same ideas of Lord B. as I *had*.

Lord B. is *threatening* all his friends with Suicide! A professed intention of this sort is rather amusing.

This affectation of truculence screened her mounting anxiety about custody of the child—irritated by her mother's conviction that Byron would insist on placing the child with his sister. Also on 15th February she was writing to Lushington:

I have thought of Terms—as you desired—and should feel so very happy to be screened from molestation with the Child, that I can scarcely think of any other advantages.

She wrote again on the 17th:

I feel confident that if I were in London I could put in action some resources which would prevent the ultimate necessity of legal proceedings —and besides, there are things which I, and I only, could explain to you in conversation, that may be of great importance to the thorough understanding of the case. I would therefore propose, unless you perceive any material objection, that I should go to London for a day or two. The Child is weaned . . . I should take my Mother's Servants, as my own would be objectionable on account of the communication with Piccadilly . . .

You might rely on my firmness in resisting all overtures for an Interview.

Has it ever been intimated to Mr. Hanson that it would be the wish of my friends rather to relieve than encrease Lord B's pecuniary embarrassments by an amicable Arrangement? For I think the release of Settlements, except £20,000 for the child, may be considered in that light and I understand . . . that Lord B. thinks very anxiously of this part of the business.

Lushington replied by return "from Mivart's Hotel where Sir Ralph, Mrs. Clermont, Col: Doyle & myself have considered your proposal to come to London before the negotiation with Lord B: has taken a decided turn."

There is one objection . . . the risque of Lord B: insisting upon a personal interview . . . We all think that no interview should take place upon any pretence . . . Your Ladyship must be aware that if in London you will necessarily be more exposed to the solicitations & appeals of Lord B: & his friends.

But Annabella had her way as usual. She was disturbed by hearing from Mrs. Clermont that "there are no delays equal to those of the *law* Lushington says he may carry it through three courts in succession if he pleases," and Sir Samuel Romilly had been retained "in the possibility of its coming into Chancery." Still more was she disturbed, as she informed Mrs. Clermont on the 15th, by Augusta's letters of the 12th and 13th:

She urges my return!—and for the weakest reasons imaginable—1. That he will kill himself if I do not—2. that he will be irrecoverably disgraced here—3. that he is determined to try the cause—4. that he intends to take away the child.

Vainly Mrs. Clermont tried to dissuade her from going to London: it was even arranged that Lushington should visit Kirkby the following week-end.

Curiously, her decision to go to London seems to have been confirmed by a further letter from Augusta, written on Saturday the 17th:

I don't presume to *urge* or to *advise*, yet I have sometimes (perhaps too often) thought it my duty to *represent*, being on the spot, seeing, hearing &

knowing what others cannot. If I have erred it is in judgement not intention. There are reports abroad of a nature *too horrible to repeat.* I had guessed them from G.B's *mysterious* manner & *excessive* annoyance for some days past. *He* GB yesterday sent for Hobhouse, who I find last night informed B. of them, & HE B has desired me to inform you of them. Of course this has added considerably to his agitations. Every other sinks into nothing before this MOST horrid one. God alone knows what is to be the end of it all. Perhaps he may write to you himself. There is a circumstance which alarms me much. I have before told you of *his hints* of self destruction. The night before last, I went as usual to his room to light his Candles & seeing a Draught on the chimney piece which looked *fermenting*, I said "What is this." "My Draught, to be sure—what did you think it was? Laudanum?" I replied jokingly that I was not even *thinking* of Laudanum & the truth—that I thought the Draught spoilt, which caused my inquiry. He immediately looked very dark & black (in the old way) & said "I have plenty of Laudanum—& shall use it." Upon my laughing & trying to turn off the subject he only repeated in the most awful manner *his most solemn determination* on the subject. I thought it but right to ask Fletcher if he could get at it, & put water to it &c., & consulted Le Mann, who said he wd change it for Extract of Hops if I could get at it. Fletcher says he has looked in the place where it used to be kept, & every where else, & that B. must have locked it up! THIS would be the means my dear A in preference to any other. This MOST dreadful report!—who knows what it may urge him to do. He said to me last night in an agony "Even to have such a thing *said* is utter destruction & ruin to a man & from which he never can recover."

In answer to yr letter I am alas! but too well convinced you are acting from *Duty*—from *Principle.* Heaven grant the consequences may be less fatal than I dread. Don't talk of reproaches from *me* my own dear A—I never could think you *wrong*, but I would save you if possible the misery I'm sure you wd feel if any one of my anticipations are realized.

I have now to mention something else which I think you *ought* & am *sure* you *cannot* know. I had yesterday information given me that a letter was read aloud by a Lady in a large party, from a friend of hers now domesticated at Kirkby[1] containing such charges of cruelty against B as to convince the person who reported this they "originated more in passion than truth." The letter ended thus—"You may make what I have now told you as public as you please but don't mention my name."

I well know my dear A—— how little you can wish or be aware of this & *the like.* Today I hear *Mrs. Harvey*[2] has been guilty of the same thing. Surely even *the truth* is better concealed if possible. . . .

Augusta added a postscript:

I wish you not to mention YE REPORT if it is not already known. I think you will not misunderstand to what I allude.

[1] Selina Doyle had been staying at Kirkby since 28th January.
[2] William Beckford's sister, Elizabeth Hervey, a friend of Judith's.

Though this letter was headed "MOST private," Annabella passed it on to Lushington along with every other letter Augusta had written to her since her departure from Piccadilly on 15th January. Can it be doubted that Annabella intended to use these letters as part of the "resources which would prevent the ultimate necessity of legal proceedings"? Vainly Augusta had sought to stimulate Annabella's jealousy of the Drury Lane actresses and of Lady Frances Webster, but she had succeeded in exciting jealousy of herself Her letters are full of her devotion to Byron: she talks to his doctor and administers his medicines, orders his food, runs his errands, writes his letters, studies his changes of mood, chooses her moments for venturing remonstration and reproach. Annabella may not have loved Byron, but she was his wife, and must have recognised that Augusta was supplying a wife's ministrations with tenderness and tact beyond her own capabilities. When she found a pistol and laudanum on his mantelpiece, Augusta "turned it off" with a laugh instead of encouraging Byron to posture like the villain of a Gothic romance; she had no thought of fear for herself, but only anxiety lest he intended injury to himself. With her vanity wounded, Annabella's jealousy awakened, and she was prepared to blackmail Byron into the separation by a threat of exposing Augusta's devotion as more than sisterly. Mrs. Clermont wrote to Judith on 21st February:

> I am sorry she [Annabella] mentions circumstances that cannot be made publick as it only increases your horrors & in my opinion confirms *him* more a Madman . . .

Annabella had still three more letters to add to her collection for Lushington. Having heard that she was "unwell," Augusta wrote a brief note on 19th February:

> This will destroy you my own dearest A . . . I know not whether I ought to write, yet—God knows I do wish from my heart for your happiness as well as that of another. My Spouse is gone home & agrees to my staying a little longer which I'm anxious to do . . .
>
> I've seen Ly Melbourne & found the best was to be explicit for otherwise she might do harm & I really think it her wish to do good . . .

Presumably Annabella received this note on the 20th, when she wrote to her father:

> I conceive it time to enquire positively & finally if Lord Byron means to accede to an amicable arrangement, as he has declared his intention of doing when fully convinced of my concurrence to the proposal of a Separation. Of this he cannot any longer have doubts.

I must therefore insist on decided measures for terminating this suspense, which is in my opinion, detrimental to all parties.

To Lushington she wrote by the same post:

Having given my authority for the requisition of a final answer from Lord Byron, I conceive this to be the critical period in which my presence might be of great use—and I therefore determine to begin my Journey tomorrow. I hope to be in Town the following day—and perhaps you might be so obliging as to afford me an hour's Conversation that Evening . . .

She proposed to take her mother's maid, Susan Morle, instead of Mrs. Fletcher—"whose communication with Piccadilly would be very disagreable," she told Mrs. Clermont:

I don't trust much in her sincerity . . . Fletcher writes to her "My dear—you know it is our *duty* to bring *man & wife* together!"—I suppose he means *themselves*.

Selina Doyle also travelled with her on 21st February, Sophy Tamworth remaining with Judith at Kirkby.

On Tuesday the 20th—the day before Annabella left for London—Augusta wrote her final appeal:

I am always wishing to speak or write to you . . . but then comes the reflexion that perhaps I *ought* NOT—that it may be deemed dishonorable in me as B's Sister to endeavor to sway you. Yet surely none can have felt more truly all *your* sufferings & unhappiness than I have. All this is my reflexion one moment. Ye next suggests another—that I never could forgive myself, if I had omitted any thing in my power to contribute to the *future* happiness of both.

I do think in my heart dearest A, that *your return* might be the *saving* & *reclaiming* of him. You could but give it a trial, & if he persisted in his ill-conduct you would be fully justified in *then* abandoning him. Your doing it now, I do think will be his *ruin*. Every good feeling will turn to hardness—he will cease to think well of *you*, the only Being who possessed his *real* & *entire* esteem & good opinion. It really appears to be his duty to the Child *not* to agree to a seperation. Your family have determined *he shall*—what then must happen? That this dreadful business is to be brought into a public Court. Do you think that even *then* you can obtain what they wish. There seems to me great doubt of it, & you will have this dreadful exposure for nothing.

Of all this my dear A you are a better judge than I am. You may know more than I do, of the charges you have to bring against him. Most likely you are aware you will have to depose against him *yrself*, & that without witnesses yr depositions will go for nothing—ye same thing in regard to those who have only heard circumstances from you.

> *You* will I know forgive all I am saying & allow for the distraction of my mind. I can't help repeating it is my opinion yr return *might* be his *salvation*—yr *abandoning* WILL inevitably be his ruin. Surely it is my duty to tell you so. I shall be blamed, but not by *you* who know my *motives*.
>
> I must add to all this *one question*—answer it or not, as you please. But *what*, my dear A, *has shaken yr opinions as to the* PRINCIPAL *cause of B's conduct?* We know—you admit yrself you left him under the impression that he was *insane* more or less. You say subsequent accts have convinced you he is not—or words to that effect. The report . . .

Here a corner of the page containing six lines is torn off. In one of her copies of the letter—not in the book into which she copied the whole series of Augusta's letters from 15th January, but in a second copy on foolscap—Annabella noted, "I received the letter with the end of that page torn off." There can be no reason to doubt this assertion; it was to Annabella's interest to preserve rather than to destroy evidence. Probably Augusta tore off what she had written—whether about the report "*too horrible to repeat*" or another—because she realised that she was committing herself to a possibly dangerous indiscretion.

On 22nd February—unaware that Annabella was then arriving in London—Augusta wrote the last of her letters lodged with Lushington—a brief note acknowledging Annabella's reassurance about her health and adding, "every hour confirms me in the opinions I have expressed to you in my last letter."

13

THE SEPARATION: ANNABELLA IN LONDON

22nd February—25th April, 1816

Annabella informed her mother of her safe arrival at Mivart's Hotel on 22nd February:

Hanson has written to say that Ld B. refuses to accede. I therefore consider everything with reference to legal proceedings.

Dr. L. thinks it of the greatest importance that you should keep the Child, and I must beg that no caution whatever may be omitted.

Ld B. now says the reports are so bad that nothing worse can be produced against him in Court—& therefore he does not care what he is accused of . . .

Next day she reported further to her mother:

I had a long conversation with Dr. Lushington last night, and was very much satisfied with himself. He has no objection whatever to my being in London—on finding how resolved I am—nor any expectations of assault, against which however there is every precaution.

Dr. L. wishes to try one more expedient (Ld Holland's mediation) before the Process is commenced. Of the success of which I have great doubts . . . At least I shall be justified to the world.

Lord B's letter[1] returned to me with others from Kirkby only contains an enquiry respecting the Child. It is thought highly advisable that he should receive constant intelligence of it. You will therefore write to Mrs. Leigh for *his* information expressly.

I have been *perfectly* confidential with Dr. Lushington and so far from thinking that the *suspicions* could do any good to me, he deprecates beyond any thing the slightest intimation of them, as having the appearance of Malice—and altogether most injurious to *me* in a social view.

The Misfortune of my Case is that so little has passed before Witnesses—and the wife's deposition *unsupported* is of no avail. The cause cannot come on till after Easter on account of the Courts breaking up . . .

Dr. Lushington *insists* upon your writing in a kind manner to Mrs. Leigh, as being most essential to my Justification *whatever she may turn out*

[1] Byron on the 21st had sent her a business paper addressed to him instead of to her, with a note explaining how it came into his hands and ending, "I hope my little Ada is well—& that you are better ever yrs. most affectly B."

—and that she should be spoken of by us in a friendly manner unless she were absolutely to forfeit her character for veracity in public. At the same time every precaution will be used against her weakness . . .

On the 24th Sir Ralph reported that Lushington had "seen Lord Holland who has undertaken to see Lord B. and endeavour to persuade him to an amicable arrangement for a separation." On the 27th Annabella was lugubrious about the means of offering any financial inducement to Byron:

The Marriage Settlement cannot be destroyed on account of the £60,000 settled on a Son, whom the Law still contemplates as possible—and my Jointure being included in this, by resigning it I should not release the Estate. So nothing can be offered from this Source . . .

The only offer which it appears possible to make at present as an inducement to him for any future provision towards my maintenance, or for allowing me control over the child (which last *I* have not however any hope of obtaining) is the payment of the rest of my Fortune, which the Trustees could otherwise withhold, and he would be entitled only to the Interest. Present gratification being so great an object, this might have weight.

In short, it is as well to see things as they are—the worst possible—except that I have escaped from the greatest Villain that ever existed. These money dealings are infamous. If *I* can be personally secure I shall think it my Salvation in this world & the next. I have no fits now—but am growing very uncharitable . . .

I had a ridiculous letter from Lord B. today—he endeavours to make a *joke* of the whole business, which inclines me to think he finds it a *bad* joke. I don't answer.

Byron had written to her on the 26th:

Dearest Pip—

I wish you would make it up—for I am dreadfully sick of all this—& cannot foresee any good that can come of it.

If you will—I am ready to make any penitential speech or speeches you please, & will be very good & tractable for the rest of my days—& very sorry for all that have gone before.

At any rate, if you won't comply with this proposition, I beg you to keep this note to yourself, & neither show it to Doctors Bailey nor Lushington nor Commons—nor any other of your present Cabinet—at least the professional part of it.

I am very sure *you* will not mistake it for anything but what it is meant to be—& I am terribly tired of the stately style of our late letters & obliged to take refuge in that which I was used to

yrs. ever

& truly

Private B.

Hanson was now taking depositions from the servants, and Annabella found she had adopted a fruitless precaution in leaving Mrs. Fletcher at Kirkby, writing at Lushington's instruction to her mother on the 23rd, "Tell Mrs. Fletcher from me that she may go to Town whenever she likes—kindly." Augusta's regular flow of letters had ceased on the 22nd, for the reason noted by Hobhouse on the 29th:

> Mrs. Leigh has been forbid all intercourse with her at her lawyer's request. A story has now got abroad against *her* (Mrs. L.) *and Byron!!!*

Can this have been the "MOST horrid" report referred to in Augusta's letters of the 17th and 20th? Would she have referred to this "story" in such terms? Hobhouse's note suggests that this rumour was new on 29th February and therefore a different report from the accusation he had noted on the 9th—that Lady Caroline Lamb accused Byron of "———". Demonstrably both rumours originated from the same source—from that "wicked and dishonorable mad-woman," as Lovelace was to describe her, "Lady Caroline Lamb"—for, apart from Lady Melbourne, so far as is known, nobody else had been favoured with Byron's confidences about his relationship with Augusta.

On hearing the news that Annabella had left her husband, Lady Caroline—like some of Byron's subsequent biographers—jumped to the conclusion that only revelations of iniquities could have impelled such a step. At first she sought to ally herself with Byron—perhaps with the idea that, finding himself ruined in reputation, he might be induced to take her with him as the companion of his exile—and she wrote to him, probably during the second or third week of February:

> . . . if letter or report or ought else has been maliciously placed in the hands of yr Wife to ruin you I am ready to swear that I did it for the purpose of deceiving her there is nothing however base it may appear that I would not do to save you or yours from this—do not oh do not believe those who would lead you for one moment to think she knows any thing for certain—be firm be guarded—resolve upon seeing her—there is nothing—nothing a Wife cannot & ought not to forgive . . .
>
> [Lady Melbourne] disbelieves every word against you—& if I tremble more than her—think not at least that I judge you—this alone I ask you—do not rashly credit any lie or invention that old Devil Lady Milbanke may invent—dont even think that Lady Biron may know because she suspects—& if it be a letter deny it at once—there are moments when to deny is a virtue & this is one—be firm & do not let mistaken friends gain your confidence . . . whatever happens insist upon seeing her . . . see your Wife—& she cannot have the heart to betray you—if she has she is a devil . . .

To Byron's publisher Murray she wrote, presumably sometime later, "For God's sake, tell me—have you breathed what I told you to any-one, and if not, have you heard the reports?" When Sir Ralph went to see Lady Melbourne on 13th February, he reported so favourably of

Lady Caroline's attitude that Annabella wrote with satisfaction to Mrs. Clermont on the 15th:

> I am very glad about Ly Melbourne. I was sure Lady C. L. would take my part. I am rather flattered by the favour of the wicked.

When Hobhouse on the 16th told Byron "the very worst I had heard against him," he confessed "astonishment" that he showed "very little discomposure." Knowing the origin of the reports, Byron doubtless assumed too optimistically that they would be discredited as coming from such a notoriously irresponsible source.

On 1st March Annabella expressed to her mother disgust at the scandalous gossip:

> I hope to be able to leave Town in a few days, being quite sick of it, and its iniquities. The tone now is to throw ridicule on me as a spoiled child.
>
> The more I think of it, the more I am convinced you ought not to *pocket that insult* . . .
>
> I hope you will be *very* cautious in regard to any correspondence with Piccadilly—and not to speak of Lord B. as if he had tender & affecte. feelings in regard to the child—nor the contrary.

Apparently she had written to Byron's Aunt Sophia suggesting that she should urge upon Augusta the desirability of her leaving Byron's house, for the old lady replied on 29th February:

> "It is a constant thorn in my side" and I know not how to relieve it—without *tearing* a Veil from her Eyes which might almost overset her *reason,* or induce her to disregard what is so contrary to it. I have written and used every argument in my power to *persuade* her to go from London. Le Sposo and her friends have been equally anxious for it . . . if I could by any means have afforded a journey and visit to L[ondon] just now I would have *spoken* to *Mrs. V[illiers]* who has great weight with her . . . I believe she remains NOW on account of The D[rawing] Room being shortly expected to take place; Her Cousins will soon be in Montague Square, *he* [Wilmot] probably tomorrow or next day, but still writing is almost impossible nor would she perhaps attend to what could be said without All could be said . . . I shall not mention to her having heard from You . . .

On 1st March Byron attempted another direct appeal:

> Dearest Bell,
>
> Although you have announced to others and by others the recommendation of "legal advisers" to hold no communication with that dangerous terrace in Piccadilly—& your adoption of this exquisite maxim of matrimonial jurisprudence: I must again urge my often repeated request that you would grant me an interview. Pray do.

. . . I have not attempted to see you (further than by so often requesting your permission) because I have no wish to agitate or intrude upon you by my sudden & unwelcome apparition—if my presence should still be important enough in your eyes to occasion such a feeling.

I have still & have always had throughout this business the most sincere & heartfelt wish for your reconciliation to me—& there is no step I am not willing to take to effect it: but—this failing—my determination is equally taken as to the course I shall pursue . . . I do not say this from any notion or wish or thought of intimidation:—nor am I ignorant of the firmness of your disposition:—I merely state the fact—that I am prepared to meet your "legal advisers" and to try what force there is "in the decrees of Venice."

I presume it is in vain to expect any answer from you or yours—except through your speaking trumpets—and perhaps not even through them:—yet I do hope you will see me—and am very sure that we should agree in any case much better by our own discussion of the subject than through the sagest of interpreters . . .

G. Byron is about to be married. I wish him as much luck & as little law as possible . . . & I think they have a very good chance of going on well.

Dearest Bell

yrs. ever most affectly

BYRON.

He added in a postscript:

I hope you will not think me flippant or unfeeling—for really I do not mean it—but in this as in many things, one must either laugh or cry—& I prefer the former (while I can) even if it should be Sardonically.

On the same day Augusta, reporting progress to Francis Hodgson, dropped a remark indicative of Byron's subsequent animosity towards Mrs. Clermont:

There has been many schemes & plans—one to go down to Kirkby to fetch ye child who has been weaned it seems this month & is left with Ly N. However that is superceded by another—of going a l'improviste to Mivarts Hotel—to Ly B. This I dread in case of the Father & Husband meeting—the idea arose from Ly B's maid (who is come up & has made an affidavit before Mr. Hanson . . .) saying that she is sure Ly B. would see him if it were not for Mrs. Clermont—the whole of her statement proves Ly B. to be under influence at least so says Mr. H. . . . Mrs. Clermont wrote to me a few days ago enclosing a letter I had misdirected in my hurry to Kirkby, saying Ly B. was forbid by her legal advisers to have any communication with *Piccadilly*—she has of course not written to me or I to her. B. desires me to tell you in answer to yr letter that he has quite made up his Mind to go into Court if they oblige him—that is, *not* to sign any articles or give up his own or his child's rights—or to shrink from an exposure as reports are *so* horrible he thinks ye *truth* even wd be better.

What that truth in its whole intent may be dear Mr. H. I rather dread. I wonder whether he deceives himself about it or is unconscious . . .

Hobhouse too was active on 1st March. He called on Lady Melbourne and "prayed" her "to ask for an interview in spite of all rebuffs —she said she would—she agreed with me that Lady Noel appeared to be coming round." In the evening at the Cocoa Tree he met Sir Ralph's attorney Wharton, "& got him to go to Sir R. Noel & state the truth—that Byron would give any guarantee for any good conduct in future—imprinted on his mind the fondness of Byron for his wife, and also the chance of his prosecuting *people* for a conspiracy or detainer of his wife."

That same day Judith was in fact again urging Sir Ralph to call in Brougham as a support to Lord Holland in mediating with Byron. Annabella replied next day that, "as there is no probability of the question coming to King's Bench," there was no reason for consulting Brougham:

> Dr. Lushington is a very intimate friend of Lord Holland's—and has communicated to him the general colour of the circumstances, and if any further Step be taken through him, he will be made acquainted with particulars. Lord Holland, in the character of an impartial Mediator, cannot, during the business, commit himself by any opinion—but will doubtless form a fair one. Lady Caroline Lamb takes my part everywhere —did I not say she would?

It may have been at this juncture that Lady Caroline wrote her impudently self-righteous appeal to Byron, so calculated to excite his derision:

> Will you generously consent to what is for the peace of both parties? and will you act in a manner worthy of yourself? I am sure in the end you will consent. Even were everything now left to your own choice, you never could bring yourself to live with a person who felt desirous of being separated from you. I know you too well to believe this possible, and I am sure that a separation nobly and generously arranged by you will at once silence every report spread against either party . . .
>
> . . . Return to virtue and happiness, for God's sake, whilst it is yet time. Oh, Lord Byron, let one who has loved you with a devotion almost profane find favour so far as to incline you to hear her . . .

On Saturday 2nd March Lord Holland called on Byron, who wrote to him next day:

> I answer *No* . . .
>
> With regard to "amicable arrangement" I am open to the MOST amicable of arrangements. I am willing & desirous to become reconciled to Lady B. & her friends—ready to make any advance or even sacrifice

for that purpose—to dismiss all & any irritation from my mind which may have arisen on this subject—to be forgiven where I may have offended—& in some points, it may be, to forgive.

But I will sign no separations . . .

To Annabella he wrote on Monday the 4th—apparently early in the day:

Dearest—If I did not believe that you are sacrificing your own happiness—as much as I know you are destroying mine:—if I were not convinced that some rash determination—&, it may be, promise—is the root of the bitter fruits we are now at the same time devouring & detesting—I would & could address you no more.

Did I not love you—were I not sure that you still love me—I should not have endured What I have already. I have rejected all propositions of separation—as I would spurn an adder—and from the same motive.

If you or yours conceive that I am actuated by mercenary motives, I appeal to the tenor of my past life in such respects. I appeal to my conduct with regard to settlements previous to your marriage. I appeal to all who know me—or who ever will know.

Whatever I may have felt (& what I feel, I often shew) in moments of pressure & distress, they were not the privations of Misfortune from which I recoiled, but its indignities.

I look upon the *manner* & statement of the proposals lately transmitted to me, as the greatest insult I have received from your family, in this struggle for moral existence . . .

I desire to see you—I request to be reconciled with you:—recollect I have done all that human being can in such circumstances to effect this object for your sake—for my child's—for mine—even for those who endeavour to prevent it. I will persevere in it—while the shadow of a hope can be distinguished—and when even that is effaced, I shall regret the sufferings which to more than *one*—or *two*—will be inevitable—there is that which will recoil upon some who may deem themselves secure.

It is difficult to understand how any wife of one year's standing could resist an appeal of such dignity and transparent sincerity, reinforced as it was by reference to his known character and past conduct. But Annabella had always prevented herself from perceiving his true character by her habit of drawing inferences to suit her own preconceptions; in all he said she looked for "art"—for hidden meanings and the intent to deceive.

With indignation doubtless whetted by consultation with Hobhouse, he wrote again later the same day:

I know of no offence—not merely from man to wife—nor of one human being to another—but of any being almost to God himself—which we are not taught to believe would be expiated by the repeated atonement which I have offered even for the *unknown* faults (for to me till stated they are unknown—to any extent which can justify such persevering rejections) I may have been supposed to committ—or can have committed against you.

But since all hope is over—& instead of the duties of a wife, and the mother of my child, I am to encounter accusation & implacability—I have nothing more to say, but shall act according to circumstances . . .

I am told that you say *you* drew up the *proposal* of separation—if so, I regret to hear it. It appeared to me to be a kind of appeal to the supposed mercenary feelings of the person to whom it was made "if you part with &c. you will gain *so* much *now*, & so much at the death of &c."—a matter of pounds shillings & pence!—no allusion to my child—a hard, dry, attorney's paper:—Oh, Bell, to see you thus stifling and destroying all feeling, all affections, all duties (for they are your first duties—those of a wife & mother) is far more bitter than any possible consequences to me.

On the same day, before receiving Byron's letters, Annabella was writing to her mother of his rejection of Lord Holland's proposal:

Well—nothing but war remains. All offers of amicable arrangement have been refused—and perhaps when you know the terms, *you* may not be sorry. Half the Noel property was offered, and only £200 per ann asked at present. It is a bad job—for I shall lose the cause, and can only obtain present Security whilst the Suit lasts. They say I shall be justified to the World. The silence of my friends has been very *dis*advantageous to Lord B. in regard to opinion—since worse than the true causes are supposed, and from all accounts I find there never was such unanimity of opinion on any subject, except at one house, and *that* is divided against itself—and if I were not a Spoiled Child *there*, I might be something worse. Lady C. Lamb & Mrs. G. Lamb warmly espouse my cause, Lady M. & Lady Cowper against me—or at least *not for me*. William Lamb maintains a becoming silence, & George Lamb declaims against me. But this is all to be kept Snug. I wish you had read Miss Eden's letter—so very kind . . .

My opinion of the best course to pursue is this—to put in the strongest statement into Court, and then to delay proceeding, so as to tire him out—and we are at liberty to make use of his conduct during the suit, if it affords ground for adultery &c. So I don't think he can well escape—and yet he is so artfull that I despond about it at times . . .

Colonel Doyle wrote to Judith the same day:

. . . I fear all hope of an amicable arrangement is at an end. As with a view to Lady Byron's keeping the child it is of the greatest importance that she shd never *lose possession* of it. I recommend you to guard it with every possible vigilance lest before the custody of it is made a legal question they might attempt by a coup-de-Main to get hold of it . . .

As a first step towards securing custody of the child, Lushington had already consulted Sir Samuel Romilly, who wrote to Annabella on 2nd March:

If the Child were made a ward of the Court of Chancery I have no doubt that the Lord Chancellor would not suffer her to be removed from you—neither at present nor I think at any future time.

On 5th March Sir Ralph assured Judith that Lushington and Wharton had "consulted about the mode of doing the *business for the Child*," and Judith wrote on the 10th, "A letter from Wharton assures me the *Chancery* business is completed, which gives me great comfort."

To the first of Byron's two letters of 4th March Lushington drafted Annabella's reply of the 5th:

I deeply regret the necessity you have imposed upon me of replying to your last letter, delivered by Milward, for anxious as I am to avoid any allusions which may irritate or wound your feelings I must not incur the Hazard of leaving an erroneous impression upon your mind by an ambiguous or undecided answer.

Most calmly & repeatedly have I weighed all that has passed & after the maturest deliberation the result is—a firm conviction that a separation is indispensable. This resolution is not formed under the impulse or at the suggestion of others.

It is mine & mine only & for the consequences I alone am responsible.

I am not less surprized than hurt at the view you have taken of the proposal Lord H sent you. The Matter & Manner were dictated & approved by me . . . I disclaim all design of Insult or offence . . .

An Interview I must decline. All my former reasons for avoiding so painful a meeting derive additional force from consideration.

Annabella added a postscript on her own account:

I have now seen Mrs. Leigh—who has heard from me the substance of this letter—and it does not appear to me that any further answer is required to her communication.

The meeting with Augusta on the 5th was the result of a letter from her friend Mrs. Villiers to Annabella on 26th February:

Tho' our acquaintance has been but of short duration, yet I will flatter myself that you are sufficiently *well inclined towards me to be convinced that nothing can be* more remote from my disposition than either impertinently to interfere in the concerns of others, or officiously to intrude on afflictions which I have not the power to soothe. So, my dear Ly B., truly and sincerely as I sympathise in your sorrows, I would have continued to do so in silence . . . had it not been for some infamous reports which have within these few last days reached my ears from various quarters . . . from the conviction I feel that your affection for Augusta is unchanged & your good opinion of her undiminished, I am persuaded you will be anxious to do her justice in the eyes of an ill-natured world; justice which *no one but yourself* can render her. The fact is that amongst the many very malicious and calumnious reports which are now most industriously circulated in London respecting your separation from Lord Byron there is *one* which is in the *highest degree* prejudicial to *Augusta's character*, and on my vehemently and indignantly resenting *such* a calumny, I was assured that the report was confirmed by *your* refusal to assign a reason for your separation. Nothing to be sure *can* be more absurd than such an inference, but as it is absolutely essential to poor Augusta's reputation that it should be contradicted, and as no one but yourself *can* do this with effect I could think of no alternative but that of suggesting to you the expediency of making known to your friends in general those sentiments of confidence, esteem and affection which I am sure you feel for her, & which I can safely assert to be reciprocal on her part. I would not for worlds add so severe a pang to Augusta's recent sufferings as I should do if I were to impart this report to her, if it can be avoided, but should it continue to be circulated her friends *must insist* I fear on her leaving London, tho' it will destroy the only *little* comfort she has remaining which is that of believing that she averts greater evils by continuing in Piccadilly.

Annabella replied immediately—doubtless writing the same day to Augusta's aunt, Sophia Byron:

I deeply regret the reports which have been circulated relative to the causes of Separation between Lord Byron & myself, and none can occasion me more sorrow than that which you mention as reflecting on Augusta's character—but as I can *positively* assert that not one of the many reports now current, have been sanctioned or encouraged by me, my family, or my friends, I cannot consider myself in any degree responsible for them.

During my residence under the same roof with Mrs. Leigh, *all* my friends have heard me express the most grateful and affectionate sense of her good offices towards me—and before I left the house I wrote of her or spoke of her in those terms, to every one who was intimate with me.

In the present state of circumstances you must be aware that a publication of the real grounds of difference between Lord B. and myself would be extremely improper—and in conformity with the advice I have received, I *must* abstain from any further disclosure. It is very painful to me to be obliged in consequence, to appear less confidential than I wish towards you . . .

This guarded answer dissatisfied Mrs. Villiers, as Annabella was soon informed by Robert Wilmot, that cousin of Augusta's mentioned in their Aunt Sophia's letter as due to arrive in Montagu Square at the beginning of March.

Wilmot was a first cousin of Byron's and Augusta's, being a son of one of their father's sisters. He was married to a Derbyshire heiress, Anne Horton, a woman of beauty and talent, much admired by Byron, who was inspired by her to write "She walks in Beauty," the first of his *Hebrew Melodies*. Three years older than Byron, he was—as Annabella was soon to learn—a person of less tact than vanity and pomposity;

he was later to have a hand in the burning of Byron's *Memoirs* and he now intervened in the separation negotiations.

In defiance of Lushington's ban on her communication with Augusta, Annabella met her on Tuesday 5th March, Augusta delivering to her Byron's second letter of the 4th. Immediately after the interview, she committed to paper the main points discussed:

Reasons for my return urged by Mrs. Leigh—

1. That Lord B. was insane during the time I was with him, and had since become sane.

Answer—If so, his friends must be convinced that my absence was desirable for him.

2. That he was at present sincerely desirous of my return—very sorry for his misconduct—not sensible of any injuries he had done me.

Answer—Evident contradictions—what hope of amendment from one who will not see his errors?

3. That no ill-consequences could ensue from my return.

Answer—First, my own destruction—next, a still more dreadful remorse to him—and no possible good.

4. Why should I not admit an Interview?

Answer—To myself it must be very cruel—and would in my opinion have a still more irritating effect on him—as I could not, & would not show any kind consideration.

5. Why I would not communicate the charges?

Answer—Because it would give him a legal advantage which he was cunning enough to use.

She also wrote immediately to Lushington:

Whilst I am expecting Lord Holland's visit I will give you the substance of an Interview between me & Mrs. Leigh, which it appeared to me that I could not avoid without greater disadvantages than it would produce. She came by Lord B's desire, having written instructions from him (besides a letter which she delivered to me) to gain my consent to his admission, or if not, to draw from me what were the charges. To both these requests my refusal was positive. The arguments to me were absurd & contradictory . . .

The most important conclusion I have formed from this interview, and from some questions I put to my Maid, is—that the impression of my being unduly influenced, prevails very strongly with every one in Lord B's house—& the accusation of a Conspiracy is to be adduced . . .

Mrs. Leigh seemed to think me quite mistaken, or rather misguided—said that there must be something more than she knew, or I could not object to return. I then recalled to her the *whole* tenor of Lord Byron's conduct, to which she could say nothing but the old excuse of Insanity. She appeared to have been terrified into this measure, as well as every other she is now adopting. No mention of *reports* on either side . . .

Lord B's last letter delivered by Mrs. Leigh is in the tone of a *Saint*—insisting on the *religious* obligation of forgiveness, &c &c.

Augusta wrote to Francis Hodgson both before and after the interview. On the 4th she made it clear that she and Byron regarded Mrs. Clermont—perhaps as Judith's trusted emissary—as a dominant influence on Annabella:

> Dear Mr. H say what you like of *the* person who made me the communication of a prohibition to communicate with Ly B. I have been quite ill humoured since yesterday afternoon—when I heard she had done her best to set Ly B. against me & Capt. B. Now, I have borne patiently & indeed laughed at all I have heard of reports against myself—& it has been a good deal for some days past. *The world* perhaps has a right to talk—but this woman who *knows* both Capt. B & I to have *devoted* ourselves to Ly B. in every possible manner considered her comfort & happiness & *both* suffered such great unhappiness on her acct.—I do think it IS abominable!

After the interview she wrote to Hodgson on the 5th:

> Alas! poor Ly B. sent for Capt. B. last night—to assure him & that he might convey to B. from her own mouth that she acted under *no* influence—that she was *perfectly determined* NEVER to return to him, happen what might—that if *her own* friends even *knelt* to her to so do she felt herself bound by every moral & religious duty to refuse—& she hinted (but this is *sacred*) that she had reasons which she hoped would die with her—why she *could never* consistently with her *duty to God* do so. This was nearly repeated to-day to me when I saw her—& I see & am convinced she will not be Shaken. What then is left but for B to consent to amicable arrangement! & I *fear* there are many who will persuade him to the contrary. I never can describe Ly Bs appearance to you—but by comparing it to what I should imagine that of a Being of another world. She is positively reduced to a Skeleton—pale as *ashes*—a deep hollow tone of voice & a *calm* in her manner quite supernatural. She received *me* kindly, but that really appeared the only SURVIVING *feeling*—all else was *death like* calm. *I* never can forget it—never!

Also on Tuesday the 5th, Wilmot wrote to Annabella:

> I hope to have the pleasure of calling upon you today, in the mean time *I give you my solemn word of honor* that it is *my opinion* that Lord Byron *may be* & *will be* induced to sign a seperation upon proper terms, without going into Court; & to assure you that you may command my services to *the utmost extent*, humble & insignificant as they may be.

Late the same evening Augusta wrote to Wilmot:

> B. has just desired me to write you word he wishes particularly to see you tomorrow . . . I fancy the object of this interview is for you to go with a message from him to Lady B. being determined to write no more—& I have *some* hopes that in the hands of so tact a person as you, *legal measures* MAY be avoided. I have been giving him my opinions on this subject, & have reason (from experience in *past* cases) to think it just possible they

may have weight tho' *at first* they appear to be rejected. Whatever happens it is my duty to tell him what I think that *she* will sink under an exposure—or longer suspense . . .

I hope you have seen poor Ly. B. this Eveg. Ld Holland has been here with a letter from her but said very little I rather believe. B. thinks you the only proper person of *all* belonging to him, friends & relatives to go to her from him . . .

Hobhouse had again addressed himself to Annabella on the 5th, asking her to return to Byron in the light of her duty to him, "to society, to God himself," but discovered that he was already out of date when he called at Byron's on the morning of the 6th. Having met Wilmot on his way, he had "argued the case—he for not bringing the matter into a court, and I, on the grounds of the rumours, for bringing it in," but at Byron's:

I found Lady Byron's letter of yesterday on the table—decisive but rather milder and claiming a promise made to her that should she prove the whole proceeding to be her own act and will, Lord Byron would consent to a private arrangement. I asked him if he ever had said so. He said his sister had said so for him.

This decided me that Lady Byron had a right to demand the performance of this promise—but I spoke to Mrs. Leigh, and asked her if she did not think Lord Byron and his friends had a right to demand, previous to any separation, a positive disavowal of all the heinous charges made against Byron, as making any part of her charge. Mrs. Leigh said yes . . .

My visit to Byron altered my views of the subject. Wilmot had seen Lady Byron, and said there was no hope of reconciliation—she was determined never to come back. Mrs. Leigh told me her persuasion of Byron's madness was so strong that she said if he was mad nothing should prevent her from nursing him. Byron wrote a note to her in which he quoted Goldsmith's mock elegy "the dog it was that died" meaning he was not mad but she. He did not send *this* note, but is perpetually sending short notes in a half serious style.

At the same time Annabella was informing Lushington:

I have now stronger reasons for thinking that we shall obtain Lord Byron's consent to our terms—but it is for this end necessary to continue hostile measures.

My Interview with Mrs. Leigh has made the desired impression. My Maid had offered to take her oath that I was detained at Kirkby *against my will*—on this false ground the family have been acting.

On Thursday 7th March Hobhouse "drew up a paper of declarations as preamble to the Separation, in which Lady Byron disavowed cruelty, systematic unremitted neglect, gross and repeated infidelities, incest and ———." Accompanied by Scrope Davies, he took the paper to Byron's:

Byron & Davies seemed to think those things had better not be put on record, and certainly not on the same paper with the Separation, as that would make the disavowal seem like the price of separation.

However, Hobhouse gave the paper to Wilmot to take to Annabella, who promptly wrote to Lushington:

I enclose for your previous [*i.e.* previous to a consultation] consideration a paper which I am required to sign as the preliminary of any Separation —I never will.

That evening Lushington, Doyle, and Wilmot conferred with Sir Ralph and Annabella at Mivart's, with the result that Wilmot met Hobhouse and Davies next day at Byron's, as Hobhouse recorded:

Wilmot took me into another room, and there in great agitation told me that I knew nothing of the case—that Byron was mad, and that something horrid would be proved against him. He adjured me therefore to advise Byron not to go into court, and said "If the matter should come out, and you should find I have misrepresented it, I will give you leave to pull my nose" . . .

He then presented me with a paper written in the form of a letter to myself from himself, in which he told me Lady Byron in a conversation had stated certain terms of arrangement.

The points of Wilmot's letter were:

With respect to the paper drawn up by you, Lady Byron *positively declines assenting* to it, or writing any letter formed upon the basis of the propositions therein contained.

With respect to the proposition made by me to her from Lord Byron, viz. for him not to retain any part of her present fortune, & to leave the Noel Property now unarranged, until Lady Byron's accession to it, he *now* giving a written promise that he will *then* consent to a fair arrangement —Lady Byron replies

That she would not be disposed to accept more of her present fortune than the £200 per annm in addition to her pin-money, already proposed to Lord Byron through Lord Holland

That she has no sort of objection to leave the Noel Property *now unarranged*, provided that Lord Byron will *now stipulate* in a *legal form* (according to the *invariable* practise in similar cases) that when the period arrives of Lady Byron's succeeding to it, he will *then* consent to an arrangement upon fair terms of arbitration.

With respect to reports, for which she is not in the slightest degree responsible—

in the event of Lord Byron's assenting to her *acceptance* of his proposal above stated

or in the event of his acceding to a separation on the terms proposed through Lord Holland, with such additions & modifications as may be deemed necessary by Arbitrators mutually appointed—

or in the event of Lord B's consenting to refer to Arbitrators (one to be appointed by each with power to call in a third in case of difference) to arrange a separation on *equitable conditions*—

In any of these events, Lady B. is ready to give the following declaration under her own hand

Declaration

Lady B. positively affirms that she has not at any time spread reports injurious to Lord Byrons character & conduct, nor have any such reports been sanctioned by her, or by those most nearly connected with her.

Hobhouse related that, having read this document, he, Byron, and Davies "at once exclaimed that the disavowal was there made clearly the *bribe* for separation and would be thought so by the whole world":

Byron was indignant . . . I said the disavowal was in itself not sufficient. Lady Byron must not only disavow the rumours having been spread, but that the specific charges—that is incest and ——— made no part of her charges. We agreed to give up the cruelty & adultery in her own house. As to the first, Wilmot told me he knew Lady Byron would not consent to disavow that—but it was agreed that Wilmot should actually specify the two grosser enormities.

Wilmot, it appeared, has been partially told Lady Byron's charge which seems to fill him with so much horror. He told me it was no enormity—indeed I told him it never could be, or she would have quitted the house, at once. He said I had not a guess at it.

That evening Lushington drafted a fresh declaration:

Lady B: positively declares that no reports injurious to Ld B's character & conduct have been spread or sanctioned by herself or by those most nearly connected with her as far as her knowledge extends, & that two Reports Specifically mentioned by Mr. Wilmot do not form any part of the charges which in the event of a separation by agreement not taking place she should have been compelled to make against Lord B:—

This declaration it is understood is to be read by Mr. W: to Lord B: but neither the original nor a copy to be delivered to Lord B: until a separation has been assented to; and further that this declaration is not to take effect unless a separation be concluded by consent.

This document was signed by Annabella and witnessed by Lushington and Doyle. But she had second thoughts overnight and wrote to Lushington on the morning of Saturday the 9th:

It is not absolutely true that "no reports injurious to Ld B's character & *conduct* have been spread or *sanctioned*" &c.—since it has been asserted in general terms by all my friends that his *ill-conduct* occasioned the Separation . . . I have therefore substituted—

"In reference to a paper communicated by Mr. Wilmot—Lady B. declares that she does not consider herself in any way responsible for the various reports injurious to Lord B's character & conduct which may be circulated in the world. They have certainly not originated with, or been spread by her, or those most nearly connected with her. And the two reports" &c. (as before).

Mr. Wilmot admits the propriety of this alteration, and has taken the paper to Piccadilly. Time being of importance, I would not delay, however anxious to have your opinion.

Hobhouse related in his Journal how Wilmot met him at Byron's house and read him the declaration; he accepted it as satisfactory and "agreed that Wilmot should keep the paper in his possession until the whole business was concluded, as a safeguard to Lady Byron in case his mediation should fail." Wilmot then produced a paper containing the articles of separation as set forth in his previous letter to Hobhouse, whereupon the two of them conferred with Byron and Scrope Davies. Byron "as it appeared to me—assented," and "Davies said he also thought the business satisfactory," so Hobhouse made a copy of the separation paper, Wilmot "took his leave in spirits," and "we all thought, at least I thought, the affair concluded."

Annabella added a postscript to her letter to Lushington:

Mr. Wilmot has returned. The enclosed paper has been acceded to—without reserve—and a copy transmitted to Hanson, it being understood that I should send one also to Mr. G. Wharton who would meet him . . . Lord B. who was *in boisterous spirits*, said "They had better not be long in signing"—& means to go abroad immediately . . .

My greatest embarassment is about Mrs. L. Mr. Wilmot was very urgent on that point and wanted me to see her tonight, which I declined on account of fatigue. Now *I know* it is still the intention to give the Child to her, and I must not compromise any power to oppose such a proceeding. This seems to be of great moment. Could such a paper as you proposed be drawn up immediately?

On 5th March, hearing that Byron had declined the separation, Judith had written to Annabella:

What can *He* be aiming at? it comes into my head that he thinks *me* in a *bad State*, I wish he could *see* me—he would fear I had taken a *new Lease* . . . what is Mrs. L. about? does She justify *my Suspicions?* I fear She does. When your Case is made out, I should suppose my Affidavit of what *She* and G. Byron said was *very essential*, as they cannot without Perjuring themselves contradict it—and Clermont heard them as well as me—they spoke *positively* to the Adultery with Miss Boyce and to *their* fears for your Life—and this repeatedly—but the *Sister* is about to *fatten* on *your Spoils*. She is as bad I believe as her Brother.

I am not very easy about Mrs. F[letche]r returning here with You. She may do some mischief about the Child—by admitting people into the House, *perhaps in the night.* Pray ask Sir S[amuel] R[omilly] about this.

To this Annabella replied on the 7th:

In regard to Mrs. Leigh you are really very gooseish. I hear from every quarter of the unreserved approbation with which she speaks of my conduct, as that of an Angel—only adding that the loss of me must ruin her brother, & therefore she wishes me to return. Now you must recollect she is the only person who can do justice to my *domestic* character, and she ought not to be disgusted by absurd & most groundless imputations. You are wholly mistaken as to her motives in the opinion both of Lushington & Doyle. I had an interview with her the day before yesterday, which is thought to have had a good effect on the intentions of the family. No one can be more friendly than Mr. & Mrs. Wilmot.

I will take care about Mrs. Fletcher.

After hearing Wilmot's good news, Mrs. Clermont wrote to Judith on the 9th:

I have at last the happiness to inform you that this Business is in a fair way to be settled without the *Law.* In the first place I must tell you that the *reports* have been as to an unnatural Crime, Incest taking women into the House with his Wife &c. Lady B: was sent to to know if she would disclaim her belief in these reports . . . All who love Lady B: have great reason to be thankful that she has escaped from him & certain misery—the Babe is not mentioned in the arrangement for they all think that with the Step that has been taken she is quite secure on that head . . .

And in regard to Mrs. Leigh you have I think been very unjust as I am confident however maliciously he may act it never has been her wish to take it from A:—nor ever will be although I fear she must have felt herself much hurt of late by a change of manner on this side. I know she has acted weakly but I do firmly believe her intentions have been good—nor can I ever forget the kindness A: experienced from her the latter part of the time she was in piccadilly even for her life I believe we may thank Mrs. Leigh . . .

Lord B: offered the whole of her present fortune but that is not thought right to take he having so little.

But Augusta still shared Annabella's anxiety about custody of the child, as she wrote to Hodgson on the evening of Saturday the 9th:

One line just to say I hope all *will* be quietly settled. Ly B. has given a *written contradiction* of the 2 principal & most horrible reports into Mr. Wilmots hands. I still dread ye combat about the poor child.

On Sunday the 10th Annabella wrote to Lushington:

My situation in relation to Mrs. Leigh becomes every day more distressing, and cannot remain without change, or my own character as well as hers must sink—for as I cannot *give sufficient* reasons, the imputation of malice would be cast upon me by her numerous connections . . .

From different causes I am convinced that Mrs. Leigh would give me the most secure promise in writing that could be required, never to accept the care of the Child whilst I lived without my consent. Would not this obviate all difficulties, and prevent the cruel necessity of stigmatizing her either directly or indirectly? I could obtain this promise without Lord B's knowledge.

Lushington replied that night:

I have just received your letter respecting Mrs. Leigh, but cannot acquiesce in your expedient at present . . . I am fully aware of the very disagreeable predicament in which you are placed . . . but I do think that it would be extremely improper to renew any intercourse with Mrs. L: until the separation is put past all doubt, & not even then until means have been taken to obviate any injurious effect in future. I have thought of a plan for that purpose more safe than what we before discussed & will mention it tomorrow evening. In the meantime I can only repeat my opinion that an interview with Mrs. L: should be avoided & if you think that avowing you do so under my advice will save you any disagreeable solicitation, pray use my name to that effect . . . if further urged you may add, that until the Separation be finally concluded, I have advised you to have no intercourse *with any one* living under Lord B's roof . . .

With callous subtlety Lushington recognised that, as Mrs. Villiers said, only Annabella's continued friendship with Augusta could silence the rumours that an incestuous relationship was the cause of the separation; without demonstration of that continued friendship, Augusta would have to leave Byron's house and the rumours would still persist. Lushington presumably regarded both results as desirable: Augusta was a restraining influence on Byron in averting "greater evils," and persistence of rumour would warn Byron's friends of the possibility of "horrid" revelations if the case was forced into the courts.

Thinking that he had settled the terms of the separation with Wilmot on the previous day, Hobhouse was surprised when he called at Byron's on Sunday the 10th, "found S. Davies and Kinnaird with him, and the whole house in a rumpus." As Byron's financial adviser and a trustee of his marriage settlement, Kinnaird objected to the last article of the separation terms relating to the Wentworth property. By the terms of Lord Wentworth's will the estate of Kirkby Mallory went to Judith for the rest of her life and then to Annabella and—subject to various contingencies—to her children. In those days before the Married Women's Property Acts Annabella's husband would control the estate during her lifetime; if Annabella died without a son, the estate then went to her cousin Nathaniel Curzon and devolved to her daughter only if Curzon died without a son. Hence Byron would not merely have controlled the estate after Judith's death, but would have been in a strong position to compel his wife's return to him if he had been so minded. To avoid a contingency that might have amounted to victimisation, the separation proposals provided—as stated in Wilmot's letter to Hobhouse—that Byron should "*now stipulate* in a *legal form*" that, on Annabella's accession to the estate, Byron would "*then* consent to an arrangement upon fair terms of arbitration."

Hobhouse remained "still of the same opinion that the principle as to the Kirkby property was equitable," and "offered to bet with Kinnaird that Sir S. Romilly would think so." He told Byron that Wilmot's paper of proposals "was nothing as a legal instrument, but that I thought he had assented positively to it." Kinnaird was "violent," so Hobhouse "differed from him, and left Byron with the notion that Romilly would be applied to."

Augusta wrote to Wilmot on Monday morning:

George & I have agreed that it is best to inform you of what *I understood* from B. last night to be ye state of things. He went to Hanson's—in ye mean time in walked Mr. Davies & Mr. Kinnaird—we had not any conversation on *the* subject, as I know the latter scarcely at all. When B returned, he said to them, "Hanson is perfectly of Kinnaird's opinion & I shall act upon it." I went away, & did not come down till the 2 *wise Men* had departed—when B informed me, Hanson would not hear of his doing ANY thing about *Kirkby* . . . Now, if this is the case, it is clear to me Hanson & others are driving B. on to *destruction*—he says in answer to my arguments "am I to give these men an advantage over me as long as I live? by saying I've been bullied into terms." Hanson is making him cavil upon a point quite unworthy of his attention—& I know acts upon *this conviction* that *Ly B* will *not* go into Court . . .

With regard to myself I have ordered fires at St. James's—but I am advised strongly not to stir from hence without an *event* to justify it—such as his quitting this house, or a Drawing room, when I should *immediately* go. This is certainly *my own feeling* too—for I think a sudden departure wd. give reason to think or say I was *afraid* to stay & face ye reports. However if B. is made to act as I have told you I *fear* he is now advised, I won't stay a moment to witness or sanction such conduct.

Hanson wrote in triumph to Byron the same morning:

I have just seen Dr. Lushington, and communicated to him the result of your determination last night, not to allow the Wentworth property to be admitted into the present consideration as an article of stipulation, and which *I most strongly advise your Lordship* not to deviate from. The doctor appeared much disappointed, and I would pledge my life on it he has no expectation of their being able to make out any case in a court. He said he could not proceed in the negotiation until he had communicated with Lady Byron on the subject of your counter project, which I think her Ladyship will accede to. It would be much more pleasant to you to allow any further increase of allowance to flow from your own spontaneous will, in case the Wentworth property should ever fall in.

Byron then wrote to Annabella the most uncharacteristic and unworthy of his letters, laboriously expounding why "the Wentworth property is no part of present consideration—it may never be the subject of consideration at all:—*you* may survive me (I hope you will) Lady Noel may survive you—or both," and asserting:

If the W. Property ever falls in—I will make what shall be fully allowed to be fair & liberal arrangements—but I will not be menaced—nor forced into any present stipulations . . .

He concluded with the disingenuous taunt, "As I do not write with a lawyer at my elbow—I must request a fair construction of what I have written." It was true that Annabella, having placed her affairs in legal hands, necessarily wrote according to lawyers' instructions, while Byron had previously written at his own inspiration, but in this instance he was interpreting the opinion expounded to him by Hanson and Kinnaird, actually with a memorandum by Hanson at his elbow.[1]

Wilmot reacted impetuously, writing to Hobhouse:

It is with feelings infinitely stronger than astonishment that I hear that Lord Byron has refused to assent to the principle of Seperation which was agreed upon last Saturday in your presence, under your sanction & with your approbation—& which *I conceive* that Lord Byron is bound to honor to me as well as to yourselves, to carry into effect.

You will oblige me by an immediate answer in writing to inform me if your opinion coincides with mine.

Scrope Davies immediately sent this letter by his groom to Whitton Park, with a note telling Hobhouse that he "had better come up to Town." Hobhouse recorded:

Very unwillingly I rode up to town, not knowing what to make of the matter, & thinking there must be some fighting . . . I told Byron my mind distinctly that I thought he was wrong—but he was positive.

I then sat down & wrote a note to Wilmot which, as Davies said it would not do, I threw into the fire. Byron then wrote a violent note which we threw into the fire! At last it was agreed that I should call on Wilmot.

He found Doyle with Wilmot at his house:

[1] A Memorandum by Hanson, undated, explaining the terms of the marriage settlement, concluded thus significantly: ". . . the Wentworth Property might never come into Possession. But if it did, it might operate as an Inducement and the Means of bringing the Parties (so young and so recently united) together again—whilst an anticipated separate Provision might tend to prevent it."

I confessed to these gentlemen my impression of the assent of Lord Byron, S. Davies & myself to the Principle of separation—but that Lord Byron had assured me on his honour that he had misconceived Mr. Wilmot, and never imagined he had not the power of receding even before the lawyers and referee were appointed to settle the business.

He then demanded from Wilmot "an avowal of his perfect satisfaction with my conduct," which "he gave me in the fullest manner, and was joined in this by Colonel Doyle," but he found "that Wilmot had made up his mind to have done with his cousin." Back at Byron's he "received congratulations," but added:

It appears that, as court is inevitable, Byron owned to Scroope Davies and me, at last, that he may have been *bereaved of* reason during his paroxysms with his wife.

It appears to me he has made some confession. I am still however in the dark utterly.

That same evening of Tuesday, 12th March, Doyle wrote a fair account of the interview to Annabella, concluding that "Wilmot has been rather incautious—looking to the end without sufficiently considering the instruments." Annabella reported to her mother on the 13th:

Wilmot conceives this to be a personal offence to himself, and has resented it in such a manner that *if* Lord B were a fighting man, worse consequences would have ensued. At present it is only a paper war. Mr. Hobhouse having been a witness of this transaction, is compelled to declare *upon his honour*, that he conceived it in the same light, *but* supposes that his friend, Lord B, acted under a complete misconception! In short that Piccadilly Coterie have no sense of Honor whatever.

The effect of the expedient proposed by Kinnaird and Hanson—so soon to be proved legally useless—was to exacerbate the temper of the negotiations. As the case seemed now destined to be fought in the courts, Lushington began taking depositions such as Hanson had already been collecting, starting with the nurse who had attended Annabella during her confinement. Already, at his bidding, Annabella had refused an interview to Augusta:[1]

In this critical moment it would be impossible for me to *speak* on the subjects which I conceive you wish to discuss—& your difficulties must be nearly equal, since we might both be called upon to answer for words

[1] Augusta wrote on Wednesday the 13th:
My dearest Annabella
I wish to have some *private* conversation with you—the sooner the better. I will leave this & call for an answer—or an interview whichever you please to grant today . . .
Yrs most affecly
AL

though uttered in the most private conversation. This has been so strongly represented to me by Dr. Lushington, that he positively forbids any such interview, which however I cannot refuse without the greatest pain.

Enclosing Doyle's account of the interview between Hobhouse and Wilmot, she wrote to Lushington:

I also enclose a note left by Mrs. Leigh, with the reply to it which in pursuance of your advice on that point I deem it necessary to give. But if you should conceive that good consequences might still result from the Interview, I do not think myself precluded from admitting it tomorrow. I am afraid the object may regard Mrs. Leigh *more particularly*.

Col: Doyle met Capt. Byron last night and formed a very favorable opinion of him. He found out what were to be the grounds of Hanson's defence. Mr. Hanson admitted the cruelty of the circumstances previous to my departure, but confidently asserted they were *legally* cancelled by the letter of the 16th and it also appears that the charge of Adultery is not expected.

I have written to Mr. Wilmot for the purpose of obtaining Capn. Byron's examination tomorrow. I despair of Mrs. Leigh's consent, since I find she will not leave the house now—but perhaps it would still be advisable to make the request.

Even as Annabella was writing thus to Lushington, Hobhouse was calling on Augusta at Byron's, where he "found her in tears and great distress indeed":

She thinks she ought in duty to her husband and children to leave Byron's house—she having staid long enough to *give the lie* to all rumours respecting herself, which Col. Leigh has most handsomely *discredited* in every way. I promised to hint this to Byron—advised Mrs. Leigh to ask for an interview with Lady Byron.

Hobhouse saw her at noon, and at two o'clock she wrote to him:

When you mention my going away, pray do it as from yourself—*your own opinion*. I have a dread of B. thinking it comes from any persecution from my husband or friends—the former particularly—and it would be unjust, as HE has never expressed the wish, but with a view to my not injuring my health, which he apprehended might suffer from anxiety and unhappiness.[1] He has never pressed my return since he quitted London, and on the subject of reports has only been indignant and vexed, as it is but natural he should feel on the subject—in short, it has *never* been wished by *any*·body from *unkind* motives towards my *brother*—and you know he is suspicious on these sort of things.

[1] Augusta's Bible thus records the birth of her fifth child: "Frederick George Leigh—born at the Six Mile Bottom May 9th 1816. Baptized there June 3 1816, by the Revd. W. Pugh. Sponsors the Earl of Jersey Lord Frederick Bentinck Countess of Jersey. Christened Oct. 22d 1818 by the Revd. Wm. Bentinck in St. James's Palace."

The next day, Thursday 14th March, Hobhouse found Byron "much affected with rage . . . inveterate against his wife & family, & no wonder." Annabella was then writing to her mother:

It may be of advantage & cannot be detrimental, that you should send very frequent accounts of the Child to Mrs. L. for Lord B. He pretends that he receives none—& keep copies with the dates.

There are yet means by which he may be compelled to accede in my opinion. In the last negociation he completely overreached all my advisers as they now admit—not having before supposed it possible that a man should so break his word of honor. There has very near been fighting. The end is a final breach between him & Wilmot—and the latter every where declares his dishonorable Conduct.

I shall leave Town very soon. I am sick of it all—a dirty job indeed—and they may make what they can of it . . .

Augusta wrote the same afternoon to Hodgson:

All going on as bad as possible—a Court inevitable I *fear* & the *Citation* will be out immediately. All owing to Mr. Hanson! Im nearly dead with worry & finding I can do no good I will not stay any longer . . .

That night she wrote at length to Hodgson:

I have been for some days *bordering* on a state of distraction. I expect to hear *every hour* of the *Citation* as it is called. I & all B's friends had hoped things were in train to be amicably—or at least *quietly* arranged—when the 2 legals met & Mr. Hanson would not hear of one of the proposed arrangements—that of B. pledging himself *legally* to do what was judged right by *Arbitrators* respecting a division of the *Kirkby* Property, whenever it may become his. I must confess that it does appear to me the most useless quibble I ever heard of—even more than that, injurious to B. for . . . it appears to me wishing to give him an *opportunity* of acting *dishonorably* by breaking his word! & on Ly B's side I should conceive that this point may be insisted on for this reason—that, if no such *legal* promise is given, B's creditors might seize the Income whenever it comes to him, & neither he she or the Child have one farthing . . . there the thing rests—Hanson is obstinate, B. ditto—tho evidently MUCH depressed by the prospect of an exposure. But what is most horrible dear Mr. H. is this—that it is intimated from Ly B's side—& I & others even think she has confided it to Mr. Wilmot—that there will come out what must *destroy him* FOR EVER in this world—even what will deprive him of all right to his Child, & so blast *his* character that neither Sister nor *Wife* who has lived under the same roof with can ever be considered as they *have* been again! What this mysterious charge can be is beyond ye utmost stretch of my imagination to guess. He *vows* HE knows not—& when I have implored Mr. Hobhouse & Mr. Davies to pause well before they advise, they answer "Can we doubt his word? he has assured us he knows of nothing." Still my mind misgives me, & I have argued thus—if (as I firmly believe) he has been subject to paroxysms of insanity for some years may he not in one of them have committed some act which he wd. not even avow to his dearest Friend—scarcely to his own soul. His manner to me makes me suspect it is so. He *now* confesses himself *insane*, seems anxious to have it established in opinion that he *was* so, & says openly it will be his *defence*. I have this Eveg. begged him to recollect Ld Ferrers's trial—I believe all *his* insanity did not save him—tho God forbid it should be ye same case, but I think it right to suggest every thing to his mind—recall all to his memory that I can.

You won't wonder at my being half mad myself—to add to all my apprehensions for the future, the last few days have been productive of a thousand. I really lived for twice 24 hours in the greatest dread of a *Duel*—between Mr. Wilmot & B or Mr. H or D. You have no idea of the pitch things rose to, in consequence of the failure of the negotiations entrusted to Mr. W—who felt hurt at B's *receding*, after having authorized him to make such proposals. Then Capt. B. was equally indignant whom I never saw indignant before, & ye same peril existed in *that* quarter. To crown all, *I* had been the person who persuaded Mr. W. to interfere!—but all is smooth as far that goes now.

It is my present intention dear Mr. H. to leave this house on Saturday. To explain *all* my reasons FOR so doing—all my GRIEF AT so doing wd. be difficult at this distance—but I am told it is positively a duty I owe myself, my Husband & Children not to stay to APPEAR to sanction B's conduct—that having staid while there was a *possibility* of reconciliation to do all I could towards it, I had better *now* go. You well know what it costs me to leave my dearest Brother, but indeed I CAN'T express one HALF of what I suffer . . .

One word more—all my fears of a *dreadful fatal event* have revived—the *dark hints* are again expressed *should any* charge be brought even without *proof* against him, that can blacken his character—he sometimes talks when viewing the subject in a fairer point of view of going abroad or to Newstead . . .

Obviously Augusta was in an overwrought state. She was aware of the "reports," and frightened by Byron's hints of suicide. But what was her idea of the terrible revelation that must destroy him for ever? Had she absorbed Annabella's fear that he had at some time committed murder? Or did she suspect that the charge would be incest, based on suspicions suggested by Byron's hints, and did she therefore hope that the idea of having committed incest might be reckoned an illusion of his insanity?

On Friday 15th March Augusta added a postscript to her letter to Hodgson:

I've seen Ly B. at her own desire—but heard nothing new—the *Citation* is to be out to day! what a business—I go to St. James's tomorrow . . .

In the course of taking depositions, making statements, and otherwise collecting her sentiments on paper, Annabella had devised a means by which Lushington could be persuaded to allow her to see Augusta. She wrote a statement of "My principles of conduct in regard to Mrs. Leigh," which Lushington then embodied in the form of a legal document, declaring that, while there had been "suspicion in Lady B's mind that an improper connection had at one time & might even still subsist between Lord B: & Mrs. L:" the causes of suspicion "did not amount to positive proof" and therefore did not justify "a direct accusation;" that "Mrs. L: had from her first acquaintance with Lady B: always manifested towards her the utmost kindness & attention endeavouring as far as laid in her power to mitigate the violence & cruelty of Lord B:" that Augusta had shown what Annabella interpreted as signs of remorse; and that Annabella had "conceived it possible that the crime, if committed might not only be deeply repented of, but never have been perpetrated since her Marriage with Lord B:". Annabella was now "anxious to avoid all possibility of doing injury to Mrs. L: & not by any conduct of her own to throw any suspicion upon Mrs. L: & it being intimated that Mrs. L:'s character can never be so effectually preserved as by a renewal of intercourse with Lady B: she does for the motives & reasons before mentioned consent to renew that intercourse."

> Now this Statement is made in order to Justify Lady B: in the line of conduct she has now determined to adopt & in order to prevent all misconstruction of her motives in case Mrs. L: should be proved hereafter to be guilty, and if any circumstances should compel or render it necessary for Lady B: to prefer the charge in order that Lady B: may be at full liberty so to do without being prejudiced by her present conduct.

The statement was devised by Lushington—as an adverse critic has remarked—"for writing 'without prejudice' over all Lady Byron's manifestations of warm affection towards her half-sister-in-law," but as Sir John Fox, a Master in Chancery, pointed out, it was also "a device for the protection of Mrs. Leigh's character," since Lushington was only compelled to its devising because Annabella wished to subdue gossip by showing that she was still on friendly terms with Augusta.

The statement also suggests—as appears from later correspondence—that incest was the "horrid" revelation feared by Wilmot, and that it would only be charged as a final resort—if Byron resisted the terms of the separation or demanded custody of the child.

It does not appear whether the meeting between Annabella and Augusta on Friday 15th March moved Byron to a more conciliatory attitude, but that same day he signed a paper empowering Hobhouse to ask Sir Samuel Romilly to act as "sole & final arbitrator" on whether the settlement of the Noel property should be included in the terms of separation. Romilly then discovered that his services had been retained by Byron many years before in the event of any legal dispute; he had therefore "done a very incorrect thing in being consulted by Lady Byron," so he withdrew from the case and declined the office of arbitrator. Thereupon, at Byron's instruction, Hobhouse wrote to Annabella, "asking her to appoint a person hitherto unemployed, to decide on the question of the legal stipulation to be made by Byron respecting the Kirkby property."

"I have no objection to the reference being made either to the Solicitor General, Sir A. Pigott, or Mr. Shadwell," replied Annabella; "The selection of the Individual is left to the option of Lord B. and his friends." She appointed Doyle to "make the preliminary arrangements before the Referee is applied to." When Hobhouse met Doyle that afternoon, he was able to inform him that Byron had chosen the Solicitor General, Sir Samuel Shepherd. Both Hobhouse and Doyle had drawn up a separation agreement, but the original agreement, signed by Byron and Annabella, and forwarded on Sunday the 17th to Sir Samuel Shepherd, was in Hobhouse's handwriting.

On Monday, informing her that Shepherd had accepted the arbitration, Hobhouse asked Annabella if, "when the affair shall be entirely terminated," she would give such "a disavowal of the more heinous rumours and charges" as that she had given to Wilmot. She began to draft such a disavowal:

> Previously to the Agreement for a Separation being concluded, Lady Byron had intended to bring a suit for Separation by reason of Cruelty & Adultery. The reports concerning charges of any other nature have not been circulated by the authority of Lady Byron or of those persons most nearly connected with her.

There she broke off, perhaps because it was considered that a guarded disavowal might irritate Byron into further obstruction, and discreetly assured Hobhouse "that I have every wish to consult the interests of others, as far as may be in my power consistently with the most candid considerations."

She had written to her mother on Sunday:

> I have just signed my name after Lord Byron's to an article of Separation which is to be submitted to Sir Samuel Shepherd, for his arbitration on a point respecting which there can be no doubt that any man of his understanding & feeling will decide in my favor. In short, it is all as well as possible, and effected at last *through Hobhouse!* There is no *possibility* of evading the business now.
>
> I am so glad the whole has been managed without Lady M's interference. She is frightened out of her senses on finding from Mrs. G. Lamb

that I knew her misdeeds towards me. On this point I want to have your opinion. I have now the fairest reasons for cutting her altogether, and I don't know what good she can ever do me. What do you think of it? I have just read "Les liaisons dangereux," which don't incline me more to cultivate her acquaintance.

Now pray "be aisy"—for I really think it is all finished in the best manner.

Every post had been bringing militant advice from Judith, who had announced as a precaution against the possible kidnapping of the child:

I have bought a pair of Pistols, which I shall have in the Room with me —for *defence*, not *Offence*—but I am more apprehensive of *Fraud* than *Force*—tho' guarded against both.

In reply to the inquiry about Lady Melbourne, she wrote to Annabella on the 19th:

I think it *incumbent* on You to *break* with her, that is, *cut her intirely*—not from *resentment* so much, as to enable You and Your Friends to *contradict* the *Lies* and aspersions She has held out *lately*—because if You *knowing them*, continue on terms with *her*, it is a *tacit* confession that they are not *unfounded*. Now I think it *best* You should openly alledge *this part of her conduct*, as a reason why *You* and Your Parents cannot notice her, *hinting* at the same time on *past* conduct. In this *Cut*, I include *Lady* C[aroline] and *G*[eorge] *L*[amb].

Lady Melbourne wrote to Annabella on 20th March:

I am inform'd that I blame You, & take Ld B's part most violently; I deny both most positively . . . & indeed I should have expected more liberality from you, than to have given credit to such an assertion without hearing what I had to say . . . I have seen Ld B *once* & that quite at first, & before I saw my Brother. I could then have form'd no opinion for I had heard nothing—& he told me nothing saying only that the whole was a Surprise upon him & that he did not even know what charges were to be brought against him. Mrs. Leigh took an oppory. at the same time to tell me, that you had just cause of complaint & that you had borne more than any other person could, with ye most exemplary patience, & she has since when ever I have seen her, held the same language. This account shock'd me very much . . . I can truly say my heart bled for you . . . I told Mrs. Leigh when she call'd upon me, yt I beg'd her to tell Ld B yt it was my decided opinion yt ye best thing for both would be to agree to an amicable Separation—to this I have had no answer & have had no communication of any sort with him either written or Verbal. I beg at ye same time to have it understood yt if Ld B had express'd a wish to see me, I should not have refused, as I am far from thinking that seeing him necessarily implies that I blame you, or think him in ye right. I believe You had been in Town ten days before I heard it & then it was told me with ye greatest injunctions of Secresy as you wish'd to remain quite private . . . I confess I thought it rather strange that after ye Letters yt had pass'd between us, & after my Brothers promise to let me hear anything yt might occur, I should not have a line from either of You . . . you may conceive my astonishment when I was told that you sd. I blame you . . . & also that I had been with Ld B last week . . . This must have been fabricated the last time I saw Mrs. Leigh & ye *Second* time yt I have been in ye House since you left it, & I most certainly did not see Ld B nor did he know I was there . . . I assure you it is not at all an indifferent thing to me to have you suppose me capable of feeling any unkindness towards You, when it is so foreign to my real Sentiments . . .

Was she aggrieved or troubled in conscience? If she did not know that Byron had shown to Annabella some of her letters, she could not know that Annabella had confided their contents to her mother, thereby reviving Judith's distrust and hostility of twenty-five years before.

Her conduct invited suspicion. On hearing reports that Byron and Annabella had parted, she had written on 5th February—not to her niece, but to Byron. Only on 10th February—the day after Hobhouse had heard "that the Melbournes are in arms against Lady Byron" —did she write to Judith to ask "the truth about ye reports that have been so prevalent about Ld. & Ly. Byron for this last week," and two days later—on the 12th—Hobhouse met her at Byron's, where she "abused Lady Noel violently." It was also on the 12th that she wrote to Sir Ralph, "I have been very much vexed at the reports which have been circulated respecting Annabella & I therefore wish very much to see you for ½ an Hour"—though Sir Ralph had then been twelve days in London. Sir Ralph called to see her on 13th February, and she wrote to Byron on the 14th, "if you wish to *see* me, or I can be of any use— I will go to you at any time . . . at all events I will call upon Mrs. Leigh tomorrow or next day."

She managed Sir Ralph as adroitly as usual: "My Brother was all kindness, & proved it by coming to me at a moment when he was oppressed & unhappy under these lamentable circumstances." She also successfully opened a correspondence with Annabella, writing on 17th February, "Your very kind Letter has given me ye greatest pleasure, & proves to me that I judged rightly in believing you would appreciate my motives for not intruding upon you at this time, to ye real cause, the fear of being troublesome." But she then lost her sense of tact in taking up a tone of admonition:

What ever passes between Husband & Wife ought to be sacred, the Strongest reasons can hardly justify a departure from this rule . . .

The relative Situation of Husband & Wife is so delicate so united & so blended together that ye World think it hardly possible that there should not be errors on both sides . . . I grieve more & more every day that this Separation had not been settled Amicably for while some people talk of Cruelty & ill Usage, others mention a bad Temper aggravated by pecuniary distress. Of course I take no part in all these differences & only wish as I told my Brother & he agreed with me that some agreement could be entered into—satisfactory to both parties, to avoid public exposure . . .

Annabella received this letter just as she was preparing to leave Kirkby for London in the hope of expediting an amicable settlement, and she replied tartly on 20th February:

I am very glad that you so fully enter into my opinion in deprecating legal measures *if possible*—and you must be surprised that Ld B. has so little consideration for his own character as not to have acceded before this time to the proposal of my Friends for a *private* & amicable arrangement. Repeated applications have been made to him for that purpose. You seem to be ignorant of this circumstance which I therefore wished to tell you. I have so much writing that you must excuse this short answer to your kind letter.

Lady Melbourne then maintained silence for a month, but Lady Caroline Lamb, having failed in her overture to Byron, was bent on making all possible mischief against him, and wrote a series of half-crazy letters to Annabella at the time of Lord Holland's mediation in the first week of March. Of Lady Melbourne she wrote:

She is infatuated about Lord B—she ever has been—& She is now more willing to think him Mad at times than wicked—besides which she has an idea that you have a *cold* character . . . therefore Dearest Lady Byron feel for yr Aunt—but never whilst you live let her think I have had any communication with you—burn these letters pray.

One other word—Lady Melbourne has a good & kind heart—it is spoilt no doubt & she is infatuated by the specious character Lord Byron has ever assumed in her presence.

She has also heard every thing against you & the cold letter you wrote offended her I think & estranged her further. Judge her not too harshly then for her personal sentiments but mistrust her also—only when sufficiently calm try & see her & say you will not for *his* sake tell—but that it is no peurile reason—above all let Lord Holland imagine that you know something which nothing but dispair will tempt you to tell—but seem assur'd of this—& it may do much good.[1]

[1] Moore wrote in his *Life of Byron*: ". . . his imagination supplied that dark colouring under which he so often disguised his true aspect from the world . . . I have known him more than once, as we have sat together after dinner, and he was, at the time, perhaps, a little under the influence of wine, to fall seriously into this sort of dark and self-accusing mood, and throw out hints of his past life with an air of gloom and mystery designed evidently to awaken curiosity and interest . . . I have little doubt that, to produce effect at the moment, there is hardly any crime so dark or desperate of which, in the excitement of thus acting upon the imaginations of others, he would not have hinted that he had been guilty; and it has sometimes occurred to me that the occult cause of his lady's separation from him, round which herself and her legal adviser have thrown such formidable mystery, may have been

Annabella did not reply to Lady Caroline's letters, nor did she attempt the suggested conciliation of Lady Melbourne. But on receiving her aunt's expostulation of 20th March, she abandoned her idea of "cutting" her, as she explained to her mother:

> I have been so hurried that I have not been able to tell you of a long letter of exculpation from Lady Melbourne, not occasioned by any communication from me. She *positively denies* having ever thought or expressed blame of my conduct, and certainly makes out a very fair statement . . .
>
> This letter of Lady Melbourne's would put me very much in the wrong if I were to cut her without further information—and I must appear to act still more unfairly by circulating such an opinion of her when she has authorized me & others in the most decided manner to contradict it. This matter is therefore still *suspended* . . .
>
> I must beg that you will hold your tongue. Lushington says the whole business might be undone, if Lord B. could trace any report of an unfavorable nature to us—my honor being pledged for silence till this arbitration is settled.
>
> The reports against Lord B. continue outrageous—and my conduct is much applauded in not endeavouring to encrease them . . .

She had already answered her aunt:

> The painful impression which you assure me is unfounded, was created in my mind by a concurrence of circumstances.
>
> First,—It had been much asserted, and confirmed to me by particular testimonies, that you expressed, or strongly implied, disapprobation of my conduct.
>
> Secondly—after the kindness of our correspondence when I was at Kirkby, you neither offered to visit me when I came here, nor explained the reasons of an appearance which I could not but think strange—and I was positively assured that you were then visiting Lord Byron, by a person who had one day been refused admission to him on that account. The mere fact of your calling at the house *in that peculiar situation of affairs*, might give a sanction to the opinions you disclaim.

---

nothing more, after all, than some imposture of this kind, some dimly hinted confession of undefined horrors, which, though intended by the relater but to mystify and surprise, the hearer so little understood him as to take in sober seriousness."

Besides this passage Hobhouse wrote in the margin of his copy of the book: "Something of this sort, certainly, unless, as Lord Holland told me, he tried to ——— her."

Lord Holland was a friend of Byron's—not of Annabella's—and in his capacity of mediator punctiliously refused to receive confidences likely to prejudice his judgment, as appears from Annabella's letter to Lushington of 5th March:

"I have seen Lord Holland, whom I found extremely kind . . . Finding him averse to hear any thing of causes, I was obliged to confine myself to the simplest outline of my motives."

Hobhouse remained always "in the dark" about Annabella's reasons for the separation, and discussing the matter with him at some subsequent time, Lord Holland may have confessed that he shared his mystification and dismissed the matter with a crude joke. Though inclined to accept humorous remarks "in sober seriousness," Hobhouse could not have interpreted this seriously, in view of his retort on 8th March to Wilmot's assurance that "it was no enormity" (see page 431).

. . . I did not mention the report till I found it so generally credited, that only your own authority could contradict it. I conceive that I shall act comfortably with your wishes by stating that authority to any one who may believe the contrary . . .

Lady Melbourne replied on 24th March that she could "certainly have no objection to your telling any of the persons who talk upon ye Subject to you, the explanation I have made":

I can not help saying yt whoever ye person was yt told you he was refused at ye door because I was with Ld B must have told a positive untruth, for ye only day I saw him Mr. Hobhouse was let in, so there could be no exclusion because I was there, & I have not seen him since.

But Surely dear Annabella it is ye first time yt any one was ever reckon'd unkind for not calling under such circumstances upon a friend of theirs, who had not inform'd them of their being in Town. In my humble opinion the unkindness was all on your Side, & your reporters must have made an impression on yr mind at that time or I am sure you would have written me a line . . .

She declared that, in a matrimonial dispute between Lord and Lady Lucan, she "was trusted by both, & never suspected by either of not acting fairly":

As to ye assertion yt I implied blame of yr conduct in my conversations, I deny it in ye Strongest manner, unless expressing for several days my disbelief of ye reports can be so construed; & I think that at that time I had good reasons for being so incredulous first from not hearing a word from Your family—Secondly from having seen Ld B when I first came to Town & from his having pass'd the greatest part of his Visit in talking of you, of your amiability, of his own happiness, & of his sincere attachment to You—& of his intention to go to Kirkby—it is not then Surprizing that four days after this Visit, when told of the report I should have sd, it can not be, it is impossible, it is an illnatur'd Story, & I remain'd under this conviction for several days, till George told me Mr. Kinnaird had heard the fact from Mr. Hobhouse . . . I never conversed on the Subject with any but my own family, & some particular friends, which with me are few in Number . . . I will call upon you to morrow or next day, & I hope You will have no objection to admit me . . .

Presumably Lady Melbourne called on Annabella, and made of that resumption of apparent cordiality an excuse to call also on Byron, for Annabella informed Lushington:

Lady Melbourne has called, and informed me of an *interview* she had with Lord B. about the letters of recommendation which he wished her to give him. I consider it as a proof that she has taken advantage of my facility in passing over the former offence—but I know of no remedy. William Lamb has been very kind indeed.

That Lady Melbourne was "*frightened*"—as Judith exultantly remarked —receives some endorsement from Hobhouse's recording on 28th March that she asked him "to get some letters of hers in Byron's possession burnt;" he promised to "hint the necessity of some such step," but on 26th April—the day after Byron's departure from England —he noted:

> Lady Melbourne is in a fright. She is sure that Lady Byron has seen some of her letters to Lord Byron, for Caroline Lambe has quoted some passages to her.

On 21st March Annabella wrote to her mother:

> I had a copy of Verses from his Lordship yesterday—very tender and so he talks of me to Every one.

Byron had written to her on the 20th:

> Dear Bell
>
> I send you the first thing I ever attempted to compose upon you—and, it may be, the last I shall compose at all. This may look at the present moment like an affectation—but it is not so.
>
> We are told that all barbarous nations are apt unwittingly to use a measured & figurative language—& that men nearest to a state of nature fall into poetical expression in saying what they think & feel.
>
> I do not know how this may be, but you know that "the lunatic the lover and the poet are of imagination all compact"—and though my conduct towards you has hitherto only indicated the two former—let me hope that the third will not add to your grievances against the first & second.
>
> Ever Yrs
> Byron

The verses enclosed were:

> Fare thee well! and if for ever,
> Still for ever, fare *thee well:*
> Even though unforgiving, never
> 'Gainst thee shall my heart rebel.
> Would that breast were bared before thee
> Where thy head so oft hath lain,
> While that placid sleep came o'er thee
> Which thou ne'er canst know again:
> Would that breast, by thee glanced over,
> Every inmost thought could show!
> Then thou wouldst at last discover
> 'Twas not well to spurn it so.
> Though the world for this commend thee—
> Though it smile upon the blow,

Even its praises must offend thee,
  Founded on another's woe:
Though my many faults defaced me,
  Could no other arm be found,
Than the one which once embraced me,
  To inflict a cureless wound?
Yet, oh yet, thyself deceive not—
  Love may sink by slow decay,
But by sudden wrench, believe not
  Hearts can thus be torn away:
Still thine own its life retaineth—
  Still must mine, though bleeding, beat;
And the undying thought which paineth
  Is—that we no more may meet.
These are words of deeper sorrow
  Than the wail above the dead;
Both shall live—but every morrow
  Wake us from a widowed bed.
And when thou would'st solace gather—
  When our child's first accents flow—
Wilt thou teach her to say "Father!"
  Though his care she must forego?
When her little hands shall press thee—
  When her lip to thine is pressed—
Think of him whose prayer shall bless thee—
  Think of him thy love *had* blessed!
Should her lineaments resemble
  Those thou never more may'st see,
Then thy heart will softly tremble
  With a pulse yet true to me.
All my faults perchance thou knowest—
  All my madness—none can know;
All my hopes—where'er thou goest—
  Wither—yet with *thee* they go.
Every feeling hath been shaken;
  Pride—which not a world could bow—
Bows to thee—by thee forsaken,
  Even my soul forsakes me now.
But 'tis done—all words are idle—
  Words from me are vainer still;
But the thoughts we cannot bridle
  Force their way without the will.
Fare thee well! thus disunited—
  Torn from every nearer tie—
Seared in heart—and lone—and blighted—
  More than this I scarce can die.

On 22nd March Hobhouse found "Byron in great spirits at the prospect of going abroad directly," and on the 25th—the day appointed by

Sir Samuel Shepherd for the arbitration—Annabella heard that "Lord B. is *really* preparing for his travels, as soon as this business is over." But later that day she received another letter from Byron:

> Dear Lady Byron—
>
> I am truly sorry to hear that you have been informed & falsely informed that—since the commencement of the proceedings which are presumed to be drawing towards a conclusion—I have spoken of you harshly or lightly. Neither are true—and no such terms, if such have been used, have originated from me—or been sanctioned by me. I have been out but little—indeed hardly at all—have seen no one with very few exceptions, but my own immediate relatives or connections—and to all these I can & do appeal for confirmation or refutation of what is here advanced. I might indeed assert—& could prove (but it matters little)—that the contrary has been the case.
>
> If in the violence & outrageous latitude of accusation which has been indulged beyond all example and all excuse in the present case by those who from friendship to you or aversion from me—or both—have thought proper to proclaim themselves assailants in your cause—any few (and but few they must have been) of those who have known me & judged less severely of me, have been provoked to repel accusation by imputation, and have endeavoured to find a defence for me, in crimination of you—I disavow their conduct, and disclaim themselves. I have interfered in no such proceedings—I have raised no party—nor even attempted it—neither should I have succeeded in such an attempt—the World has been with you throughout—the contest has been as unequal to me as it was undesired, and my name has been as completely blasted as if it were branded on my forehead.
>
> This may appear to you exaggeration—it is not so—there are reports which once circulated not even falsehood, or their most admitted & acknowledged falsehood, can neutralize which no contradiction can obliterate, nor conduct cancel. Such have since your separation been busy with my name—you are understood to say, "that you are not responsible for these—that they existed previous to my marriage, and at most were only *revived* by our differences." Lady Byron, they did not exist—but even if they had, does their *revival* give you no feeling?—are you calm in the contemplation of having (however undesignedly) raised up that which you never can allay?—& which but for you might have never arisen?—is it with perfect apathy you quietly look upon this resurrection of Infamy?

Declaring himself "very much hurt to hear that you could give credit to my having recourse to such unworthy means of defence as recrimination on you," he remarked that his first letter to Sir Ralph was "in itself sufficient to have rendered abortive such attempts had I been willing to use them." As "a parenthesis" he observed that Wilmot "should not have attempted the office of a mediator, after being biassed on one side—which he subsequently admitted that he was," before concluding:

Of whomever & whatever I have spoken, I have never blamed you—never attempted to condemn you.

The utmost I may have said, is—that I looked upon the proceedings as extreme and that I had no great faith in your affection for me. This however was only repeated by me to Augusta: and it was the conviction of *more* than myself—though *not* of *her*—on the contrary, she always combated the impression. It is not very wonderful that such a belief confirmed by events should exist in any mind—even in mine.

ever yrs. most affectly

B

P.S.—If you will name the person or persons who have attributed to me abuse of you, you will do an act of justice—& so will I. I shall at least know whom to avoid. Surely—there was bitterness enough in my portion without this addition.

He wrote again early on 26th March, enclosing three letters—from Lord Holland, Samuel Rogers, and Douglas Kinnaird—written at his request to deny that he had ever blamed Annabella in conversation with them. Rogers remembered Byron's saying "that wherever the Wrong lay, it did not lie with Lady B.—that Lady B. had been faultless in thought, word, & deed." Kinnaird "never heard you express yourself of Lady Byron but uniformly in the same tone of unquallified respect for her character & the motives of her conduct," and "the *only* act" he could remember "*ever* having heard you complain of . . . was, that her Ladyship used to keep a journal, in which your casual expressions & minutest actions were noted down." Lord Holland recalled that "you spoke of her judgment her veracity her character & her conduct with much respect," and in his capacity as impartial mediator felt it "but justice to Lady Byron to say that in the interview I had the honour of having with her she confirmed the impression which my slight acquaintance with her & your representations had given me & spoke on the painful subject on which I saw her with propriety & judgement professing great regard & interest for you."

Byron explained that he would have appealed to Hobhouse and Scrope Davies for similar assurances if they had not been out of town:

. . . to *these* alone in addition to the writers of the letters, with my sister, Sir Js. Burgess, & legal or medical advisers, have I ever spoken confidentially & without reserve on recent events, or discussed any topic connected with your name. The only levity almost with which I can charge myself is a trick upon Mrs. Clermont in sending to her "*a friendly hint*" with the address of a female author (writer of "the Bravo of Bohemia" for the stage) whom she mistook as I foresaw she would, for a female something else—& put herself or you to some expense in advertisements (which have been *carefully preserved* for the Nonce) to obtain further intelligence.[1]

[1] Byron had sent an anonymous note, postmarked 28th February, addressed to "Mrs. Clermont at Mivart's Hotel Lower Brook St." and containing the words "Miss Roberts No. 33, Orchard St Portman Square A friendly Hint."

> In the present poisoned state of your mind towards me—this may perhaps appear a heinous offence against that excellent woman Mrs. *Clermount* "Honest, Honest, Iago" but time will perhaps teach you that there was no great harm in making the person ridiculous who was endeavouring to render me wretched. I mean the woman mentioned—the person who was an attendant of your mother's, & subsequently your governess—then a spy—and subsequently a *false*-witness. I say *false*, as having misstated the evidence of another . . .

Having received from Annabella no acknowledgement of either of these letters, he wrote again later on the 26th to ask if the letter with the enclosures had been "delivered to *you*":

> One word in reply to say that in themselves—they were or were not satisfactory in this respect—would be a satisfaction to me—& surely not too much for you to accord.

He added an angry postscript:

> If these letters have been witheld (& I am told that they were taken from my servant by your father) I beg leave to say that I conceive such a proceeding will justify me in putting a stop to all proceedings for a final arrangement—to which as far as it has gone, I regard myself as strictly adherent—& bound to adhere.

Annabella now replied immediately through the medium of Augusta, to whom she wrote on the evening of the 26th:

> I do not know if it is from the misapprehension of part of the conversation between you & me yesterday that some letters which I have since recd. from Ld B. have arisen. The testimonies which he has sent me . . . are quite unnecessary, as I had not accused him of speaking of me in the manner which is denied.
>
> His letter was delivered to me immediately by my father.
>
> I beg you to communicate this note . . .

Unluckily, though Sir Samuel Shepherd did not announce his decision till 27th March, he had already intimated to Hanson what his decision would be, as Annabella heard from Augusta and reported to her mother on the 26th, "I understand from the opposite party that Sir S. Shepherd is disposed to decide in my favour—and that Hanson is absolutely *à la mort*." Hence, enclosing Byron's last letter, she wrote to Lushington on the evening of the 26th:

> I beg you to observe the P.S. as containing, in my opinion, the proof of a disposition to evade the contract. If Ld B. constitutes himself the judge of what would justify such a measure, he will easily find *another* excuse.

I answered to Mrs. Leigh, and send you a copy—it appeared to me that the less said the better . . .

I am convinced that Lord B. intends to go abroad before he has signed the articles.

Supposing that we should know of his preparations for going immediately, what measure is there to be adopted? Would it not be advisable to stamp the agreement, as you said was feasible, in order to give it legal force?

This trouble may be traced to Lady Melbourne. Only she could have confirmed Byron's feeling of "no great faith" in Annabella's affection for him. Fresh from reading her protestations that she had never sided with Byron, Annabella had seen Augusta and apparently asserted her knowledge of reports originating from Lady Melbourne and Lady Caroline. Augusta had related the conversation so that Byron conceived himself attacked—as Hobhouse noted when he called on Byron on the 28th and found, "There has been another fracas between him and Lady Byron—She accused him to Mrs. Leigh of encouraging his friends to abuse her."

Apparently Byron's pride still demanded insistence that Annabella was acting under the influence of others, for, according to Hobhouse, Byron actually sent Hanson to tell Sir Ralph that "he would be off all bargain" if his letters were not delivered. He was evidently encouraged in this belief even by Augusta, who, meeting Selina Doyle with Annabella at dinner with the Wilmots on Monday the 25th—when presumably the unfortunate conversation took place—offended her by not shaking hands with her and then told Annabella, "She did think Miss Doyle had been too forward in her interference." She wrote to Annabella from St. James's Palace on the evening of Wednesday the 27th:

I felt *particularly* anxious to have found you today, & am now almost sorry I did not leave a note as I had once thought of doing, & was prevented partly by hurry & partly thinking it better to *speak* than *write*. After I left you yesterday I saw B—— by whom I was questioned on many points—*some* I evaded answering, others I answered as little in detail as possible. But *one* thing I did repeat to him, & I really think it was but justice to do so—*as far as I did it*—which was, that you seemed to have an impression that your *late* conduct had been mentioned by *him* & *his friends* in injurious terms as springing from "*coldheartedness* & *want of affection*" towards him. I told him all I had said in his justification.

He appeared much vexed at your having such an impression & when I saw him again in the Eveg, informed me he had in consequence written 4 letters—one to you, ye rest to Ld Holland Mr. Kinnaird & Mr. Rogers, being those besides Mr. Davies & Hobhouse with whom he had principally communicated on this sad subject.

The letters you have seen. *I have* NOT—so am ignorant of their contents except from his own acct of them, & the inferences I may draw from the note I've just received from you. He *may* have *mis-apprehended* & I daresay the little I did say (for it fell very short of my *own apprehension* of yr impressions) has been magnified greatly in his imagination—but it is a natural feeling surely that he should wish to defend himself on such a point—& tho' I must confess I have very little hope, from the observations I have *lately* made, that any thing *he* can say will alter yr opinions, yet it was but *just* & *fair* in mine to give him at least a chance of undeceiving you.

You well know, I have never *screened* him where I thought him wrong, but you will allow for my anxiety that he should not be accused UN-*deservedly*. Pray forgive this long answer to yr note but I should not sleep in peace till I had given you some explanation. I will call tomorrow for ye chance of finding you at home & disengaged . . . B. read your note to me before I saw it, which I mention as you desired me to communicate it.

On Wednesday the 27th Sir Samuel Shepherd delivered his decision "that Lord Byron should *Now* bind himself on the event of Lady Noel's death to appoint an Arbitrator who together with an Arbitrator then to be appointed by Lady Byron should decide whether any and what portion of that Estate should be secured to the sole and separate use of Lady Byron during the life of Lord Byron." In sending the decision to Wharton, he wrote:

I beg to express that the grounds of my decision have not been founded upon any thing which can be supposed to reflect upon or distrust the honor of Lord Byron. I simply considered whether that which I have awarded was fit to be done, and having once decided that, I awarded that Lord Byron should bind himself to perform it; because I think it desirable that every man should bind himself to do that which is fitting to be done (if he be capable of performing it) where the interests of others depend upon his acts. It is upon a general principle therefore that I have made this award.

"I never thought Sir S. Shepherd's opinion could be otherwise," wrote Hobhouse. But Byron must have felt the decision as salt in his wounds, and he vented his brooding resentment on Mrs. Clermont in writing "A Sketch from Private Life":

. . .[1]
With eye unmoved, and forehead unabashed,
She dines from off the plate she lately washed.
Quick with the tale, and ready with the lie,
The genial confidante, and general spy—
Who could, ye gods! her next employment guess—
An only infant's earliest governess!
She taught the child to read, and taught so well,
That she herself, by teaching, learned to spell.

[1] See page 72 for the first six lines.

An adept next in penmanship she grows,
As many a nameless slander deftly shows:
What she had made the pupil of her art,
None know—but that high Soul secured the heart,
And panted for the truth it could not hear,
With longing breast and undeluded ear.
Foiled was perversion by that youthful mind,
Which Flattery fooled not, Baseness could not blind,
Deceit infect not, near Contagion soil,
Indulgence weaken, nor Example spoil,
Nor mastered Science tempt her to look down
On humbler talents with a pitying frown,
Nor Genius swell, nor Beauty render vain,
Nor Envy ruffle to retaliate pain,
Nor Fortune change, Pride raise, nor Passion bow,
Nor Virtue teach austerity—till now.
Serenely purest of her sex that live,
But wanting one sweet weakness—to forgive;
Too shocked at faults her soul can never know,
She deems that all could be like her below:
Foe to all vice, yet hardly Virtue's friend,
For Virtue pardons those she would amend.

After this somewhat fulsome flattery of Annabella, the poem concentrated in spleen against Mrs. Clermont, "this hag of hatred":

Skilled by a touch to deepen Scandal's tints
With all the kind mendacity of hints.

Thinking that the Solicitor General's award must settle the progress of the separation, Annabella prepared to leave London for Kirkby, and wrote a note of thanks to Lord Holland for his "kindness and consideration," hoping to acknowledge at some future time "to Lady Holland and yourself the obligations which I have received from both." But she received evidence of the efficiency of the Whitehall telegraph service in a note from Lady Caroline Lamb:

> I wish to see you one moment before you leave Town—but I should like it not to be known. Wm. will leave me & fetch me—any Evening after dark if that would suit you—I should like 8—or 9—if it did not appear inconvenient. I wish to say 2 words to you—that is all . . .

She was not gratified with the drama of flitting to a clandestine assignation under cover of darkness, but Annabella agreed to see her at Mrs. George Lamb's house, where she had much more than two words to say.

She began by asking for the return of her letters. Annabella replied that she would seal them up—which she duly did, along with her own notes on their conversation. Asked to explain the allusions in her letters, Lady Caroline "became greatly agitated;" though "bound by a solemn promise not to reveal those secrets," she would have done so "before my marriage in order to save me from so dreadful a fate, . . . but his protestations that he would never renew such crimes had prevailed upon her to be silent." Annabella then characteristically told her "that I conceived *her* promise was released by the infringement of *his*, and that she might now redeem all by giving me this knowledge, if as important as she signified to the preservation of my Child." So Lady Caroline confessed, "with an unfeigned degree of agitation":

> That from the time Mrs. L. came to Bennet St. in the year 1813—Lord B. had given her various intimations of a criminal intercourse between them—but that for some time he spoke of it in a manner which did not enable her to fix it upon Mrs. L. thus—"Oh I never knew what it was to love before—there is a woman I love so passionately—she is with child by me, and if a daughter it shall be called *Medora*"—that his avowals of this incestuous intercourse became bolder—till at last she said to him one day, "I could believe it of *you*—but not of *her*."

At this "his vanity appeared piqued to rage," and he assured her "that the seduction had not given him much trouble—that it was soon accomplished—and she was very willing." When Lady Caroline still declined to believe, he showed her some of Augusta's letters; some contained expressions of remorse, such as, "Oh B. if we loved one another as we did in childhood—*then* it was innocent," but in others "there were crosses + + in such positions as could not be mistaken."

> Since *that* avowal—Ly C L. never suffered any intimacy with Ld B. though she had before been prevailed on to forgive "other & worse crimes."

She then went on to declare that Byron had confessed to "the practice of unnatural crime"; he had "perverted" three of his schoolfellows, and had subsequently "corrupted" his *protégé* Rushton. She "did not believe that he had committed this crime since his return to England, though he practised it unrestrictedly in Turkey." After this confession he had threatened her "in the most terrific manner, reminding her of Caleb Williams, and saying that now she knew his secret, he would persecute her like Falkland." The reference to *Caleb Williams* must have reminded Annabella of the same threat expressed to her at Halnaby; she related, "I almost disavowed the belief of Incest—appeared so much agitated by the other subject that I suspect Ly C L. discovered her statement to be only a confirmation of my own opinions."

At the end of the interview, "Before I went, I repeated in presence of Mrs. G. Lamb—that I had declared *no* belief." But on her return to Mivart's she wrote immediately to Lushington:

> The result of my interview this morning was, I am most concerned to say, to change my strong impression relative to the 1st & 2nd reports, into *absolute* conviction.
>
> You will observe in Mr. Kinnaird's letter a passage in which Lord Byron is said to have asserted what is absolutely false about a Journal, which, as you have heard me mention, I did not keep.
>
> Ought not this to be stated to Mr. Kinnaird as it might invalidate other misrepresentations of Lord Byron's?
>
> Mrs. Leigh seems to be deeply involved on all sides. . . .
>
> Lord B. put the verses to me into the hands of Murray the bookseller *to show.*

For this last item of information she was also indebted to Lady Caroline Lamb, who sent her a copy of a protest she had written to Murray:

> I am surprised & hurt at finding that you have shewn Ld Byrons verses to a number of people . . . for God sake do any thing sooner than try & awaken one spark of interest for that Man—it is a poor paltry attempt to hide cruelty & wickedness & throw the fault on One whom yourself acknowledge He dares not blame . . .

Lushington replied to Annabella the same day:

> I return you Lord B's letter with the inclosures & entirely agree with you in thinking any reply *to him* useless. Indeed the danger of misrepresentation is so great, that it is scarcely possible to make any communication by letter or otherwise without almost a certainty of perversion . . .
>
> I have even some doubt as to negativing to Mr. Kinnaird the untruth respecting the journal. He is a very prejudiced friend of Lord B's, considering as I believe that the friendship gives him consequence . . . I believe that if you were to discredit Lord B: in twenty particulars detailed to Mr. K: you would in no degree alter the conduct of the latter . . .
>
> I hardly know what to say as to the effect of your interview this morning, except most cordially to congratulate you upon your final escape from all proximity to, or intercourse with such contamination. I cannot however avoid hinting a suspicion which has repeatedly come across my mind, that many of these letters, verses, & efforts to keep up a communication with you, are intended to draw you if possible into a correspondence of some sort; which would be argued as a species of disclaimer of all such imputations. The shewing the verses by the hands of Murray is a branch of this plan.

Annabella gave no indication of having heard such serious charges against her husband when she wrote with satisfaction to her mother next day:

Mrs. G. Lamb's friendship has been most active and zealous. To tell you a great secret—I met Lady C. Lamb at her house yesterday, by the wish of all my advisers, to receive from her some information which may be *very* important. Nothing could exceed her devoted interest for me—or William's, who has called several times, and has uniformly expressed the feelings of a gentleman & a friend—determined to support me, if it were against all his connections.

Then the Wilmots have been most kind—and judicious. So you have great reason to be satisfied—even with *ma Tante*, who is *now* become my panegyrist!

Her departure from London had to be delayed for signing the deed of separation, which was being drawn up by a conveyancer appointed by Sir Samuel Shepherd, but there was also another reason. Having been consulted on the subject of the child's custody, Henry Brougham delivered an opinion conveyed to Annabella on 29th March:

Mr. Brougham's compts to Messrs Wharton & Ford & he considers, that if Lord B. were to apply for a habeas Corpus to bring up the body of his child, and if upon the return to the writ the tender age of the child were set forth, the father could only obtain possession of it by offering to take back the mother—but if that offer were made, Mr. B. apprehends, that Lady B. could not retain possession of the child from the father.

Either this expedient did not occur to Hanson, or if it did, Byron refused to exercise it. Annabella wrote to Lushington on the 29th:

Will you at your leisure consider if an application ought not to be made to Lord B. before he goes abroad respecting the Child? The consequence of such an application I foresee to be—first—if he resigned his paternal power I should be *entirely* relieved from the future possibility of adducing painful evidence against him. Secondly—if he refused my request, I should have cause & justification for seeking the means of Security in that respect.

Lushington's comment inspired the original motive for Annabella's persecution of Augusta:

An application to Lord Byron respecting the Child requires very serious consideration, & I doubt very much whether it would be adviseable to bring forward this subject at all, until the Articles are actually signed. It will then be a question, whether Lord B: will remain in England long enough to bring the matter to a conclusion. I am fully aware of & duly appreciate the great advantages which would result from a resignation of his paternal power by Lord B: & think the end if attained worth any exertions & almost any sacrifice. The uncontrolled permanent possession of the child without any chance of future dispute would relieve you from a great anxiety, because even the remotest probability of being disturbed in this particular gives cause for anxious anticipation; and where an evil is possible, the mind cannot at all times coolly calculate the degree of improbability but is disturbed by undefined apprehensions of the future. The other reasons stated in your note are also exceedingly strong & render the object most desireable. But is it to be obtained? By what motive can Lord B's mind be influenced to the adoption of such a measure, to the concession of all power over you? By no motive I apprehend but fear, & how far that can be brought to operate appears to me very difficult to form an opinion.

Lushington took two days to consider this opinion, his letter being dated 31st March, but Annabella had already acted promptly on her own account. She had devised her Statement *AL* on 14th March to enable her meetings with Augusta and so to discountenance the rumours about her, but consideration of Augusta's reputation had now to be abandoned, for, if Byron proposed to entrust the child to his sister's care, it would then be necessary to protest that Augusta was an unfit person for its custody. Ironically she used Byron's recent letters as a pretext for avoiding Augusta when writing to Mrs. Wilmot on 29th March:

The difficulties and vexations which have, as you know, lately attended my direct intercourse with Augusta, who has been equally embarassed by questions in consequence, make me request that you will be the medium of a communication that appears absolutely necessary.

I must confess to her that under my present feelings I experience the *most* painful effects from our meetings, nor can I suppose them less distressing to her. In requesting, therefore, that she will spare me these agitations, which I find my health and spirits equally unable to support, I feel that I do not require from her a Sacrifice which I should regret to ask.

She enclosed this with a covering letter to Wilmot:

I hope you will approve the purport of the accompanying letter to Mrs. Wilmot, which is intended to convey to Augusta, with the least possible pain, the line of conduct that now appears necessary—for whatever a solitary moment of indignation may have prompted me to express, my permanent feeling will always be to soften, as far as my principles will permit, the misery that awaits her—and in regard to any influence which you may kindly allow to my wishes, I beg you to remember what I now express on this Subject.

The last sentence indicates why most of her correspondents were careful to preserve her letters; there was usually some such admonition that might be required for future reference.

Writing on 2nd April to inform Annabella that "This morning I received from Mr. Wharton the Draft Deed of Separation as settled by Mr. Butler," Lushington added:

The termination of intercourse with Mrs. L: gives me great satisfaction; as soon as the necessity for continuing upon terms ceased, every motive conspired to induce a speedy cessation of personal intercourse.

The next day Byron wrote to Augusta, who that day removed from Piccadilly on the arrival of Hobhouse to stay:

Dearest A——

As Lady B. is much better, you must write immediately about the trustees and request as a personal favour to me that *Doyle* be *not* nominated one for the reasons I gave & am prepared to give. I do not say this as an excuse to make impediments, as I am prepared to sign the articles in any case—but I beg to have this request urged—& *now* urged. It is very odd you have had no answer by Mrs. W[ilmot].

Augusta accordingly wrote on Thursday the 4th:

My dearest Annabella

I am very sorry to give you *any* trouble, but I believe *my* undertaking to send you the enclosed (just received) may be the means most likely to cause you the *least*—which is some comfort to me.

I mentioned the subject of it to Mrs. Wilmot when she gave me yr letter to her. I dined yesterday with her, but as she did not give me any answer I concluded there was none to give—& there are many subjects which I don't feel *at present* disposed to touch upon *unnecessarily*. You are aware of B's prejudice against *military men*. I don't know how far Col. D[oyle] may be considered as one, but that will account to you for his request.

I hope you hear you are much better & am ever

Yr. most affecte

A.L.

It may be supposed that Byron was less punctual than Annabella in passing on information to advisers, for not till 13th April did Hobhouse note in his journal:

Ld. Byron desired Mrs. Leigh to state that Colonel Doyle should not be one of the trustees to the separation. She did in a kind letter—and received a pencil note directed to her with only these words "Lord Byron is informed that the trustees appointed are Dr. Lushington and Mr. Ridley Colborne."

This has terminated, I believe, all correspondence between *My dearest Augusta* and *My dearest Annabella!!* Such are female friendships!

It cannot be supposed that Annabella, with her calculating eye for contingencies, did not realise how the interruption of her intercourse with Augusta, two days after her interview with Lady Caroline, would be interpreted by those who knew of that interview. Nor is it likely that Lady Caroline concealed from many of her acquaintance that the interview had taken place. After the interview—as Lushington foresaw—she tried to keep up communication with Annabella:

> Do remember that you have to oppose 2 of the greatest Hypocrites & most corrupted Wretches that were ever suffered to Exist on this earth—to do I believe all the mischief they can—the beautiful verses I consider as a cowardly attempt to make you appear barbarous & himself injured—there will fall a vengeance upon them for their treatment of you—soon or late . . .

Forgetting that she had urged Annabella to conciliate her aunt, she wrote again:

> I request you to take most particular care what you say to Lady M—you may ruin me if you chuse by shewing any one on earth this letter but you will ruin yourself if you are not extremely guarded. Take a high tone Seem sure of every thing but tell her nothing—& for God sake do not name me.
>
> I think it perfectly useless to trust her—*his* influence over her is such that I feel secure *now* nothing can shake it—pray take care—above all let her not imagine What you know—for were you ever to confide it she would only try & disprove it. I fear nothing can change her—but pray be kind should she call.

Annabella was already warned against Lady Melbourne by her mother, who wrote on 30th March, "*beware* of *La Tante*—when She is *most smooth* She is *most dangerous*."

Augusta seems to have had less regard for her own reputation than for Byron's welfare, writing to Hodgson on 28th March:

> B. talks of taking a young Physician recommended to him by Sr. W. Knighton as a travelling companion—his health is much improved but requires care—& his spirits are dreadfully depressed at times. As for Ly B she is indeed but the shadow of herself! I have seen her frequently of late but I conclude she will soon leave Town. I fear there is only unhappiness in store for both.
>
> I think of being in Town some time longer—at least till next week—particularly if the Royal Nuptials should then take place—the Household being *under orders* for the occasion. I *wish* to stay *as long* as I *can* on my dear B's account . . .[1]

A few days later she wrote to Hobhouse:

> Do not forsake your most unfortunate friend—if you do, he is lost—he has so few *sincere* friends and well judging ones. I can never express what I feel about him, but believe me, I am grateful from my heart for your friendship and friendly forbearance towards his infirmities, of whatever

[1] Princess Charlotte's engagement to Prince Leopold of Saxe-Coburg had been announced on 14th March.

kind they may be. His *mind* makes him the most unhappy of human beings. Let us hope it may not always be so. God bless you. I thank you for all your kindness . . .

Still pursued by duns, besides being persecuted by scandal and oppressed by the business of the separation, Byron cannot have been easy to live with. The loyal Hobhouse refrained even from confiding to his journal such tiffs with Byron as that which must have preceded Augusta's letter. On 9th April he and Byron dined with Scrope Davies, Lord Kinnaird, and Sir Francis Burdett; at midnight he left the others to go to the Duchess of Somerset's, where there were "great enquiries" for the "Fare thee well" and "A Sketch from Private Life," which Byron had caused to be printed—"unadvisedly," Hobhouse thought—for private circulation. Returning later, he found "the party still at it—broiled bones, punch, and a fracas succeeded which I need not set down." They sat up "till six in the morning and had a scene at home."

Poor fellow, he came into my room next morning to ask how I was. He was very sorry and so was I, but our regrets originated from different causes.

Hobhouse was frequently proved right in his judgments. He had been proved right in thinking Byron ill-advised by Hanson over the matter submitted to the Solicitor General's arbitration; he was to be proved right in disliking the choice of Dr. Polidori as the physician to go abroad with Byron; he was right in regarding as ill-advised the circulation of "Fare thee well" and "A Sketch." Mrs. George Lamb wrote to Annabella:

I am desired by the publisher of these verses to send them you, and to tell you that as he is obliged to publish them, he does not like that they should be seen by you without some apology from him. He says he could not as Ld. B's bookseller refuse to publish them, but hopes you will believe that he did so with pain & reluctance. I think I never read any thing so artful & abominable . . . If *he* publishes it releases you from all obligations of silence.

Lady Liddell wrote that Princess Mary and Lady Liverpool, the Prime Minister's wife, had spoken "of *your* conduct in terms of pity & admiration":

So do all GOOD People & indeed the abhorrence so generally expressed against him by *that class*, forms a striking contrast with the cold and measured sentences of those who *dare* not take his part, but I suppose have a sort of fellow feeling for his misconduct. I must however say that Lady *M*[elbourne] whatever she MAY have said, has *now* changed her tone. . . . Lady Harrington who is violent against Lord B. told me She had heard of the lines he had written to you—I suppose they will soon appear in the Newspapers & I am sorry to say I fear they were only written for a bad purpose . . .

Annabella wrote to her mother:

I have just seen a copy of Verses by his Lordship, which, with the others, are to be printed. These last are *blackguard* beyond belief—nothing but praise of me, but a *little aspersion on your Character*. How do you like this My Lady? . . .

Mrs. Clermont is the object of the Satire, as the confidante of your infidelities. It is very absurd . . .

On 8th April, accompanied by Hobhouse and Augusta, Byron attended a fashionable gathering at Lady Jersey's. Hobhouse recorded only that General Flahault introduced them to Benjamin Constant and his wife, but Annabella informed her mother:

Lady Jersey had a party a few nights ago, at which *he* appeared to the surprise of the Company. Mrs. G. Lamb cut both him & Mrs. Leigh—Brougham & some other Gentlemen, *him*. Lady Jersey has since called upon me. So have many people—Lady Derby three or four times.

. . . Mrs. Ellison, whose kindness has been most zealous, says that now one has an opportunity of knowing who are bad & good—that there never was a question which disclosed morals so decisively. *Exceptions*—Lady Holland & Lady Besborough—*pour moi*. Indeed I don't know any body except the Piccadilly crew of blackguards who is *avowedly* against me . . .

This expression of triumph was a reaction from a feeling of despondency. Hanson was fighting a rearguard action to delay the signing of the deed of separation, objecting to details of the financial provisions. His objections were addressed to Wharton, passed thence to Lushington, back to Wharton, thence to the conveyancer, and back again to Hanson through Wharton. Confident that Hanson could always be defeated by appeal to the Solicitor General—as eventually happened—Lushington went out of town. Deprived of his immediate support, Annabella took fright on hearing that "Fare thee well" was being circulated—she was perhaps shaken by Lady Caroline Lamb's remark, "His verses are sure to affect many"—and wrote to Lushington to ask if, as "The Tide of feeling" turned against her, she should circulate the declaration, asked for by Hobhouse, that she had authorised none of the defamatory reports about Byron. Her letter pursued Lushington on his travels, and it was not till 13th April that he reassured her of popular opinion and advised against her use of the declaration:

Until that Declaration be given to Mr. Hobhouse (which I think should not be done until he asks for it), the contents should not be made known by you, & if afterwards used, it should be with great caution. The impression that you gave a declaration, which did *not* clear up Lord B's character & that you afterwards used it *against him* (for tho' circulated for your own protection only, such must be its operation to protect you,) ought I think to be avoided for perhaps such conduct might be distorted into a species of double dealing. Honestly I would rather you were deemed a Pharisee for the next 3 months (at least six weeks longer than is possible) than that there should be a shadow of ground for impeaching the candour of your conduct in the mind of any unprejudiced person.

Witnessing Mrs. George Lamb's cutting of Augusta, Byron may well have felt deeper pain than ever before during these distressful weeks, and he wrote his tribute to her devotion in "Stanzas to Augusta":

When Fortune changed—and Love fled far,
  And Hatred's shafts flew thick and fast,
Thou wert the solitary star
  Which rose and set not to the last.
Oh! blest be thine unbroken light!
  That watched me as a Seraph's eye,
And stood between me and the night,
  For ever shining sweetly nigh.

. . . .

Still may thy Spirit dwell on mine,
  And teach it what to brave or brook—
There's more in one soft word of thine
  Than in the world's defied rebuke.
Thou stood'st, as stands a lovely tree,
  That still unbroke, though gently bent,
Still waves with fond fidelity
  Its boughs above a monument.
The winds might rend—the skies might pour,
  But there thou wert—and still wouldst be
Devoted in the stormiest hour
  To shed thy weeping leaves o'er me.
But thou and thine shall know no blight,
  Whatever fate on me may fall;
For Heaven in sunshine will requite
  The kind—and thee the most of all.

Annabella must have recognised in these stanzas a depth of feeling—of gratitude and tenderness—far beyond the flattery of herself in "Fare thee well". She never forgave Augusta for having inspired what she had been unable to inspire, though this opportunity for Augusta to be kind had been created by herself denying kindness. Thirty-five years later, in the year of Augusta's death, she was to exclaim in an agony of self-deception, "He *must* have come, had he lived, to the belief that *from first to last*, I had been his only truly devoted friend."

The time of Augusta's confinement was approaching; preparations for the royal wedding could no longer afford an excuse for remaining in London. Hobhouse—who had been staying with Byron since 3rd April—went into the country for the day on Easter Sunday, 14th April, so "that Byron might have a free leave taking of his sister." When Augusta had left him, Byron wrote to Annabella:

I have just parted from Augusta—almost the last being you had left me to part with—& the only unshattered tie of my existence—wherever I may go—& I am going far—you & I can never meet again in this world—nor in the next—let this content or atone. If any accident occurs to me, be kind to her,—if she is then nothing—to her children:—

Some time ago—I informed you that with the knowledge that any child of ours was already provided for by other & better means—I had made my will in favour of her & her children—as prior to my marriage:—this was not done in prejudice to you for we had not then differed—& even this is useless during your life by the settlements. I say therefore—be kind to her & hers—for never has she acted or spoken otherwise towards you—she has ever been your friend—this may seem valueless to one who has now so many:—be kind to her, however, & recollect that though it may be advantage to you to have lost your husband—it is sorrow to her to have the waters now, or the earth hereafter, between her & her brother.

She is gone—I need hardly add that of this request she knows nothing—your late compliances have not been so extensive, as to render this an encroachment:—I repeat it—(for deep resentments have but *half* recollections) that you once did promise me thus much—do not forget it—nor deem it cancelled—it was not a vow . . .

He enclosed a ring for his daughter and asked that news of her should be sent to him through Augusta. The letter was delivered by Mrs. Fletcher, who told Hobhouse that, on receiving it, Annabella said, "I shall answer this," went out to do so, but—as Mrs. Fletcher believed—met Mrs. Clermont, and then returned to say, "this requires no answer."

Annabella did not mention the letter when writing to her mother next day about "my dinner on Saturday at Mr. Wilmot's to meet Brougham—who has been my warmest champion throughout":

After dinner I took him into the next room to have some converse in private . . . He showed every proper & honorable feeling, and gave me his opinion on several points. The public feeling has been still more turned against Lord B. by the publication of his verses in the Champion of yesterday—and some comments were added to expose the duplicity of their author—by which a wonderful effect has been produced. So Lady Granville (ci devant Ly Harriet L-Gower)[1] has told me—She came this

[1] Lady Henrietta Elizabeth (Harriet or Hary-O) Cavendish (1785–1862), younger daughter of Georgiana Duchess of Devonshire, married in 1809 Lord Granville Leveson-Gower (1773–1846), created Viscount Granville, 1815—formerly the lover of her aunt, Lady Bessborough (see page 144).

morning, having particularly requested, by Mrs. G. Lamb, that she might wait upon me. She is a very good woman I believe.

The kindness of the Wilmots is great. He has written some very good lines, which he means to publish—in answer to the "Fare thee well."

Brougham told me that the indignation of Sir Samuel Romilly at Mrs. Clermont's Satire was so great, that he broke off a conference with Sir Arthur Pigott & Mr. Brougham to express it.

I really expect the Signature tomorrow. If it should not be given, it will be of no ultimate Consequence to me as the Chancellor would enforce the performance of the written agreement, and [it] would be the most glaring intended violation of a contract that any man ever risked.

According to the painter Haydon, it was Brougham who contrived the publication of the poems in *The Champion*, a struggling newspaper edited by John Scott, who subsequently indulged in sensation-mongering once too often and died as the result of a duel with a friend of John Gibson Lockhart's. The *Morning Post*—which had already flattered Annabella in a paragraph headed *Recent Separation in High Life*—commented on 17th April:

Lord Byron—A Correspondent observes that it was never more necessary to prove how easy it is to write artful verses, to parody sentiment, and affect feeling.

Lord Byron's new second Poem entitled *A Sketch from Private Life* is a base and unmanly attack upon a poor but worthy woman, who holds the dependent situation of Governess, and if possible, by its vulgar and insolent abuse, degrades him even still more than the gross hypocrisy, and disgusting affectation of feeling, by which his universally execrated Stanzas of *Fare thee well* are so particularly Characterized. The only Crime of this dastardly assailed poor woman appears to be, that having by her merits advanced herself from a low state of servitude to be an immediate attendant upon her Mistress, she remains faithful to her amiable Patroness. Lord Byron has indeed fallen never again to rise . . .

The *Morning Post* was then the principal rival of London's most popular newspaper, the *Morning Chronicle*, which on the same day published a defence of Byron. This was sponsored by Hobhouse, who, annoyed by the publication of the poems in *The Champion* with its "violent abuse" of Byron, wrote a paragraph which he took to James Perry, the editor of the *Chronicle*. Perry remarked that "he should add something of his own," and Hobhouse noted in his journal on the 17th, "The Chronicle's additional paragraph with a vengeance!—charge of conspiracy against Lord Byron's *domestic peace*." Annabella announced to her mother the same day:

Sir Ralph is gone with Doyle to require from Mr. Perry the contradiction of a paragraph in the Morning Chronicle respecting the "atrocious conspiracy against his Lordship's domestic peace."

All the other papers are pour moi—I send you the Champion.

At the same time she wrote to Lady Melbourne:

> The circumstances of my present Situation having, to my great regret, become the subject of the *most* public discussion, I must authorize my friends to contradict the gross falsehoods thus circulated. In regard to that of my having acted under any influence whatever, I declare that I did not admit from any person the slightest interference in regard to my Separation, until my own determination was irrevocably formed from my *personal experience* & *positive knowledge* of the facts that necessitated that measure.
>
> It cannot be necessary to make such a declaration to *you*, but you will have the satisfaction in being enabled to give so positive a refutation of this falsehood to others.

She wrote in similar terms to her mother's old friend, Mrs. Gally Knight, and to Byron's Aunt Sophia.

On 18th April Perry published an "edited" version of Sir Ralph's contradiction, saying only that "*he knew* of no conspiracy." When Sir Ralph immediately demanded publication of a letter stating that "not only *he knew* of no conspiracy, but there *is none* against Lord Byron," Perry consulted with Hobhouse, who warned him that, as the letter asserted that "Lady Byron did every thing by her own wish & inclination," its publication "might bring upon Lord Byron's friends the necessity of stating *his* case to the public." Perry accordingly wrote a long letter to Sir Ralph:

> . . . I should have no hesitation in publishing it as you desire, if I were not morally certain that it would lead inevitably to the publication of the whole correspondence from Lady Byron's first letter dated from Kirkby to the last document prepared for legal proceedings if necessary.
>
> I stop therefore for one day to enable you to reflect on the propriety of pushing the matter to this extremity. And in the meantime I beg leave to say that I published the result of the long conversation that passed between us, and not the details from motives of the most anxious concern for all parties . . .
>
> I did not wish to aggravate the unhappy difference by going into all the conversation that took place . . .
>
> If I had gone into the whole detail I must have stated the question put to you—Why no reply was given to the application made to your family to specify the charges against Lord B. that he might have an opportunity of vindicating himself from calumnies so industriously propagated against him. To this you answered that Lady Byron acted in this by the advice of Dr. Lushington! What! A Wife tears herself from the bosom of her Husband and acts by the cold caution of a Lawyer rather than by the dictates of her own heart! . . .

The letter indicates how widespread were rumours about the possible causes of the separation.

Doubtless Perry visualised a big scoop of sensational copy, but Sir Ralph merely offered his letter of contradiction to *The Courier*, the most prominent London evening paper, which published it on 19th April.

Immediately on seeing *The Courier*, Hobhouse went the same evening to Doyle and announced that, as publication seemed to be "the wish of the other party," Byron "offered to release Lady Byron from her signature and to go into court." Doyle replied "that nothing was further from the wish of the other party than any publicity—although they were quite prepared and not afraid of anything—that a court would be better than partial publication—that Lady Byron had letters from Mrs. Leigh and others, all of which would be made public—but that the whole family deprecated such a step—that Sir Ralph had interfered with Mr. Perry merely on account of his own honour." Hobhouse retorted that Perry had "merely tried to save a calumniated man;" becoming "a little angry," he "said that my friend had suffered from the basest domestic treachery."

On the 20th, when Perry published Sir Ralph's letter, Hobhouse wrote to Doyle, asking him to persuade Sir Ralph "not to proceed in his appeal to the newspapers." He was somewhat shaken when he dined at Lansdowne House and found "the run against Perry." Lord Holland asked him, "Why couldn't you stop our friend Perry's pen?" Lord Grey "did not seem pleased with it," and though Lord Kinnaird defended Perry, he was "overborne" by Lady Holland. Returning to Byron's, he felt so disturbed that he walked to Maida Vale to insist on Leigh Hunt's being "delicate" on the subject in *The Examiner*. He did not trouble to read the "violent attack" in *The Champion* on Sunday; when he was blamed by Perry a few days later for making no response to this attack, he recorded, "I have done with him—a good lesson."

Though Lushington was still out of town, Annabella was undisturbed by the threats of publicity, writing to her mother on the 20th:

> I send the Chronicle containing Perry's letter which you will think very absurd & impertinent & my Father's which I hope you will like. And there perhaps the matter will end—for I don't think they will venture on the publication of private documents.

On Sunday the 21st she wrote again:

> Our opponents are in reality confined to the Kinnairds[1] & Hobhouse—and the last is grown very timid in the Cause. The falsehoods they author-

[1] Perry and the *Morning Chronicle* were under financial obligations to Ransom's Bank, which was controlled by the Kinnairds. According to Judith, Perry was "beholden to Ld Kinnaird for intelligence from abroad—and D. Kinnaird and Hobhouse both *write* for his Paper."

ize cannot overcome the strong *feeling* on the other side of the Question. Nothing can be stronger, & it is the opinion of all the persons whose opinion is worth having that my silence has tended very much to increase the effect. How can you be so inconsiderate for me as to wish that the cause had come into Court?—for I should have died of it certainly—and now every object is attained without an exposure which revenge only could have desired, and which would have reflected some of its disgraceful consequences on myself.

Even as she was writing this letter, Byron was at last signing the deed of separation. He had always said he should sign, ever since the Solicitor General's award, but he deferred to Hanson's advice, and Hanson continued to haggle. In Hanson's company on 19th April Hobhouse talked with the Solicitor General, who listened courteously but departed, saying, "Well, Lord Byron may refuse my award if he pleases, but it will be a sad thing by all accounts." Though they agreed to wait till "the last moment," Hobhouse told Byron his opinion that he "must yield at last." The decision was reached after Wharton had submitted all Hanson's correspondence on the 18th to the Solicitor General, who then confirmed his award.

So, as Hobhouse recorded, Byron signed the deed at half-past three on the Sunday afternoon, remarking as he did so, "I deliver this as Mrs. Clermont's act and deed." The same evening Hobhouse received a note from Doyle that "Lady Byron has this day received an intimation that it is the intention of Lord Byron's friends to publish immediately her letters and other documents in the papers," and warning that "such a measure will inevitably bring upon Lady Byron the necessity, painful as it may be, of laying before the public all the circumstances of her case, from the day of her marriage to the present period." Hobhouse felt so "angry at this indiscreet threat" that he seems to have forgotten his intention of asking Annabella for her disavowal of the scandalous reports; with Byron's approval he replied tartly to Doyle, "The intimation you have received does not originate with Lord Byron or myself."

Byron had been busy with his preparations for departure. As he told Annabella, he had gone out little during February and March; he had in fact been under medical supervision from Sir William Knighton as well as from Le Mann. He seldom visited the theatre and received tearful complaints of neglect from Miss Boyce, but scandal credited him with a more glamorous conquest in the beautiful Irish actress, Mrs. Mardyn; though—as he afterwards told Medwin—he "was scarcely acquainted (to speak) with her," she was "driven with insult" from the theatre by the gossip that she was the cause of the separation. Among his sympathisers was Claire Clairmont, the half-sister of Shelley's second wife, and with her he drifted into an ill-starred affair; she followed him to the continent and became the mother of his daughter Allegra.

On Tuesday 23rd April he and Scrope Davies left for Dover in his "new Napoleonic carriage built by Baxter for 500£," Hobhouse travelling with Dr. Polidori in Davies' chaise. As soon as they left Piccadilly, the bailiffs moved in and "seized every thing"—even his "birds & squirrel." On Thursday the 25th, he embarked. As the boat tossed away "through a rough sea and contrary wind," Hobhouse "ran to the end of the wooden pier":

> The dear fellow pulled off his cap and waved it to me. I gazed until I could not distinguish him any longer.
>
> God bless him for a gallant spirit and a kind one.

He had eight more years to live—mostly in Italy—before he died on 19th April 1824 at Missolonghi on his expedition in the cause of Greek independence. He never returned to England, and he never saw Annabella again. During those eight years she was to receive twelve letters directly from him, though she heard of him frequently through Augusta.

After eight years the news of his death at the age of thirty-six came less as a shock than a blow to her self-esteem. For despite her implacability, she seems actually to have cherished an illusion that he would one day return to beg forgiveness on his knees at her feet. After reading his "Fare thee well" verses, she had written some herself, entitled "By thee Forsaken," of which these were the last two stanzas:

> But it must come—thine hour of tears,
> When self-adoring pride shall bow—
> And thou shalt own my "blighted years,"
> The fate that thou inflictest—*thou!*
>
> *Thy* virtue—but from ruin still
> Shall rise a wan and drooping peace,
> With pardon for unmeasured ill,
> And Pity's tears—if Love's must cease!

The deed of separation was safely signed, but Lushington had not ventured to ask for Byron's renunciation of his rights to his child, and Brougham had given his opinion of the means by which his rights might be claimed. So long as Byron lived, this fear must lurk. One weapon of defence lay ready to her hand—the persecution of Augusta.

Annabella's militant prudence allowed no delay in taking measures for her self-protection. On 24th April—the day after Byron left London

—she called on Augusta's friend, Mrs. Villiers, with the result that Mrs. Villiers wrote to Augusta on the evening of Thursday the 25th:

> Nothing could be more warmhearted, kind, considerate, feeling and affectionate—yes—affectionate to the greatest degree than everything she said about you . . . Lady B's declining to see you arose entirely from the difficulties and perplexities of her situation. She was aware fully of all *your* difficulties too—of the impossibility of your not answering to all the crossexaminations you underwent whenever you had seen her, and the consequent correspondences &c were as you know, very distressing to all parties. Had she answered your letters while Ld. Byron was in England hers might equally have been misunderstood or misconstrued—in short in such a situation the only safe line was absolute silence, and to that she determined to adhere till his departure. That event having taken place, the legal paper signed, and she herself returned to Kirkby today, she should now resume her intercourse with you and write to you from there.

The intercourse was resumed, as soon appeared, for the purpose of securing from Augusta an admission of guilt. While Byron lived, Annabella compelled Augusta to show her his letters to her. Though it was soon apparent that Byron had no intention of disturbing her custody of the child, she was haunted by fears of his returning to England and of Augusta's joining him in Italy.

After Byron's death she resumed the pursuit at intervals, because, as the years passed, she came increasingly to regard Augusta as having deprived her of her husband. For Augusta the pursuit ended only in 1851, when two old ladies met in the presence of an interested clergyman, the one still strong and sternly accusing, the other frail, bewildered, with but a few months to live. A year later Annabella suffered added bitterness when her daughter died, leaving directions that she should be buried beside her father. With Augusta and Ada gone, she lived more than ever with memories, and till the end of her life in 1860 continued to add to the accumulation of letters, documents, and memoranda comprised in the unique monument of self-justification known as The Lovelace Papers.

Vention Sands,
1959–62.

NOTES ON SOURCES

The source of every quotation is given—also the sources of statements of fact.

Line references are to the last line of quotations.

Where no published source is given, the source is an unpublished letter or document in the Lovelace Papers, but reference to a published source is given even if the text has been taken from the original letter or document.

The origin of a publication is London unless otherwise stated.

The names of principal correspondents are thus abbreviated: B = Byron; J = Judith Noel, who was the Hon. Mrs. Ralph Milbanke from 1777 to 1798, the Hon. Lady Milbanke from 1798 to 1815, and the Hon. Lady Noel from 1815 to 1822; AIM = Anne Isabella Milbanke before her marriage in 1815; AIB = Lady Byron, as she was from her marriage in 1815 till her mother's death in 1822; AINB = Lady Noel Byron, as she remained from her mother's death in 1822 till her own death in 1860, though she became entitled to the barony of Wentworth on the death of her cousin, Lord Scarsdale, in 1856.

The six previous works based, or partly based, on the Lovelace Papers are referred to by the following abbreviations:

Lady Noel Byron and the Leighs = *Lady Noel Byron and the Leighs: Some Authentic Records of Certain Circumstances in the Lives of Augusta Leigh, and Others of Her Family, that concerned Anne Isabella, Lady Byron, in the course of forty years after her separation . . . Strictly Private . . . Printed for the Descendants of Lord and Lady Byron . . .* 1887.

Astarte = *Astarte: A Fragment of Truth concerning George Gordon Byron, Sixth Lord Byron.* Recorded by his Grandson, Ralph Milbanke, Earl of Lovelace. New Edition, with many additional letters, edited by Mary Countess of Lovelace, 1921.
All page references to *Astarte* are to the 1921 edition, unless *Astarte*, 1905, is specified, in which case the reference is to the original edition, privately printed at the Chiswick Press, 1905.

Fox = Sir John C. Fox, *The Byron Mystery*, 1924.

Mayne = Ethel Colburn Mayne, *The Life and Letters of Anne Isabella, Lady Noel Byron*, with an Introduction and Epilogue by Mary, Countess of Lovelace, 1929.

Maurois = André Maurois, *Byron*, translated from the French by Hamish Miles, 1930.

The Late Lord Byron = Doris Langley Moore, *The Late Lord Byron: Posthumous Dramas*, 1961.

Other works frequently referred to are thus abbreviated:

Bessborough = *Lady Bessborough and Her Family Circle*, edited by the Earl of Bessborough and A. Aspinall, 1940.

Broughton = *Recollections of a Long Life*, by Lord Broughton (John Cam Hobhouse). With additional extracts from his private diaries, edited by his daughter Lady Dorchester, 6 vols., 1909–11.

Corresp. = *Lord Byron's Correspondence*, edited by John Murray, 2 vols., 1922.

Dallas = R. C. Dallas, *Recollections of the Life of Lord Byron*, 1824.

Foster = *The Two Duchesses: Georgiana Duchess of Devonshire, Elizabeth Duchess of Devonshire*, edited by Vere Foster, 1898.

In Whig Society = Mabell Countess of Airlie, *In Whig Society 1775–1818*, 1921.

Joyce = Michael Joyce, *My Friend H: John Cam Hobhouse*, 1948.

Knight = G. Wilson Knight, *Lord Byron's Marriage: The Evidence of Asterisks*, 1957.

LJ = *The Works of Lord Byron, Letters and Journals*, edited by Rowland E. Prothero, 6 vols., 1898–1901.

Lockhart's *Scott* = *Memoirs of the Life of Sir Walter Scott*, by J. G. Lockhart, Edinburgh, 2nd ed., 10 vols., 1839.

Marchand = Leslie A. Marchand, *Byron: A Biography*, 3 vols., 1957.

Medwin = Thomas Medwin, *Conversations of Lord Byron*, 2nd ed., 1824.

Memoir of Hodgson = *Memoir of the Rev. Francis Hodgson*, by his son, Rev. James T. Hodgson, 2 vols., 1878.

Memoir of John Murray = Samuel Smiles, *A Publisher and His Friends: Memoir and Correspondence of John Murray*, 2 vols., 1891.

Moore = Thomas Moore, *Life, Letters and Journals of Lord Byron*, (first published 1830), new ed., 1920.

Morgan = *Lady Morgan's Memoirs; Autobiography, Diaries and Correspondence*, 2nd ed., 2 vols., 1863.

Nicolson = Harold Nicolson, *Byron: The Last Journey*, new edition with a Supplementary Chapter, 1940.

Rogers, *Table-Talk* = *Recollections of the Table-Talk of Samuel Rogers*, first collected by the Rev. Alexander Dyce, edited, with an introduction, by Morchard Bishop, 1952.

Self-Portrait = *Byron: A Self-Portrait, Letters and Diaries*, edited by Peter Quennell, 2 vols., 1950.

Stowe = *Lady Byron Vindicated: A History of the Byron Controversy*, by Harriet Beecher Stowe, 1870.

"*To Lord Byron*" = George Paston and Peter Quennell, "*To Lord Byron*", *Feminine Profiles based upon unpublished letters*, 1939.

Wentworth Peerage Case = *Wentworth Peerage. In the House of Lords. Case on behalf of The Honourable Ralph Gordon Noel Milbanke Commonly called Viscount Ockham, the only surviving son of William Earl of Lovelace, on his claim to the honour and dignity of Lord Wentworth*, 1864.

Works = *The Works of Lord Byron, Poetry*, edited by Ernest Hartley Coleridge, 7 vols., 1898–1904.

Titles of other works quoted or cited are given fully at the reference.

Page Line

1. *MOTHER-IN-LAW, 1751–92*

23 3 B to Lady Melbourne, 21 Sept. 1812, *Corresp.*, i, 82. Byron's letters to Lady Melbourne, written in the years 1812–15 and published in *Corresp.*, i, 70–308, were left by his executor, John Cam Hobhouse, to his daughter, Lady Dorchester, who allowed them to be copied by Byron's grandson, the 2nd Earl of Lovelace (then Lord Wentworth), at intervals between 1870 and 1883. Lovelace was a meticulously exact copyist, and quotations from these letters are taken from his transcripts, though page references to *Corresp.* are given, so that students and scholars may compare the texts.

23 15 B to Augusta, 22 June 1821, *Astarte*, pp. 304–5; *Works*, vii, 75.

23 27 Lord David Cecil, *The Young Melbourne*, 1939, pp. 214–15.

24 20 Hobhouse's Journal, 30 Dec. 1814, Lovelace transcript, Broughton, i, 193. All quotations from Hobhouse's Journal are from Lovelace's transcripts, made between 1870 and 1883, though references are given where the extracts have been published in Broughton or Marchand.

35 B to Lady Melbourne, 18 Sept. 1812, *Corresp.*, i, 79.

25 1 Lord Stanhope, *History of England 1713–83*, 5th ed., 7 vols., 1858, iv, 252.

35 J's autobiographical fragment on paper watermarked 1813.

27 8 *ibid.*

28 37 MN to J, 3 Sept. 1776. The remainder of this chapter is based almost exclusively on the unpublished letters of Judith Milbanke (J) to her aunt Mary Noel (MN), and of MN, the 2nd Viscount Wentworth (W), and Sophia Susannah Curzon (SSC) to J.

29 3 W to J, 7 Nov. 1776.

8 Dated 30th December 1776—Settlement on the Marriage of Ralph Milbanke Esquire with the Honorable Miss Noel, *cf. Wentworth Peerage Case*, pp. 44–6.

15 J to MN, undated [11 Jan. 1777].

23 J to MN, 29 Oct. 1777.

34 MN to J, 6 Jan. 1778.

30 16 J to MN, 8 Jan. 1778.

24 The Reynolds portraits of both Ralph Milbanke and the 2nd Viscount Wentworth are in the possession of the Earl of Lytton.

27 Hobhouse's Journal, Broughton, i, 193.

28 Vere Foster, *The Two Duchesses*, 1898, p. 367.

29 AIM to Sir Ralph, undated [27 March 1812].

31 9 SSC to MN, 7 March 1778.

20 J to MN, 27 Apr. 1778.

29 J to MN, 9 June 1778.

31 Ralph Milbanke's commission as lieutenant-colonel in the North Riding Militia, dated 20 Feb. 1778, signed by Henry Earl of Fauconberg, Lord Lieutenant.

36 J to MN, 14 June 1778.

Page	*Line*	
32	3	J to MN, 16 July 1778.
	9	J to MN, 25 Sept. 1778.
	21	W to J, 15 Dec. 1778.
	24	Lockhart's *Scott*, vii, 313–16.
33	30	J to MN, 27 June 1779.
	40	J to MN, 5 July 1779.
34	7	J to MN, 7 July 1779.
	9	J to MN, Seaham, 21 June 1779.
	17	J to MN, 7 July 1779.
	32	J to MN, 5 July 1779.
	38	J to MN, 21 July 1779.
	43	SSC to MN, 1 Aug. 1779.
35	5	J to MN, 15 Sept. 1779.
	9	SSC to MN, 5 Dec. 1779.
	20	Edward Hulse (1744–1816), who succeeded his father as 3rd baronet of Breamore, Hants., in 1800, was a close friend of Wentworth's. Lady Bridget Tollemache was the eldest daughter of Robert Henley, Earl of Northington, former Lord Chancellor; her younger sister, Mary Countess Ligonier, married Wentworth as her second husband in 1788.
	31	J to MN, 8 July 1780.
	41	J to MN, 19 July 1780.
36	11	J to MN, 23 Oct. 1780.
	15	J to MN, 8 Nov. 1780.
	25	J to MN, 13 Nov. 1780.
37	6	W to MN, 13 Sept. 1781.
	14	J's first letter from Aycliffe Heads was on 8 July 1780.
	15	SSC to MN, 19 Oct. 1781.
	21	J to MN, 30 Aug. 1779.
	26	J to MN, 5 Sept. 1780.
	32	J to MN, 13 Sept. 1780.
38	4	SSC to MN, 17 Jan. 1782.
	15	SSC to MN, 30 Nov. 1781.
	17	Dr. Turton and George III, *Memoirs of George IV*, by Robert Huish, 2 vols., 1830, i, 498.
	28	SSC to MN, 8 Jan. 1782.
	33	SSC to MN, 1 Jan. 1782.
	39	SSC to MN, 1 March 1782.
39	2	W to J, 18 March 1782.
	5	W to J, 23 March, 11 Apr., 6, 25, 31 May, 6 June 1782.
	6	Burial certificate, *Wentworth Peerage Case*, p. 40.
	10	J to Lady Scarsdale, undated but some days before Tuesday 9 July 1782.
	14	J to MN, 10 July 1782.
	21	J to MN, 27 Aug. 1782.
	28	J to MN, 18 Nov. 1782.
	33	J to MN, 18 Nov. 1782.
40	10	W to J, 22 Jan. 1782.

Page Line

40 32 W to J, 25 May 1782.
35 W to J, 6 June 1782.
38 J to MN, 27 Sept. 1782.
41 2 J to MN, 15 July 1783.
6 W to J, 3 Jan. 1784. Philip Yorke (1757–1834) married Lady Elizabeth Lindsay, 1782, and succeeded his uncle as 3rd Earl of Hardwicke, 1796.
12 W to J, 11 March 1784.
27 J to MN, 10 July 1784.
42 2 J to MN, 11 July 1784. Harriet Meynell was the younger sister of J's close friend, Mrs. Davison (afterwards Davison Bland); she married Sir John Caldwell in 1789. Lady Balcarres was Lady Anne Lindsay's sister-in-law.
11 J to MN, 25 July 1784.
26 J to MN, 31 July 1784.
29 Diana and Susannah Clerke were sisters of Sir Francis Carr Clerke, who was killed at Saratoga in 1778, and Sir William Henry Clerke, fellow of All Souls, Oxford, who succeeded his brother as 8th baronet. They lived with their widowed mother at Waterstock, near Oxford. Diana married the Rev. E. Willes in 1785; Sukey became in 1805 the second wife of Sir Robert Peel, father by his first wife of the future Prime Minister, but her later letters to J indicate that she soon separated from her husband.
43 2 J to MN, 16 July 1782. The rich old lady was Mrs. Barnes.
3 Lord Ravensworth's barony expired at his death in 1784, his only child being a daughter Anne, who married the 3rd Duke of Grafton in 1756 and was divorced in 1769, when she married the Earl of Upper Ossory. Hearing that Lady Upper Ossory's daughter by her first marriage, Lady Georgiana Smyth, was going from Ravensworth with her husband to stay with the Duke of Grafton, J wrote to her aunt, 20 Oct. 1778, "so the old Prayer on such occasions of 'pray, pray forgive me & I'll never do so again' has succeeded in that family."
24 J to MN, 15 Aug. 1777.
28 J to MN, 1 Sept. 1784.
31 J to MN, 8 Feb. and 8 March 1785.
44 6 J to MN, 23 Nov. 1780.
9 J to MN, 26 July 1780.
10 W to J, 20 Apr. 1784.
24 J to MN, 25 July 1784.
35 J to MN, 24 Jan. 1787.
42 J to MN, 19 June 1787.
45 12 J to MN, Harrowgate, 17 July 1784.
15 J to MN, 3 Jan. 1779.
28 J to MN, 19 Aug. 1784.
30 J to MN, 1 Sept. 1784.
34 Properties cited in Ralph Milbanke's will, dated 17 Feb. 1779.
46 2 J to MN, 6 Nov. 1780.

Page	*Line*	
46	9	J to MN, 28 Jan. 1785.
	14	J to MN, 28 Jan. 1787.
	32	J to MN, 30 July 1786.
	36	J to MN, 6 Aug. 1786.
	37	J to MN, 25 Aug. 1786.
47	3	J to MN, 12 Sept. 1786.
	14	Wraxall quoted, Compton Mackenzie, *The Windsor Tapestry*, 1938, pp. 255–6.
	34	J to MN, 4 Aug. 1788.
48	13	J to MN, 10 Aug. 1788.
	19	J to MN, 5 July 1787.
49	4	Lady Scarsdale to her son, undated [Oct.]; J to Lady Scarsdale, 31 Oct., 5, 15, and 25 Nov. 1786; Lady Scarsdale to J, 1, 10 and 20 Nov. 1786.
	16	J to MN, 1 Apr. 1784.
	25	W to J, 14 Jan. 1786.
50	12	J to Sir John Eden, 15 Jan. 1786.
	14	Lady Liddell to J, 15, 18, and 21 Jan. 1786.
	32	J to MN, 9 June 1785. Richard Atkinson (1738–85), M.P. for Romney, died unmarried in May 1785. His nephew, George Atkinson, of Morland Hall, Penrith, was A.D.C. to Lady Anne Lindsay's brother, Lord Balcarres, when he was governor of Jamaica.
	35	J to MN, 1 July 1785.
51	2	W to J, undated fragment, July 1785.
	8	W to J, 19 Aug. 1785.
	9	W to J, 25 July 1784: "I hate Law & all its appendages."
	11	MN to J, 6 Jan. 1778.
	14	MN to J, 28 Jan. 1787.
	20	J to MN, 28 and 30 June 1786. Dean Rowney Noel died at Salisbury on 26 June.
	27	MN to J, 16 Oct. 1783.
	39	J to MN, 21 Dec. 1787.
52	7	Lady Ligonier to W, undated, *c.* Nov. 1787.
	15	MN to J, 15 Jan. 1790: "it is certain Ld. W is to have the Bed-chamber."
	26	J to MN, 27 Aug. 1789.
	32	J to MN, 29 Oct. 1777.
	36	J to MN, 8 Jan. 1778.
	39	J. to MN, 12 Sept. 1778.
53	4	Iris Leveson-Gower, *The Face Without a Frown*, 1944, p. 80.
	16	W to J, 20 Nov. 1783.
	18	W to J, 13 July 1784.
	n.	*In Whig Society*, p. 68; Cecil, *The Young Melbourne*, 1939, p. 33.
	24	Wraxall's *Historical Memoirs of My Own Time*, quoted, *In Whig Society*, p. 4.
54	4	Lady Melbourne to Ralph Milbanke, 20 March 1791.
55	6	J to Lady Melbourne, copy in J's hand, undated.

Page	Line	
	21	J to MN, 18 July 1791.
	26	After spending the summer and early autumn of 1783 at Seaham, J asked MN, 3 Oct. 1783, that a large order from "Coopers the China Shop in Jermyn Street" should be sent to Milbanke at The Hill, Richmond, Yorkshire.
56	14	J to MN, 21 Aug. 1791.
	15	J to MN, 24 Sept. 1791.
	37	MN to J, 12 Oct. 1791.
57	1	MN to J, 16 Nov. 1791.
	12	MN to J, 26 Nov. 1791.
	16	W to Ralph Milbanke, 30 Nov. 1791.
	31	J to MN, 14 July 1789.
	33	W to J, 23 Jan. 1792.
	35	W to J, 19 Feb. 1792.
58	3	W to J, 23 Jan. 1792.
	5	W to Ralph Milbanke, 19 May 1792.
	n.	*Wentworth Peerage Case*, p. 47.

2. *THE SPOILT CHILD, 1792–1810*

Page	Line	
59	5	W to J, 28 Oct. and 8 Nov. 1792; W to Ralph Milbanke, 10 Oct. 1792.
	7	W to J, 13 Jan. 1793: "you have forced me to own that the arguments with which you combat my wishes for your journey to Town are most forcible."
	21	Lady Gosford to J, 4 Feb. 1793.
	29	J to MN, 31 July 1793.
60	12	J to MN, 2 Aug. 1793.
	15	J to MN, undated, *c.* 12 Aug. 1793.
	19	SSC to MN, 1 Aug. 1779.
	26	J to MN, 31 Aug. 1793.
	35	J to MN, 11 Sept. 1793.
	40	J to MN, 12 Oct. 1793.
	41	J to MN, 11 Sept. 1793.
61	4	J to MN, 12 Oct. 1793.
	8	J to MN, 27 Oct. 1793.
	13	J to MN, 24 Nov. 1793.
	16	J to MN, 11 Dec. 1793.
	26	J to MN, 2 March 1794.
	32	J to MN, 24 Nov. 1793. Lord Fauconberg was lord lieutenant of the North Riding.
62	5	J to MN, 21 March 1794.
	12	J to MN, 20 Apr. 1794.
	29	J to MN, 18 Nov. 1793.
	42	J to MN, 27 Oct. 1793.
63	9	Sophy Curzon to J, 26 May 1794.
	21	J to MN, 14 June 1794.
	24	J to MN, 2 March 1794.

Page	*Line*	
63	31	W to J, 17 Dec. 1791.
	n.	*Astarte,* p. 17.
64	1	J to MN, 8 June 1794.
	12	W to J, 15 Aug. 1795.
	21	W to J, 25 Aug. 1795.
	23	J to MN, 21 Dec. 1787, quoted p. 51.
	26	J to MN, 18 July 1791.
	32	W to J, 25 Aug. 1795.
	40	W to J, 18 Oct. 1795.
	42	W to J, 14 May 1796.
65	13	J to MN, 16 July 1797.
	27	J to MN, 22 June 1794.
	36	J to MN, undated [30 May 1795].
	41	J to MN, 3 Feb. 1797.
66	4	J to MN, 27 Feb. 1797.
	9	Mrs. George Baker to MN, undated [10 March 1797].
	13	J to MN, 16 Apr. 1797.
	17	J to MN, 24 May 1797.
	22	J to MN, 30 July 1797.
	26	J to MN, 16 July 1797.
	35	J to MN, 25 Aug. 1797.
	37	J to MN, 3 Sept. 1797.
67	3	J to MN, 7 Oct. 1797.
	8	J to MN, 20 Nov. 1797.
	11	Sophy Curzon to MN, 1 Nov. 1797.
	13	J to MN, 20 Nov. 1797.
	18	J to MN, 28 Nov. 1797.
	33	J to MN, 24 Nov. 1793: "The Small-pox is now begginning in the Village . . . We have offered to Inoculate all the Children but the Obstinate fools have refused."
	43	AINB's "Early Recollections" of Seaham, on paper watermarked 1847, quoted Mayne, p. 8.
68	4	J to MN, 25 and 31 July 1784, etc.
	12	AINB's "Early Recollections."
	25	Lady Liddell to J, Tuesday Morning; Dumouriez evacuated Brussels on Monday 25 March 1793.
	36	J to MN, 31 May 1794. On 28 May 1794 Dorothy Wordsworth assured their brother Richard that she could "answer for William's caution about expressing his political opinions," as he "seems well aware of the dangers of a contrary conduct."—*Early Letters of William and Dorothy Wordsworth*, ed. E. de Selincourt, 1935, p. 117.
69	10	J to MN, 24 May 1797. Sir Robert D'Arcy Hildyard, high sheriff of Yorkshire, married Mary, daughter of Sir Edward Dering; he died 1814, she 1816.
	22	J to MN, 2 Apr. 1798.
	27	J to MN, 17 Feb. 1797.
	29	J to MN, 16 July 1797.

Page	Line	
69	34	J to MN, 4 Jan. 1785. William Beckford (1760–1844), the author of *Vathek*.
70	3	J to MN, 30 July 1797. The 3rd Earl of Darlington (1766–1842), created Duke of Cleveland 1833, was lord-lieutenant of Durham. J referred to this incident again in a letter of 23 Dec. 1797, quoted *Astarte*, pp. 26–7. Darlington was a friend and patron of Colonel George Leigh, husband of Byron's sister Augusta.
	7	J to MN, 20 Oct. 1797. The 16th Earl of Erroll died in the following June, aged thirty-one. His widow married John Hookham Frere (1769–1846).
71	2	J to MN, 19 Jan. 1798.
	7	Sophy Curzon to MN, 24 Feb. 1798.
	11	J to MN, 23 Sept. 1798.
	13	MN to J, 20 Sept. 1798.
	31	MN to J, 7 Aug. 1798.
	42	J to MN, 26 June 1798, part inaccurately quoted, Mayne, p. 4.
72	9	*Works*, iii, 540–1.
	21	MN to J, 1 Sept. 1789.
	26	MN to J, 2 Nov. 1789.
	30	MN to J, 22 Oct. 1791.
	38	MN to J, 26 Nov. 1791.
73	2	J to MN, 2 Aug. 1793, *cf.* p. 60. "From the itch-episode it does seem to emerge that Mrs. Milbanke was more or less under her [Clermont's] thumb—afraid of her, just because she was so devoted"—Mayne, p. 3. The reader may judge whether such a dominating character as J was likely ever to have been under anybody's thumb!
	23	J to MN, 26 Dec. 1793. " 'She is *resolved to go*,' moaned poor Judith in many a distracted letter to Aunt Mary"—Mayne, p. 3. This is the only occasion on which Clermont is described as "*resolved to go*."
	30	MN to J, 17 Jan. 1794.
	32	J to MN, 26 Dec. 1793.
	34	MN to J, 7 Aug. 1798, *cf.* p. 71.
	36	J to MN, 15 Aug. 1798.
	38	J to MN, 6 Feb. 1799.
	41	Mayne, p. 4, follows the caption of the frontispiece to the 1921 edition of *Astarte* (which caption did not appear in the 1905 edition under Lovelace's supervision) in stating that Annabella was ten years old when Hoppner painted her. But the sketch for the portrait is inscribed on its back, "Anne Isabella Milbanke at the Age of 7." In 1802, when Annabella was ten, her mother seems to have visited London only to attend Mary Noel's death-bed.
74	3	Sophy Curzon to MN, 1 Jan. 1799, *cf.* Mayne, p. 7.
	7	J to MN, 21 Feb. 1800.
	10	J to MN, 5 May 1801.
	13	Sophy, Viscountess Tamworth, to J, 8 May 1801.

Page	Line	
74	17	MN to J, 7 May 1801.
	25	J to MN, 23 Aug. 1801.
	32	J to MN, 4 Jan. 1802.
	38	MN to J, 9 Jan. 1802.
	40	W to J, 17 March 1803.
75	6	Sophy Curzon to MN, 15 Feb. 1800.
	18	J to MN, 11 June 1798.
	24	W to J, 22 Dec. 1794: "I went to return two visits made me last year by Lord Ferrers, & I found Betty Blue doing the Honors of the House. She looked very awkward & I confess I felt nearly as much so, but we never talked at all of former times. Her Daughter is a very well behaved Girl & seems well educated & taken care of. He introduced me to her as His Daughter Miss Shirley. Our Cousin had no name whilst I was there." Betty Mundy was the youngest daughter of Wrightson Mundy, of Markeaton, Derby, whose mother was a sister of Sir Clobery Noel, grandfather of Lord Wentworth and Judith Milbanke.
	29	J to Lord Ferrers, an undated copy, *c.* July 1800.
	31	J to MN, undated, *c.* July 1800.
	33	J to MN, 16 Sept. 1800.
	35	Mary Noel was born 8 July 1725, MN to J, 8 July 1794.
76	1	J to MN, 4 Jan. 1802.
	10	J to MN, 18 Oct. 1801. The Bishop of Durham was Shute Barrington (1734–1826).
	13	W to J, 18 Aug. 1802.
	23	"Lord Wentworth is at last made a lord of the bedchamber. He has waited a good while for it. His brother-in-law Milbanke has spent a very large sum in the Durham election. I wish Sir John may not have spent so much. It will be hard upon him to lose both his money and his election."—Anthony Morris Storer to Sir John Eden's brother, Lord Auckland, 22 Oct. 1790. *Journal and Correspondence of William, Lord Auckland*, 4 vols., 1861–2, ii, 375.
	27	G. D. H. Cole, *Life of William Cobbett*, 3rd ed., 1947, pp. 84–9.
	28	W to J, 14 Nov. 1803.
	30	W to J, 20 Feb. 1804.
	33	W to J, 10 Aug. 1804.
	37	Gen. Bowater to J, 2 Jan. 1805.
	42	J to Anne Hoar, 13 and 27 Aug. 1804.
77	8	Lady Tamworth to J, 3 Nov. 1804.
	16	Sophy Curzon to MN, 1 Sept. 1798.
	19	J to MN, 26 Dec. 1793.
	23	J to MN, 2 March 1794.
	25	J to MN, 25 Aug. 1797.
	28	J to MN, 28 Nov. 1797.
78	2	MN to J, 2 Dec. 1797.
	21	Gen. Bowater to J, 22 Feb. 1805.
	29	W to J, 5 Dec. 1803.
	32	W to J, 22 Jan. 1805.

Page	*Line*	
78	34	W to J, 10 Oct. 1807.
	41	W to J, 5 Dec. 1803.
79	14	Dated on the back of the paper in AIM's hand, 7 Nov. 1803, and inscribed, "Compliments—No. 1—praises—to be sold only to those on whom these compliments are made. Price a good deal, viz. 2s."
	16	J to MN, 26 June 1798, *cf.* p. 71.
80	4	AIM to J, 26 Oct. 1805.
	23	Sarah Siddons to J, 11 July 1810.
81	15	Sarah Siddons to AIM, 20 Jan. [? 1810].
	33	Written on paper watermarked 1811.
	38	Lady Tamworth to J, 1 Nov. 1805.
	39	W to J, 27 June 1805.
82	16	William Frend to AIM, 25 Nov. 1806.
	42	Some fifty such notebooks, of dates from 1806 to the 1850s, are preserved.
83	3	AINB's "Early Recollections" of Seaham, *cf.* Mayne, pp. 9–10.
	9	Frend to AIM, 18 Oct. 1807: "I am sorry that your essay on association goes on so slowly."
	15	J to MN, 7 Oct. 1797, from Seaham: "Doctor Paley dined here on friday & was more entertaining than ever, we sat up till One o'clock & were quite sorry to quit him even at that hour."
	22	AIB'S analysis of her religion, a fragment written on paper watermarked 1818, designated "Paper MM" by Lovelace.
	31	*Works*, i, 359.
84	7	Blacket to J, 23 Nov. 1809.
	20	AIM to Blacket, Seaham, Monday, undated.
	24	Ms. of Blacket's verses, dated "Seaham, Oct. 1809."
	25	Blacket to J, 18 Apr. 1810.
	29	Blacket to AIM, 8 March 1810.
	33	Blacket to AIM, Seaham Monday 15 [Jan. 1810]: "J Blacket hopes, most earnestly hopes, that the kind Miss Montgomery is much better." Blacket to AIM, 8 March 1810: "repeatedly have I tried to compose, for your fair friend Miss Montgomery's air; and as repeatedly have I fail'd."
	38	J to MN, 15 Aug. 1798.
	43	J to MN, 18 Oct. 1801.
85	38	Journal, 14 March 1809, a single page. The Mrs. Carter quoted was presumably Elizabeth Carter (1717–1806), the bluestocking, whose biography by Pennington was published in 1808. James Sowerby (1757–1822) was well-known for his works on botany and mineralogy.
	40	AIM'S Journal, 10 May 1810. An octavo volume contains her journal from 10 May to 20 July 1810; her Journal for 1811 starts from the other end of the volume, beginning 23 Apr. and continuing to 28 June. Earlier in 1810, from 26 Feb. to May, the Journal was kept on loose sheets of letter paper.

Page Line

3. *THE LONDON SEASONS OF 1810–11*

86 5 AINB's "Auto-description", written on paper watermarked 1831. Part quoted, Mayne, p. 14, which erroneously states that Annabella's first London season was 1811, and remarking that she stayed with Lady Gosford, expresses surprise that "her parents did not see her through the first London season." Miss Mayne consulted only a selection of Lovelace's transcripts, and he transcribed none of Annabella's memoranda before 30 July 1811.

16 Journal, 26 Feb. 1810.

87 13 *ibid*, 2 March 1810.

27 *ibid*, 3 March 1810.

n. Edward Dowden, *Life of Shelley*, 2 vols., 1886, i, 289, 324; Lockhart's *Scott*, i, 77, 208.

34 Journal, 5 March 1810.

36 *ibid*, 11 March 1810.

88 3 *ibid*, 15 March 1810.

6 *ibid*, 24 Apr. 1810.

n. Doran, *Annals of the English Stage*, 2 vols., 1864, ii, 502–9.

14 Journal, 4 May 1810.

24 *ibid*, 10 July 1810. Sarah Harrop married in 1780 Joah Bates (1741–99); she was a well-known concert singer, specialising in Handel.

27 *Reminiscences and Recollections of Captain Gronow*, 2 vols., 1900, i, 166. Byron also referred to Lady Cork's lion-hunting, *LJ*, iii, 182–3.

33 Journal, 17 July 1810.

35 *ibid*, 21 May 1810.

36 *ibid*, 15 May 1810.

89 1 *ibid*, 21 May 1810.

3 *ibid*, 3 June 1810.

7 *ibid*, 18 June 1810.

36 AIM to Lady Gosford, Seaham, Tuesday; the remark, "I am less inclined to dissent as I know you more," suggests a date before the intimacy had ripened during the summer of 1811. One sentence from another part of the letter is quoted in Mayne, p. 15.

90 3 J. R. Fenwick to AIM, Wednesday morning [5 Feb. 1812].

19 Fenwick to AIM, undated.

26 Foster, *The Two Duchesses*, p. 226.

91 8 Augustus Foster to J, 20 Sept. 1811.

16 Journal, 26 Apr. 1811.

36 AIM to J, 10 July 1811.

41 Fenwick to AIM, 12 July 1811.

42 AIM to J, 10 July 1811.

92 17 AIM to J, 11 July 1811. Mayne, p. 15, refers to "a nebulous Mr. Mackenzie" as one of Annabella's suitors, though Annabella frequently refers to him and to his mother, Lady Seaforth. He was the Hon. William Frederick Mackenzie, heir of Lord Seaforth.

Page Line

He died 28 Aug. 1814, predeceasing his father, who survived all his four sons, his pathetic condition before his death on 11 Jan. 1815 being described by Walter Scott, Lockhart's *Scott*, v, 18.

22 AIM to J, 10 July 1811.

29 AIM to J, 12 July 1811.

93 3 AIM to J, 16 July 1811.

28 *The Greville Memoirs*, ed. Henry Reeve, 8 vols., 1903–4, vi, 260–61.

35 George Eden to AIM, 26 July 1811. Two sentences misquoted, Mayne, p. 15.

94 13 Lady Auckland to AIM, 26 July 1811, not among the transcripts examined by Miss Mayne.

17 AIB'S letters to Mrs. Villiers from Eden Farm in Sept. 1816, *Lady Noel Byron and the Leighs*, pp. 51–4.

36 James Grahame to AIM, 8 and 15 Apr. 1811.

42 Mrs. Grahame to AIM, Edinburgh, undated.

95 3 Mrs. Grahame to AIM, Sedgefield, 24 Aug. 1811.

6 Mrs. Grahame to AIM, 18 Oct. 1811.

21 On the other side of the paper containing the "Character" of Mrs. Grahame is written a character of Major Dickens, whom Annabella met frequently in the spring of 1812.

30 Mrs. Grahame to AIM, Sedgefield, 7 Jan. and 9 Feb. 1812.

40 Mrs. Grahame to AIM, 18 Feb. 1812.

96 5 Mrs. Grahame to AIM, 8 March 1812.

23 Journal, 1 Jan. 1812.

26 Boothby was a guest at Seaham, with Tower and the Bakers, from 1st to 6th Jan. Recording the visit, AIM noted: "I first saw Captain Boothby in London in the Spring of 1811—Mrs. Knight's friendship for him, and the good indications of his own countenance were the recommendations that induced me to seek his acquaintance." Mayne, p. 18, suggests that Boothby "occupied her thoughts" as a suitor, but AIM's later reference (26 June 1812) to his "clergyman brother" shows that he was William Boothby (1782–1846), captain in the 15th Light Dragoons and A.D.C. to the Duke of Cumberland, who succeeded his father as 8th baronet in 1824 and was a married man of six years' standing when Annabella met him.

37 Journal, 14 Jan. 1812.

97 9 *ibid*, 20 Jan. 1812.

14 *ibid*, 20 Jan. 1812. Misquoting the verdict on *Madoc* out of context, Mayne, p. 22, cites this as an example of Annabella's "woolly kind of writing."

28 AIM to J, Elemore, Monday, remarks, "I see that Parliament is positively to assemble on the 7th Jan." Parliament re-assembled on 7 Jan. 1812.

36 J to AIM, Decr. 23d [1811].

98 9 Lady Tamworth to J, 4 Feb. 1812.

26 Fenwick to AIM, Wednesday Morning. AIM's Journal: "On the 1st I went with Ly M. to Durham and dined at Dr. F's . . .

Page Line

On the 3rd I returned to Seaham with A[nne] H[oar] & went back to Durham the next day to meet Mrs. Siddons." The rest of the entry is concerned with Mrs. Siddons' opinions on tragedy, but presumably AIM saw Fenwick with Mrs. Siddons on Tuesday the 4th and he wrote to her next morning.

99 23 AIM to J, undated. Between 4 Feb. and her arrival in London on 24 Feb. there is only one entry in her Journal, but her proposing to be in London "this day fortnight" suggests that she wrote to her mother on the 9th or 10th—the week-end following her receipt of Fenwick's letter.

32 AIM to Sir Ralph, Wetherby, 8 oclock at night.

34 AIM to Sir Ralph, Doncaster 1 o'clock; AIM to J, Grantham Sunday Morn; AIM's Journal, 24 Feb. 1812.

100 8 AIM to J, Cumberland Place, Tuesday Morn [25 Feb.].

10 AIM to J, 27 Feb.

15 AIM to J, undated [11 March]. Her letters can be readily dated, being often expanded accounts of events recorded in her Journal.

20 AIM to J, 27 Feb.

23 Fenwick to AIM, 5 March 1812.

4. THE BYRON SEASON OF 1812

101 6 AIM to J, Sunday Night [8 March].

10 AIM to Sir Ralph, undated. Her Journal records her first sitting to Hayter on Tuesday 10 March.

15 AIM to J, undated [23 March].

102 2 AIM to Sir Ralph, undated [14 March].

4 Journal, 6 Apr. 1812.

7 AIM to Sir Ralph, undated [13 Apr.].

14 Inexplicably Mayne, p. 26, asserts, "Dates seem to show that" Pakenham "was Lord Longford's eldest son." Yet his brother, the 2nd Earl of Longford, succeeded to the earldom at the age of twenty in 1794 and remained unmarried till 1817.

20 AIM to J, Thursday before Post [5 March].

22 Journal, 10 March.

23 AIM to J, 5 March.

33 AIM to J, Friday [20 March], quoted with a notable error in Mayne, p. 26.

41 *ibid.*

103 5 AIM to J, undated [23 March].

12 AIM to J, Good Friday [27 March], part quoted in Mayne, p. 26.

23 AIM to J, 20 March.

29 Journal, 24 March 1812.

34 *ibid*, 25 March.

36 AIM to J, undated [18 Apr.].

104 5 AIM to J, Monday [2 March].

14 Dorothy Margaret Stuart, *Dearest Bess*, 1955, p. 163; Bessborough p. 184.

Page	Line	
104	27	The "Character" of Mrs. George Lamb was written immediately after that of Mrs. Grahame (p. 95, l. 21) during the spring of 1812.
	34	Journal, 15 March.
105	n.	MN to J, 17 Feb. 1797.
	14	AIM to J, undated [16 March].
	16	Journal, 19 March.
	18	*ibid*, 22 March.
	22	*ibid*, 24 March, inaccurately quoted in Mayne, p. 35.
106	6	*ibid*, 25 March.
	10	*ibid.*
	42	AIM to J, Thursday [26 March].
107	6	Sir Ralph Milbanke to AIM, Seaham, 29 March. Mayne, p. 29, remarks that "scarcely any letters of Sir Ralph's" to his daughter "are to be found among the Lovelace Papers." In fact there are many, but few were among the transcripts seen by Miss Mayne because Lovelace judged few worth transcribing. Sir Ralph was not a gifted correspondent; his letters are often brief notes of his movements, with a joke or pun added. His handwriting was execrable; acknowledging a letter he had written to his brother-in-law, MN wrote to J, 22 Oct. 1791: "Ld. W bids me say Mr. Mil was very kind to tell him which was greek in his letter, otherways it would have been all greek to him. To say the truth we could not amongst us all decypher it all, & agreed that Mr. Mil was a very good sort of man, but—damn his letters."
	9	Mayne, p. 30, quotes comments on the Lord Mayor's Ball from AIM's Journal, 30 March.
	22	Journal, 31 March. The passage on Lady Caroline Lamb is quoted out of context in Mayne, p. 32. AIM went to Brocket on Easter Tuesday, 31 March, and returned to London 2 Apr.
	27	The Duchess of Devonshire to her son Augustus Foster, 29 Feb. 1812: "Caro means to see la bella Annabella before she writes to you. I don't like the last letter which you received, and I shall almost hate her if she is blind to the merits of one who would make her so happy."—Foster, *The Two Duchesses*, p. 358.
108	8	AIM to Sir Ralph, undated [9 Apr.].
	22	AIM to J, undated [10 Apr.].
	31	AIM to Sir Ralph, undated [13 Apr.].
	37	AIM to J, undated [13 Apr.].
	40	Journal, 14 Apr.
109	n.	*LJ*, i, 186, 314.
	19	AIM to J, undated [15 Apr.], part quoted as "to her father" in Mayne, p. 38, where a passage from this letter is included with that above quoted of the 13th as from the same letter.
	24	Journal, 15 Apr., quoted without date, Mayne, p. 39.
	38	AIM to J, undated [16 Apr.].
110	2	AIM to Sir Ralph, Friday, postmark 17 Apr.

Page Line

110 n. *Journals and Correspondence of Miss Berry*, ed. Lady Theresa Lewis, 3 vols., 1865, ii, 496; Hobhouse's Journal, *cf.* Marchand, i, 350.
9 AIM to J, undated [18 Apr.].
22 Journal, 18 Apr., part quoted without date, Mayne, p. 40.
28 *ibid*, 19 Apr.
29 *ibid*, 20 Apr.
33 AIM to J, undated [21 Apr.], part in Mayne, p. 40.

111 2 Journal, 23, 24, 25 Apr.
15 AIM to J, 26 Apr., Mayne, p. 41.
21 AIM to B, 17 Oct. 1814, is in Mayne, pp. 465–6, but the enclosures, including AIM's comments, are omitted.
28 AIM to J, undated [29 Apr.], one sentence in Mayne, p. 41.
36 Journal, 29 Apr.

112 6 *ibid*, 2 May, part quoted, Mayne, p. 40. "The painful acknowledgement we must suppose to have been that she had refused George Eden," Mayne, p. 42.
23 B to Lady Melbourne, 28 Sept. 1812, *Corresp.*, i, 86–7.

113 n. The text of the original—here given as far as "better much better"—differs slightly from the version in *LJ*, ii, 118–21.
7 Morgan, ii, 200.
31 Sir Ralph to AIM, Seaham, 6 May.
35 Journal, 11 May, one sentence misquoted in Mayne, p. 43.
40 *ibid*, 12 May, misquoted without date, Mayne, p. 43.

114 6 *ibid*, 20 May.

115 14 Lady Caroline Lamb to AIM, [22 May 1812], not among the transcripts used by Miss Mayne.
31 B to Lady Melbourne, 21 Sept. 1812, *Corresp.*, i, 82.

116 10 Elizabeth Duchess of Devonshire to Augustus Foster, 4 and 11 May, 2 June, Foster, *The Two Duchesses*, pp. 362, 364, 370. Foster replied perceptively on 26 May: "I see you don't like Annabella much. She is certainly rather too cold in her manners, and gives to reason too much empire over her mind, but she has good eyes, is fair, has right ideas, and sense, and mildness. I don't think she will ever be able to love very warmly; but yet I believe she thinks she ought to wait till the spirit moves her, and the spirit perhaps may never come, as I fancy happens to many of her temperament."—*ibid*, p. 365.
13 Journal, 31 May. Mayne, p. 43, refers to "a blank interval between the 12th and the 31st of May," but there is an entry in the Journal every day during that period, including mention of Byron on the 20th.
17 Hobhouse at Newstead, Broughton, i, 40; Marchand, i, 351.
20 Journal, 8 June.
26 *ibid*, 16 June.
31 *ibid*, 20 June.

117 2 *ibid*, 15 June.
5 *ibid*, 23 June, a "most agreable" ball at the Argyle Rooms.
14 *ibid*, 24 June, at Miss Johnstone's ball,

Page Line

117 20 Bankes's proposal, B to Lady Melbourne, 23 Dec. 1812, *Corresp.*, i, 121; B to AIM, August 31st 1813, *cf.* p. 169 and Mayne, p. 61.

24 Journal, 5 July: "Dined with Sir R. & Ly M. at Lord Melbourne's. Company—Mr. & Ly C. Lamb, Mr. & Mrs. Gage, Mr. Robinson, Lord & Lady Cowper." Mary, only daughter of Sir Ralph's uncle John and Lady Mary Milbanke, married in 1793 John Gage, brother of the 3rd Viscount Gage.

26 *ibid*, 6 July.

33 *ibid*, 14 July, last sentence only in Mayne, p. 43.

39 *ibid*, 16 June, after recording Byron's "propensity to coquetry."

118 4 B to Lady Melbourne, 28 Sept. 1812, *Corresp.*, 1, 86.

8 Journal, 4 Aug.: "I am just going to Tunbridge where I shall continue my journal. Last night H[ugh] M[ontgomery] went to Ireland." At Tunbridge on the 5th Miss Berry dined "with Lady Milbanke, her daughter, Mrs. Hervey, and Mrs. and Miss Chaloner. Lady Milbanke's daughter appears to have a great deal of mind, and she is said to have a good deal of information, and is not at all affected."—*Journals and Correspondence of Miss Berry*, ii, 505.

10 Journal, 15 Aug. Probably Quintin Dick, M.P.

16 Fenwick to AIM, 8 June, asked "whether Lady M. & Sir Ralph are inclined to pass this Summer in the South for the restoration of their health." On 16 Oct. he told AIM he had heard from her mother that they would not be returning to the north for the winter.

19 Mrs. Grahame to AIM, 29 Sept. 1812.

25 Mrs. Grahame to AIM, 23 Apr. 1812.

30 Mrs. Grahame to AIM, 20 Nov. 1812. "Did you see in the paper the death of Mrs. Grahame? it is a happy release for her"—J to AIB, Monday [28 Aug. 1815].

119 4 Fenwick to AIM, 8 June.

39 Dated Octr. 8, 1812, incomplete and inaccurate from Lovelace's transcript in Mayne, pp. 48–9.

5. *BYRON BEFORE HE WAS FAMOUS, 1788–1812*

120 7 Medwin, 2nd ed., 1824, p. 72.

32 *ibid*, p. 73.

121 6 B to John Murray, 16 Oct. 1820, *LJ*, v, 99.

11 Mrs. Byron to Mrs. Charles Leigh, 29 Nov. 1792, Marchand, i, 34.

14 Medwin, p. 73; Marchand, i, 46.

18 *The Problem of Byron's Lameness*, by Denis Browne, F.R.C.S. *Proceedings of the Royal Society of Medicine*, June 1960, vol. 53, No. 6, pp. 440–42.

26 Moore, *Life of Byron*, 1920 ed., p. 10.

40 *The Trial of William Lord Byron, Baron Byron of Rochdale, for the Murder of William Chaworth, Esq.* . . . Published by Order of the House of Peers . . . 1765.

Page Line

122 8 John Hanson to James Farquhar, quoted Marchand, i, 49.
21 *LJ*, ii, 325, 347.
25 *LJ*, v, 449.
29 *LJ*, v, 450.
31 Hobhouse's Journal, quoted Marchand, i, 57.
34 *LJ*, i, 10.
36 Marchand, i, 58n.
39 Lady Caroline Lamb to Medwin, ? Nov. 1824, *LJ*, ii, 453.

123 2 Hobhouse's note, quoted Marchand, i, 50.
8 Moore, p. 27.
19 Mrs. Byron to Hanson, 30 Oct. 1803, *LJ*, i, 16.
26 Pryse Lockhart Gordon, *Personal Memoirs*, 2 vols., 1830, ii, 332–3.
33 B to Augusta, 18 Aug. 1804, *LJ*, i, 31.
37 Owen Mealey, the Newstead caretaker, to Hanson, 29 Nov. 1803, quoted Marchand, i, 79–80. Mealey seems to have been landlord of Newstead Hut, which was not "a lodge in the Park" ("*To Lord Byron*", p. 25), but the local inn (W. White, *Nottinghamshire*, 1832, p. 581); the Milbankes' friend, George Baker, broke his journey there when coming from Durham to Kirkby—Sir Ralph to AIB, Octbr. 1st 1815.
43 B to Augusta, 26 March 1804, *LJ*, i, 23.

124 3 Hobhouse's note, Nicolson, p. 300; Marchand, i, 80; Knight, *Lord Byron's Marriage*, pp. 202–3.
10 B to his mother, 11 Aug. 1809, *LJ*, i, 242.
n. Hobhouse's Journal, quoted Marchand, i, 351.
21 B to Augusta, 2 and 11 Nov. 1804, *LJ*, i, 43, 46, originals Lovelace Papers.

125 7 B to Augusta, 25 Oct. 1804, *LJ*, i, 35–40.
12 B to Augusta, 2 Nov. 1804, *LJ*, i, 42–3, original in Lovelace Papers.
17 B to Augusta, 22 March 1804, *LJ*, i, 19–20, original in Lovelace Papers.
22 B to Augusta, 26 March 1804, *LJ*, i, 23.
28 Augusta to Hanson, 18 Nov. 1804, *LJ*, i, 45.
33 B to Augusta, 30 Jan. 1805, *LJ*, i, 55.
42 B to Augusta, 22 March 1804, *LJ*, i, 22.

126 16 Mrs. Byron to Hanson, 1 and 4 March and 24 Apr. 1806, *LJ*, i, 95.
22 B to Augusta, 27 Dec. 1805 and 7 Jan. 1806, *LJ*, i, 91–4, originals in Lovelace Papers.
29 Moore, p. 41; Marchand, 1, 114.
33 Nicolson, p. 300.
35 White, *Nottinghamshire*, 1832, p. 697.
37 B to Capt. J. Leacroft, 31 Jan. 1807, *LJ*, i, 114.
43 Karl Elze, *Lord Byron: A Biography*, 1872, pp. 446–50; *Works*, i, xi, 112, 38.

127 18 B to Miss Pigot, 30 June and 5 July 1807, *LJ*, i, 130–36.
29 *LJ*, v, 169.

Page	Line	
127	37	De Quincey, *Confessions of an English Opium-Eater*, ed. Malcolm Elwin, 1956, p. 202.
128	8	B to Bankes, [? March 1807], *LJ*, i, 123.
	9	B to Hanson, 2 Apr. 1807, *LJ*, i, 126.
	11	B to his mother, 26 Feb. 1806, *LJ*, i, 95.
	13	B to Hanson, 7 Dec. 1806, *LJ*, i, 111.
	27	B to Miss Pigot, 5 and 13 July 1807, *LJ*, i, 133–8.
	35	B to Hanson, 23 and 30 Nov. 1805, 2 Apr. 1807, *LJ*, i, 85–6, 125–7.
	40	Diary, 12 Jan. 1821, *LJ*, v, 168–9.
129	1	B to Miss Pigot, 30 June 1807, *LJ*, i, 130.
	10	B to Miss Pigot, 26 Oct. 1807, *LJ*, i, 146.
	14	B to John Murray, 19 Nov. 1820, *LJ*, i, 150–60.
	20	*ibid.*
	29	*ibid.*
	33	*ibid.*
	37	*LJ*, i, 155n.
	41	B to Miss Pigot, 26 Oct. 1807, *LJ*, i, 147.
130	1	B to Hanson, 25 Jan. 1808, *LJ*, i, 175.
	6	B to Augusta, 26 Apr. 1808, *LJ*, i, 187–8, original in Lovelace Papers.
	14	B to Becher, 28 March 1808, incomplete in *LJ*, i, 185–7, *cf.* Marchand, i, 152–3.
	22	B to Murray, 19 Nov. 1820, *LJ*, i, 150–60.
131	3	B to Dallas, 20 Jan. 1808, *LJ*, i, 168–71.
	16	B to Hanson, 18 Nov. 1808 and 26 Apr. 1809, *LJ*, i, 199–200, 221–2.
	20	B to Becher, 26 Feb. 1808, *LJ*, i, 182–5.
	23	Journal, 22 Nov. 1813, *LJ*, ii, 330.
	28	B to Hanson, 17 Jan. 1809, Marchand, i, 165.
	30	*LJ*, i, 236.
	40	Hobhouse, quoted Marchand, i, 199.
	43	B to his mother, 15 Sept. 1809, *LJ*, i, 243–6.
132	4	Galt, *Life of Byron*, 1830, p. 66.
	14	Hobhouse's Journal, Broughton, i, 13–14; Marchand, i, 201.
	19	Moore, p. 94.
	28	*Works*, iii, 5–12.
	30	B to Henry Drury, 3 May 1810, incomplete in *LJ*, i, 262–9, *cf.* Marchand, i, 201; *Self-Portrait*, i, 63–7.
	32	*Works*, ii, 118–21.
	40	*Corresp.*, i, 77.
133	2	*LJ*, v, 172.
	10	*Works*, iii, 15–17.
	13	p. 116.
	26	Moore, p. 119.
	31	Nicolson, p. 301.
	37	*LJ*, i, 292–3.
	40	*Self-Portrait*, i, 81.

Page	Line	
134	2	*ibid*, i, 87; Marchand, i, 258.
	11	*LJ*, ii, 311. The 2nd Marquess of Sligo (1788–1845) succeeded his father in the title in 1809; he was a boyhood friend of De Quincey's, *Confessions of an English Opium-Eater*, ed. Elwin, 1956, pp. 14, 24, 139–40, 246–7, 252, 372.
	19	C. L. Meryon, *Memoirs of Lady Hester Stanhope*, 3 vols., 1845, iii, 218–19; Ian Bruce, *The Nun of Lebanon*, 1951, p. 405; *LJ*, i, 290.
	24	B to Hobhouse, 4 Oct. 1810, *LJ*, i, 302.
	31	B to Hobhouse, 26 Nov. 1810, *Corresp.*, i, 21.
	38	B to Hodgson, 20 Jan. 1811, *Corresp.*, i, 29–30.
135	2	Byron's copy of Horace in the possession of the Earl of Lytton, a family heirloom by the 2nd Earl of Lovelace's will.
	4	B to Hobhouse, 5 March 1811, *Self-Portrait*, i, 92.
	7	B to Hobhouse, 15 May 1811, incomplete in *Corresp.*, i, 32–5, *cf.* Marchand, i, 269–70.
	16	B to Lady Melbourne, 15 Sept. 1812, *Corresp.*, i, 78.
	30	B to Davies, 7 Aug. 1811, *LJ*, i, 324–5.
	33	*LJ*, i, 339.
	38	B to Augusta, 21 Aug. 1811, *LJ*, i, 332–3.
136	8	Augusta to B, 27 Aug. 1811, *LJ*, ii, 10–11.
	20	B to Augusta, 30 Aug. 1811, *LJ*, ii, 10–12, original in Lovelace Papers.
	29	2nd letter, 30 Aug. 1811, *LJ*, ii, 13–14.
	35	Augusta to B, 31 Aug. 1811, *LJ*, ii, 16–17.
137	5	*LJ*, ii, 46.
	11	Edleston and "Thyrza": Marchand, i, 295–7; *LJ*, ii, 52–4, 57–8; *Works*, ii, 104–5; iii, 30–34.
	n.	"Detached Thoughts," 1821, *LJ*, v, 449.
	22	Susan Vaughan's letters, "*To Lord Byron*", pp. 23–39.
138	12	B to Rushton, 21 and 25 Jan. 1812, Moore, p. 153. Rushton is a not uncommon name in Nottinghamshire, but in 1832 a schoolmaster named Robert Rushton was living at Arnold, only a few miles from Newstead.—White's *Nottinghamshire*, 1832, p. 548.
	31	Though there is no indication to whom the letter was addressed, the date, January 28th 1812, suggests that it must have been written to Susan Vaughan. The original is endorsed in Lady Byron's hand, "Original letter of *B's*—To one who had deceived him."
	34	Moore, p. 152.
	35	B to Hobhouse, 10 Feb. 1812, *Self-Portrait*, i, 132.
	44	B to Hodgson, 16 Feb., *LJ*, ii, 99–100.
139	14	*Memoir of John Murray*, i, 208.
	21	B to Murray, 5 Sept. 1811, *LJ*, ii, 25–6.
	42	B to Hodgson, 3 Sept. 1811, *LJ*, ii, 18–22.
140	8	B to Hodgson, 13 Sept. 1811, *LJ*, ii, 35–6.
	21	B to Lord Holland, 25 Feb. 1812, *LJ*, ii, 103.
	31	B to Hodgson, 5 March 1812, *LJ*, ii, 104–5.
	36	Foster, *The Two Duchesses*, p. 375.

Page	Line	
140	41	Rogers, *Table-Talk*, 1952, p. 190.
141	n.	Morgan, ii, 200; John Cordy Jeaffreson, *The Real Lord Byron*, standard ed., p. 139.
142	8	Lady Caroline Lamb to B, the first dated by Byron March 9th *1812*, the second undated but received on or before 11 March. Thomas Hookham, of Old Bond Street, was the bookseller who reported to Shelley the death of his first wife—Roger Ingpen, *Shelley in England*, 1917, pp. 474–5.
	21	Dallas, pp. 226–8, 244–6. It will be seen that Dallas faithfully remembered the contents of Lady Caroline's letters.

6. PROPOSAL AND REJECTION: JULY 1812–JULY 1813

Page	Line	
143	8	Cecil, *The Young Melbourne*, 1939, p. 33.
	13	*ibid*, p. 91.
	17	*In Whig Society*, p. 71.
	19	Haydon, *Autobiography and Journals*, 1950, pp. 524–5, 528.
	24	Bessborough, p. 129.
	29	Morgan, ii, 212.
144	3	Bessborough, p. 155.
	5	Morgan, ii, 199.
	18	*In Whig Society*, p. 119.
	28	Bessborough, p. 175. Lord Wentworth wrote to his sister Judith, 27 June 1789: "I suppose you have heard of the shocking piece of Scandal which lately has been much talked of, Lord Bolingbroke's going off with his Sister Miss Beauclerck, who is in a way to make him at once an Uncle & a Father." *cf. Astarte*, p. 152n.
	37	Bessborough, p. 215.
	42	Rogers, *Table-Talk*, ed. Bishop, pp. 189–90.
145	3	Morgan, ii, 200.
	13	Dallas, p. 245.
	25	Lady Caroline Lamb to Medwin, ? Nov. 1824, *LJ*, ii, 451.
	31	Dallas, pp. 248–9.
	35	Foster, *The Two Duchesses*, p. 362.
	40	Michael Joyce, *My Friend H*, 1948, p. 37; Broughton, i, 44.
	41	Bessborough, p. 223.
146	2	Joyce, pp. 37–40, Marchand, i, 355–8.
	14	Paston and Quennell, "*To Lord Byron*", p. 190.
	43	Lady Caroline Lamb to B, undated, but the reference to Newstead suggests a few days before the auction sale on 14 Aug.
147	13	*Lord Granville Leveson-Gower: Private Correspondence*, ed. Castalia Countess Granville, 2 vols., 1916, ii, 447–8.
	19	*In Whig Society*, p. 131.
	26	Bessborough, p. 224; *Lord Granville Leveson-Gower*, ii, 452–3.
	41	B to Lady Melbourne, 10 Sept. 1812, *Corresp.*, i, 71–2.
148	43	B to Lady Melbourne, 13 Sept., *Corresp.*, i, 73–5.
149	8	B to Lady Melbourne, 15 Sept., *Corresp.*, i, 77.
	23	B to Lady Melbourne, 18 Sept., *Corresp.*, i, 79.

Page	*Line*	
149	n.	Maria Edgeworth, *Tales and Novels*, 18 vols., 1833, vol. x, *The Modern Griselda*, pp. 285, 293, 302, 347.
	35	B to Lady Melbourne, 21 Sept., *Corresp.*, i, 81–3.
150	25	B to Lady Melbourne, 25 Sept., *Corresp.*, i, 83–5.
151	6	Lady Melbourne to B, 29 Sept., *In Whig Society*, pp. 143–7. Hobhouse received from Byron all Lady Melbourne's letters to him, and apparently exchanged them in 1827 to Lady Melbourne's daughter, Lady Cowper, for Byron's letters to Lady Melbourne, *cf.* Broughton, iii, 173, 227. Lady Cowper's great-granddaughter, Lady Airlie, did not indicate how many of Lady Melbourne's letters had survived.
	27	B to Lady Melbourne, 28 Sept., *Corresp.*, i, 86–9.
	30	Dorothy Margaret Stuart, *Dearest Bess*, 1955, p. 195.
152	7	AIM Journal, Richmond, 8 Dec. 1812: "We came to this place Oct. 8 . . . Mr. William Bankes visited us on the 6th of October, to take his leave . . ."
153	20	AIM to Lady Gosford, Melbourne House, Wednesday [14 Oct.], part in Mayne, p. 50.
154	4	AIM to Lady Melbourne, n.d., *In Whig Society*, pp. 138–40, text here given from Lovelace's transcript.
	39	B to Lady Melbourne, 17 Oct., *Corresp.*, i, 90–91.
155	17	B to Lady Melbourne, 18 Oct., *Corresp.*, i, 92–4.
	26	B to Lady Melbourne, 20 Oct., *Corresp.*, i, 94–5.
	29	B to Lady Melbourne, 18 Oct., *Corresp.*, i, 92.
156	19	Lady Melbourne to AIM, Whitehall 21st Oct. 1812.
	32	AIM to Lady Melbourne, undated, *In Whig Society*, pp. 136–8.
157	17	Lady Melbourne to AIM, Whitehall 25th Octr. 1812.
	22	AIM to Lady Melbourne, undated, *In Whig Society*, pp. 138–40.
	28	B to Lady Melbourne, 24 Oct., *Corresp.*, i, 97.
	36	Journal, 8 Dec. 1812.
	40	Auto-description.
158	32	J. R. Fenwick to AIM, 26 Nov. 1812.
	42	Journal, 19 Jan. 1813.
159	11	Journal, 28 Jan. 1813.
	14	Journal, 5 Feb.
	16	Journal, 2 Apr.
	20	Journal, 21 Feb.
	27	Journal, 15 March.
	33	Journal, 26 Feb.
	44	AIM to J, 1 May 1813.
160	4	Medwin, pp. 93–4.
	13	Uvedale Price in P. W. Clayden, *Rogers and His Contemporaries*, 2 vols., 1889, i, 398.
	19	Morgan, ii, 201.
	24	Rogers, *Table-Talk*, ed. Bishop, p. 192.
	28	B to Lady Melbourne, 12 Feb., *Corresp.*, i, 134.
	34	Journal, 26 Dec. 1812.
	38	Journal, 13 Feb. 1813.

Page	Line	
160	41	Journal, 7 May.
	43	Journal, 10 May.
161	6	Journal, 19 May.
	10	" Character " of Maria Edgeworth, 1813.
	15	Journal, 2 June 1813.
	20	AIM to Viscountess Wentworth, Seaham Septr. 4 [1813].
	36	Auto-description, part quoted in Mayne, p. 55.
162	3	Narratives Q and F, the latter revised from the former in March 1817.
	19	Augusta to AIM, Thursday [20 Oct. 1814].

7. ANNABELLA IN PURSUIT: JULY 1813–SEPTEMBER 1814

163	9	B to Lady Melbourne, 2 May 1813, *Corresp.*, i, 151.
	11	Medwin, p. 94.
	14	Annabella's Statement U, so designated by Lovelace, partly dictated to Mrs. Clermont in London during March 1816.
	n.	Broughton, i, 41; *Works*, ii, 11; *Corresp.*, i, 145.
	18	Marchand, i, 396n.
164	7	Lady Caroline Lamb to Medwin, ? Nov. 1824, *LJ*, ii, 453. *cf.* an account by the Duchess of Beaufort to Lady Holland, 8 July 1813, *In Whig Society*, p. 154.
	11	AIM to Lady Melbourne, undated, *In Whig Society*, pp. 160–61.
	30	AIM to Lady Melbourne, *In Whig Society*, pp. 159–60, where the date of the letter is given as 18 July, the date of Byron's reply to Lady Melbourne.
	43	B to Lady Melbourne, 18 July 1813, *Corresp.*, i, 167.
165	4	*cf.* p. 162.
	21	B to Augusta, 4 Bennet Street St. James's, March 26th, 1813, given in *LJ*, ii, 197–8, from a copy of the original in the Lovelace Papers.
	n.	Augusta's Bible, *cf.* pp. 130, 136.
	29	*Corresp.*, i, 162.
	32	*LJ*, ii, 229–30.
166	5	AIB to J, Saturday [2 Sept. 1815].
	12	Narrative of Circumstances connected with AL, designated Narrative F by Lovelace, probably written in March 1817, as Annabella wrote to Mrs. Villiers on 24 March 1817: "did I tell you that I was composing *mon histoire?*" Paraphrased in Mayne, p. 165.
	15	B to Lady Melbourne, 9 Nov. 1812, *Corresp.*, i, 104.
	25	B to Lady Melbourne, 30 July 1813, *Corresp.*, i, 167.
	32	B to Lady Melbourne, 5 Aug. 1813, *Corresp.*, i, 168.
167	39	AIM to B, Aug. 22, though described as "much shortened," given in full in Mayne, pp. 57–9, except two sentences here included.
168	29	B to AIM, 4 Bennet Street, 25th August 1813, *LJ*, iii, 397–9. The originals of Byron's letters to Annabella are in the Lovelace Papers, whence these quotations are taken, but references are

Page	Line	
		given to the published versions, which almost always contain inaccuracies, though those in Mayne are generally accurate, having been copied from Lovelace's transcripts.
	40	AIM to B, Aug. 28, Mayne, p. 60.
169	13	B to AIM, August 31st 1813, given in full, Mayne, pp. 60–62.
	33	AIM to B, Septr. 3, part paraphrased in Mayne, p. 65.
170	10	B to AIM, Sept. 6th 1813, the first part in Mayne, p. 66, the remainder in *LJ*, iii, 399–401.
171	32	AIM to B, Septr. 16, a few sentences, one notably misquoted, in Mayne, pp. 67–8.
	37	B to Lady Melbourne, 1 July 1813, *Corresp.*, i, 162.
	45	B to Lady Melbourne, 1 May 1814, *Corresp.*, i, 257.
172	13	B to Lady Melbourne, 28 Sept. 1813, *Corresp.*, i, 183.
	17	B to Moore, 27 Sept. 1813, *LJ*, ii, 267.
	22	B to AIM, Aston Hall, Rotherham, Sept. 23rd, 1813.
	45	B to AIM, Septr. 26th 1813, *LJ*, iii, 401–4.
173	39	AIM to B, Octr. 1, a few sentences only in Mayne, p. 69.
174	3	B to Lady Melbourne, 8 Oct., *Corresp.*, i, 192.
	6	B to Lady Melbourne, 13 Oct., *Corresp.*, i, 200.
	11	B to Lady Melbourne, 23 Oct., *Corresp.*, i, 213.
	14	B to Lady Melbourne, 17 Oct., *Corresp.*, i, 204.
	18	B to Lady Melbourne, 17 Oct., *Corresp.*, i, 203.
	21	B to Lady Melbourne, 17 Oct., *Corresp.*, i, 204.
	27	B to Lady Melbourne, 10 Jan. 1814, *Corresp.*, i, 227.
	36	AIM to Lady Melbourne, undated, *In Whig Society*, pp. 161–2.
175	2	B to Lady Melbourne, 8 Oct., *Corresp.*, i, 192.
	5	B to Lady Melbourne, 23 Oct., *Corresp.*, i, 211.
	19	AIM to B, Nov. 3, part quoted in Mayne, p. 71.
176	23	B to AIM, Nov. 10th 1813, postscript Nov. 17th, postmark Nov. 18. Part in Mayne, pp. 71–2, part in *LJ*, iii, 404–8, where two consecutive paragraphs on pp. 404–5 are followed by a passage from the letter of 29 Nov., while the section on pp. 407–8, beginning "I have been scribbling" and including some errors, is attributed to 29 Nov.
177	6	AIM to B, Nov. 27, in Mayne, pp. 73–5, except one sentence.
178	14	B to AIM, Nov. 29th 1813. The first two paragraphs are in Mayne, pp. 75–6; the long third paragraph very incompletely and inaccurately in *LJ*, iii, 406–7. The remainder of the letter following the extract given here may be pieced together from Mayne, pp. 76–7 and the second paragraph (attributed to 10 Nov.) in *LJ*, iii, 405.
	39	AIM to Lady Gosford, Nov. 26, Mayne, p. 73.
179	24	AIM to Lady Gosford, Dec. 3, part in Mayne, pp. 77–8.
180	10	AIM to Lady Gosford, Dec. 5, fully, with slight inaccuracies, in Mayne, pp. 78–9.
	23	AIM to B, Dec. 26, part in Mayne, p. 80.
	31	B to Augusta, Novr. 8th 1813, *LJ*, ii, 277.
	36	B to Lady Melbourne, 25 Nov., *Corresp.*, i, 217–18.

Page	Line	
181	3	*ibid*, *Corresp.*, i, 218.
	7	Journal, 17 Nov., *LJ*, ii, 323.
	15	B to John Galt, 11 Dec., *LJ*, ii, 305.
	19	John Fox, *Vindication of Lady Byron*, 1871, quoted by Sir John C. Fox, *The Byron Mystery*, 1924, p. 85.
	21	*Astarte*, p. 263, *Works*, iii, 151.
	24	B to Augusta, Septr. 15th, *LJ*, ii, 264–5.
	25	B to Augusta, October 10th, *LJ*, ii, 276.
	28	B to Augusta, Novr. 8th, *LJ*, ii, 277.
	30	Journal, 16 Nov., *LJ*, ii, 321.
	31	Journal, 26 Nov., *LJ*, ii, 349.
	35	Journal, 24 Nov., *LJ*, ii, 343.
182	9	Augusta to B, postmarked Newmarket, 29 Nov. 1813, *Astarte*, p. 263. The hair, a natural curl, is a rich dark brown, shot with a lighter shade.
	13	Journal, 17 Nov. 1813, *LJ*, ii, 323.
	21	B to Lady Melbourne, 8 Jan. 1814, *Corresp.*, i, 223, where "my old friends the H's in By. Square" are identified as the Harrowbys in Berkeley Square. The Harrowbys were not "old friends" of Byron's, and Lord Lovelace's transcript makes the more probable suggestion of Byron's lawyer, John Hanson, who lived in Bloomsbury Square.
	25	*Squire Osbaldeston: His Autobiography*, ed. E. D. Cuming, 1927, p. 40.
	39	B to Lady Melbourne, 11 Jan. 1814, *Corresp.*, i, 228.
183	7	B to Lady Melbourne, 29 Jan. 1814, *Corresp.*, i, 241.
	20	B to Lady Melbourne, 13 Jan. 1814, *Corresp.*, i, 231–2.
	22	J to AIB, July 12 [1816].
	26	AIB to J, July 14 [1816].
	38	AIB to Mrs. Villiers, 11 May 1852, *Lady Noel Byron and the Leighs*, p. 242; *Astarte*, p. 149.
184	24	*Memoir and Correspondence of John Murray*, i, 223–4.
	n.	Augusta to AIB, Wednesday, endorsed by AIB, Jany. 17th, 1816.
	28	B to Hanson, 1 Feb. 1814, *LJ*, iii, 20.
	37	B to Murray, 7 Feb., *LJ*, iii, 27.
185	4	Journal, Feb. 18, *LJ*, ii, 383.
	7	B to Lady Melbourne, undated. Published in *Corresp.*, i, 242, as if a postscript to the letter of 6 Feb., but the Lovelace transcript shows it to be the last page of a letter, beginning, "prospect) I never shall. One of my great inducements . . ." The context suggests that its date was 19 Feb.
	26	B to Lady Melbourne, 21 Feb. 1814, differing notably in punctuation and underlining from *Corresp.*, i, 245–6.
	39	B to Lady Melbourne, 16 Jan. 1814, *Corresp.*, i, 237.
186	34	AIM to B, Seaham Feb. 10, part in Mayne, p. 84.
187	12	B to AIM, Fy. 12th 1814, complete in Mayne, pp. 84–6, except the passage quoted from AIM above.

Page	*Line*	
187	20	B to AIM, Febry. 15th 1814, in Mayne, pp. 86–7.
188	5	AIM to B, Seaham Feb. 17, in Mayne, pp. 87–8, with one notable omission.
	12	AIM to B, Seaham Feb. 18, ignored in Mayne.
	33	B to AIM, Feby. 19th 1814, in Mayne, pp. 88–9, with some inaccuracies.
189	2	B to Lady Melbourne, undated, *cf.* p. 185, l. 7 above, and *Corresp.*, i, 242.
	30	AIM to B, Seaham Feb. 24, part in Mayne, pp. 89–90.
	34	B to Lady Melbourne, undated, attributed to March in *Corresp.*, i, 247, but the rest of the letter deals with the *Courier* attack and must have been written about the same time as the letter to Moore of 26 Feb. in *LJ*, iii, 50–51.
	39	B to AIM, Fy. 25th 1814, in Mayne, p. 90, without date.
190	24	B to AIM, March 3d 1814, part in Mayne, pp. 90–91, omitting the statement on religion, given with slight inaccuracies in *LJ*, iii, 408.
191	4	AIM to B, Seaham March 12, two sentences only, without date, in Mayne, p. 91.
	8	Journal, 15 March, *LJ*, ii, 401.
	23	B to AIM, March 15th 1814, Mayne, pp. 92–3.
	27	AIM to B, Seaham March 12.
	33	AIM to Hugh Montgomery, Seaham March 10 1814.
192	9	AIM to B, Seaham April 13, a few sentences in Mayne, pp. 93–4.
	21	B to Lady Melbourne, 18 Apr., *Corresp.*, i, 250.
	31	B to AIM, Albany April 20th 1814, Mayne, pp. 94–5.
	37	Journal, March 22, *LJ*, ii, 406.
	40	Journal, March 28, *LJ*, ii, 408.
	42	B to Lady Melbourne, 8 Apr., *Corresp.*, i, 249.
193	n.	Augusta's Bible, *cf.* pp. 130, 136, 165.
	11	B to Lady Melbourne, 25 Apr., *Corresp.*, i, 251.
	21	AIM to B, Durham April 23, part in Mayne, p. 95.
	24	AIM to B, undated, but received before Byron's letter to Lady Melbourne, of 29 Apr., which mentions the verses on frowning.
194	7	B to Lady Melbourne, 29 Apr., *Corresp.*, i, 253–4.
	27	B to Lady Melbourne, 30 Apr., *Corresp.*, i, 254–5.
	38	B to Lady Melbourne, April-May 1st, *Corresp.*, i, 256.
195	2	B to Moore, 4 May, *LJ*, iii, 80.
	22	"Stanzas for Music," Lovelace ms. reproduced in facsimile in *Astarte*, 1905, differing in details from *Works*, iii, 413.
	25	B to Augusta, 9 May, *LJ*, iii, 84.
	37	*Lara*, Lovelace ms., *Astarte*, 329–30.
	40	Hobhouse's Journal, 19 May, quoted Marchand, i, 451.
196	4	AIM to B, Seaham May 17, one sentence without date in Mayne, p. 97.
	10	Lady Melbourne to AIM, Whitehall 25th May 1814. One passage indicates how well informed Lady Melbourne was of court matters: "we pass our time at Assemblys in pushing about &

Page Line

begging pardon of two Princes—one the Prince Paul of Wirtemberg the other The Prince of Orange, whom people say is a *jilted Prince*. This I do not believe & am inclined to think she (the Pss. C[harlotte]) likes him, but not enough to risk being obliged to pass her life with him *in Holland*. If they would but secure her against going there when she may not be inclined to do so, all would be quickly settled." *cf. The Autobiography of Miss Knight, Lady Companion to Princess Charlotte*, ed. Roger Fulford, 1960, pp. 168–73.

196 16 B to Moore, 8 June 1822, *LJ*, vi, 81.
20 B to Lady Melbourne, 28 May, *Corresp.*, i, 258.
31 Lady Caroline Lamb to B, undated [before 10 June], part quoted in Marchand, i, 457.
37 B to Lady Melbourne, 10 June, *Corresp.*, i, 260.

197 2 Mrs. Villiers to AIB, Saturday May 18th [1816] mentioned but not quoted in *Astarte*, p. 34.
5 Lady Caroline Lamb to Lady Melbourne, 15 Oct. 1812, *In Whig Society*, p. 148.
15 AIM to B, Seaham June 19, part in Mayne, p. 97.
23 B to Lady Melbourne, 21 June, *Corresp.*, i, 260–61.
34 B to AIM, June 21st 1814, undated in Mayne, pp. 98–9.

198 5 AIM to B, Seaham June 23, one sentence undated in Mayne, p. 99.
18 AIM to B, Seaham June 24, part undated in Mayne, p. 99.
37 Lady Caroline Lamb to B, undated, Lovelace transcript.
39 B to Lady Melbourne, 28 June, *Corresp.*, i, 262.

199 4 B to Lady Melbourne, 10 June, *Corresp.*, i, 259–60.
9 B to Lady Melbourne, 28 June, *Corresp.*, i, 262.
12 B to Lady Melbourne, 26 June, *Corresp.*, i, 261.
13 Hobhouse's Journal, Broughton, i, 157.
15 B to Lady Melbourne, 2 July, *Corresp.*, i, 263.
17 B to Lady Melbourne, 2 July, *Corresp.*, i, 265.
20 *Memoir of the Rev. Francis Hodgson*, by his son, 2 vols., 1878, i, 285–6.
23 *LJ*, iii, 102, 107.
33 Lady Caroline Lamb to Medwin, ? Nov. 1824, *LJ*, ii, 453.
39 Sir Ralph Milbanke to B, Seaham July 19th 1814.

200 20 AIM to B, Seaham July 19, misrepresented by paraphrase in Mayne, p. 100.
28 B to Lady Melbourne, 30 Apr., *Corresp.*, i, 255.
33 B to Augusta, 18 and 24 June, *LJ*, iii, 97, 100.
35 B to Rogers, 27 June, *LJ*, iii, 102.

201 2 B to AIM, Hastings, August 1st 1814, Mayne, p. 101.
21 Narrative Q, devised in July 1816 and the following months, and revised in March 1817 as Narrative F. Mistakenly described in *The Late Lord Byron*, p. 139, as "written late in life."
24 B to Lady Melbourne, 4 Oct. 1814, *Corresp.*, i, 273–4.
30 *cf.* p. 146.
32 *LJ*, ii, 406.

Page	*Line*	
202	24	AIM to B, Seaham Aug. 6, with some omissions in Mayne, pp. 102–3.
203	2	B to AIM, August 10th 1814, postmark London August 10th, Mayne, p. 103. The postmark has some importance as showing that Byron returned from Hastings to London at least a day earlier than has been supposed, *cf.* Marchand, i, 466.
	31	AIM to B, Seaham Aug. 13, cited but neither quoted nor dated in Mayne, p. 104.
	45	B to AIM, August 16th 1814, Mayne, p. 104.
204	36	AIM to B, Seaham Aug. 21, a passage on *Lara* only, undated, in Mayne, p. 105.
	45	B to AIM, Newstead Abbey, August 25th 1814, Mayne, pp. 105–6.
205	30	AIM to B, Seaham Sept. 2, postscript Sept. 3, part undated in Mayne, p. 107.
206	7	B to AIM, Newstead Abbey, 7th Septr. 1814, Mayne, pp. 108–9.
	21	AIM to B, Seaham, Tuesday [13 Sept.], a few lines quoted without date, Mayne, pp. 109–10.
	36	B to Lady Melbourne, 4 Oct. 1814, *Corresp.*, i, 274.
207	2	Narrative Q, repeated in Narrative F.
	6	Moore, p. 264.
	17	Narratives Q and F.
	42	B to AIM, Newstead Abbey, Septr. 9th 1814, postmark Mansfield Sept. 10th, Mayne, p. 111.
208	5	Narrative Q.
	22	AIM to B, Seaham, Wednesday, endorsed Sept. 14, 1814, undated in Mayne, pp. 111–12.
	n.	Sir Ralph Milbanke to B, Sepbr. 14th 1814.
	29	AIM to B, also dated Seaham, Wednesday, and endorsed Sept. 14th, 1814.
209	14	Narrative Q supplemented by Narrative F, which adds some details but, being a revised draft, is more pedantically phrased. A few sentences in Mayne, p. 112.
	37	B to AIM, Newstead Abbey, Septr. 18th 1814, Mayne, pp. 112–13.
210	16	B to AIM, Newstead Abbey, Sept. 19th 1814, Mayne, pp. 443–4.
	38	B to AIM, Newstead Abbey, Septr. 20th 1814, postmarked Mansfield 21st, Mayne, p. 444.
211	15	B to Lady Melbourne, 18 Sept. The slight differences in interpretation of punctuation in Lovelace's transcript, here given, from *Corresp.*, i, 267–8, lend emphasis in meaning, notably in the word "seriously" at the end of the sentence instead of being prefixed to its successor. The word *secret* is twice underlined.
	18	Albert Brecknock, *Byron: A Study of the Poet in the Light of New Discoveries*, 1926, p. 257.

Page	Line	
		8. FOUR MONTHS' ENGAGEMENT: SEPTEMBER—DECEMBER 1814.
214	6	AIM to B, Seaham, Thursday [22 Sept.], postscript Friday [23], part, with omissions and errors, in Mayne, pp. 444–6.
	30	AIM to Hugh Montgomery, Sept. 22nd 1814, a phrase undated in Mayne, p. 118.
	35	AIM to Lady Gosford, 28th September.
215	30	J to Hugh Montgomery, Octr. 1st, 1814.
	35	*ibid.*
	41	AIM to B, Septr. 28, Mayne, p. 450.
216	23	J to Lady Melbourne, Seaham Sepr. 25, 1814.
	47	AIM to B, Septr. 29, postscript Friday [30], with omissions not indicated in Mayne, p. 451.
217	5	Auto-description.
	11	B to AIM, Sept. 26th 1814, Mayne, pp. 446–7.
	25	B to AIM, Sept. 26th 1814, postmark 27th, Mayne, pp. 447–50.
	35	AIM to B, Septr. 28, Mayne, p. 450.
	42	AIM to B, Septr. 29, Mayne, p. 451.
218	8	B to AIM, Octr. 3rd, 1814, Mayne, pp. 452–3.
	13	AIM to B, Octr. 3, Mayne, p. 452.
	28	Selina Doyle to AIM, Saturday night 24th, received in England 30 Sept.
	43	Joanna Baillie to AIM, 3 Oct.
219	18	Emily Milner to AIM, Nun Appleton, Sunday [2 Oct.].
	n.	AIM to Emily Milner, 23 Sept. and Tuesday [4 Oct.], in *LJ*, iii, 147–9.
220	20	AIM to Lady Gosford, Octr. 8, but begun Thursday [6th], a few sentences inaccurately quoted in Mayne, p. 119.
	26	B to an unnamed correspondent, 5 Oct. 1814, *LJ*, iii, 145.
	45	B to AIM, October 9th 1814, Mayne, p. 459.
221	5	J to Lady Melbourne, Seaham Sepr. 25, 1814, *cf.* p. 216.
	11	B to Lady Melbourne, 4 Oct., *Corresp.*, i, 273; Fox, p. 75n.
	20	Augusta to AIM, Octr. 1st 1814, complete but with slight errors in Fox, pp. 75–6.
	27	AIM to B, Octr. 3, omitted in Mayne, p. 452.
222	2	B to AIM, Octr. 7, Mayne, pp. 456–7.
	6	B to Lady Melbourne, 7 Oct., *Corresp.*, i, 276.
	15	B to Lady Melbourne, 12 Oct., *Corresp.*, i, 280.
	19	B to Hobhouse, 17 Oct., *Corresp.*, i, 282.
	20	B to Lady Melbourne, 7 Oct., *Corresp.*, i, 277.
	21	B to Lady Melbourne, 17 Oct., *Corresp.*, i, 281.
	39	Augusta to AIM, Saturday Octr. 15 1814.
223	1	AIM to B, Seaham Monday [17 Oct.], Mayne, p. 465.
	27	Augusta to AIM, Thursday 20 Oct., *cf.* p. 162.
	30	AIM to B, Wednesday [19 Oct.], Mayne, p. 468.
	35	B to AIM, Octr. 22d. 1814, *LJ*, iii, 160; *cf.* Mayne, p. 469.
	42	AIM to B, *Sunday* [2 Oct.], Mayne, p. 452.

Page	Line	
224	2	B to AIM, Octr. 8th 1814, Mayne, p. 458.
	8	AIM to B, Octr. 10, Mayne, p. 460.
	15	B to AIM, October 19th 1814, Mayne, p. 466.
	21	AIM to B, Monday [17 Oct.], Mayne, p. 465.
	23	AIM to B, *Tuesday Night* [18 Oct.], Mayne, pp. 120, 466.
	26	AIM to B, Wednesday [19 Oct.], Mayne, p. 468.
	33	AIM to B, Octr. 22, Mayne, p. 470.
225	6	AIM to B, *Sunday* [23 Oct.], Mayne, p. 470.
	21	B to AIM, Octr. 25th 1814, Mayne, p. 471.
	25	B to Hanson, 25 Oct., *LJ*, iii, 162.
226	4	Augusta to AIM, Wednesday Octr. 26.
	40	Augusta to AIM, Thursday Octr. 27.
227	6	Narrative Q, repeated in Narrative F.
	8	AIB to Doyle, undated, postmark illegible, attributed by Lovelace to Feb. 1817, part in *Lady Noel Byron and the Leighs*, p. 65.
	23	Doyle to AIB, undated.
	32	B to Lady Melbourne, 31 Oct., the symbol +, here given as in Lovelace's transcript, is omitted in *Corresp.*, i, 286.
	36	*ibid.*
228	25	Statement MN.
	35	AINB to Harriet Beecher Stowe, Nov. 1st [1856].
229	5	Narrative Q.
	9	*ibid.*
	15	*ibid.*
	20	Narrative F, March 1817, revised from Q.
230	3	B to Lady Melbourne, 4 Nov., *Corresp.*, i, 287–8.
	7	*In Whig Society*, p. 139, *cf.* p. 153.
	11	J to Hugh Montgomery, Novr. 4, 1814.
	17	B to Lady Melbourne, 6 Nov., *Corresp.*, i, 288–9.
231	2	B to Lady Melbourne, 13 Nov., *Corresp.*, i, 289–91.
	33	AINB to Harriet Beecher Stowe [1856].
232	1	Harriet Beecher Stowe, *Lady Byron Vindicated*, 1870, p. 157.
	6	Statement given to my Mother, Kirkby Mallory, Jan. 18, 1816.
	20	Augusta to AIB, Saturday Eveg [22 March 1817].
	40	AIM to B, Wednesday Night [16 Nov.], undated in Mayne, pp. 127–8.
233	12	B to AIM, Boroughbridge, Novr. 16th, 1814, Mayne, p. 126.
	25	Narrative Q, slightly altered in Narrative F, March 1817. Mayne, p. 154, erroneously states that Byron was dissuaded by Augusta from breaking the engagement when he was at Six Mile Bottom on his way *to* Seaham *from* London in December.
	41	AIM to B, Thursday [17 Nov.], undated in Mayne, p. 128.
234	18	AIM to B, Saturday [19 Nov.], undated in Mayne, pp. 128–9.
235	5	J to B, Novr. 19th 1814.
	10	AIM to B, Sunday [20 Nov.], Mayne, p. 130.
	22	B to AIM, Novr. 20th 1814, postmarked Newmarket, Mayne, p. 129.

Page Line

235 30 B to AIM, Cambridge Novr. 22d. 1814, undated in Mayne, pp. 130–31.

33 B to AIM, Nover. 23d. 1814, postmarked Cambridge, Mayne, p. 132. Dating from King's College, November 23d, 1814, Hodgson wrote: "When his Lordship walked up the Senate House, to give his vote at an Election which takes place at Cambridge today, the Young Men recognized him from the Galleries, and broke out into the most ardent and cheering applause, which they repeated as he returned.

To make this hearty & honest tribute of respect for unrivalled talents more welcome, it need only be added that a few days ago the young men were forbidden to express their approbation of any person by such tokens; but on this occasion it was absolutely extorted from them, & fully felt by their elders to be not only venial but demanded."

41 AIM to B, Durham Tuesday [22 Nov.], Mayne, p. 130. The letter from Augusta mentioned seems to have been lost, but Augusta wrote again on Friday Novr. 25th: "My last letter was so hurried—so uncomfortable so every thing that it ought *not* to be . . . Of course you hear of our dearest Byron from himself, & will know that he was detained at Cambge. till yesterday to vote for some Professor or Physician, I don't exactly understand what or whom."

236 6 AIM to B, undated from Durham 23 Nov., Mayne, p. 131.

10 *cf.* p. 231.

29 AIM to Lady Gosford, Seaham Nov. 23, but postscript evidently added 25th, four sentences undated in Mayne, p. 133.

237 9 AIM to B, Thursday Night 24 Nov., postmarked 28 Nov., re-addressed by Byron to The Lady Byron, Mivart's Hotel, Lower Brook Street, 3 April 1816, *cf.* Mayne, pp. 133–4.

19 AIM to B, Nov. 26, Mayne, pp. 134–5.

21 AIM to B, undated [27 Nov.], two other sentences in Mayne, p. 135.

31 AIM to B, Nov. 30, undated in Mayne, p. 136.

36 AIM to B, Dec. 4, Mayne, p. 138.

238 13 AIM to B, Seaham Monday [5 Dec.], part in Mayne, p. 139.

33 AIM to B, Tuesday [6 Dec.], part in Mayne, p. 140.

44 B to AIM, Novr. 29th 1814, Mayne, p. 136.

239 7 B to AIM, Decr. 3d. 1814, Mayne, p. 138.

12 B to AIM, Decr. 5th 1814, Mayne, p. 139.

39 Lady Melbourne to AIM, 1st Decr. 1814, postmark 2nd.

43 AIM to B, Wednesday [7 Dec.], Mayne, p. 141.

240 2 B to AIM, Decr. 5th 1814, Mayne, p. 138.

7 AIM to B, Dec. 9, mentioned without date in Mayne, p. 142.

17 Augusta to AIM, Wednesday Novr. 30.

30 AIM to Augusta, Dec. 2.

241 6 AIM to Augusta, Dec. 9, part undated in Mayne, p. 142.

22 Augusta to AIM, Monday Night Decr. 12.

Page	*Line*	
241	28	B to AIM, Decr. 8th 1814, Mayne, pp. 141–2.
242	2	AIM to B, Dec. 10, part in Mayne, p. 143.
	14	AIM to B, Sunday Night [11 Dec.], part in Mayne, pp. 143–4.
	24	AIM to B, Dec. 12, Mayne, p. 144.
	32	B to AIM, Decr. 12th 1814, Mayne, p. 144.
243	11	AIM to B, Wednesday [14 Dec.], part undated in Mayne, p. 146.
	26	B to AIM, Decr. 14th 1814, undated in Mayne, p. 145.
	n.	AIB to Mrs. Villiers, Kirkby, March 6 [1817], cited but not quoted in *Astarte*, p. 37n.
244	4	Augusta to B, Wednesday [14], postmarked 15 Dec. 1814, reproduced precisely in *Astarte* (1905), pp. 133–4, but with the two "very" crosses misplaced in *Astarte* (1921), pp. 37–8. The signature—the monogram of twirls used habitually by Byron and Augusta—is reproduced in both editions.
	11	B to AIM, Decr. 16th 1814, Mayne, p. 146.
	13	B to AIM, Decr. 18th 1814, Mayne, p. 147.
	26	AIM to B, Friday [16 Dec.], Mayne, pp. 146–7.
	36	AIM to B, Saturday [17 Dec.], Mayne, p. 147.
245	20	AIM to B, undated [?19 Dec.], part in Mayne, pp. 148–9, and there attributed to 20 Dec.
	32	AIM to B, undated [? 20 Dec.], part in Mayne, pp. 149–50, and there attributed to 21 Dec.
	37	AIM to B, Dec. 21, Mayne, p. 149.
246	9	AIB to Sir Ralph Noel, Kirkby Mallory, Feb. 5, 1816.

9. THE HONEYMOON: 2nd to 21st JANUARY 1815

247	5	B to AIM, Decr. 23d. 1814, Mayne, p. 151.
	10	Hobhouse's Journal, 24 Dec., Broughton, i, 191. The extracts from Hobhouse's Journal are from Lovelace's transcripts, made when he was allowed access to Hobhouse's papers by Lady Dorchester from 1870 to 1883, but where they have been published, as in this instance, references are given.
	13	Augusta to AIM, Xtmas day.
	18	B to AIM, Decr. 25th 1814, Mayne, p. 153.
	21	Hobhouse's Journal, 26 Dec., Broughton, i, 191.
248	16	Hobhouse's Journal, 30 Dec., Lovelace's transcript, differing in details from both Broughton, i, 192–3, and Marchand, ii, 504, the latter being Prof. Marchand's own transcript from the original ms., now in the Berg Collection, New York Public Library.
	32	Hobhouse's Journal, 31 Dec., Broughton, i, 194–5; Marchand, ii, 504.
	35	*ibid.*, 1 Jan.
249	n.[1]	*Wentworth Peerage Case*, 1864, document no. 62, p. 48.
	31	Hobhouse's Journal, 2 Jan., Broughton, i, 195–7; Marchand, ii, 505–6.
	n.[2]	Mary G. Noel to Henrietta Jervis, Kirkby 10 Jan. 1815, franked "Wentworth", postmark Hinkley Eleventh Jany. 1815, and

Page Line

addressed to Miss H. Jervis, Argyle St., Bath. Henrietta Jervis "was about 16 & lived with her grandmother Mrs. Ricketts sister of John Jervis Earl St. Vincent before her marriage to Captain Edmund Palmer, C.B., R.N."—note by Miss Laura Palmer, of The Greenway, West Horsley, Surrey, who gave the letter to Mary Countess of Lovelace in July 1914.

250 1 Medwin, 1824, p. 47.

2 Hobhouse, review of Medwin, *Westminster Review*, Jan., 1825; Mrs. Clermont's Statement quoted in Lovelace's Digest of Lady Byron's Statements and Narratives, etc., p. xviii; F. W. Robertson's "Conversations with Ly B," January 1851; AINB's Medwin marginalia, 1851.

5 Statement to Harriet Beecher Stowe, 1856, but Jane Minns told a reporter of the *Newcastle Daily Chronicle* in 1869 that she "preceded Lord and Lady Byron, to prepare for their reception at Halnaby Hall," and Byron's valet, Fletcher, "was the only servant who accompanied the bride and bridegroom from Seaham to Halnaby, and . . . of course, sat upon the box" (unidentified news-cutting in Lovelace's scrapbook). Annabella copied into a copy of Medwin, 2nd ed., 1824, remarks by Hobhouse in his *Westminster Review* article, and wrote on p. 47: "There was nobody in the carriage that conveyed Lord & Lady Byron to Halnaby, on the day of their marriage, besides his lordship & his wife."

27 Statement T, written in March 1816. Some sentences quoted or paraphrased in Mayne, pp. 159–60, and Maurois, pp. 223–4.

35 Harriet Martineau, *Biographical Sketches 1852–68*, 2nd ed., 1869, p. 319.

251 2 News-cutting quoting *Newcastle Daily Chronicle*.

10 Statement A.

24 Narrative F, March 1817. The remark on Caroline Lamb is misquoted in Maurois, p. 224.

30 Statement T, March 1816, misquoted in Mayne, p. 161.

37 Rogers, *Table-Talk*, 1952, p. 193.

252 4 Narrative F, March 1817.

n.[1] The first version, Statement T, March 1816; the second, Statement FF, written in 1836. Mayne, pp. 161–2, paraphrases from all three versions.

12 Narrative F, March 1817.

18 *ibid.*, paraphrased in Maurois, p. 227.

23 Statement T, March 1816.

253 5 Narratives Q and F. Some sentences quoted out of context in Mayne, p. 165.

7 The dates of the statements were ignored by both Miss Mayne and M. Maurois. In his "Digest" of the statements Lovelace indicated his sources by the alphabetical symbols he allotted to every statement and separate scrap of Annabella's memoranda, but his conjectures as to dates of composition have to be sought in the files of his transcripts.

Page	Line	
253	19	Mrs. Clermont to AINB, 30 March 1830.
	29	B to Lady Melbourne, 13 Nov. 1814, *Corresp.*, 1, 290.
254	17	Augusta to AIB, Wednesday [4 Jan. 1815].
	n.[2]	*Astarte*, pp. 283, 273.
255	9	Narrative Q. *cf.* Maurois, p. 228; Mayne, p. 162.
	n.	*Works*, iii, 351.
	25	Augusta to AIB, Jany. 8th.
	34	Augusta to AIB, Monday Jany. 9th.
256	19	Augusta to AIB, Wednesday Jany. 11th.
257	11	Statement T, March 1816.
	27	Narrative Q, late 1816.
258	18	Narrative Q.
	34	Walter Raleigh, *The English Novel*, 1894, new ed. 1919, p. 228.
	38	Broughton, ii, 281.
	42	J to AIB, Janry. 9th 1815.
259	3	B to Lady Melbourne, *cf.* p. 230.
	9	Narrative F, March 1817.
	16	Narrative Q, late 1816.
	20	*ibid.*
	33	Lady Melbourne to AIB, Panshanger, 8th Janry. 1815.
260	29	Lady Melbourne to AIB, 16th Jany 1815.
	35	B to Lady Melbourne, 22 Jan., *Corresp.*, i, 295.
261	4	*cf.* pp. 185, 229, 230.
	12	B to Lady Melbourne, 7 Jan., *Corresp.*, i, 293.
	18	Narrative Q.
	22	AIB to Lord Wentworth, Halnaby, Jan. 18, 1815.
	28	J to AIB, Seaham, Janry. 9th 1815, but begun the previous day.
	42	Sir Ralph Milbanke to B, Seaham Jany. 12th, 1815.
262	3	J to AIB, Thursday night [12 Jan.].
	14	Reflections, &c. Halnaby, Jan. 13, 1815.
	30	*ibid.*
	36	Statement AA, late 1816 or early 1817.
263	3	Statement L, "Lord Byron and Literature," 1817.
	5	B to AIM, Septr. 20th 1814, *cf.* p. 210.
	9	Narrative F, March 1817.
	36	Narrative F.
264	7	*cf.* p. 259.
	37	Narrative Q, late 1816.
	n.	These mss. of *Hebrew Melodies* were among the papers received by her grandson from Lady Byron's trustees in 1868.
265	25	Augusta to AIB, Sunday Jany 15.
	35	Narrative Q, late 1816. Repeated with slight embellishments in the revised Narrative F, March 1817, with an added sentence indicative of Annabella's intention to submit the statement to lawyers if occasion arose: "I apprehend that what I have deviated from the order of time to introduce here, is not irrelevant to the subject of these melancholy recollections."
266	1	*cf.* p. 131.

Page	*Line*	
266	14	Augusta to AIB, Wednesday Jany. 18th.
	39	*ibid.*
	42	*cf.* p. 264.
267	2	*cf.* p. 257.
	6	*cf.* p. 257.
	20	Augusta to AIB, Friday, 20th [Jan.].
	29	*Astarte*, p. 139.
	33	*cf.* p. 231.
268	6	Narrative Q, repeated with slight embellishments in Narrative F, March 1817.
	n.	Unidentified newscutting in Lovelace's scrapbook, reprinting the interview from the *Newcastle Daily Chronicle*, *cf.* pp. 250–51.
269	21	Narrative Q, repeated with variations in Narrative F, March 1817.
	28	Narrative Q.
	37	Note by Lovelace in his "Digest of Lady Byron's Statements and Narratives, etc.," p. xxviii.
	42	*ibid.*
270	27	Statement L, "Lord Byron and Literature."
271	10	Narrative F, March 1817.
	22	Statement FF, 1836.
	24	AINB to Rev. F. W. Robertson, July 29th, 1850.
	42	Statement L, "Lord Byron and Literature."
272	6	Narrative F, March 1817.

10. SEAHAM AND SIX MILE BOTTOM 21st JANUARY—28th MARCH 1815

273	2	Sir Ralph Milbanke to B, Jany. 12th 1815.
	15	Narrative F, March 1817.
	20	Augusta to AIB, Friday, 20th [Jan.].
	24	Narrative Q.
	29	" Conversation with Mrs. Claremont, Oct. 11, 1846," by Henry Bence-Jones, M.D., F.R.S., who endorsed his ms., "I attended Mrs. Claremont for Lady Noel Byron for some years till she died." In 1842 Bence-Jones married Lady Millicent Acheson, second of the four daughters of Annabella's friend, Lady Gosford.
274	4	"I hope every thing is pleasantly settled with Mrs. Clermont."—J. R. Fenwick to AIM, undated, but attributed by Lovelace on internal evidence to Monday, 29 Apr. or 6 May 1811.
	6	Mrs. Clermont's Statement, March 1830, part quoted in *The Late Lord Byron*, p. 135.
	9	Jno. Ford to Lushington, Feby. 18th, 1825; Statement signed by M. A. Clermont and Sir Ralph Noel, witnessed by G. B. Wharton, 6th Aug. 1821.
	10	AINB to F. W. Robertson, Jan. 5, 1851, which mentions that Mrs. Clermont "died last year," aged "78 years."
	17	Reminiscences, 1818, designated Statement E by Lovelace.

Page Line

274 25 Mrs. Clermont's Statement, March 1830.
275 2 Mrs. Clermont to AINB, 30 March 1830.
11 Narrative R, a sequel to Q, written late in 1816 or early in 1817 on paper watermarked 1811.
14 Augusta to AIB, Thursday Jany. 26th.
23 Augusta to AIB, Saturday 28th [Jan.].
30 *ibid.*
34 Augusta to AIB, Monday Jany. 30th.
276 8 Narrative Q, late 1816.
17 Statement D, headed, "Reasons—London, March, 1816."
19 Augusta to AIB, Thursday Feby. 2d.
26 Augusta to AIB, Sunday Feb. 5th.
278 2 Lady Melbourne to AIB, Whitehall 7th Feby. 1815.
17 Narrative Q.
25 B to Lady Melbourne, 2 Feb. 1815, *Corresp.*, i, 300.
35 B to Moore, 2 Feb., *LJ*, iii, 176.
38 B to Moore, 10 Feb., *LJ*, iii, 179.
279 8 Augusta to AIB, Thursday Jany. 26th.
12 Narrative Q.
21 Augusta to AIB, Thursday Feby. 2d.
34 Augusta to AIB, Wednesday 8th Feb.
280 7 B to Lady Melbourne, 6 Feb., *Corresp.*, i, 301. For Lady Melbourne's reply of the 11th, see *Corresp.*, i, 304.
25 Augusta to AIB, Friday Feby. 10th.
281 10 Statement L, "Lord Byron and Literature."
28 Mary Anne Clermont's Statement, designated Δ by Lovelace and attributed by him to March 1816.
33 Narrative Q.
282 4 Augusta to AIB, Monday 13th [Feb.].
17 Augusta to AIB, Wednesday [15 Feb.].
n. Rogers, *Table-Talk*, 1952, p. 189. As early as April 1807 Byron reported how he had reduced his weight from 14 stone 6 lb. to 12 st. 7 lb. "by violent exercise, *much* physic, and *hot* bathing," *LJ*, i, 127.
283 n. *Works*, iii, 423; *LJ*, iii, 181, 183, 274.
12 Statement L, "Lord Byron and Literature."
27 *ibid.* On the basis of this Statement Lady Anne Blunt composed the note published by E. H. Coleridge in *Works*, iii, 30–31; her original draft is in the Lovelace Papers. According to a note in Marchand, i, 296–7, E. H. Coleridge supposed that Lady Anne's note was designed by Lovelace "to combat a theory of mine . . . that Thyrza and Edleston were one and the same person" and that "Lovelace wilfully or stupidly misunderstood the whole incident." In fact Lovelace and his sister were summarising their grandmother's evidence; it is clear that Annabella never suspected that Thyrza was *not* a woman. The reference to consumption may have led her to suppose that Thyrza was Byron's cousin, Margaret Parker. The tress of hair she supposed to have been

Page	Line	
		Thyrza's may have been that sent to Byron by Augusta on 29 Nov. 1813, *cf. Astarte*, p. 263.
284	14	*ibid*, Statement L.
	32	*Works*, iii, 399. The mss. of these two poems were among those delivered by Lady Byron's trustees to her grandson in 1868.
285	17	Mrs. Clermont's Statement, March 1830.
	22	Mrs. Clermont to Bence-Jones, 11 Oct. 1846, *cf.* p. 273.
	33	Mrs. Clermont's Statement, March 1830.
	40	This statement of Mrs. Clermont's to Bence-Jones is endorsed by Annabella's own statement, p. 264.
286	n.	Narratives Q and F.
	12	Augusta to AIB, Sunday 19th [Feb.].
	18	Unidentified reminiscences of 1818 and 1842 quoted in Lovelace's "Digest of Lady Byron's Statements and Narratives, etc."
	27	Statement to F. W. Robertson, March 1853, designated CC by Lovelace.
	37	"Statement upon which I consulted Dr. Baillie before I quitted Lord B. Piccadilly Terrace Jan. 8, 1816."
287	8	Augusta to AIB, Tuesday [21 Feb. 1815].
	15	Augusta to AIB, Wednesday 22d [Feb.].
	n.	Narrative Q.
	23	Augusta to AIB, Friday 24th [Feb.].
	29	Narrative Q.
	32	Hobhouse to AIB, Whitton Park, Feb. 27, 1815.
288	26	Statement N.
	32	B to his mother, 12 November 1809, *LJ*, i, 254.
	41	"Reflections, &c. Seaham, Feb. 1815."
289	11	Narrative R, a continuation of Q.
	16	Statement D, "Reasons—London, March, 1816."
	19	B to Moore, 8 March 1815, *LJ*, iii, 185.
	28	Lady Melbourne to AIB, 7th March 1815.
	32	Annabella's notes of 1851 in a copy of Medwin's *Conversations*, 2nd ed., 1824, repeated in the copy of Medwin annoted for F. W. Robertson, also in 1851.
290	3	Augusta to AIB, Sunday 19th [Feb. 1815].
	7	*cf.* p. 286.
	12	J to AIB, Friday Morn: [10 March 1815].
	n.	Annabella's note on p. 55 of the copy of Medwin's *Conversations*, 2nd ed., 1824, in which she copied "Hobhouse's observations, published in no. 5 of the Westminster Review."
	25	J to AIB, Saturday Morn: [11 March].
	36	Sir Ralph Milbanke to AIB, Seaham March 11th 1815.
291	6	Lady Melbourne to AIB, 11th March 1815.
	11	Lady Melbourne to AIB, undated, but begins with reference to her letter of the previous day. She added a postscript: "I forgot to mention yt all ye rooms are very light & pleasant excepting No. 4 which being carried so far back is darken'd by some buildings."

Page Line

291 15 J to AIB, Tuesday Morn: from my Pillow [14 March], addressed to "The Lord Byron, Six-mile Bottom, Newmarket."

23 J to AIB, Seaham Thursday Morn: [16 March].

292 n.[1] Statement G.

n.[2] Statement H.

n.[3] Robertson's "Conversations with Ly B," dated by Lovelace from internal evidence 15 January 1851.

293 n.[1] Statement G.

n.[3] B to Augusta, 7 Jan. 1806, *LJ*, i, 93–4.

295 n.[2] Statement H.

296 n.[1] Statement G.

19 Narrative R, written as a sequel to Q in late 1816 or early 1817, in a notebook of paper watermarked "John Hall 1811."

297 32 Narrative S, a sequel to Narrative R, written in a child's exercise-book with a print of "A Elephant" on the cover, "Published by P. Rose, Bristol."

47 Sir Ralph to AIB, Seaham March 20th, 1815.

298 4 J to AIB, Seaham, March 22d. 1815.

21 J to AIB, Saturday [25 March].

299 36 Narrative S.

11. MARRIED LIFE IN PICCADILLY: APRIL—DECEMBER 1815.

300 1 "We mean to metropolise to-morrow," Byron to Moore, 27 March 1815, *LJ*, iii, 189.

32 Augusta to AIB, 6 Mile Bottm Thursday [30 March]. Lady Harcourt is mentioned as Mrs. Harcourt in Byron's letters to Augusta from Southwell in 1804, *LJ*, i, 18, 24, 26, 30. She married in 1778 General William Harcourt, who succeeded his brother as 3rd Earl Harcourt in 1809 and was then appointed Master of the Horse to the Queen.

301 2 J to AIB, Thursday [6 Apr.].

19 J to AIB, Sunday Morn: [9 Apr.].

n. Sir Ralph and J to AIB, Newcastle 28 March 1815, March 29th, Wednesday [29 March].

26 Sir Ralph to AIB, Seaham, April 12th, 1815.

28 Wentworth's death and burial, Statement G; burial certificate, *Wentworth Peerage Case*, 1864, p. 32. Mayne, p. 182, has misled Byron's subsequent biographers by asserting that Annabella went to Kirkby Mallory to attend her uncle, who in fact died in London.

32 Viscount Wentworth's Will, dated 8 June 1805, proved 20 May 1815 by Lord Henley and Sir J. B. Burges, resulted in the Wentworth Estate Act of 4 July 1823, a copy of which was produced and printed in the proceedings of the *Wentworth Peerage Case*, 1864, pp. 33–8, in which Lord Scarsdale's burial certificate was also produced and printed, p. 41.

Page	Line	
301	38	B to Lady Melbourne, 22 Apr., of which Lovelace's transcript reads thus differently from *Corresp.*, i, 307: "& there is a good deal of Personalty besides & money &—God knows what—which will come in *half* to Lady Mil now Noel." The royal licence authorising Sir Ralph Milbanke to take the name and arms of Noel, dated 20 May 1815, was produced and printed in the *Wentworth Peerage Case*, 1864, pp. 46–7.
302	6	B to AIB, undated but attributed by Lovelace to Saturday 15 Apr., and endorsed by Annabella, "Lord B's note to me at Lord Wentworth's 1815." Incomplete in Mayne, p. 183.
	11	Sir Ralph to AIB, Seaham April 21st, 1815. "Bell is pronounced in a certain way," B to Lady Melbourne, 22 Apr., *Corresp.*, i, 307.
	36	Statement G.
	n.	Statement V, March 1816.
303	17	Narrative S.
	31	Statement K, late 1816.
304	7	Statement U, partly dictated to Mrs. Clermont, March 1816.
	12	Augusta to AIB, Saturday Eveg. [22 March 1817].
	14	B to Hobhouse, 26 January 1815, Marchand, ii, 521.
	17	The Hon. Lady Noel's Statement as to Settlements and Finance [Jan. 1816].
	20	B to Hanson, 11 Dec. 1817, mentions "house-rent to the Duchess of Devonshire" among his outstanding debts, *LJ*, iv, 188.
	30	Narrative F, March 1817.
305	12	J. R. Fenwick to AIB, May 29th [1815].
306	13	*Life, Letters and Journals of George Ticknor*, 2nd ed., 2 vols., 1876, i, 50–56.
	26	Statement G.
	43	*Astarte*, pp. 25–6.
307	12	Statement G.
	n.	Lovelace's "Digest of Lady Byron's Statements and Narratives, etc.," p. civ. *cf.* p. 136n.
	19	Statement W, March 1816.
	24	*cf.* p. 230. Mrs. Langley Moore (*Sunday Times*, 22 Feb. 1959) asserted that Lovelace in his transcripts of letters "from time to time indulged in suppression" for the purpose of "concealments," but a checking of Annabella's letters in *Lady Noel Byron and the Leighs* with the originals reveals that many of the omissions comprised comments on her ailments and prescribed treatments.
	38	Statement H, supplemented by the "Statement given to my Mother, Kirkby Mallory, Jan. 18, 1816." These instances of Augusta's courage in rebuking Byron conform with Lovelace's assessment of her character (p. 306) rather than with "her terrible cowardice about vexing anyone" (*The Late Lord Byron*, p. 152).
308	8	Statement H.
	24	Lovelace's note in his "Digest of Lady Byron's Statements and Narratives, etc.," p. xcviii.

Page	Line	
308	35	Lady Wilmot Horton to Ralph Lord Wentworth, December 2nd Thursday 1869, *Lady Noel Byron and the Leighs*, p. 47.
309	34	Augusta to Hobhouse, Six Mile Bottom, near Newmarket, 5th July 1815, Lovelace transcript, *cf.* Broughton, ii, 357–8.
	42	*cf.* pp. 204, 98–100.
310	2	Broughton, ii, 201.
	15	Lovelace's transcripts from Hobhouse's Journals, *cf.* Broughton, i, 322–3, Marchand, ii, 539–40.
	17	After transcribing Hobhouse's entry for Tuesday August 8, Lovelace noted, "Leaves London—returns in November." This evidence is at variance with the statement in Marchand, ii, 540, that "Hobhouse had much opportunity to observe Byron's growing despondency in the months that followed, for they were frequently together."
	25	Statement G.
	40	*cf. Astarte*, pp. 57–8. A large selection of the correspondence between Annabella and Mrs. Villiers was printed in *Lady Noel Byron and the Leighs*, and many letters there abbreviated were given in full in the 1921 edition of *Astarte*.
311	13	AIB to Mrs. Villiers, Friday Night, endorsed "July 1815."
	17	B to Augusta, 17 Sept. 1816, *Astarte*, pp. 272–3.
	20	Lovelace's note in his "Digest of Lady Byron's Statements and Narratives, etc.," p. xcviii.
	27	J to B, Friday Morn: [11 August 1815]. J wrote to AIB, "Kirkby 7 o'clock p.m. Augst. 14, 1815," explaining that she and Sir Ralph had stayed the weekend with Sir Robert Gunning at Horton "and only got here at 5 this afternoon."
312	1	AIB to Sir Ralph, Tuesday, postmark 15 Aug.
	18	AIB to J, Aug. 16, 1815.
	n.	Lord Rosebery, *Napoleon: The Last Phase*, 1900, p. 60.
	28	"Miscellanea. Aug. 16, 1815." For Scott's description of the vase presented to him by Byron, see Lockhart's *Scott*, 2nd ed., 10 vols., 1839, v, 41. The *Morning Chronicle* announced the marriage of Miss Mercer Elphinstone and the young Duke of Devonshire on 11 May 1815, but published a contradiction next day.—*Autobiography of Miss Knight*, ed. Roger Fulford, 1960, p. 203.
	34	AIB to J, Aug. 17, 1815.
	38	AIB to Sir Ralph, Sunday [20 Aug.].
313	10	J to AIB, Augst. 18.
	n.	Wentworth's will, *cf.* p. 301.
	35	J to AIB, undated, but same date as Sir Ralph to AIB, August 22d, 1815.
314	2	J to AIB, Monday [28 Aug.].
	12	J to AIB, Augst. 30, 1815.
	24	AIB to J, Aug. 30, 1815.
	41	AIB to J, Aug. 31.
315	3	*Astarte*, p. 273.
	5	AIB to Mrs. Villiers, *cf.* p. 311.

Page *Line*

315 10 B to AIB, Epping, August 31st, 1815, Mayne, p. 187. "Frac." for fractious, like "nau." for naughty, was an abbreviation used by Byron, Annabella, and Augusta.

31 AIB to B, Aug. 31, in Mayne, pp. 187–8.

316 n.[1] *cf.* p. 310. Hobhouse afterwards denied that he mentioned to Byron his conversation with Lady Noel.—Broughton, ii, 200.

14 Augusta to AIB, Friday [1 Sept.].

n.[2] AIB to J, Aug. 30, 1815. Augusta refers to Annabella's new maid in her letter of 15 Feb. 1815.

32 B to AIB, Septr. 1st, 1815, incomplete in Mayne, p. 188. The word "A——da" in this letter and in Annabella's of the previous day had doubtless the same significance as the name of Harriette Wilson's sister Amy when pronounced by her lover Hart-Davis, *cf. Harriette Wilson's Memoirs*, 1929, pp. 54, 76.

317 4 J to AIB, Friday [1 Sept.].

12 AIB to J, Saturday [2 Sept.].

8 14 Statement G.

19 Statement AA, a review of notes written in late 1816 or early 1817 when preparing her narratives.

22 AIB to J, Monday [4 Sept.], continuing from the previous day.

33 AIB to Sir Ralph, Sept. 5, without date in Mayne, p. 189.

37 Mrs. Siddons to B, 22 July, *LJ*, iii, 424.

40 For Byron's correspondence about his theatrical activities, see *LJ*, iii, 190–248.

319 3 AIB to J, Septr. 6, 1815.

5 J to AIB, Sepr. 7.

13 AIB to J, Septr. 8, 1815, undated in Mayne, pp. 189–90.

19 J to AIB, Sept. 21st, 1815, extensively quoted without date in Mayne, pp. 191–2.

31 Statement Y, March 1816, partly in Annabella's hand, partly dictated to Selina Doyle.

34 AIB to Sir Ralph, Sunday Night [24 Sept.].

38 AIB to J, undated, postmark 6 Oct.

320 12 AIB to Sir Ralph, Thursday Evg [14 Sept.].

15 Wharton & Ford's "Instructions for Mr. Walker to Draw Deed or Deeds as within—1815, Augst. 3." Stacks of legal documents and correspondence covering 72 years were delivered by Gerard Ford to Lovelace (then Wentworth) when he retired from practice in 1887. These are included in the Lovelace Papers, in addition to fourteen large deed boxes of documents relating to the King and Lovelace estates, dating back to the dissolution of monasteries in 1548.

24 J to AIB, Kirkby Mallory, Octr. 9, 1815.

38 AIB to J, Wednesday [11 Oct.].

42 AIB to J, Friday Morng, postmark 13 Oct.

321 9 Correspondence July to Dec. 1815 in Wharton & Ford's files.

12 AIB to J, postmark 13 Oct.

n.[1] *LJ*, iii, 191.

Page	*Line*	
321	31	Lady Caroline Lamb to AIB, Friday Morng [13 Oct.].
	n.[2]	"Dated 30th Decr. 1814—Settlement previous to the Marriage of The Right Honorable Lord Byron with Miss Milbanke—Copy made for Lord Dacre & sent to Dr. L[ushington] 1822 Mar 22. —Wharton & Ford."
322	3	AIB to Sir Ralph, Saturday [14 Oct.].
	5	J to AIB, Sunday [15 Oct.].
	6	Sir Ralph to AIB, Kirkby Octbr. 21st, 1815.
	21	AIB to J, Octr. 31.
323	25	"Reflections on Lord B's character written under a delusive feeling in its favor," dated Nov. 1, 1815.
324	4	AIB to Augusta, n.d. The first part of the letter is missing. Lovelace suggested its date as 8 Nov.; it must have been then or earlier. The fragment here given in full is incomplete in Mayne, p. 194, which omits the passage on "pursuits of Fashion" and Lady Melbourne.
	38	AIB to Augusta, Thursday [9 Nov.], given with notable omissions in Mayne, pp. 194–5.
325	25	AIB to Augusta, undated but enclosed with a note postmarked 10 Nov.
	29	AIB to Augusta, postmarked 10 Nov., accompanying the foregoing letter.
	40	AIB to John Ford, Piccadilly Terrace, Nov. 11, 1815.
326	5	AIB to Augusta, Sat. [11 Nov.].
	12	Hobhouse's Journal, 11 Nov., Lovelace's transcript, *cf.* Marchand, ii, 547–8.
	22	Medwin, 2nd ed., 1824, pp. 52–3. Against this passage Annabella noted in 1851, "No such words uttered by either, if the Survivor's Memory may be trusted."
	24	*cf.* p. 323.
	33	Statement given to my Mother, Kirkby Mallory, Jan. 18, 1816.
	37	*cf.* p. 320.
	38	*cf.* p. 325.
327	13	G. B. Wharton to C. Cookney, 12 Oct. 1815.
	17	"The Hon. Lady Noel's Statement as to Settlements and Finance," drafted for Lushington's information about 25 January 1816.
	24	Moore, 1920 ed., p. 295.
	31	B to Murray, 14 Nov., *LJ*, iii, 249.
	35	Moore, p. 295.
	37	*ibid.*
328	n.[1]	Lushington's "Notes to Statement given to Lady Byron's Mother."
	23	Statement given to my Mother, Kirkby Mallory, Jan. 18, 1816.
	n.[2]	For account and letters of Susan Boyce, see "*To Lord Byron,*" by George Paston and Peter Quennell, 1939, pp. 177–87.
329	10	Lushington's "Notes to Statement given to Lady Byron's Mother."
	19	*Detached Thoughts*, 1821, *LJ*, iii, 236–7.

Page	*Line*	
329	24	"*To Lord Byron*," p. 179.
	26	*cf*. p. 324.
	32	B to Kinnaird, 23 Aug. 1821, Marchand, ii, 550.
	35	Hobhouse's Journal, 12 March 1816, Lovelace's transcript.
	38	*ibid*, 9 Feb. 1816.
330	3	Statement Y, March 1816.
	11	Statement B, " Additions "—*i.e.* to her Statement of Jan. 18, 1816.
	28	Statement G.
	32	G. Wilson Knight, *Lord Byron's Marriage*, 1957.
	39	Mrs. Villiers to AIB, 9 May 1816, *Astarte*, p. 202.
331	10	AIB to Mrs. Villiers, 12 May 1816, *Astarte*, p. 203.
	32	Statement U, "Desultory", March 1816, partly in Annabella's hand, partly dictated to Mrs. Clermont.
	35	"I had seen Lady Byron almost every day since the middle of April."—Mrs. Clermont's Statement of 22 Jan., 1816.
332	2	Mrs. Clermont's Statement, designated *Θ* by Lovelace, lodged with the lawyers in March 1816.
	13	Memorandum by the Hon: Lady Noel, 23 Jan. 1816.
	45	Narrative F, March 1817.
333	48	Statement G.
334	22	Mrs. Clermont's Statement of 22 Jan. 1816.
	30	Statement given to my Mother, Kirkby Mallory, Jan. 18, 1816 [actually written 19th].
	44	Lushington's "Notes to Statement given to Lady Byron's Mother."
335	17	Statement W, March 1816.
	22	Hobhouse's Journal, 25 Nov. and 2 Dec., Lovelace's transcript, cf. Broughton, i, 324; Marchand, ii, 552.
	30	Hobhouse's Journal, 5 Feb. 1816.
	35	Hanson to Wharton & Ford, 16th Decr. 1815.
	40	Wharton & Ford to Hanson, Temple, Decr. 22d, 1815.
336	11	Statement given to my Mother, Kirkby Mallory, Jan. 18, 1816.
	18	Mrs. Clermont's Statement of 22 Jan. 1816.
	27	AIB to Lushington, Kirkby, Feb. 11, 1816.
	34	Broughton, ii, 279.
337	10	Statement XY, March 1816, part dictated to Selina Doyle.
	14	Augusta to Hodgson, Dec. 11, *LJ*, iii, 291.
	18	Statement H.
	20	Broughton, ii, 280.
	36	Lady Anne Barnard's narrative, quoted in Lord Lindsay's letter, dated Dunecht, Sept. 3, in *The Times*, 7 Sept., 1869; reprinted in *Lady Byron Vindicated*, by Harriet Beecher Stowe, 1870, p. 306.
338	7	Statement UV, March 1816, dictated to Mrs. Clermont.
	14	Mrs. Clermont's addition to Statement UV.

Page	Line	
		12. THE SEPARATION: ANNABELLA AT PICCADILLY AND KIRKBY—DECEMBER 1815–20th FEBRUARY 1816
339	11	Hobhouse's Journal, 21, 22, 29 Dec. 1815, Lovelace's transcripts, *cf.* Broughton, i, 324, 330–31; Marchand, ii, 554.
	27	Hobhouse, "The Byron Separation," Broughton, ii, 201–2.
340	24	Endorsed by AIB, "Statement upon which I consulted Dr. Baillie before I quitted Lord B.—Reperused April 1824," dated Piccadilly Terrace, Jan. 8, 1816.
341	4	AIB to Lushington, Kirkby, Feb. 11, 1816.
	10	Jane Austen's *Northanger Abbey*, chapters xxi–xxv.
	n.	Statement T, March 1816.
	27	Statement V, March 1816. The passage omitted is not a "suppression," but repeats references to the stay at Six Mile Bottom and to Augusta's first visit to Piccadilly, more fully related in other statements (pp. 295, 302).
	34	Statement AA.
342	11	Statement Y, March 1816, partly dictated to Selina Doyle.
	30	Memorandum by the Hon: Lady Noel, 23 Jan. 1816.
343	3	J to AIB, undated [28 Dec. 1815].
	21	J to B, Dec. 28, *cf.* Fox, pp. 100–101.
344	n.	Lushington's "Notes to Statement given to Lady Byron's Mother."
	16	Statement given to my Mother, Kirkby Mallory, Jan. 18, 1816.
	22	Additions [to the foregoing Statement, probably written on the following day]. The same words are repeated in further additional notes, designated Statement Z by Lovelace.
	38	Statement VX, summarising the nurse's evidence, probably written on 13 March 1816, according to Mrs. Clermont to J of that date: "we have the Nurse here."
	42	AIB to J, undated, postmarked 2 Jan., written the previous evening; part quoted without date, Mayne, p. 200.
345	2	AIB to Sir Ralph, postmarked 4 Jan., part quoted without date, Mayne, p. 200.
	9	AIB to Lady Melbourne, Jan. 4, part quoted without date, Mayne, p. 200.
	11	Statement given to my Mother, Kirkby Mallory, Jan. 18, 1816.
	25	B to AIB, January 6th, 1816, *cf. Astarte*, p. 39; Mayne, pp. 200–201.
	26	Statement given to my Mother, Kirkby Mallory, Jan. 18, 1816.
	28	AIB to B, undated [7 Jan.].
	33	Mrs. Clermont's Statement Δ, March 1816.
346	10	Statement H.
	41	Statement upon which I consulted Dr. Baillie before I quitted Lord B. Reperused April 1824. Piccadilly Terrace, Jan. 8, 1816.—The passages on pp. 286 and 340, inserted in that order, complete the full statement.
	44	In her *Remarks occasioned by Mr. Moore's Notices of Lord Byron's Life*, 1830, p. 8 (reprinted in Moore, 1920 ed., p. 662), Annabella

Page	Line	
		stated that it was Dr. Baillie who "enjoined that in correspondence with Lord Byron I should avoid all but light and soothing topics," but her contemporary statement (p. 363) shows that this was Le Mann's advice.
347	48	Hobhouse's Account of Lady Byron's Interview with John Hanson, here given from Lovelace's copy of the original; the differences from Broughton, ii, 252–4, are mainly the spellings of "practice" and "extravagancies" and some underlinings. A note from Annabella to Hanson of 12 Jan. (*LJ*, iii, 293) indicates that she sent the marked copy of the "Medical Journal" *after* the interview.
348	6	AIB to Sir Ralph, undated, but received at Kirkby on 10 Jan.
	13	Sir Ralph to AIB, Kirkby, Jany. 13th, 1816.
	32	Statement G.
	38	Statement given to my Mother, Kirkby Mallory, Jan. 18, 1816.
349	33	Statement U, "Desultory", March 1816, part dictated to Mrs. Clermont.
	40	"Additions", probably written on 20 Jan. 1816.
350	21	Statement B, "Additions". The passage here omitted has been already quoted on p. 330.
	29	Mrs. Clermont's Statement Θ, March 1816.
	43	AIB to Mrs. Clermont, at Mrs. Kelly's (Milliner), North Audley St., London—Wooburn, Jan. 15, 1816.
351	11	AIB to B, Jan. 15, 1816. The letter, as altered from the draft, is in Fox, p. 98.
	26	The "Dearest Duck" letter was dated Kirkby, Jan. 16, 1816, but, as Lovelace noted in his transcript, this must be an error for the 17th. The maid, Ann Fletcher, stated in her "Deposition" (Broughton, ii, 264) "That they reached Woburn the first night, and arrived at Kirkby Mallory about six o'clock the next evening."
352	13	AIB to Selina Doyle, Jan. 15, 1816, Wooburn.
353	2	Augusta to AIB, Monday ¼ before 4, endorsed by AIB "No. 1 Jany. 15th 1816" and initialled "G.J." This was the first of a sequence of twenty-eight letters which Annabella apparently handed to Lushington shortly after her return to London on 22nd February. They were returned to her on 8th April with a note from Lushington's proctor, George Jenner: "Mr. Jenner has placed his Initials to all the papers, in case at any time, it may become necessary for him to identify them."
	34	Augusta to AIB, Tuesday, endorsed "2/Jany. 16th. 1816".
	n.	The complete sequence of Augusta's letters to her from 15th January to 11th April were copied, with some slight omissions and inaccuracies, by AIB into an octavo notebook of paper watermarked 1819.
354	7	Mrs. Clermont to AIB, Tuesday [16 Jan.].
	30	Augusta to AIB, Wednesday, endorsed "No. 3—Jany. 17th. 1816".

Page	Line	
354	35	Hobhouse's Journal, 17 Jan., Lovelace's transcript, *cf.* Marchand, ii, 567, which gives the reading, "drank brandy & water till two in the morning."
355	7	Augusta to AIB, Thursday Mng, wrapper dated by Augusta "London January Eighteenth", endorsed AIB "No. 4".
	20	AIB to Capt. George Byron, K.M., Jan. 17, 1816, as in Fox, p. 100, but Lovelace points out in his transcripts that Annabella was evidently one day behind the calendar in her datings during the first week after her arrival at Kirkby.
356	19	Augusta to AIB, Thursday Mng, continued from above, the final postscript "5 o'clock".
	38	Augusta to AIB, Thursday Night, endorsed "No. 5 Jany. 19th. 1816".
357	7	*ibid*, "Friday ½ past 4".
	16	Augusta to J, Friday 19th, endorsed by AIB as No. 6 and so copied in her book of copies, but not certified by Jenner.
	33	Augusta to AIB, Friday Eveg, endorsed by AIB "No. 7 20th Jany. 1816".
358	7	*ibid.*
	36	*ibid.*
	44	AIB to Francis Le Mann, Jan. 17, 1816 [18 Jan.], Fox, p. 101.
359	13	Mrs. Clermont to AIB, thursday evening [18 Jan.].
360	4	Selina Doyle to AIB, undated, but ascribed by Lovelace to 18 Jan., for though Annabella dated her "Statement given to my Mother" Jan. 18, her other correspondents' letters show that during this week her dates were in error, and the Statement must have been written on the 19th.
	43	AIB to Mrs. Clermont, misdated Jan. 18, 1816, evidently written 19th.
361	12	Statement dated Jan. 19, 1816, therefore probably written on 20th.
	22	AIM to B, 3 Sept. 1813, 24 Feb. and 14 Sept. 1814, *cf.* pp. 169, 189, 208.
	36	Mrs. Clermont to AIB, Friday [19 Jan.].
362	16	AIB to Mrs. Clermont, Jan. 19, 1816, attributed by Lovelace to 21st; postscript in Mayne, p. 205; *The Late Lord Byron*, p. 138.
363	18	AIB to J, undated [21 Jan.].
	30	Statement C, one of the "Additions" to the "Statement given to my Mother".
	33	Walter Raleigh, *The English Novel*, 1919, p. 193.
	42	*Works*, ii, 7–8.
364	11	AIB's "Notes on Childe Harold—*Duomo. Edition 1815.*"
	46	AIB to Mrs. Clermont, Jan. 20, 1816. The postscript dated Monday shows that the letter was written on Sunday night and posted Monday 22nd.
365	6	Augusta to AIB, Friday Eveg, p. 357 above, postscript dated "Saturday".
	13	AIB to Mrs. Clermont, Jan. 20, 1816. See above.

Page	Line	
365	17	AIB to Augusta, misdated Jan. 20, its postscript being dated "Monday" [22nd], *LJ*, iii, 299.
366	7	AIB to J, undated [22 Jan.].
	46	Selina Doyle to AIB, Sunday night [21 Jan.].
367	34	J to AIB, Monday [22 Jan.].
368	6	Mrs. Clermont to AIB, undated [22 Jan.].
	24	Augusta to AIB, Sunday, dated by Augusta on wrapper, "London January twenty second", endorsed by AIB as No. 8.
	31	AIB to Augusta, January 18th, probably 19th, *LJ*, iii, 296.
369	19	Augusta to AIB, Sunday, continued "Monday", dated 22nd as above and endorsed No. 8.
	44	Augusta to AIB, Tuesday, dated by Augusta on wrapper "London January Twenty third", endorsed by AIB No. 9.
370	4	*ibid.*
	37	Augusta to AIB, Wednesday, wrapper dated by Augusta "London January Twenty fourth", endorsed by AIB No. 10.
371	21	Augusta to AIB, Wednesday Night, finished Thursday, wrapper dated by Augusta "London January Twenty fifth", endorsed by AIB No. 11.
	30	AIB to Augusta, January 23rd, *LJ*, iii, 299.
	33	Augusta to AIB, Thursday, continuation of that begun Wednesday Night, No. 11 above.
	36	*ibid.*
	40	Hobhouse's Journal, Jan. 25, Lovelace transcript.
372	25	Augusta to AIB, Thursday Night, wrapper dated by Augusta "London January Twenty Sixth", endorsed by AIB No. 12.
	28	Augusta to AIB, Tuesday [23rd], No. 9 above.
	31	AIB to Augusta, January 25th, *LJ*, iii, 300.
	37	AIB to Augusta, Jan. 28, *LJ*, iii, 302.
	44	Augusta to AIB, Tuesday [23rd], No. 9 above.
374	34	J to AIB, Tuesday 23d Janry, part undated in Mayne, pp. 205–6.
	n.[1]	*LJ*, iii, 255–8; *Memoir of John Murray*, i, 355.
375	13	AIB to J, Jan. 23, 1816 [24th].
	25	Memorandum, designated MP by Lovelace, probably written late in 1816.
	37	"No doubt Dr. Lushington will intrigue against us . . . I feel great distrust of Dr. Lushington's influence as his mind is long ago made up on this matter & in a sense quite opposed to my grandmother's wishes," Ralph Lord Wentworth to his sister, 7 Nov. 1866; and of a conversation with Major R. R. Noel, son of Rev. Thomas Noel, he reported on 5 Nov. 1868, "he agreed with me as to Dr. L's infamy in preventing any reconciliation" (a parenthetical euphemism is substituted for the word "infamy" in *Ralph Earl of Lovelace, A Memoir*, by Mary Countess of Lovelace, 1920, p. 19). Statements of Annabella's account with Drummond's Bank from Feb. 1822 to Jan. 1853 are preserved in the Lovelace Papers.

Page	*Line*	
376	40	J to AIB, undated [24 Jan.], postscript Thursday Morn: [25th], part undated in Mayne, p. 206.
377	18	Mrs. Clermont to AIB, Wednesday [24 Jan.].
378	3	Selina Doyle to AIB, Thursday Morg. [25 Jan.].
	26	Selina Doyle to AIB, Friday Morg. [26 Jan.].
	29	"I shall set out tomorrow about eleven o'clock and get to Woburn —do not wait dinner on Sunday for the roads are so bad."—J to AIB, Friday [26 Jan.].
	37	AIB to J, Jan. 25 [26], part undated in Mayne, p. 207.
379	15	J to AIB, Friday [26 Jan.].
	21	Lushington to J, Friday night ten oclock [26 Jan.]; Jany. 27, 1816.
	37	Memorandum dated Kirkby, Jan. 27, 1816.
380	1	*cf.* p. 375.
381	15	AIB to Augusta, Jan. 27, 1816. Not Sent.
	29	"A Sister's Sentiments", following some verses dated Sept. 1815 in one of AIB's notebooks.
	39	AIB to Augusta, Jan. 28, *LJ*, iii, 301–2.
	44	AIB to Augusta, Jan. 25, *LJ*, iii, 300.
382	5	Augusta to AIB, Saturday; "No. 13 Jan. 27th" in AIB's hand.
	30	*ibid.*
	42	Sir Ralph to B, Kirkby Mallory, Jany. 28th, 1816.
384	6	Augusta to AIB, Monday, endorsed by AIB, "No. 14. Jany. 29th. 1816".
	44	Augusta to AIB, Tuesday Evg. In AIB's book of copies this letter is headed in her hand, "No. 15 (30th Jany) sent to Lady B by Capt. G. Byron."
385	6	Lady Byron's Objections to a Passage in Sir Ralph Noel's Letter to Lord Byron.
	10	Sir Ralph to B, Mivarts Hotel 44 Lower Brooke Street, Febry. 2d. 1816, endorsed "Copy of a letter sent to Lord Byron". In this copy the words of the substitution quoted are in Lushington's hand.
	35	J to Augusta, uncompleted draft undated [30 Jan.].
386	15	J to Augusta, uncompleted draft undated [31 Jan.].
387	3	J to Mrs. Clermont, postscript dated Febry. 1st.
	16	Enclosure with preceding.
	37	J to Sir Ralph, Febry. 2nd, 1816.
388	7	Mrs. Clermont to J, undated [1 Feb.].
	13	Mrs. Clermont to AIB, undated [1 Feb.], endorsed "Recd. Feb. 2".
	35	Mrs. Clermont to AIB, undated, attributed by Lovelace to 2 Feb., part quoted in *The Late Lord Byron*, p. 138.
	42	Mrs. Clermont to AIB, Saturday [3 Feb.].
389	4	Mrs. Fletcher to her husband, Broughton, ii, 220.
	14	J to Sir Ralph, Febry. 3d.
	40	AIB to Mrs. Clermont, Feb. 1, 1816 [2 Feb.].
390	24	Augusta to AIB, *private* Friday 5 o clock; with enclosure dated Feby 2d, 1816; wrapper dated by Augusta "London February

Page	Line	
390		Second". Though this letter bears Jenner's initials, Annabella omitted to number it in the sequence.
	44	Augusta to AIB, Saturday 4 o'clock; wrapper endorsed by AIB, "No. 18 Piccadilly Feby 3d 1816".
392	2	B to Sir Ralph, February 2d, 1816, with some inaccuracies in Broughton, ii, 211–13.
	25	B to AIB, February 3d, 1816, undated in Mayne, pp. 209–10.
	33	AIB to Augusta, Kirkby, Feby. 3, 1816, AIB's copy, *cf. LJ*, iii, 302.
	37	AIB to Augusta, undated copy [4 Feb.], *cf. LJ*, iii, 303.
393	9	Mrs. Clermont to J, undated [4 Feb.].
	35	AIB to Mrs. Clermont, Feb. 4, 1816; one sentence misquoted in *The Late Lord Byron*, p. 138.
394	8	AIB to Lushington, Feby. 4, 1816, postscript Feb. 5.
395	10	AIB to Sir Ralph, Feb. 5, 1816.
	17	Mrs. Clermont to J, undated [5 Feb.].
	26	Mrs. Clermont to AIB, Monday [5 Feb.].
	36	B to AIB, February 5th, 1816, *cf.* Mayne, p. 210.
396	5	Hobhouse's Journal, 17 and 25 Jan., Lovelace transcripts; *cf.* pp. 354, 371, and Marchand, ii, 567.
	13	Hobhouse's Journal, 5 Feb., Lovelace transcript, *cf.* Marchand, ii, 573.
	19	Hobhouse to AIB, Whitton Park, Hounslow, undated [5 Feb.]. For his second and longer letter, Tuesday [6 Feb.], see Broughton, ii, 221–7.
	27	AIB to Hobhouse, Feb. 6, 1816.
	36	Lushington to AIB, Febr. 6, 1816.
397	19	AIB to B, Kirkby Feb. 7, 1816, *cf.* Broughton, ii, 235–6; Mayne, pp. 211–12.
	35	B to Sir Ralph, February 7th, 1816, *cf.* Broughton, ii, 237–8.
398	13	B to AIB, February 8th, 1816, complete but with slight inaccuracies in Broughton, ii, 239–41.
	36	Augusta to AIB, Private Friday, dated on wrapper "February Ninth", endorsed by AIB No. 19.
399	2	Augusta to AIB, Feby. 12th, endorsed by AIB No. 20.
	8	AIB to Mrs. Clermont, Feb. 8, 1816.
	29	AIB to Mrs. Clermont, Feb. 11, 1816.
401	11	AIB to Mrs. Clermont, Feb. 13, 1816: "I enclose some Comments on Lord B's last letter, which comments I wish you to show to Dr. Lushington."
	42	J to Sir Ralph, Tuesday Febry. 6.
402	17	J to Sir Ralph, postscript Wednesday Morn: [7 Feb.].
	34	Mrs. Clermont to J, Wednesday [7 Feb.].
	41	Lady Melbourne to B, 5 Feb., *Corresp.*, i, 307.
403	3	Hobhouse's Journal, 9 Feb., Lovelace transcript, *cf.* Marchand, ii, 576.
	30	Mrs. Clermont to J, Sunday [11 Feb.].
	35	Mrs. Clermont to AIB, Monday [12 Feb.].

Page	Line	
403	37	Hobhouse's Journal, 12 Feb., Lovelace transcript.
	42	Mrs. Clermont to AIB, Monday [12 Feb.].
404	9	AIB to Mrs. Clermont, Feb. 11, 1816.
	36	Mrs. Clermont to AIB, Tuesday [13 Feb.].
	42	AIB to B, Kirkby, Feb. 11, 1816, Mayne, p. 213.
405	29	Lushington to AIB, Febr. 10, 1816.
	42	Lushington to AIB, Thursday night [8 Feb.], continued Friday.
406	22	AIB to Lushington, Feb. 11, 1816; this letter contains the passage already quoted on pp. 340–41.
	24	Augusta to AIB, Private Friday, *cf.* p. 398.
	28	AIB to Lushington, Feb. 7, 1816.
	31	AIB to Lushington, Feb. 8, 1816.
	34	AIB to Augusta, Feb. 12, *cf. LJ*, iii, 308.
	42	AIB to Lushington, Feb. 11, 1816.
407	3	AIB to Augusta, Feb. 11, 1816, headed *Not Private*, misdated Feb. 21 and with variants in *LJ*, iii, 315.
	31	Hobhouse's Journal, 12 Feb., *cf.* Marchand, ii, 576–7.
408	12	Augusta to AIB, Monday, wrapper dated and postmarked "February Twelfth", endorsed by AIB No. 21.
	40	Augusta to AIB, Tuesday, wrapper dated and postmarked "February Thirteenth", endorsed by AIB No. 22.
409	10	AIB to B, Kirkby, Feb. 13, 1816, complete in Mayne, pp. 213–14.
	18	AIB to Lushington, Feb. 14, 1816, a sentence in Fox, pp. 109–10.
	29	Statement A, mainly in Lady Noel's hand [14–15 Feb.].
410	9	AIB to Lushington, Feb. 15, 1816.
	43	B to AIB, Fy. 15th, 1816, given from an apparently inaccurate copy in Broughton, ii, 257–8.
411	7	Augusta to Francis Hodgson, Thursday 15 [Feb.].
	9	*LJ*, iii, 303–6.
	15	Hodgson to AIB, Bradden near Towcester, February 13th, 1816, complete but with inaccuracies and without date in *Memoir of the Rev. F. Hodgson*, ii, 24–7, and *LJ*, iii, 306–8.
	16	AIB to Hodgson, Kirkby Febry. 15, 1816, in *Memoir of Hodgson*, ii, 28–30, and *LJ*, iii, 312–13.
	35	AIB to Sir Ralph, Feb. 15, 1816.
	42	AIB to Lushington, Feb. 15, 1816, Fox, p. 110, and *cf.* pp. 409–10.
412	15	AIB to Lushington, Feb. 17, 1816, one sentence in Fox, p. 110.
	24	Lushington to AIB, Febr. 18, 1816.
	29	Mrs. Clermont to AIB, Wednesday [14 Feb.].
	35	AIB to Mrs. Clermont, Feb. 15, 1816.
	38	Mrs. Clermont to AIB, undated [20 or 21 Feb.]: "Dr. Lushington will endeavour to be at Kirkby on Saturday next his stay cannot be long as he must be in court at ten on Monday morning but he does not like your coming to London at present & is anxious to meet your wishes of an interview."
413	45	Augusta to AIB, MOST private Saturday; dated "February Seventeenth", postmarked 17th, and endorsed by AIB No. 24. Initialled "G:J" by Jenner.

Page	Line	
414	6	See p. 412.
	16	See pp. 354 and 413.
	25	Mrs. Clermont to J, Wednesday [21 Feb.].
	34	Augusta to AIB, Monday; wrapper dated "February Nineteenth", postmarked 19th, and endorsed by AIB No. 25.
415	2	AIB to Sir Ralph, Kirkby Feb. 20, 1816.
	9	AIB to Lushington, Kirkby Feb. 20, 1816.
	15	AIB to Mrs. Clermont, Feb. 17, 1816.
	17	Selina Doyle to J, enclosed with AIB to J, undated [22 Feb.]; Sir Ralph to J, Feby. 23d 1816; J to AIB, Sunday [25 Feb.].
416	9	Augusta to AIB, Tuesday; dated by AIB "Feb. 20". The wrapper is missing, Annabella having substituted the wrapper of a note from Augusta to Lady Noel, thanking her for news of the baby to be conveyed to Byron, postmarked the 20th; it is endorsed by AIB "No. 27 Feby. 20th 1816".
	14	The paper of the foolscap copy is watermarked 1813, that of the book of copies 1819.
	23	Augusta to AIB, 5 o clock Thursday; wrapper dated "February Twenty second", postmarked 22nd, and endorsed by AIB "No. 28 Piccadilly Feby 22d. 1816". After the copy of this letter in AIB's book of copies, she wrote, "Here ends the letters certified by Mr. Jenner—Proctor of Doctors Commons."

13. THE SEPARATION: ANNABELLA IN LONDON 22nd FEBRUARY–25th APRIL, 1816

Page	Line	
417	9	AIB to J, undated [22 Feb.], postscript by Selina Doyle.
	n.	B to AIB, February 21st, 1816. Lady Noel reported on the 25th: "I have written to Mrs. L. very kindly, with that excellent account of Augusta, which with truth I can give." Byron acknowledged the message personally on the 27th with an ironic note [*The Late Lord Byron*, p. 133], which Lady Noel forwarded to Annabella on 29th Feb. as "the *Acme* of impudence, but . . . I shall take it *quietly* and *civilly* as if I thought it was meant so."
418	3	AIB to J, Feb. 23, 1816.
	6	Sir Ralph to J, Feby. 24th, 1816.
	26	AIB to J, undated [27 Feb.].
	43	B to AIB, February 26th, 1816.
419	3	AIB to J, Feb. 23, 1816.
	6	Hobhouse's Journal, 29 Feb., Lovelace's transcript, *cf.* Marchand, ii, 583.
	8	*cf.* pp. 413, 416.
	12	*cf.* p. 403.
	14	In a draft of the first (unpublished) version of *Astarte*, p. 1a.
	38	Lady Caroline Lamb to B, undated [Feb. 1816].
	41	"*To Lord Byron*", p. 70.
420	4	AIB to Mrs. Clermont, Feb. 15, 1816.

Page	Line	
420	7	Hobhouse's Journal, 16 Feb., Lovelace's transcript, *cf.* Marchand, ii, 579.
	18	AIB to J, March 1, 1816.
	34	Sophia M. Byron to AIB, Thursday Feby. 29, *cf.* p. 348.
421	27	B to AIB, March 1st, 1816, *cf.* Broughton, ii, 286–7.
422	2	Augusta to Hodgson, Friday March 1.
	11	Hobhouse's Journal, 1 March, Lovelace transcript.
	13	J to Sir Ralph, Friday 1 March: "I want to know if *Brougham* has been with You and whether *he* knows the Circumstances, I think he *ought*—both as to influence in Society, his intimacy with Ld Holland, and as a LEGAL Man."
	23	AIB to J, March 2, 1816.
	35	Lady Caroline Lamb to B, undated, *LJ*, ii, 449.
423	4	B to Lord Holland, March 3d, 1816.
	31	B to AIB, March 4th, 1816, delivered by Milward.
424	14	B to AIB, March 4th, 1816, delivered by Augusta, *cf.* Broughton, ii, 288–9.
	35	AIB to J, March 4, 1816.
	41	Doyle to J, Monday [4 March].
425	3	Sir Samuel Romilly to AIB, Mar. 2, 1816.
	5	Sir Ralph to J, March 5th, 1816.
	7	J to Sir Ralph, Sunday Morn: [10 March].
	28	AIB to B, March 5, 1816, draft in Lushington's hand, except the postscript and two phrases added by AIB.
426	17	Mrs. Villiers to AIB, Febry. 26th, 1816.
	35	AIB to Mrs. Villiers, Mivart's Hotel [26 Feb.], first published *Quarterly Review*, Jan. 1870, with the impossible date, 20 Feb., when AIB was still at Kirkby. *Lady Noel Byron and the Leighs*, p. 26, suggested 29 Feb., but arranging his transcripts ten years later, Lovelace realised that AIB would have replied immediately on receiving Mrs. Villiers's letter on the 26th.
	39	*cf.* p. 420.
	44	*Works*, iii, 381, where Wilmot's wife is correctly identified as Anne Horton, though elsewhere in the *Works* and *LJ* she is confused with Barbarina Ogle, who married firstly Valentine Wilmot, secondly Lord Dacre.
	45	AIB on Wilmot's character, *Lady Noel Byron and the Leighs*, pp. 51–2, 60–61: "His defect certainly is Vanity . . . He requires to be softened himself, and has not the *tact* which makes good intentions acceptable to people's feelings," to Mrs. Villiers, Eden Farm, September 14th 1816; "He appears to me never to have any repose from the constant efforts to attain a standard of reputation which either his talents or his application are unequal to sustain," to Mrs. Villiers, Kirkby, Nov. 2, 1816.
427	5	*cf.* pp. 433 and 424.
	25	"March 5, 1816. Reasons for my return urged by Mrs. Leigh."
	46	AIB to Lushington, undated [5 March].
428	13	Augusta to Hodgson, Monday, postmark 4 March.

Page	*Line*	
428	30	Augusta to Hodgson, Tuesday March 5.
	36	Wilmot to AIB, Montagu Square Tuesday [5 March].
429	7	Augusta to Wilmot, Tuesday Evg. 8 o'clock.
	10	Hobhouse to AIB, March 5, Broughton, ii, 293–4.
	32	Hobhouse's Journal, 6 March, Lovelace transcript, *cf.* Marchand, ii, 584–5.
	39	AIB to Lushington, March 6.
430	3	Hobhouse's Journal, 7 March, Lovelace transcript, *cf.* Marchand, ii, 586.
	8	AIB to Lushington, Thursday [7 March].
	10	"Lushington Doyle & Mr Wilmot were here last night in consultation," Sir Ralph to J, March 8th, 1816.
	20	Hobhouse's Journal, 8 March, Lovelace transcript, *cf.* Marchand, ii, 587–8.
431	11	Wilmot to Hobhouse, Friday 8th March, 1816.
	25	Hobhouse's Journal, 9 March, Lovelace transcript, *cf.* Marchand, pp. 587–8.
	36	Disclaimer by Lady Byron, signed Anne Isabella Byron, S. Lushington, F. H. Doyle, March 8, 1816.
432	9	AIB to Lushington, March 9, 1816. For the revised declaration witnessed by Wilmot, see Fox, p. 112.
	20	Hobhouse's Journal, 9 March, Lovelace transcript, *cf.* Marchand, ii, 588. For the articles of separation, see Broughton, ii, 303–4.
	32	AIB to Lushington, March 9, 1816.
433	2	J to AIB, March 5, postscript March 6.
	14	AIB to J, undated [7 March].
	34	Mrs. Clermont to J, Saturday [9 March].
	39	Augusta to Hodgson, Saturday.
434	8	AIB to Lushington, March 10, 1816.
	22	Lushington to AIB, Sunday night March 10.
	35	Hobhouse's Journal, 10 March, Lovelace transcript, *cf.* Broughton, ii, 305–6.
435	8	*cf.* p. 430; Lord Wentworth's Will, p. 301; The Hon. Lady Noel's Statement as to Settlements and Finance, *c.* 25 Jan. 1816, *cf.* p. 327.
	15	Hobhouse's Journal, 10 March, Lovelace transcript.
	36	Augusta to Wilmot, Monday Morng. [11 March].
436	4	Hanson to B, Bloomsbury Square, 11th March, 1816.
	15	B to AIB, March 11th, 1816, part quoted in *The Late Lord Byron*, pp. 128–9.
	n.	Paper by John Hanson, undated.
	27	Wilmot to Hobhouse, Monday [11 March].
	30	Hobhouse's Journal, 11 March, Lovelace transcript.
437	15	*ibid*, 12 March.
	19	Doyle to AIB, undated [12 March].
	27	AIB to J, Wednesday [13 March], finished by Mrs. Clermont.
	33	Statement VX, the nurse's deposition, *cf.* p. 344.
	n.	Augusta to AIB, Wednesday Mar. 13th.

Page Line

438 3 AIB to Augusta, undated [13 March].
20 AIB to Lushington, March 13, 1816.
28 Hobhouse's Journal, 13 March, Lovelace transcript, *cf* Marchand, ii, 590.
n. Augusta's Bible, *cf.* pp. 130, 136, 165, 193.
39 Augusta to Hobhouse, Wednesday 2 o'clock [13 March], attributed to Feb. in Broughton, ii, 360.
439 3 Hobhouse's Journal, 14 March, Lovelace transcript.
14 AIB to J, March 14, 1816.
18 Augusta to Hodgson, Thursday March 14th.
440 31 Augusta to Hodgson, Thursday night, postscript Friday [15].
43 *ibid.*
44 Lovelace attributed to this period of March 1816 Statements VX, W, U, UV, Y, XY, T, VW, V, X, D, and two statements by Mrs. Clermont, Δ and *Θ*, as well as the sealed and dated Statement *AL*.
441 3 For "My principles of conduct in regard to Mrs. Leigh," see Fox, p. 113.
26 Statement *AL*, in Lushington's hand, complete in *Astarte*, pp. 46–8.
29 R. E. Prothero, quoted Fox, p. 114.
31 Fox, p. 114.
442 8 Hobhouse's Journal, 15 March, Lovelace transcript; for Romilly, *cf. LJ*, iii, 324–5; Broughton, ii, 365–6.
13 AIB to Hobhouse, March 16, 1816, *cf.* Broughton, ii, 309–10.
18 Hobhouse's Journal, 16 March; Hobhouse to AIB, undated [16 March]; Lushington to Sir S. Shepherd, March 16; AIB to Shepherd, draft by Lushington; AIB to J, 16 March 1816; The Original Agreement between Lord & Lady B: (so endorsed by Lushington), *cf.* Broughton, ii, 310–12.
22 Hobhouse to AIB, Mivart's, Monday [18 March], *cf.* Broughton, ii, 313–14.
28 A fragment, touching the *disclaimer*, in AIB's hand.
33 AIB to Hobhouse, March 18, 1816, *cf.* Broughton, ii, 315.
443 8 AIB to J, Sunday [17 March].
13 J to AIB, Friday [15 March].
23 J to AIB, undated [19 March].
444 11 Lady Melbourne to AIB, 20th March 1816.
18 Lady Melbourne to B, February 5th, 1816, see p. 402.
19 Hobhouse's Journal, 9 Feb., see p. 402.
21 Lady Melbourne to J, 10th Febry. 1816.
23 Hobhouse's Journal, 12 Feb., see p. 407.
26 Lady Melbourne to Sir Ralph, Febry. 12th, 1816.
27 See p. 404.
30 Lady Melbourne to B, 14th Febry. 1816, *Corresp.*, i, 308.
33 Lady Melbourne to AIB, 17th Feb. 1816.
445 6 *ibid.*
17 AIB to Lady Melbourne, Febry. 20, 1816.

Page	Line	
445	37	Lady Caroline Lamb to AIB, undated [5 March]. This and two other undated letters of Lady Caroline's are extensively quoted in *The Late Lord Byron*, pp. 231–9, and there ascribed to "shortly after the middle of March". But the reference to Lord Holland indicates that the first two letters were written at the time of his mediation, and Lovelace was probably correct in ascribing them to 4 and 5 March. The third letter, urging Annabella to "try & conciliate yr Aunt", advises, "pray take care & do not tell her Mrs. Lamb called on you—as I think it would vex her if she knew that *she* had seen you before her." In an undated letter to her mother, received at Kirkby on 7th March and probably written on the 5th, Annabella wrote, "I saw Mrs. G Lamb yesterday Evening—kind to the greatest degree."
	n.	Moore, 1920 ed., pp. 647–8; Joyce, *My Friend H*, p. 101; Nicolson, p. 303; Knight, *Lord Byron's Marriage*, p. 222; AIB to Lushington, undated [5 March].
446	2	The statement in *The Late Lord Byron*, p. 239, that "Lady Byron thereupon took Caroline's advice and wrote Lady Melbourne the conciliatory letter recommended", seems to be without foundation—likewise the statement on the same page that "Lord Holland too was duly interviewed and had the bones of the skeleton rattled at him from the cupboard." For Lord Holland's own account of Annabella's behaviour at their interview, see p. 451.
	19	AIB to J, March 23, 1816.
447	4	AIB to Lady Melbourne, March 21, 1816.
	35	Lady Melbourne to AIB, 24th March 1816.
	43	AIB to Lushington, April 1, 1816.
448	1	J to AIB, Monday Morn: [25 March].
	5	Hobhouse's Journal, 28 March, Lovelace transcript.
	9	*ibid*, 26 Apr.
	12	AIB to J, 21 March.
	27	B to AIB, March 20th, 1816, from Lovelace's transcript of Mary Millicent Montgomery's copy of the original, which seems to have been lost before the Papers came into Lovelace's hands, *cf.* Broughton, ii, 316.
449	46	*Works*, iii, 537–40.
	48	Hobhouse's Journal, 22 March, Lovelace transcript.
450	2	AIB to J, undated [25 March].
451	14	B to AIB, March 25th, 1816, part quoted in *The Late Lord Byron*, p. 246.
	20	Rogers to B, Tuesday Evg. [26 March], *cf.* Broughton, ii, 319–20.
	25	Kinnaird to B, March 26, 1816, *cf.* Broughton, ii, 320–1.
	32	Lord Holland to B, March 26, 1816, *cf.* Broughton, ii, 318–19, and note to p. 446 above.
	n.	The anonymous note was sealed with a key, written in two different hands, and posted unpaid from Great Russell St., C.G. Byron's use of Emma Roberts's name is explained in Broughton, ii, 291.

Page	*Line*	
452	8	B to AIB, March 26th, 1816, *cf.* Broughton, ii, 321.
	20	B to AIB, March 26th, 1816, second letter.
	29	AIB to Augusta, March 26, 1816. Broughton, ii, 321–2, asserts that the letter was sent on Thursday the 28th, but Hobhouse's Journal for that date shows that it had already been received before then, as does the date of Augusta's reply below. On Kinnaird's reference to her keeping a journal, AIB noted, "I kept no such journal," against which statement Hobhouse argued in Broughton, ii, 322, but there is no evidence that she kept any journal during the year of her marriage.
	35	AIB to J, March 26th, 1816.
453	8	AIB to Lushington, March 26, 1816—Evg.
	10	*cf.* p. 451.
	18	Hobhouse's Journal, 28 March, Lovelace transcript.
	22	*ibid.*
	27	*ibid.*
454	15	Augusta to AIB, March 27. 1816 St. James's Palace Wedy. Eveg.
	21	Dated 27 March 1816—The Solicitor General's Award, signed Samuel Shepherd—Wharton & Ford's files.
	31	Sir Samuel Shepherd to G. B. Wharton, Serjeants Inn, March 27, 1816.
	32	Hobhouse's Journal, 28 March.
455	26	*Works*, iii, 540–44.
	31	AIB to Lord Holland, March 27, 1816. Both Lord and Lady Holland replied on 29 March; to Lord Holland's courteous note a curious significance is attached in *The Late Lord Byron*, p. 239.
	37	Lady Caroline Lamb to AIB, undated.
457	1	"Minutes of Conversation with Ly CL. *March 27. 1816*". Completely quoted, with very slight errors, in *The Late Lord Byron*, pp. 240–45.
	13	AIB to Lushington, March 27, 1816, one sentence quoted in both Mayne, p. 223, and *The Late Lord Byron*, p. 244.
	20	Lady Caroline Lamb to John Murray, undated [27 March].
	39	Lushington to AIB, March 27th, 1816, one sentence quoted in *The Late Lord Byron*, p. 244.
458	10	AIB to J, misdated March 27, 1816 [28 March].
	12	The conveyancer appointed by the Solicitor General was Charles Butler, of Lincoln's Inn.
	21	Brougham to Wharton, Temple Tuesday morning, endorsed by Wharton 29 March 1816.
	30	AIB to Lushington, March 29, 1816.
459	8	Lushington to AIB, March 31, 1816.
	27	AIB to Anne Wilmot, March 29, 1816.
	36	AIB to R. J. Wilmot, March 29, 1816.
460	3	Lushington to AIB, April 2d, 1816.
	12	B to Augusta, April 3d, 1816.
	27	Augusta to AIB, Thursday morning.

Page	Line	
460	36	Hobhouse's Journal, April 13, Lovelace transcript, *cf.* Marchand, ii, 599.
461	8	Lady Caroline Lamb to AIB, undated, but written later on the day of their interview, 27 March, extensively quoted in *The Late Lord Byron*, p. 245.
	20	Lady Caroline Lamb to AIB, undated, but between 28 and 31 March, as Lady Melbourne had called before 1 Apr., *cf.* p. 447—part quoted in *The Late Lord Byron*, p. 247.
	23	J to AIB, Saturday Morn: [30 March].
	35	Augusta to Hodgson, Thursday Eveg, March 28th.
	n.	*Autobiography of Miss Knight*, ed. Roger Fulford, 1960, p. 208.
462	3	Augusta to Hobhouse, St. J.P. Jany. 3rd, 1816, so dated in Broughton, ii, 359, and in Lovelace's transcript, but the context and the dating from St. James's Palace suggest a slip for 3 *April*, the day when Hobhouse arrived to stay at Piccadilly Terrace with Byron: "Rode up to London and settled at Ld Byron's—No. 13 Piccadilly Terrace."—Hobhouse's Journal, Wednesday April 3.
	18	Hobhouse's Journal, 9 Apr., Lovelace transcript, *cf.* Marchand, ii, 599.
	32	Mrs. George Lamb to AIB, undated [? 8 Apr.].
463	3	Lady Liddell to AIB, undated, but mentioned in AIB to J, misdated March 27 for 28, *cf.* p. 458.
	10	AIB to J, undated [? 8 Apr.].
	14	Hobhouse's Journal, 8 Apr., Lovelace transcript, *cf.* Marchand, ii, 598.
	24	AIB to J, Friday [12 Apr.].
	30	Legal correspondence in Wharton & Ford's files.
	35	Lady Caroline Lamb to AIB, [27 March]: "His verses are sure to affect many—& is it not a mean & paltry act to give them to a Bookseller to show."
	36	AIB's letter to Lushington is missing; the phrase quoted occurs in his reply.
464	9	Lushington to AIB, Cheltenham, April 13, 1816, part quoted in *The Late Lord Byron*, p. 164.
	37	*Works*, iii, 544–6.
	45	AIB to F. W. Robertson, Janry. 23, 1851.
465	5	Hobhouse's Journal, 14 April, Lovelace transcript, *cf.* Marchand, ii, 599.
	26	B to AIB, Sunday April [14] 1816, *cf.* *Astarte*, pp. 51–2; Mayne, pp. 221–2.
	31	Hobhouse's Journal, 14 April, Lovelace transcript, *cf.* Broughton, ii, 330.
466	11	AIB to J, Monday [15 Apr.].
	12	*The Diary of Benjamin Robert Haydon*, ed. Willard B. Pope, 2 vols., 1960, ii, 482–4.
	31	Extracts from *Morning Post* enclosed with Sir Ralph to J, April 17th, 1816.
	33	H. R. Fox Bourne, *English Newspapers*, 2 vols., 1887, i, 273, 279.

Page	Line	
466	37	Hobhouse's Journal, 15 April, Lovelace transcript.
	38	*ibid*, 16 April.
	40	*ibid*, 17 April.
467	1	AIB to J, April 17.
	13	AIB to Lady Melbourne, April 17, 1816.
	15	Selina Gally Knight to AIB, Friday [19 Apr.]; Sophia M. Byron to AIB, Windsor Monday April 22.
	17	Hobhouse's Journal, 18 April, Lovelace transcript.
	19	*ibid*, *cf*. Broughton, ii, 333.
	23	*ibid*.
	43	James Perry to Sir Ralph, Strand 18 April—11 o'clock.
468	5	Hobhouse's Journal, 19 April, Lovelace transcript.
	18	*ibid*.
	21	Hobhouse to Doyle, April 20, Broughton, ii, 343.
	27	Hobhouse's Journal, 20 April, Lovelace transcript.
	28	*ibid*, 21 April.
	30	*ibid*, 26 April.
	36	AIB to J, April 20.
	n.	Fox Bourne, *English Newspapers*, i, 261; J to AIB, April 18.
469	8	AIB to J, April 21.
	17	Hobhouse's Journal, 19 April, Lovelace transcript. Hobhouse's account of his interview with the Solicitor General in Broughton, ii, 340, has subtle differences from the facts recorded in his Journal at the time.
	19	Chas. Hanson to Wharton, 11 April; Wharton to B, 13th April; John Hanson to Wharton & Ford, 15th Apl., enclosing Hobhouse to Hanson, undated; Wharton to Hanson, 15th April; Wharton to Hanson, 17 Apl.; Hanson to Wharton, 17th April and 18th Apl.; Wharton to Hanson, 18 April.
	22	Hobhouse's Journal, 21 April, Lovelace transcript, *cf*. Marchand, ii, 605.
	28	Doyle to Hobhouse, Sunday [21 Apr.], Broughton, ii, 345.
	29	Hobhouse's Journal, 21 April.
	33	Hobhouse to Doyle, undated [21 Apr.], Broughton, ii, 346. This correspondence seems a contradiction of the inference in Broughton, ii, 337, that Sir Ralph was deterred from further newspaper controversy by the threat of publishing private letters. As Doyle told Hobhouse, Sir Ralph's concern was with securing publication of his denial of any conspiracy against Byron; having secured that publication, he had no motive for pursuing the matter further. Hobhouse's published account of the press controversy—as of his interview with the Solicitor General—in Broughton, ii, 331–47, shows subtle differences from the facts recorded in his Journal. It should be noted that the account in *The Late Lord Byron*, pp. 162–6, quotes from the published version in Broughton, ii, 332, 334, 336–7, though the source is given as "Hobhouse, *Contemporary Account*."
	35	See p. 450.

Page	Line	
469	37	"B. has been consulting Sr Wm. Knighton with Mr. Le Mann (the Apothecary) & both agree as *he* tells me in thinking he must *have been* insane—& to recommend *quiet* & *caution* in future."—Augusta to Hodgson, Monday Night [18 March], postmark 19 March 1816.
	38	"*To Lord Byron*", pp. 182–6.
	42	Medwin, 1824, pp. 55, 62. Against the reference to "Mrs. Mardyn, who was a beautiful woman, and might have been a dangerous visitress," Annabella noted in the margin of the copy of Medwin sent to F. W. Robertson in Jan. 1851, "No such *visits* to Lord Byron were known to Lady Byron nor was she aware of any visits made *by* him *to* Actresses, except in one instance (not Mrs. M.) from his own information only."
470	3	R. Glynn Grylls, *Claire Clairmont: Mother of Byron's Allegra*, 1939, pp. 53–69.
	6	Hobhouse's Journal, 23 April, Lovelace transcript, *cf.* Marchand, ii, 607.
	8	*ibid*, 24 and 25 April.
	13	*ibid*, 25 April, *cf.* Marchand, ii, 608.
	33	"By thee Forsaken—March 1816," from a notebook, "Verses, 1809–1816." AINB to F. W. Robertson, Janry. 23, 1851: "Towards the close of his life his feelings towards me were softening—but evil influence had not yet lost its hold entirely. He *must* have come, had he lived, to the belief that *from first to last*, I had been his only truly devoted friend. It was not permitted!"—undated in Mayne, p. 405.
	37	See p. 458.
471	15	Mrs. Villiers to Augusta, Thursday evg. [25 Apr.], her own copy enclosed with Mrs. Villiers to AIB, Friday April 26. For AIB's reply from Kirkby, April 27, 1816, but postmarked 29 Ap., see *Lady Noel Byron and the Leighs*, pp. 29–30.
	21	*Lady Noel Byron and the Leighs* presents a selection of the vast correspondence illustrating the pursuit of Augusta; it has been supplemented by *Astarte*, pp. 199–262 (though many letters are given more fully in the earlier book), and by some additions in Mayne and in *The Late Lord Byron*.
	27	AINB's "Memorandum of my Interview with Mrs. Leigh at Reigate, Ap. 8, 1851", *Lady Noel Byron and the Leighs*, pp. 220–21; *cf.* Mayne, pp. 408–11, *The Late Lord Byron*, pp. 336–7.
	28	Ada, Countess of Lovelace died 27 November 1852; she was buried at Hucknall Torkard on 3 December, *Wentworth Peerage Case*, p. 64, *cf.* Mayne, p. 436.

The author apologises if the foregoing Notes suggest pedantry, but he has had to bear in mind that, pending fuller publication of the documents in the Lovelace Papers, the present book must be used by scholars for reference. The utmost care has been taken in transcription of letters; idiosyncrasies of spelling have been scrupulously preserved, but as these are frequent, it has not been thought necessary to disfigure the text with the parenthetical [*sic*].

INDEX

INDEX